CONTEMPORARY FAMILIES and
ALTERNATIVE LIFESTYLES

CONTEMPORARY FAMILIES and ALTERNATIVE LIFESTYLES

handbook on research and theory

edited by

ELEANOR D. MACKLIN
ROGER H. RUBIN

Published in cooperation with the
Groves Conference on Marriage and the Family

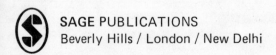

SAGE PUBLICATIONS
Beverly Hills / London / New Delhi

For information address:

SAGE Publications, Inc.
275 South Beverly Drive
Beverly Hills, California 90212

SAGE Publications India Pvt. Ltd.
C-236 Defence Colony
New Delhi 110 024, India

SAGE Publications Ltd
28 Banner Street
London EC1Y 8QE, England

Printed in the United States of America

Library of Congress Cataloging in Publication Data

Main entry under title:

Contemporary families and alternative lifestyles.

1. Family—United States—Addresses, essays,
lectures. 2. Family—Addresses, essays, lectures.
3. Sex customs—United States—Addresses, essays,
lectures. 4. Sex customs—Addresses, essays,
lectures. I. Macklin, Eleanor D. II. Rubin,
Roger Harvey.
HQ536.C749 1982   306.8'5   82-10717
ISBN 0-8039-1053-3

FIRST PRINTING

Lovingly dedicated to my folks
Pearl Berger Rubin
and
Joseph Rubin
and the rest of my family
— Roger

And to Harold Feldman, who inspired
me, and Joan Liversidge,
who made it possible
— Ellie

Contents

Acknowledgments   9

Foreword *by Robert G. Ryder*   13

Prologue: The 1970s and American Families (A Comitragedy)
    CATHERINE S. CHILMAN   15

PART I: LIFESTYLE ALTERNATIVES

1. Singlehood
    PETER J. STEIN   27

2. Nonmarital Heterosexual Cohabitation: An Overview
    ELEANOR D. MACKLIN   49

3. Voluntary Childlessness: A Critical Assessment of
the Research
    JEAN E. VEEVERS   75

4. Single-Parent Families: In the Mainstream of
American Society
    EDWARD H. THOMPSON, Jr., and PATRICIA A. GONGLA   97

5. Divorce: A Frequent "Alternative" in the 1970s
    SHARON PRICE-BONHAM, DAVID W. WRIGHT, and
    JOE F. PITTMAN   125

6. Remarriage and Stepfamilies: Research Results
and Implications
    CATHERINE S. CHILMAN   147

7. Dual-Career/Dual-Work Families: A Systems Approach
    MARY W. HICKS, SALLY L. HANSEN, and
    LEO A. CHRISTIE   164

8. Commuter Marriage: Couples Who Live Apart
    NAOMI GERSTEL and HARRIET GROSS   180

9. "Open" Marriage and Multilateral Relationships:
The Emergence of Nonexclusive Models of
the Marital Relationship
    DAVID L. WEIS   194

10. Gay Male and Lesbian Relationships
      JOSEPH HARRY   216

11. Radical Community: Contemporary Communes and
    Intentional Communities
      GERRY BRUDENELL   235

12. Contemporary Traditional Families:
    The Undefined Majority
      SARA B. TAUBIN and EMILY H. MUDD   256

PART II: LIFESTYLE PERSPECTIVES AND ISSUES

13. Alternatives for the Elderly
      PAULA L. DRESSEL and BETH B. HESS   271

14. The Present and Future of Alternative Lifestyles
    in Ethnic American Cultures
      MARIE F. PETERS and HARRIETTE P. McADOO   288

15. Alternative Lifestyles from an International Perspective:
    A Trans-Atlantic Comparison
      BRAM BUUNK   308

16. Clinical Issues in Alternative Lifestyles
      ROBERT A. PHILLIPS, Jr.   331

17. The Law and Alternative Lifestyles
      NOEL MYRICKS   343

18. Teaching About Alternative Family Forms and Lifestyles
      ANTHONY P. JURICH and CATHERINE A. HASTINGS   362

19. Religious Reactions to Alternative Lifestyles
      ROBERT T. FRANCOEUR   379

Epilogue: Families and Alternative Lifestyles in an Age of
    Technological Revolution
      ROGER H. RUBIN   400

About the Contributors   410

Acknowledgments

This volume is the product of the 1981 Groves Conference on Marriage and the Family held in Mt. Pocono, Pennsylvania. The conference title was "The Pursuit of Happiness: Progress and Prospects." It followed by ten years the "The Future of Marriage and Parenthood" theme of the 1971 Groves Conference held in Puerto Rico, during which scholars were alerted to the rapidly evolving alternative lifestyles and the significant changes that were occurring in the American family. "Letting Many Flowers Bloom," theme of the 1973 meetings, further examined the growing pluralism and the need for research on its implications.

The years since then have been a time of dramatic social change and of frantic activity by students of the family as they have scurried to keep up with these changes. It seemed appropriate that the 1981 meetings be devoted to a critical assessment of what had been learned during this very fertile period. To this end, researchers, scholars, and practitioners were brought together to sift through the accumulated knowledge of the past decade. Papers growing out of the conference were specifically solicited and prepared for this volume. It is a statement of what we have learned and of what remains to be learned, a benchmark from which to measure further progress, and a guide for those who seek direction for future policy and research. It is produced in keeping with the mission of the Groves Conference.

Established in 1934 by Ernest R. Groves, Professor of Sociology at the University of North Carolina at Chapel Hill, the Groves Conference on Marriage and the Family meets for five days on an annual basis in various parts of the United States and elsewhere. It is an international organization serving to bring together professionals concerned with marriage and the family so that they may share their knowledge and their ideas, and be a source of stimulation to one another. Ernest Groves was among the first academicians to promote the scientific study of the family. His vision and leadership still live through the Conference and its members, as they seek to remain on the cutting edge of theory development and empirical research, using interdisciplinary perspectives and fostering the application of findings to the public arena.

The Groves Conference limits membership to a select number of family scholars, practitioners, and policy specialists who are invited to meet each year to share observations and recent findings with fellow members and guests. In contrast to most traditional scientific meetings, Groves is organized around in-depth workshops focused on some facet of the theme, with much of the substantive information coming from interaction among attendees. This format allows for the exploration of issues, as well as a free exchange of information and experiences among scholars. It creates an intellectual "hothouse," conducive to the conception of ideas that may in time develop into further research, intervention programs, and public policy.

It is evident that the success of the Groves Conference stems from the vitality and contributions of its participants and organizers. This was no less true of the 1981 Conference. We especially recognize the skill and ability of the Conference Coordinator, Joan (Mills) Liversidge and her assistants, Nancy Coleman, Carol Love, Robin Saipe, and Sherry Starr. We thank Sylvia and Walter Clavan, Eileen Hepburn, and Richard Hess for local arrangements. Joan Constantine and Richard Dunham, as associate chairpersons, were responsible for helping to conceptualize the format and the focus of the program and shared the responsibility for the Conference's success. We salute the creativity of those bulwarks of the family field whose innovative thinking in the earlier conferences formed the basis for this one, in particular: Marvin Sussman (president during the 1971 meetings); Catherine Chilman (program chairperson for the 1971 meetings); Harold Feldman (workshop chairperson for the 1971 meetings and president during the 1973 meetings); and Robert Ryder (program chairperson for the 1973 meetings and president during the 1981 meetings).

The development of this volume has been the result of inestimable hours of personal and professional effort. The contributors to it have donated their time and incurred expenses, putting aside other pressing obligations to meet deadlines and rewriting innumerable drafts with patience and good humor, in an impressive display of professionalism. Appreciation is extended to Cathy Howard for her yeoman editing and to Kassy Hargadon and Lynne Tylee for their loyal assistance. The contribution of graduate assistance, postage, telephone, xeroxing costs, and secretarial services by the Department of Family and Community Development at the University of Maryland made this project possible, as did the support and encouragement of Mitch Allen of Sage Publications.

Finally, Roger Rubin acknowledges his mentors, Arthur Gravatt and Carlfred Broderick, whose nurturance brought him into the family field and whose intelligence led him to appreciate it; and David H. Olson, who provided him the opportunity to pursue this profession. Ellie Macklin wishes to express her deep appreciation to Harold Feldman, whose unflagging enthusiasm and support gave her the impetus she needed to weather many years as a graduate student and a fledging academician and whose role model inspired her to risk the study of the unconventional; to

Joan Liversidge, without whose dedication and expert assistance she could not have prevailed; and to her family, who have been a constant source of encouragement and understanding.

— Eleanor D. Macklin, Ph.D.
— Roger H. Rubin, Ph.D.

Foreword

It was my great privilege to be associated with the Groves Conference during the 1970s. As many of the chapters in this volume will point out, this was a period of great change — real and/or intended. Change was the focus of attention at one conference after another, with small groups discussing what was actually happening and what might happen, from many different perspectives. Macklin and Rubin have now done us all a great, and I think unique, service in bringing together a collection of retrospective views of this strange and dramatic period, providing a mix of perspectives that are interdisciplinary and cross-cultural and that represent varying value orientations and ideologies.

I am almost, but not quite, tempted simply to express my personal happiness at the publication of this book. After all, I think that the book is important and valuable not just from the point of view of social science, but also as a historical document. However, my happiness is tempered by sadness, because there is a sense in which this book is an epitaph to a decade and hence suggests that something has died. The various authors will express differing degrees of optimism or pessimism about the present and future of social change, depending on whether or not the changes that came about in the 1970s seem real and stable, and whether or not the authors themselves are fond of these changes. However, there seems to be little doubt that the optimism and hope that still characterized such broad segments of the American population in 1971 were less evident in 1981.

Optimism of the late 1960s received many severe blows in the following decade. The oil embargo forced us to consider our national dependence on petroleum and demolished at one stroke the myth of unlimited American affluence. The final acts of the Vietnam tragedy left little for anyone to cheer over. We celebrated our 200th national anniversary with the nation's first appointed president, elected by no one. In personal lives, those who experimented with allegedly new and different ways found the sailing not as smooth as some might have expected, and the gentle tug of conventions to be persistent and ultimately forceful.

Cynicism seems to have grown greatly. Many people seem much more certain about the identity of their enemies than of their friends, and even less sure of their heroes.

On the other hand, mixed feelings are part of the human condition. If there is a sense in which this volume is an epitaph, there is also a sense in which it represents a refusal to let something die and be forgotten. Whether one favors or abhors the various ideologies described and represented in these pages, there must be lessons to be learned from these ideologies and from the fact that they have existed. When the ferment and excitement of the 1920s died in the Great Depression, the social ideas of the time seemed partly to have gotten lost in recollections of fun and frivolity. Macklin and Rubin are interested in this not happening again. They present a series of views by professionals who want to go beyond the superficial and beyond recollections. These essays call for work to be done at present and in the future. I earnestly hope, without ambivalence, that this call will be heeded.

— *Robert G. Ryder*
President, Groves Conference on
Marriage and the Family, 1979-1981

Prologue:
The 1970s and American Families
(A Comitragedy)

CATHERINE S. CHILMAN
University of Wisconsin — Milwaukee

I would like to review with you some major trends of the 1970s and how these trends affected families. We really are not far enough away from that decade to know much about it. In fact, we still have not digested the 1960s, by any means. Moreover, many historians would say that we must wait at least 100 years before we will have any real perspective on this recent time. Very likely this is so, but, nevertheless, let us undertake a short-range view of the amazing period we have only recently left. Not left, really, because the past decade will affect wives and husbands, fathers and mothers, sons and daughters for a long time to come. Moreover, the tragicomic events of the 1970s have endowed us with many unresolved problems for the 1980s — a decade that threatens to be an especially dreary one for the majority of American families.

Much of what I will say here is based on my earlier analysis of recent social history and its effects on adolescent sexual behavior (Chilman, 1979). It also builds on my experience as program chair of the 1971 Groves Conference on Marriage and the Family, during which most of the members were startled and delighted to learn that alternative family lifestyles had definitely emerged from their various closets. What adventurers we,

Author's Note: This introduction is adapted from an after-dinner plenary session address given by the author at the 1981 Annual Meetings of the Groves Conference on Marriage and the Family. As an after-dinner speech it was meant to be light-hearted and informal in style, though serious in purpose. It continues to follow this form in keeping with its subtitle: a comitragedy.

and others like us, thought we were! So enlightened, brave, honest, sincere, possessors of a higher morality in which we did everything we had ever wanted to do about sex but had not dared to do, or if we had done it, we had not dared to go public about it. Now it was authentic and "in" to announce our personal good news to the world.

I had also attended the White House Conference on Youth in April 1971. This conference was held in Estes Park, Colorado, because President Nixon could not bear the thought of all those dangerous young radicals coming to Washington. This conference, for me, was a cram course in the new youth culture. I met gay rights activists who wanted homosexuals to have the right to adopt children and young philosophers who pronounced that all past history was dead and that nothing before 1970 applied to the present or the future. Youthful historians announced that the entire past of the United States was nothing but betrayal and genocide and that all vestiges of American civilization needed to be destroyed by nice, clean fires. A totally new world of personal freedoms had suddenly emerged. Petitions were drawn up to demand that President Nixon support the right of all people of all ages to engage in any kind of consensual individual and group sex they wished. Even a sudden spring blizzard, ordered, perhaps, by the White House, failed to cool the brave new leaders of the youth conference.

The early 1970s saw the end of the social protest movement of the 1960s and the launching of the psychological "me first" protest movement of the following years. The social protestors had pursued the ancient and ever-glorious, ever-elusive utopian dream of liberty, justice, and peace for all. They sought various routes to this utopia: civil rights, academic freedom, escape from poverty, freedom of speech. The mid-sixties had been heady days, with vast numbers marching together to build a "great society," a community of free and equal citizens. History will not forget the Freedom March led by Martin Luther King, Jr., the man with a dream, or a bit later, the March on the Pentagon to demand an end to the Vietnam War.

But 1967 was the year in which great screws were turned on peace movements, the youth movement, academic reform, the flower children, and the War on Poverty — a war that went, instead, to Vietnam. Nineteen sixty-seven! Surely a turnaround year for U.S. society. Here are some of the major things that happened:

- Race riots broke out in most of the big cities.
- Numerous campuses resounded with student protests.
- Many people announced they had discovered that the family was "irrelevant."
- The divorce rate started its long climb upward.
- The marriage rate dropped.

- The incidence of nonmarital intercourse among White adolescent girls rose from about 10 percent by age 18 to 30 percent or so. (Data for Black adolescent girls are not available for this time period.)
- The birthrate continued to decline from its 1948-1958 boom years, but the rate of births outside of marriage started to rise rapidly, especially for teenagers.
- The women's movement was reborn.
- The economy began its inflationary spiral as the Johnson administration expanded war industries but failed to increase taxes to meet heavy defense spending and economic growth.
- Family "real" income continued to rise markedly and the rate of poverty declined, especially for Black families.
- College and university students demanded the right to live in coeducational dormitories.

The enormous changes of 1967 were followed in 1968 by similar but in many instances more devastating changes. This was the year in which Robert Kennedy and Martin Luther King, Jr., were assassinated and the inner cities were burned, the year in which a violence-torn nominating presidential convention revealed a fragmented and demoralized Democratic party. This was the year in which conservatives, reacting against the explosiveness of change-oriented, left-wing liberals elected Richard Nixon on a traditionalist platform that called for, among other things, a return to "old-fashioned decency and morality." It was a morality supposedly desired by the silent majority and loudly proclaimed by Vice-President Agnew until he was silenced when he was forced to resign from office for his numerous fiduciary delinquencies.

Thus partly through their own excesses and dissensions, and partly through conservative reactions, societal reform movements had been all but annihilated by the end of the 1960s. As I see it, the reformers, depressed and disillusioned by the defeat of their efforts, turned away from the concept of utopian attainment through community to a new dream: realization of paradise through the self as a freed individual. With the twilight of *social* change came the dawning of *individual* change — individual change based on the theories and therapies of such psychological high priests as Rollo May, Abraham Maslow, Carl Rogers, and Fritz Perls. Defeated in the larger world, millions of utopia seekers turned from the quest for fulfillment through the liberated community to fulfillment through the liberated self. Thus was born the age of narcissism as Christopher Lasch (1979) has termed it, or, in the words of Yankelovich (1981), the duty-to-self culture. Adopted initially by youth in the "better" universities ("better" meaning universities peopled particularly by privileged students who could afford to be in revolt against the conventions), the authentic search for the "real me" diffused to blue-collar youth and other segments of the population in a few years (Yankelovich, 1974).

According to a recent analysis by Yankelovich (1981), about 80 percent of the people in this country were involved in the search for self-fulfillment during the 1970s: 17 percent of the population as especially ardent in this quest. The avant-garde-dedicated searchers tended to be under age 35, professionals, possessors of some college education, children of parents who had been to college, and liberal Democrats. Less than half of them were married. This was the group that especially questioned all authority and especially sought their "true individual identity."

This identity or "real me" was often sought in an exotic variety of encounter groups, especially when families proved unsympathetic to the "only me" orientation. There was a vast flowering of confrontation therapies, weekend communal retreats, total pornography sessions, group sex, self-help support groups, communes, hot tubs, and the like. There seems to be a certain illogic in searching for the special individual "me" through so many group activities, but if you are going to explore your true, autonomous self independently of family ties, it is important to have good, dependable friends who can join you. The group search was not a search of altruistic sharing, but rather a matter of individualized activities rather like those carried out in nursery schools where 3- and 4-year-olds engage in "parallel play."

People (especially women, because men already knew) were learning how to be "number one," to "take charge of their own lives," to be good to themselves, to be responsible for their own orgasms. They were also learning to be assertive, slim, and trim, and to discover peak religious experiences in the process of jogging. There was a move away from an older culture that had an ethic of self-denial to a new culture that had an ethic of denying itself nothing. This ethic held that you should make no commitments and keep all your options open. This included a move from an emphasis on procreational sex to one on recreational sex.

The new psychological utopians mistakenly thought they could cure themselves through do-it-yourself, off-the-couch therapeutic methods. If you could find your true self in therapy, cast off your inhibitions and defenses on the therapist's couch, why not go forth, psychologically naked, to the family and the community? There are major flaws in this reasoning. Therapists are paid to accept the "real you" for an hour or so a week; families have to take the "real you" all the time and they are not paid for this arduous work. And communities have a hard time being communities when everyone is focused on self-discovery.

Is it any wonder that, as these changes went on, more and more families were involved in a series of disasters or, as some optimists would have it, growth-producing experiences? These included rising rates of divorce and separation, nonmarital births, and abortion. Until 1975 or so, both the marriage rate and the birthrate continued their declines. There was an apparent rise in domestic violence (both child and spouse abuse), child neglect, parent/youth conflicts, incest, and rape within the family as well as in the outside community. Violence was also rampant in the community: in the schools, on the streets, in the market place, and more recently, even in the Vatican.

These responses were understandable. For most people in the country, former cultural patterns were being swept away: patterns that emphasized denial of personal feelings and impulses; submergence of the self to the needs of the family, work, and community; rigid differentiation of clearly defined sex roles; fear of God, dirty dishes, and economic failure.

In many ways these cultural patterns were "out of sync" with the kind of highly technological, urbanized, overpopulated country we had become. The constraints of these patterns were as uncomfortable and outdated as an old-time corset. And by 1970, even pantigirdles were passé. The difficulty was, and is, that most of us need *some* normative, as well as figurative, support. Left totally on our own, we tend to lose control. Encouraged to seek self-actualization and hassle-free self-expression, most of us find it difficult to think simultaneously in altruistic, empathetic terms: to act with self-control and generosity in relating to our mates, our children, and other kinfolk, not to mention our peers on the job and in the community.

One culture had been shredded, and a new one, better adapted to both the times and socialized living, had yet to evolve in any coherent, integrated way. Its evolution was not made any easier by the behavior of then president, Richard Nixon. Nationwide morale was all but destroyed in 1973 when he, the sovereign leader of traditional morality, was found to be a master innovator of spying, bribery, thievery, and bold-faced lying from the inner sanctum of the White House.

Why should we be astonished after the Watergate proceedings, then, to find that old-time fundamentalist religion, with its rigid insistence on absolute rights and wrongs, revived in strength across the land? Not only was there the alarm caused by a disintegration of old ways and by the Nixon debacle, but there was the economic recession of 1974 and 1975. A profound shock to one's morality is bad enough, but when it is coupled with an invasion of the pocketbook, there is a double-jeopardy effect that leads many a straying lamb back to the fold, or even converts new ones to traditional religion.

The rising tide of evangelism found a media-perfect name, "the Moral Majority" — a moral majority that was out to "save" the traditional family. Politically astute morality majors used popular dismay over familial tribulations to build a conservative power base that played a large part in electing a strongly reactionary president and Congress in 1980.

By 1981, it became painfully clear that so-called profamily forces were destroying most of the government programs that had protected and supported the majority of the nation's families. It soon became obvious that, according to this group, a profamily position served primarily the white, conservative, well-heeled, politically "correct" families. Profamily measures, in the moral majority dialogue, meant programs that abolished job training and placement programs for the poor (especially minority youth and single mothers), subsidies for housing of low-income families, nutritional and medical programs for these same families, child care centers for children of poorly paid working mothers, special education programs for children with learning disabilities, assurances of child and family social services, affirmative action programs to enhance the opportunities for minority families, and family planning and abortion resources for people of limited income. And as of spring 1982 the Moral Majority program, at least President Reagan's "save America, profamily" platform, called for shattering the social and economic security of virtually every family in the country except for those few who were happily blessed with the bulging incomes of the very rich.

The profamily platform also called for a return to the "happy homes" of nostalgic yesterdays when women fulfilled their "natural roles" as family-centered wives and mothers unsullied by the world's work and politics; when "unnatural" types such as gays and lesbians were decently kept in closets; when children learned to fear God and father both at home and at school; and when sex was only for reproduction within the bonds of holy matrimony or for males away from home on "important business ventures."

Excuse me if I sound faintly partisan. If you detect certain political overtones you are absolutely right. This is no time for cool neutrality. The tides of today threaten to carry the social programs of this country and its families back 100 years or more. These tides threaten to destroy the nation, for they carry with them the flotsam and jetsam of the nineteenth century: a century heavy with its own lurid Gothic tales, its social, political, economic, and familial horrors.

But that is a somewhat different story. Rather, let us turn again to the late 1970s and recall the excitement many family specialists felt when there was growing presidential interest in public policy and families. Many hoped that the forthcoming 1980 White House Conference on Families would incorporate such relatively new concepts as family ecology, family policy impact analysis, and the development of supportive family environments. More specifically, many hoped that governmental programs would be designed that would address themselves to building family strengths by recognizing and planning ways to meet basic family needs: family income supports, family-sensitive employment policies that included part-time and flex-time working hours, child care assistance, maternity and paternity leave, family health insurance, comprehensive assistance services for families caring for handicapped, aged and chronically ill members, increased subsidies for family housing, and guaranteed equal rights between the races and between the sexes. In short, the United States might actually join, at last, other industrialized, modern countries that have progressive policies designed to provide a solid foundation on which families might safely build their lives.

However, it soon became clear that the hopes of many social scientists and political liberals were to be denied. Most of what these groups had seen as essential to family well-being was viewed by right-wing enthusiasts as damaging to families or, as they self-righteously proclaimed, antifamily.

Perhaps the extreme turn to the right in the early 1980s was a temporary reaction to the enormous social changes of the 1960s and 1970s. Perhaps the pendulum had swung too far, or at least too fast, to the left during the 1960s and, to some extent, during the 1970s. Perhaps the country was due for a more middle-of-the-road approach to many individual and family values and norms. Even before the election of Republican majorities in 1980, there had been signs that the liberals, too, were becoming somewhat conservative. As demographic data show, as human service programs and some research indicate, and as personal experience all too often confirms, the costs of "freedom and fulfillment now" were often too severe. Did, perhaps, the costs outweigh the benefits?

For some people, yes; for some, no. At any rate, demographic data plus the 1980 elections showed that many Americans, not just the members of the so-called Moral Majority (which is actually less than 20 percent of the population), had become somewhat less individualistic and nontraditional in their behaviors. As of 1975 or so, the marriage rate and birthrate were somewhat higher than in the previous five years, the divorce rate leveled off briefly, and concepts of altruism and community were heard in the land. We were told that families were "here to stay" (Bane, 1976), and family researchers were busy developing meanings and measurements of love and commitment.

Had the liberal half of the country crossed over to the conservative side, ready to give up many of its hard-won freedoms of the past 15 or 20 years? It hardly seems likely. According to Yankelovich (1981), who carried out a 30-year analysis of national public opinion polls and attitude surveys, there had been a definite change in many of our norms and values and these were unlikely to be reversed in the near future. For example, at the end of the 1950s, 80 percent of the population surveyed thought people who did not marry were neurotic, sick, or immoral. By the mid-1970s, almost the same proportion of people took a neutral view of singlehood. Getting married was something that you did or did not do according to your own desires. By 1975, three-fourths of the respondents thought it was okay if a woman had an illegitimate child and raised the child by herself. And half of the nation's adults gave an okay to cohabitation among the young. Whereas in 1967, 85 percent of parents of college-age students thought that premarital intercourse was wrong for their youngsters, by the late 1970s, two-thirds of the parents condoned this behavior.

Until the late 1960s, public opinion averred that mothers should stay out of the work force and remain at home to take care of their children. A man's first duty was to work and to support his family. By the late 1970s, the majority thought that mothers enhanced their womanly status by employment outside of the home, and priorities for men moved into the realm of high-quality family relationships. But there is some confusion. Simultaneously with the above attitudes, 77 percent of the population said that women should put the well-being of their husbands and children ahead of their own careers. Whereas the majority of 1978 survey respondents yearned for the warmth and closeness of family life associated with "the good old days," few wanted to give up their new-found sexual and sex role freedoms in order to attain this.

Even so, by the mid-1970s, the word "conservative" or at least "conservation" had developed a certain appeal. The country was well into the energy crisis, and there were serious problems of air and water pollution as well as severe economic difficulties. Whether or not conservative steps will save the economy in the future is one of the crucial questions of the 1980s. Surely inflation and accompanying high rates of unemployment are an economic conundrum and both are devastating to families.

Some social commentators see the social revolutions of the 1960s and early 1970s as having been based on a boom economy. Until recently, for instance, a rising economy made flexi time and dual careers for spouses possible. It was an age of economic growth and demand for recently trained, highly skilled professionals and technicians. However, by 1981 the massive entry of the 1948-1958 baby-boom generation into the labor market, plus a number of other factors, had sharply decreased employment opportunities. What effect this would have on families was not clear, but 1982 reports indicated rising rates of alcoholism, family violence, mental illness, and marital breakdown along with a rising tide of unemployment.

It became increasingly apparent, moreover, that divorce and separation were leading causes of poverty, especially for female-headed families with children. Women's liberation from oppressive marriages all too often meant women's oppression by low wages, unemployment, child care problems, and lack of child-support payments from angry ex-husbands (Hill et al., 1981). As the late Angus Campbell (1981) reported in his analysis of attitude trends from 1957 to 1978, young single people of the 1970s were the unhappiest age group in the population and the unhappiest people of all ages were the separated, divorced, widowed, and never married (also Veroff et al., 1981).

The growing housing shortage and costs also tightened, and frequently strained, family bonds. Many young singles, for instance, found they could not afford to live alone: The swinging apartment scene was too expensive and, alas, for all concerned, the young often needed to return to the once-empty family nest. Moreover, many older people who had maintained their separate homes were being forced to double up with elderly friends or with their kin. In a word, alternative family lifestyles often proved to be too expensive in an age of dwindling economic opportunity and soaring inflation.

We are gradually realizing that the long period of American prosperity that included steadily rising real family income from the end of World War II to about 1975 has come to what may be a permanent end. The affluence of this period gilded a large segment of our sociey. Many Americans actually lived like the tiny minority of privileged royalty in the past. We could *afford* the sweet agony of perfervid trips into our own psychological interiors. We could *afford* premarital and extramarital affairs and experimentation with a heady variety of alternative lifestyles. We could *afford* divorces and new marriages. We at least thought we could afford to risk our jobs by assertively proclaiming our own treasured identity.

Is the search for freedom, equality, self-determination, honesty, creativity, and continuing growth throughout the human life span merely an artifact of economic prosperity? Does it dissipate in hard times? Or are the quests of the 1960s for a more just and democratic society, and of the 1970s for a more egalitarian and humane personal and family life, indicative of a more basic search that will not end? Do these quests perhaps reflect the enduring aspirations of people to add significance and meaning to life, to deny the assertion that life is simply a "tomorrow and tomorrow and tomorrow that creeps in this petty pace from day to day to the last syllable of recorded time" (Shakespeare, 1605). Surely all our yesterdays have not simply "lighted fools to dusty death."

To move from Shakespeare to Yankelovich (1981), a welcome trend may be emerging, an ethic of commitment away from focus on the self to connectedness to the outer world. His analysis of public opinion polls and surveys leads him to believe that there may be a popular yearning to devote more of the self to human relationships and less to material and instrumental selfish goals. Yankelovich discerns that many people long for closer and deeper human relationships, a sense of community, and a reverential approach to living.

He writes that the 1980s will demand that we live far more practical lives than we have in the recent past. We will need to pay more attention to economic realities such as jobs, homes, food, and personal safety. We will have acute battles over issues like abortion, prayer in the schools, sex education, racism, and the struggle between the "haves" and the "have nots." We need to strive for a new social ethic, not one of gloom and despair or nostalgia for the good old days, but one directed toward building a more balanced society that combines elements of the self and community, freedom and responsibility, autonomy and commitment. Having paid obesiance to Shakespeare, I now reach even further back to the Greeks, who passed on to us the wisdom of attempting to devote our lives both to ourselves and to the community, of striving for balance in all things, of seeking the "golden mean."

Can we find altruism, commitment, and a sense of community again? Can we achieve responsibility toward others as well as toward the self?

Can we find and hold onto these qualities without giving up large measures of our own arduously achieved freedoms? Can we develop bonded families that do not bind too tightly? Can we take responsibility, as concerned and informed citizens, to turn back the dangerous forces of today's reactionary politics? Perhaps personal *and* social commitment, autonomy and connectedness, are almost impossible to achieve at any time. Perhaps they are impossible in the 1980s. I do not really know. What do you think?

References

BANE, M. J. (1976) Here to Stay. New York: Basic Books.

CAMPBELL, A. (1980) The Sense of Well-Being in America. New York: McGraw-Hill.

CHILMAN, C. (1979) Adolescent Sexuality in a Changing American Society. Washington, DC: Government Printing Office.

HILL, M. S., D. H. HILL, and J. N. MORGAN (1981) Five Thousand American Families: Patterns of Economic Progress, Vol. 9. Ann Arbor: University of Michigan Press.

LASCH, C. (1979) The Culture of Narcissism: American Life in an Age of Diminishing Expectations. New York: W. W. Norton.

SHAKESPEARE, W. (1605) Macbeth. London: Oxford University Press.

VEROFF, J., E. DOUVAN, and R. KULKA (1981) The Inner American: A Self-Portrait from 1956-1976. New York: Basic Books.

YANKELOVICH, D. (1981) "A world turned upside down." Psychology Today 15, 4: 35-91.

PART I

LIFESTYLE ALTERNATIVES

CHAPTER 1

Singlehood

PETER J. STEIN
William Paterson College

In 1980, more than 58 million American adults over the age of 18 were unmarried. This is about 34 percent of American men and more than 40 percent of American women. The unmarried population varies with respect to age, previous marital status and nature of the termination of that status, living arrangements, sexual preferences, educational, occupational, and income levels, class background and identification, ethnic and racial identification, religion, and parental status.

Some statistics from the 1980 Census help point out why this group is important and how it is growing:

(1) The median age at first marriage for women increased from 20.8 years in 1970 to 22.1 years in 1980; for men it increased from 23.2 years in 1970 to 24.6 years in 1980.

(2) Fully 50 percent of all women between the ages of 20 and 24 have never been married (compared with fewer than 30 percent in 1960).

(3) There are 1.5 million unmarried couples living together, more than three times the number in 1970.

(4) Divorce has continued to increase so that the ratio of divorced persons to married persons living with their spouses increased from 47 per 1000 in 1970 to 100 per 1000 in 1980.

(5) In 1980, 20 percent of children under the age of 18 lived with only one parent.

(6) The number of persons living alone increased by more than 60 percent in the 1970s so that presently, 23 percent of all American households are composed of a single person.

Statistics also show an increase in the number of women attending college and postponing age of first marriage, as well as an increase in the numbers of men and women who actively are choosing the single life.

Author's Note: This is a revised version of a paper presented at the 1981 Annual Meetings of the Groves Conference on Marriage and the Family. The author gratefully acknowledges the editorial and typing assistance of Ellen Rope and Jeanne Bradshaw.

Despite the great variety in lifestyles and life chances found among unmarried adult men and women, singles continue to be regarded as a global residual category. The term "single" continues to mean the absence of marriage and therefore has meaning only when compared with marriage. Other terms, such as "bachelor," "spinster," or "old maid," bring specific, often negative, images to mind. At its best, single as a term is more useful for those who write about singles than it is for the singles themselves, as it does not denote the many categories of singleness, or the variety existing within each category. As a group, singles are at least as diverse as is the married population. Within this broad spectrum of singlehood, several major categories emerge: the never married, the separated, the divorced, and the widowed (see Table 1.1).

The Never Marrieds

The largest category in the singles population is the never marrieds. The U.S. Bureau of the Census reports that in 1980 never marrieds made up more than 23 percent of the male and 17 percent of the female population of this country. Yet never-married persons have been consistently treated as members of an insignificant and deviant group, worthy of study primarily for their departure from the normal, married state.

Stereotypes die hard, and it has taken years of shifts in population, as well as a new wave of sociologists, to bring an awareness of the positive, as well as the problematic, aspects of singleness to professionals and to the population at large. It is true that not everyone who wants to be married will be. But it is also true that some people (more every year) are freely choosing to be part of the never-married group.

What accounts for the increase in the numbers of young adults who are choosing to postpone marriage and for the accompanying dramatic shift in the age of first marriage? Some of the contributing social developments include:

(1) the increase in the number of women enrolled in colleges and in graduate schools;

(2) expanding employment and career opportunities for women;

(3) the impact of the women's movement;

(4) the excess of young women at the currently "most marriageable" ages;

(5) greater ambivalence regarding the desirability of marriage among both college and noncollege young people;

(6) conflict between marriage and the desire for individual development and personal growth;

(7) the increasing divorce rate, which has led some young people to question the appeal of marriage and family life; and

(8) the increasing availability and acceptability of birth-control methods.

TABLE 1.1 Marital Status of the U.S. Population, Age 18 and Over, 1980 (in thousands of persons)

	Total	Married	Never Married	Divorced	Widowed	Separated
Men	74,101 (100)[a]	48,752 (65.8)	17,434 (23.5)	3,871 (5.2)	1,972 (2.7)	2,071 (2.8)
Women	82,054 (100)	48,627 (59.3)	13,977 (17.0)	5,831 (7.1)	10,479 (12.8)	3,140 (3.8)

SOURCE: U.S. Bureau of the Census, Marital Status and Living Arrangements: March, 1980. Current Population Reports, Series P-20, No. 365, Washington, DC: Government Printing Office, 1981.

a. Numbers in parentheses indicate percentage distribution.

In addition to the young singles waiting for later marriage, there are those for whom marriage is either not desirable or not possible. These include older singles who will never marry, either because they have not found eligible partners or because they are satisfied with singlehood and/or are opposed to marriage. There are priests and nuns whose career choices preclude marriage. Some men and women prefer homosexual and lesbian relationships to traditional marriage, and are precluded by law from same-sex marriage. Other individuals may have physical or physiological impairments that prevent them from finding mates. Because of the increased number of persons electing to remain single, it is predicted that 8 to 9 percent of adults now in their twenties will experience a lifetime of singlehood as opposed to 4 to 5 percent of those now 50 years old (Glick, 1979).

The Separated, Divorced, and Widowed

The number of marriages ending in divorce in the United States continues to increase so that today marriage partners have about a one-in-three chance of becoming divorced. The ratio of currently divorced persons per 1000 married persons has doubled during the past decade so that in 1980, for every 10 currently married persons there was one person who had divorced but not remarried. Children have about a one-in-two chance of spending part of their lives in a single-parent home. Even persons who avoid divorce themselves may end up in a marriage with a divorced partner.

Social scientists, family practitioners, and educators all express concern over the increasing rate of divorce. Some emphasize what they perceive as a decline in the quality of life and the weakening of family bonds. Others see greater opportunities for self-expression, the exercise of choices, and increased individual freedom. These data tell more of the story:

(1) The ratios of divorced to married vary considerably between men and women (79 per 1000 for men and 120 per 1000 for women). The

number of divorced women at any one time is greater than the number of men because men are more likely than women to remarry, and are likely to remarry more quickly. As of 1980, about five out of every six divorced men remarried compared with about three of every four divorced women.

(2) The median age for divorce after a first marriage is 27 years for women and 29 years for men. However, the median age for those currently in the divorced category is about 45. Since young divorcees are more likely to remarry, more older divorcees remain in the divorced category.

(3) The most common age for remarriage after a first divorce is 25 to 34 years for men and 20 to 34 years for women.

(4) The divorce rate for remarriages is higher than for first marriages. If present trends continue, about 40 percent of Americans in their late twenties and early thirties who remarry after a divorce can expect their second marriage to also end in divorce. For both men and women, 35 to 44 is the most common age for a second divorce.

(5) Because women in the United States tend to live about eight years longer than men, women are more likely than men to experience the death of a spouse. Wives outnumber husbands as survivors by a ratio of about five to one. To add to the inequity, widowers are more likely than widows to remarry. Fewer than one-third of widows remarry.

While these data indicate the magnitude of separation and divorce within society as a whole, it is the individuals themselves who must struggle with the private trauma that divorce brings them, their families, and their friends. For example, when a group of psychologists conducted a telephone survey of households in the Boulder, Colorado, area to determine the community's need for marriage and divorce counseling and for community intervention programs, they found that the likelihood of any married couple experiencing a separation was nearly 5 percent in one year (with the highest risk among the young), and that most separations, after lasting for about a year, ended in divorce. Since the separation period is known to be quite stressful, and the stress is manifested in many forms of disorders and diseases, the authors concluded that community services were sorely needed (Bloom et al., 1977).

The Typology of Singlehood

Before one can adequately research the topic of singlehood, one must have a way of categorizing the many types of singles. Table 1.2 presents a typology developed by the author in an attempt to group the heterogeneous population of singles according to the nature of their single state: voluntary/involuntary and stable/temporary. The use of these categories, of course, assumes that researchers will be able to determine the extent to which single people want to be or do not want to be single at a particular time, and the extent to which their single state is temporary or relatively stable. The typology provides a way of classifying different groups of single

TABLE 1.2   A Typology of Singlehood

	Voluntary	Involuntary
Temporary	Never married and formerly married who are postponing marriage by not actively seeking mates, but who are not opposed to the idea of marriage (ambivalents).*	Those who have been actively seeking mates for shorter or longer periods of time, but have not yet found mates; those who were not interested in marriage or remarriage for some period of time but are now actively seeking mates (wistfuls).*
Stable	Never marrieds and formerly marrieds who have chosen to be single; persons who for various reasons oppose the idea of marriage; religionaries (resolveds).*	Never marrieds and formerly marrieds who wanted to marry or remarry, have not found a mate, and have more or less accepted being single as a probable life state (regretfuls).*

*Terms developed by Shostak (in press).

adults and the extent of their probable commitment to a single life. Membership in these categories, of course, will change over time as a result of social influences and personal decisions.

Voluntary/Temporary Singles

Among those who have chosen to be single on a temporary basis are the younger never marrieds and the divorced who are postponing marriage or remarriage for some limited period of time. They remain open to the possibility of marriage, but the search for a mate has lower priority than other activities such as continued education, work, career, politics, and personal development. Also included in this category are men and women who live together in order to try out marriagelike arrangements. However, not all of the voluntary/temporary singles will marry "on time" since some will not find appropriate mates and others will marry at a later date than had been desired.

Voluntary/Stable Singles

Among those who have chosen to be single as a stable condition of life are those who have never married and are satisfied with that choice, those who have been married but do not want to remarry, cohabitors who do not intend to marry, and those whose lifestyles preclude the possibility of marriage (e.g., priests and nuns). Also included are single parents, both never marrieds and formerly marrieds, who are not seeking mates and who are raising their children alone or with the help of relatives and/or friends.

Involuntary/Temporary Singles

This category consists of singles who would like to be married and who expect to marry within some finite period of time. It also includes younger never marrieds who do not want to be single and who are actively seeking mates, as well as somewhat older men and women who were previously not interested in marriage but are now actively seeking mates. It includes the widowed and divorced seeking remarriage as well as single parents seeking mates. These are men and women who believe in marriage and who would like to be married.

Involuntary/Stable Singles

This category consists primarily of older divorced, widowed, and never-married people who wanted to marry or to remarry, have not found mates, and have come to accept being single as a probable ongoing life situation.

It is important to note that classifications within the typology will vary according to the stage of life occupied by the individual at any time. For example, as younger never marrieds who regarded singlehood as a voluntary state grow older, some marry. Others, unable to find an appropriate mate, remain single involuntarily and become increasingly concerned about the possibility that they may never find a mate. Still others may enjoy their single state and begin to see it as a stable rather than a temporary condition. One individual may identify singlehood as a voluntary/temporary status before marriage, then marry and divorce and become single again. This person may then be a voluntary/stable, involuntary/stable, or involuntary/temporary single, depending on his or her preference, opportunity, and resources.

This typology has been applied, tested, and critiqued by Elizabeth Higginbotham (1981, 1982) and Edward Kain (1981). Higginbotham (1982) suggests that singlehood for college-educated, single Black women results from "their commitment to upward mobility rather than a commitment to singlehood as an alternative life style." Higginbotham identified three groups: voluntary/temporary singles, voluntary/stable singles, and involuntary singles. She reports that a majority of the unmarried respondents say that they would prefer to be married, either with or without children, yet 30 percent of her sample, in response to a question on life plan preference, indicated a choice of career with an active, single social life. She reports that single Black women tend to develop peer support networks because "they as a group participate less in the leisure activities directed towards singles" (1982: 1).

Kain (1981), in a further refinement of the typology, suggests that the decision to postpone marriage may affect one's chance of marriage. For example, if "a young woman decides to pursue her education and delay marriage, the market of eligible partners who are of the 'correct' ages will be considerably smaller by the time she completes school . . . and if she plans to marry someone with more education . . . the field of eligibles will be even smaller" (1981: 1). Kain argues that what at first was a voluntary "decision" about delaying marriage may in turn become an involuntary choice to remain unmarried. Kain points out that there is a "complex causal structure of marital decisions and the unclear boundaries between voluntary and involuntary decisions must be kept in mind" (1981: 3).

Using a National Opinion Research Center sample of 6760 men and women over the age of 35, Kain tested the hypothesis that factors that increase the age at first marriage also increase the probability of remaining never married. Kain found that males, Catholics, Blacks, persons with more education, and those who lived in urban areas had higher rates of nonmarriage. Of the five dichotomous variables, the most important one in predicting nonmarriage is education (1981: 12).

Major Tasks Faced by Single Adults

Included among the major tasks faced by single adults are: achieving and maintaining friendships, intimacy, and fulfilling sexuality; maintaining emotional and physical well-being; making satisfactory living arrangements; seeking and finding productive work; becoming successful parents; and adjusting to aging. These issues are faced by all adults and they require decision making, the expenditure of physical and emotional energy, value and goal clarification, and resource allocation. The accomplishment of these tasks yields varying degrees of satisfaction, pleasure, discord, stress, and happiness. The discussion that follows is not meant to be exhaustive, but rather to highlight the major tasks and issues for single persons.

Friendship, Intimacy, and Sexuality

All humans need intimacy, yet the experiences of intimacy differ for single and married people, and among singles. Society today is undergoing a well-publicized revolution with regard to sexual attitudes and behaviors, and gender roles. One product of this is the growing acceptance of sexual relationships outside marriage, thus increasing the options available to single men and women (Libby, 1977).

Increased social and sexual availability presents both opportunities and problems. Personal enrichment, access to a variety of ideas and encounters, and the opportunity to select associates and activities consistent with one's own needs and goals are obvious advantages. Problems include limited access to the world of the married, the stress of juggling ever-shifting emotional commitments, the uncertainty of the commitment of others, and the lack of role clarity and social endorsement.

An important sexual outlet for singles, as well as for married people, is masturbation. Though there are no data regarding whether singles masturbate more or less than the general population, it can be assumed that its incidence is at least as high as the adult average, that is, 95 percent of men and 63 percent of women (Hunt, 1974).

Some single men and women choose celibacy (Brown, 1980), either as a long-term voluntary state, or as a temporary, perhaps difficult, state between relationships. Celibacy may be a religious requirement, may arise out of moral conviction, may be a means of conserving energy for creative endeavors, or may represent a flight from intimacy. The celibate person's degree of satisfaction with this lifestyle depends on the degree of motivation and on the freedom of choice.

Some singles have elected to be part of a new movement called the "New Celibacy." Its proponents argue that they are celibate by choice, not through default, often because of the disappointments, displeasures, and stresses of one-night stands. Some, such as Gabrielle Brown in *The New Celibacy* (1980), discuss the value of taking a vacation from sex. Critics argue that if celibate singles had a choice, they "would prefer a loving, sexual relationship with a partner" (Shostak, forthcoming). This debate will undoubtedly continue.

For many singles, sexual experimentation is a part of their single identity, enjoyed for itself or used as a stage leading to marriage or choice of a single sexual partner. Those who try a variety of relationships can learn much about the world and about themselves. They may avoid commitment in order to work on a career or on personal growth, or to recover from a painful past relationship. Some set up a hierarchy of relationships involving special obligations to a primary partner and lesser responsibilities to others. Personal enrichment is a possible benefit of this style of relationship, but the stress of managing conflicting commitments and a lack of clarity about one's role are potential problems (Clayton and Bokemeier, 1980).

There are two other sexual lifestyles that bear mention. Casual sexuality — whether heterosexual or homosexual — is more frequently practiced by single men than by single women. Many women find it difficult to be assertive enough to find a variety of partners, and women's commonly held ideas of love are more likely to be violated by this seeming promiscuity. "Relationship" sexuality is a more popular choice with women, whether as part of a monogamous or a sexual experimental lifestyle. A relationship is considered to be "leading somewhere" and sexual intercourse symbolizes a degree of caring between the partners (Laws and Schwartz, 1977).

Many singles believe that an individual cannot love more than one person at a time. Those who adhere to the Judeo-Christian ethic often prefer a monogomous relationship — a single sexual partner — even if it is without the obligations and daily responsibilities of marriage. As needs and desires change, these persons may move on to new partners, in a kind of serial monogamy.

Nonmarital cohabitation is a major source of intimacy for growing numbers of singles. Most cohabitors consider their relationship important, affectionate, supportive, and exclusive of other sexual involvements. Those who live together often claim to gain deeper self-understanding and emotional growth. Many homosexual as well as heterosexual couples choose cohabitation as a shorter- or longer-term alternative to marriage (Macklin, 1980).

Persons who elect a homosexual lifestyle often remain single because of legal constraints on gay marriage. Same-sex relationships may be just as diverse as heterosexual relationships. Some gay people prefer a permanent partner in a marriagelike arrangement, while others prefer living a single lifestyle. Public acceptance of homosexuality is an increasingly important issue for gays, as is active participation in the gay subculture. Political consciousness of the gay community is growing as are various gay and lesbian support systems (Vida, 1978; Levine, 1979).

Emotional and Physical Health

Historically, studies have shown that married people live longer than unmarrieds and that they use health care facilities less often. The complex cause-and-effect relationship between marital status and better health has been acknowledged, but more recent studies suggest that this relationship may no longer be as strong.

In a comprehensive review based on data from two national health surveys, Verbrugge (1979) writes that limiting chronic and work-disabling conditions are rather low for "noninstitutionalized single people." Among singles, the divorced and separated have the worst health status, followed by the widowed and the never married. Noninstitutionalized never marrieds "are the healthiest of all marital groups. . . . They take the least time off for health problems and have lowest utilization of physician and hospital services" (Verbrugge, 1979: 270). However, institutionalization rates for the never married are relatively high, and the total singles population is, in fact, less healthy than the total married population.

What happens to singles when they become ill? The lucky ones have a support group to which they can turn: family, neighbors, fellow communards, or roommates. Indeed, the crucial factor may not be marriage versus singlehood, but the strength of the support network. As the single state comes to be seen as less deviant, and more friends and groups become available to single adults, their general health and well-being should improve. Today, however, as single people grow older and their health deteriorates, they enter institutions more readily than do the married, having fewer opportunities for home care and fewer social responsibilities (Verbrugge, 1979).

A recent study of 400 single adults (Cargan and Melko, 1982) found no differences between marrieds and singles in terms of reported nightmares or crying spells, but did find that more singles worry and/or feel guilty, despondent, worthless, or lonely. However, it is the divorced that report feelings of despondency, worthlessness, sexual apathy, and loneliness more often than the never married. They note that if frequent contemplation of suicide is used as a measure, the figures are highest for the divorced (20 percent), followed by the never married (10 percent), and the married (7 percent).

In an important article examining the relationship between social class, marital status, life strains, and depression, Pearlin and Johnson (1981) reject the traditional interpretation that the poorer physical and mental health of singles reflects the unmet inner needs and emotional frustrations of never-married and formerly married people. Rather, this study examines the consequences of economic hardship, social isolation, and obligations of parents. These are three basic conditions of life to which unmarried people are both more exposed and more vulnerable. However, Pearlin and Johnson find that the greater life hardships of the unmarried only partly explain their greater incidence of depression. Even when hardships of married and unmarried persons are equally severe, the effects of these hardships are more devastating among the unmarried. "The combination most productive of psychological distress is to be simultaneously single, isolated, exposed to burdensome parental obligations, and most serious of all, poor." To what extent does marriage help fend off the psychological assaults of economic and social problems? Is its protective function the reason for the continued survival of marriage as an institution?

Living Arrangements

Among the important decisions single men and women face is where to live. This involves not only such fundamental matters as one's financial resources and the availability of housing, but also such questions as with whom to live, for what period of time, and what these decisions say to the world about oneself. Living arrangements are a central issue of single life, since each alternative involves many possibilities and limitations.

Shostak (forthcoming: 25) cites a recent MIT-Harvard Joint Center for Urban Studies report indicating that in the 1980s "only 50 percent of households will be headed by married couples compared with 80 percent in 1950. People will spend more years living alone or with roommates or partners. They will increasingly delay marriage, divorce more, remarry more slowly."

A single person may live alone, with friends or family, as head of a household, or as part of an unmarried couple. He or she may choose a commune, a single-family home, an apartment, or a dormitory. The most common trends in living arrangements for singles are the following.

Living Alone

In 1980 there were 17.8 million people living alone, an increase of 61 percent from the 10.9 million of 1970. Over those years the number of single residences maintained by persons under the age of 35 more than tripled, from 1.4 million to 4.8 million. A majority of these men and women are living in urban areas. New York City, Chicago, Los Angeles, Houston, and San Francisco are the most prominent. In each of these cities, and in others, there are areas that are occupied primarily by single adults living alone. But the greatest number of people living alone are not younger singles. Persons over the age of 45 constitute 65 percent of all those living alone, the largest group of which is elderly widows. Of all women living alone, more than half are widows over the age of 65.

While ideally single adults might choose living arrangements that reflect their needs and values, it is more likely that their household situations will reflect their economic status. For example, census data show that in 1977 the median income of women living alone was $3412, which means that half of these women actually received less than that figure. Since "housing choices will be somewhat limited, even for those with incomes up to $8000 . . . the wonder is not that so few aged parents share a home with an adult child, but that so many do not" (Hess and Markson, 1980).

Heading Households

About six out of ten single adult households are headed by single women. The number of single-parent households headed by women is now about 8.2 million, or 10.6 percent of the population, while only 1.6 million, or 2.1 percent of the population, are headed by men in the absence of a woman.

Cohabiting

Cohabitation is defined as a "more or less permanent relationship in which two unmarried persons of the opposite sex share a living facility without legal contract" (Cole, 1977: 67). Cohabitation has been around for a long time, but has become increasingly popular in the last ten years (Macklin, 1978, 1980). In 1980, some 3.2 percent of all "couple households" were unmarried men and women living together. In 1980 there were 1.56 million unmarried couples living together — three times as many as in 1970, when there were 523,000. Unmarried couples with no children represent about three-fourths of all unmarried couples. Some 63 percent of all unmarried couples were composed of two adults under the ages of 35. In 20 percent of all households, both partners were under age 25.

Why are so many singles choosing to live together as unmarried couples? The following factors are influential:

(1) financial considerations such as the higher cost of living alone;

(2) housing shortages in urban areas;

(3) greater social tolerance of alternative living arrangements;

(4) greater tolerance and support for cohabitation among undergraduates and graduate students and among postcollege adults;

(5) greater acceptance of premarital sex;

(6) changing gender role definitions; and

(7) the sheer force of greater numbers of singles.

Paul Glick and Graham Spanier (1981) used data from the U.S. Bureau of the Census to estimate the prevalence of cohabitation in the United States. "Rarely does social change occur with such rapidity," they write. "Indeed, there have been few developments relating to marriage and family life which have been as dramatic as the rapid increase in unmarried cohabitation" (1981: 65). They mention the trend toward smaller families and the increase in age at which women begin childbearing as contributing to this phenomenon. They report that unmarried cohabitation is more common in large cities, more common among Blacks than among Whites, and most likely to end for any given couple within two years.

Work, Careers, and Occupations

Income and wealth derived from paid work is, for most of us, a central resource. Society places a high value on what we do for a living; so do the people we meet; so do we ourselves. Work provides the means for obtaining the goods and pursuing the activities that are the essence of the single lifestyle. Marketing experts recognize the impact of singles' consumption patterns in the marketplace and they create product lines and selling strategies to lure singles' dollars. From townhouses to sports cars, from tape decks to vacations in Mexico, goods are created and singles work to obtain the money to enjoy them.

Beyond the marketplace, work provides a crucial source of identity. Power, prestige, and privilege all flow from occupational involvement, as does a sense of self-worth. Single people are far more likely to place their career goals above interest in family. Some devote longer hours to work than their married colleagues, and many feel that they receive significant emotional support from their co-workers (Stein, 1976).

Though single women and men can make superior employees, some continue to receive lower wages than married colleagues and are sometimes passed over for promotion on the basis of their single status. A survey of fifty major corporations found that in 80 percent of the responding companies, the official corporate position was that marriage was not essential to upward mobility within the corporation. However, in a majority of these same companies, only 2 percent of their executives, including junior management levels, were single. Over 60 percent of the replies stated that single executives tend to make snap judgments, and 25 percent said that singles are "less stable" than married people (Jacoby, 1974). Discrimination may range from overt cases to more subtle ones involving the complex networks that exist in every institution: business-related friendships, luncheon conversations, and other informal contacts that affect job retention and promotion. Since race, sex, ethnic origin, and religion are also bases for discrimination, discrimination based on single-ness is often difficult to isolate. Whatever its cause, such discrimination victimizes many men and women who hope to get ahead in their work, or hope just to get by.

The marital status and the socioeconomic status of women and their families are particularly influential in determining choices of occupation. Natalie Sokoloff's 1981 study of woman college graduates showed that single and married women differed in their early career activities and in their occupational choices. The differences in career activities were due less to marital status than to socioeconomic status. Some of Sokoloff's findings were:

(1) Almost all single women from all socioeconomic classes were employed, and 25 percent were involved in postbachelor's studies.

(2) Married women were less likely to be employed or in school three years after graduation from college.

(3) A larger percentage of women from lower socioeconomic status families remained single three years after graduation. This was true even when the women had children.

(4) The largest percentage of single and married women were employed in professions traditionally considered "female."

For many women, obtaining a good education and entering a profession take priority over marrying and establishing a family, at least for a period of time. This is true of Black and White women from lower-middle-class families. Higginbotham's studies (1981, 1982) of middle- and lower-middle-class Black, college-educated women compared the relevant emphasis placed on marriage by the two groups. The upwardly mobile women from lower-middle-class backgrounds had parents who did not see future marriage prospects as assuring the desired mobility for their daughters. They therefore focused on educational success to the exclusion of other goals, including marriage. On the other hand, women from Black middle-class homes were expected to integrate careers with family life.

The problem of successfully integrating personal and professional life is compounded for many gay men. Keeping one's job often means hiding one's homosexuality. How this is accomplished, what happens when one is found out, and the extent of discrimination against gays throughout the working world are the focus of Martin Levine's "Employment Discrimination Against Gay Men" (1981). Public opinion polls report strong support for barring gays from high-status occupations; application forms are constructed to weed out gays; there is discriminiation even in government licensing and security clearances. The struggle to conceal their sexual orientation from co-workers often leaves gay people feeling alienated and anxious, and if they fail to conceal it, the situation can be worse. Many companies enforce a policy of firing gays upon discovery. Others keep employees at a low level or transfer them to a "more suitable" job.

Parenting

Single parents may be separated, divorced, or widowed, or may never have been married at all. They tend to be older than most singles and their social lives are shaped by the daily responsibilities of child care. They may be independent and self-sufficient, but most are overburdened and financially strained (Benjamin, 1981).

There were 5.7 million one-parent families in 1978, an increase of 9 percent over 1977. More than 90 percent of these families are maintained by women. In 1980, 11.1 million children were living with their mothers alone, while about 1 million were living with their fathers alone. Overall, 19.7 percent of all children under 18 were living in one-parent families (U.S. Bureau of the Census, 1981).

Single parents experience three major worries: loneliness, children, and money. Their problems evolve over time. The first months after the breakup of a marriage are the most traumatic. The newly divorced person must deal with disputes over child support and custody as well as personal problems of depression, self-doubt, desire for revenge, and the need for new emotional involvements. Then come financial worries (Weiss, 1979). The median income in two-parent families is two to three times that of one-parent families. The economic hardships faced by single parents reflect the lower wages paid all women, particularly minority women, who make up 35 percent of all single mothers. Less than 30 percent of families headed by women report incomes as high as $10,000, compared with 70 percent of two-parent families. These single parents need skilled child care, part-time jobs with benefits, and easily available health care facilities (Stein, 1981).

The difficulties of providing for their own and their children's physical, social, and emotional needs often result in role overload and fatigue. It is difficult to develop and maintain a satisfying social/sexual life. Nonparents often consider single parents, with their attached responsibilities, less than "marriageable." Many single parents are reluctant to expose their children to dates who spend the night, and getting away for weekends or vacations requires child care arrangements. Not surprisingly, single mothers are somewhat less likely to remarry than other single women (Duberman, 1975).

How do women heading families feel about their situations? "Rarely is the concept put forward that the female-headed family is an acceptable family form or that, once divorced, it is all right for a mother to stay divorced," report Kohen, Brown and Feldberg (1981: 288). But presumptions in favor of the male-headed family have begun to be questioned as the advantages of singlehood emerge. When a couple divorces, the woman not only loses most of her right to the man's resources, but she also loses her personal dependence and obligations of service. For some women, the experience of heading a family may be more rewarding than were their marriages.

Rosenthal and Keshet (1981) found that young single fathers experience role conflicts between work and child care similar to conflicts experienced by single mothers. Moreover, full-time and half-time fathers averaged considerably less income than did men in intact marriages. Yet at home, men who learned to meet children's practical daily needs began to feel better about themselves and their relationship with their children. Bringing the criteria of work performance to the parenting role made them more at ease with their new obligations.

Aging

Only 12 percent of the 11 million single persons over the age of 65 have never married; 3 percent are separated, 77 percent widowed, and 7 percent divorced. There are dramatic differences in the statistics for men and women. Most notably, 75 percent of men over the age of 65 are married and 14 percent are widowed, while only 37 percent of the women in this age group are married and 52 percent are widowed. The number of older never-married people is significant and their characteristics are varied.

What do we know about singles and aging? One of the few analyses done on the elderly never married tells us that they are not especially lonely in old age. They are similar to the married elderly in that both groups are more positive in outlook than the divorced or widowed elderly. Moreover, having never been married means that one avoids the desolation of bereavement following the death of one's spouse (Gubrium, 1975). A study of older women points out that the never marrieds had the best physical and psychological health and were the best able to cope in terms of facing up to problems and taking action. Experience with living alone appears to increase independence and autonomy and to have some beneficial effects for coping effectively (Wood, 1979).

Black Singles

While most studies of the never married have focused on Whites, studies of Black singles are increasing. *The World of Black Singles* (Staples, 1981), a comprehensive study of 500 Black, urban, college-educated singles between the ages of 25 and 45, examines the complex worlds of middle-class, single Blacks. The importance of studying this population is dramatized by the fact that singles constitute a substantial portion of the Black adult population, and if current trends continue, by the year 2000 a majority of Black adults will be unmarried.

Middle-class, single Blacks tend to have difficulty establishing a satisfactory social life. Staples (1981) notes that changes in residence patterns have increased the isolation of Black middle-class singles from each other. Black singles tend to live in predominately White areas and thus do without facilities that might cater to their special needs. There is a lack of settings where they can meet one another. Blacks, unlike White singles, are less frequent visitors to singles bars, most of which cater to Whites. The large cities offer bars that are frequented by both Blacks and Whites, but these are almost exclusively used by Black men and White women. There are few Black organizations where singles are likely to meet, few formal dating services, single organizations, or newspaper and magazine ads. Work settings, a major place for single, middle-class Whites to meet persons of the opposite sex (Starr and Carns, 1972), do not serve the same function for Blacks.

Staples (1981) notes that "most Blacks do not see their singleness as a viable choice but as a condition forced upon them by certain vicissitudes of life in America." He indicates that basic reasons for the increase in singleness are the dramatic shortage of eligible men for middle-class Black women as well as tension and conflict found in male-female relationships, reflecting perceived differences in values, interests, and goals. Unlike White women, among whom the percentage of never marrieds drops dramatically in the 25-29 and 30-34 age brackets, Black women remain unmarried for longer periods of time (see Table 1.3). In both of these age categories, the percentage of Black women who have never married is double that for White women.

The research of both Staples (1981) and Higginbotham (1981, 1982) reminds us of the importance of examining sociohistorical factors when seeking to understand singlehood. Higginbotham concludes that "the particular cities in which women live, occupations and other structural factors might be as influential as history of interpersonal relationships in shaping the course single women pursue" (1982: 32).

Coping Styles of Never-Married Adults

Margaret Adams (1976), in a pioneering study of single women who had made successful life adjustments, cited three major factors responsible for making singleness a viable lifestyle for them: economic independence, social and psychological autonomy, and a clear intent to remain single by choice.

In his summary of the literature, Shostak (forthcoming) identifies six major coping mechanisms employed by singles. Three are traditional coping mechanisms for singles: permissive social attitudes, same-sex friendships, and marriage-deriding attitudes. The three more recent coping mechanisms are: assertive social attitudes, dating support systems, and prosinglehood options.

TABLE 1.3   Percentage of Never-Married Black and White Men and Women, by Age, 1980

	18-19	20-24	25-29	30-34	35-44	45-64	Over 65
Single Men							
Black	97.7	79.0	42.7	26.7	14.4	9.6	5.7
White	93.6	66.9	31.1	14.6	6.5	5.7	4.8
Single Women							
Black	90.9	68.7	37.2	19.0	10.5	6.7	4.6
White	81.5	47.2	18.3	8.2	4.8	4.4	6.2

SOURCE: U.S. Bureau of the Census. Marital Status and Living Arrangements: March, 1980. *Current Population Reports,* Series P-20, No. 365. Washington, DC: Government Printing Office, 1981, Table 1.

Citing a 1976-1977 Harris poll for *Playboy* of 684 never-married men, Shostak reports that "about twice as large a proportion of the never-married as the married males were designated 'innovators,' the most liberal of the four possibilities,[1] and less than half as many singles as married men were labeled conservative 'traditionalists' " (forthcoming: 19).

Single women have similar liberal attitudinal profiles, according to the 1980 Virginia Slims Poll. Though cautious about the incomplete data, Shostak indicates that single women and men "stand out . . . in their comparative permissiveness, liberality and acceptance of change" (forthcoming: 19).

Singles stress the importance of close, caring friendships, based on free choice and developing into a sense of mutuality. Stein (1976) interviewed sixty single men and women between the ages of 25 and 45, mostly college graduates employed and living in New York and Boston. In their departure from traditional family structures, they expressed a strong need for substitute networks of human relationships that provide the basic satisfactions of intimacy, sharing, and continuity.

Intimacy for these women and men came from both opposite or same-sex friendships. Groups of friends, formal or informal, are especially well suited to meeting the needs of single people, helping them to deal with life choices and to pursue personal growth. For many of the single people interviewed, friendships meant survival.

Marriage-deriding attitudes may be used to justify the unwed state. Some take a very critical stance with reference to marriage, feeling that "it is better to be single than caught in an unfulfilling marriage." There is a need among singles to develop a consistent and supportive world view.

Assertive social attitudes are apparent in the emergent ideology of positive singlehood, which is now documented in a number of magazines, journals, seminars, and the like. The positive aspects of singlehood are stressed in such titles as "Living Alone and Liking It," "Single Can Be Fun," and so on. The traditional appeal of marriage as a conveyor of respectability has been considerably weakened by the recent liberalizing of our social norms, and having children is no longer considered necessary for either full adulthood or for a full and happy marriage relationship (Burnley and Kurth, 1981: Cheung, 1982: Greenwood, 1978).

Dating support runs the gamut from singles' magazines and clubs catering to singles, to computer dating services, singles' bars, and vacation resorts. More formal structures are also emerging to provide intimacy and continuity among adults. They frequently take the form of group living arrangements, one type of "experimental family" (Cogswell and Sussman, 1972). While communal homes might include the socialization of children, they also focus on the needs for identity, intimacy, and interaction of adult members. Other structures include women's and men's groups, therapy and encounter groups, and organizations formed around specialized interests. Although not restricted to singles, they are particularly well adapted to meeting the needs of single people and were cited by the singles interviewed as examples of positive experiences in their lives (Stein, 1976). Such group interactions foster friendships and spur personal growth by providing a supportive context.

Shostak indicates the need to alter certain public policies that affect singles. "Nonmarried Americans need a fair hearing and positive changes in their roles as learners, as citizens, as renters, as cohabitors, as parents, as purchasers of 'singles only' services, and especially as the subjects of social science research" (forthcoming: 38). Shostak echoes the need for further research (see also Stein, 1978). For example:

(1) What are the similarities and differences between voluntary and involuntary, temporary and stable singles (Shostak's ambivalents, wistfuls, resolveds, and regretfuls)?

(2) How do women and men make decisions regarding preferred marital status and how committed are they to these choices?

(3) To what extent are people "embedded" in their present married or single state?

(4) How do singles opt for transitory versus long-term single life?

(5) How does the experience of singlehood differ for men and women?

(6) How do gender differences coupled with age intersect with work experiences, life arrangements, and social supports?

(7) How much variation is there in the singlehood experiences of different ethnic, religious, and racial groups?

(8) To what extent do existing social support systems provide help for singles, and what new forms of support are still needed?

(9) What kinds of adults cope well and enjoy the single experience and who are those who are discontent? What social and psychological factors seem to account for these similarities and differences?

(10) Have the stereotypes of single life changed to reflect its heterogeneity?

(11) What are the work and career experiences of today's singles?

A crucial need also exists for a systematic comparison of cohorts of nonmarried and married men and women based on both aggregate and individual data that would lead to the development of concepts, typologies, and theories. Testable hypotheses must be generated and existing statistics need to be replicated. Interested social scientists will find many research opportunities; social practitioners and those concerned with social policy will find much to consider.

Conclusion

Singles are an important segment of the adult population. Their interests, their activities, and their lifestyles are often in the forefront of social trends. Singles take risks; they experiment; they consume; they set trends. Any one of us may some day belong to the singles population, if we are not now single. Statistics show that about one-third of young adults currently marrying will divorce; three out of four married women will become widows; many people will live together without marriage. There are many styles of adulthood in our society. Different people may choose different styles, or one person may adopt various styles in the course of a lifetime.

Although personal statements provide us with insight into single experiences, little has been done to provide a systematic examination of singlehood. Singles have often been regarded as a somewhat deviant group, different from "normal" married adults, and until very recently they have been avoided as a subject of serious research. Recognition of the variations that exist within the singles population, and of the goals and concerns they hold in common with other people, such as meaningful work, friendship, financial security, health care, a comfortable and secure home, and self-esteem, is a result of recent research on this lifestyle. The interested researcher and practitioner will find many opportunities to do creative and constructive work.

Note

1. The other three categories were traditionalist, conventional, and contemporary.

References

ADAMS, M. (1976) Single Blessedness. New York: Basic Books.

BENJAMIN, E. (1981) "It's not easy being single after years of marriage: the social world of separated and divorced parents." Presented at the Annual Meetings of SSSP.

BLOOM, B., W. HODGES, R. CALDWELL, L. SYSTRA, and A. CEDRONE (1977) "Marital separation: a community survey." Journal of Divorce 1 (Fall): 7-19.

BROWN, G. (1980) The New Celibacy. New York: McGraw-Hill.

BURNLEY, C. and S. KURTH (1981) "Never married women's perceptions of adult life transitions." Presented at the Annual Meetings of the SSSP.

CARGAN, L. and M. MELKO (1982) Singles. Beverly Hills, CA: Sage.

CHEUNG, L. M. (1982) "Single Chinese-American women." Presented at the Annual Meetings of the Eastern Sociological Society.

CLAYTON, R. R. and J. L. BOKEMEIER (1980) "Premarital sex in the seventies." Journal of Marriage and the Family 42 (November): 759-775.

COGSWELL, B. and M. SUSSMAN (1972) "Changing family and marriage forms." Family Coordinator 21 (September): 505-516.

COLE, C. L. (1977) "Cohabitation in social context," pp. 62-79 in R. Libby and R. Whitehurst (eds.) Marriage and Alernatives. Glenview, IL: Scott, Foresman.

DUBERMAN, L. (1975) The Reconstituted Family. Chicago: Nelson-Hall.

GLICK, P. C. (1979) "Future Americans." Washington COFO Memo 2 (Summer/Fall): 2-5.

——— and G. SPANIER (1981) "Cohabitation in the U.S.," pp. 194-209 in P. J. Stein (ed.) Single Life: Unmarried Adults in Social Context. New York: St. Martin's.

GREENWOOD, N. A. (1978) "Safely single or wisely wed? A sociological analysis of singleness as a positive lifestyle." Master's thesis, California State University, Sacramento.

GUBRIUM, J. F. (1975) "Being single in old age." International Journal of Aging and Human Development 6 (Fall): 29-41.

HESS, B. and E. MARKSON (1980) Aging and Old Age. New York: Macmillan.

HIGGINBOTHAN, E. (1982) "Educated single Black women: marital options and limits." (unpublished).

——— (1981) "Is marriage a priority? Class differences in marital options of educated black women," pp. 259-267 in P. J. Stein (ed.) Single Life: Unmarried Adults in Social Context. New York: St. Martin's.

HUNT, M. (1974) Sexual Behavior in the 1970s. Chicago: Playboy.

JACOBY, S. (1974) "49 million singles can't all be right." New York Times Magazine (February 17): 41-49.

KAIN, E. (1981) "Social determinants of the decision to remain never-married." (unpublished)

KOHEN, J., C. BROWN, and R. FELDBERG (1981) "Divorced mothers," pp. 288-305 in P. J. Stein (ed.) Single Life: Unmarried Adults in Social Context. New York: St. Martin's.

LAWS, J. L. and P. SCHWARTZ (1977) Sexual Scripts: The Social Construction of Female Sexuality. Hinsdale, IL: Dryden.

LEVINE, M. (1981) "Employment discrimination against gay men," pp. 268-273 in P. J. Stein (ed.) Single Life: Unmarried Adults in Social Context. New York: St. Martin's.

——— [ed.] (1979) Gay Men: The Sociology of Male Homosexuality. New York: Harper & Row.

LIBBY, R. (1977) "Creative singlehood as a sexual lifestyle: beyond marriage as a rite of passage," pp. 37-61 in R. W. Libby and R. N. Whitehurst (eds.) Marriage and Alternatives. Glenview, IL: Scott, Foresman,

MACKLIN, E. D. (1980) "Nontraditional family forms: a decade of research." Journal of Marriage and the Family 42 (November): 905-922.

——— (1978) "Nonmarital heterosexual cohabitation." Marriage and Family Review 1 (March/April): 1-12.

PEARLIN, L. I. and J. S. JOHNSON (1981) "Marital status, life strains, and depression," pp. 165-178 in P. J. Stein (ed.) Single Life: Unmarried Adults in Social Context. New York: St. Martin's.

ROSENTHAL, K. and H. KESHET (1981) "Childcare responsibilities of part-time and single fathers," pp. 306-324 in P. J. Stein (ed.) Single Life: Unmarried Adults in Social Context. New York: St. Martin's.

SHOSTAK, A. (forthcoming) "Singlehood: the lives of never-married employed Americans," in M. Sussman and S. Steinmetz (eds.) Handbook on Marriage and the Family. New York: Plenum.

SOKOLOFF, N. (1981) "Early work patterns of single and married women," pp. 238-259 in P.J. Stein (ed.) Single Life: Unmarried Adults in Social context. New York: St. Martin's.

STAPLES, R. (1981) The World of Black Singles. Westport, CT: Greenwood.

STARR, J. and D. CARNS (1972) "Singles in the city." Society 9 (October): 43-48.

STEIN P.J. [ed.] (1981) Single Life: Unmarried Adults in Social Context. New York: St. Martin's.

——— (1976) Single. Englewood Cliffs, NJ: Prentice-Hall.

U.S. Bureau of the Census (1981) Marital Status and Living Arrangements: March 1980. Current Population Reports, Series P-20, No. 365. Washington, DC: Government Printing Office.

VERBRUGGE, L. (1979) "Marital status and health." Journal of Marriage and the Family 41 (May): 267-285.

VIDA, V. [ed.] (1978) Our Right to Love: A Lesbian Resource Book. Englewood Cliffs, NJ: Prentice-Hall.

WEISS, R. (1979) Going It Alone. New York: Basic Books.

——— (1975) Marital Separation. New York: Basic Books.

WOOD, V. (1979) "Singles and aging." Presented to the Annual Meetings of the National Council on Family Relations.

CHAPTER 2

Nonmarital Heterosexual Cohabitation: An Overview

ELEANOR D. MACKLIN

Syracuse University

Prevalence

The 1970s saw a dramatic increase in the number of couples living together unmarried (see Table 2.1). The U.S. Bureau of the Census (1981: 5, Table F) reported that as of March 1980 there were 1,560,000 unmarried couple households (i.e., "households occupied by two unrelated adults of the opposite sex, with and without the presence of children under 15 years of age"), three times the number reported in 1970 (523,000). Although census figures (1979) show that unmarried couples represent only about 3 percent of all households at any give time, "currently cohabiting" figures tend to be much lower than "ever cohabited" figures, and numbers of other persons from this population are likely to have previously lived with or will live with someone to whom they are not married. It is increasingly clear that we are dealing with a living arrangement that affects a significant portion of the population (see also Newcomb, 1979). Comments by Glick and Spanier (1980: 20), after a review of census data, are indicative:

> Rarely does social change occur with such rapidity. Indeed there have been few developments relating to marriage and family life which have been as dramatic as the rapid increase in unmarried cohabitation.

Unmarried couples include persons of all ages (U.S. Bureau of the Census, 1981: 5, Table G), with the majority under 35 years of age and the men somewhat older than the women. In 1981, 38 percent of the women and 25 percent of the men were under 25, 36 percent of the women and 41

Author's Note: The term "cohabitation" will be used throughout this chapter in reference to unmarried couples living together unless otherwise noted.

TABLE 2.1   Trends in Unmarried Heterosexual Cohabitation in the United States, 1960-1980

Date	Number of Unmarried Couples of Opposite Sex Living Together		Percentage of All Households	Ratio to 1970
1980	1,560,000[a]			2.98[a]
	children present	424,000		2.16
	no children present	1,136,000		3.47
1979	1,346,000[b]			2.57[b]
	children present	360,000		1.84
	no children present	985,000		3.01
1978	1,137,000[e]			
	children present	272,000		
	no children present	865,000	3.1[c]	
1977	957,000[b]			
	children present	204,000		
	no children present	754,000		
1976	no children present[d]	660,000		
1975	886,000[e]			
	children present			
	no children present		2.3[c]	
1970	523,000[c]			
	children present	196,000		
	no children present	327,000	1.7[c]	
1960	no children present[d]	242,000	1.6[c]	

a. U.S. Bureau of the Census, 1981: 5.
b. U.S. Bureau of the Census, 1980: 4.
c. U.S. Bureau of the Census, 1979: 1.
d. U.S. Bureau of the Census, 1977: 4-5.
e. Glick and Spanier, 1980: 20-21.

NOTE: 1980 and 1981 editions of the above Census reports referred to " 'unmarried-couple' households," i.e., "households occupied by two unrelated adults of the opposite sex with or without the presence of children under 15 years of age"; 1979 edition referred to "other nonfamily households," i.e., households occupied by "two or more persons including no one related to the persons maintaining the household" (included companions, partners, or roommates); 1977 edition referred to "two-person households in which the household head shared the living quarters with an unrelated adult of the opposite sex" (included partners, resident employees, and roomers).

percent of the men were aged 25 to 34, 20 percent of the women and 28 percent of the men were aged 35 to 64, and 6 percent of both sexes were 65 years or older. One in every five households of unmarried couples included two partners under 25 years of age. Unmarried couples can be roughly divided into three categories (extrapolated from U.S. Bureau of the Census, 1981: 45-46, Table 7): those composed of two never-married persons (37 percent), those composed of one never-married and one currently or previously married person (31 percent), and those composed of two persons currently or previously married to others (32 percent). In 1981, about 50 percent of both men and women had not been previously married. About one-quarter of the households (27 percent) included one or more children under 15 years of age; it is not known how many others included children who visited periodically.

It is interesting to compare the above statistics with those from other countries. The following information is taken from Trost, (1979, 1981): In *Iceland* in 1971, it was estimated that two-thirds of all persons marrying had lived together before marriage. In *Norway* in 1973, almost 3 percent of couples living together were unmarried, and in 1977, 5 percent of women aged 18 to 44 were living with a man without being legally married to him. In *Finland* in 1971, 3 percent of all cohabiting couples in the 18 to 54 age bracket were unmarried; the rate varied greatly with age, and in 1978, was 33 percent for those aged 15 to 24 and 8 percent for those aged 25 to 44, with few over 45. In *Denmark* in 1977, 10 percent of all cohabiting couples were unmarried; of those 20 to 24 years old, 57 percent were cohabiting without marriage in 1977 compared to 46 percent in 1974. In *Sweden* in 1975, 11 percent of all couples cohabiting were unmarried (it is estimated that this figure increased to 19 or 20 percent in 1980), more than half of the cohabitants aged 20 to 24 were unmarried, and all those persons married and younger than 30 had cohabited prior to marriage. In 1977 in *The Netherlands,* 7 percent of all cohabiting couples were unmarried (Straver, 1981), and in *France,* 44 percent of a sample of 18- to 29-year-olds who married in 1976-1977 had cohabited prior to marriage (Trost, 1979: 34).

The trend toward nonmarital cohabitation has been accompanied by decreasing marriage rates in the above countries (e.g., the marriage rate decreased 25 to 30 percent in Finland from 1970 to 1977, corresponding with the increase in unmarried cohabitation). The rate of children born to unmarried mothers has simultaneously increased (e.g., from 1900 to 1965, the rate in Sweden was relatively stable at 10 to 15 percent, while in 1979, 38 percent of all children born in Sweden were born to unmarried mothers.) Increasingly, the pattern in Sweden is for couples to marry *after* having children. "Instead of being a rite de passage, the marriage ceremony seems to be a rite de confirmation, confirmation of being a unit, a family, with a relatively high degree of stability" (Trost, 1981: 415).

Living patterns have changed somewhat more slowly in the United States than in northern Europe. When making comparisons, one must adjust for the facts that European figures for unmarried cohabiting couples are usually reported as percentages of all cohabiting couples, whereas U.S. figures are usually percentages of all households, and that European figures sometimes include homosexual as well as heterosexual couples, whereas recent U.S. reports have made an effort to differentiate. However, it is clear that the United States is only now at the point where Scandinavia was in the early 1970s. Whether the gap will ever close is not known. It seems unlikely that it will do so in the near future, given our conservative religious heritage and the continuing emphasis placed on marriage in this country, both as a symbol of commitment and as a basis for legal and economic decisions.

Living together without marriage is obviously not a new phenomenon. Nonlegal marital unions and common-law marriages have long been accepted in many cultures, particularly among low-income persons (see, for example, Rodman, 1966, for a discussion of the "value-stretch" that can occur when environmental circumstances make it difficult to live by dominant cultural values). What is new is the increasing prevalence of nonmarital cohabitation among the middle class, the fact that many of the participants (at least in this country) do not consider themselves married, and the increasing acceptance of this living pattern by the majority culture. Although the concepts of trial or two-stage marriage were a topic of debate as early as the late 1920s (see Lindsey and Evans, 1927/1929; Mead, 1966, 1968; Russell, 1929), it has only been in the last ten years that there has been any serious popular consideration given to them. The years 1966-1975 appear to have been watershed years in U.S. culture with regard to sexual values and associated lifestyles. Prior to this time, only the most avant garde or the most impoverished, or those otherwise considered to be on the social periphery of society, were to be found openly cohabiting outside of marriage, and unmarried persons known to be living together could expect to be referred to derogatorily as "shacking up."

The first hints of change came in the late sixties via the popular media (Newsweek, 1966; Esquire, 1967; Grant, 1968; McWhirter, 1968; Schrag, 1968; Time, 1968; Block, 1969; Karlen, 1969; Sheehy, 1969), a series of published interviews with cohabiting college students (Ald, 1969), and two professional papers delivered by Whitehurst (1969a, 1969b). It was in college towns that increasing cohabitation was first noted and here that the first research was done — a master's thesis at the University of Iowa, based on 28 cohabiting couples (Johnson, 1968). Suddenly, sociologists on campuses all over the country were noting the growing tendency for student couples to be living together (e.g., Arafat and Yorburg, 1973; Bower and Christopherson, 1977; Clatworthy, 1975; Henze and Hudson, 1974; Huang, 1976; Macklin, 1972b, 1976; Peterman et al., 1974; Thorman, 1973). Nonmarital cohabitation became the new "hot" topic for graduate theses and dissertations (among the early ones were: Bower, 1975; Budd, 1976; Danziger, 1976; Ganson, 1975; Gavin, 1973, Kieffer, 1972; Lautenschlager, 1972; McCauley, 1977; Olday, 1977, Petty, 1975; Polansky, 1974; Segrest, 1975; Steiner, 1975; Stevens, 1975, and Storm, 1973).

In 1972, the first professional articles were published (Lyness, Lipetz, and Davis, 1972; Macklin, 1972b), and the first issue of the *Cohabitation Research Newsletter* appeared (Macklin, 1972a). At the 1973 meetings of the Groves Conference on Marriage and the Family, a special invited workshop of researchers on nonmarital cohabitation was held, to coordinate research efforts and to stimulate study in this pioneer area. Society soon found that it had to take note of the growing trend, and the topic appeared frequently on the 1970s agendas of professional meetings of student personnel administrators, clergy, bankers, physicians, counselors and therapists, lawyers, and others whose work required that they respond intelligently to the changing patterns (see, for example, Mace and Mace, 1981).

By 1978, evidence from accumulated surveys at large university settings suggested that about one-quarter of current U.S. undergraduates, taking the country as a whole, had had a cohabitation experience, with the percentage on any given campus varying with whether the campus was coed and with its particular norms and regulations (Macklin, 1978a). Surveys of systematic samples found, for instance, that 29 percent of the males and 18 percent of the females at Arizona State (Henze and Hudson, 1974), 33 percent of the males and 32 percent of the females at Penn State (Peterman et al.,1974), and 31 percent of the combined sophomores and seniors at Cornell (Macklin, 1976) had cohabited at least once, with definitions of cohabitation varying somewhat from study to study. Interviews in 1974-1975 with a national sample of 2510 20- to 30-year-old men who had registered for the Selective Service in 1962-1972 revealed that 18 percent had lived nonmaritally with a woman for a period of six months or more, with 5 percent still doing so at the time of the survey (Clayton and Voss, 1977), indicating that the pattern was also evolving among noncollege samples.

Further evidence of the prevalence of cohabitation comes from various studies of couples. Yllo (1978), in a review of data collected from a 1976 national area-probability sample of 2500 adults living with a member of the opposite sex, found that 1.9 percent of the couples were unmarried, a figure comparable to the estimated 1.8 percent based on census data at that time (Glick and Spanier, 1980). Risman and colleagues (1981), in a 1972 study of college dating relationships, found on initial interview that 17 percent of their 231 couples were cohabiting "most or all of the time." In a 1974-1975 study of married students at a southern university, 65 percent of the 84 respondents reported having had at least one cohabitation experience prior to marriage, and about half of these reported that they had cohabited more than once (Jacques and Chason, 1979). In a sample of 159 recently married couples in Los Angeles (Newcomb and Bentler, 1980b), 47 percent reported having lived together for some time before their marriage (35 percent for three months or more).

Attitudes

Research on attitudes has shown that students, in general, approve of nonmarital cohabitation. Almost 80 percent of respondents in a large survey at City College of New York in the early 1970s said that they would live with someone of the opposite sex if given the opportunity to do so (Arafat and Yorburg, 1973). Almost 60 percent of the men and 35 percent of the women who had not cohabited at Arizona State answered "yes" when asked if they would want to (Henze and Hudson, 1974). In a 1975 survey of sixteen state universities, more than 50 percent of those who had not cohabited said they would consider doing so (Bower and Christopherson, 1977). In a systematic sample of sophomores and seniors at Cornell in 1972, only 7 percent of those who had not cohabited said it was because of moral reasons; more common reasons were not having yet found an appropriate partner or being geographically separated from partner (Macklin, 1976).

When asked what kind of relationship should exist before persons cohabit, most students indicate that cohabitation is acceptable as long as there is an affectionate, preferably monogamous, relationship between the two persons. Data from four collegiate institutions in the early 1970s indicated that about 5 percent of the undergraduates thought a couple should be married before living together; 15 percent said should be formally or tentatively engaged; 40 percent said should have a strong, affectionate, monogamous relationship; 25 percent said should at least be good friends or have a strong, affectionate relationship but could be dating others; and 15 percent said that persons should be able to live together if expedient to do so even if there were no emotional involvement (Macklin, 1978b).

Attitudes of the general public have changed more slowly than those of youth, but just as definitively. Three early 1970s studies of parents of college students showed a large generation gap: The great majority of parents indicated that cohabitation outside of marriage was either immoral, emotionally unhealthy, or unwise, and said that they would work to prevent or stop such behavior (Macklin, 1974a; Smith and Kimmel, 1970; Steiner, 1975). However, when Yankelovich and associates (1981) did a survey for *Time* in 1978, 52 percent of the respondents said that they did *not* believe it to be "morally wrong for couples who are not married to be living together."

Why this fairly sudden change in social values and behaviors? What has allowed us to accept today that which was unthinkable only a generation ago? Myriad factors have combined to create an atmosphere conducive to the change. A major factor has been technology and the increased availability of effective contraception, which gave a fresh boost to the gradual evolution in sexual values and behaviors that began in the early part of the century. Since the 1920s, increasing urbanization, mobility, and education of women, and the resulting opportunities for anonymity and privacy, have led to gradually increasing nonvirginity rates for women and a growing acceptance of sexual involvement before marriage. By the late

1960s, sexual intercourse among college students in a "going steady" relationship was taken for granted, and in 1972, it was estimated that 70 percent of single students of both sexes were nonvirginal by their senior year (Guttmacher and Vadies, 1972).

For couples to want to spend the night together, and to want to increase the number of such nights, seems a natural extension of the above changes. This was soon made possible by the social movements of the 1960s, and by the growing demands that women and men be granted equal rights and that students be treated as adults. The result, on most campuses, was a fairly rapid elimination of in loco parentis, the initiation of coed dorms and 24-hour visitation privileges, new freedom for women to live off campus, and a gradual reduction in the double standard. Simultaneously, the increasing divorce rate caused persons to move more cautiously into both first and second marriages and created large numbers of persons who felt a need to try out a relationship before making a permanent commitment. A new emphasis on quality of relationships and on personal growth caused persons to question the superficiality of traditional dating and to search for a lifestyle that would allow both individual freedom and more genuine intimacy. As more and more persons experienced cohabitation and found the personal benefits to outweigh the costs (see, for example, Macklin, 1972b), and as society observed few of the anticipated debilitating effects, attitudes relaxed and the behavior spread. Found functional for many and congruent with other simultaneous changes within the culture, the structure was fairly rapidly incorporated into the broader institutions of society.

Nature of the Relationship

Agreeing on an operational definition of nonmarital cohabitation has been a major dilemma for students of the phenomenon, making it difficult to describe with any consistency the nature of the relationship. When one looks at the range of existing relationships between two unmarried persons of opposite sex cohabiting in the same household, it is possible to place them on a continuum from "low emotional and physical involvement/ minimal commitment" to "high emotional and physical involvement/ maximum commitment," and to distinguish at least five types (e.g., see Petty, 1975; Storm, 1973):

(1) *temporary casual convenience* (including "contract cohabitation" as described by Van Deusen, 1974), where two persons share the same living quarters because it is advantageous to do so, with interaction ranging from friendly companionship to none;

(2) *affectionate, going-together relationship,* where the couple live together because they enjoy being together and will continue to live together as long as this is true;

(3) *"trial marriage,"* where the couple are together because they are seriously contemplating a permanent commitment and wish to test the wisdom of it;

(4) *temporary alternative to marriage,* where the couple have made a commitment to marry but are living together until it is more convenient to do so;

(5) *permanent or semipermanent alternative to marriage,* where the couple are living together in a long-term committed relationship similar to marriage but without the legal and religious sanctions.

Couples may pass through various points on this continuum during the evolution of their relationship, and with differing degrees of behavioral commitment at the same point (e.g., some type 5s may own property in common, have children, share joint bank accounts, and name each other as insurance beneficiary, while other 5s may have none of these).

Because of the complications, some researchers have resorted to phenomenological definitions (i.e., if the respondent thinks of him- or herself as cohabiting, he or she is counted as such), and so use some version of the question, "Have you ever lived with someone of the opposite sex to whom you were not married?" They have then limited their analysis to persons who have lived together for certain specified lengths of time (e.g., three months or more, six months or more). Because of the desire for a more precise definition and the fact that the initial research was done on college campuses, one of the first attempts at definition was Macklin's (1972b) "sharing a bedroom and/or bed for four or more nights a week for three or more consecutive months with someone of the opposite sex to whom one is not married" (thus the better part of a week for the better part of a term). Many have considered this too similar to contemporary dating and have pushed for the more stringent criterion of common residence or common residence under marriagelike conditions (e.g., "two adult persons of different sex living together under marriagelike conditions in the same household without having officially confirmed their relationship through marriage"; Cole, 1977: 65). The latter fits with the definition most commonly used by European researchers (e.g., Trost, 1981). As one can see in Table 2.1, the U.S. Bureau of the Census has gone through a decade of struggle to find a definition with which it can be comfortable. It is important to recognize the wide degree of variation among cohabiting couples, and the high degree of ambiguity implicit within the current terminology, even when one limits the term to "living together under marriagelike conditions."

With the above in mind, it is difficult to say what percentage of the 1.5 million cohabiting couples counted by the U.S. Census fall into each of the above categories, and there are few data to help us. When college cohabitants have been asked to describe their relationship, most designate themselves as being in a "strong, affectionate, monogamous" type 2 relationship (Macklin, 1978b). They share a deep emotional relationship with each other, but have not yet reached the point of long-term commitment (women being somewhat more likely than men to indicate plans to marry their partner; Lyness et al., 1972; Risman, 1981). However, it is not at all clear that this would be the case for older couples, and it is certainly not true of those couples designated as cohabiting nonmaritally in Europe. Of the unmarried Swedish cohabitants reported by Trost (1981), about two-thirds intended to or believed that they would marry each other (with many others intending to stay together unmarried).

Data to date of U.S. couples indicate that few choose to cohabit on a long-term basis without marriage, and that most nonmaritally cohabiting relationships either terminate or result in marriage. For example, Clayton and Voss (1977) found that while 18 percent of their national probability sample of 20- to 30-year-old men had cohabited nonmaritally for six months or more, only 5 percent were currently doing so. A study of 231 unmarried college couples (Risman et al., 1981) found that the vast majority of those who were cohabiting planned to eventually marry someone (93 percent of the women and 85 percent of the men), although not necessarily each other, and that after two years, college cohabiting couples were not significantly less likely to have married than dating couples. It is this kind of data that has led researchers to conclude that cohabitation in the United States is part of courtship and mate selection rather than an alternative to marriage (e.g., Bower and Christopherson, 1977; Danziger, 1976; Henze and Hudson, 1974; Johnson, 1968; Macklin, 1974b, 1978a; Risman et al., 1981). Length of time together may well be more indicative than cohabitation per se of a couple's stage in the courtship process or of their point on the commitment continuum.

Characteristics of Nonmarital Cohabitants

Who are those persons who have experienced living with someone to whom they are not married, and in what way are they different from persons who have not? Initially answers to these questions were based on surveys of college students and a comparison of the responses of persons who had and had not cohabited (e.g., Arafat and Yorburg, 1973; Henze and Hudson, 1974; Macklin, 1976; Peterman et al., 1974). More recently, information has become available on cohabitants within the general population, based on national probability samples (Clayton and Voss, 1977; Glick and Spanier, 1980; Yllo, 1978) and an analysis of marriage license applicants (Hanna and Knaub, 1981; Newcomb and Bentler, 1980b). It must be remembered that it is sometimes impossible to determine from available data the extent to which certain differentiating characteristics were present *before* or are a consequence *of* the cohabitation experience.

The following variables have been found to differentiate between people who have and have not cohabited nonmaritally:

(1) *Age.* As a group, cohabitants tend to be somewhat younger than were married people. In an analysis of the 1975 Census data, 60 percent of currently cohabiting persons and 33 percent of married persons were under 35 (Glick and Spanier, 1980). In a 1976 national probability sample, 60 percent of the cohabitants and 27 percent of the marrieds were under 30 (Yllo, 1978).

(2) *Religiosity.* Researchers have consistently found cohabitants to have lower rates of church attendance and higher rates of no religious affiliation (Arafat and Yorburg, 1973; Clayton and Voss, 1977; Henze and Hudson, 1974; Newcomb and Bentler, 1980b; Yllo, 1978). There has been no consistency in findings with regard to the relationship between cohabitation and specific religious affiliation.

(3) *Race.* 1975 Census data showed cohabitation rates among Blacks to be three times those among Whites, and interracial couples were more frequent among currently cohabiting than among currently married couples, especially in the younger age groups (Glick and Spanier, 1980). Of males 20 to 30 years old in 1974-1975, 29 percent of the Blacks and 16 percent of the Whites had cohabited for six months or more (Clayton and Voss, 1977). However, Blacks make up a very small percentage of the total number of cohabitants.

(4) *Geographic area.* Cohabitants are more likely to be living in large metropolitan areas and in the Northeast and the West (Clayton and Voss, 1977; Glick and Spanier, 1980).

(5) *Socioeconomic status.* Findings have been somewhat inconsistent with regard to social class. As a group, couples living together unmarried have tended to be characterized by relatively low income levels and high unemployment. On the other hand, unmarried cohabiting women are more likely to be employed and to have had more education than married women, and cohabiting couples are more likely than married couples to have both partners employed (Clayton and Voss, 1977, Glick and Spanier, 1980). The economic differences may well be explained by the fact that large numbers of cohabiting persons are young, students, low income persons, or separated/divorced persons. A study of marriage license applicants in Los Angeles found no significant educational or occupational differences between persons who had and had not cohabited prior to marriage (Newcomb and Bentler, 1980b), and a 1976 national probability study of couples found no relationship between cohabitation and parents' educational background (Yllo, 1978).

(6) *Unconventionality.* Cohabitants as a group have been more likely to engage in unconventional behavior (e.g., drug usage, oral sex, participation in meditation, attendance at rock concerts, intercourse prior to 15) and to espouse more liberal attitudes (Clayton and Voss, 1977; Henze and Hudson, 1974; Newcomb and Bentler, 1980b).

(7) *Personality.* Cohabitants tend to perceive themselves as more androgynous and more liberated from traditional sex role characteristics than do noncohabitants. Cohabiting males are more likely to describe themselves as less managerial and competitive and as warmer and more emotionally supportive, while cohabiting women are likely to describe themselves as more extroverted, assertive, independent, and intelligent than do noncohabiting women (Arafat and Yorburg, 1973; Guittar and Lewis, 1974; Newcomb and Bentler, 1980b). Cohabitants are *not* more likely to come from unhappy or divorced homes, do not perform less well academically, and are not significantly less likely to want to marry eventually (Macklin, 1976; Risman et al., 1981; Yllo, 1978).

(8) *Age of children.* In the case of divorced persons, incidence of cohabitation tends to decline with age of the children involved. Of 80 remarriage families, 14 percent of those who had cohabited before remarriage had children aged 11 to 17 compared to 30 percent of those who had not (Hanna and Knaub, 1981). This may reflect the fact that adolescent children tend to have more problems with being part of a stepfamily than do younger children.

Researchers of college populations have consistently emphasized the similarities between cohabitants and noncohabitants:

> On campuses where a large percentage of persons engage in cohabitation at some point in their undergraduate life, persons who cohabit do not appear to be dramatically different from those who do not. As people, cohabiting students seem representative of the general undergraduate population, with their cohabitation more a consequence of the opportunity for such a relationship than a result of any demographic characteristics, although they are likely to be persons whose personal and religious values are congruent with this lifestyle, and they must possess sufficient interpersonal skills to initiate such a relationship [Macklin, 1978a: 5].

As cohabitation becomes more widespread within the general population, it seems likely that the differences between persons who have and have not cohabited premaritally will become increasingly insignificant. Recent studies seem to indicate this trend (Hanna and Knaub, 1981; Newcomb and Bentler, 1980b).

Comparisons of Couples Who Are and Are Not Cohabiting Nonmaritally

Much research to date has been devoted to investigating the similarities and differences between couples who are and are not living together unmarried. In some cases, the latter have been married; in others, they have been dating or engaged. The focus has been on differences in commitment, sex roles and division of labor, and degree of expressed satisfaction. It is crucial in this kind of research that the comparison groups have been appropriately matched for such variables as age, social class, length of time together, presence of children, and whether or not previously married (i.e., it makes much more sense to compare separated/divorced cohabitants with separated/divorced noncohabitants or remarried couples than with first marrieds or never marrieds). Researchers are becoming more sensitive to these issues.

Commitment

Cohabitation researchers have seen commitment as having two distinct components (see Cole, 1977; Johnson, 1973): (1) personal commitment, or the extent to which one is personally dedicated to continuing the relationship; and (2) behavioral or structural commitment, i.e., acts, and the consequences of those acts, that tend to bind one into a relationship (e.g., the extent to which others know of the relationship and support its continuing, the number of possessions owned in common, and the changes one would have to make in one's life were one to leave). The general finding from research to date on U.S. samples has been that unmarried cohabiting persons report significantly less commitment than do married persons, with marrieds expressing more commitment to continue the relationship and more external constraints on its termination (Budd, 1976; Johnson, 1973).

The above is not surprising, given that most unmarried cohabiting relationships in the United States are still at the courtship phase of their relationship. One would not expect similar findings in Europe, where a large proportion of nonmaritally cohabiting couples are in a marriedlike relationship (Straver, 1981; Trost, 1981). If one wishes to separate effects of unmarried cohabitation per se from effects of stage in the courtship process, it will be necessary to control for degree of personal and behavioral commitment to the relationship. This would allow for more meaningful cross-cultural comparisons as well as more definitive research on the cohabitation relationship within this culture.

When nonmarital cohabitants have been compared to noncohabiting engaged persons, the cohabitants as a group have been as committed to their partners and to the relationship, but less committed to marrying their partners, with degree of commitment of engaged couples best predicted by such variables as length of time together and of cohabiting couples by present quality of the relationship (Lewis et al., 1977).

In an intensive study of 231 unmarried cohabiting and dating college couples (Risman et al., 1981), cohabiting women were more likely than dating women to think that they would marry their partner, but there was no significant difference between cohabiting and noncohabiting men. (This gender difference in degree of expressed commitment has also been noted by other cohabitation researchers: Budd, 1976; Johnson, 1973; Kieffer, 1972; Lyness et al., 1972; Lewis et al., 1977). However, neither gender held high expectations of marriage — about 50 percent probability in the case of men and 60 percent in the case of women. In point of fact, after a two-year period, almost 50 percent of both the dating and the cohabiting couples had broken up, suggesting minimal differences in functional commitment between college cohabiting and noncohabiting couples.

Data suggest that while more likely to espouse permissive attitudes, cohabiting couples tend to be as sexually exclusive as those in other relationships of similar duration (Bower, 1975; Clatworthy and Scheid, 1977; Huang, 1976). In a study of 31 cohabiting couples, Montgomery (1973) found that while persons might support an individual's right to sexual freedom, most voluntarily restricted their own sexual activity with increasing commitment to the relationship.

Division of Labor

Cohabitants tend to hold more liberal attitudes and to see themselves as more androgynous than do others (an exception is the research by Segrest and Weeks, 1976, which found married males held significantly more egalitarian role expectations than did cohabiting males and no difference among women). However, there is little evidence to suggest that their relationships are any less traditionally sex roled, especially if one controls for age, previous marital history, and presence of children. Using a sample of currently cohabiting married and unmarried students, Stafford and colleagues (1977) found no significant differences between groups with regard to division of household labor. Men and women in both samples exhibited very traditional assignment of tasks, and women took most of the responsibility for, and performed most of, the household chores.

In a 1976 national probability sample of couples, Yllo (1978) found no significant differences between married and unmarried cohabitants regarding who had final say on family decisions or in division of household labor, with both reporting fairly traditional sex roles. Although unmarried cohabiting women under 30 reported carrying somewhat less of the responsibility for household chores than did married women under 30, there was no difference with age of men and no difference between married and unmarried women over 30. In a study of 231 unmarried cohabiting and dating students, Risman et al. (1981) found that whereas both groups of women held relatively nontraditional attitudes, and the attitudes of cohabiting males were less traditional than those of dating men, cohabiting relationships were not in fact more egalitarian. In fact, cohabiting college women were more likely to report male dominance than noncohabiting dating women, perhaps because living together required more household tasks and daily decision making.

Most researchers have concluded that unmarried cohabiting couples are characteristic of the society about them and engage in behaviors typical of others of their age group. The many years of role scripting are difficult to counteract, and although couples in general are more egalitarian than previously, there are many forces that operate to maintain conventional modes of interaction, even among those who on the surface might appear less traditional (Whitehurst, 1974).

Communication and Satisfaction

Risman and colleagues (1981) reported significant differences between dating and living-together couples on measures of couple intimacy. Even though they had gone together for a shorter period of time, cohabiting students saw each other more often, had intercourse more often, saw their relationship as closer, indicated greater love for each other, and reported more mutual self-disclosure and fewer problems in the relationship. Whether the greater intimacy preceded or resulted from the cohabitation is not clear. It is interesting to note that, given these findings, there was little difference in rate of termination.

When married and unmarried cohabiting couples are compared on degree of satisfaction and problems experienced, few differences have been noted (Budd, 1976; Cole and Bower, 1974; Cole and Vincent, 1975; Olday, 1977; Polansky et al., 1978; Stevens, 1975). Cole and Vincent, in summarizing their research on a matched sample of twenty married and twenty cohabiting couples, state it well:

> Apparently it is not so much the legal nature of the relationship that encourages or discourages satisfaction. Instead, it is more likely a factor of how the partners behave toward each other and define their roles that is predictive of happiness within an individual relationship [Personal communication, 1975].

Internal Dynamics

Initiation

Writers have generally agreed that couples tend to drift into living together unmarried, with little initial discussion of the evolving nature of their relationship (e.g., Macklin, 1972b; Trost, 1981). The typical pattern has been to spend increasing numbers of nights together and to gradually accumulate possessions at one residence. The actual conscious decision to live together is often prompted by some external event, such as graduation, termination of a lease, or a geographic move. Trost (1981) notes that in Europe there are two prevailing patterns: The couple commits to the relationship but has to wait until there is available housing, or they live together and the commitment gradually grows.

It should be noted that couples do not necessarily agree as to when it was that they began cohabiting, perhaps dating it from when the one who moved in gave up his or her other residence, or from when they both moved together into a new apartment, or from when they made some public acknowledgment of their relationship. It is impossible to say how long couples typically date before cohabiting, given the great variation among couples and the differing definitions as to when cohabitation officially begins.

Maintenance

There has been little study of the internal dynamics of the cohabiting relationship as it evolves over time. It has been hypothesized that because of the relatively few external and symbolic supports for a nonmarital cohabiting relationship, more effort must be expended by the couple themselves to sustain the relationship. Montgomery (1973) has suggested a hierarchy of behavioral indices of the gradually evolving mutual commitment that must occur if a cohabiting relationship is to last.

Hennon (1981) has explored the way in which nonmarital cohabiting couples manage conflict and has noted that "commitment balance" (i.e., equal commitment to the relationship from both partners) is an important factor. "Symmetrical couples" characteristically demonstrate more consensus regarding the process by which they deal with their conflicts. Thus, in addition to being open to experiencing conflict, they are better able to manage such conflict and to keep it from threatening the relationship. This may be due to the fact that, because they are equally invested emotionally, they are willing to invest equal energy in conscious effects at maintenance.

Cole and Goettsch (1981) studied self-disclosure among nonmarital cohabiting couples and found that the greater the degree of self-disclosure, the greater the degree of relationship satisfaction. The achievement of depth within the relationship appears to be dependent on a couple's willingness to risk disclosure and their ability to then deal constructively with any ensuing conflict. To accomplish this, couples need both a high degree of commitment to working on the relationship and the communication and problem-solving skills to do so. There is no reason to think that these findings are unique to nonmarital couples.

Termination

A nonmarital cohabitation can either continue or terminate in marriage or breakup. It is difficult to say what proportion of cohabiting couples fall into each category. Lyness (1978) found, in an 8-month follow-up of 23 dating couples and 15 living-together couples who had been involved in a serious relationship for 8 to 9 months when first interviewed in 1969, that the latter had experienced less change of status. Only two of the cohabiting couples had separated and two had married, while 30 percent of the dating couples had married. In their two-year follow-up of 231 college couples, Risman et al. (1981) found no significant difference in rate of marriage or breakup between cohabiting and dating couples.

Only two studies provide data on termination from national probability samples. Clayton and Voss (1977) found that three-quarters of their 20-30-year-old men who had cohabited six months or more had terminated their cohabitation as of 1974-1975, either through marriage or breakup. For 37 percent of the men who had experienced one cohabitation and one marriage, cohabitation had apparently led to marriage. This corresponds closely to the finding by Risman et al. (1981) that approximately 40 percent of their college cohabiting couples had married (after an average period of two years from first date to marriage). The study by Yllo (1978) of a national probability sample of 2500 adults in couple relationships indicated that while cohabiting couples were more likely than married couples to have contemplated separating, there was no significant difference in the numbers who actually did.

Cole, reporting on a follow-up of forty noncollege cohabiting couples, concluded that "of those relationships able to work through initial adjustment problems, there is as good a chance that the relationship will continue, with the same chance of success, as found among the married population" (1976: 13-14). He lists the following reasons why unmarried cohabiting relationships might fail: emotional immaturity, insufficient or unequal commitment, crises external to the relationship (e.g., physical separation or external interference), and differences in lifestyle, such as use of money or division of labor.

Ganson (1975) studied the reasons given by cohabitants for breaking up, noting that the most commonly expressed reasons were "grew apart," overdependency, and loss of identity, with women reporting more problems than men (see also Risman et al., 1981). This may be because women are more sensitive to relationship issues, are more emotionally invested in the relationship and, hence, more emotionally dependent on it, or are likely to wish a more egalitarian relationship.

One can conclude that unmarried cohabiting couples are as likely to stay together as others who are at the same point on the courtship continuum, and that of those U.S. couples who cohabit for six months or more, probably 35 to 45 percent will eventually marry (although this estimate is based on very limited data). There has been some indication that when they do marry, couples who have lived together before marriage tend to have less elaborate marriages and fewer guests, and are less likely to take a honeymoon (Risman et al., 1981; Rank, 1981).

Although some researchers have suggested that one advantage of living together unmarried is the relative ease of termination, this is probably an overstatement. Although there are few data on the effects of termination on the individuals involved, anecdotal evidence suggests that the dynamics are similar to those associated with divorce: denial, anger, grief, and gradual reintegration into single life, with the amount of stress experienced proportional to the degree of emotional involvement and the length of time together. Because there is less social stigma, less legal hassle, and usually less initial expectation of permanence, and cohabiting relationships are generally of shorter duration than marriage, there will probably be less guilt, less sense of failure, and a quicker adjustment to separation.

Effects of Nonmarital Cohabitation

There are few published longitudinal studies on the effect of nonmarital cohabitation on the relationship or the persons involved. The one exception is a four-year follow-up of 77 couples applying for marriage licenses in Los Angeles, half of whom had cohabited for an average of eight months before marriage (Newcomb and Bentler, 1980a). Most other data come from retrospective self-reports of participants and from a comparison of married couples who have and have not cohabited before marriage.

Personal Growth

The great majority of persons who have cohabited nonmaritally tend to give very positive ratings to the experience and to report that it facilitated their self-understanding and their understanding of relationships. Students who have cohabited have said that they would elect to do it again, and would not wish to marry without living together first (Bower, 1975; Lautenschlager, 1972; Macklin, 1976; Peterman et al., 1974; Shuttlesworth and Thorman, 1973). Whether cohabitation leads to more growth than would be achieved in a non-living-together couple relationship has not been established.

Marital Quality

For many social critics, the crucial question is: What effect does living together before marriage have on the later marital relationship? Proponents have argued that it should serve as a more effective screening device and give persons a more realistic relationship experience, hence, providing for better mate selection and marriage preparation. Because the only available data come from comparisons of married couples who report that they did or did not live together before marriage, it is never clear to what extent any observed differences are due to the cohabitation experience itself or to preexisting personality characteristics.

The general findings suggest little difference between married couples who have and have not lived together premaritally. When Lyness (1976) compared eleven married couples who had cohabited before marriage with thirteen who had not, on sixteen variables representing characteristics of open marriage, she found few differences. Olday (1977) compared 184 married students who had cohabited with their spouses before marriage and 524 who had not and found premarital cohabitation unrelated to degree of marital satisfaction, conflict, egalitarianism, or emotional closeness. Budd (1976) compared 48 married couples who had cohabited before marriage and 49 who had not and found no differences on problems experienced, self-disclosure, or degree of commitment. Jacques and Chason (1979) studied 84 married students, of whom 54 had cohabited with someone before marriage, and found little difference between the two after a year of marriage, with both groups indicating fairly high levels of marital satisfaction and intimacy. Risman et al. (1981) similarly found that, at this early point in marriage, virtually all of their student couples who had married reported high levels of satisfaction, irrespective of prior cohabiting history.

Unlike the above studies, Clatworthy and Scheid (1977) noted some significant differences between couples who had and had not lived together before marriage: Those who had cohabited premaritally more frequently disagreed, were less dependent on their spouses and their marriages, and were more likely to have sought marriage counseling. However, it is quite possible that these persons, because of their values and predispositions, would have had such marriages irrespective of their premarital cohabitation. Clatworthy and Scheid conclude that there is no evidence that couples who live together before marriage have any better or less conventional marriages, or that they select more appropriate partners.

The one study that has found cohabitation before marriage to be positively related to marital quality was done on remarriage families, forty of whom had cohabited prior to marriage and forty of whom had not (Hanna and Knaub, 1981). Remarried couples who had lived together before marriage reported significantly higher degrees of happiness, closeness, concern for partner's welfare, and positive communication, gave higher ratings to their remarrying family's adjustment, and perceived more environmental support than did remarrieds who had not cohabited. The fact that those families who had lived together before marriage tended to have somewhat younger children, and that adolescent children experience more problems with remarriage than do younger children, could explain the finding that those who had lived together before marriage experienced better remarried family adjustment.

Newcomb and Bentler (1980a), in their four-year follow-up of 68 couples first interviewed soon after marriage (34 who had cohabited premaritally, and 34 who had not), found no significant differences on measures of marital adjustment or on divorce rate, although a higher percentage of the cohabitants were divorced (26 percent of the noncohabitants and 36 percent of the cohabitants). Divorce was highly related to length of premarital cohabitation, with couples who had cohabited less than three months or more than ten months having the highest divorce rates, and those cohabiting three to ten months having the lowest (21 percent), suggesting that there may be an optimum length of time to cohabit before marrying.

Premarital cohabitants in the above study who had the more successful marriages tended to be older, previously divorced, more educated, and more traditional on some measures (findings were often reversed for the noncohabitants, where being less traditional and not previously divorced was predictive of more positive marital outcome). Perhaps the older, more educated, once-married individuals are more likely to have the maturity and the motivation to better utilize premarital cohabitation as a learning experience. It is also interesting that premarital cohabitants who later divorced tended to have higher marital adjustment scores than did noncohabitants who divorced. A number of explanations are possible: Persons who have cohabited premaritally may be less motivated to "hang in there" and work on marital problems, women who cohabit before marriage are more independent and hence have more options available if marriage does not work out, or couples who cohabit before marriage are able to deal with dissolution with less interpersonal deterioration and animosity. In any case, it is clear that the relationship between premarital cohabitation and marital success is highly complex and will not be easily understood.

There has been some concern about the effect of the transition from living together unmarried to living together married. Berger (1974), after interviews with 21 married couples who had cohabited premaritally, concluded that, in general, marriage did not lead to any dramatic change in the relationship, with the quality of the relationship after marriage reflecting the reported quality before marriage. In a study of married and divorced relationships, some of which had involved living together before the marriage, Rank (1981) found greater differences between the married and the divorced groups than between those who had and had not cohabited premaritally. Marriages that had ended in divorce tended to have one member who saw his or her marriage as having caused a significant change in the premarital relationship, with new and undesired demands and expectations that had not been present before marriage. In the case of those couples who were still married two to five years after the wedding, partners were reported as having similar expectations of married life and as having made a special effort to minimize the transition and to treat the marriage as a natural continuation of the cohabiting relationship.

Rank's data support Clatworthy and Scheid's (1977) contention that premarital cohabitation is not an effective screening device. Those who later divorced were more likely to report that they had inaccurately predicted how their partner would behave after marriage, had married for inappropriate reasons (e.g., parental pressure, fear of losing partner, or insecurity), and had assumed that marriage would solve their relationship problems. Because the data are from retrospective interviews and the sample is very small, often with only one member of the couple reporting, findings must be considered as merely suggestive.

Ridley, Peterman, and Avery (1978) have argued that premarital cohabitation will affect various individuals and couples differently, depending on the goals, expectations, and skills of the persons involved:

> It would seem unfortunate to conclude that cohabitation is inherently good or bad preparation for marriage, but rather it should be viewed as having the potential for both, with the characteristics of the individual and of the relationship being of critical importance in determining the long-range effects of cohabitation (1978: 134).

They hypothesize that cohabitation will provide more positive learning and better preparation for marriage when the participants: (a) have as a goal greater understanding of self and of intimate day-to-day living; (b) have realistic and mutually agreed-on expectations for the relationship; (c) do not have strong "deficiency needs"; (d) have good interpersonal skills; (e) have had serious dating relationships in the past that made them developmentally ready for cohabitation; (f) see themselves as heterosexually desirable; and (g) have a fairly extensive network of same and opposite-sex friends so that they do not become overly dependent on the relationship and, hence, unable to be objective.

Ridley and colleagues (1978) suggest that by posing appropriate questions to unmarried couples, counselors can help them assess the extent to which their proposed cohabitation is likely to be a growth-producing and positive experience. Couple growth groups, especially designed for unmarried cohabiting couples, could presumably serve an important function by helping participants discuss and assess their relationship and by providing the necessary communication and conflict-negotiation skills. Some couple enrichment specialists have already moved in this direction, but efforts are, by and large, "too little for too few."

Society

There has been as yet no evidence that increased nonmarital cohabitation will lead to reduced marriage rates in the United States as it has in the Scandinavian countries. Scandinavian couples report few perceived economic or legal advantages to being married in Sweden and Denmark (Trost, 1981), but the institutional supports for marriage are still strong in this country, and the great majority of youth still indicate a desire to eventually marry (e.g., Bower and Christopherson, 1977).

What is clear is that there is a trend toward postponement of first marriage (U.S. Bureau of the Census, 1981). This is evidenced by an increase in median age at first marriage (20.8 years for women in 1970 and 22.1 in 1980) and an increase in the percentage of young women who have never married (36 percent of women aged 20 to 24 in 1970, 50 percent in 1980). Whether this trend is a function of persons adding a period of cohabitation to their courtship or to some other set of factors such as the changing roles of women is not clear. It seems likely that it is more the latter, since studies of persons who have and have not cohabited before marriage indicate similar lengths of time between their first date and marriage, with nonmarital cohabitation often not lasting more than a year or so (e.g., Hanna and Knaub, 1981; Newcomb and Bentler, 1980a, 1980b; Rank, 1981).

It is also unclear what effect cohabitation will have on the birthrate. In the Newcomb and Bentler study (1980a), persons who had cohabited before marriage were significantly less likely to have children within the first four years of marriage (53 percent of those who had not cohabited had children versus 21 percent of those who had cohabited). This is consistent with the findings by Bower and Christopherson (1977) that students who had cohabited planned to have significantly fewer children. Whether this will hold as cohabitation becomes more widespread, or as these respondents become older, is not known.

At the moment it seems unlikely that cohabitation before marriage will lead to any dramatic change in divorce rates — either up or down. Research findings to date tend to emphasize the similarities between married couples who have and have not cohabited before marriage, with premarital cohabitation per se having little significant effect on marital quality. There are currently too many factors contributing to the increased divorce rate, and too little effort being made to help couples utilize their cohabitation in ways which would enhance their functioning, to expect premarital cohabitation to affect divorce in any significant fashion. If norms were to change to the point where society made a concerted effort to encourage couples to use the living-together phase of their courtship as a time to examine their relationship and provided them with easily available instruction in relationship skills, premarital cohabitation might indeed come to have a positive impact on later marriage.

The effect of cohabitation on other societal institutions has been more profound, requiring in some cases important changes in policy and procedures. The most publicized has been the increasing judicial recognition being given to nonmarital relationships. Issues have included protection against discrimination, the legal rights of children of cohabitors, the effect of cohabitation on custody and alimony decisions, extension of insurance benefits, and the division of property at termination (e.g., see Bernstein, 1977). A precedent was set in 1976 with the famous Marvin v. Marvin case, in which the California Supreme Court stated that courts should uphold oral or written agreements between nonmarital partners regarding property distribution (Marvin v. Marvin, 1976; see discussion of palimony by Myricks, 1980, and his chapter in this volume; Macklin, 1978a). Numerous volumes have been published to help persons deal with the legal ramifications of their living-together experience (e.g., Douthwaite, 1979; Fels, 1981; Hirsch, 1976; King, 1975; Lavori, 1976; Massey and Warner, 1974).

Conclusion

It is obvious that nonmarital cohabitation, which became highly visible less than fifteen years ago, is rapidly becoming part of the normative culture. The number of persons living in unmarried-couple households grows with each year, and it is increasingly predictable that individuals who are going together — before either a first marriage or a remarriage — will also be living together. Although there is a growing trend in Europe for nonmarital cohabitation to replace formal marriage, at least during the early years of a relationship, most nonmarital cohabitation in the United States is still part of the courtship process and relatively temporary. No one has yet attempted to predict the lifetime prevalence of nonmarital cohabitation for those who are now under thirty. However, given the incidence among young unmarried couples, the high divorce rate, and the incidence of nonmarital cohabitation among separated and divorced persons, it is likely that a substantial majority (perhaps three-fourths) will cohabit nonmaritally at some point in their lives.

Many of the concerns about nonmarital cohabitation have been put to rest during the past ten years. Societal experience, substantiated by research, has indicated that the benefits tend to outweigh, or at least balance, the costs, and that there are few deleterious effects. Participants tend to report cohabitation as having been a positive experience that they might well repeat another time, and later relationships do not seem to suffer. On the other hand, there have not been the gains that were anticipated by some. Mate selection has not improved, marriages are not significantly better, and divorce has not been reduced.

Research on nonmarital cohabitation has been prolific since the early 1970s, and although samples have often been small and nonrandom, findings have been sufficiently consistent to seem reliable. The early research was almost entirely on college or college-aged populations, and on cohabitation before first marriage and without children present. Only within the last five years have there been published data on national probability samples (albeit selected initially for other purposes) or on cohabitation among once-married persons. Most of the research on couples has been based on the report of one member of the couple, and much of the data have been retrospective in nature. There is an urgent need for longitudinal analyses designed to give some perspective on how cohabitation fits into the developmental sequences and relationship histories of the participants and to see whether hypotheses based on short-term studies hold up over time.

It is increasingly clear that nonmarital cohabitation is not a sufficiently definitive concept to be meaningful, explanatory, or predictive. To know that a couple is living together unmarried, at least in the United States, tells one little about them, their relationship, or their probable future. To explain more of the variance, attention must be paid to such factors as: the meanings that the participants attach to the relationship (at the very least, where it falls on the courtship continuum); the age, educational level, marital history, values, and interpersonal competencies of the participants; and relationship variables such as length of time together, commitment balance, self-disclosure, and conflict management.

It is interesting to note that some of the most recent research using samples of nonmaritally cohabiting couples (Cole and Goettsch, 1981; Hennon, 1981) has focused on relationship dynamics and only incidentally on the fact that the sample was unmarried. One is tempted to suggest that society might also do well to focus less attention on cohabitation per se and more on ways to facilitate the functioning of couples irrespective of marital or residential status.

References

ALD, R. (1969) Sex Off Campus. New York: Grosset & Dunlap.

ARAFAT, I. and B. YORBURG (1973) "On living together without marriage." Journal of Sex Research 9: 97-106.

BERGER, M. E. (1974) "Trial marriage followup." (unpublished)

BERNSTEIN, B. E. (1977) "Legal problems of cohabitation." Family Coordinator 26, 4: 361-366.

BLOCH, D. (1969) "Unwed couples: do they live happily ever after?" Redbook (April): 90+.

BOWER, D. W. (1975) "A description and analysis of a cohabiting sample in America." Master's thesis, University of Arizona, Tucson.

——— and V. A. CHRISTOPHERSON (1977) "University student cohabitation: a regional comparison of selected attitudes and behavior." Journal of Marriage and the Family 39, 3: 447-453.

BUDD, L. S. (1976) "Problems, disclosure, and commitment of cohabiting and married students." Ph.D. dissertation, University of Minnesota, Minneapolis.

CLATWORTHY, N. (1975) "Couples in quasi-marriage," pp. 67-90 in N. Glazer-Malbin (ed.) Old Family/New Family: Interpersonal Relationships. New York: Van Nostrand.

——— and L. A. SCHEID (1977) "A comparison of married couples: premarital cohabitants with non-premarital cohabitants." Ohio State University. (unpublished)

CLAYTON, R. R. and H. L. VOSS (1977) "Shacking up: cohabitation in the 1970s." Journal of Marriage and the Family 39, 2: 273-283.

COLE, C. L. (1977) "Cohabitation in social context," pp. 62-79 in R. W. Libby and R. N. Whitehurst (eds.) Marriage and Alternatives. Glenview, IL: Scott, Foresman.

——— (1976) "Living together as an alternative life style." Iowa State University. (unpublished)

——— and D. W. BOWER (1974) "Cohabitation pair-bond intimacy requirements and love-life development differences." Presented at the Annual Meetings of the National Council on Family Relations, St. Louis, Missouri.

COLE, C. L. and S. L. GOETTSCH (1981) "Self-disclosure and relationship quality: a study among nonmarital cohabiting couples." Alternative Lifestyles 4, 4: 428-466.

COLE, C. M. and J. P. VINCENT (1975) "Cognitive and behavioral patterns in cohabitive and marital dyads." (unpublished)

DANZIGER, C. (1976) "Unmarried heterosexual cohabitation." Ph.D. dissertation, Rutgers University, New Brunswick, New Jersey.

DOUTHWAITE, G. (1979) Unmarried Couples and the Law. Indianapolis: Allen Smith.

Esquire (1967) "Room-Mates." September: 94-98.

FELS, L. (1981) Living Together: Unmarried Couples in Canada. Toronto: Personal Library.

GANSON, H. C. (1975) "Cohabitation: the antecedents of dissolution of formerly cohabiting individuals." Master's thesis, Ohio State University, Columbus.

GAVIN, M. (1973) "The living together phenomenon." Master's thesis, Washington State University, Pullman.

GLICK, P.C. and G.B. SPANIER (1980) "Married and unmarried cohabitation in the United States." Journal of Marriage and the Family 42, 1: 19-30.

GRANT, A. (1968) "No rings attached: a look at premarital marriage on campus." Mademoiselle 66 (April): 208+.

GUITTAR, E.C. and R.A. LEWIS (1974) "Self-concepts among some unmarried cohabitants." Presented at the Annual Meetings of the National Council on Family Relations, St. Louis, Missouri.

GUTTMACHER, A.F. and E.E. VADIES (1972) "Sex on campus and the college health services." Journal of the American College Health Association 21: 145-148.

HANNA, S.L. and P.K. KNAUB (1981) "Cohabitation before remarriage: its relationship to family strengths." Alternative Lifestyles 4, 4: 507-522.

HENNON, C.B. (1981) "Conflict management within cohabitation relationships." Alternative Lifestyles 4, 4: 467-486.

HENZE, L.F. and J.W. HUDSON (1974) "Personal and family characteristics of cohabitating and non-cohabitating college students." Journal of Marriage and the Family 36, 4: 722-726.

HIRSCH, B.B. (1976) Living Together: A Guide to the Law for Unmarried Couples. Boston: Houghton Mifflin.

HUANG, L.J. (1976) "Some patterns of nonexclusive sexual relations among unmarried cohabiting couples." International Journal of Sociology of the Family 6 (Autumn): 265-274.

JACQUES, J.M. and K.J. CHASON (1979) "Cohabitation: its impact on marital success." Family Coordinator 28, 1: 35-39.

JOHNSON, M.P. (1973) "Commitment: a conceptual structure and empiricial application." Sociological Quarterly 14: 395-406.

———— (1968) "Courtship and commitment: a study of cohabitation on a university campus." Master's thesis, University of Iowa, Iowa City.

KARLEN, A. (1969) "The unmarried marrieds on campus." New York Times Magazine (January 26): 29+.

KIEFFER, C.M. (1972) "Consensual cohabitation: a descriptive study of the relationships and sociocultural characteristics of eighty couples in settings of two Florida universities." Master's thesis, Florida State University, Tallahassee.

KING, M.D. (1975) Cohabitation Handbook: Living Together and the Law. Berkeley, CA: Ten Speed Press.

LAUTENSCHLAGER, S. Y. (1972) "A descriptive study of consensual union among college students." Master's thesis, California State University, Northridge.

LAVORI, N. (1976) Living Together, Married or Single: Your Legal Rights. New York: Harper & Row.

LEWIS, R.A., G.B. SPANIER, V.L. ATKINSON, and C.F. LeHECKA (1977) "Commitment in married and unmarried cohabitation." Social Focus 10: 367-374.

LINDSEY, B.B. and W. EVANS (1927/1929) The Companionate Marriage. Garden City, NY: Doubleday.

LYNESS, J.F. (1978) "Happily ever after? followup of living-together couples." Alternative Lifestyles 1, 1: 55-70.

———— (1976) "Open marriage among former cohabitants — we have met the enemy: is it us?" Texas Tech University. (unpublished)

———— M.E. LIPETZ, and K.E. DAVIS (1972) "Living together: an alternative to marriage." Journal of Marriage and the Family 34, 2: 305-311.

MACE, D. and V. MACE (1981) "What is marriage beyond living together? Some Quaker reactions to cohabitation." Family Relations 30, 1: 17-20.

MACKLIN, E.D. (1978a) "Non-marital heterosexual cohabitation: a review of research." Marriage and Family Review 1, 2: 1-12.

———— (1978b) "Review of research on non-marital cohabitation in the United States," pp. 197-243 in B. I. Murstein (ed.) Exploring Intimate Life Styles. New York: Springer.

———— (1976) "Unmarried heterosexual cohabitation on the university campus," pp. 108-142 in J.P. Wiseman (ed.) The Social Psychology of Sex. New York: Harper & Row.

———— (1974a) "Comparison of parent and student attitudes toward non-marital cohabitation." Presented at the Annual Meetings of the National Council on Family Relations, St. Louis, Missouri.

———— (1974b) "Students who live together: trial marriage or going very steady?" Psychology Today (November): 53-59.

———— (1972a) Cohabitation Research Newsletter 1 (October).

———— (1972b) "Heterosexual cohabitation among unmarried college students." Family Coordinator 21, 4: 463-472.

Marvin v. Marvin (1976) 18 Cal.3d 660, 134 Cal. Reptr. 815, 557 P.2d 106.

MASSEY, C. and R. WARNER (1974) Sex, Living Together and the Law: A Legal Guide for Unmarried Couples and Groups. Berkeley, CA: Nolo.

McCAULEY, B. (1977) "Self-esteem in the cohabiting relationship." Master's thesis, University of Delaware, Newark.

McWHIRTER, W. A. (1968) "The arrangement at college." Life (May 31): 56+.

MEAD, M. (1968) "A continuing dialogue on marriage: why just living together won't work." Redbook 130 (April): 44+.

———— (1966) "Marriage in two steps." Redbook 127 (July): 48+.

MONTGOMERY, J. P. (1973) "Commitment and cohabitation cohesion." Presented at the Annual Meetings of the National Council on Family Relations, Toronto.

MYRICKS, N. (1980) " 'Palimony': the impact of Marvin v. Marvin." Family Coordinator 29, 2: 210-215.

NEWCOMB, M. D. and P. M. BENTLER (1980a) "Assessment of personality and demographic aspects of cohabitation and marital success." Journal of Personality Assessment 44, 1: 11-24.

———— (1980b) "Cohabitation before marriage: a comparison of married couples who did and did not cohabit." Alternative Lifestyles 3, 1: 65-85.

NEWCOMB, P. R. (1979) "Cohabitation in America: an assessment of consequences." Journal of Marriage and the Family 41, 3: 597-605.

Newsweek (1966) "Unstructured relationships: students living together." 68 (July 4): 78.

OLDAY, D. (1977) "Some consequences of heterosexual cohabitation for marriage." Ph.D. dissertation, Washington State University, Pullman.

PETERMAN, D.J., C.A. RIDLEY, and S.M. ANDERSON (1974) "A comparison of cohabitating and non-cohabitating college students." Journal of Marriage and the Family 36, 2: 344-354.

PETTY, J. A. (1975) "An investigation of factors which differentiate between types of cohabitation." Master's thesis, Indiana University, Bloomington.

POLANSKY, L. (1974) "A comparison of marriage and cohabitation on three interpersonal variables." Master's thesis, Ball State University, Muncie, Indiana.

POLANSKY, L. W., G. McDONALD, and J. MARTIN (1978) "A compairson of marriage and heterosexual cohabitation on three interpersonal variables: affective support, mutual knowledge, and relationship satisfaction." Western Sociological Review 9 (Summer): 49-59.

RANK, M. R. (1981) "The transition to marriage: a comparison of cohabiting and dating relationships ending in marriage or divorce." Alternative Lifestyles 4, 4: 487-506.

RIDLEY, C.A., D.J. PETERMAN, and A.W. AVERY (1978) "Cohabitation: does it make for a better marriage?" Family Coordinator 27, 2: 129-136.

RISMAN, B.J., C.T. HILL, Z. RUBIN, and L.A. PEPLAU (1981) "Living together in college: implications for courtship." Journal of Marriage and the Family 43, 1: 77-83.

RODMAN, H. (1966) "Illegitimacy in the Caribbean social structure: a reconsideration." American Sociological Review 31: 673-683.

RUSSELL, B. (1929) Marriage and Morals. New York: Liveright.

SCHRAG, P. (1968) "Posse at generation gap: implications of the Linda LeClair affair." Saturday Review 51 (May 18): 81.

SEGREST, M. A. (1975) "Comparison of the role expectations of married and cohabiting students." Lexington: University of Kentucky.

———— and M. O. WEEKS (1976) "Comparison of the role expectations of married and cohabiting students." International Journal of Sociology of the Family 6 (Autumn): 275-281.

SHEEHY, G. (1969) "Living together: the stories of four young couples who risk the strains of non-marriage and why." Glamour (February 1): 136+.

SHUTTLESWORTH, B. and G. THORMAN (1973) "Living together unmarried relationships." (unpublished)

SMITH, P.B. and K. KIMMEL (1970) "Student-parent reactions to off-campus cohabitation." Journal of College Student Personnel 11: 188-193.

STAFFORD, R., E. BACKMAN, and P. diBONA (1977) "The division of labor among cohabiting and married couples." Journal of Marriage and the Family 39, 1: 43-57.

STEINER D. (1975) "Non-marital cohabitation and marriage: questionnaire responses of college women and their mothers." Master's thesis, North Dakota State University, Fargo.

STEVENS, D. J. H. (1975) "Cohabitation without marriage." Ph.D. dissertation, University of Texas, Austin.

STORM, V. (1973) "Contemporary cohabitation and the dating-marital continuum." Master's thesis, University of Georgia, Athens.

STRAVER, C. J. (1981) "Unmarried couples: different from marriage?" Alternative Lifestyles 4, 1: 43-74.

THORMAN, G. (1973) "Cohabitation: a report on couples living together." Futurist 7, 6: 250-253.

Time (1968) "Linda, the light housekeeper." April 26: 51.

TROST, J. (1981) "Cohabitation in the Nordic countries: from deviant phenomenon to social institution." Alternative Lifestyles 4, 4: 401-427.

——— (1979) Unmarried Cohabitation. Vasteras, Sweden: International Library.

VAN DEUSEN, E. L. (1974) Contract Cohabitation: An Alternative to Marriage. New York: Grove.

U.S. Bureau of the Census (1981) Marital Status and Living Arrangements: March 1980. Current Population Reports, Series P-20, No. 365. Washington, DC: Government Printing Office.

——— (1980) Marital Status and Living Arrangements: March 1979. Current Population Reports, Series P-20, No. 349. Washington, DC: Government Printing Office.

——— (1979) Household and Family Characteristics: March 1978. Current Population Reports, Series P-20, No. 340. Washington, DC: Government Printing Office.

——— (1977) Marital Status and Living Arrangements: March 1976. Current Population Reports, Series P-20, No. 306. Washington, DC: Government Printing Office.

WHITEHURST, R. N. (1974) "Sex role equality and changing meanings in cohabitation." Presented at the annual meetings of the North Central Sociological Association, Windsor, Canada.

——— (1969a) "The Unmalias on campus." Presented at the Annual Meetings of the National Council on Family Relations.

——— (1969b) "The double standard and male dominance in non-marital living arrangements: a preliminary statement. Presented at the annual meetings of the National Council on Family Relations.

YANKELOVICH, D. (1981) "New rules in American life: searching for self-fulfillment in a world turned upside down." Psychology Today (April): 35-91.

YLLO, K. A. (1978) "Non-marital cohabitation: beyond the college campus." Alternative Lifestyles 1, 1: 37-54.

CHAPTER 3

Voluntary Childlessness:
A Critical Assessment of the Research

JEAN E. VEEVERS

University of Victoria, Canada

Although presumably there have always been some couples who did not want to have children, and who were successful in avoiding them, the deliberate rejection of parenthood did not become a visible alternative until the early 1970s. Before that time, if the possibility of voluntary childlessness was considered at all, it was assumed to be an atypical pathology that fortunately affected only a few persons. The neglect by social scientists of the study of voluntary childlessness reflected not only their own biases, but also its lack of visibility and subsequent lack of public concern (Veevers, 1973a).

The social upheavals of the 1960s and the emergence of various counter-cultures were associated with an increasing pluralism of nontraditional family forms (Macklin, 1980). Puritanical restrictions on sexuality were modified or ignored, conventional definitions of marriage were called into question, and the traditional assumptions about sex roles were irrevocably challenged. Tangential to these major changes was a redefinition of the nature and meaning of parenthood. The injunction to be fruitful and multiply gave way to admonitions concerning responsible parenthood and freedom of choice, with the inevitable consequence of smaller families. The separation of sex from procreation, made possible by the birth control revolution, led to the increased possibility of a separation of marriage from procreation. The result was that, after centuries of pronatalism, the motherhood mandate could for the first time be successfully challenged.

During the 1970s, voluntary childlessness received increasing attention, with over 100 feature articles on it appearing in national magazines (McKirdy and Nissley, 1980). Recently, this attention expanded from publications predominantly concerned with so-called women's issues, to those with a broader base of appeal, such as *Psychology Today* (Albin, 1979),

U.S.A. Today (Benson, 1979), and *Newsweek* (Francke, 1980). The National Alliance for Optional Parenthood (NAOP) mounted a vigorous compaign for childlessness as a viable alternative to conventional family life.[1] Voluntary childlessness emerged "out of the closet" and now appears well established as a topic for debate and, at least for some, as a viable alternative lifestyle.

Of all couples, between 10 and 20 percent never have children (Freshnock and Cutright, 1978; Mattessich, 1979). Among women born at the turn of the century, childlessness rates were remarkably high, especially among Blacks, a phenomenon usually attributed to subfecundity. Careful examination of the data, however, suggests that even in the 1920s and 1930s, low parity was facilitated by widespread use of contraception and abortion (Davis, 1979). During the 1950s and 1960s, childlessness reached an all-time low (Mattessich, 1979), and the incidence of voluntary childlessness was conservatively estimated at about 5 percent of all married couples (Veevers, 1979). With declining fertility, the incidence of childlessness is increasing and is almost certain to continue to do so (Schapiro, 1980), with differentials in childlessness attributable mainly to choice rather than to fecundity problems (Freshnock and Cutright, 1978). In some instances, rates of childlessness can be remarkably high. Den Bandt (1980) estimates that of all marriages contracted in the Netherlands in 1980, as many as 20 percent may be deliberately childless. In the United States in 1978, among young single women aged 18 to 24, 18 percent expected to remain childless throughout their lives, a cohort that would be unlikely as yet to be aware of fecundity problems (Blake and del Pinal, 1981: 236).

While it seems likely that voluntary childlessness will continue to increase with increased contraceptive sophistication and increased permissiveness, it also seems likely that such an increase has intrinsic limitations. In the face of a millennium of pronatalism and a continuing cultural endorsement of the social significance of parenthood, most people are unwilling to relinquish parenthood as a life goal (Blake, 1979). Taking into account these various factors, the available evidence suggests support for Benson's (1979: 46) prediction that "in the medium-range future, the percentage of intentionally childless couples will not likely go below 6 percent or above 17 percent of all married couples."

In 1979, *Marriage and Family Review* published a review of more than 200 articles on voluntary childlessness, including a synthesis of 40 relevant research projects (Veevers, 1979). Rather than reiterate these materials, the present review will be limited to two further queries: First, what additional evidence has been forthcoming; and second, how does this evidence suggest that the meaning of childlessness may be changing? To answer these questions we have attempted to incorporate most of the remaining literature on voluntary childlessness published in English up until 1982, including 42 additional empirical research projects of direct relevance.[2]

The Social Meanings of Childlessness: Assessing Pronatalism

Early discussions of the subject of childlessness began with the assumption that American society was basically pronatalist. They were replete with anecdotal evidence illustrating pejorative views of nonparenthood, in which the deliberately childless were described as maladjusted, immature, unhappy, unfulfilled, lonely, selfish, immoral, unhappily married, and prone to divorce. Assertions of the existence of pronatalism have subsequently been documented in a number of empirical research studies, as summarized in Table 3.1.

Gallup polls reveal a "virtual unanimity" of opinion that childlessness is disadvantageous, especially for men (Blake, 1979: 249). There is an explicit rejection of nonparenthood as allowing a more interesting, glamorous, and personally satisfying existence. The indirect costs of children are viewed as unimportant, and only about 11 percent of adults consider that direct costs outweigh the benefits (Blake and del Pinal, 1981).

Studies based on projective techniques (Peterson, 1975, 1977) or on surveys (Bierkens et al., 1978) establish the existence of a negative image of childless persons. Those opting out of parenthood are perceived to experience negative presures and rejection, and to be likely to change their minds (Peterson, 1982). Jamieson et al., (1979: 226) report a stereotype of childless women as "less sensitive and loving, less typical of American women, more active in women's liberation, less happy, less well adjusted, less likely to get along with her parents, and less likely to be happy and satisfied at age 65." Ratings of childless men were more unfavorable than were those of women, a finding surprising in its contravention of the expected double standard.

Comparing images of voluntary and involuntary childlessness, Calhoun and Selby (1980) found that among wives, the deliberately childless were less well liked and less well adjusted than the subfecund; among husbands, fathers were viewed as less psychologically disturbed than nonfathers regardless of their circumstances. They offer the novel contention that "it may be that with respect to children, men are judged in terms of effects of their actions while women are judged in terms of the reasons for their actions" (Calhoun and Selby, 1980: 183). Contrary to expectations, Calhoun and Selby did not find childlessness perceived as related to divorce. Conclusions of this study and of Jamison et al. (1979) must be treated with caution, however, since both are based on small groups of undergraduates, an atypical segment of the population that, by unfortunate necessity, still remains the mainstay of research in social science.

TABLE 3.1 Summary of Selected Empirical Research on Pronatalism

Author, Publication Date, and Place of Research	Size of Sample and Nature of Design	Area of Concern
Peterson (Chicago: 1975)	178 undergraduates in 1971 and 290 undergraduates in 1973 asked to draw a picture of a happy couple married 2 or 5 years.	Extent to which presence of children is seen as essential for a happily married couple.
Peterson (Chicago and Australia: 1977)	Both sexes; 128 undergraduates in Chicago; 149 clinical psychologists randomly selected from Australian Psychological society; evaluation of bogus case histories identical except for parental and employment status.	Perceived happiness and emotional health of 39-year-old wife, described as either childless or with two children, and as either a housewife or working.
Bierkens et al. (Holland: 1978)	153 inhabitants of Nijegen; mailed questionnaire with low response rate of 65 percent for females, 37 percent for males.	Perceived traits of persons who do or do not want children.
Strong (Connecticut: 1978)	354 undergraduates, both sexes, randomly selected; questionnaires involving attitudes toward 12 alternative marriage and family forms.	Correlates of positive attitudes to alternative family forms and of willingness to participate in them, including voluntary childlessness.
Blake (USA: 1979)	1600 respondents: nationwide Gallup Poll of adults; 7-item Likert and scale of attitudes toward childlessness.	Correlates of responses to five items concerning disadvantages of childlessness and two items concerning advantages.

Study	Description
Jamison et al. (San Diego: 1979)	156 undergraduates and 61 high school students; structured questionnaire to evaluate two hypothetical case histories.	Perceived traits of sterilized childless wives compared with sterilized mothers with two children.
Jamison et al. (San Diego: 1979)	116 undergraduates; structured questionnaire ratings of persons with and without children.	Perceived traits of voluntarily childless men and women compared with fathers and mothers.
Calhoun and Selby (Southeast USA: 1980)	113 undergraduates; structured questionnaire to rate social paradigms of couples with and without children.	Perceived traits of voluntarily and involuntarily childless couples compared with parents of two.
Blake and del Pinal (USA: 1981)	1555 respondents; nationwide Gallup Poll of adults; 14-item Likert scale on consequences of parenthood.	Correlates of balance of perceived costs and benefits of having children or being childless.
Patterson and Defrain (Nebraska: 1981)	29 major textbooks, copywrited 1969 or later, used in high school classes in family, home economics, or related subjects.	Pronatalism in family studies texts.
Peterson (Chicago: 1982)	203 undergraduates, both sexes, asked to complete stories about persons who did or did not intend to have children.	Outcomes of decisions of single and married persons to have or to avoid children.
Peterson (Perth, Australia: 1982)	64 clerks and 75 school teachers, aged 18 to 44; Likert-type scale of attitudes toward childlessness.	Correlation of positive attitude toward childlessness with other liberal values.

Documentation of the existence of pronatalism as a cultural theme suggests a next logical focus of inquiry, namely: What are the social characteristics that are associated with being more or less pronatalistic in one's views? Blake and del Pinal (1981) report that the perception that the costs of children exceed the benefits is more likely among nonparents than among parents, and among those with no religion and who live in large cities. However, they stress that the data do *not* vary significantly according to the major social and demographic characteristics. Young women are more concerned with the costs of children than are young men: However, among persons aged 25 to 34, men are more antinatalist. Blake and del Pinal speculate that men and women may be "out of sync" because male support for nonparenthood has been related to antiestablishment ideology, which is becoming more conservative, whereas female support has been related to feminism, which is accelerating. Assessment of the costs and benefits of parenthood seems more closely related to sex role attitudes and anxieties than to any single background characteristic. A major component of antinatalist views is the suspicion that parenthood is a potent force for inducing conventional sex roles in marriage (Blake and del Pinal, 1981: 260).

Demographic Correlates of Childlessness

Generally, the characteristics of voluntarily childless couples are similar to those of persons who have only one or two children. Compared with others, childless couples are more likely to live in *large urban areas.* Childlessness in general, and voluntary childlessness in particular, is strongly associated with relatively *late age at first marriage.* Compared with other women, deliberately childless wives tend to have *above-average education,* often having university degrees. One of the most consistent findings is that voluntary childlessness is associated with *low religiosity,* as measured by self-designation as an atheist or agnostic, by an absence of religious affiliation, or by irregular church attendance.

Although a willingness to stay childless may have some relation to parental rejection and dissatisfaction (Strong, 1978), most evidence suggests that the childless come from *conventional family backgrounds* without distinctive traits (Feldman, 1981; Levine, 1979; Magarick and Brown, 1981). Some researchers suggest that voluntary childlessness is disproportionately common among *only children* (Baum and Cope, 1980; Deven and Last, 1980), but other studies have failed to substantiate such differences (Levine, 1979; Magarick and Brown, 1981). A *small family of origin* is known to be associated with low fertility aspirations, and controlling for this variable may mitigate the effects of birth order (Stokes and Johnson, 1979).

Childless women are two to three times as likely as other women to be *gainfully employed* (Grindstaff et al., 1981: 344). Since they are relatively well educated, and since they tend to show *above average career commitment,* when they work they are disproportionately involved in *high-status occupations* in management and the professions. Consequently, they tend to earn relatively *high incomes,* with the result that their total family income is especially high. The cause/effect relationship implicit in these correlates of childlessness remains unresolved. Some women doubtless forego having children in order to pursue a career; others may become involved in a career and subsequently feel a diminished desire for parenthood. The key to predicting future trends in childlessness may be the labor force opportunities that become available (Freshnock and Cutright, 1978), especially the prestigious, well-paid jobs available to young women (Knox, 1980: 148). However, the intense labor force involvement of most childless wives should not obscure the fact that there are always some women who neither work nor have children (Mattessich, 1979). Opting out of both these preoccupations is a truly variant lifestyle worthy of special attention in future research (Baum and Cope, 1980).

With the marked increase in women's labor force participation and the concomitant decline in fertility there has been a general decline in differential fertility. Discrepancies in the characteristics of mothers and of voluntarily childless wives are still extant, and still vary in the expected directions, buy they are less pronounced than they were. Contrary to the findings for North America, studies in the Netherlands fail to report the expected associations with education or social class (den Bandt, 1980; Deven and Last, 1980), suggesting that voluntarily childlessness there is less restricted to an elite group. In the foreseeable future, fertility in general is expected to remain low, and childlessness is expected to become an increasingly acceptable option. Under these circumstances, the demographic profile of the voluntarily childless will become less distinctly different from the profile of married couples who plan to have small families.

Childlessness and Adjustment

A critical issue in the study of childlessness is the fundamental question of the beneficial or the deleterious effects of having or not having children. There are not yet sufficient comparative data to formulate definite conclusions regarding the effects of parenthood or its absence on psychological and social adjustment. However, over the past several years, some additional work has been done that contributes suggestive, albeit inconclusive, evidence for the ongoing debate concerning the consequences of parenthood. Some research is concerned with childlessness per se, and hence is less than ideal in that it does not distinguish between the subfecund and the deliberately childless. Research projects in this category are summarized in Table 3.2. Other research, summarized in Table 3.3, is of direct relevance since the respondents involved are clearly those who are childless by choice. Although adjustment in one area usually has consequences

(text continues on p. 88)

TABLE 3.2 Summary of Selected Empirical Research on Childlessness: Involuntary Undifferentiated from Voluntary

Author, Publication Date, and Place of Research	Size of Sample and Nature of Design	Characteristics of Respondents
Hargens et al. (USA: 1978)	96 research scientists; 16 childless wives and 7 childless husbands compared with 41 mothers and 32 fathers; systematic random sample from *Directory of Graduate Research*, supplemented by data from *American men and Women of Science* and mailed questionnaires.	Married persons employed in universities or government research laboratories; evaluated as more-or-less successful by publication and citation indexes; most males married to housewives; most females in two-career households.
Heath (USA: 1978)	28 childless men compared with 40 fathers; longitudinal study of intensive interviews and testing from adolescence to early thirties.	Respondents originally selected to represent mature, intermediate, and immature college freshmen; respondents later primarily in professional-managerial class; childless men included eight who never married.
Bachrach (USA: 1980)	428 childless persons compared with 2566 persons with one or more living children; national probability sample of persons over 65.	Caucasians and Blacks; excluded never-married persons.

Gibson (England and Wales: 1980)	297 wives childless at the time of their divorce compared with 848 divorcing mothers; one in fifty random sample of all couples divorcing in England and Wales during first six months of 1972; data as recorded by the Registrar General.	Most divorces were granted to women under age 45 emerging from primary marriages; definitions of children include adopted children; considers both duration of cohabitation and duration of legal marriage.
Kivett and Learner (North Carolina: 1980)	66 childless men and women compared with 315 with one or more living children; representative sample of adults aged 65 to 99; secondary analysis of structured questionnaire.	Caucasians and Blacks; rural; mean age 73; 40 never married; 26 married.
Halkiw (Toronto, Canada: 1981a)	1971 Census of Canada Public Use Sample Tape: intact families (N = 3314) of whom 14.2 percent (N = 470) were childless.	Wife aged 35 to 64.
Singh and Williams (USA: 1981)	968 persons, subsample of NORC national surveys 1974-1978.	Noninstitutionalized White and Black persons 65 years and older.

TABLE 3.3 Summary of Selected Empirical Research on Voluntary Childlessness

Author, Publication Date, and Place of Research	Size of Sample and Nature of Design	Characteristics of Respondents
Delleman et al. (Netherlands: 1975)	100 childless couples drawn from 1978 self-selected respondents; no control group; mailed questionnaire.	Married and unmarried couples; mean age 33; upper middle class; mostly working wives.
Tiecholz (Boston: 1977, 1978)	70 childless wives; 38 committed to permanent childlessness; 32 planning their first child; self-selected respondents, matched for age, education, and SES; structured questionnaire with psychological tests plus interview.	Urban, well-educated employed women aged 23 to 38, judged to be well adjusted and feminine.
Denniston (Seattle, Washington: 1978)	From 1971 to 1974, 165 childless men requested vasectomies; 157 received them; follow-up interviews were done on 23.	Mostly young men under 30; half single; working class; patients reported no undue complications or regrets.
Brown and Magarick (1979) and Magarick and Brown (Maryland: 1980)	44 voluntarily vasectomized, childless men and 51 vasectomized fathers; purposive sample from a vasectomy clinic; mailed questionnaire.	Caucasians; urban; middle class; mostly working wives; mean age 30; geographically mobile.
Houseknecht (Ohio: 1979a)	51 wives explicitly childless by choice; availability sample selected by modified network approach; in-depth interviews.	Caucasians; aged 25 to 40 with mean age of 30; married minimum of five years; no known fecundity impairments; most employed in upper-middle-class positions.

Source	Method	Sample
Houseknecht (Ohio: 1979b)	50 wives explicitly childless by choice; availability sample selected by modified network approach; precision matched by education, religion, and labor force status with 50 mothers; in-depth interviews plus structured questionnaire.	As above; mean marriage duration of 7 years for childless wives; 13 years for mothers; half of sample were nonreligious; detailed assessment of marital adjustment.
Inazu (Cincinnati: 1979)	92 childless couples; random survey of currently childless married couples selected by random digit dialing and interviewed by telephone.	Urban; included persons involuntarily, voluntarily, and temporarily childless; both husband and wife responded.
Jones (Los Angeles and Florida: 1979)	36 voluntarily childless wives compared with 55 voluntary mothers; purposive samples; mailed questionnaire.	All of the childless and 33 of the mothers were employed; childless drawn from NON.
Levine (Michigan: 1979)	25 deliberately childless wives, matched by age, birth order, and education with 25 mothers of planned families; in-depth interview plus psychological tests.	Women at least 25, in primary marriages of at least 5 years duration, living with their husbands.
Nijhuis-Nell (Netherlands: 1979)	45 voluntarily childless wives compared with 57 undecided, 544 postponers, and 3010 mothers; random sample of wives from 1963-1973 marriage cohorts; structured questionnaire.	Wives in first marriages, under 40 years of age, with no known fecundity problems.
Baum and Cope (Britain: 1980)	161 voluntarily childless wives plus 71 childless wives undecided about motherhood or postponing it; mailed questionnaire to self-selected volunteers.	Middle class and working class; aged 28 to 62; married at least one year; most gainfully employed.

(continued)

TABLE 3.3 Continued

Author, Publication Date, and Place of Research	Size of Sample and Nature of Design	Characteristics of Respondents
Benjamin et al. (Los Angeles: 1980)	Of 45 childless women electing sterilization, 35 were followed up after 1-1/2 to 4 years with a self-administered questionnaire; of these, 21 gave nonmedical reasons.	Average age 28; 17 single, 8 married, and 10 divorced.
den Bandt (Netherlands: 1980)	65 voluntarily childless wives compared with 41 undecided, 23 postponers, and 29 mothers; random sample supplemented with purposive sample of voluntarily childless wives; mailed screening questionnaire plus in-depth interviews.	Urban; wives under 35 married a minimum of three years; first child under 2 years of age to exclude "forced" marriages from control group.
Deven and Last (Belgium: Dutch-speaking 1980)	48 childless wives compared with 3081 mothers, both from a random sample of all women; focused interviews plus psychological tests.	Wives aged 20 to 44, living with their husbands, using contraceptives, no known history of sterility; rural and urban areas; 94 percent employed; average education; above-average incomes.
Peterson (Illinois: 1980)	23 adolescents intending to remain childless compared with 216 intending to have children; availability sample; anonymous questionnaire plus psychological tests.	Urban freshmen and sophomores from a junior college and a university psychology class.
Peterson (Illinois: 1980)	18 adolescents intending to remain childless compared with 196 intending to have children; independent sample of students with known GPAs; questionnaire.	Urban freshmen and sophomores from a junior college and a university psychology class.

Study	Sample	Characteristics
Peterson (Illinois: 1980)	14 adolescents intending to remain childless compared with 112 intending to have children; availability sample of students involved in a MMPI testing project.	Urban university freshmen; mostly Caucasian.
Polonko (Mid-western USA: 1980)	95 wives intending to be childless compared with 530 wives intending to be mothers; stratified random sample of marriage bureau applicants; questionnaire.	Caucasian wives currently in primary marriages, married after age 21.
Pupo (San Diego: 1980)	Sample size not given; committed childless couples differentiated from undecided couples and from future parents.	Caucasians; heterosexuals; cohabiting minimum of five years; middle class; aged 24 to 32.
Feldman (USA: 1981)	37 intentionally childless couples randomly selected from NON membership compared with 42 intentional parents; parents interviewed separately in second trimester and 6 months after birth, childless sent separate mailed questionnaires.	Matched for age (late twenties) and husband's education and occupation; childless wives had higher education and employment levels; marriage duration 34 months for parents, 62 months for childless.
Halkiw (Ontario Canada: 1981b)	38 voluntarily childless couples married minimum of 5 years; purposive sample, no control group; structured telephone interview.	Average age 38; average marriage duration 8.7 years; highly educated; both working with high career commitment and income; low religiosity.
Beckman and Houser (Los Angeles: 1982)	719 women in approximately equal groups: widowed and married, with and without children; individual interviews.	Women aged 60 to 75.

for adjustment in all areas, for the purposes of analysis it is convenient to consider separately six dimensions: mental health, androgynous sex roles, divorce, marital morale, occupational success, and finally, senescence.[3]

Mental Health

In assessing the relationship of childlessness and mental health, some few researchers consider the desire to avoid parenthood de facto evidence of psychological maladjustment and a prodromal indicator of various pathologies (Peterson, 1980). Although labeling theory suggests that the experience of being considered deviant should have negative effects, severe consequences have not been observed, and a number of studies report no difference in the general adjustment of childless persons compared with parents (Feldman, 1981; Jones, 1979; Levine, 1979; Magarick and Brown, 1981). Thus Tiecholz (1977: 1865) concludes that "the popular and professional opinions holding voluntary childlessness to be associated with poor social adjustment, poor mental health, or lack of appropriate sexual identity do not receive support." Persons opting for childlessness appear to be more independent than others and generally well defended against disapproval.

Some theorists hold that being deprived of responsibility for children and interaction with them detracts from the development and maturation of adult personality. In an exceptionally thorough longitudinal study comparing fathers and nonfathers, Heath (1978) found that although they did not differ in adolescence, they did differ significantly on 11 percent of measures of adult personality: fathers were more physically and psychologically healthy, more mature, and more competent. Unfortunately, Heath did not differentiate men in terms of marital status, thereby confounding the effects of marriage and of parenthood. The number of childless men was small, and there was no distinction between deliberate and biological childlessness.

Androgynous Sex Roles

Positive attitudes toward childlessness appear to be associated with nontraditional sex role attitudes (Feldman, 1981; Polonko, 1980; Strong, 1978). In addition, the circumstances of the childless dyad facilitate the enactment of egalitarian roles. However, childless couples are not clearly more egalitarian than parents (Feldman, 1981), and while some studies suggest that childless women are more androgynous (Tiecholtz, 1978), others have failed to document a difference (Jones, 1979; Levine, 1979).

Divorce

Although the relationship of childlessness and divorce has been a topic of debate for at least a quarter of a century, the available data still do not allow a definite conclusion as to whether or not marriages with children are intrinsically less prone to divorce than are those that are childless (Leete,

1976). One problem is that the critical variable of marriage duration has been interpreted in terms of the de jure length of marriage, as measured from legal marriage to legal divorce; in reality, the de facto length of marriage, as measured by the actual time a couple cohabits, may be the more relevant component. Gibson (1980: 130) reports an increase in England and Wales in the proportion of divorcing couples who are childless. However, he argues successfully that when controls are introduced for the wife's age at marriage and for the de facto marriage duration, there is "little difference" in the levels of infertility of divorced and still-married couples (Gibson, 1980: 125).

Marital Morale

Evidence on the relationship of marital adjustment and parenthood remains contradictory. Several studies have failed to find any systematic differences between parents and childless couples (Feldman, 1981; Magarick and Brown, 1981; Pupo, 1980; Tiecholz, 1978). In contrast, one study of fathers reported them more satisfied with their marriages and their sexual relations than were nonfathers (Heath, 1978). A Canadian study found childless persons, especially childless wives, more likely than parents to report their marriages to be "very happy" (Lupri and Frieders, 1981). Another researcher found voluntarily childless wives to have higher overall marital adjustment scores than did a matched control group of mothers, and concluded that "the relationship between childlessness and enhanced marital adjustment satisfaction found by earlier investigators . . . is not spurious" (Houseknecht, 1979b: 264).

Occupational Success

Among working wives, childless women have a competitive advantage over mothers in that they are better educated and are likely to be more committed to their careers and to have continuous rather than interrupted employment histories. An absence of child care demands means, in most instances, that the childless woman has a relative surplus of time and energy that, in individualistic and creative occupations, can be manifest in increased productivity and recognition. For example, among women of eminence listed in Who's Who, a disproportionate number are childless (Veevers, 1979: 12). Research on scientists suggests that the childless are more productive (Hargens et al., 1978), although this finding cannot be generalized to all academics (Hamovitch and Morgenstern, 1977). The edge available to the childless is most clearly manifest at the upper levels of the most prestigious occupations, where virtuoso performance involves both exceptional demands and exceptional rewards.

Senescence

One issue of concern to persons considering childlessness is the impact it may have upon their happiness and well-being in old age. Several studies have recently addressed themselves to this question. Singh and Williams (1981) found childlessness among old persons to be associated with negative reports of satisfaction with family life, a relationship especially pronounced among women and among persons over 70. Unfortunately for our purposes, it is not clear if low satisfaction with family life per se is necessarily associated with general dissatisfaction with one's circumstances. Beckman and Houser (1982) found that, while widowed, childless, older women had lower psychological well-being than did widowed mothers, among married older women childlessness had no significant effects on well-being. In a nationwide study, Bachrach (1980) found that although the childless were more likely than others to live alone, except for manual workers and for those with serious problems, they were no more likely to be socially isolated. Kivett and Learner (1980) found little association with the presence or absence of children and loneliness, health, or general quality of life for old persons. Although children are a sustaining force for many old persons, it is apparent from the data that they are not irreplacable sources for everyone. Many elderly childless persons appear either to manage effectively in relatively isolated situations, or to find alternative sources of interaction and support. Unfortunately, none of the studies of senescence have differentiated the deliberately childless from the subfecund, a distinction that presumably is strongly associated with perceived satisfaction at all stages of the life cycle.

Deciding to be Childless

The timing of the decision to forego parenthood provides a convenient dichotomy of childless couples. Some of the deliberately childless decided before they were married that they would never have children: They were, in effect, *early articulators* of an antinatalist ideology (Houseknecht, 1979a). Others were *postponers,* in that they started marriage intending to have children and later changed their minds. The proportion of early articulators has been variously reported from about one-third of all couples (Houseknecht, 1979a; Veevers, 1973a) to one-half or more (Baum and Cope, 1980; Magarick and Brown, 1981; Niphuis-Nell, 1979).

When couples decide to be childless is relatively easy to determine, at least in general terms; why they do so is more complex; and how the decision is made is the most difficult of all. Reasons for wanting to avoid parenthood are difficult to document in that respondents are unskilled at verbalizing their motivations. Moreover, in the absence of longitudinal studies, respondents are required to formulate retrospective accounts, with some unknown distortion due to forgetfulness or to rationalization. Moreover, the initial reasons for deciding to postpone parenthood may be quite different from the reasons for continuing to postpone it.

Although verbalized concerns of childless couples do not constitute a consistent pattern, they do involve a number of recurrent themes. Not surprisingly, they view children as relatively costly in terms of their impact on the wife's career and on their standard of living. They express an intolerance for debt (Polonko, 1980) and an appreciation of the relative affluence of the two-income household. Financial themes are often secondary to concern with freedom, independence, and the pursuit of an adult-centered lifestyle, which may preclude an interest in children or an involvement in childish things. Some persons who value the dyadic intensity of their marriages may be reluctant to have it diluted by the presence of children (Inazu, 1979; Levine, 1979; Polonko, 1980). Houseknecht (1979b) suggests that the decision process and background factors involved may be systematically different for early articulators than for postponers, with the former being more distant from their parents and more achievement oriented.

Childlessness and Social Policy

The pronatalism that is pervasive in virtually all cultures is functional for the continued recruitment of married couples to the difficult and often demanding tasks of childbearing and child rearing. Protests concerning pronatalism are appropriate when they focus not upon its existence per se, but pressure that is deemed coercive. Unfortunately, pronatalism (like sexism) is to some extent a judgment extant in the eye of the beholder. The National Alliance for Optional Parenthood has been instrumental in raising subtle pronatalist messages to the level of awareness. Having done so, it is important not to become hypersensitive to pronatalism in any of its manifestations. Platitudes and policies supporting an explicitly antinatalist perspective are as inappropriate as are pronatalist manifestos. Ideally, what is desired is a situation that would maximize individual options by outlining objectively the pros and cons of parenthood and leaving couples to their own decisions in light of their other priorities.

An increasingly laissez-faire attitude toward parenthood is well on the way to being achieved as childless marriages become more acceptable (den Bandt, 1980; Knox, 1980). A number of lay self-help books offer guidance for the couple considering remaining childless (Bombardieri, 1981; Burgwyn, 1981; Harper, 1980; Shealy and Shealy, 1981). Educators are beginning to present childlessness as a legitimate choice (Patterson and Defrain, 1981) and to advocate the formation of support groups (Prochaska and Coyle, 1979). The medical profession, including nurses (Rosenthal, 1980), is becoming more cognizant of its role in facilitating the childless option, with special attention being directed toward the right of childless men and women, married or not, to elect to be sterilized (Benjamin et al., 1980; Denniston, 1978; Lieberman et al., 1979).

Barnett makes a strong case for the appropriateness of child exclusion policies in housing, arguing that compelling considerations in the promotion of adults-only apartments and condominiums include "protection of the childfree lifestyle, with a concomitant increase in individual freedom and creativity, and promotion of population control" (Barnett, 1979: 983).

Although pronatalist pressures still exist, there is increasing sympathy for the idea that parenthood should be the result of conscious planning rather than of sexual happenstance. The childfree movement began, as nascent social movements frequently do, with the upper middle class. With the general decline in fertility, the disparaging concern with childlessness per se is less vehement and pejorative than it once was. Once the prospect of free choice is offered, it is inevitable that the number of persons opting for it will increase. There is some evidence that what began as an option for elite career women may filter down to become a viable option at all socioeconomic levels.

Implications for Future Research

Being unable to eschew the venerable tradition of calling for additional research, we shall at least specify some parameters of it. The distinction between voluntary and involuntary childlessness is of paramount importance and must be scrupulously incorporated into every research design. Theoretically and pragmatically, the consequences of a phenomenon must be assumed to be quite different if it involves the achievement of a major life goal, or the frustration of one. "Choice may well be one of the most significant determinants of satisfaction with a particular life-style" (Feldman, 1981: 593). The issue is further complicated by the possibility that a couple who initially intended merely to postpone childbearing may ultimately find that they have become subfecund or even sterile. At this point, they are involuntarily childless. One spouse may desire children while the other does not, so that even if both are fecund, childlessness is in a sense "involuntary" on the part of the reluctant but compliant partner. The critical question for research purposes is: *On the issue of childbearing, are the persons involved getting what they want?*

The issue of self-determination of parental status also raises issues regarding appropriate control groups. Those few studies that do have control groups often use samples of parents that include both those who entered the role willingly and an unknown but not insubstantial proportion of people who were "conscripted" through unwanted pregnancies. Conclusive studies of voluntary childlessness should compare persons who elected to stay childless with those who planned to have children (Feldman, 1981; Jones, 1979; Levine, 1979).

Most work on childlessness has been done on wives (Schapiro, 1980). The next necessary step is to broaden the base of inquiry to include husbands. In addition, on issues such as fertility the couple, rather than the individual, may prove the most relevant unit of analysis (Insazu, 1979). Ultimately, it would also be desirable to extend the study of childlessness to include single persons, whose decision to not marry may or may not interface with their decision not to procreate.

Having differentiated deliberate from unintentional childlessness, the next step is to distinguish among kinds of childless couples. Childless wives in dual-career marriages need to be compared with working mothers (Houseknecht, 1979b; Jones, 1979). The unusual childless wife who elects to stay at home has been ignored and needs be compared with other housewives. Houseknecht (1979a) makes a valuable beginning of a typology by comparing persons who are early articulators with persons who are postponers. There is some suggestive evidence that differences in these two kinds of childlessness may go beyond the timing of the decision. Early articulators may be predominantly concerned with the disadvantages attendant upon parenthood: They view themselves as different from others and are more militant in their dislike of children and their presentation of an antinatalist philosophy. In contrast to these rejectors, postponers may be less concerned with the disadvantages of parenthood than with the advantages of the childfree lifestyle; they are aficionados of some other interest and tend to view themselves as not intrinsically different from their more conventional counterparts (Veevers, 1980: 157-159). Future research might usefully be concerned with the development and documentation of this preliminary typology.

Deliberate childlessness still clearly violates the dominant family and fertility mores of our culture, and persons opting for it are still stereotyped and sanctioned for their unusual preferences. However, the social saliency of childlessness as a flawed identity is markedly less than it was even a few years ago, and persons choosing this alternative are not subject to the same degree of pronatalist pressure. Voluntary childlessness has increased both in prevalence and in visibility, and it is clear that this trend will continue for the foreseeable future, perhaps to a maximum rate of 15 or 20 percent of all married couples. While voluntary childlessness will never become a dominant lifestyle, it is increasingly gaining in acceptability as one viable alternative lifestyle, ideally suited for some persons who would find the rigors of parenthood an undue and perhaps unnecessary burden and strain. At the present, empirical knowledge of the causes and consequences of deliberate childlessness remains scanty and inconclusive. An expansion of research on this topic would go a long way in providing answers to the critical question for would-be parents: What kinds of persons under what circumstances are likely to find parenthood a worthwhile and rewarding experience? Conversely, what kinds of persons under what circumstances would be best advised to live out their lives without children?

Notes

1. The National Alliance for Optional Parenthood (NAOP) formerly the National Organization for Nonparents, is now located at 2010 Massachusetts Avenue, Washington,

D.C. 20036. Its publication, *Optional Parenthood Today,* presents a potpourri of research reports, mass media coverage, and personal testimonials from childless persons.

2. Because of space limitations, not all materials concerning childlessness could be mentioned in this review or in the previous one (Veevers, 1979). A more exhaustive bibliography including materials of peripheral relevance is available from the author on request.

3. For a more detailed presentation of research concerning the possible consequences of voluntary childlessness see "The Choice of Childlessness: Researching the Repercussions" (Veevers, 1982).

References

ALBIN, (1979) "The healthy adjustment of the childless woman." Psychology Today 13: 29-30.

BACHRACH, (1980) "Childlessness and social isolation among the elderly." Journal of Marriage and the Family 42: 627-636.

BARNETT, L. D. (1979) "Child exclusion policies in housing." Kentucky Law Journal 67: 967-986.

BAUM, F. and D. R. COPE (1980) "Some characteristics of intentionally childless wives in Britain." Journal of Biosocial Science 12: 287-299.

BECKMAN, L. J. and B. B. HOUSER (1982) "Consequences of childlessness on the social-psychological well-being of older women." Journal of Gerontology 37: 243-250.

——— (1980) "Elective sterilization in childless women." Fertility and Sterility 34: 116-120.

BENSON, D. E. (1979) "Intentionally childless couples." U.S.A. Today 107: 45-46.

BIERKENS, P. B. et al. (1978) "Attitude tegenover vrijwillige kinderloosheid: een onderzoek." Medisch Contact 33: 1045-1050.

BLAKE, J. (1979) "Is zero preferred? American attitudes toward childlessness in the 1970s." Journal of Marriage and the Family 41: 245-257.

——— and J. H. del PINAL (1981) "The childlessness option: Recent American views of nonparenthood." p. 235-261 in Gerry Hendershot and Paul Placek (eds.) Predicting Fertility: The Validity and Reliability of Birth Expectations. Lexington, MA; D. C. Heath.

BOMBARDIERI, M. (1981) The Baby Decision. New York: Rawson, Wade.

BROWN, R. A. and R. H. MAGARICK (1979) "Psychologic effects of vasectomy in voluntarily childless men." Urology 14: 55-58.

BURGWYN, D. (1981) Marriage Without Children. New York: Harper & Row.

CALHOUN, L. G. and J. W. SELBY (1980) "Voluntary childlessness, involuntary childlessness, and having children: a study of social perceptions." Family Relations 29: 181-183.

DAVIS, N. J. (1979) "The political economy of reproduction." Dissertation Abstracts 40.

DELLEMAN, I. et al. (1975) Motieven voor Vrijwillige Kinderloosheid. Groningen: Instituut voor Algemene Psychologie.

den BANDT, M. L. (1980) "Voluntary childlessness in the Netherlands." Alternative Lifestyles 3: 329-349.

DENNISTON, G. C. (1978) "The effect of vasectomy on childless men." Journal of Reproductive Medicine 21: 151-152.

DEVEN, F. and L. LAST (1980) Data on Voluntary Childlessness: A Technical Note. Brussels, Belgium: Population and Family Study Center, Ministry of Public Health.

FELDMAN, H. (1981) "A comparison of intentional parents and intentionally childless couples." Journal of Marriage and the Family 43: 593-600.

FRESHNOCK, L. and P. CUTRIGHT (1978) "Structural determinants of childlessness: a non-recursive analysis of 1970 U.S. rates." Social Biology 25: 169-78.

FRANCKE, L. B. (1980) "Childless by choice." Newsweek (January 14): 96.

GIBSON, C. (1980) "Childlessness and marital instability: a re-examination of the evidence." Journal of Biosocial Science 12: 121-132.

GRINDSTAFF, C.F., T.R. BALAKRISHNAN, and G.E. EBANKS (1981) "Socio-demographic correlates of childlessness: an analysis of the 1971 Canadian census." Canadian Journal of Sociology 6: 337-352.

HALKIW, W. (1981a) "Voluntary childlessness in Canada (Part I: census)." Master's thesis, Queen's University, Kingston, Ontario.

——— (1981b) "Voluntary childlessness in Canada (Part II: interviews)." Master's thesis, Queen's University, Kingston, Ontario.

HAMOVITCH, W. and R.D. MORGENSTERN (1977) "Children and the productivity of academic women." Journal of Higher Education 48: 633-645.

HARGENS, L.L., J.C. McCANN, and B.R. RESKIN (1978) "Productivity and repro-ductivity: fertility and professional achievement among research scientists." Social Forces 57: 154-163.

HARPER, K. (1980) The Childfree Alternative. Brattleboro, VT: Stephen Greene.

HEATH, D.H. (1978) "What meaning and effects does fatherhood have for the maturing of professional men?" Merrill-Palmer Quarterly 24: 265-278.

HOUSEKNECHT, S.K. (1979a) "Timing of the decision to remain voluntarily childless: evidence for continuous socialization." Psychology of Women Quarterly 4: 81-96.

——— (1979b) "Childlessness and marital adjustment." Journal of Marriage and the Family 41: 259-265.

INAZU, J.K. (1979) "Perceptions of the effects of a newcomer as a factor in voluntary childlessness." Dissertation Abstracts 40: 1957.

JAMISON, P.H., L.R. FRANZINI, and R.M. KAPLAN (1979) "Some assumed characteris-tics of voluntarily childfree women and men." Psychology of Women Quarterly 4: 266-273.

JONES, S.L. (1979) "Towards a psychological profile of voluntary childfree women." Dissertation Abstracts 40: 895B.

KIVETT, V.R. and R.M. LEARNER (1980) "Perspectives on the childless rural elderly: a comparative analysis." The Gerontologist 20: 708-716.

KNOX, D. (1980) "Trends in marriage and the family — the 1980s." Family Relations 29 (April): 145-150.

LEETE, R. (1976) "Marriage and divorce." Population Trends 10: 17.

LEVINE, J.O. (1979) "Voluntarily childfree women and mothers: a comparative study." Dissertation Abstracts 39: 3524.

LIEBERMAN, R.G. et al. (1979) "Vasectomy for the single childless man." Journal of Family Practice 8: 181-184.

LUPRI, E. and J. FRIDERES (1981) "The quality of marriage and the passage of time: marital satisfaction over the family life cycle." Canadian Journal of Sociology 6: 283-305.

MACKLIN, E.D. (1980) "Nontraditional family forms: a decade of research." Journal of Marriage and the Family 42: 905-922.

MAGARICK, R.H. and R.A. BROWN (1981) "Social and emotional aspects of voluntary childlessness in vasectomized childless men." Journal of Biosocial Science 13: 157-167.

MATTESSICH, P.W. (1979) "Childlessness and its correlates in historical perspective." Journal of Family History 4: 299-307.

McKIRDY, G. and D. NISSLEY (1980) A Decade of Voluntary Childlessness: A Bibliog-raphy. Washington, DC: National Alliance for Optional Parenthood.

NIPHUIS-NELL, M. (1979) "Kenmerken van vrijwillig kinderloze vrouwen in Nederland." Bevolking en Gezin 2 (February).

PATTERSON, L.A. and J. DeFRAIN (1981) "Pronatalism in high school family studies texts." Family Relations 30, 2: 211-217.

PETERSON, R.A. (1982) "Attitudes toward the childless spouse." Sex Roles: A Journal of Research.

——— (1980) "Intended childlessness in late adolescence: personality and psychopathology." Journal of Youth and Adolescence 9: 439-448.

——— (1977) "Attitudes toward the 'childless wife' life style." Presented to the Australian Psychological Society, Adelaide, South Australia, August.

——— (1975) "Change in college students' attitude toward child-bearing from 1971 to 1973." Journal of Personality Assessment 39: 225-227.

POLONKO, K. A. (1980) "Accounting for the conditions of voluntary childlessness." Dissertation Abstracts 40: 4261.

PROCHASKA, J. and J. R. COYLE (1979) "Choosing parenthood: a needed family life education group." Social Casework: Journal of Contemporary Social Work 60: 289-295.

PUPO, A. M. (1980) "A study of voluntarily childless couples." Dissertation Abstracts 41: 1095B.

ROSENTHAL, T. (1980) "Voluntary childlessness and the nurse's role." American Journal of Maternal Child Nursing 5: 398-402.

SCHAPIRO, B. (1980) "Predicting the course of voluntary childlessness in the 21st century." Journal of Clinical Child Psychology 9: 155-157.

SHEALY, N. and M. C. SHEALY (1981) To Parent or Not. Norfolk, VA: Donning.

SINGH, B. K. and J. S. WILLIAMS (1981) "Childlessness and family satisfaction." Research on Aging 3: 218-227.

STOKES, S. C. and N. E. JOHNSON (1979) "Birth order, size of family of orientation, and desired family size." Journal of Individual Psychology 33: 42-46.

STRONG, L. E. (1978) "Alternative marital and family forms." Journal of Marriage and the Family 40: 493-503.

TIECHOLZ, J. G. (1978) "Psychological correlates of voluntary childlessness in married women." Presented to the Annual Meetings of the Eastern Psychological Association, Washington, D.C., March.

——— (1977) "A preliminary search for psychological correlates of voluntary childlessness in married women." Dissertation Abstracts 48: 1865B.

VEEVERS, J. E. (1982) "The choice of childlessness: researching the repercussions." (unpublished)

——— (1980) Childless by Choice. Toronto: Butterworths.

——— (1979) "Voluntary childlessness: a review of issues and evidence." Marriage and Family Review 2: 1-26.

——— (1973a) "Voluntary childlessness: a neglected area of family study." Family Coordinator 22: 199-205.

——— (1973b) "Voluntarily childless wives: a exploratory study." Sociology and Social Research 57: 356-366.

CHAPTER 4

Single-Parent Families:
In the Mainstream of American Society

EDWARD H. THOMPSON, Jr.

Holy Cross College

PATRICIA A. GONGLA

University of California, Los Angeles

The single-parent family has recently become a renewed topic of national concern. Much of the attention has resulted from the dramatic increase in the proportion of American families maintained by a single mother or single father. By the end of the 1970s, however, a conflict between lifestyle choice and cultural scripts also called attention to these families. Some of this attention is due to the emergence of single parenting as a more deliberately intentional and less transitional lifestyle for many than has previously been the case. Some is due to the recent shift in cultural scripts and family policy from tacit concern for the welfare of all families to intentional support of the conventional two-parent family, a shift that may presage the increased vulnerability of single-parent families in the 1980s. The combined effect of these changes has been to arouse some concern with regard to how mainstreamed single-parent families have and will become. The question is raised: Are single-parent families a viable, legitimate, albeit still alternative, family form in contemporary American society?

Uncertainty about the status of single-parent families is in part due to the inconsistency and inadequacy of much of the available research literature. For four decades research has disputed the effectiveness of this family's ability to serve its basic functions, but methodological flaws invalidate or seriously limit the validity of these findings (Blechman, 1982; Sprey, 1967). The recent efforts of researchers to reconceptualize the single-parent family as a normal family system have produced findings that challenge earlier investigations on the quality of life inside these families

(Rosenthal and Keshet, 1980; Weiss, 1979), underscored that there is as yet no coherent theoretical conceptualization of the single-parent family system (Ambert, 1982; Blechman and Manning, 1976; Mahoney and Mahoney, 1974), and made us aware of how little attention has been paid directly to the single-parent family within the broader societal context. Extensive literature exists in both the academic community and the public marketplace on the individuals comprising the single-parent family household — the children, the custodial parent, and the absent parent (e.g., Atkin and Rubin, 1976; Hetherington et al., 1976; Hunt and Hunt, 1977; Levitin, 1979; Klein, 1973; Roman and Haddad, 1978). However, with few exceptions most studies reporting on single-parent families have not directly examined the family as a total unit. If we are to understand this family form, "What is sorely needed from here on in is a shifting of our research focus from the conduct of individual spouses and children toward families as systems" (Sprey, 1979: 156).

This review refocuses attention on the single-parent family system, with primary emphasis on three interrelated themes. First, the current status of single-parent families will be examined in the context of the question: Are these families a contemporary family form within the mainstream of society, or are they outside the mainstream, still considered to be a deviant, alternative lifestyle? Second, we look inside the families, focusing on the diversity of their organization and the quality of life within these families. Third, the interface between single-parent families and their social environment will be explored, in particular, the relationships that these families maintain with their support systems and with major social institutions.

Contemporary Families or Alternative Lifestyle?

Demographic Reality

The 1980 Census data identifies the last decade as an epoch period during which the single-parent family emerged as a significant and highly visible family form. The single-parent family is, of course, a rather traditional family system in this country (Seward, 1978: 89-92), with the proportion of single-parent families in America in 1970 about the same as it was in 1870. In fact, available estimates suggest that from the mid-nineteenth century to 1970, nearly one in ten families was maintained by either the mother or the father (e.g., Bane, 1976; Farley and Hermalin, 1971; Sennett, 1974; Seward, 1978). This consistent pattern ended, however, with the 1970 Census. By 1980, the *proportion* of single-parent families had doubled (U.S. Bureau of the Census, 1971, 1981b). Single-parent families now represent 21.4 percent of the families with dependent children at home.

Barring extraordinary changes, the proportion of single-parent families will become even greater. The single-parent family is the second-fastest growing family lifestyle in America today (after cohabiting couples), having grown at 21 times the rate of the traditional two-parent family during the 1970s (Glick and Spanier, 1980; U.S. Bureau of the Census, 1971, 1981a, 1981b). Over the course of the decade, the *number* of single-parent families increased by 107 percent to an unprecedented 6.7 million families, whereas the number of two-parent families actually decreased by 4 percent, down to 24.8 million. The net result was a dramatic increase, both in the absolute and relative number of families maintained by one parent as well as in the single-parent family's visibility.

Perhaps one of the best illustrations of the single-parent family's increased visibility is the fact that, in 1980, 8.7 percent of the people in the United States were members of single-parent families. This is one and a half times the proportion of the population represented by all persons of Spanish origin, and nearly three-fourths the size of the Black population (U.S. Bureau of Census, 1981b). Moreover, these figures do not even begin to estimate the percentage of people who as of 1980, had lived in a single-parent family at some time in their lives (see Bohannon, 1970), or the number of households in which an unmarried adult assumes responsibility for an unrelated child.

There is every indication that the percentage and number of families headed by single parents will continue to grow. It is estimated that a quarter of the mothers and fathers who have still-immature children at home will be single parents sometime in the 1980s, and that half of the children born in the 1980s will spend part of their childhood living with either their mothers *or* their fathers (see Norton and Glick, 1979; Weiss, 1979). If current trends continue, it is conceivable that a majority of Americans will at some point in their lives experience living for some time in a single-parent family.

Thus, far from being an aberration, the single-parent family is fast becoming a very common family pattern, already representing nearly half of the families in the Black community and over one-fifth of the families in the White community (Staples, 1980; U.S. Bureau of the Census, 1981b). The demographic reality is that single-parent families are part of the mainstream of American society and are likely to become even more prevalent. Any expected decline in the total number of single-parent families created by the slowdown in divorce (Glick, 1979) is likely to be replaced by an upsurge of families maintained by never-married mothers (U.S. Bureau of the Census, 1981a). Thus, proportionally fewer single-parent families will be maintained by the father, even though the absolute number of single-father families will continue to rise (U.S. Bureau of the Census, 1980a: 3); single parents will be younger than in the past (Glick and Norton, 1977) and more likely to have responsibility for younger, yet fewer children (U.S. Bureau of the Census, 1978); and single-parent families will continue the trend of "going it alone" as opposed to moving in with relatives (Bianchi and Farley, 1979; U.S. Bureau of the Census, 1981b).

TABLE 4.1   Distribution of Family Households by Type and Presence of Children, and Parent-Child Families by Type, 1980 (numbers in thousands)

Family Households
(58,426)

Married-Couple Family Households (48,180)		Female-Headed Family Households (8,540)		Male-Headed Family Households (1,706)	
Without Children (22,973)	With Children (25,207)	Without Children (2,622)	With Children (5,918)	Without Children (970)	With Children (736)
With Related but not Own Children (639)	With Own Children (24,568)	With Related but not Own Children (578)	With Own Children (5,340)	With Related but not Own Children (127)	With Own Children (609)
	Plus		Plus		Plus
	Married Couples[a] with Own Children Living with a Nonrelative (12)		Mothers[a] with Own Children Living with a Nonrelative (264)		Fathers[a] with Own Children Living with a Nonrelative (18)
	Plus		Plus		Plus
	Married Couples[b] with Own Children Living with a Relative (254)		Mothers[b] with Own Children Living with a Relative (194)		Fathers[b] with Own Children Living with a Relative (55)
	Totals		Totals		Totals
	24,834 Married-Couple Families with Own Children		6,098* Single-Parent Mothers with Own Children		672* Single-Parent Fathers with Own Children

SOURCE: U.S. Bureau of the Census, Current Population Reports, Series P-20, No. 366, Household and Family Characteristics: March 1980 (Tables 1, 14 and 21), U.S. Government Printing Office, Washington, D.C., 1981.

* It is this group that shall be referred to as single-parent families.

a. These families do not maintain their own households; rather, they share a house or apartment with a nonrelative, who is head of the household. Formerly called secondary families, the Bureau of the Census now identifies them as "unrelated subfamilies," because they are embedded within someone else's household. A very common example is a single-parent mother and her child(ren) living with a friend in whose name the home is owned or rented.

b. "Related subfamilies," however, share a relative's house or apartment. A very common example is a single-parent mother and her child(ren) living in her parents' home.

When reporting estimates for the number of single-parent families, it is important to be clear about how these families are counted in our society, since it is possible to misinterpret data from the Bureau of the Census and overestimate their number. As can be seen in Table 4.1, a distinction must be made between *female-headed family households* (or male-headed family households) and *single-parent households.* The former category can include households without children and households in which the children present are not the sons or daughters of the person who heads the household. In some cases these adults may be assuming the social role of parent (e.g., a grandmother who has the unshared responsibility for raising a grandchild), or they may be the head of a household that includes a two-parent subfamily (e.g., a daughter, son-in-law, and grandchild). To unwittingly confuse these categories can result in an inflated estimate of the number of single-parent families. Mendes (1976), Lewis (1978), and Katz (1979), for example, overestimated the number of single fathers by unintentionally reporting the generic category *male-headed families with children.* In this chapter, single-parent families are thus strictly defined as those *families* — and not family households — in which there is a single-parent father or single-parent mother raising his or her own children (see Weiss, 1979). Although some single-parent families live with a relative or with a nonrelative (see Table 4.1), in the vast majority of cases, these families do not share their house or apartment with others. It should also be noted that many single parents share the parenting role with the nonresidential parent, who may or may not share custody of the children.

Societal Reaction

The most significant commonality across single-parent families is the structural characteristic that only one parent lives with the children. Because the other parent is "absent," and perhaps because nearly 90 percent of the single-parent families have been "headed" by women for over a century (Seward, 1978), single-parent families have long been thought to be in trouble. Whether trouble is defined as mothers managing a family unit alone and unattached, or as "father absence" depriving children of the necessary experiences and role models for satisfactory adult moral behavior, public interest in single-parent families has manifested itself as concern. The common belief is that these families are "broken" and "disorganized" (Burgess, 1970), and that the presence of both a mother and a father are prerequisites for a child's normal development (Blechman, 1982; Levitin, 1979). Benson's 1909 article, entitled "Alarming Changes in American Homes," called attention to the turn-of-the-century "social problem" (cited in Blechman and Manning, 1976: 62), and Malinowski's (1930/1974) proposed sociological law that "no child should be brought into the world without a man — and one man at that — assuming the role

of sociological father" underscored the professional community's concern
with father absence.

Early public and professional interest in single-parent families focused
on the children growing up in these "partial" families. Although the single
parent was usually widowed, at worst deserted, and also a "victim," public
sympathies and worries focused almost exclusively on the children.

By 1980, however, death of a parent has become the least frequent
factor in the establishment of a single-parent family. Separation and divorce are now the most common causes of single-parent families, although
since the 1970s, there has been a major increase in the number of families
created by single women having babies. In effect, Americans are increasingly choosing single parenthood over unhappy marriages, to remain
single parents rather than quickly remarrying (Brown et al., 1976; Staples
1980; Weiss. 1979), to create a single-parent family rather than aborting an
unplanned pregnancy or releasing the baby for adoption (Grow, 1979
Haring, 1975), and to create single-parent families through adoption of
planned premarital conception (Doughtery, 1978; Kadushin, 1970
Shireman and Johnson, 1976).

These lifestyle choices can probably be attributed to a variety of
factors, among them the diminished moral stigma associated with divorce
parenting alone, and premarital conceptions. However, despite the diminished stigma attached to individuals, public concern with the single
parent family has not diminished. Indeed, as the number of single-parent
families increased throughout the 1970s, so did public alarm (e.g., The
Consortium for the Study of School Needs, 1980; Goldstein et al., and
Solnit, 1979; Hatch, 1981; Lynn, 1974). There is still concern that single
parent families are "partial" and "broken" and thus are harming children
(Anthony, 1974). In addition, there is now widespread alarm about the
future of the traditional nuclear family. Social critics suggest that the choice
to single parent is threatening the legitimacy of the traditional two-parent
family and thus the stability of society. Rather than viewing the single-
parent family as one type of family in American society, these families are
defined as deviant family systems (Bernard, 1979; Levitan and Belous,
1981; Schorr and Moen, 1979). Social policymakers are often encouraged
to reform existing family policy on the *assumption* that single-parent family
systems are detrimental to the welfare of both the children and the
economy (e.g., Senate bills 1070 and 1378, 97th Congress).

In hindsight, Ross and Sawhill's (1975) proposal for a neutral family
policy, which would neither encourage nor discourage various kinds of
family organization, clearly forecasted these trends and presently would
seem too liberal. The 1980s have begun with a rise in a family protec-
tionism ideology that does not speak well for family pluralism or for the
welfare of all families (see Fox, 1981; Wiseman, 1981). Rather, this new
wave of familism appears to support only the "neoclassical" family of

Western nostalgia, where the married individuals are in their first marriage, living together, and natural parents to their children. Whether intended or not, governmental bureaucracies are thus likely to become increasingly involved in the lives of single-parent families (Hawkins, 1979; Schorr and Moen, 1979; Zimmerman, 1976, 1979).

Characteristics of Single-Parent Families

The paths along which single-parent families evolve are varied. Some begin as two-parent families, and as a result of separation, divorce, desertion, or death, the family becomes single parent. Others begin as one-parent families, as when a single person chooses to adopt a child or when a single woman delivers and keeps her own child. Despite the different routes to the single-parent situation, single-parent families are frequently viewed as alike and collectively referred to as *the* single-parent family. The assumption is made that single-parent families are more similar to one another than to other family types, and that they share a common lifestyle and common problems (Billingsley and Giovannoni, 1971). In some aspects of everyday life these families *may* share certain experiences. For example, they commonly experience a major reduction in family income (Bane and Weiss, 1980), a sense of isolation and loneliness (Greenberg, 1979; Katz, 1979; Nock, 1981; Smith, 1980), role overload (Glasser and Navarre, 1965; Weiss, 1979), and unequal access to the material and social resources more easily available to two-parent families (Cherlin, 1981; Schorr and Moen, 1979).

Nonetheless, it is impossible to discuss "the single-parent family" since the concept covers a wide variety of types of families. One must distinguish between single-father and single-mother families (which differ in composition) the paths along which the family system evolved, the extent to which an outside parent is involved in child care and consultation, manner and level of functioning, patterns of interaction, and subjective well-being. Furthermore, they differ in economic lifestyles, opportunities and resources, social class, racial and ethnic background, and age of parent. The conclusion to be drawn is deceptively simple: Single-parent families are not a homogeneous group. Failure to see the diversity among families, however, has been a frequent conceptual error and, until recently, has hindered our understanding of these families. To paraphrase Billingsley and Giovannoni (1971) and Sprey (1967), understanding the diversity across single-parent families may be more important theoretically, clinically, and politically than the search for the common denominators of single-parent family life.

Several recent attempts have been made to develop typologies that capture the diversity among the families (Ahrons, 1979; Boss, 1977; Mendes, 1979; Rosenfeld and Rosenstein, 1973), primarily using the precipitating cause or the absent parent's degree of presence as the basis of classification. There are at least four types of family systems involving the children's natural parents, if one considers just the interactive and psychological presence or absence of the nonresidential parent (Gongla and Thompson, forthcoming). If a parental substitute enters the family boundary (e.g., a live-in housekeeper, grandparent, cohabitant), the variation in types increases dramatically (Boss, 1974; Mendes, 1979; Rosenthal and Keshet, 1978, 1980; Weiss, 1979). It is as yet impossible to say how many types of single-parent families exist in fact or what proportion of families fall within each category.

Recently, comparisons between single-father and single-mother families have also become a topic of inquiry, largely because there has been an increase in the absolute number of fathers acquiring custody of their children. Contrary to the impression fostered by the mushrooming literature on single-parent fathers, Census data show single-fathers heading proportionately fewer families in 1980 than in 1970, and fewer still in 1970 than in 1960 (U.S. Bureau of the Census, 1980b, 1981b), although the absolute number has continued to grow. The share of single-parent families maintained by fathers, however, may very well begin to increase as a by-product of the following:

(a) men's changing lifestyles (Lynn, 1974; Pleck, 1979);

(b) normative shifts favoring single fatherhood (Cordell et al., 1980; George and Wilding, 1972; Gersick, 1979; Katz, 1979; Keshet and Rosenthal, 1978; Mendes, 1976; Orthner et al., 1976; Rossi, 1977; Schlesinger, 1978);

(c) noncustodial fathers' desire to continue their parenting role (Atkin and Rubin, 1976; Earl and Lohmann, 1978; Fischer and Cardea, 1981; Hetherington et al., 1976; Wallerstein and Kelly, 1980);

(d) single fathers' greater access to economic resources and better economic well-being than single mothers' (Orthner et al., 1976);

(e) research findings that suggest single fathers and single mothers can effectively function as custodial parents (Ambert, 1982; Bartz and Witcher, 1978; Gasser and Taylor, 1976; Lowenstein and Koopman, 1978; Orthner et al., 1976; Rosenthal and Keshet, 1980; Smith and Smith, 1981); and

(f) research that suggests that the positive and negative experiences of being a single parent are similar for both fathers and mothers (Ambert, 1982; DeFrain and Eirick, 1981; Greenberg, 1979; Weiss, 1979).

Despite the possibility of many more single-father families, research to date on these families has generally been limited to small nonprobability samples, and there have been very few comparative studies matching single fathers with single mothers. Life inside the two family "types" remains virtually uncharted.

Equally uncharted are three spheres of single-parent family life that have bearing on how these families manage, sometimes even thrive: the extent to which the nonresidental parent is involved in the family, the nature of the parent/child boundary, and the home environment. Research findings related to each will be discussed in some detail.

Family Systems

The everyday reality of single-parent families suggests a wide variety of interaction patterns and family boundaries, ranging from the noncustodial parent being minimally present as in the "sole executive" family system (Mendes, 1979) to being maximally involved as in the "binuclear" family system (Ahrons, 1979). The extent to which the nonresidential parent is *psychologically* and *interactively* present in the family system depends to a large extent on the person's availability and freedom of access (Abarbanel, 1979; Boss, 1977, 1980a; Fulton, 1979; Hetherington et al., 1978; Wallerstein and Kelly, 1980; Weiss, 1979), and on the extent to which the noncustodial parent was "inside the family system" prior to the onset of single parenthood (Kantor and Lehr, 1975; Kelly and Wallerstein, 1977; Minuchin, 1974; Rosenthal and Keshet, 1980).

A number of studies suggest that parents living apart from their children may still be *interactively* inside the single-parent family boundary for some time (Clapp and Raab, 1978; Earls and Siegel, 1980; Fischer and Cardea, 1981; Furstenberg and Talvitia, 1980; Hetherington et al., 1976). This parent may frequently visit the child(ren), babysit for the custodial parent, and share responsibility in decision making. Mendes (1979) identified this type of parent as an "auxiliary parent," and several authors have previously addressed this phenomenon within their discussion of the part-time father (Atkin and Rubin, 1976) or visiting parent (Wallerstein and Kelly, 1980). In cases in which both parents desire to continue their parenting roles, two interrelated households can form one family system, the binuclear family system (Ahrons, 1979). This pattern can occur whether joint custody has been awarded or not, as long as a coparenting relationship is maintained. Ahrons (1980a) and other observers of custody arrangements (Abarbanel, 1979; Galper, 1978; Greif, 1979; Newsome, 1977; Roman and Haddad, 1978) estimate that this coparenting pattern may soon be the rule rather than the exception.

However, with few institutional supports for the noncustodial parent's role, the nonresidential parent/child subsystems that emerge vary considerably, usually falling between the extremes of an "empty shell" relationship involving erratic and infrequent interaction and a "vital" relationship involving recurring interaction and cohesiveness. Tentative findings suggest that the quality of the noncustodial parent/child(ren) relationship initially improves, at least for a while (Earl and Lohmann, 1978; Earls and Siegel, 1980; Greif, 1979; Hetherington et al., 1976). Over time, though, this relationship often decomposes as the frequency of interaction decreases. The absent parent's interactive presence is often diminished when custody is not shared (Abarbanel, 1979; Ahrons, 1980a), when loss of everyday contact with family rituals and routines is either blocked by visitation restrictions or a strained relationship with the custodial parent (Benedek and Benedek, 1979; Cline and Westman, 1971; Fulton, 1979; Weiss, 1979), or when the noncustodial parent was only marginally involved inside the family in the first place (Keshet, 1980; Minuchin, 1974).

Even when strained interaction characterizes the ex-marital subsystem, "most single-parents do what they can to foster their children's relationships with their noncustodial parents. They do so despite their own feelings, because they believe it important for the children" (Weiss, 1979: 159). Goldsmith (1979) and Wallerstein and Kelly (1980) corroborate this finding, reporting that the majority of parents (both fathers and mothers) felt it important for the noncustodial parent to stay involved with the child. Thus the absent parent may be *psychologically* inside the single-parent family boundary for some time, even in families where the parent is *physically* absent (Boss, 1980a; Lopata, 1979). It would also be misguided to assume that the "absent parent" diminishes in saliency in the eyes of the child even if the interaction is reduced. Children frequently continue to think of themselves as children of two parents, despite the degree of interaction with the "absent parent." Based on their study of children of divorce, Wallerstein and Kelly (1980: 307) comment: "Although the mother's caretaking and psychological role became increasingly central in these families, the father's psychological significance *did not* correspondingly decline."

Evidently there is good reason to question the stereotype of "parent absence." Yet a perspective commonly found in the literature (see Burgess, 1970, for a review and critique) appears to be: When a marriage dissolves, the family dissolves; and if a marriage was never present, as is the case for many single mothers, a family never existed. But as Sprey (1979: 155) says: "Divorce [or any other form of marital dissolution] ends a marriage but not a family. It removes one parent from the household." It changes the relationship between the parents, it does not end the relationship; psychological and interactive ties continue to connect all family members, but under widely different circumstances.

There are apparent risks, however, with the noncustodial parent's active involvement in the family's life. Inability to manage the conflict within the ex-spouse subsystem can add subjective stresses to the lives of all family members (Atkin and Rubin, 1976; Fischer and Cardea, 1981; Fulton, 1979; Hetherington et al., 1976, 1978; Wallerstein and Kelly, 1980; Weiss, 1979), and an interactively absent but psychologically present parent can increase boundary ambiguity and jeopardize the family's ability to reorganize (Boss, 1980a; Keshet, 1980). As Boss (1980b: 449) has suggested, "Stress continues in any family until membership can be clarified and the system reorganized regarding (a) who performs what roles and tasks, and (b) how family members perceive the absent parent."

Internal Family Boundaries

Until recently, there was no systematic research on the single-parent family as a system with its own authority structure, norms, processes of conflict management and boundary maintenance, patterns of exchange and reciprocity, and decision-making rules. The second, albeit corollary, sphere of family life that remains virtually uncharted thus has to do with the concept of "boundary redefinition" and life inside single-parent families over the course of the family career.

When one parent leaves the family household, two dramatic changes follow. First, as Weiss (1979) noted, the loss of a parent tends to decrease the social distance, and open the normal boundary between the custodial parent and the child(ren). More specifically, the authority structure in a two-parent family is grounded on the implicit coalition of two adults aligned against the child(ren). In single-parent families, this superordinate/subordinate "echelon structure" collapses. Weiss suggests that the children are promoted: The custodial parent relinquishes some decision-making control and then begins to engage the children "as if" they were junior partners. "The parent wants to be able to rely on the children as fully participant in the functioning of the family," and "once children accept the increased responsibility, it becomes natural for the single-parent to consult the children regarding household decisions" (Weiss, 1979: 75, 76).

Second, decomposition of the authority structure and group size, to paraphrase Simmel (Wolff, 1950), increases communication and disclosure. Given this and the fact that single-parent families are often more isolated from friends and community groups (Burgess, 1970; Kitsen et al., 1980; Smith, 1980; Weiss, 1975, 1979), a type of parent/child(ren) "dyad" forms, which is markedly different from the traditional parent/child bond. Characterized by greater equity, more frequent interaction, more discussion, and heightened cohesiveness (i.e., greater intimacy and companionship), the relationship fosters a wholly different affective structure (see Blechman and Manning, 1976; Hess and Camara, 1979; Keshet, 1980). "The condition of intimacy consists in the fact that the participants in a given relationship see only one another, and do not see, at the same time, an objective, super-individual structure which they feel exists and operates on its own" (Simmel, cited in Wolff, 1950: 127-128).

There has been as yet little in-depth study of this single-parent/child relationship. Assuming that the dyad shares household tasks, problems, feelings, and often recreational activities (Keshet and Rosenthal, 1978; Klein, 1973; Weiss, 1979; Wallerstein and Kelly, 1980), one could predict a higher level of parent/child intimacy than exists in most two-parent families. But one is left at the moment with more questions than data. Do statements of affection increase and hostile statements decrease (see Blechman and Manning, 1976)? Does parent/child communication improve in terms of the openness, depth, and breadth of topics discussed and issues shared (Kieffer, 1977)? Is the situation a type of "fox-hole" intimacy, eroding once the crisis situation passes, or does the relationship gradually increase in closeness? Does the "intimacy drain" on the parent translate into further emotional and social isolation from other adults, thus helping to explain the fact that many single parents never remarry (Greenberg, 1979; Weiss, 1979)? Or, does the closeness of the family make singlehood less painful and thus contribute to the tenure of single parenting (Adams, 1978; Libby, 1977)? Do these children, who Weiss (1979) suggests grow up a little faster, fare better in their own ability to develop intimate relationships?

Simmel noted that when the dyad is expanded, as when the parent begins to date, the parent/child dyad completely changes its sociological character. A new oligarchical, adult clique emerges, competitive conditions follow, and coalitions replace solidarity. In effect, when the custodial parent begins dating, the parent/child(ren) dyad once again becomes a *sub*system within the total family structure. Both the parent and the child(ren) must relinquish some of the closeness and time shared (Rosenthal and Keshet, 1980; Staples, 1980; Walker and Messinger, 1979), leading some children to report jealousy (Staples, 1980; Weiss, 1979). Much more systematic research is needed to understand the nature, extent, and effects of this boundary reorganization. When there are two or more children in the family, does the presence of an "outsider" prompt the children to coalesce into a partisan, competitive power, or does the fact there are two reduce the likelihood of enmeshment with the mother, and hence the possessiveness? Does the addition of another adult inside the family boundary cause a redistribution of power, reestablishing an echelon authority structure? Do changes in the dyad alter the affective bonds between parent and child, and do the changes provide members more or less autonomy?

It is clear that there are both theoretical and empirical reasons to begin to conceptualize single-parent families as family systems with their own structure, norms, and internal process of boundary reorganization. Recent research, albeit scanty, has offered some suggestion of what life is like inside these families. Parents are often overloaded (Weiss, 1979), and children are precariously occupying a junior partner status (Weiss, 1979; Wallerstein and Kelly, 1980). Although the amount of research is still small, there is a growing awareness among researchers that we must concentrate on the single-parent family as a family unit, examining its own unique internal organization and its reorganization over time.

Quality of Family Life

Although "pathology is a prominent element of the public view of single parenthood" (Schorr and Moen, 1979: 15), research suggests that single-parent family systems are not inherently disorganized nor necessarily detrimental to individual members. Rather, they simply differ in structure and internal organization (Blechman and Manning, 1976; Burgess, 1970; Mendes, 1979). Just as there are variations within the two-parent system, some single-parent families effectively meet the needs of family members and society and some do not.

Until very recently, only those single-parent families seeking help for problems in living were studied. Because single parents are more open to seeking help (Blechman and Manning, 1976; Guttentag et al., 1980) and clinicians are socialized to anticipate pathology, many studies reported that single-parent family life was producing troubled children and anxious, if not neurotic, parents. Kalter's (1977) review of the clinical "research" found only five studies that systematically attempted to compare two-parent and single-parent family systems. However, these five also fall into the long tradition of research on the "single-parent condition," with the standard conceptual biases and methodological limitations (for reviews and critiques, see Biller, 1970; Herzog and Sudia, 1968, 1971; Lamb, 1977; Sprey, 1967).

Much of the research purportedly examining the single-parent family system has instead focused on the individual family member(s). It assumed living in a single-parent household was at best problematic and at worst the source of major social problems, and thus sought to identify what negative effects the single-parent condition had on which family members. The single-parent condition was assumed to be the cause of a family member's inappropriate sex role behavior, achievement problems, low self-esteem, depression, immaturity, and sexual precocity (see Goetting, 1981; Blechman, 1982, for reviews). Few studies controlled for other casual explanations, such as the family's socioeconomic status and degree of access to social supports, the custodial parent's sex and employment opportunity, the child's age, sex, and involvement with the noncustodial parent, or the relationship between the parents before and after the single-parent family's formation.

Billingsley and Giovannoni (1971: 368) noted at the beginning of the decade, "The unfortunate assumption that there is a one-to-one relationship between this type of family structure and all kinds of social and psychological pathology has resulted in almost total ignorance about [those single-parent] *families* — the majority — who somehow circumvented this 'inevitable' pathology." During the last decade, however, investigators have begun the necessary systematic comparison of families, assessing whether interaction within single-parent and two-parent family systems differentially affects individual members. Some have examined the mother/child relationship (e.g., Hetherington, 1972; Hoffman, 1971), while others have focused on the psychosocial climate within the families (e.g., Berg and Kelly, 1979). Although most of this research still focuses on the individual and does not directly assess family systems, it is nonetheless important, for it substantiates the idea that family processes supersede family structure. Studies have examined the interaction patterns and coorientation between mothers and children (Aldous, 1972; Longabaugh, 1973); the degree of inaccessibility of both parents in two-parent systems (Blanchard and Biller, 1971; Kagel et al., 1978; Minuchin, 1974; Reuter and Biller, 1973); the quality of parent/child relationships before and after marital separation (Hess and Camara, 1979; Wallerstein and Kelly, 1980); the quality of the marital relationship across families (Raschke and Raschke, 1979); and the emotional quality of the home environment (Herzog and Sudia, 1971; Ney, 1957; Raschke and Raschke, 1979). Results suggest that it is the psychosocial characteristics of the family unit, independent of the number of parents, that affect the individuals. Living in a single-parent family need be no more harmful than living in a two-parent family.

However, there is as yet little evidence indicating the *comparative effects* of living in a single-parent family. Single-parent life is probably less detrimental for children than living in an unhappy, conflict-ridden two-parent system (Nye, 1957; Staples, 1980), and less permanently troubling than previously anticipated (Kulka and Weingarten, 1979; Loge, 1977; Luepnitz, 1979). But at present there is little information grounded in methodologically sophisticated work. For the time being, conclusions must remain tentative.

Research needs to move ahead in new directions. First, more extensive comparison of a broad range of families (both single-parent and two-parent systems) would test the validity of the notion that the single-parent family system is inevitably pathological and its family members disadvantaged. Second, it is important for researchers to untangle the effects of the crisis period that begins the single-parent family situation from the family system's pattern of interaction following the "crisis event." Are the problems so often experienced by single parents and their children a result of life in a single-parent family per se or of the trauma of family formation (Boss, 1980b; Hansen and Johnson, 1979; Levitin, 1979; Luepnitz, 1979)? Research is needed on both the short- and long-term impact of the crisis event (Berkman, 1969; Bloom et al., 1978; Luepnitz, 1979) and on life at various stages in the single-parent family's career. Third, a typology of the different stages in the single-parent family career is needed, one that captures the changing patterns of interaction and conflict management. Fourth, the effects of family formation and reorganization need to be separated from the effects of the family's place in the larger society. To what extent are the problems commonly attributed to single-parent families a consequence of the dynamics of living in that family or of the discrimination these families often encounter in a two-parent society ("stress pile-up"; Dill et al., 1980; McCubbin et al., 1980)?

Single-Parent Families in Society

The interface between single-parent families and their larger social environment has largely gone undiagnosed. Reviewing titles listed in the *Inventory of Marriage and Family Literature,* it is as if single-parent families exist in a vacuum, unattached to major social institutions, service organizations, or personal support systems.

Economics and Employment

One obvious exception to the above is the research on the interface between single-parent families and the economy. Evidence has accumulated to conclusively document the low economic status of single-parent families — their low incomes, high rates of poverty, and fewer employment opportunities than two-parent families (Bane and Weiss, 1980; Bianchi and Farley, 1979; Bradbury et al., 1979; Brandwein et al., 1974; Dinerman, 1977; Espenshade, 1979; Hoffman, 1977; Ross and Sawhill, 1975; Sawhill, 1976; Wattenberg and Reinhardt, 1979). As Cherlin (1981) and Colletta (1979a) have summarized, the major problem faced by single-parent families is not the lack of a male's presence, but the lack of a male income.

Nowhere is the linkage between major social institutions and single-parent families as pointed as it is in the areas of economics and employment. Throughout most of the 1970s, the income of single-mother families remained less than one-third the income of two-parent families, and the income differential appears to be increasing. By the end of the decade, single mothers commanded half the income of single fathers, and half again the average income of the two-parent family. The most recent figures for family incomes show that in 1979, single mothers raising two children had a median income of $8,314, whereas a married couple with two children had $23,000 (U.S. Bureau of the Census, 1981c).

With such an income differential, it is no surprise that families maintained by a single mother are over three times more likely than those headed by single fathers, and six times more likely than two-parent families, to have incomes below the poverty threshold (U.S. Bureau of the Census, 1980: Table 19). A major reason of the single parent's poor economic status, especially the single mother's status, is the sizable reduction in family income most families experience following marital disruption. In recent years the magnitude of this reduction has become even more severe; it is the single most important factor explaining the economic gap between single-parent and two-parent families (Bane and Weiss, 1980; Bianchi and Farley, 1979; Espenshade, 1979; Hoffman, 1977).

Reexamining the data on single-parent families within the Institute of Social Research's study of 5000 U.S. families, Bane and Weiss (1980: 13) found the average income of widowed mothers falls 31 percent after the death of a spouse, while divorced mothers and separated mothers experience 43 and 51 percent drops in family income, respectively. One would expect that the economic plight of the never married would be worse, given the generally younger age, lower education, and higher percentage of minority families that this group comprises (Wattenberg and Reinhardt, 1979). These data strongly suggest that reduced economic circumstances are an inevitable condition of single parenthood, especially in the case of families maintained by single mothers.

A number of other factors contribute to the poor economic conditions of the single-parent family: the father's inability or unwillingness to contribute to the family's income (U.S. Bureau of the Census, 1981d; Wattenberg and Reinhardt, 1979); the costs of child care (Sawhill, 1976; Schorr and Moen, 1979); the "Catch-22" governing policies of public assistance and "workfare" (Dinerman, 1977); the labor market "squeeze," which results in younger single mothers receiving the lowest income, experiencing the highest rate of unemployment, and obtaining the fewest benefits (Schorr and Moen, 1979; Wattenberg and Reinhart, 1979); and the recurring problem of discrimination against women in the workplace (Sawhill, 1976; Schorr and Moen, 1979).

Links to Other Institutions

Policymakers who would consult family specialists for more comprehensive information regarding single-parent families vis-à-vis other institutions discover little systematic research. One finds only scattered references, indicating that the flow of influence and control between single-parent families and major social institutions is unidirectional, from institutions to families, but little systematic data exist to support this contention. It is therefore difficult to describe with any certainty the present societal status of single-parent families. With this in mind, what can be said about the linkages between single-parent families and their environment? Are these families viewed as within the mainstream by the major social institutions, such as education, government, religion, and medicine?

Burgess (1970) and Schorr and Moen (1979) contend that many organizations and their programs view single parenthood as a temporary condition and transitional phase in a family career. The conventional wisdom is that the single-parent family will "go away" when the single-parent (re)marries. With marriage, never-married mothers will form a complete family, and with remarriage, broken families will be reconstituted or blended. In this sense, then, single-parent families are not recognized as "real" families. The conventional standard that a marriage is necessary before a social group will be defined as a legitimate family system (Sprey,

1979) may inhibit major social institutions from seeing a family nucleus when just a father/child or mother/child bond exists.

This assumption, like most common-sense assumptions, is in part justified. The reality is that the median interval between divorce and the second marriage is three years for those 35 to 54 years old (Glick, 1980). In recent years, the interval has been increasing, and the remarriage rates for both widowed and divorced single parents have been dropping (U.S. National Center for Health Statistics, 1980a, 1980b). When the unit of analysis is shifted from each to all single-parent families, however, the common-sense asssumption is not justified. The reality is that by the time (re)marriage ends the single-parenting experience for one family, another has taken its place. Single-parent families are one family type in American society. The view that single parenthood is temporary can thus become a powerful though tacit policy where a lack of accommodation to and recognition of these families is acceptable (Blechman and Manning, 1976; Hawkins, 1979; Hulme, 1976; Moroney, 1980; Parks, 1981; Schorr and Moen, 1979; Wilk, 1979). Paraphrasing Simmel, when the plurality of organizations in a society tacitly defines a group as being outside the mainstream, members of that group will fare badly. With the plurality of institutions believing that "two parents are better than one," single-parent families face not only discrimination but attendant feelings of humiliation as well (Wolff, 1950: 224-265).

Cogswell and Sussman (1972: 513) noted a decade earlier that the interface between single-parent families and institutional systems was as Simmel would predict: dictated by institutions failing to support or acknowledge single-parent family systems as legitimate or viable families. Instead, institutional systems

> make certain assumptions about the family. They gear their services toward an ideal of what the family ought to be, namely, a nuclear traditional one. . . . Because agencies idealize the traditional family, their programs are aimed at restoring this form and, thus, are ill-equipped to provide relevant supportive services to variant family forms.

Lindahl's (1979) analysis of the interface between local churches and single-parent families, for instance, concludes with such a restorative approach: "The church . . . must provide a message and an experience of reconciliation and redemption to its members who suffer the anguish of broken human relationships." Horowitz and Perdue (1977: 508) found that when health professionals come into contact with single-parent families, the institutional approach often ignores their unique group composition and indiscriminately offers solutions designed for two-parent families, or it recognizes the one-parent structure as "abnormal" and provides treatment aimed at helping the family members accept a regrettable situation (see Blechman and Manning, 1976; Wilk, 1979). Discussing single mothers who may have problems with external social service agencies and schools, Moroney (1980: 49) points out: "She may have a problem, but, if so, it often is with the system which tends to be rigid."

Although individual family members may benefit from their contact with specific organizations and their programs, organizations continue to provide a rather inimical climate for single-parent families *as families* (Blechman and Manning, 1976; Hawkins, 1979). Given the slow rate of change in large-scale organizations, it is not surprising that there have been few accommodations to single-parent families since Cogswell and Sussman wrote the above quote. For example, they noted that health care services for children are organized for the convenience of the medical care professionals and not around the availability of adults to accompany children to the agency. A decade later, clients are still supposed to adjust to the schedules of the health care agencies (Hulme, 1976; Moroney, 1980; Wilk, 1979). Yet the single parent may lose income and even jeopardize a job by having to accommodate the health organization's schedule (Brandwein et al., 1974).

Thus, institutions actually discriminate against one-parent families in two ways: by indiscriminately treating them as similar to two-parent families (Hawkins, 1979; Horowitz and Perdue, 1977) and by viewing the one-parent structure as "abnormal" (Blechman and Manning, 1976). Both approaches are dysfunctional for single-parent families. In the first case, they are obliged to fulfill the same functions and conditions as two-parent families, yet the limitations on their ability to do so are ignored (Brandwein et al., 1974; Horowitz and Perdue, 1977; Schorr and Moen, 1979). In the second case, the institutionalized view of the single-parent family as both temporary and deviant generates a daily barrage of subtle discrimination, for example, banks demanding cosigners for loans, landlords unwilling to rent housing (Brandwein et al., 1974), lack of easily available and affordable child care options (Rossi, 1977; Sawhill, 1976; Woolsey, 1977), and reduction in employment opportunities (Bane and Weiss, 1980; Bradbury, et al., 1979).

There is a social psychological analogue to the subtle, albeit formal, discrimination that single-parent families encounter. Because many families are treated as "nonfamilies" or are stigmatized as deviant, and a social distance is erected between "normal" and "abnormal" families, a self-fulfilling prophecy is put into operation. Schorr and Moen (1979: 18) state that all single-parent family members suffer from public images of the ideal and the single-parent family: "The most moving effect of misrepresentation is that many single parents believe what is said of them and add belief to the problems they face. The stereotypes involved are about as legitimate as most that are involved in discriminatory behavior — and as destructive."

Links to Other Support Networks

The relationships single-parent families maintain with friends and kin can only be obtained by piecing together studies that have focused on the parent's social ties or the child's kin relationships. Because we must borrow bits and pieces from the available information, the linkage between single-parent families and their social networks cannot be clearly defined.

Some literature suggests that single parents maintain or increase their exchange and affectional ties with their own relatives (consanguine kin) after the single-parent family evolves (Anspach, 1976; Clapp and Raab, 1978; Gongla, 1977; Spicer and Hampe, 1975). Relatives basically feel a commitment to help, and that commitment provides the family a sense of continuity and security whether help is actually given or not (Weiss, 1979). This is particularly true in the case of the never-married mother (Clapp and Raab, 1978; Grow, 1979). Nonetheless, turning to the child(ren)'s grandparents for help can create a "Catch-22." Returning home for services and support often results in tension and dependant feelings (Clapp and Raab, 1979; Colletta, 1979b; Dell and Applebaum, 1977; Weiss, 1975, 1979). Particularly acute are the problems of boundary ambiguity when grandparents offer unsolicited advice about child rearing or when children fail to turn to the custodial parent for emotional support.

Interaction with in-laws usually diminishes with divorce, unless the noncustodial parent continues to maintain contact with the family and thus provides a pathway to the in-laws (Anspach, 1976; Gongla, 1977). In effect, relationships with in-laws remain contingent upon the interactive presence of the noncustodial parent and generally worsen as the noncustodial parent withdraws from the single-parent family.

Ties to friends seem to follow a different pattern. As the single-parent family emerges, defines, and reorganizes itself, so too does the family's community of friends. For both the previously married and never married, the first reaction is a sense of being marginal to the family's former community and a sense of social, if not emotional, isolation (Clapp and Raab, 1979; Hetherington et al., 1979; Kitson et al., 1980; Rosenthal and Keshet, 1980; Smith, 1980; Weiss, 1979). Unlike single fathers, many single mothers are nonetheless able to maintain or increase their intimacy pattern with their old friends (Clapp and Raab, 1979; Gongla, 1977). As time goes on and the family is able to more clearly define itself, a new community of friends is often formed (Clapp and Raab, 1979; McLanahan, Wedemeyer and Adelberg, 1981; Rosenthal and Keshet, 1980; Weiss, 1979). Loge (1977) contends such friends may be more effective than kin, providing more support for the single parent and respecting the family's external boundaries (see Greenberg, 1979). However, this finding may only be valid for those custodial parents who strongly identify with the role of single parent and who are attempting to reorganize their lives in a way that increases their independence (McLanahan et al., 1981).

The importance of different kinds of networks cannot be understated: Serving as a buffer to external stresses and providing emotional and instrumental assistance as needed, social supports do seem to have an effect on the *fact* and the *feeling* of going it alone (Bloom et al., 1978; Chiriboga et al., 1979; Kurdek and Siesky, 1980; McLanahan et al., 1981; Wilcox, 1981).

Implications and General Discussion

The intent of this chapter has been to examine public views and research traditions regarding single-parent families in American society. Demographically, it is clear that single-parent families are now within the mainstream of American society. Moreover, after at least four decades of work that emphasized their deviation from the two-parent family and the pathological effect on individual members (Shaw and McKay, 1932), single-parent families are now gradually coming to be recognized and studied as whole, often healthy, families.

Some manage to adapt and reorganize easily, even to thrive, coping effectively with stresses from both within and outside the family unit. Others do not. Research findings suggest that the factors directly associated with successful families are the age of the single parent and child(ren) (Clapp and Raab, 1978; Wallerstein and Kelly, 1980), family income (Colletta, 1979a; Ross and Sawhill, 1975; Wattenberg and Reinhardt, 1979), residential stability (Bane and Weiss, 1980), development of an adaptive informal support system (McLanahan et al., 1981), systematic separation of marital and parenting roles (Keshet, 1980; Weiss, 1979), the interactive *and* psychological presence of the nonresidental parent (Boss, 1977), ability to manage conflict (Goldsmith, 1979; Raschke and Raschke, 1979; Weiss, 1979), abandoning old rules and rituals and establishing new family norms (Ahrons, 1980b; Weiss, 1979), and access to child care alternatives (Sawhill, 1976; Schorr and Moen, 1979).

Before proceeding, a caveat is in order. This summary of factors associated with single-parent families' success must be interpreted cautiously. Few studies have been designed to compare families, and our knowledge is too limited to suggest what resources have an ameliorative effect on the life in a single-parent family in a two-parent society. Most, if not all, of the factors mentioned above also probably apply to the maintenance of well-functioning two-parent families. Data suggest that there are more variations within single-parent and two-parent families than between them. Hence continued concern with the structural variable of number of parents within the household may be less helpful than a search for those characteristics all well-functioning families share.

Single-parent families desperately need to be studied as family systems that involve internal and external boundaries and some degree of embeddedness in a social environment. There must be a continued focus on single-parent *families,* with attention to the diversity of their internal organization and boundary reorganization over time, the degree of involvement with kin and friends outside the household, and their interaction with the large social environment. Recent research strongly suggests that new investigations of single-parent families recognize the possible existence of a second parent who continues to be present within the family system. While findings are at present tentative, the second parent continues to play an important role in the family after separation, divorce, or death, and when unmarried mothers keep their babies. The interactive and/or psychological presence of the second parent must certainly have its attendant benefits and costs, but it is difficult to specify when benefits will outweigh costs.

Although most single-parent families will continue to experience the effect of their low economic status, and although the full impact of the change in economic lifestyle is far from fully explored, families appear to differ in their degree of vulnerability and with regard to the stage in their family career at which they are most vulnerable. There is increasing evidence that individuals and family systems are often at greater risk immediately following a transition than they are after a period of reorganization. Thus while most single-parent families will experience some degree of burden, it may not necessarily accompany them throughout their careers. More work is needed on the developmental career of the single-parent family. Research suggests that the single-parent family career is a several-stage process, that single-parent families often functionally exist *before* the crisis event (Bohannon, 1970), that the "absent" parent continues to be present at least for a while (Clapp and Raab, 1979; Earls and Siegel, 1980; Hetherington et al., 1976; Mendes, 1979), and that the family system continually renegotiates its boundaries to include or exclude the absent parent (Ahrons, 1979; Rosenthal and Keshet, 1980; Wallerstein and Kelly, 1980; Weiss, 1979), as well as kin and friends (Colletta, 1979b; McLanahan et al., 1981). These findings are consistent with the notion that the postdivorce adjustment process for individuals involves several stages, but much remains to be understood.

In the emergence of a more conservative era, when the 1980s "hands-off families" mandate seems instead to be an appeal for a "hands-on" policy to support and restore the traditional, two-parent family system, single-parent families seem increasingly vulnerable to challenges from outside forces. For family specialists, the 1980s offer the challenge of coming to understand the particular needs and dynamics of single-parent families, and how best to facilitate their effectiveness. It is time that researchers and policymakers alike acknowledge the prevalence of the single-parent family, and welcome it within the mainstream of American society.

References

ABARBANEL, A. (1979) "Shared parenting after separation and divorce: a study of joint custody." American Journal of Orthopsychiatry 49 (April): 320-329.

ADAMS, M. (1978) Single-Blessedness. New York: Viking.

AHRONS, C. (1980a) "Joint custody arrangements in the postdivorce family." Journal of Divorce 3 (Winter): 189-205.

———— (1980b) "Divorce: a crisis of family transition and change." Family Relations 29 (October): 533-540.

———— (1979) "The binuclear family: two households, one family." Alternative Lifestyles 4 (November): 499-515.

ALDOUS, J. (1972) "Children's perceptions of adult role assignment: father-absence, class, race, and sex influences." Journal of Marriage and the Family 34 (February): 55-65.

AMBERT, A. (1982) "Differences in children's behavior toward custodial mothers and custodial fathers." Journal of Marriage and the Family 44 (February): 73-86.

ANSPACH, D. (1976) "Kinship and divorce." Journal of Marriage and the Family 38 (May): 323-330.

ANTHONY, E. J. (1974) "Children at risk from divorce: a review," in E. J. Anthony (ed.) The Child and His Family: Children at Psychiatric Risk, Vol. 3. New York: John Wiley.

ATKIN, E. and E. RUBIN (1976) Part-Time Father. New York: Signet.

BANE, M. (1976) Here to Stay: American Familes in the Twentieth Century. New York: Basic Books.

———— and R. WEISS (1980) "Alone together: the world of single-parent families." American Demographics 2, 5: 11-15.

BARTZ, K. and W. WITCHER (1978) "When fathers get custody." Children Today 7, 5: 206, 235.

BENEDEK, R. and E. BENEDEK (1979) "Children of divorce: can we meet their needs?" Journal of Social Issues 35, 4: 155-169.

BERG, B. and R. KELLY (1979) "The measured self-esteem of children from broken, rejected and accepted families." Journal of Divorce 2 (Summer): 363-369.

BERKMAN, P. (1969) "Spouseless motherhood, psychological stress and physical morbidity." Journal of Health and Social Behavior 10 (December): 323-334.

BERNARD, J. (1979) "Forward," in G. Levinger and O. S. Moles (eds.) Divorce and Separation: Context, Causes, and Consequences. New York: Basic Books.

BIANCHI, S. and R. FARLEY (1979) "Racial differences in family living arrangements and economic well-being: an analysis of recent trends." Journal of Marriage and the Family 41 (August): 537-551.

BILLER, H. (1970) "Father absence and the personality development of the male child." Developmental Psychology 2: 181-201.

BILLINGSLEY, A. and J. GIOVANNONI (1971) "Family: one parent," in R. Morris (ed.) Encyclopedia of Social Work, Vol. 1. New York: National Association of Social Workers.

BLANCHARD, R. and H. BILLER (1971) "Father availability and academic performance among third-grade boys." Developmental Psychology 4: 301-305.

BLECHMAN, E. (1982) "Are children with one parent at psychological risk? A methodological review." Journal of Marriage and the Family 44 (February): 179-195.

———— and M. MANNING (1976) "A reward-cost analysis of the single-parent family," in E. Mash (ed.) Behavior Modification and Families. New York: Brunner/Mazel.

BLOOM, B., S. ASHER, and S. WHITE (1978) "Marital disruption as a stressor: a review and analysis." Psychological Bulletin 85 (July): 867-894.

BOHANNON, P. (1970) Divorce and After. Garden City, NY: Doubleday.

BOSS, P. (1980a) "The relationship of psychological father presence, wife's personal qualities and wife/family dysfunction in families of missing fathers." Journal of Marriage and the Family 42 (August): 541-549.

———— (1980b) "Normative family stress: family boundary changes across the life-span." Family Relations 29 (October): 445-450.

———— (1977) "A clarification of the concept of psychological father presence in families experiencing ambiguity at boundary." Journal of Marriage and the Family 39 (February): 141-151.

—— (1974) "Psychological absence in the intact family: a systems approach to a study of fathering." Presented at the Theory Construction Workshop, National Council on Family Relations, St. Louis.

BRADBURY, K., S. DANZIGER, E. SMOLENSKY, and P. SMOLENSKY (1979) "Public assistance, female headship and economic well-being." Journal of Marriage and the Family 41 (August): 519-535.

BRANDWEIN, R., C. BROWN, and E. FOX (1974) "Women and children last: the social situation of divorced mothers and their families." Journal of Marriage and the Family 36 (August): 498-514.

BROWN, C., R. FELDBERG, E. FOX, and J. KOHEN (1976) "Divorce: chance of a new life-time." Journal of Social Issues 32, 1: 119-134.

BURGESS, J.K. (1970) "The single-parent family: a social and sociological problem." Family Coordinator 19 (April) 137-144.

CHERLIN, A. (1981) Marriage, Divorce, Remarriage. Cambridge, MA: Harvard University Press.

CHIRIBOGA, D., A. COHO, J. STEIN, and J. ROBERTS (1979) "Divorce, stress and social supports: a study in help-seeking behavior." Journal of Divorce 3 (Winter): 121-135.

CLAPP, D. and R. RAAB (1978) "Follow-up of unmarried adolescent mothers." Social Work 23 (March): 149-153.

CLINE, D. and J. WESTMAN (1971) "The impace of divorce on the family." Child Psychiatry and Human Development 2: 78-83.

COGSWELL, B. and M. SUSSMAN (1972) "Changing family and marriage forms: complications for human service systems." Family Coordinator 21 (October): 505-515.

COLLETTA, N. (1979a) "The impact of divorce: father absence or poverty?" Journal of Divorce 3 (Fall): 27-35.

—— (1979b) "Support systems after divorce: incidence and impact." Journal of Marriage and the Family 44 (November): 837-846.

Consortium for the Study of School Needs of Children from One-Parent Families (1980) The Most Significant Minority: One-Parent Children in the Schools. Arlington, VA: National Association of Elementary School Principles and the Institute for Development of Educational Activities.

CORDEL, A., R. PARKE, and D. SAWIN (1980) "Father's views on fatherhood with special reference to infancy." Family Relations 29 (July): 331-338.

DEFRAIN, J. and R. EIRICK (1981) "Coping as divorced single parents: a comparative study of fathers and mothers." Family Relations 30 (April): 265-274.

DELL, P. and A. APPLEBAUM (1977) "Trigenerational enmeshment: unresolved ties of single parents to family of origin." American Journal of Orthopsychiatry 47 (January): 52-59.

DILL, D., E. FELD, J. MARTIN, S. BEUKEMA, and D. BELLE (1980) "The impact of the environment on the coping efforts of low-income mothers." Family Relations 29 (October): 503-509.

DINERMAN, M. (1977) "Catch 23: Women, work and welfare." Social Work 22 (November): 472-477.

DOUGHTERY, S. (1978) "Single-adoptive mothers and their children." Social Work 23 (September): 311-314.

EARL, L. and N. LOHMANN (1978) "Absent fathers and Black male children." Social Work 28 (November): 413-415.

EARLS, F. and B. SIEGEL (1980) "Precocious fathers." American Journal of Orthopsychiatry 50 (July): 469-480.

ESPENSHADE, T. (1979) "The economic consequences of divorce." Journal of Marriage and the Family 41 (August): 615-625.

FARLEY, R. and A. HERMOLIN (1971) "Family stability: a comparison of trends between Blacks and Whites." American Sociological Reveiw 36 (February): 1-17.

FISCHER, J. and J. CARDEA (1981) "Mothers living apart from their children: a study in stress and coping." Alternative Lifestyles 4 (May): 218-227.

FOX, G. (1981) "Family research, theory and politics: challenges of the eighties." Journal of Marriage and the Family 43 (May): 259-261.

FULTON, J. (1979) "Parental reports of children's post-divorce adjustment." Journal of Social Issues 35 (4): 126-139.

FURSTENBERG, F., Jr. and K. TALVITIE (1980) "Children's names and paternal claims bonds between unmarried fathers and their children." Journal of Family Issues (March): 31-57.

GALPER, M. (1978) Co-parenting. Philadelphia: Running Press.

GASSER, R. and C. TAYLOR (1976) "Role adjustment of single parent fathers with dependent children." Family Coordinator 25 (October): 397-403.

GEORGE, V. and P. WILDING (1972) Motherless Families. London: Routledge & Kegan Paul.

GERSICK, K. (1979) "Fathers by choice: divorced men who receive custody of their children," in G. Levinger and O. Moles (eds.) Divorce and Separation. New York: Basic Books.

GLASSER, P. and E. NAVARRE (1965) "Structural problems of the one-parent family." Journal of Social Issues 21, 1: 98-109.

GLICK, P. (1979) "Future American families." COFO Memo 2 (Summer/Fall): 1-7.

——— (1980) "Remarriage: some recent changes and variations." Journal of Family Issues 1 (December): 455-478.

——— and A. NORTON (1977) "Marrying, divorcing, and living together in the U.S today." Population Bulletin 32, 5. Washington, DC: Population Reference Bureau.

——— and G. SPANIER (1980) "Married and unmarried cohabitation in the United States." Journal of Marriage and the Family 42 (February): 19-30.

GOETTING, A (1981) "Divorce outcome research: issues and perspectives." Journal of Family Issues 2 (September): 350-378.

GOLDSMITH, J. (1979) "Relationships between former spouses: descriptive findings." Presented at the Annual Meeting of the National Council on Family Relations, Boston.

GOLDSTEIN, J., A. FREUD, and A. SOLNIT (1979) Before the Best Interests of the Child. New York: Macmillan.

GONGLA, P. (1977) "Social relationships after marital separation: a study of women and children." Ph.D. dissertation, Case Western Reserve University.

——— and E. THOMPSON, Jr. (forthcoming) "Single-parent families," in M. Sussman and S. Steinmetz (eds.) Handbook of Marriage and the Family. New York: Plenum.

GREENBERG, J. (1979) "Single-parenting and intimacy: a comparison of mothers and fathers." Alternative Lifestyles 2 (August): 308-330.

GREIF, J. (1979) "Fathers, children and joint custody." American Journal of Orthopsychiatry 49 (April): 311-319.

GROW, L. (1979) "Today's unmarried mothers: the choices have changed." Child Welfare 58 (July): 363-371.

GUTTENTAG, M., S. SALASIN, and D. BELLE (1980) The Mental Health of Women. New York: Academic.

HANSEN, D. and V. JOHNSON (1979) "Rethinking family stress theory: definitional aspects," in W. Burr, R. Hill, F.I. Nye, and I. Reiss (eds.) Contemporary Theories About the Family, Vol. 1. New York: Macmillan.

HARING, B. (1975) "Adoption trends, 1971-1974." Child Welfare 54 (July): 524-525.

HATCH, O. (1981) "Family issues and public policy." COFO Memo 3 (Winter/Spring): 4-5.

HAWKINS, L. (1979) "The impact of policy decisions on families." Family Coordinator 28 (April): 264-272.

HERZOG, E. and C. SUDIA (1971) Boys in Fatherless Families. Washington, DC: U.S. Department of Health, Education and Welfare, Office of Child Development, Publication No. (OCD) 72-33.

——— (1968) "Fatherless homes: a review of research." Children 15: 177-182.

HESS, R. and K. CAMARA (1979) "Post-divorce family relationships as mediating factors in the consequences of divorce for children." Journal of Social Issues 35 (4): 79-96.

HETHERINGTON, E. (1972) "Effects of father-absence on personality development in adolescent daughters." Developmental Psychology 7: 313-326.

——— M. COX, and R. COX (1979) "The development of children in mother-headed families," in D. Reiss and H. Hoffman (eds.) The American Family: Dying or Developing. New York: Plenum.

——— (1978) "The aftermath of divorce," in J. Stevens and M. Mathews (eds.) Mother-child, Father-child Relations. Washington, DC: National Association for the Education of Young Children.

——— (1976) "Divorced fathers." Family Coordinator 25 (October): 417-428.

HOFFMAN, L. (1971) "Father absence and conscience development." Developmental Psychology 4: 400-406.

HOFFMAN, S. (1977) "Marital instability and the economic status of women." Demography 14 (February): 67-76.

HOROWITZ, J. and B. PERDUE (1977) "Single-parent families." Nursing Clinics of North America 12 (September): 503-511.

HULME, T. (1976) "Health concerns of the single-parent family," in S. Burden, P. Houston, E. Kriple, R. Simpson, and W. Stultz (eds.) Proceedings of the Changing Family Conference V: The Single-Parent Family. Iowa City: University of Iowa.

HUNT, M. and B. HUNT (1977) The Divorce Experience. New York: McGraw-Hill.

KADUSHIN, A. (1970) "Single-parent adoptions: an overview and some relevant research." Social Service Review 44, 3: 263-274

KAGEL, S., R. WHITE, and J. COYNE (1978) "Father-absent and father-present families of disturbed and nondisturbed adolescents." American Journal of Orthopsychiatry 48 (April): 342-352.

KALTER, N. (1977) "Children of divorce in an outpatient psychiatric population." American Journal of Orthopsychiatry 47 (January): 40-51.

KANTOR, D. and W. LEHR (1975) Inside the Family: Toward a Theory of Family Process. New York: Harper & Row.

KATZ, A. (1979) "Lone fathers: perspectives and implications for family policy." Family Coordinator 28 (October): 521-528.

KELLY, J. and J. WALLERSTEIN (1977) "Part-time parent, part-time child: visiting after divorce." Journal of Clinical Child Psychology 6, 2: 51-54.

KESHET, H. and K. ROSENTHAL (1978) "Fathering after marital separation." Social Work 23 (January): 11-18.

KESHET, J. (1980) "From separation to stepfamily: a subsystem analysis." Journal of Family Issues 1 (December): 517-532.

KIEFFER, C. (1977) "New depths of intimacy," in R. Libby and R. Whitehurst (eds.) Marriage and Its Alternatives: Exploring Intimate Relationships. Glenview, IL: Scotts, Foresman.

KITSON, G., H. LOPATA, W. HOLMES, and S. MEYERING (1980) "Divorcees and widows: similarities and differences." American Journal of Orthopsychiatry 50 (April): 291-301.

KLEIN, C. (1973) The Single-Parent Experience. New York: Avon.

KULKA, R. and H. WEINGARTEN (1979) "The long-term effects of parental divorce in childhood on adult adjustment." Journal of Social Issues 35, 4: 50-78.

KURDEK, L. and A. SIESKY, Jr. (1980) "Sex role self-concepts of single divorced parents and their children." Journal of Divorce 3 (Fall): 249-261.

LAMB, M. (1977) "The effects of divorce on children's personality development." Journal of Divorce 1 (Winter): 163-174.

LEVITAN, S. and R. BELOUS (1981) What's Happening to the American Family. Baltimore: Johns Hopkins University Press.

LEVITIN, T. (1979) "Children of divorce: an introduction." Journal of Social Issues 35, 4: 1-25.

LEWIS, K. (1978) "Single-parent fathers: who they are and how they fare." Child Welfare 57 (December): 643-651.

LIBBY, R. (1977) "Creative singlehood as a sexual life-style: beyond marriage as a rite of passage," in R. Libby and R. Whitehurst (eds.) Marriage and Alternatives: Exploring Intimate Relationships. Glenview, IL: Scott, Foresman.

LINDAHL, A. (1979) "An evaluation of divorced single parents' views of local church ministries." Dissertation Abstracts 40(A): 1708.

LOGE, B. (1977) "Role adjustments to single parenthood: a study of divorced and widowed men and women." Dissertation Abstracts 38(A): 4647.

LONGHAUGH, R. (1973) "Mother behavior as a variable moderating the effects of father absence." Ethos 1: 456-465.

LOPATA, H. (1979) Women as Widows: Support Systems. New York: Elsevier-North Holland.

LOWENSTEIN, J. and E. KOOPMAN (1978) "A comparison of the self-esteem between boys living with single-parent mothers and single-parent fathers." Journal of Divorce 2 (Winter): 195-208

LUEPNITZ, D. (1979) "Which aspects of divorce affect children?" Family Coordinator 28 (January): 79-85.

LYNN, D. (1974) The Father: His Role in Child Development. Monterey, CA: Brooks/ Cole.

MALINOWSKI, B. (1930/1974) "Parenthood, the basis of social structure," in R. Coser (ed.) The Family: Its Structure and Functions. New York: St. Martins.

MAHONEY, K. and M. MAHONEY (1974) "Psychoanalytic guidelines for child placement." Social Work 19 (November): 688-696.

McCUBBIN, H., C. JOY, A. CAUBLE, J. COMEAU, J. PATTERSON, and R. NEEDLE (1980) "Family stress and coping: a decade review." Journal of Marriage and the Family 42 (November): 855-871.

McLANAHAN, S., N. WEDEMEYER, and T. ADELBERG (1981) "Network structure, social support, and psychological well-being in the single-parent family." Journal of Marriage and the Family 43 (August): 601-612.

MENDES, H. (1979) "Single-parent families: a typology of lifestyles." Social Work 24 (May): 193-200.

——— (1976) "Single-fathers." Family Coordinator 25 (October): 439-444.

MINUCHIN, S. (1974) Families and Family Therapy. Cambridge, MA: Harvard University Press.

MORONEY, R. (1980) Families, Social Services, and Social Policy: The Issue of Shared Responsibility. Washington, DC: U.S. Department of Health and Human Services, DHHS Publication No. (ADM) 80-846.

NEWSOME, O. (1977) "Postdivorce interaction: an explanation using exchange theory." Dissertation Abstracts 37(A): 8001.

NOCK, S. (1981) "Family life-cycle transitions: longitudinal effects on family members." Journal of Marriage and the Family 43 (August): 703-714.

NORTON, A. and P. GLICK (1979) "Marital instability in America: past, present and future," in G. Levinger and O. Moles (eds.) Divorce and Separation. New York: Basic Books.

NYE, F.I. (1957) "Child adjustment in broken and unhappy unbroken homes." Marriage and Family Living 19 (November): 356-361.

ORTHNER, D., T. BROWN, and D. FERGUSON (1976) "Single-parent fatherhood: an emerging family life style." Family Coordinator 25 (October) 429-437.

PARKS, A. (1981) "Single-parent families: meeting the challenge of the 1980s." Presented at The Groves Conference on Marriage and the Family, Mt. Pocono.

PLECK, J. (1979) "Men's family work: three perspectives and some new data." Family Coordinator 28 (October): 481-488.

RASCHKE, H. and V. RASCHKE (1979) "Family conflict and children's self-concepts: a comparison of intact and single-parent families." Journal of Marriage and the Family 41 (May): 367-374.

REUTER, M. and H. BILLER (1973) "Perceived paternal nurturance — availability and personality adjustment among college males." Journal of Consulting and Clinical Psychology 40, 3: 339-342.

ROMAN, M. and W. HADDAD (1978) The Disposable Parent: The Case for Joint Custody. New York: Holt, Rinehart & Winston.

ROSENFELD, J. and E. ROSENSTEIN (1973) "Towards a conceptual framework for the study of parent-absent families." Journal of Marriage and the Family 35 (February): 131-135.

ROSENTHAL, K. and H. KESHET (1980) Fathers Without Partners: A Study of Divorced Fathers and Their Families. Totowa, NJ: Rowman & Littlefield.

——— (1978) "Childcare responsibilities of part-time and single-fathers." Alternative Lifestyles 1 (November): 465-491.

ROSS, H. and I. SAWHILL (1975) Time of Transition: The Growth of Families Headed by Women. Washington, DC: Urban Institute.

ROSSI, A. (1977) "A biosocial perspective on parenting." Daedalus 106 (Spring): 1-32.

SAWHILL, I. (1976) "Discrimination and poverty among women who head families." Signs 1 (1-3): 201-211.

SCHLESINGER, B. (1978) "Single-parent fathers: a research review." Children Today 7, 3: 12, 18-19, 37-39.

SCHORR, A. and P. MOEN (1979) "The single-parent and social policy." Social Policy 9 (March/April): 15-21.

SENNETT, R. (1974) Families Against the City. New York: Vintage.

SEWARD, R. (1978) The American Family: A Demographic History. Beverly Hills, CA: Sage.

SHAW, C. and H. McKAY (1932) "Are broken homes a causative factor in juvenile delinquency?" Social Forces 19: 514-525.

SHIREMAN, J. and P. JOHNSON (1976) "Single-persons as adoptive parents." Social Service Review 50 (March): 103-116.

SMITH, M. (1980) "The social consequences of single-parenthood: a longitudinal perspective." Family Relations 29 (January): 75-81.

SMITH, R. and C. SMITH (1981) "Child rearing and single-parent fathers." Family Relations 30 (July): 411-417.

SPICER, J. and G. HAMPE (1975) "Kinship interaction after divorce." Journal of Marriage and the Family 37 (February): 113-119.

SPREY, J. (1979) "Conflict theory and the study of marriage and the family," in W. Burr, R. Hill, F. I. Nye, and I. Reiss (eds.) Contemporary Theories About the Family, Vol. 2. New York: Macmillan.

——— (1967) "The study of single-parenthood: some methodological considerations." Family Coordinator 16 (January): 29-34.

STAPLES, R. (1980) "Intimacy patterns among black, middle-class single parents." Alternative Lifestyles 3 (November): 445-462.

U.S. Bureau of the Census (1981a) Marital Status and Living Arrangements: March 1980. Current Population Reports, Series P-20, No. 365. Washington, DC: Government Printing Office.

——— (1981b) Household and Family Characteristics: March 1980. Current Population Reports, Series P-20, No. 366. Washington, DC: Government Printing Office.

——— (1981c) Money Income and Poverty Status of Families and Persons. Current Population Reports, Series P-60, No. 127. Washington, DC: Government Printing Office.

——— (1981d) Child Support and Alimony. Current Population Reports, Series P-23, No. 112. Washington, DC: Government Printing Office.

——— (1980a) Marital Status and Living Arrangements: March 1979. Current Population Reports, Series P-20, No. 349. Washington, DC: Government Printing Office.

——— (1980b) Household and Family Characteristics: March 1979. Current Population Reports, Series P-20, No. 352. Washington, DC: Government Printing Office.

——— (1978) Marital Status and Living Arrangements: March 1977. Current Population Reports, Series P-20, No. 323. Washington, DC: Government Printing Office.

——— (1971) Household and Family Characteristics: March 1970. Current Population Reports, Series P-20, No. 218. Washington, DC: Government Printing Office.

U.S. National Center for Health Statistics (1980a) Remarriages of Women 15-44 Years of Age Whose First Marriage Ended in Divorce, 1976. Monthly Vital Statistics Report Advance Data, No. 58. Washington, DC: Department of Health, Education and Welfare.

——— (1980b) Births, Marriages, Divorces, and Deaths for 1979. Monthly Vital Statistics Report Vol. 28, No. 12. Washington, DC: Department of Health, Education and Welfare.

WALKER, K. and L. MESSINGER (1979) "Remarriage after divorce: dissolution and reconstruction of family boundaries." Family Process 18 (June): 185-192.

WALLERSTEIN, J. and J. KELLY (1980) Surviving the Breakup: How Children and Parents Cope with Divorce. New York: Basic Books.

——— (1979) "Children and divorce: a review." Social Work 24 (November): 468-475.

WATTENBERG, E. and H. REINHARDT (1979) "Female-headed families: trends and implications." Social Work 24 (November): 460-467.

WEISS, R. (1979) Going It Alone: The Family Life and Social Situation of the Single-Parent. New York: Basic Books.

——— (1975) Marital Separation. New York: Basic Books.

WILCOX, B. (1981) "Social support in adjusting to marital disruption: a network analysis," in B. Gottlieb (ed.) Social Networks and Social Support. Beverly Hills, CA: Sage.

WILK, J. (1979) "Assessing single-parent needs." Journal of Psychiatric Nursing 17, 6: 21-22.

WISEMAN, J. (1981) "The family and its researchers in the eighties: retrenching, renewing, and revitalizing." Journal of Marriage and the Family 43 (May): 263-266.

WOLFF, K. (1950) The Sociology of Georg Simmel. New York: Macmillan.

WOOLSEY, S. (1977) "Pied piper and the child care debate." Daedalus 106 (Spring): 127-145.

ZIMMERMAN, S. (1979) "Policy, social policy, and family policy: concepts, concerns, and analytical tools." Journal of Marriage and the Family 41 (May): 487-495.

——— (1976) "The family and its relevance for social policy." Social Casework 57 (November): 547-554.

CHAPTER 5

Divorce:
A Frequent "Alternative" in the 1970s

SHARON PRICE-BONHAM

DAVID W. WRIGHT

JOE F. PITTMAN

University of Georgia

This country witnessed a precipitous increase in divorce during the 1970s. For example, divorces increased from 2.5 per 1000 population in 1965 to 5.3 in 1979 (National Center for Health Statistics, 1980). Furthermore, it is projected that 40 percent of all marriages of persons born in the 1970s will end in divorce (Glick and Norton, 1977). Several factors have contributed to this increase, including: (1) increased education and employment of women, (2) smaller families, (3) higher incomes, (4) free legal aid, (5) the Vietnam War, (6) greater social and religious acceptance of divorce, (7) reform of the divorce laws, and (8) the growth and age distribution of married persons (National Center for Health Statistics, 1978).

Compared to other family phenomena there is still a paucity of systematic research or theoretical work in this area (see reviews by Kitson and Rashke, 1981; Price-Bonham and Balswick, 1980). Prior to the 1970s, the major projects that focused on divorce included Lichtenberger's in 1909 (1931) and Waller's in 1930 (1967), and Goode's (1956) study of divorced women. However, the recent increase in divorce has been accompanied by a similar increase in interest from social scientists. This is evidenced by the number of articles on divorce that were published in professional journals and by the establishment of the *Journal of Divorce*. Other indices include the creation of a Task Force on Divorce and Divorce Reform by the National Council on Family Relations, compilation of bibliographies on divorce (e.g., Sell and Sell, 1978) and the establishment of the Research and Information Network for Divorce Research.[1]

This increased interest is also evident in the American populace; i.e., divorce is a dominant theme in movies, TV shows, and popular literature. Books on how to initiate and survive divorce are challenging sex manuals in popularity, divorce insurance is discussed, divorce greeting cards are available, and organizations that offer counsel and support to divorcing/ divorced people are increasingly popular.

For the purpose of this review, divorce is defined as the legal dissolution of a socially and legally recognized marital relationship between a man and a woman that alters the obligations and privileges of the two persons involved. It is also a major life transition that has far-reaching social, psychological, legal, personal, economic, and often parental conse-quences. Due to space restrictions, this review will be limited to research published in the United States in the last decade, and will focus primarily on divorce as it affects the adults involved.

Divorce Adjustment

The integration of the divorce experience into one's total life experience, such that the individual lives by the daily and future demands of his or her new social position rather than by constant reference to the ties defined by the previous marriage [Goode, 1956: 241].

Divorce, a public and private event, is viewed as painful and stress producing (Bloom et al., 1978; Epstein, 1975; Hetherington et al., 1978; Hunt and Hunt, 1977; Weiss, 1975). Although attempts have been made to delineate the processes involved in adjusting to divorce, research has been limited by a lack of consistent definitions and measures and a lack of empirical evidence documenting the postulated "stages" of coping (Price-Bonham and Balswick, 1980; Rashke, 1977). Measures of "divorce adjustment" are not included in Straus and Brown's *Family Measurement Techniques* (1978).

However, several authors have described the various phases that one may experience in the process of divorce adjustment (see Table 6.1). The phases of adjustment, which have been developed from work in clinical settings with divorced persons, often parallel the reaction to death. They need not occur one after the other, but rather may be concurrent or may overlap. In addition, a person could reach one point of adjustment and then "revert" to a previous phase. Researchers on divorce adjustment should seek to specify the stage of the divorce process being explored.

The Separation

The divorce process starts before the decision to divorce is reached, and it continues through the separation, legal action, and resolutions a couple must come to about their relationship, their children, and the larger society (Wiseman, 1975). However, the time of separation has been described as the period of greatest stress and should be distinguished from the divorce per se as it may precipitate very different reactions. The stress precipitated by separation has been evidenced by psychophysiological symptoms including headaches, dizziness, skin rashes, asthma, loss of appetite, pains in the chest and stomach, weight change, sleep difficulties, heavier drinking and smoking, tiredness, and self-neglect (Bloom et al., 1978).

There are few empirical data on the separation period because, in general, separations are not recorded. However, Weiss (1975) estimates that approximately one-half of all married couples separate at least once. Kitson et al. (1977) report that 42 percent of the divorced persons in their longitudinal study had separated and reconciled before initiating a final divorce action. Bloom et al. (1979) conducted a telephone survey in Boulder, Colorado, and found that 90 percent of the separations ended in divorce. Therefore, for most couples, separation is part of the divorce process. However, there are couples who select the state of separation instead of divorce, i.e., those persons who cannot afford a divorce and/or who belong to religious groups that oppose divorce.

The stress experienced during separation may be the result of several factors (some or all of which may be occurring at the same time), including life changes in habits and patterns, legal problems, concern over jobs, economic stresses, children, family, and friends (Salts, 1979). In addition, separation is a public declaration of marital discord (Chiriboga et al., 1978; Kessler, 1975), a loss of familiar activities and habit systems, a time of learning new roles and behaviors, and the loss of a love object (Krantzler, 1973; Weiss, 1976). The status ambiguity of this time could also contribute to the stress, i.e., one is not really married nor is one really single.

Pearlin and Johnson (1977) studied 2300 married, separated, and divorced persons and found the separated were the most depressed and experienced the greatest economic hardships. (They also found economic strain was more predictive of depression than social isolation and parental responsibilities.) Chiriboga et al. (1978) collected data from 309 newly separated men and women and found men were significantly less happy than women, older persons unhappier than younger persons, and women were angrier, prouder, and more anxious while men were more restless. These authors concluded men and women may react differently to separation. When Chiriboga (1979) compared recently separated persons with persons experiencing normative family transitions, he found that the divorcing persons experienced heightened preoccupation with both negative stresses and positive stresses.

Divorce and Stress

Bloom et al. (1979) reviewed the literature that deals with divorce and various health disorders. They concluded that divorced/divorcing persons are at greater risk for psychiatric disorders, suicide, homicide, accidents

TABLE 5.1 Characteristic Phases Associated with Separation and Divorce (organized by author)

Time Sequence	Authors and Phases									
	Bohannon 1970	Herman 1974	Kessler 1975	Wiseman 1975	Weiss 1975	Brown 1976	Froelaid/ Hozeman 1977	Levy/ Joffee 1977	Kraus 1979	Smart 1979
Before separation	Emotional divorce	Denial Anger	Disillusionment Erosion Detachment	Denial Loss Depression	Erosion of love	Decision making	Denial Anger Bargaining		Denial	Trust versus Mistrust Autonomy versus Shame and Doubt
Separation		Bargaining Depression	Physical separation	Anger Ambivalence		Physical separation	Depression	Separation	Anger/ Guilt/ Regret	Initiative versus Guilt
After separation to legal divorce	Legal divorce Economic divorce Coparental divorce		Mourning	Reorientation of lifestyle and identity	Transition	Restructuring: Phase (1) Emotional (2) Legal (3) Parent/ child (4) Economic (5) Social			Focus on one's own present functioning	Industry versus Inferiority

Post-divorce	Community divorce	Acceptance	Recovering	Acceptance and new level of functioning	Recovery (Persistance of attachment)	Restructuring;	Acceptance	Individuation	Acceptance of new lifestyle	
	Psychic divorce		A. Second adolescence B. Hard work			Fairly stable and autonomous lifestyle		Reconnection		Identity versus Role Confusion
										Intimacy versus Isolation
										Generativity versus Stagnation
										Ego Integrity versus Despair

SOURCE: Adapted from Salts (1979) and Price-Bonham and Balswick (1980).

and disease, morbidity, and mortality. Gove (1973) reported similar data
for divorced persons (men more than women). Three basic theories have
been presented in an attempt to explain these findings (Bachrach, 1975;
Bloom et al., 1978):

(1) *theory of selectivity* (persons who divorce had more psychopathology to
begin with),

(2) *role theory* (marriage enhances health and well being), and

(3) *stress theory* (changes in marital status cause stress).

Kitson and Rashke (1981) addressed the theory of selectivity, pointing
out that a common thread in the divorce literature is that people who
divorce are psychologically less fit than those who do not. For example,
Briscoe and Smith (1973), Briscoe et al. (1973), and Rushing (1979)
reported that some people who divorce have diagnosed psychiatric diseases. If one adheres to this theory, the research should examine the
impact of these disorders on initial mate selection and the differential
impact of an unhappy marriage on persons with various degrees of mental
and physical health.

The differences in the physical and emotional health of married and
divorced persons were explained by Brown (1978) using stress theory. She
viewed divorce as a crisis involving social and psychological stressors.
Similarly, Kraus (1979) explained the reaction to divorce using crisis
theory, dividing reaction into *short-term* and *long-term* reaction. Short-
term reactions are temporary states of personality disorganization and are
often mistaken for psychopathology, while long-term reactions culminate
in a continuum of outcomes — ranging from psychopathology to enhanced functioning.

Persons often report improved health after divorce, depending on the
stress of the marriage (Kraus, 1979; Spanier and Lachman, 1979). Renne
(1971) found unhappily married persons were less healthy than divorced
or happily married ones; Brown et al. (1976) reported positive consequences of coping successfully with divorce; and Meyers et al. (1972)
emphasized that divorce often resolved a stressful situation rather than
increasing the symptomology. Divorce can lead to a new sense of competence and control, development of better relationships, and freedom of
time to develop one's own interests.

It cannot be assumed that divorce is a traumatic event for everyone.
For example, Albrecht (1980) found 17 percent of the 207 men and 293
women in his study reported divorce was relatively painless, and Kitson
and Sussman (1977) found 20 percent of their sample reported no, or only
one, symptom of psychological disturbance. There is a need to distinguish
between those people for whom divorce is a crisis and those for whom it is
not (Bloom et al., 1978).

Definitions and Measurements of Adjustment

One of the more recent definitions of divorce adjustment is that given by Kitson and Rashke (1981: 16):

> An ability to develop an identity for oneself that is not tied to the status of being married or to the ex-spouse and an ability to function adequately in the role responsibilities of daily life — home, work, and leisure time.

Other definitions include that of Rashke and Barringer (1977), who described divorce adjustment as adequate family functioning, satisfaction with the divorce, and a reduction in stress and problems attributed to the divorce. Similarly, Spanier and Hanson (1978) and Spanier and Anderson (1979) described adjustment as involving the dissolving of the marriage as well as the beginning of a new life.

Several authors have operationalized divorce adjustment, including Rashke (1977), who tested her 68-item scale for reliability and validity. She divided adjustment into the areas of emotional states, relationship with former spouse, dating, children, home, withdrawal and guilt, and new roles with people in jobs and organizations. Spanier and Hanson (1978), instead of computing an overall adjustment score, used four measures: Satisfaction with Life, Rosenberg's Self-Esteem Scale, Bradburn and Caplority's Measure of Positive and Negative Feelings, and Kitson's Measure of Adjustment to Separation. Granvold et al. (1979) defined adjustment as high self-acceptance and the absence of anxiety or avoidance reactions in social situations and measured it using the Expressed Acceptance of Self Scale and the Social Avoidance and Distress Scale.

In summary, adjustment to divorce involves several concurrent developmental processes, including breaking away from the former marriage, accepting new roles, building a new lifestyle, and regenerating one's sense of self-concept and trust of others. (Remarriage is not assumed to necessarily indicate successful adjustment to divorce.)

Variables Related to Adjustment

Variables that have been found to be related to divorce adjustment include, among others:

Who wanted the divorce. One spouse may want a divorce before the other. In fact, the other spouse may never reach the point of concluding the relationship is unworkable (Federico, 1979). Research has indicated this situation contributes to greater stress during the divorce process (Spanier and Casto, 1979; Weiss, 1975). The person taking the initiative has the distinct advantage of being in control of the decision, may experience more guilt (Weiss, 1976), and has worked through much of the detachment stage prior to separation: "Learning autonomy within the comfort of marriage is like learning to ride a bike with the help of training wheels" (Kessler, 1975:

30). In addition, the initiator may have evaluated the alternatives outside the present relationship as superior to the relationship while the other spouse sees fewer outside rewards or has not evaluated possible alternatives.

Economics. Divorce has a more adverse economic impact on women than on men (Bane, 1976; Brandwein et al., 1974). Economic problems are, however, inversely related to divorce adjustment for both women and men (Spanier and Casto, 1979; Spanier and Lachman, 1979). In fact, the higher the expected or real income, the lower the trauma (Bould, 1977; Kitson and Sussman, 1977; Marroni, 1977; Pais, 1978; Rashke, 1974). Pearlin and Johnson (1977) reported 69 percent of the association between marital status and depression was attributable to differential exposure and vulnerability of the unmarried to the life strains of economic hardships, parental responsibilities, and social isolation.

Hetherington et al. (1978) did not find a relation between the amount of income and feelings of economic stress in their middle-class sample, but did find financial conflicts were a major source of disagreement among divorced couples. They also found divorced fathers were more likely to increase their workload because of economic pressures.

There has been little agreement regarding the impact of education on adjustment to divorce. Barringer (1973), Marroni (1977), and Rashke (1974) found it had little or no effect on trauma, distress, or adjustment. In contrast, Everly (1978) found higher education was related to less strain and easier role transition.

Children. The findings are not consistent regarding the impact of children on adult adjustment to divorce. Reported findings include: (1) the more children a woman has, the greater her trauma (Pais, 1978); (2) the younger the children, the greater the depression (Pearlin and Johnson, 1977); (3) adjustment was not affected by the number of children (Barringer, 1973); (4) women's distress was not influenced by children (Rashke, 1974); (5) the more children, the less the stress for men without custody (Rashke and Barringer, 1977); and (6) fathers' separation from their children contributed to their stress (Hetherington et al., 1978).

Research investigating the association between children and divorce adjustment should control for the impact of variables such as economic resources, degree of contact with and support from the former spouse, availability and use of other support systems, and attitudes toward children. Until the influence of such variables is clarified, findings such as those reported are only suggestive.

Social networks and support. It has been assumed that individuals and groups that provide emotional and material resources may aid a person in adjusting to a crisis (Kitson and Rashke, 1981). Friends and relatives are generally supportive (Spanier and Casto, 1979), especially during the first two months following the divorce (Hetherington et al., 1978), and families often give support through child care, companionship, and money (Colletta, 1979; Weiss, 1975). Support such as this has been found to be related to lower stress, particularly among lower-income, single mothers (Hynes, 1979). In contrast, although Spanier and Hanson (1979) found a high incidence of interaction with and support from kin, it did not appear to be related to post-separation adjustment.

Hetherington et al. (1978) reported that as a result of the disengagement from friends (greater for women than men), divorced persons increased their contact with divorced, separated, or single friends. This network of "formerly marrieds" is a vital force in promoting stability through the divorce process (Hunt and Hunt, 1977; Wiseman, 1975).

Divorced people are more likely to date other divorced people and, in general, the more they date, the better the adjustment (Rashke and Barringer, 1977; Spanier and Casto, 1979). In fact, the most important factor in raising the divorced person's self-concept two years after the divorce is the establishment of a satisfying, intimate, heterosexual relationship (Hetherington et al., 1978).

Hunt and Hunt (1977) estimated that 75 percent of separated/divorced individuals dated within the first year after divorce and 90 percent before the end of the second year. However, "formerly marrieds" tend to view dating a variety of people somewhat ambivalently: While enjoyable and exciting, it is also viewed as more sophomoric and less prestigious than having an exclusive intimate relationship.

Taibbi (1979) warned against certain transitional relationships. Divorced persons, because of vulnerability and sensitivity, are often attracted to those persons who overtly have opposite qualities of the former spouse but covertly have identical psychological construction. There is also a tendency to become involved in a relationship in which the other person is viewed as a "saviour," the result being feelings of helplessness when the relationship ends. Weiss (1975) also cautioned that, because of the divorced person's feelings of vulnerability, the greatest danger in dating is the possibility of rejection. (Other problems include expense, time and energy, and the contrived quality of dating.)

Sex is often a part of the relationships of the "formerly married," and Hunt and Hunt (1977) concluded that in spite of the sexual anxiety experienced during this time, sex, for the most part, had a positive influence on adjustment. Hunt and Hunt (1977) developed a typology of sexual styles: (1) abstainers, (2) users (using others sexually without commitment), (3) addicts (casual and indiscriminate sex). This typology provides a model for investigating the sexual aspects of postdivorce life (Kitson and Rashke, 1981).

Scarf (1980) contended it was not unusual for women to use sex after divorce in order to cover up depression, although they may not be consciously aware of the dynamic. Being physically close to someone provides a sense of security and a feeling of being cared for.

Other variables. Several additional variables have been found to be related to divorce adjustment:

(1) A higher tolerance for change and lower dogmatism are associated with lower stress (Rashke, 1974; Rashke and Marroni, 1977).

(2) Higher religiosity and higher church attendance have been found to be related to better adjustment and lower stress (Barringer, 1973; Brown, 1978).

(3) Women with more traditional sex role attitudes reported greater psychological distress and lower self-esteem (Brown and Manela, 1978).

(4) High anxiety and low self-esteem were related to poorer postdivorce adjustment (Blair, 1970; Pais, 1978).

(5) Independence has been found to be related to better adjustment (Colletta, 1979).

(6) Internal locus of control is associated with better adjustment (Bould, 1977; Pais, 1978).

(7) The longer the period of time since physical separation, the better the adjustment (Barringer, 1973; Chester, 1971; Chiriboga and Cutler, 1977; Pais, 1978; Rashke and Barringer, 1977).

(8) The longer one had been married, the more difficult the adjustment (Pais, 1978) as well as the easier the adjustment (Granvold et al., 1979).

(9) Divorced women over 40 have been found to be less happy (Chiriboga et al., 1978) as well as more happy (Granvold et al., 1979) after divorce.

Relationship Between Gender and Divorce Adjustment

There is an ongoing debate regarding who "has it worse" in divorce. Findings in this area have been somewhat confusing. For example, Rashke and Barringer (1977) found that in their urban sample, females reported greater stress than the males while the opposite was true of their small-town/small-city sample. Chiriboga and Cutler (1977) reported that women experienced greater distress than men in the predivorce decision-making period. Deckert and Langelier (1978) reported no differences between men and women in the *separation* period after 20 or more years of marriage, but found women experiencing more long-term divorce stress.

Although it is difficult to specify the degree of stress experienced, it may be assumed that men and women will experience the divorce process differently. For example, for many women, a divorce means the departure of the major or only financial contributor to the family, and hence, for these women, poverty may be a result of divorce (Brandwein et al., 1974). Women are often left with the sole or major responsibility for child care, economic support, and household maintenance thereby leaving little time for social life — a variable related to better adjustment to divorce (Rashke,

1977). In addition, the stigma of divorce may be greater for women than men (Brandwein, et al., 1974: 499): "Societal myths of the gay divorcee out to seduce other women's husbands lead to social ostracism of the divorced woman and her family."

Several authors have reported differences by race for women experiencing divorce. For example, Black and White mothers reported significantly large decreases in income, but Black mothers perceived themselves as experiencing significantly less distress than white mothers. White mothers are more likely to report feelings of loneliness, being hassled, and having inadequate time, while Black mothers reported greater social supports and were more likely to view religion as a factor helping to integrate them into the community (Geerken and Gove, 1974; Rashke, 1979). Brown et al. (1977) studied 253 Black and White Detroit women in the process of marital dissolution and reported that a nontraditional sex role ideology served an adaptive coping function for White women, but not for Black women. The more traditional White women more often reported low self-esteem, high distress, high external control, and little personal growth.

There is also evidence to substantiate the fact that divorce constitutes an emotional upheaval for men. For example, Gove (1973) found that divorced men have more symptoms of mental illness than divorced women, and Bloom (1975) found admission rates to public and private inpatient facilities for males with disrupted marriages were nine times higher than for men in nondisrupted marriages. These findings have been attributed to a lack of social support for divorced men as well as to their tendency to deny their dependency needs and feelings (Dreyfus, 1979).

Hetherington et al. (1976) compared divorced fathers to married fathers and found the former (1) spent less time at home and more time at work, (2) experienced a "frenzied" social and recreational life, and (3) decreased contact with the former spouse and children over time. These men also experienced problems in establishing a new lifestyle in practical (everyday living) issues, their interpersonal life (developing social and intimate relationships), and changes in their self-concept and identity. They were more disorganized than men in intact families, were less likely to eat at home, slept less, and had more erratic sleep patterns. While these men reported a higher level of social life than their former wives, this social life was cyclical: It was restricted at two months after the divorce, followed by a surge of activity at one year after the divorce and a decline to the former wife's level at two years. If still unmarried at the end of two years, these men reported intense loneliness. However, their happiness, self-esteem, and feelings of competence in heterosexual behavior increased over the two-year period.

Rosenthal and Keshet (1978) studied 128 separated/divorced fathers who had at least one child aged 3 to 7. The fathers who had custody of their children reported conflict between their work role and their parental role, feelings of persistent tiredness, being rushed, and being burdened with child care. Pearlin and Johnson (1977) also studied men who had custody of children. They reported that the experiences of men were very similar to those of their female counterparts; they were more disposed to depression than married men with parental responsibilities or single men free of these responsibilities.

Gender differences with regard to the experience of separation and divorce may be the consequence of differential socialization for social roles and coping styles. It is expected that as sex role socialization becomes less rigid and social roles become available to both sexes, there will be fewer differences and more similarities in the ways divorced men and women cope with their experience (Brown, 1976).

The Relationship with Former Spouse

Divorced persons often remain bound to one another by children, love, hate, friendship, business matters, dependence, moral obligations, the need to dominate or rescue, or habit. For example, former spouses may continue contact because of residual emotional involvements that are based on tangible connections. This contact may continue as long as obligations are in force, thereby preserving some trace of the former relationship. If a couple is not particularly hostile, this quasi-familial interaction can promote feelings of friendship and facilitate adjustment (Hunt and Hunt, 1977). It is increasingly recognized that divorce does not necessarily dissolve a family unit and, in the case of children, may result in a "binuclear" family (Ahrons, 1979).

Krantzler (1973: 51) described the former spouse relationship as the "hardest to understand and, once understood, the most difficult to overcome." It consists of four people, "a man and woman suddenly strangers to each other, and the familiar husband and wife (they) once had been" (Krantzler, 1973: 53). Weiss (1976) described this relationship as characterized by the "persistence of attachment," and reported that separated persons often felt compelled to reestablish contact with their former spouses. These feelings existed even if a new and satisfactory relationship had been established; they were unrelated to liking, admiration, or respect, and appeared to be independent of an individual's conscious desire. This attachment appears to fade over time, but seeing the former spouse (even after the passage of years) may still evoke a resurgence of fondness, anger, bitterness, and yearning.

Many persons experience ambivalent feelings toward their ex-spouse, e.g., the desire to rejoin the former spouse coupled with anger because of that spouse's role in the separation distress (Weiss, 1976). Hunt and Hunt (1977) reported that many of their respondents alternated between hostility and seductiveness toward their former spouses. (This seductive mode of relating was viewed as the least successful way of coping as it is generally a continuation of a pattern that existed toward the end of the marriage.)

Some former ex-spouses continue to relate sexually to one another. The Hunts (1977) reported that love for, or sexual attraction to, the former mate lingers for some people. Weiss (1975) found it is not unusual for former spouses to see one another as lovers. Although usually indicative of a friendly relationship, there can be danger in a continued sexual involvement, especially if one person may interpret the relationship as implying reconciliation.

Hetherington et al. (1976) found divorced spouses had difficulty breaking customary patterns of interaction, even though this occupied much time and energy, and two-thirds of the interchanges were a continuation of previous patterns. However, old affection patterns also persisted in this period, and one-eighth of their sample had sexual intercourse during the first two months after divorce.

Authors do not agree regarding the feasibility of friendship between former spouses. Krantzler (1973) stated that the "chances are slim," especially at first, that they can really be good friends. However, the "amicable divorce" was proposed by Blood and Blood (1979). This divorce offers a minimum of conflict and develops through a process of gradual deescalation from a marital to a friendship relationship. Men and women may differ as to their desire for a continued relationship with the former spouse. Goetting (1979) found women preferred greater social distance from their former spouses than did men.

Goetting's (1979) study of 180 divorced and remarried men and women emphasized the lack of prescribed roles for former spouses. Her respondents indicated a high degree of consensus with regard to the following: (1) former wives should inform former husbands (and vice versa) of emergency situations involving the children; (2) former spouses should not discuss current marriage problems, and (3) it was appropriate for a father to periodically request and be given extra time with his children. In contrast, there was low consensus regarding: (1) extra financial support, (2) willingness to socialize, (3) perpetuation of rapport, (4) reciprocal influence in child-rearing behavior, and (5) the former husband caring for the children.

There are professionals who discourage relationships with former spouses. Kressel et al. (1978) reported that, in general, psychotherapists expressed the sentiment that former spouses who were friends, business partners, or lovers were actually experiencing separation distress rather than realistic caring. They contended that these continuing attachments drain energies that could be more productively spent in forming new relationships. Some argue that the best policy is for childless couples to sever all ties.

Divorce Counseling, The Legal Process, and Divorce Mediation

Divorce Counseling

Marriage and family therapists as professionals have had to reexamine their roles in relation to divorce during the 1970s. Whereas traditionally the primary purpose of the therapist had been to preserve a marriage, the emergence of divorce counseling during this decade implied that divorce was now to be seen as a viable option (Brown, 1976).

Kressel et al. (1978: 433), after interviewing 21 highly experienced therapists, concluded divorce counseling can have different meanings to different practitioners and that "we are in a transitional stage in the emergence of this therapeutic specialty." However, there are common elements in divorce counseling. For example, Brown (1976: 400) stated that the purpose was to

> provide assistance to the couple or to the individual spouses as they consider divorce, and as they are faced with the rapid and massive change which is triggered by physical separation.

Fisher (1973: 55) described it as

> a therapeutic process by which those who experience and continue the pain and humiliation of divorce can be helped towards personal growth and adjustment, enabling them to move away from egocentricity toward altruism and a desire to contribute to society.

According to Brown (1976), divorce counseling should take place during the *decision-making period* and the *restructuring period*. Similarly, Fisher (1973) delineated three periods of divorce counseling: (1) predivorce (time of decision), (2) during litigation (when the legal divorce is obtained), and (3) postdivorce (after the decree of divorce). Areas considered in divorce counseling are the legal divorce, economic readjustment, restructuring the parent/child relationship, social readjustment, and the emotional and psychological aspects of divorce. Dreyfus (1979) contended that counseling divorced fathers was unique because of their special concerns, i.e., loss of their homes, loss of children, loss of friends, loss of familiar possessions, loss of status, and unconscious dependency needs.

There are no training programs specifically for divorce counseling as part of their practice. However, data suggest that people are more likely to consult a member of the clergy than a therapist. In general, the clergy view divorce as a traumatic experience and their role is characterized as being informal, practical, emotionally supportive, and concerned with reconciliation, the viability of the family unit, and the welfare of the children. The clergy also tend to place a high priority on facilitating psychological adjustment (Weinglass et al., 1978).

The Legal Aspects of Divorce

The original divorce statutes in this country were heavily influenced by English divorce laws whose basic premise was that although people could voluntarily enter marriage they could not voluntarily leave it. Marriage was viewed as a contract between two persons in which they promised to fulfill certain responsibilities to each other. However, unlike other contracts, a marriage contract could not be broken simply by mutual consent; the state maintained the right to decide when and if someone could divorce. Divorce was to be granted only for grave and serious reasons and only one party could be "guilty." These premises provided the basis for the "fault" system of divorce in which one spouse had to bring charges against the other.

The 1970s witnessed sweeping changes in the divorce statutes of many states. California, with the California Family Act of 1969, effective January , 1970, was the first state to eliminate the concept of fault from the divorce process. California legislators abolished the term "divorce" and substituted "dissolution of marriage." Other states have used terms such as "irremediable breakdown," "irreconcilable differences," "irretrievable breakdown," and "no reasonable likelihood of preserving the marriage." By 1976, 47 states allowed couples to declare the marriage irretrievably broken and granted divorces on the basis that there had been a voluntary separation or a given period of time (Cavanagh and Rhode, 1976).

The cause and effect relationship between increased divorce rates and more liberal divorce laws is not clear. Some have hypothesized that divorce laws became increasingly flexible in response to society's changing attitudes toward marriage and divorce. Fain (1977) explained these changes as a reflection of a fundamental transition in human values, a decline in the influence of social institutions, a changing system of morals, and increased mobility, urbanization, and industrialization. He also stated that past assumptions about family law, women, divorce, and alimony had changed, and that divorce laws were forced to follow these changing societal attitudes. Other researchers have suggested that the more liberal divorce laws have contributed to the higher divorce rates.

Sell (1979) analyzed divorce rates for 32 states that changed their grounds for divorce between 1968 and 1978 and 15 states that did not. He concluded that divorce rates increased for both groups of states and that changes in the grounds for divorce did not substantially influence the change in divorce rates. He cautioned that those who see the legal changes as a causal factor may fail to note that states that have not changed their laws also show substantial increases in their divorce rates.

Mazur-Hart and Berman (1977) investigated the divorce rates in Nebraska from January 1969 to December 1974 (a no-fault divorce law was enacted July 6, 1972). They concluded that divorce was increasing systematically, but, in general, the inception of no-fault divorce was not associated with an increase in the overall number of divorces granted in Nebraska for White couples. (However, the level of divorces did increase significantly for Black couples, at least partially because no-fault divorce made divorce less expensive.)

We cannot conclude that no-fault divorce laws have a direct impact on rates of divorce. Gunter (1977) compared persons who filed for divorce in Hillsborough County, Florida, before and after a no-fault law was effective in Florida (January 1, 1972). He reported that the proportions of the sexes initiating divorce reversed from the first to the second period: before no-fault divorce two-thirds of the spouses who filed were women, while after the no-fault law, two-thirds of the spouses who filed were men.

The Legal Process and Attorneys

The legal system is frequently viewed as responsible for increasing the trauma experienced by divorcing persons. Grounds for divorce must be molded to fit the grounds in any given state, and the laws often require the spouses to become adversaries. The rational-logical approach of the legal system does not provide an environment for the resolution of interpersonal conflict and may even result in increased hostilities (Bass and Rein, 1976; Bohannan, 1970; Brown, 1976; Rose and Price-Bonham, 1973).

In Spanier and Anderson's (1979) study of separated and divorced persons, 5 percent of the respondents indicated that they were dissatisfied with the entire legal process, 74 percent indicated satisfaction with their attorneys, 20 percent reported that their attorneys advised them to exaggerate their marital problems more than they wanted to, and 29 percent reported that their lawyer advised them to do things (not pay bills, not talk to spouse, take money out of savings, move out of house) that might aggravate their spouse. However, Spanier and Anderson did not find these factors influenced postseparation adjustment.

Herrman et al. (1979) investigated how attorneys perceived their role in the divorce process. They interviewed 22 Georgia lawyers who had had substantial experience with divorce cases. These respondents reported that, in general, clients were very uninformed about the legal aspects of divorce, seldom understood the basic obligations of a settlement agreement, and did not consider the long-term consequences of divorce. They expressed ambivalence over their inability to reduce conflict and strain in the divorce process and suggested: (1) attorneys need formal training in counseling, (2) a better knowledge of referral services is needed, and (3) attorneys must increase their sensitivity to the trauma of divorce.

Kressel et al. (1978) conducted in-depth interviews with 17 attorneys, and on the basis of their responses, identified six major approaches to their role in the divorce process:

(1) *The undertaker:* general cynicism, assumes clients are in a state of emotional derangement; lawyer's job is a thankless, messy business;

(2) *The mechanic:* pragmatic, technically oriented; assumes clients are capable of knowing what they want;

(3) *The mediator:* oriented toward negotiated compromise and rational problem solving; emphasis on cooperation with other side;

(4) *The social worker:* concerned for client's postdivorce adjustment and overall social welfare;

(5) *The therapist:* assumes legal aspects of a divorce can be dealt with if the emotional aspects are engaged by the lawyer ;

(6) *The moral agent:* rejects neutrality; assumes the lawyer should not hesitate to use her or his sense of "right" and "wrong."

In summary, there are emotional factors in addition to the legal factors that attorneys deal with when working with divorcing persons. Some attorneys view dealing with these factors as part of their legal-professional role, but many, due to crowded schedules and feelings of inadequacy, do not.

Divorce Mediation

In 1976, the American Arbitration Association promulgated its "Family Dispute Services," which provide: rules and procedures designed to facilitate possible conciliation, aid to separated parties in arriving at the terms of a separation agreement, a referee for final and binding determination of those items on which the parties could not agree, and "arbitration" of disputes arising under separation agreements. This model, along with the later Mediation Model, evolved because of an increased recognition that divorcing spouses often have difficulty working out the details of a divorce settlement (in particular, alimony, child support, property division, and custody). Mediation was viewed as more desirable than the traditional legal process because it avoids the adversary posture associated with attorney-negotiated agreements.

The Mediation Model, developed by Coogler, Lightman, and Irving, is viewed as an adjunct and alternative to court processing of disputes (Coogler et al., 1979). Developed by the Family Mediation Association, it requires that the divorcing spouses pursue a rational approach to the resolution of the conflictual issues surrounding divorce. The spouses do not abdicate the decision making, but are helped under the guidance of a

mediator to decide for themselves (Coogler, 1978). Other modes of di
vorce mediation have since evolved (e.g., Haynes, 1981). One can readily
see advantages in mediation. Research is now needed to determine the
feasibility of the approach and the characteristics of couples able to
mediate issues.

The legal system is attempting to humanize the process of divorce
through such changes as no-fault divorce, conciliation courts, family cour
systems, and mediation. One can only applaud any efforts to develop a
system that encourages "nonconflictual conflict" during the divorce proc
ess.

Summary

Although divorce was an alternative lifestyle for an unprecedented
number of people in the 1970s, it often took place without guidelines
helping agencies, status, or recognition. Most family life takes place in the
context of institutionally defined norms. In contrast, divorce lacks clearly
defined norms resulting in divorced persons moving from a structured
defined, and institutionalized marriage to a noninstitution in which few
ideals and expectations are present. This phenomenon is assumed to add
to the stress created by divorce. Therefore, in order to alleviate at least par
of the trauma associated with divorce, our society needs to develop norm
regarding divorced persons in the areas of financial security, companion
ship, sexual fulfillment, and parenting.

Research that focused on the processes of divorce and, in particular, or
divorce adjustment increased in the 1970s. However, methodological and
theoretical issues that should be emphasized in the 1980s include: (1) lon
gitudinal research, including men, women, and children, (2) clear defini
tions of concepts and standardization of measurements, (3) the continuing
family system, (4) internal processes leading to the decision to divorce and
divorce adjustment, (5) comparison of those people that do and do no
experience a crisis as a result of divorce, (6) utilization of appropriate
theoretical frameworks for the purposes of guiding research, (7) compari
son of couples who divorce with married couples, and (8) multivarian
analyses of variables related to divorce and adjustment to divorce.

Note

1. For information about the Information Network for Research on Divorce contact
Dr. Dorothy S. Huntington, Center for the Family in Transition, 5725 Paradise Dr.
Building A, Suite 100, Corte Medera, CA, 94925.

References

AHRONS, C.R. (1979) "The binuclear family: two households, one family." Alternative Lifestyles 2, 4: 499-515.
ALBRECHT, S.L. (1980) "Reactions and adjustments to divorce: differences in the experiences of males and females." Family Relations 29: 59-68.
BACARACH, L.L. (1975) Marital Status and Mental Disorder: An Analytical Review. U. S. Department of Health, Education and Welfare Publication No. (ADM) 75-217. Washington, DC: Government Printing Office.
BANE, M.J. (1976) Here to Stay: American Families in the Twentieth Century. New York: Basic Books.
BARRINGER, K.D. (1973) "Self-perception of the quality of adjustment of single parents without partners organizations." Ph.D. dissertation, University of Iowa.
BASS, H.L. and M.L. REIN (1976) Divorce or Marriage: A Legal Guide. Englewood Cliffs, NJ: Prentice-Hall.
BLAIR, M. (1970) "Divorcees' adjustment and attitudinal changes about life." Dissertation Abstract International 30: 5541-5542. (University Microfilms, No. 70-11, 099.)
BLOOD, R.O. and M.C. BLOOD (1979) "Amicable divorce." Alternative Lifestyles 2, 4: 483-498.
BLOOM, B.L. (1975) Changing Patterns of Psychiatric Care. New York: Human Sciences.
——— S.J. ASHER, and S.W. WHITE (1978) "Marital disruption as a distressor: a review and analysis." Psychological Bulletin 84 (July): 867-894.
BLOOM, B.L., W.F. HODGES, R.A. CALDWELL, L. SYSTRA, and A.R. CEDRONE (1979) "Marital separation: A community survey." Journal of Divorce 3 (Fall): 7-19.
BOHANNAN, P. (1970) "The six stations of divorce," pp. 33-62 in P. Bohannan (ed.) Divorce and After. Garden City, NY: Doubleday.
BOULD, S. (1977) "Female-headed families: personal fate control and the provider role." Journal of Marriage and the Family 39 (May): 339-349.
BRANDWEIN, R.A., C.A. BROWN, and E.M. FOX (1974) "Women and children lost: the social situation of divorced mothers and their families." Journal of Marriage and the Family 36 (August): 498-514.
BRISCOE, C. and J.B. SMITH (1973) "Depression and marital turmoil." Archives of General Psychiatry 29 (December): 811-817.
——— E. ROBINS, S. MARTIN, and F. GASKIN (1973) "Divorce and psychiatric disease." Archives of General Psychiatry 29 (July): 119-125.
BROWN, B.B. (1978) "Who shall I turn to? Social and psychological determinants of helpseeking among urban adults." American Journal of Community Psychology 6 (October): 425-439.
BROWN, C.A., R. FELDBERG, E.M. FOX, and J. KOHEN (1976) "Divorce: chance of a lifetime." Journal of Social Issues 32 (Spring): 119-134.
BROWN, E.M. (1976) "Divorce counseling," pp. 394-429 in D.H.L. Olson (ed.) Treating Relationships. Lake Mills, IA: Graphic Publishing.
BROWN, P. (1976) "Sex differences in divorce," pp. 101-123 in E. Gomberg and V. Franks (eds.) Gender and Disordered Behavior. New York: Bruner/Mazel.
——— and R. MANELA (1978) "Changing family roles: women and divorce." Journal of Divorce 1 (Summer): 315-328.
BROWN, P., L. PERRY, and E. HARBURG (1977) "Sex role attitudes and psychological outcomes for Black and White women experiencing marital dissolution." Journal of Marriage and the Family 39 (August): 549-561.
CAVANAGH, R.C. and D.L. RHODE (1976) "The unauthorized practice of law and pro se divorce: an empirical analysis." Yale Law Journal 85 (November): 104-184.
CHESTER, R. (1971) "Health and marriage breakdown: experience of a sample of divorced women." British Journal of Preventive and Social Medicine 25: 231-235.
CHIRIBOGA, D.A. (1979) "Marital separation and stress." Alternative Lifestyles 2 (November): 461-470.

———— and L. CUTLER (1977) "Stress responses among divorcing men and women." Journal of Divorce 1 (Winter): 95-106.

CHIRIBOGA, D.A., J. ROBERTS, and J.A. STEIN (1978) "Psychological well-being during marital separation." Journal of Divorce 2 (Fall): 21-36.

COLLETTA, N.D. (1979) "Support systems after divorce: incidence and impact." Journal of Marriage and the Family 41 (November): 837-846.

COOGLER, O.J. (1978) Structured Mediation in Divorce Settlements. Lexington, MA: D.C. Heath.

———— R.E. WEBER, and P.C. McKENRY (1979) "Divorce mediation: a means of facilitating divorce and adjustment." Family Coordinator 28 (April): 255-259.

DECKERT, P. and R. LANGELIER (1978) "The late-divorce phenomenon: the causes and impact of ending 20-year-old or longer marriages." Journal of Divorce 1 (Summer): 381-390.

DREYFUS, E.A. (1979) "Counseling the divorced father." Journal of Marital and Family Therapy 5 (October): 79-85.

EPSTEIN, J. (1975) Divorced in America: Marriage in an Age of Possibility. Baltimore: Penguin.

EVERLY, K. (1978) "Leisure networks and role strain: a study of divorced women with custody." Ph.D. dissertation, Syracuse University, Syracuse, New York.

FAIN, H.M. (1977) "Family law — whither now?" Journal of Divorce 1 (Fall): 31-41.

FEDERICO, J. (1979) "The marital termination period of the divorce adjustment process." Journal of Divorce 2 (Winter): 93-106.

FISHER, E.O. (1973) "A guide to divorce counseling." Family Coordinator 22 (January): 55-61.

GEERKEN, M. and W.R. GOVE (1974) "Race, sex, and marital status: their effect on morality." Social Problems 22 (April): 567-580.

GLICK, P.C., and A.J. NORTON (1977) "Marrying, divorcing, and living together in the U.S. today." Population Bulletin 32, 5. Washington, DC: Population Reference Bureau.

GOETTING, A. (1979) "The normative integration of the former spouse relationship." Journal of Divorce 2 (Summer): 395-414.

GOODE, W.J. (1956) After Divorce. New York: Macmillan.

GOVE, W.R. (1973) "Sex, marital status and morality." American Journal of Sociology 79 (September): 45-67.

GRANVOLD, D.K., L.M. PEDLER, and S.G. SCHELLIE (1979) "A study of sex role expectancy and female post divorce adjustment." Journal of Divorce 2 (Summer): 383-394.

GUNTER, B.G. (1977) "Notes on divorce filing as role behavior." Journal of Marriage and the Family 39 (February): 95-98.

HAYNES, J.M. (1981) Divorce Mediation. New York: Springer.

HERRMAN, M.S., P.C. McKENRY, and R.E. WEBER (1979) "Mediation and arbitration applied to family conflict resolution: the divorce settlement." Arbitration Journal 34 (March): 17-21.

HERRMAN, S.J. (1974) "Divorce: a grief process." Perspectives in Psychiatric Care (Spring): 108-112.

HETHERINGTON, E.M., M. COX, and R. COX (1978) "The aftermath of divorce," pp. 149-176 in J.H. Stevens, Jr., and M. Mathews (eds.) Mother-Child, Father-Child Relations. Washington DC: National Association for the Education of Young Children.

———— (1976) "Divorced fathers." Family Coordinator 25 (October): 417-428.

HUNT, M. and B. HUNT (1977) The Divorce Experience. New York: McGraw-Hill.

HYNES, W.J. (1979) "Single parent mothers and distress: relationships between selected social and psychological factors and distress in low-income single parent mothers." Ph.D. dissertation, Catholic University of America, Washington, D.C.

KESSLER, S. (1975) The American Way of Divorce: Prescriptions for Change. Chicago: Nelson-Hall.

KITSON, G.C., W.M. HOLMES, and M.B. SUSSMAN (1977) "Predicting reconciliation: a test of the exchange model of divorce." Presented at the Annual Meetings of the American Sociological Association, Chicago, Illinois.

KITSON, G.C. and H.J. RASHKE (1981) "Divorce research: what we know; what we need to know." Journal of Divorce 5 (Fall): 1-37.

KITSON, G. C. and M. B. SUSSMAN (1977) "The impact of divorce on adults." Concilia-
tion Courts Review (December): 20-24.
KRANTZLER, M. (1973) Creative Divorce: A New Opportunity for Personal Growth. New
York: Evans.
KRAUS, S. (1979) "The crisis of divorce: growth promoting or pathogenic." Journal of
Divorce 3 (Winter): 107-119.
KRESSEL, K., M. LOPEZ-MORILLAS, J. WEINGLAS, and M. DEUTSCH (1978) "Pro-
fessional intervention in divorce: a summary of the views of lawyers,
psychotherapists, and clergy." Journal of Divorce 2 (Winter): 119-156.
LEVEY, T. M. and W. JOFFE (1977) "Counseling couples through separation: a develop-
mental approach." Presented at the Annual Meetings of the National Council on
Family Relations, San Diego, California.
LICHTENBERGER, J. P. (1931) Divorce: A Social Interpretation. New York: McGraw-Hill.
MARRONI, E. L. (1979) "Factors influencing the adjustment of separated or divorced
Catholics." Master's thesis, Norfolk State College.
MAZUR-HART, S. F. and J. J. BERMAN (1977) "Changing from fault to no-fault divorce:
an interrupted time series analysis." Journal of Applied Social Psychology 7
(October): 300-312.
MEYERS, J. K., J. J. LINDENTHAL, M. P. PEPPER, and D. R. OSTRANDER (1972) "Life
events and mental status: a longitudinal study." Journal of Health and Social Behavior
13 (December): 398-406.
National Center for Health Statistics (1980) "Births, marriages, divorces, and deaths for
1979." Monthly Vital Statistics Report 28, 12.
——— (1978) Mortality from Selected Causes by Marital Status: United States (Parts A &
B), Department of Health, Education and Welfare Publication No. (PHS) 1000-Series
20- No. 8. Washington, DC: Government Printing Office.
PAIS, J. P. S. (1978) "Social-psychological predictions of adjustment for divorced
mothers." Ph.D. dissertation, University of Tennessee.
PERLIN, L. I. and J. S. JOHNSON (1977) "Marital status, life strains and depression."
American Sociological Review 42 (October): 704-715.
PRICE-BONHAM, S. and J. O. BALSWICK (1980) "The non-institutions: divorce and
desertion, and remarriage." Journal of Marriage and the Family 42
(November): 959-972.
RASHKE, H. J. (1979) "Social-psychological consequences of divorce: a comparison of
Black and white low-income single parent mothers." Presented at the Annual Meetings of the American Sociological Association, Boston, Massachusetts.
——— (1977) "The role of social participation in postseparation and postdivorce adjustment." Journal of Divorce 1 (Winter): 129-139.
——— (1974) "Social and psychological factors in voluntary postmarital dissolution
adjustment." Ph.D. dissertation, University of Minnesota.
——— and E. MARRONI (1977) "Adjustment of marital dissolution." Presented at the
Annual Meeting for the Study of Social Problems, San Francisco, August.
——— and K. D. BARRINGER (1977) "Postdivorce adjustment among persons participating in Parents-Without-Partners organizations." Family Perspective 11 (Winter): 23-
34.
RENNE, K. S. (1971) "Health and marital experience in an urban population." Journal of
Marriage and the Family 33 (May): 338-350.
ROSE, V. L. and S. PRICE-BONHAM (1973) "Divorce adjustment: a woman's problem?"
Family Coordinator 22 (July): 291-297.
ROSENTHAL, K. N. and H. S. KESHET (1978) "The impact of child care responsibilities
on part-time or single fathers — changing patterns of work and intimacy." Alternative
Lifestyles 1 (November): 465-491.
RUSHING, W. A. (1979) "Marital status and mental disorder: evidence in favor of a
behavioral model." Social Forces 58 (December): 540-556.
SALTS, C. J. (1979) "Divorce process: integration of theory." Journal of Divorce 3
(Spring): 233-240.
SCARF, M. (1980) Unfinished Business: Pressure Points in the Lives of Women. Garden
City, NY: Doubleday.
SELL, K. D. (1979) "Divorce law reform and increasing divorce rates," pp. 290-308 in
J. G. Wells (ed.) Current Issues in Marriage and the Family. New York: Macmillan.

————— and B. H. SELL (1978) Divorce in the United States, Canada, and Great Britain: A Guide to Information Sources. Detroit: Gale Research Company.

SPANIER, G. B. and E. A. ANDERSON (1979) "The impact of the legal system on adjustment to marital separation." Journal of Marriage and the Family 41 (August): 605-613.

SPANIER, G. B. and R. CASTO (1979) "Adjustment to separation and divorce: an analysis of 50 case studies." Journal of Divorce 3 (Spring): 241-253.

SPANIER, G. B. and S. HANSON (1978) "The role of extended kin in the adjustment to marital separation." Presented at the Annual Meetings of the Southern Sociological Society, New Orleans, Louisiana.

SPANIER, G. B. and M. E. LACHMAN (1979) "Factors associated with adjustment to marital separation." Presented at the Annual Meetings of the Eastern Sociological Society, New York, New York.

STRAUS, M. and B. W. BROWN (1978) Family Measurement Techniques: Abstracts of Published Instruments, 1935-1974. Minneapolis: University of Minnesota Press.

TAIBBI, R. (1979) "Transitional relationships after divorce." Journal of Divorce 2 (Spring): 263-270.

WALLER, W. W. (1967) The Old and the New: Divorce and Adjustment. Carbondale, IL: Southern University Press.

WEINGLASS, J., K. KRESSEL, and M. DEUTSCH (1978) "The role of the clergy in divorce: an exploratory study." Journal of Divorce 2 (Fall): 57-82.

WEISS, R. (1976) "The emotional impact of marital separation." Journal of Social Issues 32 (Winter): 135-145.

————— (1975) Marital Separation. New York: Basic Books.

WISEMAN, R. S. (1975) "Crisis theory and the process of divorce." Social Casework 56 (Spring): 233-240.

CHAPTER 6

Remarriage and Stepfamilies: Research Results and Implications

CATHERINE S. CHILMAN

University of Wisconsin — Milwaukee

Remarriage brings with it a diversity of family sizes and structures. Two main categories of remarriages are those that occur after widowhood and those that occur after divorce. The first type was the most common in this country before the 1940s but, increasingly, the more usual kind of remarriage has become one that follows divorce: over 80 percent of all remarriages today (Glick, 1980).

Major Forms of Remarriage

Wife	Husband
• No children	• No children
• One or more biological children by former spouse. Children live with wife in new family; wife has custody.	• No biological children by former spouse. Is stepfather to wife's children; the biological father (has or has not) visiting rights and pays (or does not pay) support.
• No biological children by former spouse but stepmother to current husband's one or more children. Children's biological mother has custody and children live with her but husband pays (or does not pay) support and visits (or does not visit) children.	• Biological father to one or more children by former spouse. Children do not live in his new home but he does (or does not) support them and does (or does not) visit them.
• One or more biological children by former spouse.	• One or more biological children living with him in new family; has custody.

Author's Note: The following persons were resource people for the Remarriage Workshop at the Groves Conference on Marriage and the Family, May 1981, on which this

Children living with her in new family; has custody.

- Has no stepchildren living in new family but new wife has previously born biological children living with her former spouse.

- One or more previously born biological children living with former spouse who has custody. She has (or has not) visiting rights.

- Previously born biological children in home; also a biological child as a product of this remarriage.

- Previously born biological children in home; has a biological child as a product of this remarriage.

Further variations of reconstituted family structures revolve around such factors as whether or not divorced former spouses are remarried, cohabiting, or single and whether children of the former marriage have been adopted by the stepparent. It is also important to consider variations associated with socioeconomic status, race, ethnicity, and religion.

Trends in Divorce and Remarriage

The divorce rate per 1000 married women between the ages of 14 and 44 peaked following World War II and dropped during the family-oriented 1950s and early 1960s. By 1965, however, it began to rise and continued to do so at a rapid rate through 1975. Between 1975 and 1980, the ascent of the divorce rate was more gradual (Carter and Glick, 1976; Spanier and Glick, 1981). The remarriage rate per 1000 widowed and divorced women between the ages of 15 and 54 rose steadily from a low in the 1930s to a high in 1945. It then dropped, but experienced a steep climb again between the early 1960s and 1970s. However, the remarriage rate has shown a gradual decline during the 1970s (Carter and Glick, 1976).

The most recent figures indicate that about 32 percent of all marriages in the United States today are remarriages, about 13 percent of the nation's children under the age of 18 are in reconstituted families, over 17 percent are in single-parent families (divorced, separated, or never married), and about 67 percent are in two-parent, first-married households (Visher and Visher, 1979). About 16 percent of the nation's women are remarried, most for the second and a few for the third time. Over two-thirds of those who divorce remarry, but this is true for less than 20 percent of widows — most of whom are over age 40 at the time of marital dissolution.

chapter is based: Rignoor Asmundsson, University of Connecticut; David Baptiste, University of New Mexico; William Doherty, University of Iowa; Barbara and Phillip Newman, Ohio State University. Important substantive content for this chapter was added by the following participants: Helen Kearney, Robert Rice, Virginia Sibbison, and Jane Tybring.

Factors Associated with Remarriage

The following factors are associated with remarriage within five years of marital divorce or widowhood (Glick, 1980; Price-Bonham and Balswick, 1980; Spanier and Glick, 1980):

For women

- education less than college or graduate levels but more than eighth grade
- few, but some, children
- being divorced rather than widowed (age factor operates here as older women are more apt to be widowed — 87 percent of women widowed at age 40 or older do not remarry)
- being under age 40, preferably age 30 or less
- not being in the labor force
- having a low income but not being a recipient of AFDC.

For men

- Men, more than women, are apt to remarry, partly because there are more women over age 25 in the population than men.
- On the average, men who remarry wed women seven years younger than themselves.
- having an adequate to good income

Remarriage: How Problematic for the Remarried Couple Relationship?

Carter and Glick (1976) write that census data show that second marriages following divorce are somewhat more likely than first marriages to dissolve: 38 percent of first marriages of women in their thirties campared to 45 percent of these women if they remarry. In actuality, this difference is not exceedingly large, but some commentators make a great deal of it. For instance, Cherlin (1978, 1981) interprets this kind of data to suggest that remarriage, as a marital form, is exceptionally vulnerable. His 1978 essay is frequently quoted to the effect that remarriages have special problems because they are not recognized as a social institution and thus there are almost no normative guidelines for remarried couples, their children, and stepchildren. This lack of norms creates problems because remarriage is a markedly complex family form, especially when children are involved.

Along these lines, Furstenberg (1980: 443) writes,

This structural difference between the two forms of remarriage (after divorce or after death) is far from trivial for it introduces a host of issues not provided for in our nuclear-based kinship system. We have no set beliefs, no language, and no rules for a family form that has "more than

two parents," yet a substantial minority of the United States will participate or already is participating in such a system.

The somewhat higher rate of marital dissolution for second marriages
might well be caused, at least in part, by the characteristics of people who
remarry. For example, as shown above, the remarrying man tends to wed a
woman who is about seven years younger than himself, has relatively little
education, few employment skills, and little in the way of financial resources.

It is essential that a pathology model be avoided in conceptualizing
remarriage and stepfamilies. Clinicians particularly tend to view this family
form as traumatic because they see the selected group of troubled people
who come for counseling. They do *not* see those who are making a
relatively trouble-free adjustment to their remarriage.

Along these lines, Campbell (1980) reports on 1971 and 1973 national
surveys of the quality of life in the United States. These surveys showed
that the majority of remarried men and women, both those who had been
previously widowed and those who had been divorced, viewed their
marriages as highly satisfying. Their responses to marital satisfaction items
were quite similar to those of people in their first marriages. Divorced
people who had not remarried were singularly dissatisfied with many
aspects of their lives, more so than any other group of respondents.

Important insights about remarriage issues are furnished by Weingarten (1980), who carried out an analysis of data obtained in 1976 by a
University of Michigan national survey of many aspects of family and
individual life in the United States. In analyzing the responses of men and
women in their first marriages compared to those who had been divorced
and were in their second marriage, a number of interesting similarities and
differences were obtained. Controls were used in this analysis for sex of the
respondent, education (which also tends to measure income), and length
of current marriage (which tends to also indicate age).

There were no statistically significant differences for either the male or
female groups on the following variables:

- Self-perceived happiness, self-esteem, sense of well-being, and
  self-acceptance were all at generally high levels for both groups.

- Both groups had low self-assessments of anxiety and worry.

- Self-reported marital happiness was lower for the remarried group in an
  early analysis, but this difference disappeared when controls were used for
  the effects of education.

Remarried women, as a group, were significantly more likely than
those in first marriages to say they were happy with their present lives.
Remarried men, compared to those in first marriages, were more apt to say
they were not "too happy" (only 14 percent gave this rating, however). The
remarried respondents were more likely to say that they had experienced a
lot of trauma in their lives and to have used professional help with their

personal problems. They were also more likely to report physical symptoms associated with chronic stress.

The residual effects of earlier divorce trauma (Bohannon, 1970; Brown, 1976; Chiriboga, 1979; Coletta, 1979; Wallerstein and Kelly, 1980; Weiss, 1975) may be indicated in part by the finding that remarried women were especially apt to think they got a great deal out of the partnership in their second marriage. Perhaps this perception also reflects the personal growth and altered concept of marital and parental roles that often appear to be associated with the after effects of divorce (Kulka and Weingarten, 1979; Visher and Visher, 1979). Some observations of clinical practitioners are:

- Divorce is often associated with an extramarital affair *preceding* the broken first marriage. Remarriage may be between the partners in this affair, or the affair may have been used as a mechanism for precipitating a divorce.

- Divorce may be perceived by marital partners as a process of "dumping" or being "dumped" by the spouse. Clinical observation suggests that it is a complex question as to which person "dumped" the other. Ideally, reactions to the "dumping" processes should be confronted and resolved before the person remarries. If not, these reactions may negatively affect the new relationship.

- Other projected attitudes or feelings from the past are apt to adversely affect the remarriage in a number of ways, especially if too little time (two years or so) is given to the adjustment and mourning processes following divorce or widowhood. Even in poor first marriages, a certain amount of bonding has occurred that needs to be loosened.

- Remarriage often follows a period of cohabitation with one or more partners, including the new spouses. Experiences from these relationships also require considerable reworking.

- Remarriages are more complex than first marriages. Conflict is to be expected; open communication about past and present, personal and family issues appears to be essential.

- Remarriage often involves changing jobs and moving one's residence for at least one partner. These upheavals are apt to have their traumatic aspects, as will be discussed later when the effects of remarriage on children are presented.

- The complexities of remarriage, especially of the reconstituted family, are so numerous that flexibility of the partners seems essential.

The strengths, as well as difficulties, of remarriage should be recognized:

- Remarriage presents an opportunity for mid-career change in accordance with personal growth that may have occurred and that may be enhanced by a new marriage.

- With advanced age and experience, remarried couples may bring greater maturity, knowledge, and skills to the new situation.

- The woman's financial situation is often improved through remarriage, although the burdens for the man may be increased, especially if he is

obligated to pay alimony and/or child support for the children of his
former marriage.

Furstenberg (1980: 449), in noting the strengths of remarried couples,
remarks on the Pennsylvania study he conducted with Spanier:

> There is a clear indication that most remarried couples regard their
> second marriage as distinctively different from their first. Remarried
> people report greater flexibility in the division of household tasks, more
> shared decision-making, and a greater degree of emotional exchange.

Weingarten (1980) compared remarried parents with children to parents in their first marriages. When controls were used for the effects of sex,
education, and length of marriage, no significant differences were found in
parent perceptions on the following items: the effect of having children on
changes in one's life, feeling that having children would fulfill important
personal values, and feeling that having children does not interfere with
what one wants to do. However, significantly more of the remarried
parents (68 percent), compared to first-married ones (50 percent), agreed
that they felt inadequate about their ability to maintain close physical-
emotional contact with their children (probably referring to stepchildren,
especially). Also, the remarried couples were significantly more likely to
say that they felt children are apt to draw married couples apart (37 percent
of remarried and 20 percent of first married).

In summarizing her analysis of national data, Weingarten writes that
although she found some indication of extra problems for reconstituted
families, on the whole remarried couples seem to do as well as those in first
marriages. Faced with a difficult and complex task, most appeared to
demonstrate the ability to develop a satisfying, "successful" marriage, over
a period of time (Weingarten, 1980).

Earlier studies, using mainly middle-class, small samples, reported
high levels of satisfaction among the remarried (Bernard, 1956; Goode,
1956). Later, Glenn and Weaver (1977) obtained only slightly different
results when they analyzed 1973, 1974, and 1975 data from National
Opinion Research Center Surveys of national probability samples of the
White population. A comparison of the self-reports of divorced, remarried
persons, and first-married persons showed few differences between the
two groups. Virtually no differences were found when a small group of
short-lived remarriages was withdrawn from the sample.

Spanier and Furstenberg (in press) have taken a welcome approach to
the study of marital adjustments among the remarried in a rural-urban
Pennsylvania county. Important elements include: a longitudinal research
design, the use of a number of criteria of "marital and life adjustments,"
and a comparison of the divorced/still single to the divorced/remarried.
This comparison is far more logical than the usual one, which compares the
first married to the remarried. Such a comparison is fallacious because
remarriage is *not* an analogue of first marriage. Remarriage is available

only to those who become single *after* the dissolution of a first marriage through death or divorce. The logical alternatives to the possibility of remarriage are:

- an unhappy marriage that is *not* dissolved by divorce (about one-third or fewer first marriages are self-rated as somewhat or very unhappy),
- staying single and living alone or only with one's children following the dissolution of a marriage (the most usual arrangement for those who do not remarry),
- staying single but cohabiting following marital dissolution, or
- staying single but living with relatives or friends following marital dissolution.

Despite a huge sample loss (only about 20 percent of the possible sample consented to participate in the original study), Furstenberg and Spanier obtained interesting results through structured interviews at two different time periods (immediately after divorce and 2 years later). At time 2, 32 percent of the divorced group had remarried. Comparing remarried, single, and cohabiting persons, it was found that there were no significant differences among groups in such areas as self-reported well-being and self-esteem, satisfaction with health, smoking, and drinking habits, work satisfaction, kin support, and marital or life adjustment.

Effects of Divorce and Remarriage on Children

Effects of Divorce

As mentioned earlier, a number of studies show that separation and divorce impose severe strains on men and women, and that recovery from the traumatic effects usually takes two or three years. Studies also indicate that divorce is extremely stressful for children (Hetherington et al., 1978; Wallerstein and Kelly, 1980). In their five-year longitudinal study, Wallerstein and Kelly (1980) made many important clinical observations based on intensive interviews with all members of divorcing families.[2] They found that the initial period of divorce and parental separation was profoundly difficult for all of the children and adolescents in their sample. Even when parents had been caught in severely unhappy marriages, their children usually did not want the divorce to occur. Five years after the divorce, the researchers observed that one-third of the children were judged to have made a good adjustment to the event, one-third showed both positive and negative symptoms, and one-third remained in deep trouble. Even those who were assessed as having made a good adjustment recalled the past five years as a sad and frightening time in their lives.

The divorcing parents, especially the women, appeared to recover more rapidly and completely from the event than the children did. "Only those children who were physically separated by the divorce from a rejecting or demeaning or psychiatrically disturbed father showed post divorce improvement comparable to that of the adult" (Wallerstein and Kelly, 1980: 306). The investigators go on to say that there is no supporting evidence in their study for the commonly stated argument that divorce is better for children than an unhappy marriage (see also Hetherington et al., 1978). Wallerstein and Kelly (1980: 307) conclude that the divorced family was "neither more nor less beneficial or stressful for children than the unhappy marriage. But unfortunately neither unhappy marriages nor divorces are especially congenial for children."

They also found that, despite the divorce, the children in the sample retained a deep identification with, and attachment to, both sets of biological parents. This was true even if the parent without custody (usually the father) rarely contacted his children and even if the parent (or parents) remarried and stepparents were added to the family. Even when a child formed a positive relationship with the stepfather, she or he continued to yearn for the "real Dad."

Wallerstein and Kelly (1980), among others, have found that their divorcing families were extremely vulnerable to psychological, physical, and economic stress. The triple burden of sole child care, homemaking, and (frequently) full-time employment often proved too heavy for the custodial parent and seriously eroded her (usually it was the mother) ability to provide sufficient guidance and nurturance to the children.

Effects of Remarriage

Large-scale research with adequate samples is relatively scanty regarding the effect of remarriage on children. In a 1964 study, Burchinal used questionnaires and test scores from the Minnesota Multiphasic Personality Inventory (MMPI), to study 1500 Iowa high school students. In general, no significant differences were found between adolescents in first marriage, broken, or remarriage families.

Bohannon and Yahraes (1979) report on a survey questionnaire sent to 190 volunteer families (84 with biological fathers and 106 with stepfathers). The families were matched with respect to race, religion, income, education of the parents, and age and sex of the children. No significant differences were found between the two groups with respect to achievement, school behavior, interactions within the family, and relationships with peers.

Langer and Michael (1963) studied the mental health status of a large New York City sample. They concluded that children from remarried families had poorer mental health ratings than those from intact nuclear families (however, their assessments have been frequently criticized). Both Bernard (1956) and Goode (1956) failed to find adverse effects of stepfamilies for children in their nonrandom, largely White and middle-class samples. These studies also indicated that stepfamilies were less likely to encounter problems if the parents were of high socioeconomic status (Bernard, 1956; Langer and Michael, 1963).

Bernard pointed out long ago (1956) that it was illogical to compare the adjustments of children in remarried families to children in first-married families. As noted above, when studying marital adjustment and remarriage, it is necessary to use the correct comparison groups. For children, one needs to compare their development and adjustment in (a) stepfamilies (separately considering stepmother and stepfather effects), (b) single-parent families (divorced, widowed, separated, cohabiting or communal, never married), and (c) first-marriage families in which there is a high degree of marital dissatisfaction.

Duberman (1975) conducted a small study of stepfamilies in Cleveland, Ohio, with the criterion of good family adjustment being that of a high level of family integration as judged by both trained interviewers and study participants. Using questionnaires and interviews, she found that only 21 percent of the families were judged to be poorly integrated. A high level of family integration seemed to be heavily dependent on a close, satisfying relationship between the husband and wife. Also, the higher the social class membership, the higher the integration level.

Messinger (1976) interviewed, in depth, 76 remarried couples in Toronto who volunteered to take part in her study. She concluded that stepfamilies were at high risk of numerous stresses. Problems with children and finances (including child support) were seen as the most frequent difficulties.

Spanier and Furstenberg (1980) investigated the impact of remarriage on the relationships between grandchildren and grandparents, using responses from their Pennsylvania sample of divorced, cohabiting, and remarried couples. They found that stepgrandparents were usually quick to accept their "instant" grandchildren, partly as a way of giving support to their reconstituted family. Some of the grandchildren were found to have active, warm relationships with three or four sets of grandparents.

Visher and Visher (1979) and other clinicians provide useful insights concerning frequently observed problematic behavior of children in stepfamilies. Children in such families must deal with the loss brought on by divorce or death of a biological parent. In both instances there is mourning, grief, anger, guilt, fear, and despair. Mourning for a dead parent can be particularly acute because he or she can be fantasized as an ideal, all-loving, all-giving mother or father, far different from the substitute parent.

As Wallerstein and Kelly (1980), among others, note, a child (or children) may have built a special bond with the solo parent following marital dissolution and feel betrayed when that parent remarries. Then, too, when parents remarry soon after dissolution of the former marriage, they may not have given either their children or themselves enough time to finish the grieving process. Thus, the reconstituted family may be damaged by unfinished business from earlier relationships.

According to Visher and Visher (1979), children seem to rarely welcome a remarriage: Most feel split apart by the need to be loyal to two sets of parents. Many harbor the continuing wish that their divorced parents will mend their marriage, and a new marriage undermines this possibility.

The addition of stepsiblings may come as a shock to children. The age, sex, and role structure of the family is profoundly disturbed. Moreover, sharing with stepsiblings may be particularly difficult at a time of special psychological vulnerability. In addition, when older children of the opposite sex are thrown together in a new family, the situation may complicate problems of overstimulation and identity confusion already aroused by dating and related sexual activities of the parents.

Unhappy youngsters in remarried families often seek to manipulate their parents and stepparents as a way of expressing their hurt, anger, fear, and dependency needs. Guilty, anxious, insecure, or competitive biological parents are vulnerable to such manipulations. Sibling and stepsibling rivalries are often another feature in the double family drama. The possibilities for conflict are mind-boggling.

Visher and Visher (1979) point out that children must not be used as scapegoats in parent conflicts. It is far too easy to use children as a weapon against a former spouse in battles over such issues as custody, support, inheritance, and visiting privileges. With regard to visitation, the Vishers recommend that parents speak of the child as living with different sets of parents at different times rather than as visiting the former parent. This concept avoids the unfortunate connotation that the child is the guest of one parent (and as such should be entertained and coddled) and the live-in son or daughter of the other parent (and, as such, expected to adapt responsibly to the everyday business of family life).

Older children in the Wallerstein and Kelly (1980) sample were especially slow to accept their stepfathers. Coming to terms with the new family situation usually took several years and, in some instances, it seemed unlikely that the children would ever accept the stepfather as a real family member. However, most of the children expressed relief at having two parents in the home and became extremely anxious if they sensed conflict in the new marriage. Having experienced one divorce, they were supersensitive to the possibility of another.

As Duberman (1975) and Visher and Visher (1979) have observed, difficulties with respect to relationships with stepparents and biological parents were most likely to arise when the remarried couple were in conflict with each other. Unresolved conflicts between a stepfather and the child's biological father were a major source of trouble for children caught in these hostile rivalries, especially when the child's mother joined the fray. The Vishers, among others, warn against a too common practice by harassed parents and stepparents: that of seeking to shift the custody and usual home of the child from one biological parent to the other when the children have problems or the families encounter difficulties.

Further points derived from clinical practice[3] include:

- Discipline is a particularly thorny issue in many stepfamilies. The stepparent (usually a stepfather) often moves into the new marriage eager to play the role of an effective dad. He tends to strive for instant love and intimacy as well as for firm control over the children's behavior. During courtship preceding the marriage, he probably tried to be popular with the youngsters, as an easy-going "pal," but with marriage his perceptions of his role tend to change. Children are apt to strongly resent the stepfather's discipline, especially if the norms and methods are different from those practiced by the mother and biological father. Particularly in the early months of remarriage, it is usually helpful for the stepfather to discuss his concepts of family rules and discipline with the biological mother and ask her to be the leader in this respect, a position that is legitimated both by custom and by law.

- Open communication between the marital pair *and* the children regarding many issues, including discipline, seems to be essential. Too frequently, the newlyweds are so focused on their relationship that they overlook the needs and feelings of the children. These needs and feelings are apt to be acute and complex. This is particularly so when the reconstituted family consists of two sets of children from the former marriages. Rivalry between the two sets of youngsters, value conflicts, and psychological incompatibility are some of the common difficulties.

- Difficulties are apt to intensify if there are shifts or deficits in the physical environment. For example, a remarriage means that either the bride or groom (or both) move to a new residence. When children are involved, this may mean changes in neighborhoods and schools, as well as housing. Especially if family finances are limited and the combined family has a large number of children, living conditions can become cramped. If a child is displaced as sole possessor of his or her room and play equipment, there can be a strong sense of invasion and loss of "turf."

- A close, positive relationship within the marital dyad generally reduces conflicts between the stepsiblings and within the stepparent-stepchild relationship. When marital conflicts are unresolved, the children tend to act out the problems of the marriage.

- It is recommended that reconstituted families use open discussions with all members and set superordinate goals for the family as a whole. Without such goals, the remarried family is apt to disintegrate into two separate families, returning to their earlier premarriage systems.

- Although the Spanier and Furstenberg (1980) study quoted above indicated that grandparent-grandchild relationships were generally harmonious in stepfamilies, clinical observers often find otherwise. Biological grandparents who resent the divorce and the remarriage may seek to form a coalition with their grandchildren against the new family. They may especially resent the remarriage of their biological child who has no youngsters to a spouse who already has children and does not want to have any more. Then, too, some grandparents discriminate between their biological grandchildren and their stepgrandchildren. Grandparents can make an important contribution of security and stability to their grandchildren, especially during stressful periods of death, divorce, and remarriage. However, it is usually best if they reach out to their grandchildren through discussions with the biological parents rather than attempting to bypass the primary parent-child relationship. Of course, many contemporary grandparents do not offer the stable model of the traditional family: They, too, may be involved in divorce and remarriage. Moreover, many are widowers or widows, especially the latter.

- Grandparents and their grown children may be interacting in a continuing troubled relationship of unresolved dependencies, rivalries, and ambivalences. It should be recognized that reconstituted families may be especially haunted by ghosts of the past, not only of earlier marriages but of the various families of origin. Children can, therefore, become the battlegrounds for the earlier family wars of both their biological parents and their stepparents.

Stepfathers and Stepmothers

Wallerstein and Kelly (1980) studied all members of their sample who remarried. The stepfathers were mainly older, serious men who were eager for a home and wanted to do a good job as both husbands and fathers. Visher and Visher (1979) discuss commonly observed problems of stepfathers. Men in remarriages often feel caught between the demands of two wives and various sets of children. Then, too, it is usually they who join an already functioning family group. They often feel guilty over the plight of their previous family and the need of both families for their attention and their money. The sexuality of their stepchildren, especially the adolescent girls, may be troublesome and the issue of discipline is often difficult, especially before children form bonds of affection with their stepfathers.

Visher and Visher (1979) write that remarried men and women frequently try for unrealistic perfection as parents. They want to make up to their stepchildren and their biological children for the trauma that the youngsters have experienced in the past. Women, particularly, tend to take on the burden of trying to make an emotionally perfect family life. They yearn to disprove common myths about "the wicked stepmother." They attempt to deny the reality of their reconstituted family and to create the image of the traditional intact nuclear family. Stepparents, perhaps especially stepmothers, often try too hard to achieve "instant intimacy and love" from their stepchildren. Guiltily, they try to deny the anger and disapproval they may feel toward some of their stepchildren. It takes time for the remarried couple to develop its private and public identity as a marital pair; it takes even more time for the reconstituted family to develop its special private and public identity.

The Reconstituted Family as a Whole: Some Theoretical Perspectives

As mentioned above, the reconstituted family needs its own norms and guidelines. Attempts to fit it into the traditional pattern inevitably create problems. It appears that some families, fearful of rejection from neighbors and various social institutions such as the school, church, and youth organizations, attempt to conceal their status and pose as first-married families. They often expect criticism and therefore tend to deny any marital or parent/child problems. Conversely, many social institutions expect stepfamilies to be problem laden. Most do not know how to deal with them and, hence, these organizations also engage in denial and issue avoidance.

Walker and Messinger (1979) carefully examine the differences between the remarried family system and the first-marriage system. They find that there is particular confusion about family subsytems and various dyadic and larger family group transactions that may be formed between the different sets of parents and children, present and former marital pairs, sets of biological siblings and stepsiblings, and so on.

Visher and Visher (1979), along with other clinicians, observe that reconstituted families need to take time to learn the separate family histories that the various members bring to the new situation. First-marriage couples develop their own family history slowly from the time of their courtship and marriage, through the birth of their children and the children's growth. The first-marriage couple and their children have developed a complex system of shared memories, role perceptions, communication patterns, customs, tastes, and preferences. The remarried couple and their children need a "cram course" from each other concerning various perceptions of the different members as to what a family should be and do. Open, frequent, and clear communication between family members appears to be a "must" for the well-being and gradual integration of the reconstituted family.

Reconstituted families start at a different "developmental stage" (Duvall, 1976) than do first-marriage families:

> The initial formation of a remarried family requires a dramatic compression of developmental stages, with coupling and parenting occurring simultaneously rather than sequentially . . . individual developmental needs of individual members may be out of step with the new family's development. Most obvious is the need of an adolescent to separate and emancipate just at the time when the remarried family needs its members to integrate or join the new intimate group [Asmundsson, 1981].

Comment on Research to Date

The various clinical studies reported here are largely based on observations of people who have sought help from a counseling program or have volunteered to participate in intensive studies. The problems that these parents and children presented seemed to be highly predictable given the fundamenal nature of reconstituted families that include children. However, the specialists in this field have not drawn on similar (probably available) clinical literature that presents observations of parents and their children in unhappy first marriages (including marriages that may involve substance-abusing parents, family violence, psychotic disturbance, mental retardation, and so on). Nor have these specialists explored in depth the clinical literature that may well be available concerning never-married parenthood or single parenthood after divorce, separation, or death. All in all, life may be better, in the long run, for some children who live in reconstituted families than for those who live in other, more customary family forms.

Clinical studies and observations seem to yield far different results from the research and systematic data analyses reported in this chapter. The

systematic studies seem to say that although reconstituted families (especially those with children) may present a range of complex problems, these
problems can be surmounted. Overall, people in reconstituted families
score as high on various measures of satisfaction and well-being as do
people in first-marriage families. Moreover, when appropriate statistical
controls are used, remarriages seem to be no more inherently prone to
divorce than first marriages.

On the other hand, clinical studies and observations with their small
samples of volunteer participants reveal a number of serious difficulties
associated with the trauma of the marital dissolution that precedes the
remarriage and with the exceptional complexities experienced by stepparents, biological parents, and children in the formation of reconstituted
families. Do these intensive clinical studies provide more valid information
than the larger, more formal surveys? Are the problems revealed by clinical
observation mainly a result of the nature of the sample used? Are these
problems also present in the larger, more representative remarried samples
(strongly hinted at, particularly in the Weingarten analysis) but viewed by
subjects as being difficulties they can readily accept and handle, difficulties
that are outweighed by the positives in their remarriage situations? The
answers to questions such as these are far from clear. As the saying goes,
much more research is "urgently needed."

Some Implications for Further Research and Program Development[4]

There is a pressing need for sophisticated cost/benefit analysis for
human services for all families, including those who are in remarried
structures. This is an "age of accountability" and it is crucial that both
researchers and practitioners sharpen their evaluation research skills.[5]
Moreover, it is essential that the results of these studies be reported in brief,
clear, understandable form to such decision makers and influentials as
program administrators, legislators, lobbyists, and leaders of the mass
media.

There is an increased interest in prevention of problems. Thus, early
identification of difficulties and the mounting of low-cost, effective programs to prevent their escalation might be a useful strategy. Education and
counseling for couples who are considering remarriage should stress:

- the importance of thoroughly discussed and written prenuptial
  agreements, including issues of inheritance for both children and
  parents, custody and child-support arrangements, and financial plans;

- the importance of not expecting a remarriage to be like a first marriage;
  it is a different, but not deviant or pathological, family form;

- the development of communication skills for all family members and
  development of integrative goals and guidelines for the new family;

- understanding of legal provisions in the localities in which the remarriage will take place and the reconstituted family will live;

- recognition that feelings and attitudes about former spouses need to be shared and worked through before remarriage.

Whether or not such education and counseling services before remarriage would prevent later difficulties should be carefully tested with a modified experimental longitudinal design. The same suggestion applies to postmarital educational and counseling services.

There are no really satisfactory studies at present with respect to the outcomes of remarriage and stepfamilies over a period of time. Research is needed that has the following characteristics: (1) an adequately large national probability sample that can take into account a large number of variables that are apt to influence remarriage outcomes (see the family typologies at the start of this chapter plus the statements that appropriate controls are needed for demographic characteristics of the study populations); (2) a longitudinal, life-course design; (3) multiple measures of personal and marital satisfactions, happiness, and well-being in a number of life domains (see, especially, the Weingarten study reported above); (4) assessment of outcomes for children with various demographic characteristics and in a variety of family typologies, with measures including educational achievement, evidence of deviant or disturbed behavior, adolescent dating behavior (including early nonmarital pregnancy), and the like; (5) comparisons of remarried couples and children in reconstituted families with the appropriate analogues: people in conflict-ridden first marriages or single-parent families (widowed, divorced, separated, never married, cohabiting). Results of studies such as these should also be reported in clear, direct terms to decision makers and others.

More interaction between the social scientists and the military and private business and industry is also called for. All of these sectors are becoming more sensitive to the needs of families for enlightened programs and services that strengthen family well-being. They have found that such services are essential in recruiting and retaining competent personnel. Although the increasing trend of social and community service provisions for members of the military and employees in the private sector is encouraging, serious gaps in these services for poor families (those who need services the most) are rapidly escalating because of withdrawal of federal and state funds. It is essential that these inadequacies and the outcomes of service deprivation be monitored so that a cogent case can be made for service restoration.

A question is raised as to whether the present training for academics will allow for the more pragmatic approach to services and research suggested above. These activities may be particularly appropriate for the professional schools, but traditional social science academics must also reassess their priorities, interests, values, and skills if they are to deal effectively with the current crisis in human service programs, including those directed toward understanding and assisting reconstituted families.

Notes

1. Based on contributions made by participants in the above workshop.

2. As in the case of other intensive clinical studies, some of which have been reviewed here (for example, Duberman, 1975; Messinger, 1976), the Wallerstein and Kelly study is open to criticism because of the small sample size (60 families). Moreover, the method of sample selection may have elicited a disproportionate number of troubled parents: divorcing parents who responded on their own initiative, or through referrals, to a public announcement of a free divorce counseling service that was child centered, preventive planning oriented, time limited, and voluntary. The composition of the sample was mainly White, middle-class residents of Marin County, an avant garde, generally wealthy suburb of San Francisco.

3. Based on contributions made by participants in the above workshop.

4. This section was greatly enriched by contributions from Drs. Helen Kearney, Robert Rice, and Virginia Sibbison.

5. For an excellent instruction manual providing expert guidance for program and practice development, needs assessment, and evaluative procedures for services to families of separation, divorce, and remarriage, see Helping Youth and Families of Separation, Divorce and Remarriage, a 1980 publication of the U.S. Department of Health and Human Services.

References

ASMUNDSSON, R. (1981) Personal correspondence.

BERNARD, J. (1956) Remarriage: A Study of Marriage. New York: Holt, Rinehart & Winston.

BOHANNON, P. [ed.] (1970) Divorce and After. New York: Doubleday.

BOHANNON, P. and H. YAHRAES (1979) "Stepfathers as parents," pp. 347-362 in E. Corfman (ed.) Families Today: A Research Sampler on Families and Children. NIMH Science Monograph. Washington, DC: Government Printing Office.

BROWN, E. M. (1976) "Divorce counseling," pp. 394-429 in D.H.L. Olson (ed.) Treating Relationships. Lake Mills, IA: Graphic Publishing.

BURCHINAL, L. (1964) "Characteristics of adolescents from unbroken, broken and reconstituted families." Journal of Marriage and the Family 26, 1: 44-51.

CAMPBELL, A. (1980) The Sense of Well-being in America. New York: McGraw-Hill.

CARTER, H. and P. GLICK (1976) Marriage and Divorce: A Social and Economic Study. Cambridge, MA: Harvard University Press.

CHERLIN, A. (1981) Marriage, Divorce, Remarriage. Cambridge, MA: Harvard University Press.

——— (1978) "Remarriage as an incomplete institution." American Journal of Sociology 84: 634-650.

CHIRIBOGA, D. (1979) "Marital discord and stress: a life-course perspective." Alternative Lifestyles 2, 3: 461-470.

COLETTA, N. (1979) "Support systems after divorce: incidence and impact." Journal of Marriage and the Family 41, 4: 837-846.

DUBERMAN, L. (1975) The Reconstituted Family. Chicago: Nelson-Hall.

DUVALL, E. (1976) Family Development. Philadelphia: Lippincott.

FURSTENBERG, F. (1980) "Recycling the family: perspectives for a neglected family form." Marriage and Family Review 2, 3: 1, 12-21.

GLENN, N. and C. WEAVER (1979) "The marital happiness of remarried divorced persons." Journal of Marriage and the Family 39, 2: 331-337.

LICK, P. (1980) "Remarriage, some recent changes and variations." Journal of Family Issues 1: 455-478.

OODE, W. (1956) After Divorce. New York: Macmillan.

ETHERINGTON, M., M. COX, and R. COX (1978) "The aftermath of divorce," pp. 149-176 in J. Stevens and M. Matthews (eds.) Mother-Child, Father-Child Relations. Washington, DC: National Assoication for Education of Young Children.

ULKA, R. and H. WEINGARTEN (1979) "The long-term effects of parental divorce in childhood and adult adjustment." Journal of Social Issues 35, 4: 50-78.

ANGNER, L. and S. MICHAEL (1963) Life Stress and Mental Health. New York: Macmillan.

ESSINGER, L. (1976) "Remarriage between divorced people with children from previous marriages." Journal of Marriage and Family Counseling 42, 4: 193-200.

RICE-BONHAM, S. and J. BALSWICK (1980) "The noninstitutions: divorce, desertion, and remarriage." Journal of Marriage and the Family 42, 4: 959-972.

PANIER, G. and F. FURSTENBERG (forthcoming) "Remarriage after divorce: a Longitudinal analysis of well-being." Journal of Marriage and the Family.

PANIER, G. and P. GLICK (1980) "Paths to remarriage." Journal of Divorce 3, 3: 283-297.

.S. Department of Health and Human Services (1980) Helping Youth and Families of Separation, Divorce and Remarriage. Washington, DC: Government Printing Office.

ISHER, E. B. and J. S. VISHER (1979) Stepfamilies: A Guide to Working With Stepparents and Stepchildren. New York: Bruner/Mazel.

ALKER, K. and L. MESSINGER (1979) "Remarriage after divorce: dissolution and reconstruction of family boundaries." Family Process 18: 185-192.

ALLERSTEIN, J. and J. KELLY (1980) Surviving the Break-up: How Children and Parents Cope with Divorce. New York: Basic Books.

EINGARTEN, H. (1980) "Remarriage and well-being." Journal of Family Issues 1, 4: 533-559.

EISS, R. (1975) Marital Separation. New York: Bantam.

CHAPTER 7

Dual-Career/Dual-Work Families: A Systems Approach

MARY W. HICKS

SALLY L. HANSEN

LEO A. CHRISTIE

Florida State University

One of the most important recent developments in American families has been the dramatic increase in women's labor force participation. Wife employment is not a new phenomenon. Women have always had worke roles in every type of human society, but it is only within our own time tha substantial proportions of women began to work away from the home and be paid for it. The sheer number of women involved in the labor force — the fact that the employment is physically removed from the home, tha women can earn money (and that some can earn substantial amounts) and that for many women there are significant career possibilities — all c these factors taken together portend considerable stress on the family a we have known it.

It cannot be otherwise since these trends mean there will be more pressure toward egalitarian roles, as well as a continuation of the family pressures that already exist for women when they pursue a career. Any change that occurs in women's roles automatically demands concomitan changes in men's roles. Children are also affected and children living in families in which both the husband and wife are employed perform many household tasks (Hicks and Hansen, 1981). As wives enter the labo market, it may often be the children, and not the husbands, who take ove the chores wives no longer have time for.

Currently, nearly 21 million married women are working in jobs outside the home. The participation of women with young children has increased to the point where nonworking mothers of young children are now in the

sional commitment, and is not simply a way to earn supplemental income for the family. In the "dual-work" or "two-paycheck" family, both husband and wife work but the wife's work is classified as a job rather than a career.

There are a number of features that make the dual-career family an important subject for sociological exploration. First, its increasing incidence demands some attention. While only a small percentage of employed women are actually career women, this percentage is likely to increase along with growing rates of higher education and equal employment opportunities for women (Hicks and Hansen, 1981). Second, on the heels of the "women's movement" of the 1970s, there appears to be something of a normative shift in the direction of truly equal occupational and familial roles for women (e.g., Bayer, 1975; Scanzoni, 1976, 1978). Third, the change from a family form in which the husband's central role is clearly occupational and the wife's is clearly familial is certain to have significant structural consequences for families. In addition to having an impact on the family's social status, standard of living, and role responsibility assignment (Scanzoni, 1978), a major consequence of the shift to a dual-career family is the amount of stress with which the family must deal.

In a recent literature review on stress and coping in dual-career families, Skinner (1980) classified a number of sources of stress delineated by previous research into internal and external types of strain. The former arises within the family itself and includes issues of work overload, role identity confusion, career and family cycling difficulties, and nuclear family limitations. Stated more simply, these internal sources of stress include the difficulties spouses may have balancing career and home life, feeling all right about stepping outside traditional husband and wife roles, meshing individual career cycles with family cycles, and finding satisfactory child care arrangements. External strains are those resulting from conflict between the dual-career family and other societal structures. Examples of these strains can be found in the disparity between dual-career lifestyles and traditional family norms, the demands of the occupational structure for geographic mobility when there is continuous career advancement, and the dilemma of finding time for interaction with friends and relatives in addition to career and family. Both internal and external strains are alluded to in Scanzoni's (1978) observation that as women continue to push for equality with men, they come increasingly into conflict with men's efforts to maintain a privileged position. This appeared to be the case in a recent study that found that married couples with more modern/egalitarian role preferences experienced more conflict than couples with traditional preferences (Christie, 1981). As yet, there are few societal solutions to these problems and dual-career families are forced to seek their own answers.

Research continues to emphasize the stress associated with women combining jobs and family. Scanzoni (1978) suggests that as the meaning of work changes for women, so will the way in which women negotiate family conflicts with husbands. The change in the meaning of work for women and the consequences that employment has for her and her family will influence marital roles, bargaining, power, and conflict.

Another important observation is that women are moving toward modern roles, including an acceptance of women's career commitment, faster than are men (Scanzoni, 1978). If wives prefer to give significant amounts of their time and energy to their careers, this change is certain to have some impact upon their marital and family relationships, and one of the results will very likely be increased stress.

Keith and Schafer (1980), in a study on role strain and depression, found women in two-job families experienced significantly more work/family role strain than did the men in these families, and that women were significantly more depressed than men. It is not clear, however, whether women in two-job families experience more or less stress than those in dual-career families, and whether the male/female stress differential is greater in these families.

Gilbert et al. (1981) found that for career-motivated women who derive high life satisfaction from both their professional and maternal roles, combining work and family can be very rewarding. Although considerable stress was caused by conflicts between their professional and maternal roles, this is often more than offset by the increased resources and privileges and the enhanced sense of personal growth accrued from professional roles. It may be that the cost for dual-career and dual-job women is the same, but the payoff is greater for career women, hence, less depression.

The 1960s were responsible for much of the ground-breaking research in the area, and the 1970s have served to substantiate earlier findings, pointing to the complexities and potential for stress and noting that by and large the husband's career still takes priority over the wife's. Popular literature, e.g., *The Two Pay-Check Marriage* (Bird, 1979), has added little to our knowledge; and *The Two-Career Family: Issues and Alternatives* (Petersen et al., 1978), the outcome of a recent symposium on two-career families, is disappointing since it relies heavily on a nonempirical approach.

The research needs are clear: researchers need to locate more representative dual-career and dual-work samples, improve response rates, examine life-cycle variations, develop scales to enable data collection from large representative samples (see Pendleton et al., 1980), and avoid "wife-only" samples. It is time to move beyond exploratory studies and to view the family as a system, gathering data from children as well as from parents.

Cross-Cultural Literature

Although the initial formulation of dual-career families was rooted in a British study (Fogarty et al., 1968, 1971), it was explicitly put in an international perspective. It took into consideration Scandinavian works on the changing roles of women (Dahlstrom and Lilijestrom, 1967; Myrdal and Klein, 1956), and efforts by East European sociologists, as well as American studies (Rossi, 1964; Nye and Hoffman, 1963; Yudkin and Holme, 1963).

In 1978, a special issue of the *Journal of Comparative Family Studies* was devoted to the study of women in family and work from a cross-cultural perspective. Cross-culturally, family research on working women appears to emphasize female "employment" rather than female "careers," and the effect of women's employment on family decision making, role sharing, and bargaining rather than on family stress and coping (Kim and Kim, 1977; Cunningham and Green, 1979; Fuse, 1981; Hultaker, 1981). Primarily, the focus is on opinions and attitudes about women's work and how female labor force participation affects conjugal bargaining.

Gibbins et al. (1978) studied the emergence of egalitarianism within the family in Canada. Based on their Canadian public opinion data, they report a mixed reaction by Canadians to women's liberalism and employment. Liberalism on women's issues was positively related to liberalism on other issues (e.g., support for environmental protection and support for native Indians), so it appears that acceptance of egalitarian roles for women was part of a generalized liberal attitude.

Cross-cultural data are limited but appear to confirm that wives working outside the home is a common phenomenon throughout the world. There is essentially no research comparing dual-career families cross-culturally.

Development of a Model of Role Transition

Since role conflicts appear to be a major source of stress in dual-career/dual-work families, a conceptual model will be developed to aid in our understanding of role transitions within such families. There are many types of dual-career/dual-work families (e.g., commuter, long distance, and part-time work families) and the ideas presented can be applied to all of them. For purposes of illustration the model will focus on dual-career families, because of their increasing incidence, because of the changing norms implied by this emerging lifestyle, and because research and public interest has focused more sharply on this lifestyle.

The schema presented emphasizes the patterns common to these families, with an eye to understanding and assisting people entering such families. It is hoped the resulting model will be of interest and use to clinicians, educators, researchers, and dual-career families themselves as they explore this lifestyle. We hope it is a model that can be applied to any family dealing with role difficulties across a variety of family/work combinations.

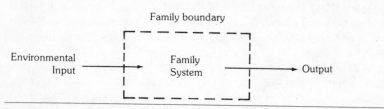

Figure 7.1   Family Interactive with Environment

A System Theory Approach

The role of theory in studying an area like dual-career lifestyles is to provide a set of guidelines to limit, organize, and explain relevant information. The overall theoretical perspective suggested here will be that of systems theory, although at various points in the development of the model some ideas from social exchange theory will be introduced. By combining the relevant parts of both theories, it should be possible to gain a more complete understanding of stress in dual-career families.

Essentially, the position of systems theory is that families, like other social structures, are dynamic rule-governed systems that affect and are affected by the environment in which they live. In other words, a family's structure and activities are influenced by the society (neighborhood, city, country) in which it lives, and at the same time, the society is influenced by the activities of the families that make up that society. This is a particularly useful perspective from which to study work/family linkages.

The interaction between family and environment is represented in Figure 7.1. The broken line representing the family boundary is an expression of the fact that the lines that set the family apart from the rest of society are permeable to some extent, ranging from a low to a high degree of communication with the external environment. Families vary greatly with regard to the relative openness of their external boundaries and their willingness to accept ideas from outside (e.g., Olson et al., 1979). A family's degree of openness to outside influence may in turn be related to the degree of stress it experiences as a result of these outside pressures.

The simplicity of Figure 7.1 neglects the fact that once a family receives some input from the environment, it performs certain internal processes on the new information before it returns some output to the environment. All families have a hierarchy of "rules," that is, characteristic patterns of how they respond to inputs from the outside (Broderick and Smith, 1979). There are several levels, or hierarchies, of rules, the lowest level being each individual family member's typical responses to external stimuli. For example, one member may typically react to external inputs with hysteria, while another may be relatively unmoved. The next level of rules is referred to as "family rules," and is the family's typical response to external stimuli. Family rules evolve from the combined members' rules. The third and highest level of rules is known as "meta-rules" (Broderick and Smith, 1979), or those family policies that evolve over time, based on individual and family rules and the family's prior responses to external events. Meta-rules are different from individual and family rules, primarily because of their overriding and persistent nature. Individual and family rules are more amenable to change than meta-rules, which are more abstract and include a wider spectrum of behaviors. For example, a family policy on who earns the income is more fundamental and hence more enduring and more powerful than the opinions the family may have about what particular job the individual worker(s) should take.

At this point, a substantive illustration might serve to clarify some of these concepts and place them into the realm of dual-career families. Figure 7.2 illustrates the process of a family's response to input from the external environment. The process is known as "rule transformation" (Broderick and Smith, 1979), and is the way in which a family adapts old rules or forms new rules in response to novel situations. It is essential to keep in mind the interactive nature of this process. That is, the family reacts to input from the environment, which is then processed and sent back to the environment as output, which then becomes input for itself and other families. Since the process is circular, there is no beginning and no end (Watzlawick, 1967), and it is unproductive to attempt to determine where an interaction begins. For example, one might ask whether a wife's desire to have a career began in her own rules, in the family's rules, or in the environment. Since the three components are in perpetual interaction with each other, and since the output of each is input for all others, the focus must be on the process of the interaction rather than on any static component. Only in this way, according to systems theory, can family functioning be understood.

Family rule transformation under traditional norms. The process of rule transformation illustrated in Figure 7.2 may be more clearly understood in the context of dual-career families by applying specific messages to each of the components in the model. Listed below are possible environmental input, rules, and output for a family in a society in which traditional male and female roles are the norm. At the risk of belaboring the point, let it be said once again that there is no beginning and no end to this process. The order in which the messages are listed does not imply temporal sequencing, but is used only for convenience in following the illustration in Figure 7.2.

- *Environmental input:* "Women should be subordinate to men."
- *Wife's rule:* "Wife should do whatever is necessary to support husband's career."

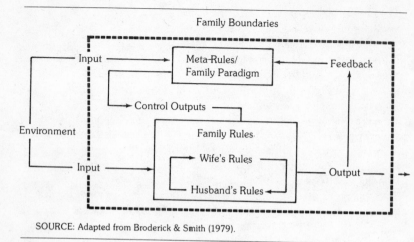

SOURCE: Adapted from Broderick & Smith (1979).

Figure 7.2   Family Rule Transformation Process

- *Husband's rule:* "Husband should give full energy to career and wife should support him."
- *Family rule:* "Husband should work and wife should have responsibility for child care and housekeeping."
- *Meta rule:* "Husband is primary, wife is subordinate."
- *Family system output:* "Husband provides income, wife supports husband through child care and housekeeping."

The message given above may be thought of as one "cycle" of family rule transformation, in which the environment and all rules within the family are in relative harmony. In their interaction with each other, wife, husband, the family unit, and the environment all agree that the husband should provide the income and the wife should take care of the house and care for the children. The above list is essentially an expression of the way things were before societal norms for male and female roles began to change.

Family rule transformation as norms begin to change. But what would happen if someone started doing things differently, if a wife somewhere decided to have a career of her own? Suddenly all the rules in the hierarchy and all the components in the system in Figure 7.2 would be thrown into imbalance. The messages associated with each component in this second cycle are:

- *Environmental input:* "Women should be subordinate to men."
- *Wife's rule:* "Wife should be able to have a career and get help from husband on family work."

- *Husband's rule:* "Husband should give full energy to career and wife should support him."
- *Family rule:* "Husband should work and wife should have a responsibility for child care and housekeeping."
- *Meta rule:* "Husband is primary, wife is subordinate."
- *Family system output:* "Husband provides income, wife supports husband through child care, housekeeping, and supplemental income."

This list of rules differs from the preceding one in only two places. First, the wife's rule has changed to include the possibility of a career for herself and the expectation of getting help from her husband on child care and housekeeping. Second, the output from the family system has changed incrementally to add supplemental income earning to the wife's support activities. The husband's rule, family rule, and meta-rule have not changed at all, and it would probably take many cycles of family rule transformation before they would change even a little. But at this point, the wife is out of step with the rest of the system, a fact that is likely to result in some stress in the family. One other change that has taken place is that the family's output to the environment now includes a modest statement that it may be all right for a wife to work. This output may become another family's input, making it somewhat easier for the wife in that family to begin having career aspirations.

Family rule transformation as egalitarian norms continue to evolve. The preceding list illustrates what may be the first small step in a society in transition from traditional to egalitarian roles. After many cycles and over an extended period of time, the combination of inputs, rule transformations, and outputs may result in a situation such as the one that exists in contemporary Western societies, in which an egalitarian norm is evolving, but with husbands' and families' rules still slow to change. This situation might be characterized by the messages listed below:

- *Environmental input:* "Men and women should be equal."
- *Wife's rule:* "Wife should be able to have a career and get help from husband on family work."
- *Husband's rule:* "Wife should be able to work; husband's career should be primary."
- *Family rule:* "Wife can work and husband will share family work to the extent that it does not interfere with his career."
- *Meta rule:* "Husband is senior partner, wife is junior partner."
- *Family system output:* "Increased participation by wife in providing, increased participation by husband in child care and housekeeping."

The striking features of this list are that (a) some change has occurred in all components and (b) the husband's, family, and meta-rules are still

resistant to a completely egalitarian ethic. Since there is a disparity between the components, stress is likely to be generated in the family and
society. Thus, it can be seen that one of the by-products of the functioning
of the system, as illustrated in Figure 7.2, is stress within families.

What has been demonstrated thus far is something about how normative changes may take place in family systems within society. What has not
been demonstrated is how this process occurs between husbands and
wives. In other words, how does a married couple make the transition from
a traditional, single-earner family to a dual-career family? What happens
within the husband-wife component of Figure 7.2 that transforms environmental input into new family rules and output? Answers to these
questions must be sought within the "black box."

The Black Box

The term "black box" is borrowed from communications theory
(Watzlawick et al., 1967: 43) and refers to the mysterious, unseen area
within which input is transformed into output. Within the present context,
the black box is the component of Figure 7.2 wherein a family uses the
input "men and women should be equal" and makes the decision to
become, over a period of time, a dual-career family. The input, an egalitarian norm, and the output, dual-career behavior, can be seen. But what
happened in between the two has been shrouded in mystery. One of the
purposes of this theoretical model is to penetrate the "black box" as with
x-ray vision and demystify how families change.

Scanzoni and Szinovacz (1980) have made significant inroads into this
previously uncharted area. Using an adaptation of social exchange theory,
in which each spouse's cost/reward ratio as well as their maximum joint
profit are the central focus, Scanzoni and Szinovacz have sketched what
may take place in marital decision making. What is involved is a series of
exchanges in which one spouse proposes an idea and the other responds.
As seen in Figure 7.3, the other's response can take one of three forms:
(a) yes, (b) yes, but . . . , and (c) no. In the first instance, the couple
discovers that they agree and have reached "spontaneous consensus." In
case b, further discussion and/or negotiation may be called for, and in case
c, conflict is likely to result.

In the context of dual-careers, the proposition may be the wife's
declaration that "I want to have a career." The husband's response may
then be: (a) "Yes, that's all right with me"; (b) Yes, but you're going to have
to keep up with the housework as well"; or (c) "No, I like our life the way it
is."

Two essential points may be derived from this exchange perspective of
what occurs within the black box. First, in every case — whether the
response to a proposition is yes, yes but, or no — the spouses will be acting
on what they see as their own best ratio of rewards to costs and their

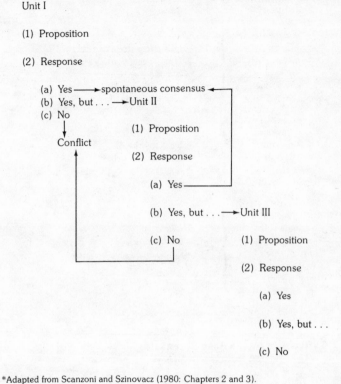

Unit I

(1) Proposition

(2) Response

    (a) Yes ⟶ spontaneous consensus

    (b) Yes, but . . . ⟶ Unit II

    (c) No

        Conflict   (1) Proposition

                    (2) Response

                    (a) Yes

                    (b) Yes, but . . . ⟶ Unit III

                    (c) No   (1) Proposition

                                     (2) Response

                                     (a) Yes

                                     (b) Yes, but . . .

                                     (c) No

*Adapted from Scanzoni and Szinovacz (1980: Chapters 2 and 3).

Figure 7.3 Ongoing Process of Marital Bargaining

maximum joint profit as a couple. Over a period of interacting in this way, they will eventually produce an output, which may be to continue as a single-earner family, to change to a dual-career family, or to adopt any of the possibilities in between. The second point to be made is that regardless of the husband's response — be it yes, yes but, or no — the family will have to cope with stress. If the response is yes and the family embarks on a dual-career lifestyle, they will have numerous sources of strain in making that change (Skinner, 1980). If the husband's response is yes but, then husband and wife have some differences to resolve, and the process of negotiation may be stressful. If the husband says "no, I don't want you to have a career," then the wife's ambitions are frustrated, and the ongoing conflict that results will cause family tension. The point is, regardless of the husband's response to his wife's desire to have a career, the family is likely to be subjected to new stress as a result of dealing with the idea of a dual-career lifestyle.

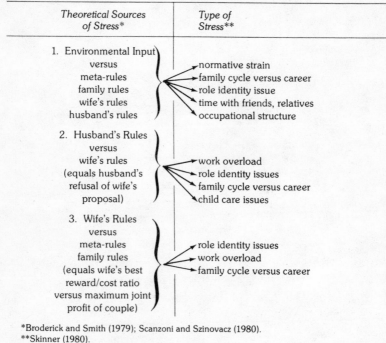

*Broderick and Smith (1979); Scanzoni and Szinovacz (1980).
**Skinner (1980).

**Figure 7.4   Types of Stress Associated with
                Theoretical Sources of Stress**

In summary, we have illustrated how dual-career lifestyles may evolve
in family systems within society and have briefly suggested a framework for
viewing how husbands and wives may interact to make the change to dual
careers. As a means of unifying the two under the theme of "stress
generation" in dual-career families, it may be useful to organize the types
of strain categorized by Skinner (1980) into the theoretical frameworks
proposed above. In Figure 7.4, it can be seen that conflicts among any of a
number of components of the family/social systems can lead to the various
types of internal and external strains listed by Skinner.

Societal and Personal Implications

What effect will the dual-career/dual-work lifestyle have on marriage
and divorce patterns? Unless efforts are made to reduce the predictable
sources of stress and to help persons cope more effectively with such stress,
increasing dual-career involvement and economic self-sufficiency are
likely to combine and translate into a continuation of the trend toward high
divorce rates. The need for increased family services such as marital
counseling and day care is obvious. If the direction of the 1980s continues

to be toward less funding of such social services, one can expect the cycle of escalating family and individual stress to be exacerbated.

There are several implications of the model presented here for clinicians dealing with families. First, as dual-career/dual-work lifestyles proliferate and the associated strains are experienced by more families, the numbers of such cases in therapy will continue to multiply. Second, since higher-order meta-rules and family rules are slow to change, and often represent the traditional norms more nearly than the evolving ones, rules governing relationships are likely to be in conflict. Finally, the schema of husband/wife negotiation proposed by Scanzoni and Szinovacz (1980) illustrates the need for married couples to learn and practice new bargaining strategies, and it offers the potential to teach these strategies.

The implication for family life education for all age groups is clear: Attention must be given to the preparation of persons for dual-career/dual-work as an emerging lifestyle. Since so many families are likely to be participating in dual-career/dual-work lifestyles in the near future, educators must begin to train their students to deal with the problems they are likely to encounter. Exploring role strain and new family roles and responsibilities, such as parenting when both parents work, is but one of the tasks facing educators.

In addition to the research needs mentioned earlier, there must be more in-depth examination of what goes on within the "black box" as families adjust to normative shifts in the direction of egalitarian marital relationships. And before we can answer the question, "How do rules change?" we must develop a method for identifying the particular rules of any given family. The complexity of family functioning demands careful observation of the process of change, guided by a theoretical framework to limit and organize the research effort. The phenomenon of dual-career/dual-work lifestyles provides an excellent opportunity for such observation because it is happening both visibly and commonly, and because the families who are experiencing this transition are in need of assistance in coping with the associated stresses.

The gradual increase in dual-career/dual-work families raises many policy issues and indicates a need for some fairly profound change. We have already suggested change in the family institution, i.e., role modification through negotiation and bargaining supplemented by normative shifts in cultural role definitions. In addition, there must be improvement in child care facilities, after-school care for the young school-aged or latch-key child, increased employment opportunities for teenagers, greater flexibility in work schedules, time off for childbearing without loss of promotional opportunities, and new attitudes at the administrative/managerial level regarding the hiring of women.

Future Directions

It is clear that the dual-career/dual-work lifestyle is here to stay, and there is little doubt that it will exert an increasingly profound effect on social and family structures. An understanding of the processes involved in lifestyle transition and a conscious adaptation of structures to facilitate that transition may serve to reduce the stress inherent in such change. As new age cohorts approach the marrying age, they may be better prepared to cope than were their parents, since their socialization may have been toward more egalitarian role prescriptions. Undoubtedly, families will be smaller, for even in dual-work situations child care is still a wife's primary responsibility and one way to manage is to have fewer children.

The innovators of the 1960s and 1970s—the individuals and the families—have made their contribution to change. It is now time for the larger social institutions to change in response.

Note

1. The above data are compiled from Department of Labor Statistics, "Perspective on Working Women: A Data Book," October 1980, as summarized in Resource Center for Women's Programs (1981).

References

BAYER, A. (1975) "Sexist students in American colleges: a descriptive note." Journal of Marriage and the Family 37: 146-154.
BIRD, C. (1979) The Two-Paycheck Marriage. New York: Rawson, Wade.
BRODERICK, C. and J. SMITH (1979) "The general systems approach to the family," pp. 112-129 in W. C. Burr, G. K. Leigh, R. D. Day, and J. Constantine (eds.) Contemporary Theories about the Family, Vol. 2. New York: Macmillan.
CHRISTIE, L. A. (1981) "Antecedents and consequences of role sharing: a study of sex role preferences and marital interaction from a conflict theory perspective." Ph.D. dissertation, Florida State University.
CUNNINGHAM, C. M. and R. T. GREEN (1979) "Working wives in the United States and Venezuela: a cross-national study of decision making." Journal of Comparative Family Studies 10, 1: 67-80.
DAHLSTROM, E. and LILIJESTROM [eds.] (1967) The Changing Roles of Men and Women. London: Duckworth.
FOGARTY, M. P., R. RAPOPORT, and R. N. RAPOPORT (1971) Sex, Career, and Family. Beverly Hills, CA: Sage.
——— (1968) Women and Top Jobs: An Interim Report. London: PEO.
FUSE, A. (1981) "Role structure of dual career families (Japan)." Journal of Comparative Family Studies 12, 3: 329-336.
GIBBINS, R., J. R. POINTING, and C. L. SYMONS (1978) "Attitudes and ideology: correlates of liberal attitudes towards the role of women." Journal of Comparative Family Studies 9, 1: 19-40.

GILBERT, J., C. HOLAHAN, and L. MANNING (1981) "Coping with conflict between professional and maternal roles." Family Relations 30, 3: 419-426.

HICKS, M. W. and S. L. HANSEN (1981) "Dual careers: the issue of conflicting commitments for women." Florida State University, Tallahassee, Florida. (unpublished)

HULTAKER, O. E. (1981) "Attitudes toward maternal employment and child care in Sweden." Journal of Comparative Family Studies 12, 1: 95-109.

KEITH, P. and R. B. SCHAFER (1980) "Role strain and depression in two-job families." Family Relations 29: 483-488.

KIM, O. L. and K. D. KIM (1977) "A casual interpretation of the effect of mother's education and employment status on parental decision-making role patterns in the Korean family." Journal of Comparative Family Studies 8, 1: 117-131.

MYRDAL, A. and V. KLEIN (1956). Women's Two Roles. London: Routledge & Kegan Paul.

NYE, R. E. and L. W. HOFFMAN [eds.] (1963) The Employed Mother in America. Chicago: Rand McNally.

OLSON, D. H., D. H. SPRENKLE, and C. S. RUSSELL (1979) "Circumplex model of marital and family systems I: cohesion and adaptability dimensions, family types, and clinical applications." Family Process 18, 1: 3-28.

PENDLETON, B. F., M. M. POLOMA, and T. N. GARLAND (1980) "Scales for investigation of the dual-career family." Journal of Marriage and the Family 42, 2: 269-276.

PETERSEN, S. S., J. M. RICHARDSON, and G. V. KREUTER [eds.] (1978) The Two-Career Family: Issues and Alternatives. Washington, DC: University Press of America.

RAPOPORT, R. and R. N. RAPOPORT (1969) "The dual career family." Human Relations 22: 3-30.

RAPOPORT, R. N. and R. RAPOPORT (1978) "Dual career families: progress and prospects." Marriage and Family Review 1, 5: 1-12.

Resource Center for Women's Programs (1981) Research Modules for Women's Centers. Tallahassee: Florida State University.

ROSSI, A. (1964) "Equality between the sexes: an immodest proposal." Daedalus 93: 638-646.

SCANZONI, J. (1978) Sex Roles, Women's Work, and Marital Conflict. Lexington, MA: D. C. Heath.

——— (1976) "Sex role change and influences on birth intentions." Journal of Marriage and the Family 38: 43-60.

SCANZONI, J. and M. SZINOVACZ (1980) Family Decision-Making. Beverly Hills, CA: Sage.

SKINNER, D. A. (1980) "Dual-career family stress and coping: a literature review." Family Relations 29, 4: 473-481.

SWEET, J. N. (1973) Women in the Labor Force. New York: Seminar.

VAN DUSEN, R. A. and E. B. SHELDON (1976) "The changing status of American women: a life cycle perspective." American Psychologist 21, 2: 106-116.

WATZLAWICK, P., J. H. BEAVIN, and D. H. JACKSON (1967) Pragmatics of Human Communication. New York: W. W. Norton.

YUDKIN, S. and A. HOLME (1963) Working Mothers and Their Children. London: Michael Joseph.

CHAPTER 8

Commuter Marriage: Couples Who Live Apart

NAOMI GERSTEL

University of Massachusetts, Amherst

HARRIET GROSS

Governors State University

Until recently, everyday use of the term "marital separation" referred only to that period, usually preliminary to divorce, in which the marital bond was in the process of dissolution. Unthinking acceptance of the connection between the viability of marriage and continued coresidence reveals the tenacity of the cultural ideal that links "intact" marriage with spouses' occupancy of a single household. Acceptance of this connection has been no less characteristic of social scientists whose conceptualizations of the family contain common residence as a defining characteristic (Murdock, 1949: 1; Schneider, 1968: 33).[1] Moreover, no matter how they might differ in other respects, most sociological models of the relation between labor force participation and the family — from Parsons (1959) to Laslett (1979) — have assumed that the presence of both husband and wife in a single household is the irreducible minimum of the viable marriage. In treating this conjugal unit as such a minimum, these theorists neglect the possibility that labor market demands may affect husbands and wives differently. Although highly sensitive to the strains that the creation of national labor markets place on the maintenance of multigeneration households, such macrosocial theorizing about the economy and family reveals a remarkable insensitivity to the possibility that labor markets may also strain the ability of the conjugal unit itself to maintain a single household.

However, the existence of marriages in which spouses separate in the service of divergent career demands at least suggests a need to question both the presupposition that coresidence is necessary for marital viability and its corollary that husbands and wives necessarily share economic fates. Dubbed "commuter," "long-distance" or "two-location" families, these marriages entail the maintenance of two separate residences by spouses who are apart from one another for periods ranging from several days per week to months at a time. In this chapter we undertake (1) to place such marriages in the context of other similar contemporary and historical arrangements, (2) to summarize research findings about the commuting experience, and (3) to compare commuter couples with another contemporary variant of couples who live apart, Merchant Marine families.

Classification of Couples Who Live Apart

No doubt journalistic, popular, and even scientific interest in commuter marriage stems from its break with the traditional marital norms requiring spousal coresidence. But an examination of the circumstances that separate spouses shows that living apart per se is not its most novel characteristic. Table 8.1 is an attempt to categorize known historical and contemporary circumstances that require that couples live apart.[2]

As Table 8.1 reveals, marital separation in its broader sense is by no means without precedent: War, imprisonment, and illness are the most notable examples of previous circumstances that required spouses to separate, typically involuntarily, for significant periods of time. Table 8.1 also points to the many contemporary instances of formally voluntary separations resulting from labor market demands placed on spouses who presumably consider their marriages intact. Merchant Marines, construction workers, professional athletes, politicians and entertainers all practice occupations that call for regular periods of separation.

However, these examples differ in significant respects from the commuter couples who are the primary subject of this chapter. In all these other cases, it is typically the husband's occupation that occasions the separation, while the wife, who may or may not work, remains in the "family" home. In contrast, among commuters — by definition, dual-career families — it is the presence of two careers pursued simultaneously rather than the character of work in any one occupation that requires that couples live apart. It is the *wife's* voluntary participation in, and even commitment to a career that has led to an interest in this marital structure and generated the label "alternative lifestyle." In the following discussion, then, we focus primarily on commuter couples, bearing in mind that this is only one of the many possible variants of couples who live apart.

The Commuting Experience

Characteristics of Commuters

Commuter couples have been defined operationally as dual-career couples who set up separate residences and live apart at least three

**TABLE 8.1   Classification of Couples Who Live Apart
by Sources of Separation**

Sources of Separation	
Characteristics of the Labor Market* (formally voluntary)	Other Reasons (formally involuntary)
A. One Spouses's Work as the Source	Illness
Merchant Marines	Military Conscription
Construction Workers	
Professional Athletes	Imprisonment
Politicians	
Entertainers	
Migrant Workers	
B. Both Spouses' Careers as the Source	
Commuter or Long-Distance Marriage	

*Refers to occupations that require the maintenance of separate, at least quasi-permanent, residences, as distinguished from occupations in which traveling is a regular feature but does not require the maintenance of a separate residence for each spouse.

(Gerstel, 1977) or four (Gross, 1980a) days per week. Analyses of couples studied to date (Farris, 1978; Gerstel, 1977, 1978c; Gross, 1980a; Kirschner and Wallum, 1979) suggest the following demographic profile:

(1) *high educational levels* — over 90 percent had completed at least some graduate work,

(2) *high-ranking occupations* — almost all were professionals or executives and a very high proportion were academics (over half of the respondents in every study held faculty positions or were in graduate school preparing for professional occupations);

(3) *high income levels* — median family income was between $30,000 and $40,000.

Although small, nonrandom samples, it is believed that the couples studied are representative of commuter couples in general.

Although these professional occupations yield relatively high family incomes, the expenses of this lifestyle (travel, telephone bills, two residences) are still a burden for most of these families. In any case, it is not financial gain that prompts them to set up two homes. Gerstel (1978b) demonstrated this by a cost/benefit analysis of the couples in her sample. She found that the added income produced by the job occasioning the couples' separation typically did not compensate fully for all the added costs of commuting. The absence of economic gain suggests that commuters do not work primarily for wages but rather because they view their work as a "central life interest." We should note, however, that this intense commitment to work does not preclude an equally intense commitment to their marriage. In fact, it is not only in the service of career demands that they live this way, but also because they want so much to remain married. That is, they value the marriage so highly that they are willing to invest the time, money, and effort that separations and reunions require. This latter point speaks also to the contention that these people are individuals unable to maintain an intense marital commitment. Instead it must be stressed that they live apart primarily in response to the structural tensions between the traditional family and work demands rather than because of some interpersonal failing.

In terms of familial characteristics, more than half of these couples had been married for nine years or longer. They ranged in age from 25 to 67 years, with a mean age in the mid- to late thirties. Moreover, 40 to 50 percent in each sample had children.

All of these studies suggest that the absence of children facilitated living apart, as did length of marriage: The longer the couples were married, the less stressful they found separation. Moreover, the career stage of each spouse influenced the couples' adjustment. Older couples, married longer, with at least one spouse's career (usually the husband's) well established, fared better than younger couples who were more likely to be contending with the demands and uncertainties of new professional and marital identities. On the basis of these distinguishing characteristics, Gross (1980a) characterizes these couples as either "adjusting" or "established." Younger couples, married too few years to have yet developed a long, shared history and beleaguered by the demands of early careers are still "adjusting." By contrast, older couples, having endured as a marital unit, possess a backlog of experiences that cushion the impact of separation on their relationship. Furthermore, the more established couples are able to draw a measure of comfort unavailable to the younger couples. These older established couples see themselves correcting a previous imbalance in which the husband's career demands had priority. Now it is the "wife's turn" — a perception that helps mitigate the strains of living apart.

The younger couples, because they did not perceive this previous imbalance, do not see the current balance as a compensation for previous inequities in their own lives. Thus, they are less likely to gain as much satisfaction from the departure from conventional norms that their separation implies.

Commuting Patterns

There is much more variation in the conditions under which these spouses separate and reunite than in their demographic characteristics. The number of years couples have sustained their commute ranges from three months to fourteen years. The range of distance spouses traveled varied from as little as 40 to 2700 miles. Couples came together as often as every weekend (at least as many as half in each sample) to as little as a few days every few months.

As we would expect, the longer the distance traveled, the more difficult the commuters found the arrangement. Increased distance requires both greater costs (for phone and travel) and more time and energy. And, most importantly, the increased cost, time, and energy required for the greater distance traveled tended to mean that spouses spent more time apart (Gerstel, 1977; Kirschner and Wallum, 1978). When the time apart increases, so too does the dissatisfaction with commuter marriage. Gerstel (1978a) suggests that there seems to be a boundary on the amount of time that can be spent apart without serious cost to the relationship. Most couples who were apart only a week, or even two, found the situation tolerable (and even in some ways beneficial). Those who lived apart for more than a month at a time were much more likely to find the situation extraordinarily stressful. The commuters seemed to feel that if they were apart a month or more, they began to develop "separate worlds," or that their mariages began to resemble nonmarriages. They no longer felt in touch with their spouses or that they had a unique relationship that provided an order to their lives.

Gross (1980b) suggests that in addition to the *duration* of separation, the *pattern* of separation also affects the quality of the commuting experience. Irregular regrouping, or reuniting when either spouse's schedule permits, challenges the relationship in a way that a regular regrouping (e.g., every weekend) does not. Gross's analysis suggests that couples who see each other every weekend not only have the obvious advantage of seeing each other more often, but they also have a pattern of separation and regrouping that roughly parallels the work/leisure pattern for most of the society. That is, they are away from each other while others are working and together for the weekend, which they, like other couples, are able to devote to activities they can do together. Without this regular pattern, which resembles the lives of their dual-career counterparts, commuter spouses report that they feel "awkward" or "strange" when they come together (see Gerstel, 1978a, for similar findings with regard to the important symbolic meaning attached specifically to weekend reunions). Finally, couples who can reunite every weekend do not build up impossible expectations for their time together and adapt more readily to their routines, even taking comfort in their regularity.

Consequences of Commuting

In the preceding section we focused on the characteristics of couples and their commutes. In this section we focus on the more general consequences of commuting. First, commuting influences career opportunities and the pattern of daily work lives. Second, living apart affects the relationship between the spouses. And third, commuting changes the couple's relationship with kin, friends, and lovers.

The effect of commuting on career opportunities must be viewed in light of the couple's previous career histories. Typically, the couples had previously given priority to the husband's career and in so doing had disregarded the wife's career objectives. She had followed him, and as a result, usually had remained un- or underemployed (Gerstel, 1978b).[3] Since spouses chose to establish two homes so that they could both pursue orderly careers, it is not surprising that both spouses, but especially wives, report that the ability to pursue occupational opportunities is the chief advantage of this marital structure (Gerstel, 1979; Gross, 1980a; Kirschner and Wallum, 1978). Living apart extends to the wife an advantage that only the husband previously enjoyed — an advantage consistent with both spouse's views of themselves and each other as committed professionals.

There is also a daily, work-related advantage that accompanies this long-range career benefit. Free from family pressures and daily constraints, such as shared mealtimes, recreation, and sleep patterns, these spouses are able to concentrate more fully on their work. Given their intense professional identification, they view this freedom to work as long as they wish, without interruption, as a real "plus." Kirschner and Wallum (1978) have an interesting perspective on this advantage. They suggest that commuters intensify their focus on work and achievement as justification for their unorthodox living arrangements. Thus commuting reinforces the very orientations that are likely to promote it as a marital form.

To understand changes in commuter couples' relationships resulting from the commuting experience, we must view their lifestyle from the perspective of coresident marriage, in terms of what living together provides. This is necessary because commuters themselves take conventional marriage as the point of reference from which to assess their own nontraditional marriages. We recognize their implicit comparison to traditional marriage by what they say they miss in their current relationship. They tell of missing "trivial," everyday talk. They find they are unable to discuss family matters and cannot share and interpret one another's daily experiences or relate impressions of the day's events, since telephone conversations or letter writing are poor substitutes for face-to-face interaction. They lament, as well, their inability to take walks with their spouses or be together at mealtimes or simply to sit quietly in the same room with one another. Without these everyday routines, Gross (1980b) suggests that commuters lose the confirmation that helps produce the ordered (and ordering) world typically entailed in a marital relationship. As a result, some commuter couples — especially young couples without a solid base — fear they will move apart or that they are placing their relationship in jeopardy (Farris, 1978; Gross, 1980b). The absence of both daily conversation and joint nonactivity jeopardizes the taken-for-granted quality of their relationship.

Even more fundamentally, commuters miss the common base that is their "home," where the sharing of daily trivia and activity/non-activity typically occurs. Gross (1980b) suggests that the place-irregularities of these marriages contribute to the awareness that someting is awry — out of order. When they reunite away from their old shared "turf," they are unable to relax. Their reference to "reentry problems" is evidence that they miss the familiarity, the sense of being "in place," that a shared home or living together implies. The home provides a sense of spatial interconnectedness; its absence calls into question the order-constructing quality of the marital relationship.

Such emotional responses to living apart suggest ways in which physical separation induces psychological distance in the marital relationship. The other side of these limitations, however, is the absence of boredom or dullness that conventional partners so often report. When commuter spouses reunite, both view their time together as "special." They speak of a sense of rediscovery and heightened communication. But here again there is a dark side to even these valued consequences. Because their time together is so separated from "other time," their periods together are more vulnerable to inflated expectations, which when not met, mar the comfort of reunions. Their sexual relationship may also suffer. They tell of the need to readjust when they get together and their sense of pressures for time. Thus says Gross (1980b), these mates are more aware of "spoiled time" together than are their coresident counterparts.

These nuances in the variety of emotional reactions show clearly how benefits perceived from one perspective become costs perceived from another. As Gerstel (1978b) points out, commuter marriage and conventional marriage are mirror images. By living together couples obtain intimacy but such intimacy may yield disenchantment or frustration. By living apart, couples rediscover each other at the cost of daily intimacies. Here the costs and rewards of residential separation expose a basic, perhaps irreconcilable, dilemma of conventional marriage.

Most commuter couples also experienced transformations in their division of labor. They became less traditional in their handling of domestic chores (Farris, 1978; Gerstel, 1978b; Pour-El, n.d.). The redistribution of chores, which largely freed the wife from the primary responsibility for housework and child care, was an equalizing force in the couple's relationship. Simultaneously, these spouses found some satisfaction in being able to manage previously sex-linked jobs. For example, wives learned to perform household repairs and car maintenance, while their husbands reported new competence in preparing meals, sewing buttons, or ironing shirts. Previously, before living apart, many had felt dependent in these areas, defining them as their spouse's area of expertise. Here too we see the implicit comparison to traditional marriage. By promoting a specialized division of labor, the single home becomes a training ground for incapacitation. Precisely because the domestic division of labor breaks down in commuter marriages, the alternative arrangement produces a new sense of effectiveness.

In concert with emotional changes and transformations in their own relationship come changes in the ways in which these couples respond to kin, friends, and lovers. Relations with extended family members sometimes become strained, largely because their relatives also take conventional marriage as a standard, and, in so doing, see their commuter children as negligent. Farris (1978) found that, for some, the greatest strain in the social network occurred in relationship to the husband's parents, who were overtly disapproving, especially when they lived close by and when young children were involved.

Constraints in forming and maintaining relationships with friends also troubled these couples (Farris, 1978; Gerstel, 1977; Gross, 1980a). Besides needing to dispel friends' doubts about the solidity of their marriages, they also needed to contend with other married couples' reluctance to include them at social gatherings. When spouses are apart, many married couples exclude them because they are a threat or simply do not fit in (Gerstel, 1977; Kirschner and Wallum, 1978). Friendships with singles are also problematic. As "married singles" (Kirschner and Wallum, 1978), they are less able to form independent ties (Farris, 1978) and more likely to steer away from opposite sex friendships (Gerstel, 1979).

This latter finding sharply contradicts the popular image, as well as much sociological thought (Maykovich, 1976; Laws and Schwartz, 1977; Cuber, 1969), that spouses will reject monogamy when their behavior is beyond their partner's scrutiny. Contrary to such images, commuters were not more likely to have affairs after they set up two homes than they were before they did so (Gerstel, 1979; Ortner et al., 1979). Most of those who had affairs while apart had also done so while still sharing a home with their spouses. Most who had not taken lovers while they shared a single home did not do so when they moved apart. That is, though many suggested that they were more likely to fantasize about affairs when they were alone, the large majority of couples continued to act as they had before commuting. For most, fantasies were not translated into sexual activity. These findings suggest that it is not physical proximity — or an ability for regular observation — that allows marriage to serve as a mechanism of social control. Instead, the constraints that marriage imposes on sexual affairs are a result of an internalized value system (which precedes residential separation) advocating fidelity that many spouses can, and do, carry with them.

In sum, commuter marriages affect the careers and daily work patterns of individual spouses, their marital relationship, and the social networks in which they are embedded. But these changes do not have the same impact on men that they have on women. Women are the prime beneficiaries of the commuter arrangement (Gerstel, 1978b; Gross 1980a). It is women who gain orderly careers by living apart. It is women who no longer need to accommodate others' needs as they did in their traditional nurturing role. It is women who no longer must bear the responsibility for household work and management. It is women who experience gains in self-esteem by finally fulfilling career aspirations. Nevertheless, these women do not usually view these distinct gains as adequate compensation for the considerable stress that separation produces. Most would prefer a world in which it was possible to obtain these benefits while sharing a home with their husbands.

Commuter and Merchant Marine Families: A Comparison

All of the researchers who have studied commuter couples make passing reference to other circumstances that require marital separation. These researchers seemed to assume that the very existence of these other cases testifies to the viability of such a way of life. Thus, the logic goes: Commuting, too, must be viable.

A closer look at such reasoning reveals a hidden premise — that commuter marriage, usually viewed as an accommodation to wives' newly found career prospects, somehow needs defending. It is almost as if students of this new variant of separated living anticipated censure for the study of a lifestyle that breached the marital norm requiring coresidence, if the breach reflected a newly achieved equality between spouses. But the zeal to defend commuter marriage by locating precedents for separated living in situations resulting from men's mobility requirements (see classification scheme presented earlier) presumed what should have been left to investigation: the viability of such precedents.

Such an investigation is currently underway. One of the authors of this chapter has completed in-depth interviews with 26 wives of husbands in the Merchant Marines who work as captains, mates, and engineers of commercial sailing fleets in the Great Lakes region. These couples regularly separate for months at a time during the long, nine-month sailing season. For many, reunions during this period may be limited to the eight-hour periods when the husbands are not on duty — and then only when they happen to be in ports near home where their wives can come to them. Though they do live together for three uninterrupted months of each year in the winter (when the seas are not navigable), these families regularly endure lengthy separations. And they have been separating in this fashion for many years. For most of their married lives together, which ranged from 3 to 41 years, they had lived apart for the nine months that the husband was working and together for only the three months he was not.

Such a marked departure from conventional marital interaction exacts its toll. While it is not possible to describe the findings in detail at this time, preliminary analysis of the interviews suggest interesting contrasts as well as parallels with dual-career commuter couples. Though each is a viable lifestyle in the sense that these marriages endure, in both cases accommodation to the lifestyle depends on the balance of trade offs each group is willing to make. In either case, mere endurance is not equivalent to viability if viability is to be defined in terms of a mutually rewarding and satisfactory marital life.

A diversity of consequences follows from the distinctive pattern of separation and regrouping that characterizes the Merchant Marine families, or "sailing families," as they describe themselves. Just as would be expected from the considerable time these wives spend alone, loneliness and boredom are concerns with which they have to contend continually. Unlike commuters, however, who also say loneliness is a problem, these women do not have absorbing work demands to fill their time. Only about a third work and the jobs they hold are typically neither full time nor highly absorbing. The counterpart to work involvement for them is investment in their children's lives. Recognizing that they are the dominant parental presence for their sons and daughters, they structure their own activities around their children — making the children's schedules the focus of their own. This intense involvement with children in conjunction with the father's limited presence makes it difficult to incorporate him into the family authority structure. They tell of conflicts with their husbands over how they are raising the children and managing the household. The wife, in turn, attributes her husband's criticism to his lack of first-hand experience with the day-to-day demands of child rearing and household management. As one wife puts it, "Husbands don't understand what things cost because they are rarely in stores." Others suggest that since their husbands do not see their children on a regular basis, they hold unreal expectations for them.

Moreover, the time these couples do share is fraught with frustration. When the husband does come home for the extended period they spend together, he has no regular work to do. Having him around "all the time" when he has been around so little takes "getting used to" (reminiscent of the newly retired husband). Perhaps the most stressful adjustment for these wives is the restrictions they feel their husbands place on their previous freedom to come and go as they please and to control family matters.[4] Many tell of curtailing social engagements, for example, club meetings or luncheon appointments with friends, when their husbands are home. Or, if they feel compelled to keep such appointments, they speak of "feeling guilty" about leaving him.

Much more significant than the need to cancel social engagements is the need to reorient themselves to a coupled relationship, especially if the husband calls on the wife to relinquish control and subordinate herself to his direction. For some, real bitterness accompanies the awareness that their husbands do not realize how independent they have had to become. They not only chafe at having to accept the scrutiny of another person, but also at the expectation that they can easily give up the control over family matters they have previously been required to exercise:

> It's like I said one time, "You can't be smart nine months and stupid three." I said, "You can't become a robot at the end of nine months and let somebody put you in a jar and screw the lid down," and then emerge when they leave and start taking over again.

Just as there are benefits that commuter couples recognize as the counterparts of the costs that accompany their lifestyles, so too do seamen's wives juxtapose perceived benefits against such sources of strain. Most important are the financial rewards their husband's work provides. They recognize that their husband's limited formal education and typically working-class background would, in all probability, have consigned them to much lower salaries had they not gone into this line of work. So their relatively high income levels, which average around $50,000 a year, are a distinct benefit. Thus at least some wives exchange a materially secure existence for a seemingly troubled marital relationship. Moreover, they sense that their husbands love their work. Several commented upon previous attempts to break away from sailing in order to have more time with their families. These attempts failed because their husbands really enjoyed their work and missed it when they tried something else. To the wives personally, the independence their way of life has brought them is a valued outcome. Most admit to a previous period in their lives when they were much more dependent and are glad for the change.

This brief overview of themes in the lives of these seamen's wives shows that they, like commuter wives, identify tradeoffs that are the basis of their accommodation to the requirements of separated living. In this sense, their lives are similar. Both groups are aware of balancing the good with the bad points of a difficult lifestyle. But on balance, lives of seamen's wives seem bleaker than the lives of commuter wives. For one thing, they have fewer resources. Typically they do not finish high school and the few who do work hold low-skilled, low-paying jobs as clerks, waitresses, beauty shop operators, and the like. They do not convey the sense of self-assurance and personal satisfaction of the better-educated professional women. In addition, their mates, unlike commuter husbands, do not look upon them as social equals. Moreover, the seamen's wives generally share their husband's traditional views about marriage and women's place, though they wrestle with encroachments on their autonomy and sometimes question the legitimacy of their husband's expectations.

Resources and expectations, then, play a large part in the adjustment to living apart. Relative to seamen's wives, commuter wives have educational and occupational advantages, high self-esteem, as well as more egalitarian marital expectations, that help them cope with the strains of separation. They can depend on the more stabilizing and regenerative effect on their marital relationship of, at least, regular reunions on weekends and of more predictable family gatherings. And the husband's more continuous work obligations mean that the wife does not have to contend with his boredom when he comes home. Most importantly commuter couples' shared assumptions about greater marital equality mean that the commuter wives do not feel required to revert to a more dependent posture when they do reunite with their husbands.

A comparison of the circumstances surrounding the adjustment of these two kinds of families shows that the effect of the common fact of separated living cannot be assessed independently of the expectations or resources mates bring to their relationship. Moreover, one cannot isolate the effects of separation per se without taking into consideration ways in which shared values and job characteristics mitigate and temper such living patterns.

Conclusion

This chapter has presented a scheme for classifying couples who reside in separate residences because of the work situation(s) of one or both spouses. We have attempted to specify the impact of coresidence on the spouses, their marital relationship, and the social networks in which they are embedded.

Findings to date suggest that commuting is likely to be least stressful when: (1) couples have moderate to high incomes or financial resources; (2) spouses have intense career motivations or view work as a central personal commitment; (3) couples have been married enough years to share a history that provides a "taken-for-granted" stability; (4) children are not yet or no longer in the home; and (5) spouses reunite regularly on weekends.

Through a comparison of dual-career and Merchant Marine families, we have shown that separation of residence must be analyzed in concert with other couple characteristics if one is to understand the effect of the separation on the couples' lives. The costs of residential separation may be more burdensome for nonprofessional couples than for dual-career professional couples who have more material resources and less traditional values, which together mitigate the impact of living apart. Although both commuters and Merchant Marines experience difficulties with their lives, findings confirm that it is possible to maintain a marriage even in the absence of a single shared residence.

Notes

1. In diverse sources, social scientists defined the family as a unit that necessarily involved residential unity. Murdock (1949: 1), in his classical formulation, defined the nuclear family as a "Social group characterized by common residence, economic cooperation, and reproduction." Schneider (1968: 33) wrote: "A condition which is part of the definition of American kinship: the family, to be a family, must live together." And even according the the U.S. Bureau of the Census (1976: 3): "The term family refers to a group of two or more persons related by blood, marriage or adoption and residing together in a household." For a critique of the presumption that the family unit necessarily implies common residence see Skolnick, 1978, and Leibowitz, 1978.

2. Two qualifications are necessary with regard to this subcategory, "One Spouse's Work as the Source." First, although we refer to the source of separation here as one spouse's work, it should be noted, of course, that this is still typically the husband's work. Second, although we refer to all of these as formally voluntary, some of these occupations

preclude spousal coresidence, e.g., Merchant Marines' wives cannot regularly accompany their husbands to work. However, these separations are formally voluntary in that the decision to enter these occupations in the first place is a personal choice.

3. For discussions of family mobility patterns among dual-career couples, see Duncan and Perucci, 1976; Ferber and Huber, 1979; Holmstrom, 1973; Linn, 1971.

4. See Hill, 1949; Burr, 1973; and McCubbin et al., 1976, for similar findings about the reintegration of families after war-induced separations; see also McCubbin, 1979.

References

BURR, W. (1973) Theory Construction and the Sociology of the Family. New York: John Wiley.

CUBER, J. (1969) "Adultery: reality vs. stereotype," pp. 190-197 in G. Neubeck (ed.) Extramarital Relations. Englewood Cliffs, NJ: Prentice-Hall.

DUNCAN, R. and C. C. PERUCCI (1976) "Dual occupation families and migration." American Sociological Review 41 (April): 252-261.

FARRIS, A. (1978) "Commuting," pp. 100-107 in R. Rapoport and R. N. Rapoport (eds.) Working Couples. New York: Harper & Row.

FERBER, M. and J. HUBER (1979) "Husbands, wives, and careers." Journal of Marriage and the Family 41 (May): 315-325.

GERSTEL, N. (1979) "Marital alternatives and the regulation of sex." Alternative Life- styles 2 (May): 145-176.

——— (1978a) "The residential basis of social networks: commuter marriage as a test case." Presented at the Annual Meetings of the Eastern Sociological Society, Philadelphia, Pennsylvania.

——— (1978b) "Commuter marriage: constraints on spouses." Presented at the Annual Meetings of the American Sociological Association. San Francisco, California.

——— (1978c) "Commuter marriage." Ph.D. dissertation, Columbia University, New York.

——— (1977) "The feasibility of commuter marriages," pp. 357-367 in P. J. Stein, J. Richmond and N. Hannan (eds.) The Family: Functions, Conflicts and Symbols. Reading, MA: Addison-Wesley.

CROSS, H. (1980a) "Dual career couples who live apart: two types." Journal of Marriage and the Family 40 (August): 567-576.

——— (1980b) "Couples who live apart: time/place disjunctions and their conse- quences." Symbolic Interaction 3 (Fall): 69-81, 93-94.

——— (1978) "Couples who live apart: the dual-career variant." Presented at the Annual Meeting of the American Sociological Association, San Francisco, California.

HILL, R. (1949) Families Under Stress. Westport, CT: Greenwood.

HOLMSTROM, L. L. (1973) The Two Career Family. Cambridge, MA: Schenkman.

KIRSCHNER, B. and L. WALLUM (1978) "Two-location families: married singles." Alter- native Lifestyles (November): 513-525.

LASLETT, B. (1979) "Production, reproduction and social change: a theory of family in history." Presented at the Annual Meetings of the American Sociological Association, Boston, Massachusetts.

LAWS, J. L. and P. SCHWARTZ (1977) Sexual Scripts. Chicago: Dryer.

LEIBOWITZ, L. (1978) Females, Males, Families: A Biosocial Approach. North Scituate, MA: Duxbury.

LINN, E. L. (1971) "Women dentists: career and family." Social Problems 18 (Winter): 393-403.

MAYKOVICH, M. K. (1976) "Attitude vs. behavior in extra-marital sexual relations." Journal of Marriage and the Family 38 (November): 693-699.

McCUBBIN, H. (1979) "Integrating coping behavior and family stress." Journal of Mar- riage and the Family 41 (May): 237-244.

———— B. DAHL, G. LESTER, D. BENSON, and M. ROBERTSON (1976) "Coping repertories of families: adapting to prolonged war-induced separation." Journal of Marriage and the Family 38 (August): 461-471.

MURDOCK, G. P. (1949) Social Structure. New York: Macmillan.

ORTNER, J., J. SULLIVAN, and S. M. CROSSMAN (1979) "Long distance marriage." (unpublished)

PARSONS, T. (1959) "The social structure of the family," pp. 173-201 in R. Anshen (ed.) The Family, Its Function and Destiny. New York: Harper & Row.

POUR-EL, M. B. (n.d.) "Spatial separation in family life — a mathematician's choice." (unpublished)

SCHNEIDER, D. (1968) American Kinship: A Cultural Account. Englewood Cliffs, NJ: Prentice-Hall.

SKOLNICK, A. (1978) The Intimate Environment. Boston: Little, Brown.

U.S. Bureau of the Census (1976) Household and Family Characteristics: March 1975. Current Population Reports, Series P-20, No. 291. Washington, DC: Government Printing Office.

CHAPTER 9

"Open" Marriage and Multilateral Relationships: The Emergence of Nonexclusive Models of the Marital Relationship

DAVID L. WEIS

Rutgers University

The popular view of the 1960s is that it was a decade of rapid social change and tremendous social conflict. To this day, the mass media and print journalism emphasize these elements and portray the sixties as the decade of the civil rights movement, the rebirth of feminism, the sexual revolution, and the anti-Vietnam War movement. The sixties are seen as a decade of sweeping shifts in the normative character of American society. Frequently, the forces resisting change are overlooked in discussions of that period. Whatever the real changes might have been and whatever their ultimate impact on American society may be, the 1960s can be characterized as a time of critical examination of existing institutions. Although it would be inaccurate to infer that all Americans participated, it is true that large segments of the population were involved in this reassessment of values, lifestyles, and relationships.

This was as true for the marriage and family institutions as for others. Criticisms of traditional marriage and family relationships abounded in the late sixties and early seventies. This criticism came from all quarters—feminists and nonfeminists, gays and heterosexuals, Blacks and Whites, liberals and conservatives (Melville, 1980). Of special interest were the attacks directed against the sexually exclusive and monogamous character

Author's Note: This chapter is a revised version of a presentation made at the Annual Meetings of the Groves Conference on Marriage and the Family, Mt. Pocono, Pennsylvania, May 28-29, 1981. The author would like to thank Remi Clignet, Larry L. Constantine, and J. Kenneth Davidson for their helpful comments.

of the marital institution (McMurty, 1977; Roy and Roy, 1977; Schwartz, 1977). Several writers went so far as to predict the "death" of marriage and family as institutions (Cadwallader, 1966; Cooper, 1970; Keller, 1971). The validity of such criticisms and predictions is not a concern here. What is important to the present discussion is that the perception of social change, the critical examination of basic institutions, and the predictions of a decline of marriage and family all helped to create a social environment in the late sixties that led writers to present new models of the marital relationship. It was during this period that nonexclusive intimate lifestyles such as swinging, "open" marriage and group marriage began to receive widespread attention in print.[1]

Of course, nonexclusive lifestyles did not emerge for the first time in the late 1960s, nor was this the first time writers advocated nonexclusivity. As just one example, Bertrand Russell (1929) argued that extramarital sexual relations could be incorporated into a successful marriage. However, the past fifteen years are significant because, for the first time, many writers began to articulate the scripts for nonexclusive patterns, and American society witnessed serious debate over exclusivity. One of the more prolific advocates of what has been labeled "alternative" marriage is Robert Rimmer, whose novels (1964, 1966, 1969a, 1972, 1977) and essays 1969b, 1971, 1973) have explored a variety of alternatives to sexually exclusive, monogamous marriage. Rimmer has continually argued that structural changes in the family are necessary for the fulfillment of many individuals. He has urged a reconceptualization of love by arguing that jealousy and possessiveness can and should be eliminated and that love is not exclusive. Toward this end he has presented models of group marriage 1964, 1966, 1969a), synergamous marriage (1972), and consensual extramarital sex (1977). Another well-known work in this vein is *Open Marriage* by Nena and George O'Neill (1972a). The O'Neills' book is frequently and mistakenly construed as a simple rationalization for extramarital sex. Actually, the portions of the book concerned with extramarital sex represent only a small part of the work. The major thrust of *Open Marriage* indicates a concern with the role of autonomy and independence in intimate and marital relationships and with the ability of couples to build individualized, but mutually agreeable, rules for their relationships. The term "open" marriage, which has become a buzzword for nonexclusive lifestyles, was first used by Ron Mazur (1970).

It is not this writer's intention to thoroughly review the literature presenting the alternative marriage philosophy. Rather, the purpose is to suggest that an extensive literature has developed and that writers in this area view intimate relationships in a unique way, particularly with respect to the issue of exclusivity in marriage. In addition to the works already cited as representing alternative marriage philosophies, one could readily find a host of books (see Francoeur and Francoeur, 1974; Lobell and Lobell, 1972; Mazur, 1973; Ramey, 1976; Roy and Roy, 1968), numerous edited collections (DeLora and DeLora, 1972; Gordon and Libby, 1976; Libby and Whitehurst, 1977; Otto, 1970; Skolnick and Skolnick, 1971; J. R. Smith and Smith, 1974), special issues of professional journals (e.g., Sussman, 1972, 1975; Walters, 1977), and an extensive array of articles in professional and popular periodicals. It would be erroneous to assume that all these writers completely share the philosophy of Rimmer or the O'Neills. There are, in reality, a number of alternative philosophies. What unites them for purposes of discussion here is not so much their uniformity as the fact that they all represent departures from the traditional model of sexually exclusive marriage. What they share is their attempt to portray the various aspects of sexuality, love, and marriage in a new way.

During roughly the same period of time that the various alternative marriage philosophies appeared, a wave of traditionally oriented publications presented a strikingly different philosophy of marriage. *The Total Woman* by Marabel Morgan (1973) is one of the more widely publicized examples. The main thrust of Morgan's presentation is an advocacy of traditional sex roles. However, Morgan also argues that true love is exclusive and that marital happiness is achieved through sharing and not through autonomous activities. While she does not specifically oppose or argue against the development of friendships outside the marital dyad, the focus of her presentation is experience within the marriage. Other writers (Andelin, 1974; Decter, 1972; Rosner and Hobe, 1974; Schnall, 1976) have presented similar marital philosophies. All seem to emphasize the exclusivity of love in marriage. The traditional philosophies have also supported a romantic view of love relationships (Andelin, 1974; Morgan, 1973; Rosner and Hobe, 1974; Schnall, 1976), shunned or ignored the development of intimate relationships outside the marriage, and notably, made no recommendations for structural changes in the nuclear family.

Many of the traditionalists have argued that the alternative philosophies are nothing more than an attempt to license adulterous behavior (Banashek, 1978; Rosner and Hobe, 1974; Schnall, 1976). Within the last several years, claims have been made that "open" marriages are never successful and that such marriages mask underlying problems (Banashek, 1978). Nena O'Neill's more recent book, *The Marriage Premise* (1977), has even been used by some to buttress this argument. Unfortunately, there are no data that indicate how many persons try "open" marriage, how many successfully incorporate nonexclusive patterns into their marriages, or what the social forces leading to nonexclusive scripts may be.

While this historical overview has been necessarily short and, as a result, oversimplified, it does highlight several factors that help to develop a sociohistorical perspective for the various nonexclusive intimate relationships. First, in comparison to the traditional model of marriage, models of nonexclusive and/or nonmonogamous relationships have been available to a wide segment of the American population for a very short period. In

act, it would be interesting to see what percentage of Americans have
ctually been exposed to such models. It is probably fair to suggest that
elatively few Americans have been able to model or to witness such
onexclusive relationships. Second, the reaction of traditionalists to
onexclusive models is, in light of the recent introduction of these models,
uite understandable. Proposals to transform the exclusive and
nonogamous character of marriage represent radical shifts in the institu-
on. It is only reasonable to expect widespread opposition to such shifts.
inally, given the recent appearance of nonexclusive models and the
egree of change they represent, it is also reasonable to expect that many
f those who have attempted to live nonexclusive lifestyles have encoun-
ered great difficulties in doing so.[2]

This chapter will review the models presented by writers for the follow-
ng nonexclusive lifestyles:

(1) open marriage

(2) extramarital sexuality (ES)

(3) nonsexual extramarital relationships (NER)

(4) sexually open marriage/comarital sex (SOM)

(5) intimate friendship networks

(6) swinging

(7) group marriage/multilateral relationships

The chapter will also present an overview of previous research on these
ifestyles, assess the research needs, and explore social psychological
actors that may influence the future incidence of nonexclusive patterns.

Social Scripts for Nonexclusivity

The use of the term "marital philosophy" in the previous section
eflects the distinct metaphysical and epistemological differences between
he traditionalists and the advocates of alternative marriage. The positions
aken by the two groups are much more than simple differences of opinion.
Nena O'Neill's (1977) discussion of the importance of sexual fidelity is a
ood example. This has been interpreted by some as a reversal in the
osition on extramarital sexuality taken in *Open Marriage* (1972a). In fact,
he more recent discussion of sexual fidelity illustrates the strikingly differ-
nt ways in which people view marriage and sexuality. While some may
ee the term "sexual fidelity" as referring to sexual exclusivity in marriage,
t is quite clear that O'Neill is using the term to describe faithfulness to a
mutually agreeable marital contract that may or may not include
greements to permit ES.

These divergent philosophies can be conceptualized as social scripts
epresenting distinct ways of defining marriage. A social script may be

defined as a complex cognitive organization of beliefs and values pertaining to a particular referent (Weis, 1979; Weis and Slosnerick, 1981). Humans employ social scripts to define and organize experience in the same way that an actor uses a script on the stage (Gagnon and Simon, 1973; Gecas and Libby, 1976; Laws and Schwartz, 1977; Sprenkle and Weis, 1978). These scripts are developed through social interaction and are used to guide and assess behavior in particular situations. Weis (1979) notes that social scripts are both internalized by individuals and institutionalized within groups. Cazenave (1979) has criticized work in the area of alternative lifestyles for its emphasis on ideological preference and its failure to explore how such structural variables as gender, age, and race may impose external constraints on the selection of an intimate lifestyle. Cazenave's criticisms are serious and legitimate; the special issue of *Alternative Lifestyles* on Black alternate lifestyles (Cazenave, 1980) represents one of the few efforts by social scientists to study the influence of social structure on lifestyle selection. The issue is raised here because some readers may be tempted to view social scripts as simple ideological choices unrelated to social structure. While scripts are internalized through a process of modeling, reinforcement, and rehearsal, Weis (1979) emphasizes that this process occurs within and is limited by one's social environment. Researchers must assess both the individual character of script formation *and* the limits imposed by the social environment if they are to succeed in explaining the development of social scripts (Weis, 1979). Although one cannot point to specific research depicting the variables (ideological, structural, and interactional) influencing the internalization of nonexclusive scripts, a social scripting perspective does maintain that such variables do need to be studied (Weis, 1979; Weis and Slosnerick, 1981).

For purposes of discussion, two fundamental scripts regarding exclusivity in intimate/love relationships can be identified. The first of these basically maintains that intimate relationships should be exclusive; it is expected that emotional needs, as well as sexual needs will be met by the spouse (Clanton and Smith, 1977; Laws and Schwartz, 1977; Whitehurst, 1977). This script emphasizes mutuality and sharing within the marital relationship while shunning extramarital relationships of various kinds. In the extreme, this includes disapproval of nonsexual as well as sexual involvements outside the marriage (Weis and Slosnerick, 1981). Marriage is seen as "settling down" (Laws and Schwartz, 1977). Heterosocial, nonsexual extramarital relationships (NERs) are viewed as potential avenues to ES involvement (Cuber and Harroff, 1965) and as a destructive force in marital relationships (Bell et al., 1975; Cuber, 1969; Johnson, 1970b; Sprenkle and Weis, 1978). Consequently, heterosocial NERs are regarded as a threat to marital stability and as a source of jealousy and conflict (Clanton and Smith, 1977; Gagnon and Greenblat, 1978; Lopata, 1971). Moreover, a high interest in NERs and/or ES is thought to reflect a lack of love and marital commitment (Laws and Schwartz, 1977; Libby and Whitehurst, 1977; Whitehurst, 1977). Of course, the traditional American script prohibits all ES. ES is seen as a deviant behavior that is indicative of marital problems and likely to lead to divorce. It is viewed as one of the most serious violations of the marital contract. Because no proscription is totally effective, the traditional script also includes guidelines for those who transgress the basic prohibition of ES. These guidelines encourage the "adulterer" to be secretive and discreet, suggest that guilt will be a consequence, and maintain that the spouse will react with feelings of jealousy and rejection if the ES is discovered (Sprenkle and Weis, 1978). The key point here is that some behavior that is clearly nonexclusive stems from and is reflective of a social script that advocates exclusivity in marriage.

At the opposite end of the continuum is a social script based on nonexclusivity. This script values individual autonomy and independence, as well as mutuality and sharing (O'Neill and O'Neill, 1972a). Persons using this script do not view love as exclusive, and they negatively evaluate jealousy and possessiveness within marriage (Francoeur and Francoeur, 1974; Lobell and Lobell, 1972; Rimmer, 1966, 1969a). As Clanton and Smith (1977) note, this approach to marriage does not necessarily mean that feelings of jealousy and possessiveness are entirely absent from relationships based on this social script. However, they are discouraged rather than promoted. The script suggests that all of one's emotional needs cannot be met by the spouse (Gagnon and Greenblat, 1978; Neubeck, 1969; Neubeck and Schletzer, 1962). Consequently, NERs are seen as appropriate for married persons and are viewed as a supportive resource for marriage, a source of personal growth, an expansion of intimacy, and a legitimate means of meeting needs (Francoeur and Francoeur, 1974; Gagnon and Greenblat, 1978; Libby and Whitehurst, 1977; O'Neill and O'Neill, 1972a; Ramey, 1976; Rimmer, 1966, 1969a; Roy and Roy, 1968; J. R. Smith and Smith, 1974). Heterosocial NERs are not seen as motivated by marital dissatisfaction or loss of love (Gagnon and Greenblat, 1978), and ES involvement either is not feared or is viewed as an acceptable outcome of NERs (Francoeur and Francoeur, 1974; Ramey, 1976).

Having considered the broad ways in which the nonexclusive lifestyles addressed in this chapter share similar scripting, it is important to recognize their scripting differences. One of the better known alternative scripts is the concept of open marriage presented by Nena and George O'Neill (1972a, 1972b, 1974). In their view, an open marriage is characterized by: (1) living in the "here-and-now" with realistic expectations, (2) respect for personal privacy, (3) role flexibility, (4) open and honest communications, (5) open companionship (an openness to personal relationships outside the marriage that *may or may not* include an agreement to allow ES), (6) equality of power and responsibility, (7) pursuit of personal identity, and (8) mutual trust. In the only empirical study of the degree of "openness" in marriages, Wachowiak and Bragg (1980) report that marital openness is correlated with fewer children, less frequent church attendance, younger age, and higher marital adjustment for wives (as measured by the Locke-Wallace Scale). Strictly speaking, the O'Neill model is not necessarily a script for nonexclusivity. Although they do maintain that ES can be successfully incorporated into a marriage if it is mutually agreeable to a couple and although they do support the establishment of a network of intimate friends outside marriage, the clear focus of their approach is self-determination. The O'Neills urge couples to set their own mutually agreeable rules for marriage. They would be as disturbed by the suggestion that married persons should have ES as by the dictate that such behavior be avoided. Despite this, the term "open" marriage is frequently taken to imply a marriage in which there is an agreement for consensual ES, although this is a gross misuse of the term.

This has led to some confusion in the years since the model first appeared. One is never certain when an author uses the term open marriage whether he or she is referring to the concept presented by the O'Neills or to the more widely held notion that open marriage means "playing around." This has led some writers (Buunk, 1980b; Knapp, 1975, 1976; Knapp and Whitehurst, 1977; Watson, 1981) to use the term "sexually open marriage" to refer to those marriages with a consensual agreement permitting ES. Others (Cole and Spanier, 1974; Knapp, 1975; Libby, 1977; L. G. Smith and Smith, 1974; Ziskin and Ziskin, 1975) use the term "comarital sex" to refer to consensual ES.

While it is certainly important to distinguish extramarital behavior that is acknowledged and approved of by the spouse from that which is not, one must also recognize that many different types of behavior and agreements are subsumed under the rubric of comarital experiences. As one example, not all couples agree to permit the same type of extramarital experiences. Some couples establish agreements to permit friendships outside of marriage as long as they are not sexual. Some agree to permit ES if the ES relationship is temporary (like a fling on a business trip) or nonintimate. Some agree to allow ES "as long as I don't know about it." In short, couples make agreements that permit and also rule out various kinds of nonexclusive behavior. Each of these various agreements represents a slightly different scripting for nonexclusivity. Discussions of and research on comarital agreements must recognize that these scripts can vary on dimensions such as the degree of sexual involvement desired, the degree of intimate involvement desired, the degree of openness with the spouse, and the amount of time spent with the extramarital partner (Buunk, 1980b; Sprenkle and Weis, 1978).

An example of a particular comarital script is the pattern Ramey (1972, 1975, 1976) calls "intimate friendship networks." The focus of Ramey's model is the creation of an interpersonal network of close, loving friends. Within this context, married persons might conceivably have sexual relations with another member of the network. However, sex per se is not the ocus of the interaction; intimacy is. Many couples involved in an intimate riendship network would not accept casual ES with a person outside of hat network—the very opposite of many consensual agreements.

A very different example of a comarital script is provided by the lifestyle known as swinging or mate sharing. Swinging is a pattern in which couples share sexual interaction with others in a social context defined by the participants as recreational play (Bartell, 1970, 1971; Gilmartin, 1974, 1977, 1978). Swinging is something married couples do together. The formation of an extramarital sexual relationship by either of the spouses alone is a violation of the script. Whereas intimate friendship networks are designed to allow sexual contact between intimate friends, swinging is specifically structured to prevent intimacy (Bartell, 1970, 1971). Some writers have used terms such as "utopian swinging" (Symonds, 1970) or "interpersonal swinging" (Varni, 1972, 1973) to describe types of mate sharing oriented toward interpersonal intimacy rather than recreation, but such intimate arrangements are more in line with Ramey's model than with what is typically called swinging.

Thus far, two basic social scripts for nonexclusivity have been identified: (1) nonconsensual extramarital experiences and (2) consensual extramarital experiences. Both of these scripts are part of a larger script that views monogmous marriage as the primary intimate relationship. The last social script to be considered here concerns relationships that are nonmonogamous as well as nonexclusive. In general, the scripting for such lifestyles is similar to that for other nonexclusive patterns with respect to such beliefs as the diffusion of love/intimacy, the negative evaluation of jealousy, the multilateral character of need meeting, and the view of multilateral intimacy as growth enhancing (Constantine and Constantine, 1973; Ramey, 1972; Rimmer, 1966, 1969a). According to Ramey (1972), the primary difference between group marriage and open marriage or intimate friendship networks is the degree of commitment required of individuals. Multilateral involvements also challenge the notion of primacy in intimate relationships.

A few notes of caution must be added to this scripting perspective. The social scripts depicted here reflect the opinions and beliefs of various writers. There is little, if any, empirical verification that individuals actually internalize scripts as outlined here. Future research will need to determine the specific factors that constitute the various scripts for nonexclusivity. The present framework may be appropriately viewed as a set of hypotheses to be tested. Another issue concerns the very nature of social scripts at a theoretical level. Scripts are cognitive organizations of behavior. They are not, however, the behaviors themselves. It is not necessarily the case that individuals will establish lifestyles consistent with their scripts. For example, it cannot be assumed that someone who exhibits swinging behavior ipso facto has a swinging script. This person may have been coerced. Scott's (1980a) study of man sharing is another example. Man sharing is clearly a multilateral relationship, but apparently one that many Black women enter because of structural constraints rather than to express a multilateral script. In fact, it would be enlightening to see what types of scripts the various participants of man sharing have as they enter such relationships and how those scripts change as the relationship proceeds. Quite clearly, more attention needs to be directed at the relationship between nonexclusive scripts and nonexclusive behavior.

A Selective Review of Research on Nonexclusivity

The previous section suggested that, while much has been written about the belief structures characterizing nonexclusive lifestyles, there has been little empirical investigation of how those belief structures are related to the actual experience of nonexclusive lifestyles.

Overview of Cross-Cultural Evidence

In his study of family patterns in 148 societies, Murdock (1949) reported that five (3 percent) societies freely allowed ES, nineteen (13 percent) conditionally permitted ES, and four (3 percent) disapproved ES, though they did not strictly forbid it. The remaining 120 (81 percent) societies had taboos on ES behavior. Murdock did add, however, that "a substantial majority" of societies permitted extramarital sexual relations with specified relatives. In the same study, 195 (85 percent) of 243 societies allowed some form of plural marriage. Polygyny was more common than polyandry or group marriage, and monogamy was the most common marital form even in societies allowing plural marriage (Murdock, 1949). In a similar ethnographic study, Ford and Beach (1951) reported that 39 percent of 192 societies permitted some form of ES, although this was usually restricted to special occasions or specified relatives. Ford and Beach (1951) also reported that 84 percent of the societies in their analysis permitted men to have several wives.[3]

Comparisons of nonexclusive patterns in contemporary societies with data from the United States are difficult because of sampling differences, methodological differences, and differences in the time period of data collection. However, data are available on ES attitudes or behavior for England (Chesser, 1956), France (French Institute, 1961), the Netherlands (Buunk, 1980a), Greece (Safilios-Rothschild, 1969), Sweden (Zetterberg, 1969), Denmark (Christensen, 1962, 1973), and Japan (Maykovich, 1976). The reports by Christensen and Maykovich are of special note because they involve direct comparisons of samples drawn from different cultures. Christensen (1962, 1973) found that Danish college students were more likely to approve ES than American students. Students in both cultures were more permissive in the 1973 study. Maykovich (1976) reported that a sample of Japanese women were less likely to approve ES but not significantly less likely to experience ES than a group of American women.

The available cross-cultural data are indicative of two major trends in research on nonexclusivity. First, researchers have overwhelmingly focused on the sexual aspects of nonexclusivity. Second, there has been little recognition in research of the differing scripts for nonexclusivity. Research on ES, for example, has tended to ask respondents to indicate whether they approve or disapprove ES or whether they have had ES. Typically, the methods utilized have ignored the fact that there are several different types of ES occurring in a variety of social contexts.

Extramarital Sexual Relationships

One major avenue of research on ES has been the assessment of attitudes toward ES. Results with a variety of samples have consistently indicated that approximately 70 percent of American adults continue to disapprove of ES (Blum, 1966; Bukstel et al., 1978; Glenn and Weaver, 1979; Levitt and Klassen, 1974; Reiss et al., 1980; Singh, 1976). Approval of ES has been found to be related to: (1) being male, (2) young age, (3) low religiosity, (4) high education, (5) gender egalitarianism, (6) political liberality, (7) unhappiness with marriage, and (8) premarital sexual permissiveness. The Reiss research group (1980) has presented a theoretical model of extramarital permissiveness (see Reiss et al., 1980) and, although much of it still needs to be tested, it represents a major step in thinking about nonexclusivity. Finally, Buunk (1980a) found with a Dutch sample that the intent to engage in ES is related to a need for intimacy, marital need deprivation, a facilitative social context, approval by the spouse, and gender egalitarianism. Unfortunately, because of the failure to assess attitudes toward specific types of ES, one cannot be certain that the relationships identified by previous research will also appear for specific types of ES.

Another major focus of research on ES has concerned the possible relationship between ES and marital happiness. Although several studies have found that ES involvement (usually assessed in terms of whether the respondent had ever had ES or not) is significantly related to marital unhappiness, these same studies indicate that many ES participants have happy marriages (Atwater, 1979; Bell et al., 1975; Cuber and Harroff, 1965; Edwards and Booth, 1976; Hunt, 1969, 1974; Johnson, 1970a, 1970b; Levin, 1975; Roebuck and Spray, 1967). Dissatisfaction with marriage is commonly thought to be a major motive for ES (Sprenkle and Weis, 1978). However, such variables as curiosity, desire for personal growth, and desire for new experience also appear to be motivating factors (Atwater, 1978, 1979; Buunk, 1980a; Ellis, 1969, 1972; Kinsey et al., 1948; Kinsey et al., 1953). Glass and Wright (1977) have provided evidence that the relationship between ES and marital satisfaction varies with the length of marriage and is different for men than it is for women.

Researchers have also explored the relationship between ES and structural variables,[4] equity (Walster et al., 1978), alienation (Whitehurst, 1969), and family violence (Whitehurst, 1971). Other topics of research have included extramarital sexual fantasy (Neubeck and Schletzer, 1962) and the formation of ES liaisons in a cocktail lounge (Roebuck and Spray, 1967).

Once again research on the behavioral aspects of ES has been weakened by the failure to distinguish types. Kinsey et al. (1948, 1953) reported that 50 percent of American men and 26 percent of American women experience ES at least once. It would appear that the rate for women has increased (Anthanasiou et al., 1970; Bell et al., 1975; Hunt, 1974; Levin, 1975; Maykovich, 1976) possibly because of the increased number of women working outside the home (Levin, 1975). It does appear that most ES is still of the nonconsensual and secretive variety and that it is more likely to be short term in nature (Hunt, 1974). However, few researchers have actually assessed such variables as length of the ES relationship or the degree of openness with the spouse.

Swinging

Of the various forms of consensual ES, the one that has received the most research attention is swinging. It has been estimated that 2 percent of the American population has participated in swinging (Athanasiou et al., 1970; Hunt, 1974). Comparisons of swingers with nonswingers reveal that swingers tend to be: (1) less religious, (2) overwhelmingly middle class, (3) predominantly White, and (4) quite "normal" except for their swinging behavior (Bartell, 1970, 1971; Breedlove and Breedlove, 1964; Denfeld and Gordon, 1970; Gilmartin, 1974, 1977, 1978; Twichell, 1974; Varni, 1972; Walshok, 1974). Bartell (1970, 1971) reported that the swingers in his study (from the midwest) tended to be politically conservative and were unlikely to have gone to college. Moreover, the wives in the Bartell study were unlikely to be employed outside the home. These findings stand in contrast to other studies, which have found swingers to be politically liberal and more likely to have gone to college, with the husbands likely to be employed in professional or white-collar positions and the wives employed outside the home (Denfeld and Gordon, 1970; Gilmartin, 1974, 1977; Twichell, 1974).

In a comparison of swinging and nonswinging couples, Gilmartin (1974, 1977, 1978) found that the swingers have less rewarding relationships with their parents; interact more frequently with their friends, but less with neighbors and relatives; are less attached to agents of social control like the church; gain heterosexual experiences at a younger age and with more partners; have sexual relations more frequently; marry younger; and are more likely to have been divorced in a previous marriage. The swinging couples did not significantly differ in marital happiness in comparison to the control couples, although they did report higher ratings than those control couples engaging in secretive ES (Gilmartin, 1977, 1978).

Husbands tend to initiate swinging behavior (Bartell, 1970, 1971; Henshel, 1973; Varni, 1972), and wives usually respond negatively to the suggestion (Varni, 1972). For those couples who overcome their initial anxieties, swinging can contribute positively to the marriage by increasing openness and sharing between the husband and wife (Bartell, 1971; Denfeld and Gordon, 1970; Varni, 1972). It must be noted, however, that this is a view expressed by active swingers. In a study of couples who had dropped out of swinging and gone to a marriage counselor, Denfeld (1974a, 1974b) found that such problems as jealousy, guilt, emotional attachments, boredom, and perceived threats to the marriage were common reasons for dropping out of swinging. Unfortunately, there has been no research identifying the factors that differentiate couples who are satisfied with swinging from those who are not.

Sexually Open Marriage (SOM)

In contrast to swinging, which is a behavior shared by husbands and wives, some couples establish mutual agreements to allow each other to have openly acknowledged, independent sexual relationships with other partners (Macklin, 1980). There have been very few empirical investigations of such consensual agreements. Beltz (1969) reported that none of the five clinical couples he studied had been able to successfully incorporate ES into their marriages. Knapp (1976) and Whitehurst (Knapp and Whitehurst, 1977) found their White, middle-class samples to be highly individualistic, noncomformist, stimulated by complexity, and motivated by personal value systems. These couples reported such problems as: (1) jealousy, (2) loneliness, (3) complex negotiations, (4) lack of social support, and (5) conflict over free time. They also cited increased self-esteem and increased awareness of self and others as benefits derived from pursuing a sexually open marriage. Most were unwilling to return to a more traditional relationship. Knapp and Whitehurst (1977) suggested that this lifestyle required: (1) the desire to maintain the primacy of the marriage, (2) a high degree of affection between spouses and a mutual agreement over the choice of lifestyle, (3) the skills needed to manage complex relationships, and (4) the selection of extramarital partners who would not compete with the spouse.

Buunk (1980b) has studied the ground rules or strategies that SOM couples evolve to reduce potential threats to the marriage. Buunk identified five types of couple strategies: (1) primary value placed on maintaining the marriage, (2) limiting the intensity of the ES involvements, (3) keeping the spouse fully informed of ES relationships, (4) approving ES only if it involves mate exchange, and (5) tolerating ES if it is invisible to the spouse. Buunk's research represents an important step in our understanding of nonexclusivity. It would be enlightening to explore the relationship between type of strategy and the consequences of extramarital behavior.

The only longitudinal evidence of effect of SOM on marriage comes from a two-year study of persons who had experienced such a relationship

(Watson, 1981), some of whom were divorced at time of first interview and some of whom were still in an ongoing SOM relationship. Those who were divorced indicated that the SOM experience had been motivated by an unfulfilling marriage, that their outside relationship had been more satisfying, and that they did not desire to return to an SOM relationship. After two years, members of the ongoing group were still married but, with one exception, had adopted an exclusive relationship although they still saw SOM as a possible future choice. Watson concludes that SOM may be a stage in a relationship rather than an ongoing lifestyle.

Intimate Friendship Networks (IFN)

Ramey (1975, 1976) has studied 380 individuals participating in IFN. In general, these persons seem to have the same kinds of personal characteristics and experience similar costs/benefits as the couples studied by Knapp and Whitehurst. The overwhelming majority reported being satisfied with their primary relationship, but it must be noted that Ramey focused his investigation on persons participating in IFN for ten years. Ramey maintains that IFN develop from the practice of sexually open marriage over an extended period of time.

Multilateral Marriage/Relationships

Multilateral or group marriage has probably been the least studied of the lifestyles addressed in this chapter, and it is probably the least common as well. Joan and Larry Constantine's research (1973) on group marriages in the United States is virtually the only source of data on American groups, and their various publications constitute the bulk of the empirically grounded literature (Constantine, 1978; Constantine and Constantine, 1972, 1973, 1974, 1977; Constantine et al., 1972). The Constantines report that the typical multilateral marriage consists of four adults. Most persons enter a multilateral marriage with their spouse, and if the group dissolves, most of the original pair bonds survive. In fact, the original pair bonds appear to retain some semblance of primacy after the formation of the group, and this may be a factor working against the success of the group.

Scores on the various personality profiles employed by the Constantines indicate that participants tend to have a high need for change and autonomy and low need for order, guilt, and deference. Common motives for entering a group marriage include a desire for more companionship, sexual variety, love, and personal growth. Few of the groups studied by the Constantines lasted more than a year. The major problems leading to a break-up seemed to be communication difficulties, jealousy, and interpersonal conflict.

Scott (1980a, 1980b) has studied the phenomenon of man sharing in contemporary Black American communities by interviewing eleven consensual and eleven legal wives. Man sharing is a pattern where two (or conceivably more) women living in separate dwellings each maintain an intimate relationship with one man. Scott refers to this pattern as a form of Black polygamy, although other writers (Allen and Agbasegbe, 1980; McAdoo, 1980) deny this claim largely on the basis that the lifestyle is not voluntarily chosen by women and is not socially legitimated. It would appear that the imbalanced sex ratio among Blacks and the economic deprivation of Blacks compel Black women to accept man-sharing arrangements (Allen and Agbasegbe, 1980; McAdoo, 1980; Scott, 1980b). Scott counters such criticisms by noting that Black women do consent to man sharing and that these relationships are socially recognized in the Black community. This study can be applauded for its focus on a group that is not representative of the white middle class usually studied by researchers of nonexclusivity.

Extramarital Nonsexual Relationships

As noted earlier, relatively little attention has been given to the nonsexual relationships established outside of marriage. Weis and Slosnerick (1981) report the results of a study of the attitudes of college students toward a range of male/female extramarital interactions. Approximately 30 percent of the students disapproved of ES. However, one-half of the students indicated approval of such activities as dancing or eating dinner when the spouse was absent, and nearly 80 percent approved of going to a movie. Approval of the various extramarital situations was related to: (1) disassociation of sex, love, and marriage, (2) premarital sexual permissiveness, and (3) being male. Approval was not related to marital status or length of marriage. These findings indicate that exclusivity is a multidimensional construct influencing scripting for nonsexual as well as sexual interactions. The fact that a majority of the students approved several of the nonsexual extramarital situations also suggests that researchers who have been interested in studying changing attitudes toward exclusivity may be focusing on the wrong end of the continuum. Because sexuality is viewed by Americans as the most intimate of behaviors, it seems likely that attitudes toward sexual exclusivity would be the last to change.

An Assessment of the Future

What can research to date tell us about future trends? Many writers argue that American society is about to experience a shift toward nonexclusive values, but few of these claims are substantiated by data. Glenn and Weaver (1979) maintain that the greater permissiveness of young, highly educated persons in a national study of ES attitudes may lead to an increased acceptance of ES in the future. However, other studies raise some doubts about this. Strong (1978) reported that consensual ES, spouse swapping, and group marriage were ranked as the least desirable of a group of twelve lifestyles in a study of 354 college students. They were also the only nonexclusive lifestyles included in the study. In a study comparing Black/White and Male/Female college students, Ericksen (1980) reported that White males were the group most likely to indicate they would participate in a marriage with consensual ES, but only 17 percent of them were willing to participate in such a marriage. Rao and Rao (1980) conducted a similar study of Black students' willingness to participate in various lifestyles. They found 13 percent willing to have consensual ES, 7 percent willing to swap spouses, 8 percent willing to participate in a group marriage, 7 percent in polyandry, and 14 percent in polygyny. None of these studies provides much evidence that nonexclusive lifestyles will be viewed as more acceptable in the foreseeable future.

This does not necessarily mean, however, that American society will continue to maintain the norm of exclusivity. Reiss (1980) notes that, with respect to premarital sexual norms, behavior changes preceded attitudinal changes. There are several factors that suggest that a similar shift may occur in extramarital experiences during the next several decades. The growth of technology and the growth of female participation in the labor force is already leading to an increase in male/female interactions involving married persons. While it is certainly not the case that all or even most of these interactions will result in a sexual exchange, it is certainly true that opportunities will develop. The growing divorce rate is resulting in increases in what is sometimes called serial monogamy. It could just as easily be called serial nonexclusivity. One result will be that increasing numbers of Americans will experience multiple (though not at the same time) intimate/sexual realtionships, and they will be exposed to the benefits of multiple intimacy. The decreases in age of first intercourse will have similar impact on premarital experience by increasing the probability that young people have several intimate/sexual relationships before marriage.

Each of the above factors, plus the growth of singlehood as a lifestyle (Libby and Whitehurst, 1977), will mean that America will increasingly be characterized by what Farber (1964) calls permanent availability. The increased isolation of the nuclear family, the growing egalitarianism of male/female relationships, the greater acceptability of premarital sex, the increasing mobility of American society, the advent of contraceptive technology, and the increased alienation of contemporary society have all been offered as possible factors leading to increases in nonexclusive behavior. As these factors converge, more Americans are likely to have at least minimal experience with multiple intimacy and sexuality. In effect, it is being suggested here that there will be increases in nonexclusive behaviors over the next fifty years, even though most people today do not want those changes. As a consequence, it seems reasonable to predict that most nonexclusive behavior will continue to follow the secretive, nonconsensual mode for some time to come. It seems premature to make any predictions about the various consensual models discussed in this chapter. After all, those models have only recently emerged; they are still being "tested for suitability," and Americans are still a long way from acknowledging that many of us will not lead exclusive lives.

The prediction that there will be increases in nonexclusive behaviors in the next several decades must be viewed as highly speculative at best. Unfortunately, there has been little research on the factors cited here as likely to influence increases in nonexclusivity. This can be viewed as one of the major weaknesses of research on nonexclusive lifestyles. Sadly, little is known about the social factors that are related to nonexclusive lifestyles—the very type of knowledge we need to make precise predictions of future behavior.

What are the future research needs? Although the following list is by no means exhaustive, it is presented with the hope that it will help to influence the direction of future research.

(1) As the discussion above implies, there is a need for research that identifies the social and psychological factors leading to the emergence of and expression of nonexclusivity.

(2) There is still a need for basic descriptive data on the various nonexclusive patterns in the American population at large. What groups are likely to support or oppose nonexclusivity? What percentage actually participate in these lifestyles?

(3) Researchers need to utilize more broadly constructed samples and make more effort to study non-White, non-middle-class groups, in order to identify the differences in patterns and the significance of these patterns within a given cultural context.

(4) More attention needs to be directed to the development and testing of theoretical models of nonexclusivity, particularly frameworks that acknowledge the influence of structural and interactional variables as well as ideological variables.

(5) Future research needs to focus on the nonsexual, as well as sexual, aspects of nonexclusivity.

(6) A recognition of the various types of extramarital sexuality needs to be incorporated into the design of research. Researchers need to move beyond asking respondents whether they have had extramarital sex in order to tap the social and relational contexts surrounding the behavior.

(7) Research needs to determine the process by which nonexclusive scripts are internalized and the key variables influencing the process at various stages of the life cycle. It would also be of interest to know the extent to which Americans have been exposed to script models for nonexclusivity and determine how those models influence individuals. The composition of the nonexclusive scripts outlined in this chapter needs to be subjected to empirical verification.

(8) Efforts should be directed toward identifying the various types of consensual extramarital agreements and their relationship to the consequences of extramarital behaviors.

(9) There is a need to identify the variables associated with success in the various nonexclusive patterns. For example, there should be a test of the

hypothesis that the ability to maintain an open marriage may be related to level of ego development of the participants (Ryals and Foster, 1976).

(10) Empirically grounded models of therapy need to be developed for persons experiencing nonexclusive relationships, given the incidence of cases dealing with nonexclusivity (Sprenkle and Weis, 1978; Ziskin, 1975) and the evidence that many therapists have negative biases against nonexclusive lifestyles (Constantine et al., 1972; Hymer and Rubin, forthcoming; Knapp, 1975).

Clearly, there is still much to be done. The study of nonexclusive models of marriage is still in its infancy.

Notes

1. This leaves open the question of whether there has been a corresponding increase in the percentage of Americans actually experiencing these lifestyles.

2. Lest anyone think that this implies that such relationships have "failed," it must be noted that, by whatever criteria, many persons who seek the traditional pattern of monogamy and sexual exclusivity also experience great difficulties (divorce, secretive affairs, alcoholism, marital unhappiness, family violence).

3. More detailed discussions of cross-cultural patterns of extramarital behavior can be found in Neubeck (1969) and Reiss (1980).

4. Given the length of this chapter, it is not possible to review that research here. In essence, results are similar to those with ES attitudes (for more detailed reviews of ES research, see Libby, 1977; Macklin, 1980; Reiss, 1980).

References

ALLEN, W. R. and B. A. AGBASEGBE (1980) "A comment on Scott's 'Black polygamous family formation.'" Alternative Lifestyles 3, 4: 375-381.

ANDELIN, H. B. (1974) Fascinating Womanhood. New York: Bantam.

ATHANASIOU, R., P. SHAVER, and C. TAVRIS (1970) "Sex." Psychology Today 4 (July): 39-52.

ATWATER, L. (1979) "Getting involved: women's transition to first extramarital sex." Alternative Lifestyles 2, 1: 38-68.

——— (1978) Women in Extramarital Relationships: A Case Study in Socio-sexuality. New York: Irvington.

BANASHEK, M. (1978) "Infidelity: what it can and can't do for your love life." Mademoiselle (March): 210-219.

BARTELL, G. D. (1971) Group Sex: A Scientist's Eyewitness Report on the American Way of Swinging. New York: Wyden.

——— (1970) "Group sex among the mid-Americans." Journal of Sex Research 6: 113-130.

BELL, R. R., S. TURNER, and L. ROSEN (1975) "A multi-variate analysis of female extramarital coitus." Journal of Marriage and the Family 37, 2: 375-384.

BELTZ, S. E. (1969) "Five-year effects of altered marital contracts: a behavioral analysis of couples," pp. 162-189 in G. Neubeck (ed.) Extramarital Relations. Englewood Cliffs, NJ: Prentice-Hall.

BLUM, S. (1966) "When can adultery be justified or forgiven?" McCall's (May).

BREEDLOVE, W. and J. E. BREEDLOVE (1964) Swap Clubs: A Study in Contemporary Sexual Mores. Sherbourne Press.

UKSTEL, L. H., G. D. ROEDER, P. R. KILMANN, J. LAUGHLIN, and W. M. SOTILE (1978) "Projected extramarital sexual involvement in unmarried college students." Journal of Marriage and the Family 40, 2: 337-340.

UUNK, B. (1980a) "Extramarital sex in the Netherlands." Alternative Lifestyles 3, 1: 11-39.

—— (1980b) "Sexually open marriages: ground rules for countering potential threats to marriage." Alternative Lifestyles 3, 3: 312-328.

ADWALLADER, M. (1966) "Marriage as a wretched institution." Atlantic Monthly (November): 62-66.

AZENAVE, N. A. (ed.) (1980) Black Alternative Lifestyles. Special issue of Alternative Lifestyles 3 (November): 371-504.

—— (1979) "Social structure and personal choice: effects on intimacy, marriage and the family alternative lifestyle research." Alternative Lifestyles 2 (November): 331-358.

HESSER, E. (1956) The Sexual, Marital and Family Relationships of the English Woman. Watford, England: Hutchinson's Medical Publications.

HRISTENSEN, H. T. (1973) "Attitudes toward infidelity: a nine-culture sampling of university student opinion." Journal of Comparative Family Studies 4 (Autumn): 197-214.

—— (1962) "A cross-cultural comparison of attitudes toward marital infidelity." International Journal of Comparative Sociology 3: 124-137.

LANTON, G. and L. G. SMITH [eds.] (1977) Jealousy. Englewood Cliffs, NJ: Prentice-Hall.

OLE, C. L. and G. B. SPANIER (1974) "Comarital mate-sharing and family stability." Journal of Sex Research 10: 21-31

ONSTANTINE, L. L. (1978) "Multilateral relations revisited: group marriage in extended perspective," pp. 131-147 in B. I. Murstein (ed.) Exploring Intimate Life Styles. New York: Springer.

—— and J. M. CONSTANTINE (1977) "Sexual aspects of group marriage," pp. 186-194 in R. W. Libby and R. N. Whitehurst (eds.) Marriage and Alternatives: Exploring Intimate Relationships. Glenview, IL: Scott, Foresman,

—— (1974) "Sexual aspects of multilateral relations, " pp. 268-290 in J. R. Smith and L. G. Smith (eds.) Beyond Monogamy. Baltimore: Johns Hopkins Press.

—— (1973) Group Marriage: A Study of Contemporary Multilateral Marriage. New York: Macmillan.

—— (1972) "Dissolution of marriage in a non-conventional context." Family Coordinatior 21, 4: 457-462.

—— and S. K. EDELMAN (1972) "Counseling implications of comarital and multilateral relations." Family Coordinator 21 (July): 267-273.

OOPER, D. (1970) The Death of the Family. New York: Vintage.

UBER, J. F. (1969) "Adultery: reality versus stereotype," pp. 190-196 in G. Neubeck (ed.) Extramarital Relations. Englewood Cliffs, NJ: Prentice-Hall.

—— and P. B. HARROFF (1965) Sex and the Significant Americans. Baltimore: Viking.

ECTER, M. (1972) The New Chastity. New York: Berkley Medallion.

eLORA, J. S. and J. R. DeLORA [eds.] (1972) Intimate Life Styles: Marriage and Its Alternatives. Pacific Palisades, CA: Goodyear.

ENFELD, D. (1974a) "Dropouts from swinging." Family Coordinator 23 (January): 45-59.

—— (1974b) "Dropouts from swinging: the marriage counselor as informant," pp. 260-267 in J. R. Smith and L. G. Smith (eds.) Beyond Monogamy. Baltimore: Johns Hopkins Press.

—— and M. Gordon (1970) "The sociology of mate swapping." Journal of Sex Research 6: 85-100.

DWARDS, J. N. and A. BOOTH (1976) "Sexual behavior in and out of marriage: an assessment of correlates." Journal of Marriage and the Family 38, 1: 73-81.

LLIS, A. (1972) The Civilized Couple's Guide to Extramarital Adventure. New York: Pinnacle.

—— (1969) "Healthy and disturbed reasons for having extramarital relations," pp. 153-161 in G. Neubeck (ed.) Extramarital Relations. Englewood Cliffs, NJ: Prentice-Hall.

ERICKSEN, J. A. (1980) "Race, sex, and alternate lifestyle choices." Alternative Lifestyles 3, 4: 405-424.

FARBER, B. (1964) Family: Organization and Interaction. San Francisco: Chandler.

FORD, C. S. and F. A. BEACH (1951) Patterns of Sexual Behavior. New York: Perennial.

FRANCOEUR, A. K. and R. T. FRANCOEUR (1974) Hot and Cool Sex. New York: Harcourt, Brace, Jovanovich.

French Institute of Public Opinion (1961) Patterns of Sex and Love: A Study of the French Woman and Her Morals. New York: Crown.

GAGNON, J. H. and C. S. GREENBLAT (1978) Life Designs: Individuals, Marriages, and Families. Glenview, IL: Scott, Foresman.

GAGNON, J. H. and W. SIMON (1973) Sexual Conduct: The Social Sources of Human Sexuality. Chicago: Aldine.

GECAS, V. and R. Libby (1976) "Sexual behavior as symbolic interaction." Journal of Sex Research 12 (February): 33-49.

GILMARTIN, B. G. (1978) The Gilmartin Report. Secaucus, NJ: Citadel.

——— (1977) "Swinging: who gets involved and how?" pp. 161-185 in R. W. Libby and R. N. Whitehurst (eds.) Marriage and Alternatives: Exploring Intimate Relationships. Glenview, IL: Scott, Foresman.

——— (1974) "Sexual deviance and social networks: a study of social, family and marital interaction patterns among co-marital sex participants," pp. 291-323 in J. R. Smith and L. G. SMITH (eds.) Beyond Monogamy. Baltimore: Johns Hopkins Press.

GLASS, S. P. and T. L. WRIGHT (1977) "The relationship of extramarital sex, length of marriage, and sex differences on marital satisfaction and romanticism: Athanasiou's data reanalyzed." Journal of Marriage and the Family 39 (November): 691-703.

GLENN, N. D. and C. N. WEAVER (1979) "Attitudes toward premarital, extramarital, and homosexual relations in the U.S. in the 1970's." Journal of Sex Research 15: 108-118.

GORDON, S. and R. W. LIBBY [eds.] (1976) Sexuality Today — And Tomorrow. North Scituate, MA: Duxbury.

HENSHEL, A. (1973) "Swinging: a study of decision-making in marriage." American Journal of Sociology 78 (January): 885-891.

HUNT, M. (1974) Sexual Behavior in the 1970's. New York: Dell.

——— (1969) The Affair. New York: World.

HYMER, S. M. and A. M. RUBIN (forthcoming) "Therapists' attitudes and clinical experiences with alternative lifestyle clients." Small Group Behavior.

JOHNSON, R. E. (1970a) "Extramarital sexual intercourse: a methodological note." Journal of Marriage and the Family 32 (May): 279-282.

——— (1970b) "Some correlates of extramarital coitus." Journal of Marriage and the Family 32 (August): 449-456.

KELLER, S. (1971) "Does the family have a future?" Journal of Comparative Family Studies II (Spring): 1-14.

KINSEY, A. C., W. B. POMEROY, and C. E. MARTIN (1948) Sexual Behavior in the Human Male. Philadelphia: Saunders.

KINSEY, A. C., W. B. POMEROY, C. E. MARTIN, and P. A. GEBHARD (1953) Sexual Behavior in the Human Female. Philadelphia: Saunders.

KNAPP, J. J. (1976) "An exploratory study of seventeen open marriages." Journal of Sex Research 12: 206-219.

——— (1975) "Some non-monogamous marriage styles and related attitudes and practices of marriage counselors." Family Coordinator 24 (October): 505-514.

——— and R. N. WHITEHURST (1977) "Sexual open marriage and relationships: issues and Prospects," pp. 147-160 in R. W. Libby and R. N. Whitehurst (eds.) Marriage and Alternatives: Exploring Intimate Relationships. Glenview, IL: Scott, Foresman.

LAWS, J. L. and P. SCHWARTZ (1977) Sexual Scripts: The Social Construction of Female Sexuality. Hinsdale, IL: Dryden.

LEVIN, R. J. (1975) "The Redbook report on premarital and extramarital sex: the end of a double standard?" Redbook (October): 38-44, 190-192.

LEVITT, E. E. and A. D. KLASSEN (1974) "Public attitudes toward homosexuality: part of the 1970 national survey by the Institute for Sex Research." Journal of Homosexuality 1, 1: 29-43.

BBY R. W. (1977) "Extramarital and comarital sex: a critique of the literature," pp. 80-111 in R. W. Libby and R. N. Whitehurst (eds.) Marriage and Alternatives: Exploring Intimate Relationships. Glenview, IL: Scott, Foresman.

—— and R. N. WHITEHURST [eds.] (1977) Marriage and Alternatives: Exploring Intimate Relationships. Glenview, IL: Scott, Foresman.

OBELL, J. and M. LOBELL (1972) John and Mimi: A Free Marriage. New York: St. Martin's.

OPATA, H. Z. (1971) Occupation Housewife. New York: Oxford University Press.

ACKLIN, E. D. (1980) "Nontraditional family forms: a decade of research." Journal of Marriage and the Family 42 (November): 905-922.

AYKOVICH, M. K. (1976) "Attitude versus behavior in extramarital sexual relations." Journal of Marriage and the Family 38 (November): 693-699.

AZUR, R. (1973) The New Intimacy. Boston: Beacon.

—— (1970) "Beyond morality: toward the humanization of the sexes." Presented at the Annual Meetings of the National Council on Family Relations.

cADOO, H. P. (1980) "Commentary on Joseph Scott's 'Black polygamous family formation.'" Alternative Lifestyles 3, 4: 383-388.

cMURTY, J. (1977) "Monogamy: a critique," pp. 3-13 in R. W. Libby and R. N. Whitehurst (eds.) Marriage and Alternatives: Exploring Intimate Relationships. Glenview, IL: Scott, Foresman.

ELVILLE, K. (1980) Marriage and Family Today. New York: Random House.

ORGAN, M. (1973) The Total Woman. Old Tappan, NJ: Revell.

URDOCK, G. P. (1949) Social Structure. New York: Macmillan.

EUBECK, G. [ed.] (1969) Extramarital Relations. Englewood Cliffs, NJ: Prentice-Hall.

EUBECK, G. and V. SCHLETZER (1962) "A study of extramarital relationships." Marriage and Family Living 24, 3: 279-281.

'NEILL, N. (1977) The Marriage Premise. New York: M. Evans.

—— and G. O'NEILL (1974) "Open marriage: a conceptual framework," pp. 56-67 in J. R. Smith and L. G. Smith (eds.) Beyond Monogamy. Baltimore: Johns Hopkins Press.

—— (1972a) Open Marriage: A New Life Style for Couples. New York: M. Evans.

—— (1972b) "Open marriage: a synergic model." Family Coordinator 21, 4: 403-409.

TTO, H. A. [ed.] (1970) The Family in Search of a Future. New York: Appleton-Century-Crofts.

AMEY, J. W. (1976) Intimate Friendships. Englewood Cliffs, NJ: Prentice-Hall.

—— (1975) "Intimate groups and networks: frequent consequences of sexually open marriage." Family Coordinator 24 (October): 515-530.

—— (1974) "Communes, group marriage and the upper-middle class," pp. 214-229 in J. R. Smith and L. G. Smith (eds.) Beyond Monogamy. Baltimore: Johns Hopkins Press.

—— (1972) "Emerging patterns of innovative behavior in marriage." Family Coordinator 21, 4: 435-456.

AO, V. V. and V. N. RAO (1980) "Alternatives in intimacy, marriage, and family lifestyles: preferences of Black college students." Alternative Lifestyles 3, 4: 485-498.

EISS, I. L. (1980) Family Systems in America. New York: Holt, Rinehart & Winston.

—— R. E. ANDERSON, and G. C. SPONAUGLE (1980) "A multivariate model of the determinants of extramarital sexual permissiveness." Journal of Marriage and the Family 42, 2: 395-411.

IMMER, R. H. (1977) Come Live My Life. New York: Signet.

—— [ed.] (1973) Adventures in Loving. New York: Signet.

—— (1972) Thursday, My Love. New York: Signet.

—— (1971) You and I . . . Searching for Tomorrow. New York: Signet.

—— (1969a) Proposition 31. New York: Signet.

—— (1969b) The Harrad Letters. New York: Signet.

—— (1966) The Harrad Experiment. New York: Bantam.

—— (1964) The Rebellion of Yale Marratt. New York: Avon.

OEBUCK, J. and S. L. SPRAY (1967) "The cocktail lounge: a study of heterosexual relations in a public organization." American Journal of Sociology 72: 388-395.

ROSNER, S. and L. HOBE (1974) The Marriage Gap. New York: McGraw-Hill.

ROY, R. and D. ROY (1977) "Is monogamy outdated?" pp. 22-34 in R. W. Libby and R. N. Whitehurst (eds.) Marriage and Alternatives: Exploring Intimate Relationships. Glenview, IL: Scott, Foresman.

———— (1968) Honest Sex. New York: Signet.

RUSSELL, B. (1929) Marriage and Morals. New York: Liverright.

RYALS, K. and D. FOSTER (1976) "Open marriage: a question of ego development and marriage counseling." Family Coordinator 25, 3: 297-302.

SAFILIOS-ROTHSCHILD, C. A. (1969) "Attitudes of green spouses toward marital infidelity," pp. 77-93 in G. Neubeck (ed.) Extramarital Relations. Englewood Cliffs, NJ: Prentice-Hall.

SCHNALL, M. (1976) Your Marriage. New York: Pyramid Books.

SCHWARTZ, P. (1977) "Female sexuality and monogamy," pp. 229-240 in R. W. Libby and R. N. Whitehurst (eds.) Marriage and Alternatives: Exploring Intimate Relationships. Glenview, IL: Scott, Foresman.

SCOTT, J. W. (1980a) "Black polygamous family formation: case studies of legal wives and consensual 'wives.' " Alternative Lifestyles 3, 4: 41-64.

———— (1980b) "Reprise: conceptualizing and researching American polygny — and critics answered." Alternative Lifestyles 3, 4: 395-404.

SINGH, B. K., B. L. WALTON, and J. J. WILLIAMS (1976) "Extramarital sexual permissiveness: conditions and contingencies." Journal of Marriage and the Family 38, 4: 701-712.

SKOLNICK, A. J. and J. H. SKOLNICK [eds.] (1971) Family in Transition: Rethinking Marriage, Sexuality, Child Rearing, and Family Organization. Boston: Little, Brown.

SMITH, J. R. and L. G. SMITH [eds.] (1974) Beyond Monogamy. Baltimore: John Hopkins Press.

———— (1970) "Co-marital sex and the sexual freedom movement." Journal of Sex Research 6: 131-142.

SMITH, L. G. and J. R. SMITH (1974) "Co-marital sex: the incorporation of extramarital sex into the marriage relationship," pp. 84-102 in J. R. Smith and L. G. Smith (eds.) Beyond Monogamy. Baltimore: Johns Hopkins Press.

SPRENKLE, D. H. and D. L. WEIS (1978) "Extramarital sexuality: implications for marital therapists." Journal of Sex and Marital Therapy 4: 279-291.

STRONG, L. (1978) "Alternative marital and family forms: their relative attractiveness to college students and correlates of willingness to participate in non-tradtional forms." Journal of Marriage and the Family 40, 3: 493-503.

SUSSMAN, M. B. [ed.] (1975) The Second Experience: Variant Family Forms. Special issue of Family Coordinator 24, 4.

———— [ed.] (1972) Variant Marriage Styles and Family Forms. Special issue of Family Coordinator 21, 4.

SYMONDS, C. (1970) "The utopian aspects of sexual mate swapping: in theory and practice." Presented at Annual Meetings of the Society for the Study of Social Problems, Washington, DC

TWICHELL, J. (1974) "Sexually liberality and personality: a pilot study," pp. 230-245 in J. R. Smith and L. G. Smith (eds.) Beyond Monogamy. Baltimore: Johns Hopkins Press.

VARNI, C. A. (1973) "Contexts of conversion: the case of swinging," pp. 166-181 in R. W. Libby and R. N. Whitehurst (eds.) Renovating Marriage. Danville, CA: Consensus.

———— (1972) "An exploratory study of spouse swapping," Pacific Sociological Review 15: 507-522.

WACHOWIAK, C. and H. BRAGG (1980) "Open marriage and marital adjustment." Journal of Marriage and the Family 42, 1: 57-62.

WALSHOK, M. L. (1974) "The emergence of middle-class deviant subcultures: the case of swingers," pp. 159-169 in J. R. Smith and L. G. Smith (eds.) Beyond Monogamy. Baltimore: Johns Hopkins Press.

WALSTER, E., J. TRAUPMANN, and G. W. WALSTER (1978) "Equity and extramarital sexuality." Archives of Sexual Behavior 7 (March): 127-142.

WALTERS, J. [ed.] (1977) The Family and the Law. Special issue of Family Coordinator 25, 4.

David L. Weis   215

WATSON, M. A. (1981) "Sexually open marriage: three perspectives." Alternative Life-
    styles 4, 1: 3-21.
WEIS, D. L. (1979) "Toward a theory of social scripting: the measurement of extramarital
    sexual scripts." Ph.D. dissertation, Purdue University.
——— and M. SLOSNERICK (1981) "Attitudes toward sexual and nonsexual extramarital
    involvement among a sample of college students." Journal of Marriage and the Family
    43, 2: 349-358.
WHITEHURST, R. N. (1977) "Jealousy and American values," pp. 136-139 in G. Clanton
    and L. G. Smith (eds.) Jealousy. Englewood Cliffs, NJ: Prentice-Hall.
——— (1971) "Violence potential in extramarital sexual responses." Journal of Marriage
    and the Family 33: 683-691.
——— (1969) "Extramarital sex: alienation or extension of normal behavior," pp. 129-
    145 in G. Neubeck (ed.) Extramarital Relations. Englewood Cliffs, NJ: Prentice-Hall.
ZETTERBERG, H. (1969) On Sexuallivet: Sverige. Stockholm: SOV.
ZISKIN, J. and M. ZISKIN (1975) "Comarital sex agreements: an emerging issue in sexual
    counseling." Counseling Psychologist 5: 81-84.

CHAPTER 10

Gay Male and Lesbian Relationships

JOSEPH HARRY

Northern Illinois University

A decade review of the literature on lesbian and gay couples and family relationships is particularly appropriate since it is only within the last 10 years that there has been reported research on the topic. Prior to the 1970s, the literature arose principally out of two sources: (a) occasional but infrequent pieces by scholars who wrote a single article on gays or lesbians (Leznoff and Westley, 1956; Reiss, 1961), and (b) publications by professionals, such as psychiatrists or psychologists, or by research institutions, such as the Kinsey Institute (Pomeroy, 1972), who had a social license to write about homosexuality without the usual stigma attached to homosexuality rubbing off on them. Most of the pre-1970 writings on homosexuality either dealt with disembodied sexual activities with no concern for their relationship context or explored those relationships as instances of psychopathology.

The rise of the study of gay and lesbian relationships is intimately linked to the rise of the gay and women's movements. The gay caucuses that arose within the academic professions during the early and mid-1970s were successful in influencing their respective professions to provide forums for the presentation and publication of social-scientific analyses of gay and lesbian lives. The members of these caucuses have also been the principal persons conducting and publishing analyses of gay men (e.g., Harry, 1979; Miller, 1979; Peplau, 1981). Rather than publishing a lone piece on the topic of homosexuality, as in earlier decades, the members of these caucuses have formed continuing and interacting communities of scholars pursuing research on the topic as a career.

The above does not hold for analyses of lesbians, however. Most of the major nonpopular studies of lesbians appear to be by self-identified heterosexual women (e.g., Ponse, 1978; Tanner, 1978; Wolf, 1979; Peplau, 1981). This asymmetry appears to be due to the fact that the female members of the lesbian/gay caucuses seem more identified with the women's movement than with the lesbian movement per se. For example,

f the women members of the Sociologists' Gay Caucus who provided
nembership information regarding their areas of academic interest, 62
ercent named "sex roles" or "the family," while only 10 percent of the
nale members mentioned these areas.

Gay Couples

The Butch/Femme Hypothesis

Tripp (1975: 152) has observed that persons unfamiliar with gay male
elationships often tend to heterosexualize them by viewing one partner as
nasculine (i.e., doing the masculine household chores, being dominant in
exual activities and decision making, and financially supporting the part-
er) and the other as engaging in complementary feminine activities.
However, the one thing that the literature most clearly shows about inti-
nate gay relationships is that they infrequently approximate this version of
usband and wife roles. Bell and Weinberg (1978: 323-325) found
pecialization in sex-typed tasks to occur in fewer than 10 percent of their
86 interviews of gay male respondents in San Francisco. Westwood
(1960: 119), in a study of 127 English homosexuals, reported little evi-
ence that masculine and feminine gay men were mutually attracted to
ach other and found that the large majority preferred masculine partners.
imilarly, Saghir and Robins (1973: 74-75), in a study of 89 homosexual
nales, found that few gay couples pattern their relationships according to a
aditional husband/wife model. Although a few gays may organize their
elationships in a "butch/femme" manner, the literature strongly indicates
nat gay relationships are more likely to be patterned after a "best friends/
pommates" model than after a heterosexual sex role model.

Only one study has reported support for a butch/femme pattern in gay
elationships (Haist and Hewitt, 1974). When gay men were divided into
nsertors and insertees in their preferences in anal intercourse, and then
ompared on their preferences for fellating others versus being fellated,
pllowing a partner's suggestions versus giving the suggestions, and having
masterful partner versus being masterful, differences on the order of 20
p 30 percent were found in support of a butch/femme hypothesis. How-
ver, these differences overstate the degree of support for the butch/
emme hypothesis because the respondents were apparently not permit-
ed to say whether they liked both or neither of the activities in question.
)ther data (Bell and Weinberg, 1978: 328) report considerable flexibility
n sexual behaviors. Bell and Weinberg found that 80 percent of their gay
nale respondents had performed anal intercourse in the past 12 months,
rhile 69 percent had received anal intercourse in that time period. Clearly
nere is considerable overlap between insertors and insertees, and
ichotomizing gay subjects into these two groups does violence to the
ata.

Harry and DeVall (1978b: 104-108) analyzed preferences among 241 Detroit gay men for erotic techniques, using questions that did not oblige respondents to make forced choices. Exploring preferences for the ac tivities of oral insertee, oral insertor, and anal insertee, and anal insertor they found that the most popular combination was a liking for all of these activities, again indicating greater flexibility than a simple insertee/insertor dichotomy would suggest. When respondents were asked, "If I lived with a lover (or do live with), I would probably make most of the decisions' (Harry and DeVall, 1978b: 112), responses to this item showed no signifi cant association with the four sexual techniques. However, among those who preferred inegalitarian forms of decision making, the associations among the four sexual techniques were consistent with the butch/femme hypothesis. It thus seems that the butch/femme hypothesis, while not completely lacking in empirical support, may hold only for those gay men who bring expectations or values of inegalitarianism to a relationship. Further evidence that the butch/femme hypothesis may hold only for a small minority of gay relationships is reflected in findings from Harry's (1982a: 213) study of 1556 gay men in Chicago who responded by mailback questionnaire. Gay men who rated their hypothetical preferred erotic partners as "very masculine" were about 40 percent more likely to agree that "it is very important for me to look masculine." Thus masculinity, when valued in the self appears to be also valued in erotic partners. Since masculinity of appearance is positively evaluated by many gay men, it is suggested that a butch/butch pattern may be the more dominant pattern.

Equality in Relationships

Peplau and her associates (Peplau, 1981; Peplau and Cochran, 1981) have compared the values and relationship expectations of 128 gay men, 127 lesbians, and 130 unmarried heterosexual men and women. Of their gay male respondents 92 percent said that both partners to a relationship should "have exactly equal say," although only 37 percent of the currently coupled reported that their relationship was exactly equal. Peplau (1981) found that, regardless of sexual orientation, women were somewhat more likely than men to value equality, emotional expressiveness, and similarity of attitudes between partners. Peplau concluded that gender of respon- dent rather than sexual orientation was the major predictor of differences in relationship values, with the exception that heterosexuals were some- what more likely than homosexuals to value sexual exclusivity than gays. Only 13 percent of the coupled lesbians versus 54 percent of the coupled gays had been sexually nonexclusive in the preceding six months.

Peplau and Cochran (1981) also indicate that a large majority of persons value equality in relationships regardless of sex or sexual orienta- tion, although in practice there often may be departures from equality. A common reason for departure from equality in relationships is differential access to resources outside of the relationship (Blood and Wolfe, 1960: 29-30). This also seems to hold in gay relationships, since it has been found that income differences between gay partners are associated with self-reported differences in decision making (Harry and DeVall, 1978b: 99). However, in gay and lesbian relationships such income differences seem to be considerably less than in the case of heterosexual couples. Housepersons in gay relationships are quite rare, and most couples are dual-worker, dual-career units. Harry (1979; 1982b) found that only 1 percent of his Detroit gay respondents and none of his Chicago respondents were economically supported by another man. Since the analogue of a housewife is unusual among gay couples, and typically both parties work, the economic basis for inequality in relationships is virtually absent. Income differentials in gay or lesbian relationships are also reduced due to the fact that both parties are of the same sex and hence likely to be subject to the same degree of sex discrimination in jobs and income. In contrast, working wives in heterosexual couples are likely to earn considerably less than their husbands and hence are more likely to be somewhat economically dependent on them. These two factors — the general absence of housepersons and the approximate similarity of incomes — suggest that gay relationships often may be more egalitarian than heterosexual ones.

A major source of potential inequality in relationships is age difference between partners. Blood (1972: 526) has reported that older partners in heterosexual relationships tend to be dominant in decision making, although the age difference must be fairly large, e.g., 10 or more years, to have an effect. Harry (1982a: 209) also reports that older partners in both past and present gay relationships say they were more likely to make the decisions in the relationship. He summarizes, (1982a: 209): "If a gay relationship is inegalitarian in decision making, it is likely to be one between age-different persons, although age differences predict less well to decision making."

Age-Related Characteristics

The extant data indicate that there is more variability in the age difference between gay partners than among heterosexual couples. While the age difference between heterosexual partners is approximately two years, Harry (1982b) reported the median age difference between gay male partners to be 4.9 years. (This corrects his earlier, erroneously reported figure of zero years; Harry, 1979.) Cotton (1972) also reported age differences between gay partners in a majority of his 36 gay men, but did not indicate the extent of the age difference. Bell and Weinberg (1978: 319) found an age difference of six or more years in 49 percent of their coupled gay male respondents. While Blood (1972: 523) found that 58 percent of his married heterosexual respondents were within three years of their spouses' age, the comparable statistic from Harry's Chicago data is 36 percent among gay partners.

The greater variability of age differences among gay partners may arise for two reasons. First, there are fairly widely agreed upon norms concerning preferred age differences for heterosexual couples while there are no corresponding norms for gay coupies. Second, age segregation in institutions containing large percentages of young heterosexuals in their marrying years (e.g., universities and leisure organizations) may be greater than in the gay world. While the gay world is often young and youth oriented and does display tendencies toward age segregation of settings (Gagnon and Simon, 1973: 149-150; Harry and DeVall, 1978a; Harry, 1974), it does not seem to be as greatly divided into settings for the young and unmarried versus those for the older and married as among heterosexuals. For these reasons, there may be greater leisure-time interaction between age-different partners, and hence greater age differences in subsequent couplings, in the gay world than in the heterosexual world.

Being in a coupled state — whether the couple lives together or not — seems curvilinearly related to age among gay men. Based on their Detroit data, Harry and DeVall (1978b: 85) reported that 35 percent of gay men 18 to 29 years of age had been currently coupled for at least a year; 46 percent of those 30 to 39 and 39 percent of those 40 and older had been coupled for a year. Similar findings were reported from his Chicago data (1982a: 221), with 47 percent of those under 24 years of age being currently coupled, approximately 55 percent of those aged 25 to 40, 44 percent of those aged 41 to 54, and 32 percent of those 55 and older. The higher percentages of currently coupled found in the Chicago data are likely due to the fact that the question for the Detroit data required that the respondent had been going with a partner for at least a year. Saghir and Robins (1973: 56-57) reported a similar curvilinear association between age and current involvement with another man. Bell and Weinberg (1978: 282) found no significant association between age and current involvement, although their measure of association would not have detected a curvilinear association. When respondents are asked whether they were *currently involved with another man*, the percentages were as follows: 51 percent (Harry, 1982a: 221), 59 percent in West Germany (Schafer, 1977), 41 percent (Peplau and Cochran, 1981); *currently involved for at least one year*: 32 percent (Westwood, 1960: 114-115), 40 percent (Harry and DeVall, 1978b: 85); *currently living with a lover*: 31 percent (Robinson et al., 1982); *currently living with a lover among those over 40*: 43 percent (Berger, 1980). The studies suggest that at any given time 40 to 50 percent of gay men are currently involved with someone else, and that being involved is curvilinearly related to age with a peak at about 40 years of age.

While the literature is in substantial agreement on the extent to which gay men may be currently coupled and on the relationship between being coupled and age, one must raise the question of the extent to which these findings may be artifacts of sampling. The principal places from which gay men have been sampled are gay bars, gay organizations, and gay friendship networks (Weinberg and Williams, 1974; Bell and Weinberg, 1978; Harry and DeVall, 1978b; Harry 1982a). Since older gay men are less likely to attend gay bars and clubs (Weinberg and Williams, 1974: 314), they are less likely to be included in the studies of gay men. Also, if one assumes that the age distribution of gay men should approximate that of heterosexual men, it is clear that all of the studies have systematically underrepresented the older age groups. If, as the data suggest, those over 50 are less likely to be coupled, the extent of coupledness may be overestimated in the published data while, if the coupled avoid the typical settings where gay men are sampled, the published data may have underestimated the extent of coupledness.

To explore these contradictory possibilities, the relationship between being currently coupled and going to gay bars, being a member of a gay organization, and having mostly gay friends was explored by Harry in a sample of 1556 gay men located in a variety of settings in the Chicago area (see Harry, 1982a, for a description of sampling procedures). Findings from mailback questionnaires indicated that men currently involved with another man were somewhat less likely to attend gay bars once or more a week (46 percent versus 56 percent) and somewhat more likely to have all or mostly gay friends (54 percent versus 44 percent); they did not differ from the uncoupled on membership in gay organizations. Among the currently coupled, those in relationships of greater duration were less likely to go to gay bars. Of those in relationships of less than a year duration, 57 percent went to gay bars once or more a week; 43 percent of those in relationships of one year to less than five years duration and 35 percent of those in relationships of five or more years duration went to gay bars once or more a week. The Chicago data also show that the curvilinear relationship between age and being coupled is largely confined to those who go to gay bars less than once a week.

The implications of these data appear to be that: (1) The studies of gay men may have underrepresented the frequency of long-term relationships because men in such relationships are less likely to go to bars, older men are less likely to go to bars, and, among the coupled, it is the older who are more likely to be in long-term relationships. (Among the coupled, the percentage who are in relationships of five or more years duration rises from 4 percent of those under 25 years of age to 60 percent of those 45 and over.) (2) The strength of the curvilinear relationship between being coupled and age has been somewhat underestimated in the literature because that relationship is largely confined to the less frequent bar goers, and such men are less likely to be included in surveys. (3) The extent of coupledness among gay men remains uncertain because, although the coupled and especially the long-term coupled are less likely to go to gay bars, the older are both less likely to go to bars and are less likely to be coupled. It is hoped that someday these questions may be answered through the inclusion of a question on sexual orientation in general probability surveys.

Sexual Exclusivity

The literature clearly shows that gay male relationships are considerably less sexually exclusive then heterosexual ones or lesbian relationships. Peplau (1981) found that 46 percent of her coupled gay males had been sexually exclusive during the last six months compared to 87 percent of the lesbian counterparts. Schafer (1977) reported similar findings when comparing West German gay and lesbian couples. Harry and DeVall (1978b: 88) found that a quarter of their coupled gay males had been exclusive during the last year, a finding that supports figures reported by Saghir and Robins (1973: 57). Sexual exclusivity has been found to be negatively related to the duration of a relationship. Harry and DeVall (1978b: 92) found that 46 percent of their coupled gay men in relationships of less than three years duration had been exclusive during the last year versus 16 percent of those in longer-term relationships. The Chicago data replicate this finding and show complete exclusivity to have been the case for 39 percent of persons in relationships of one to less than five year's duration, and 9 percent of those in relationships of five or more years duration. Apparently, exclusivity is more common during the honeymoon stage of gay relationships.

Hoffman (1968: 154-177) has interpreted the common nonexclusivity of gay relationships as a major problem, often leading to jealousy and termination of relationships. However, Warren (1974: 72-76) has suggested that exclusivity may be nonnormative and problematic principally in the heterosexual community. She has suggested that, although it may be characteristic of the honeymoon stage of gay relationships, nonexclusivity often becomes accepted as the most common expectation for "mature" relationships and represents an adjustment to reality. Harry and DeVall (1978b: 91-92) found support for Warren's hypothesis in that in longer-term relationships there was greater agreement between partners on either fidelity or infidelity, while disagreement decreased with length of relationships. Couples in relationships of three or more years duration were divided into three roughly equal groups: those who were agreed on exclusiveness, those who agreed on nonexclusiveness, and those who disagreed. It would seem that since gay couple relationships lack the conventional cultural guidelines that govern heterosexual relationships, they develop in more diverse directions and exclusivity may be either approved or disapproved. Since Peplau (1981) found that sexually exclusive coupled gay men did not differ from nonexclusives on measures of relationship intimacy or satisfaction, both of these adaptations seem workable.

Perhaps the major problem encountered by gay couples is reaching an agreement regarding exclusivity. Silverstein (1981: 140) has suggested that "at some point in the life of every gay couple, the monogamy battle will be fought." Dividing gay men into "excitement seekers" and "home builders" 1981: 113-138), he suggests that gay relationships are more workable when both parties to a relationship are of the same type, since their eventual choice of lifestyle is more likely to flow from their personal predispositions than from the imposition of the heterosexual cultural norm of monogamy. An emphasis on exclusivity by one partner when paired with a partner seeking excitement may be perceived to be too constraining to the latter, who would prefer an open relationship. Some suggestive data consistent with Silverstein's hypothesis have been reported by Harry and Lovely (1979), who found that those who formerly had been coupled for at least a year — "the divorced" — were more likely to favor sexual exclusivity than the currently coupled or the single, thus suggesting that their emphasis on exclusivity may have been a barrier in their own couple-forming attempts. This group was also the only group for which there was a significant association between intimacy scores and the item "gay lovers should be completely faithful to each other." Thus it may be that an emphasis on exclusivity, possibly borrowed from the heterosexual marriage model, may interfere with the relationships of gay men.

Gay Fathers

Because a percentage of gays have been heterosexually married, many gay men are also fathers. The percentages of gays who have ever married, as reported in the literature, are: 25 percent (Dank, 1972); 18 percent (Saghir and Robins, 1973: 11); 17 percent (Weinberg and Williams, 1974: 128); 20 percent (Harry and DeVall's Detroit data); 19 percent (Bell and Weinberg, 1978: 374); 16 percent (Harry, 1982a: 42); 14 percent (Robinson et al., 1982). Thus it is safe to say that about 20 percent of gay men have been heterosexually married. Of these marriages, about half (52 percent) resulted in children (Bell and Weinberg, 1978: 391); a similar percentage (56 percent) was found for lesbians who have been married (Bell and Weinberg, 1978: 391). In a few cases children have been adopted by gay or lesbian couples through marginally legitimate channels (Miller, 1979).

The reasons that gay men have married include a lack of awareness of their own homosexuality, a belief that their homosexuality was a peripheral part of their lives, or an assumption that marriage would help them overcome their homosexuality (Dank, 1972). In a third of the cases it appears that the spouse was aware of the gay man's homosexuality before the marriage but believed that the marriage would eliminate the husband's homosexuality (Bell and Weinberg, 1978: 386). The marriages, which lasted three or four years (Bell and Weinberg, 1978: 388), were typically full of problems, especially sexual problems. In over half of the cases the men fantasized about other men during sexual relations with the wife (Bell and Weinberg, 1978: 384). The majority of gay men who either have been or currently are married tend to give negative descriptions of these marriages (Ross, 1971). Reporting on thirteen currently married gay men, Ross (1971) found many of these marriages filled with resentment and bitterness over the infrequency of sexual relations, the nonexclusivity of the husband due to his search for male sexual partners, and the feeling that the husband had deceived the wife at time of marriage.

During the course of the marriage, as the husband's need for sexual fulfillment through sex with other men became more conscious and pressing, most resorted for a period to furtive sexual encounters in a variety of places. Many such encounters are described in Humphrey's classic study, *Tearoom Trade* (1970). Of the men who had had sex in restrooms, 54 percent were heterosexually married (1970: 112). This period of their lives was one in which the husbands engaged in quick sex at the sleazy periphery of the gay world, hated themselves for doing it, and lied to their wives about where they had been and what they had been doing. Men in occupations permitting greater freedom in their movements and control over their time commitments appear to have managed this phase with less worry and more grace. Movement from this lifestyle to an acceptance of one's own homosexuality, becoming socially active in the gay world, and, usually, getting a divorce, was motivated principally by coming to see gay men and homosexuality in a more positive light and falling in love with another man (Miller, 1978).

All of the forty gay fathers interviewed by Miller (1979) feared disclosure of their homosexuality to their children and most feared disclosure to their wives. When they did disclose to their wives, the wives, after a period of initial shock, sometimes agreed to arrangements that permitted the marriage to continue while allowing the husband to pursue homosexual activities outside of the marriage (Bozett, 1981). These included allowing a "night out with the boys," understanding that the husband would only have sex with other men when in other cities, and an occasional *menage à trois* (Bozett, 1981; Ross, 1971). While Bozett (1981), reporting on eighteen gay fathers, has described these arrangements as mutually consensual "permission giving," they also appear to have been last-minute attempts to keep a marriage that was near collapse together. Virtually all of the gay fathers studied stated that the principal reason they remained in their marriages as long as they did was because they loved their children (Miller, 1979; Bozett, 1980).

Those gay fathers who disclosed to their children, either before or after a divorce, reported that, after the initial surprise, the children generally responded quite acceptingly. Although the numbers involved in the various studies are small, there is the suggestion that acceptance by female children is more forthcoming than by male children. Both Miller (1978) and Bozett (1980) report that relationships with children tended to improve after disclosure. "Children who showed the greatest acceptance were those who, prior to full disclosure, were gradually introduced by their parents to homosexuality through meeting gay family friends, reading about it, and discussing the topic informally with parents" (Miller, 1979).

While a number of gay men are fathers, the large majority of these fathers do not retain custody of the children at the time of divorce. This arises because the couple often decides that the children are to live with the mother, the courts have traditionally preferred to give custody to the mother, and, when custody is contested and the father's sexual orientation is an issue in the case, gay fathers rarely win custody (Maddox, 1982). In contested custody cases where a parent's sexual orientation is an issue, lesbian mothers win in about 15 percent of the cases with gay fathers winning less frequently. Indeed, the courts are so averse to giving custody to gay fathers that the contested issue is usually visiting rights while for lesbian mothers the issue is usually custody (Hitchens, 1980).

Another way in which gay men sometimes become fathers is through becoming foster fathers. During the 1970s, there arose a number of gay foster homes in some large cities (New York Times, May 7, 1974: 47). Gay adolescents who had either run away from home or been thrown out by parents after learning of the child's homosexuality have been occasionally placed with gay male couples. Of course, the foster parents have been carefully screened to eliminate the inappropriately motivated. Such placements, typically done by private agencies, often encounter a number of legal problems since the natural parents usually retain legal custody. Such placements seem a promising development since gay adolescents often do not fare well in institutions for juveniles or in heterosexual foster homes. For some young gays the relationship with the gay foster father may be the first positive relationship with an adult male in their life.

Lesbian Couples

Lesbian partners are somewhat more likely to live together than are gay male partners (Bell and Weinberg, 1978: 319; Schafer, 1977; Cotton, 1975) and to value the importance of living together (Bell and Weinberg, 1978: 322). Approximately three-quarters of lesbian couples live together compared with somewhat more than half of all gay male couples. Lesbian couples are also more likely to be sexually exclusive than are gay couples (Peplau et al., 1978; Peplau, 1981; Cotton, 1975). Exclusivity seems to be characteristic of 75 to 85 percent of the cases. The differences in degree of exclusivity between lesbians and gay men have been attributed by Simon and Gagnon to their respective gender role socialization and are said to parallel the differences in exclusivity among heterosexual males and females (Kinsey et al., 1948: 585; Hunt, 1974: 257-258; Kinsey et al.,

1953: 435-438). Males are socialized to engage in sexual behaviors both with and without affection while women are more expected to combine the two. As a result, when two men enter a partnership, nonexclusiveness can be expected, while when two women enter a relationship, exclusiveness could be expected. Aside from exclusivity, men and women do not seem to differ in the values, e.g., romanticism, that they bring to a relationship (Peplau, 1981). Laner (1977) reported great similarity among student samples of gay men, lesbians, heterosexual men, and heterosexual women in what they expect in a partner. The great majority (89 to 92 percent) of all four groups wanted a permanent partner with little difference among groups. It thus seems that the principal sex difference is not in relationship values but in how sexuality is combined with those values.

The butch/femme hypothesis has also been applied to lesbian couples (Jensen, 1974). While a small minority of lesbian couples do play gender roles, role playing is relatively rare (Tanner, 1978: 99-101; Ponse, 1978: 114-116; Wolf, 1979: 49-43). The division of household tasks is typically done by turns or by talent and both parties to the relationship are usually employed. Both Ponse and Wolf report that role playing seems to have been more common in the 1950s and 1960s and is somewhat more common among older lesbian couples. This seems supported by the one study that found gender-typed division of household tasks in the large majority of the 17 couples studied (Jensen, 1974). It should be noted that these seventeen couples were interviewed in the mid-1960s and the majority were Mormons living in Salt Lake City and Denver, highly gender-conservative environments.

Role playing as a relationship style has become quite unpopular in lesbian circles, probably due to the fact that a large percentage of lesbian women became affiliated with the women's movement of the late 1960s and the 1970s (Wolf, 1979: 85). One goal of the lesbian/feminist movement has been to create identities as women rather than in relationship to men. Toward this end, one fairly large segment of the lesbian world advocates and practices separatism from men. Such separatism sometimes extends to advocating that lesbian mothers should give up their male children to the father, although the voluntary practice of this is rare (Wolf, 1979: 156-158). The rise of the women's movement and of feminist theory has had the effect of creating a quite varied spectrum of lesbian circles, ranging from traditional and often closeted role players on the "right" to lesbian/feminists in the "center" to lesbian/feminist/separatists on the "left." At the left may be found communal households containing one to three pairs of lovers plus a few single women (Wolf, 1979: 98-101). Household boundaries tend to coincide with political boundaries and having the proper political credentials may be a condition for admission to a household.

While gay couples tend to interact within such gay institutions as the gay bar, the gay church, and gay organizations, lesbian couples tend to live within social networks of lesbians, although there is some overlap between the gay world and that of lesbians (Ponse, 1978: 89-90; Tanner, 1978: 66-70). The lesbian bar plays a much smaller role in the world of lesbians than does the gay bar in the gay world (Tanner, 1978: 67-68). The principal forms of socializing in the lesbian world include inviting other lesbian couples to one's home, attendance at lesbian coffee houses and theater, and participation in women's organizations. The lesbian bar seems somewhat more significant in the lives of unattached women (Tanner, 1978: 67; Cotton, 1975), although some lesbians disparage lesbian bars as places for socializing because of the "role-playing, fighting, or drug use" that may occur there (Chafetz et al., 1974). Since roughly three quarters of lesbians are currently coupled compared to 40 to 50 percent of gay men (Bell and Weinberg, 1978: 318; Schafer, 1977; Harry and DeVall, 1978b: 85; Peplau and Amaro, 1982), the social world of lesbians tends to be a world of couples whereas the world of gay men is one of singles *and* couples.

Lesbians tend to meet their partners through lesbian friendship networks (Tanner, 1978: 66-71). There subsequently follows a period of courtship lasting from one to nine months. In contrast, the courtship period for gay men is considerably truncated and may be preceded by sexual relations. Thus among lesbians a sexual relationship usually arises out of a developing affectional relationship while among gay men affection may develop out of a sexual relationship.

The literature is inconsistent regarding whether lesbian or gay relationships last longer. While (Schafer (1977) found that lesbian relationships last longer than gay ones, Bell and Weinberg (1978: 320) reported that 38 percent of their currently coupled gay men were in relationships of four or more years duration compared with 30 percent of the comparable lesbian respondents. Saghir and Robins (1973: 225) found no difference in the length of gay and lesbian relationships. For both groups, the average length of a relationship appears to be approximately two to three years (Peplau and Amaro, 1982). It appears that the gender difference in relationship longevity has been exaggerated and that a principal difference between the two groups is in the amount of one's life that is spent in relationships (i.e., the between-partner time spent outside of relationships seems to be shorter for women). This interpretation is supported by Bell and Weinberg's (1978: 315) finding that among lesbians romantic involvement with another woman was the most commonly mentioned reason for the breakup of their first affair, while this reason was fourth among gay men (29 percent versus 14 percent). Hence it seems that more lesbians go directly from one relationship to another. It should be noted that the studies of lesbian couples, even more so than for gay couples, have been largely based on samples of persons in their twenties and thirties and that the duration of lesbian relationships in general may be greater than is estimated from these studies.

Satisfaction in lesbian relationships has been found to be positivel associated with equality in decision making (Peplau et al., 1982). This als seems to hold for gay relationships. Of the currently involved gay me studied by Harry (1982a), 72 percent of those who said that decisions wer made equally reported that they and their partner got along "very well, compared to 50 percent of those who said that they made the decision and 43 percent of those who said that the partner made the decisions Being low in decision-making power in lesbian relationships is, in turn associated with having less education and less income than one's partne (Caldwell and Peplau, 1982). Relationship satisfaction has also bee found to correlate strongly ($r = +.63$) with the expectation that the curren lesbian relationship would continue for another five years and with equal ity of emotional involvement (Peplau et al., 1982). Factors negativel associated with relationship satisfaction include differences in interests conflicting attitudes about sex, conflicting attitudes about exclusivity, an desire for independence (Peplau et al., 1982). No significant association were found between satisfaction and scores on a Sex-Role Traditionalism Scale, age, number of previous relationships, education, and the extent o closetedness. While satisfaction was not found to be related to closeted ness, it would be useful to explore whether differences in closetednes between partners may create problems for a couple. Since few lesbians o gay men are totally uncloseted toward all the heterosexuals with whom they may interact, differing degrees of closetedness could be expected t create tensions in a relationship.

In recent years there appear to have been some changes in lesbia relationships induced by the women's movement. As an expression o indentification with women, a number of bisexual or heterosexual wome have come to have affairs with lesbian women (Ponse, 1978: 122-124) Sometimes referred to as "political lesbians," these women are ofte distrusted in lesbian circles because there is always the chance that th political lesbian may end a relationship and return to men or to the husbands. "Political gay men" seem unheard of, although a few migh exist. Another effect of the women's movement has been some decline i sexual exclusivity and an increase in "cruising," i.e., the search for brie sexual encounters at lesbian bars and by younger lesbians (Lewis, 1979 178-180). Since much feminist writing is directed toward the elimination o gender roles and the traditionally structured inegalitarian heterosexua family, this sometimes is extended in lesbian writing to include the elimina tion of romanticism and monogamy (Lewis, 1979: 168-171), customs tha are seen to hold women in emotional dependency. Among lesbians acceptance of nonexclusivity in relationships tends to be associated wit less traditional attitudes toward women (Peplau et al., 1978). It thu appears that the nonexclusivity and the cruising found among gay me have made an appearance on the lesbian scene.

esbian Mothers

Lesbian households are considerably more likely to contain children han are gay households. This is largely due to the fact that a higher ercentage of lesbians have been heterosexually married: approximately ne-fifth of gay men have been married versus one-third of lesbians (Bell nd Weinberg, 1978: 374; Saghir and Robins, 1973: 255; Cotton, 1975; chafer, 1977). Also contributing to the greater presence of children in esbian households is the tradition of the courts awarding custody to the nother *as long as the mother's homosexuality is not an issue in the divorce* Maddox, 1982). A further reason for the greater presence of children is nat lesbians tend to "come out" a few years later than gay men. While gay nen usually come out during late adolescence at approximately 18 or 19 ears of age (Dank, 1971; Harry and DeVall, 1978b: 65; Saghir and Robins, 1973: 67), lesbians do so during their early 20s (Schafer, 1977; aghir and Robins, 1973: 232). One effect of this is that lesbians are at risk f marriage for a longer time than are gay men, particularly at the age when large percentage of their heterosexual peers are getting married.

Courts give two primary reasons for their reluctance to grant custody or ven visiting rights to lesbian mothers and gay fathers. First is the possibility nat the children might become homosexual if raised in a lesbian or gay ousehold. The extant data show that there is little ground for this concern. ireen (1978) examined the erotic fantasies of 37 children raised in lesbian, ay male, and transsexual households and found all of the children, with ne possible exception, to be heterosexual. Hoffer (1981) examined the >y preferences of 20 children of lesbian mothers and 20 children of eterosexual mothers and found no differences between the two groups of hildren. (Toy preferences seem to be the best childhood indicator of future dult gender atypicality (Green, 1976; Bell et al., 1981: 75-76, 147; Vhitam, 1980). From the reports of 40 gay fathers on their 21 sons and 27 aughters who were old enough for their sexual orientations to be as- essed, it was found that one of the sons and three of the daughters were omosexual (Miller, 1979). Hotvedt and Mandel (1982) compared the 56 hildren of 50 lesbian mothers with the 48 children of 40 heterosexual ngle mothers while controlling on ages of mother and children, race, ncome, time since separation, education, and religion. For boys, there as no difference in toy preferences, with boys of both groups consistently hoosing masculine toys. The daughters of lesbian mothers chose some- hat less feminine toys than did the daughters of heterosexual mothers, ut they did not choose masculine ones. These data suggest no dispropor- onate amount of homosexuality among the children of homosexual arents, although more research clearly needs to be done.

The second concern of the courts is that the children of homosexual arents will be harrassed by others because of their parents. Children in three of the thirteen families studied by Green (1978) had been teased by other children, e.g., "Your mother is a lezzie," "Your mother is a queer," "homoson." However, Bruce Voeller, former president of the National Gay Task Force and a person whose homosexuality has been quite visible through appearances on numerous television shows, reported that his children who live with him have never been teased about their father (Voeller and Walters, 1978). Of the eighteen gay fathers studied by Bozett (1980), one reported that his child had been teased. Hotvedt and Mandel (1982) reported from interviews with the children of lesbian and heterosexual single mothers that the two groups of children did not differ in their popularity with other children of either sex. Interviews with the mothers on the children's popularity also showed no differences.

Like gay fathers, lesbian mothers often advise their children to be guarded in providing information about the home life to neighbors and school teachers (Wolf, 1979: 153). It appears that in those cases in which a gay father has disclosed his gayness to a child a common tactic has been for the father to suggest that the child practice discretion (Bozett, 1980). For example, the father's live-in lover is referred to as an "uncle" in the presence of other children. The evidence suggests that, while the lives of the children of gay and lesbian parents are not problem free, harrassment is not common and seems typically manageable.

Because of the court's strong propensity not to accord custody of children, and especially male children, to lesbian mothers, these mothers are often fearful of losing their children and attempt to conceal their homosexuality from ex-husbands, grandparents, welfare workers, landlords, neighbors, and school personnel (Pagelow, 1980). In a study of 20 lesbian and 23 nonlesbian single mothers, Pagelow (1980) reported that lesbian mothers may be somewhat more likely to live in houses rather than apartments since the former housing permits greater privacy. They were also more likely to be self-employed, thus permitting a greater measure of both privacy and freedom.

There has been some question about whether male children are out of place or unwelcome in lesbian circles. Hall (1978) described a situation in which persons planning a mother's day celebration for lesbians and their children questioned the appropriateness of allowing male children to participate and yet hesitated to exclude them. However, it seems that lesbian mothers are usually aware of the needs of their male children and are more likely than single heterosexual mothers to be concerned about providing adult male figures for their boys (Kirkpatrick et al., 1981). Nungesser (1980) reported that 80 percent of the male children of lesbian mothers had adult male figures involved in their lives, including a number of gay men. Some have suggested that lesbian mothers may, because of their relatively unique situations, bend over backwards to assure that male children have exposure to adults of both sexes. It does seem fairly clear that lesbian mothers in general attempt to raise their children in nonsexist ways and to bring them up without the constraints of traditional gender roles (Kirkpatrick et al., 1981: Wolf, 1979: 152).

Kirpatrick et al., (1981) compared ten boys and ten girls living with lesbian mothers to a similar sample of boys and girls living with single heterosexual mothers and found no differences with regard to emotional disturbance, toy preferences, or gender identifications. While they did find a high level of problems in both groups of children, they attributed this to the fact that both groups had experienced parental divorces in recent years. As in the case of stepfamilies, children of lesbian mothers may require a period of adjusting to the mother's lover (Hall, 1978; Lewis, 1979: 120). The scanty literature suggests that most such children come to accept and love the mother's lover, although Lewis (1977) found in a study of 21 children of lesbian mothers that older adolescent boys reacted negatively to their mother's homosexuality.

Future Research and Policy Questions

Although much remains to be explored, the studies do permit a few policy suggestions. Sometimes judges have imposed on a lesbian mother the condition that she can have custody only if she does not live with, or sometimes even associate with, her lover (Hall, 1978). This condition may do serious damage to the household functioning, since two-income and two-adult households typically have superior financial resources and more personpower for child care arrangements. Judges thereby condemn the household to poverty. Similarly, gay fathers have usually been denied custody and often visiting rights. Yet since the extant evidence negates the hypothesis that the father's sexual orientation will rub off on the children, and suggests that parent/child relations may improve once the father discloses to the child, such court actions seem both to deprive the child of a father and to tell the child that his or her father is bad.

Although there have been a number of attempts by gay and lesbian couples to obtain legal marriages, no court to date has recognized such unions (Rivera, 1979). The acquisition of legal marriages by gays and lesbians would bring with it the advantages of symbolic equality, spouse social security benefits, spouse health insurance benefits, lower car insurance, family membership in various organizations, and inheritance rights. In the case in which there are children in the lesbian or gay household, the lack of these benefits also accrues to these children. However, there are also disadvantages to the acquisition of legal marital status. The termination of the relationship would obligate the parties to undergo the bother and expense of legal and financial disentanglements. A legal marital status would also grant to the state a right to regulate relationships that are essentially private, and a major thrust of the gay/lesbian movement has been to get the state out of the bedroom.

Because of the limited research to date, many questions remain to be answered. If, as Peplau and Amaro (1982) suggest, lesbian relationships typically last approximately three years, they can be characterized by a pattern of serial monogamy. Since most children in lesbian households have already experienced a heterosexual divorce, what is the effect on the child of a subsequent series of homosexual divorces? Do male children in lesbian households feel comfortable living in social circles so heavily populated with women? Does the heterosexual model of monogamy and sexual exclusivity create problems when gay men attempt to pattern their relationships after it? Has the advent of gay/lesbian liberation had the effect of lowering the age at which homosexual persons come out and thus reduced the frequency with which homosexual persons attempt heterosexual marriages? It is hoped that as these questions and others are answered, counselors to lesbians and gays of the future will be able to give more accurate and useful information to their counselees and parents, and relatives of gays and lesbians will be able to relate to the latter in a more positive manner.

References

BELL, A. and M. WEINBERG (1978) Homosexualities. New York: Simon & Schuster.
———— and S. HAMMERSMITH (1981) Sexual Preference. Bloomington: Indiana University Press.
BERGER, R. (1980) "Psychological adaptation of the older homosexual male." Journal of Homosexuality 5: 161-175.
BLOOD, R. (1972) The Family. New York: Macmillan.
———— and D. WOLFE (1960) Husbands and Wives. New York: Macmillan.
BOZETT, F. (1981) "Gay fathers: evolution of the gay-father identity." American Journal of Orthopsychiatry 51: 552-559.
———— (1980) "Gay fathers: how and why they disclose their homosexuality to their children." Family Relations 29: 173-179.
CALDWELL, M. and L. PEPLAU (1982) "The balance of power in lesbian relationships." Sex Roles.
CHAFETZ, J., P. SAMPSON, P. BECK, and J. WEST (1974) "A study of homosexual women." Social Work 19: 714-723.
COTTON, W. (1975) "Social and sexual relationships of lesbians." Journal of Sex Research 11: 139-148.
———— (1972) "Role playing substitutions among male homosexuals." Journal of Sex Research 8: 310-323.
DANK, B. (1972) "Why homosexuals marry women." Medical Aspects of Human Sexuality 6: 14-23.
———— (1971) "Coming out in the gay world." Psychiatry 34: 180-197.
GAGNON, J. and W. SIMON (1973) Sexual Conduct. Chicago: Aldine.
GREEN, R. (1978) "Sexual identity of 37 children raised by homosexual or transsexual parents." American Journal of Psychiatry 135: 692-697.
———— (1976) "One hundred ten feminine and masculine boys." Archives of Sexual Behavior 5: 425-426.
HAIST, M. and J. HEWITT (1974) "The butch-fem dichotomy in male homosexual behavior." Journal of Sex Research 10: 68-75.
HALL, M. (1978) "Lesbian families: cultural and clinical issues." Social Work 23: 380-385.
HARRY, J. (1982a) Gay Children Grown Up: Gender Culture and Gender Deviance. New York: Praeger.
———— (1982b) "Decision making and age differences among gay couples." Journal of Homosexuality.

—— (1979) "The marital liaisons of gay men." Family Coordinator 28: 622-629.
—— (1974) "Urbanization and the gay life." Journal of Sex Research 10: 238-247.
—— and W. DeVALL (1978a) "Age and sexual culture among homosexually oriented males." Archives of Sexual Behavior 3: 199-209.
—— (1978b) The Social Organization of Gay Males. New York: Praeger.
HARRY, J. and R. LOVELY (1979) "Gay marriages and communities of sexual orientation." Alternative Lifestyles 2: 177-200.
HITCHENS, D. (1980) "Social attitudes, legal standards, and personal trauma in child custody cases." Journal of Homosexuality 5: 89-95.
HOFFER, B. (1981) "Children's acquisition of sex-role behavior in lesbian-mother families." American Journal of Orthopsychiatry 51: 536-544.
HOFFMAN, M. (1968) The Gay World. New York: Bantam.
HOTVEDT, M. and J. MANDEL (1982) "Children of lesbian mothers," in J. Weinrich and B. Paul (eds.) Homosexuality: Social, Psychological, and Biological Issues. Beverly Hills, CA: Sage.
HUMPHREYS, L. (1970) Tearoom Trade. Chicago: Aldine.
HUNT, M. (1974) Sexual Behavior in the 1970s. New York: Dell.
JENSEN, M. (1974) "Sexual differentiation in female quasi-marital unions." Journal of Marriage and the Family 36: 360-367.
KINSEY, A., W. POMEROY, and C. MARTIN (1948) Sexual Behavior in the Human Male. Philadelphia: W. B. Saunders.
—— and P. GEBHARD (1953) Sexual Behavior in the Human Female. Philadelphia: W. B. Saunders.
KIRKPATRICK, M., C. SMITH, and R. ROY (1981) "Lesbian mothers and their children." American Journal of Orthopsychiatry 51: 545-551.
LANER, M. (1977) "Permanent partner priorities: gay and straight." Journal of Homosexuality 3: 21-39.
LEWIS, K. (1977) "Lesbian mother survey results." Boston: Gay Community News (September 6): 7.
LEWIS S. (1979) Sunday's Women. Boston: Beacon.
LEZNOFF, M. and W. WESTLEY (1956) "The homosexual community." Social Problems 3: 257-263.
MADDOX, B. (1982) "Homosexual parents." Psychology Today 16: 62-69.
MILLER, B. (1979) "Unpromised paternity: the life-styles of gay fathers," pp. 240-252 in M. Levine (ed.) Gay Men. New York: Harper & Row.
—— (1978) "Adult sexual resocialization." Alternative Lifestyles 1: 207-232.
NUNGESSER, L. (1980) "Theoretical bases for research on the acquisition of social sex-roles by children of lesbian mothers." Journal of Homosexuality 5: 177-187.
PAGELOW, M. (1980) "Heterosexual and lesbian single mothers." Journal of Homosexuality 5: 189-204.
PEPLAU, L. A. (1981) "What homosexuals want in relationships." Psychology Today 15: 28-38.
—— and H. AMARO (1982) "Understanding lesbian relationships," in J. Weinrich and W. Paul (eds.) Homosexuality: Social, Psychological, and Biological Issues. Beverly Hills, CA: Sage.
PEPLAU, L. A. and S. COCHRAN (1981) "Value orientations in the intimate relationships of gay men." Journal of Homosexuality 6: 1-19.
—— K. ROOK, and C. PADESKY (1978) "Loving women: attachment and autonomy in lesbian relationships." Journal of Social Issues 34: 7-27.
PEPLAU, L. A., M. HAMILTON, and C. PADESKY (1982) "Satisfaction in lesbian relationships." Journal of Homosexuality.
POMEROY, W. (1972) Dr. Kinsey and the Institute for Sex Research. New York: Harper & Row.
PONSE, B. (1978) Identities in the Lesbian World. Westport, CT: Greenwood.
REISS, A. (1961) "The social integration of queers and peers." Social Problems 9: 102-119.
RIVERA, R. (1979) "Our straight-laced judges: the legal position of homosexual persons in the United States." Hastings Law Journal 30: 799-955.

ROBINSON, B., P. SKEEN, C. HOBSON, and M. HERRMAN (1982) "Gay men's and women's perceptions of early family life and their relationships with parents." Family Relations 31: 79-83.

ROSS, L. (1971) "Mode of adjustment of married homosexuals." Social Problems 18: 385-393.

SAGHIR, M. and E. ROBINS (1973) Male and Female Homosexuality. Baltimore: Williams & Wilkins.

SCHAFER, S. (1977) "Sociosexual behavior in male and female homosexuals." Archives of Sexual Behavior 6: 355-364.

SILVERSTEIN, C. (1981) Man to Man. New York: William Morrow.

SIMON, W., and J. GAGNON (1967) "Femininity in the heterosexual community." Social Problems 15: 212-221.

TANNER, D. (1978) The Lesbian Couple. Lexington, MA: D.C. Heath.

TRIPP, C.A. (1975) The Homosexual Matrix. New York: Signet.

VOELLER, B. and J. WALTERS (1978) "Gay Fathers." Family Coordinator 27: 149-157.

WARREN, C. (1974) Identity and Community in the Gay World. New York: John Wiley.

WEINBERG, M. and C. WILLIAMS (1974) Male Homosexuals. New York: Viking.

WESTWOOD, G. (1960) A Minority. London: Longmans.

WHITAM, F. (1980) "The prehomosexual male child in three societies: the United States, Guatamala, Brazil." Archives of Sexual Behavior 9: 87-99.

WOLF, D. (1979) The Lesbian Community. Berkeley: University of California Press.

CHAPTER 11

Radical Community: Contemporary Communes and Intentional Communities

GERRY BRUDENELL

Florida State University

Living groups are enduring, changing, purposive, and various. From social experiments to "imperfect alternatives" (Wernick, 1974) to "nontraditional family forms" (Macklin, 1980) to "family by choice" (Raimey, 1979), options for group living exist. Rose, a woman living in an intentional community, describes one choice:

> When I first moved out to the land [in 1974] . . . I was filled with pioneer spirit. We lived without water and electricity in a small shelter for a few months. . . . An overriding feeling that I experience today is that our community is a healthy one. . . . We are a land co-operative. . . . This fosters a feeling of equality. Thus, there is no hierarchy and there are no leaders. . . . There is a feeling . . . that we are all powerful, capable people. . . . Often we have worked together on the building [of homes] or have included our neighbor's works of art and craft in them. There is an easy flow from one household to another because of this and our children have the sense that the whole community really is their home. . . . I have found that we need not fear private property, individuality and diversity in community. Rather, these aspects lead to a wholeness, an organic building process that fosters stability in a very rich life [Van Oss, 1980: 26].

The lifestyle of Rose and other communitarians helps to focus this review. To better understand that lifestyle, it is necessary to establish a terminology to describe the elements of radical community. Radical community, a lifestyle not chosen by most Americans, has goals compatible with those of more traditional families. Persons not attracted to radical communities may adapt their lifestyles to experience some of the benefits discovered by families working together in community. A look to the future suggests that families acting in community may better adapt their lives to our evolving society than those who do not.

Diversity of Terminology

The variety of terms used by social scientists to refer to radical communities reflects the diversity in types of living groups. Labels for members include "communalists" (Dammers, 1974), "freaks" (Jerome, 1974), "communitarians" (Zablocki, 1980), and "communards" (Berger, 1981). Group-living households have also been variously labeled: "new extended family" (Raimey, 1979), "multi-adult" (Ramey, 1976), and "multi-lateral marriage" (Constantine and Constantine, 1973). Raimey (1979) cites other terms frequently used in the literature: cooperative household, communal household, collective household, shared household, hippie crash pad, alternative family, commune, and intentional community. These same ventures may also appear in the public records under such designations as nonprofit corporation, business, church, or family. In the literature, the terms "communes" (Berger, 1981; Kanter, 1972; Zablocki, 1980) and "intentional communities" (Bouvard, 1975; Johnson and Deisher, 1973; Raimey, 1979) are frequently interchanged and appear to encompass many of the attributes of the other terms. Thus no distinctive terminology has yet evolved, probably due to the changing nature of terminology and the lack of research done on intentional communities.

Some working definitions have been attempted. Zablocki (1980) defines *commune* as any group of five or more adults, plus any children, who live together by choice, indefinitely, with an ideological goal. To avoid including monastic communities, Zablocki studied only communes that had both sexes or one sex with children. While Zablocki (1980) does not refer to "intentional communities" specifically, his category of cooperative communes hints at such a distinction, as does Johnson and Deisher's (1973) description of communal environments. Bouvard (1975) reports that in the 1950s the Federation of Intentional Communities defined *intentional community* as three families (or five individuals) with shared or adjacent housing. Rural examples are outgrowths of the back-to-the-land movement of the 1960s.

The major distinctions between communes and intentional communities appear to be whether or not the locus of control lies with the individual household or with the community as a whole (Macklin, 1982), and in the extent to which monies are pooled (Conover, 1975). Commune members place the living community ahead of the nuclear family unit and decisions are made as a total community group. In contrast, members of intentional communities, although they see themselves as members of an identifiable group, live in individual households; the decisions that affect household functioning are made within that unit. Conover (1975) observes that in a commune, incomes and expenditures are "melded" into a "common purse," but in an intentional community there is "double" accounting with both common community and separate household economies.

Still another factor of definition is interpreting the essence of family. Sociologists usually define communes as communities that are usually exclusive alternatives to the nuclear family (Adams, 1980). However, persons living in radical communities consider their households as families (Berger, 1981; Jerome, 1974), whether in a commune that functions as a family (Raimey, 1979; Wernick, 1974; Zablocki, 1980), or in an intentional community that is an interactive collection of variant family forms (Brudenell, 1982; Kanter, 1972).

Research on Radical Communities

Among radical communities, scholars report and research communes more often than intentional communities. These writers describe antecedents to contemporary communal living from the first century A.D. (Mayer, 1978; Zablocki, 1980) through the nineteenth century (Bestor, 1950; Kanter, 1972) and the twentieth century (Bouvard, 1975; Zablocki, 1980). This review focuses on contemporary radical communities studied within North America during the past decade. It is drawn from studies of the following populations: West Coast communes by Berger et al. (1972); 20 intentional communities by Johnson and Deisher (1973); 30 urban communes by Levine et al. (1973); numerous intentional communities by Bouvard (1975); 35 urban/suburban communal households by Kanter and her students (Jaffe and Kanter, 1976; Kanter, et al., 1975; Weisberg, 1977); 50 urban communal households by Raimey (1979); 156 nonconventional families (54 communal) of the UCLA interdisciplinary Family Styles Project (Eiduson and Alexander, 1978; Eiduson, 1980, 1981; Weisner and Martin, 1979); 60 urban communes by Zablocki and his associates (1980). Additionally, Berger's (1981) eight-year ethnographic study of one rural commune offers a comprehensive look at communal evolution.

Data for these studies were typically obtained through questionnaires, personal interviews, and participant observation. The advantage of this approach was the accumulation of voluminous qualitative reports of communal life, useful for the generation of hypotheses. The disadvantage was that the data are not comparable through statistical analyses, with the exceptions of the projects led by Eiduson, Kanter, and Zablocki.

Attempts to classify communal groups have been made many times (Berger et al., 1972; Bouvard, 1975; Jerome, 1974; Kanter, 1972; Raimey, 1979). Zablocki (1980), while compiling data for his historical review of

TABLE 11.1   Eight Types of Commune Ideologies

Categories of Attention	Strategic Philosophy	
	Consciousness Oriented	Action Oriented
Spiritual locus	Eastern (22)[a]	Christian (15)
Individual locus	Psychological (9)	Rehabilitational (4)
Community locus	Cooperative (16)	Alternative family (11)
Society locus	Countercultural (29)	Political (14)

SOURCE: Adapted from Zablocki (1980: 205, 208, 209).

a. Numbers in parentheses indicate numbers of communes studied.

communal life and the results from studying 120 communes, developed a categorical system so comprehensive that it merits presentation here.

Zablocki grouped the communes he studied by their (1) strategic philosophy (i.e., whether primarily reflective and consciousness raising or action oriented) and (2) locus of attention (i.e., whether primarily focused on the spirit, the self, the commune, or the secular society). This classification scheme resulted in eight types of commune ideologies (see Table 11.1).

Zablocki found the most pronounced differences between religious (Eastern and Christian) communes and secular (psychological, rehabilitational, cooperative, alternative-family, countercultural, and political) communes. The distinction between consciousness-raising and action-oriented groups did not appear as significant. Considerable overlapping of categories was noted. Ten of the communes were closely associated with two of the categories, and an additional thirty, though clearly associated with one category, had at least one element of another.

According to Zablocki's classification, the *Eastern Communes* derive their beliefs primarily from the cultural traditions of India, Tibet, and Japan, Native American religions, and astrology. Each pays homage to a future-oriented guru, and followers are subjected to a severely disciplined life often symbolized by distinctive clothing or markings. *Christian Communes* are not as neatly grouped. Members focus on reviving the early Christian virtues of love, honesty, and forgiveness, and pursue personal salvation through Christ, who is seen as the ultimate guru.

Psychological Communes tend to have members who have had extensive experience in a variety of settings, and who experiment with the use of drugs, therapies, mystical practices, and nonconventional sexual relationships. *Rehabilitational Communes* are therapeutic groups of former drug addicts, prostitutes, or criminals. Compared to other categories, members of these communes have the least contact with mysticism, individual psychotherapy, political radicalism, and sexual experimentation. *Coopera-*

ive Communes facilitate the achievement of individual goals by serving as collective support groups and emphasizing freedom. There is much diversity among members of these groups. *Alternative-Family Communes,* their members claim, are "prototypes" of the non-blood-related families of the future, with members developing what they believe to be superior family forms. *Countercultural Communes* reflect the hippie ideals of the 1960s. Members protest the conventions of society: civil obedience, marriage, monogamy, wealth, and traditional religion. *Political Communes* work toward anarchy or socialism, experimenting with new forms of social organization while destroying old ones. Members often struggle toward such goals as the abolition of private property and the elimination of discrimination based on age or sex.

The overlapping of terms and the newness of Zablocki's classification system limits accuracy in the enumeration of contemporary radical communities. Although commune populations, as such, are rarely counted (Zablocki, 1980), Jerome (1974) estimated that over 750,000 persons (3 percent of the national population at the time) were living communally, 500,000 in urban areas. In spite of the uncertainty of number and the wide variation in form and terminology, observers have been able to describe some common qualities and activities of alternative living groups.

Components of Radical Community

One way to report what is now known about radical communities is to examine, organize, and discuss research findings in terms of the various components of communal living. The scheme used here has been adapted from the elements identified by Mayer (1978) as components of radical (in his case, Christian) community during the first century: witness, worship, service, *koinonia* (community building), and nurture (a complex of three components). To the early Christians, witness was expressing values through actions rather than words; worship was coming together as a group to celebrate spiritual life; service was sharing one's talents, time, and treasures with others; *koinonia* was building a togetherness and a community identity distinct from other groups; nurture was providing a sense of knowledge, care, and order within the community (Mayer, 1978).

Although the early Christian communities were intentionally formed for the mutual support and protection of members with a new spiritual belief, these five elements, translated into seven core components, apply to contemporary group living as well (see Table 11.2).

Reflecting Values

Communal groups reflect experimental, evolutionary, small and interdependent, "here and now," meaningful, and egalitarian values in action. Members of communes and intentional communities often *experiment* with "mindblowing" activities such as drug use, sexual involvement, nud-

TABLE 11.2   Elements of First-Century Christian Radical Communities Compared with Core Components of Twentieth-Century Communal Life

Elements of Radical Christian Community	Core Components of Communal Life
Witness	Reflecting Values
Worship	Celebrating life
Service	Working (by choice) (by design)
Koinonia (community building)	Achieving group identity and group cohesion
Nurture	Sharing knowledge Demonstrating concern Evolving rules

SOURCE: Adapted from Mayer (1978).

ity, and spirituality. Berger (1981) calls this a "desocialization of sensibility" (a desensitizing to what is radical), which, as Coffman (1979) suggests, does not necessarily provide easy answers to problems in life, but provides a supportive context for seeking them.

Kanter (1972) describes communes as *evolutionary,* or willing to learn from mistakes. Communes have evolved, in Coffman's (1979) opinion, from the "naivete of utopias" (rigid thinking) to the "natural pattern" (of evolution). As Kemplar (1976) remarks, you "just have to let some things happen." Change is the norm (Bouvard, 1975).

Church, clan, and racial groups often get too large for members to know each other personally (Bane, 1976), so radical communities emphasize *small size* (Bouvard, 1975). This promotes *interdependence,* since members encounter each other more often, even though they sacrifice privacy and self-determination in the process (Kemplar, 1976). When Schumacher wrote *Small is Beautiful* (1973), communitarians gained another guru.

Kanter (1972) observed that communards value the *here and now.* The past blends with a thrust toward the future (Bouvard, 1975). The present is a fulcrum, balancing the old ways of self-sufficiency, small economic units, natural childbirth, and organic farming with the future goal of personal and community growth.

Communitarians seek a more *meaningful* life (Alexander, 1976; Bouvard, 1975). Meaningful life comes from families and family relationships (Masnick and Bane, 1980), in that closeness and intimacy develop in the identifiable family; Eiduson (1981) labels this value "humanism." Zablocki (1980) considers meaningfulness as a kind of collective charisma;

members see themselves as integral parts of a group in that they make or help to make choices within that group.

Communes and intentional communities espouse *egalitarian* values, seeking the liberation of both sexes from limited roles (Bouvard, 1975), except those united by a creedal (particularly Christian) ideology (Eiduson, 1981; Weisner and Martin, 1979; Zablocki, 1980). In many communes, gender role differentiation has evolved from "blatantly sexist" (Berger, 1980) to a concern of "highest priority" (Zablocki, 1980). In Zablocki's study, women spent twice as much time as men cooking, cleaning, dishwashing, laundering, and minding children. Men spent more time each week on home and car maintenance, keeping account books, spreading the communal message, and counseling other commune members. As Coffman (1979) notes, even the most androgynous groups must struggle to express egalitarian values in action.

Celebrating Life

Celebration is the continuing spirit that energizes group living. Celebrating may occur spontaneously or be carefully planned as in the case of a festival. A home-birthed baby (Berger et al., 1972), visitors (as opposed to "tourists"; Berger, 1981), home construction, and Thanksgiving all give cause to celebrate.

Normally unpleasant and overwhelming tasks become enjoyable "work parties" (Raimey, 1979). One group of over thirty persons "dried in" (i.e., built the foundation, framework, and roof but no siding) a neighbor's house in fourteen hours, using alternate work crews so that everyone could take breaks; others provided beer, food, and music. In addition to spontaneous socials and work parties, communities also plan festivals that are often distinctive to their groups such as observations of solstices, equinoxes, and various phases of the moon.

Working

Work may be by personal choice (voluntary, cooperative work; Zablocki, 1980) or by design (tasks assigned to members; Kinkade, 1973; Bouvard, 1975). The pattern in any given commune expresses the values of that group. Communes work toward a flexible division of labor (Kanter, 1972; Levine et al., 1973; Bouvard, 1975); the older (Kanter, 1972) and larger (Zablocki, 1980) the commune, the more formal the structure. The more organized the work effort is, the more smoothly the commune operates (Levine et al., 1973). In more efficient communes, those jobs that require real skill and dedication, such as cooking and bookkeeping, are rotated the least.

Members of radical communities typically resist *alienated* (i.e., contrary to communal) work (Zablocki, 1980; Berger, 1981). They seek work primarily on the land. Although Zablocki (1980) reported that working "outside" was usually a factor of urban communal life, no rural commune members worked outside their communes.

Achieving Group Identity and Group Cohesion

Community building results from individuals affiliating with an identifiable entity and bonding together. Communitarians seek an identity as members of a group distinct from other groups. Members clearly see their boundaries: the edge of their land and the roster of members (Kanter, 1972). Each commune and intentional community expresses uniqueness; the inside and outside of the community are definable.

Group cohesiveness evolves as group members achieve togetherness. Togetherness is "commitment" (Kanter, 1972), "integration" (shared values; Dammers, 1974), "closeness" (a blend of companionship, close friendship, and intimate sharing; Raimey, 1979), or cohesion. Zablocki (1980) decided that the concept of cohesion was inadequate to describe the communal process since bonding was more an accumulation of couplings than a group aggregate. More useful was the concept of *cathexis* from the psychoanalytic literature, which is used to describe emotionally invested relationships. In Zablocki's use, *dyadic cathexis* is an index of the density of "reciprocated loving relationsips. He noted that in "any given group of population N, there will be $N(N-1)/2$ possible connections linking any one person with any other" (Zablocki, 1980: 163). The more love or cathexis, he concluded, the greater the turnover of least loved commune members will be, except in the presence of charisma. Charisma is a variable component of any social system in which individuals identify themselves with the group (Zablocki, 1980). Whatever the terminology, Constantine and Constantine (1973) emphasized that group identity and group cohesion are essential to the survival of communes.

Sharing Knowledge

In communes, members place major emphasis on helping individual gain skills and knowledge. Communes and intentional communities are actually life schools for all members. Members usually come literate and skilled, or enthusiastic about developing skills, with the spirit of sharing. Those with knowledge of planting gardens, building homes, or repairing automobiles train willing but unskilled volunteers. Children and adult alike benefit from this, the ultimate of free schools. Although non formalized education surrounds the lives of all communards, most group invest considerable energy in schooling for children.

Kinkade (1973) reported on the efforts at Twin Oaks to structure full-time controlled environment for children with a child manager charge. Blanton (1980) described the Synanon experience for children - a controlled educational environment in which the community ideolog and the tasks of the child's full day, both at home and at school, form th basis for the curriculum. Berger (1981) described a commune he studie during the 1970s in which children were educated on the land in a free school that developed such a reputation for excellence beyond the commune that the majority of the students were noncommune children, and the local education agency funded its program. Although this commune was much less structured than those described by Kinkade and Blanton, all three curricula were similar: a blend of teacher's expectations, parent's wishes, and children's requests, including such topics as reading, writing, arithmetic, arts and crafts, and practical skills such as blacksmithing and bicycle repair.

These free schools, outgrowths of the counterculture of the 1960s, are typically learner structured and nongraded. Teachers tie practical activities to the more traditional academic subjects. They were influenced by the writings of A. S. Neill, particularly *Summerhill,* and the earlier "infant schools" of Robert Owen, which were patterned on Pestalozzi's schools of the 1800s (Bouvard, 1975).

Demonstrating Concern

Caring in the communal setting is expressed through interpersonal relationships: among members, children and adults alike; between spouses; between children and their parents, biological and otherwise. These relationships have an effect on the children living communally.

Communal parenting demonstrates concern and caring in the community. The functional parent is most often the adult who happens to be at hand when a need arises (Berger, 1981; Johnson and Deisher, 1973). Although much diversity in child rearing exists (Eiduson and Alexander, 1978), Zablocki (1980) found generally favorable reports of communal parenting. Because communal parenting is usually shared parenting, and communal membership tends to be transient, communal children experience great fluctuation in parenting (Eiduson and Alexander, 1978). Weisberg (1977) warns that a "Cinderella effect" may be operating in communes, particularly where there are young children and high adult/child ratios. Even though shared parenting provides many talented adults among whom the children find companions, teachers, chauffeurs, and storytellers, it also provides many, sometimes contradictory, bosses. Thus communal life for children is a "mixed bag" of both good and bad parenting. In a sense, a commune is a typical family, only magnified (Weisberg, 1977). What appears to matter, Marotz-Baden et al. (1979) concluded, is not so much the family structure as the family process (i.e., the quality of the interactions of the members).

By the age of four or five, children are seen as equal members of the communal family (Berger, 1981; Blanton, 1980). Hackett has commented that children are recognized "by lowering one's line of vision rather than one's level of discourse" (Berger, 1981: 59). The emphasis on egalitarianism in communes increasingly results in agelessness (Berger, 1981). Consequently, while children in communes appear like any other

children, they are rarely shy or withdrawn and seem "saltier," more sel
possessed, and more confident than noncommunal children (Berge
1981; Johnson and Deisher, 1973). They express ideas freely and willingl
especially in times of unfamiliar and traumatic experiences (Johnson an
Deisher, 1973).

Relationships among spouses in most communal settings are, gener
ally, much like those in conventional families. A continuing state of tensio
exists as partners strive to overcome jealousy and possessiveness. Mem
bers routinely face the crises of courtship, coupling, uncoupling, an
recoupling as each seeks personal freedom (Berger, 1981). Commune
that do not advocate celibacy most often support marriage. Some com
munes instill an "incest" taboo, discouraging sexual relations between th
"sisters" and "brothers" of the communal family, but allowing individual
to seek sexual relationships elsewhere.

Communal life, according to Jaffe and Kanter (1976), presents either
risk of separation or an opportunity for egalitarian relationships. Whil
studying 29 couples from 17 middle-class, urban communes, they foun
that communal life often leads to divorce, with "traditional" couples mor
likely to separate than "innovative" couples. A tension exists betwee
couple identity and group identity, with the emphasis being on the coupl
sharing their private lives with the group. Couples then learn that whe
one partner cannot meet a particular need, another member of the house
hold may be able to help.

Evolving Rules

Except for the legal structures that govern the corporate aspects c
radical communities, rules are usually implied rather than explicit. Regula
tions do evolve, however, especially as problems fester and the grou
matures. Issues that can become problems requiring discussion and rul
making may include: vegetarianism, decor (neatness in common rooms)
nudity, smoking, children, pets, drugs, sexual practices, noise, visitors, an
the use of common possessions (Levine et al., 1973; Woodrow, 1981)
Over time, an increasingly complex set of procedures usually become
codified in order to guide current members and orient new ones (Kante
1972).

Intentional Community: A Case Analysis

Rose, quoted at the beginning of this chapter, lives in an intentiona
community that was built upon the core components of radical communit
discussed in the preceeding section. Rose's community was analyzed usin
ten criteria of success (Levine et al., 1973): longevity, group cohesion
individual satisfaction, stability, spirit, commitment, common ideology
degree of organization, emergent leadership, and well-integrated indi
viduals. Sources of data used in this analysis included biweekly newsletter

nd governance meeting agenda items accumulated over eight years, nterviews with community residents from 1973 to 1982, and publications y community residents.

The community evolved from a weekly night class in a "free university" 1 1973 when over 200 individuals, representing a variety of family struc- ures, met to explore possible ways of organizing to meet their common reams. A social experiment was under way. A concrete show of strength nd unity came in August when at one of their weekly meetings they eclared that they were ready to buy land. That evening $116,000 were ollected in money and loan commitments. With those funds, 240 acres of nd were purchased.

The class deliberations had helped people to become better ac- uainted. The common threads that linked these "strangers" together ere commitments to: (1) buy land cheaply, (2) help others buy land heaply, (3) preserve the land, and (4) construct a life as ecologically sane s possible. From the beginning, much diversity marked the group. Ages nged from newborn babies to persons in their seventies; occupations epresented every classification listed in the *Occupational Outlook Hand- ook* (U.S. Department of Labor, 1980). Incomes varied from subsistence unemployed) to substantial (wealthy heirs of southern plantation for- nes). Education ranged from high school to postdoctoral training, with e majority of persons being college-educated adults with graduate de- rees or advanced specialized training.

Gradually, household after household settled. In 1979, 53 (of 98) ouseholds actually settled on the land (Frese, 1979). Of 43 households urveyed, 55 percent were a first marriage, 59 percent represented a uclear household, 17 percent were single-person households, and 15 ercent were housemate and multi-adult with children households. The 982 community census recorded 188 individuals living in 72 households. mong these, increasing numbers of bloodline family units had settled ithin the community. One couple, their three sons, their three sons' ives, and their grandchildren all live in proximity to one another.

ongevity

How long a communal group exists is important, but not crucial in self. This rural alternative community continues to grow and develop in its inth year of operation. Besides an increase in membership and the urchase of 84 additional acres, members appear to grow more closely ogether.

roup Cohesion

This community demonstrates cohesion by the way it functions as a roup. What started as a loosely knit collection of separate households has volved into an increasingly intimate community of friends. This unity esults primarily from community rituals and traditions. One such tradition

requires that everyone who moves onto the land must fulfill four require
ments: (1) be on a waiting list until land is available, (2) take a walk throug
the community, interacting with land residents whenever possible, (3) a
tend at least one Town Council meeting, and (4) attend at least one soci
event, of which there are many. Membership is self-selected. Those wh
do not like the community and its norms do not choose membership.

In addition to initiation rituals, the community plans various festiva
and socials including New Moon festivals, fire department benefits, an
astrological birthday parties. Generally, not every person participates i
every event; each event attracts a different clustering from the total mem
bership.

In 1982, an important indicator of cohesion surfaced as membe
decided to construct a new community center. Despite insufficient func
and busy schedules, different individuals emerged as leaders to energiz
volunteer clusters for the different components of the project. On
member, a former Wall Street broker, developed a loans program (fror
members) to generate capital; another orchestrated the building desigr
another arranged the construction sequence; another organized food an
entertainment to accompany the work parties. Other clusters negotiate
the project with county building inspectors, sold postholes to raise money
built cabinets, planned landscaping, and organized the rituals to celebrat
completion.

The building — in terms of its design, time frame, and work crew
represents consensus in action. Different people with different talents an
different conceptions of the finished product completed their respectiv
contributions to the common good while achieving individual satisfaction.

Individual Satisfaction

Individuals indicate satisfaction by remaining in the community a
active members. If member expectations are met, they stay. If not, the
leave. Only one couple who did not like communal life stayed on for mor
than six months. During their 5-year stay, the dissatisfied couple becam
an island to themselves. A survey of 43 of the 53 households living on th
land in 1979 revealed that 95 percent of those households considered th
community as meeting or surpassing member expectations (Frese, 1979)
Respondents were particularly satisfied with the (1) community newslette
(2) cooperation among households, (3) concept of a land cooperative
and (4) concern for the environment.

Stability

Stability describes the frequency of changes in membership and direc
tions. The community still includes a majority (59 percent) of the individu
als who began with the group in 1973. Members expect and accep
turnover of both people and ideas. Those who leave keep in touch an
return. Old ideas reappear as appropriate. As members see a time fo

change in direction, the community moves toward greater stability by changing to be consistent with the new direction. For example, two years ago some individuals saw governance as increasingly "labor intensive" as more households became established on the land. A cluster developed to draft a reorganization that specified more clearly realistic operating procedures for a larger population. Guided by community spirit, this plan is being realized.

Spirit

Spirit is what one experiences when in the presence of community members. People curious about the community are invited to visit in order to feel and understand the spirit. Overnight visitors are common. Spirit can best be demonstrated by residents' claims to have found their "home base" and by their handling of conflicts in the community. The spirit of affiliation helps residents to be "up front" in times of conflict. Provocations include barking dogs, offensive exterior lights, loud stereos (on which the "wrong" album is being played), or goats that break through fences to eat neighbors' gardens. If one member is upset by another, the offending member is informed. A sense of spirit carries the group through (Peace, 1980).

Commitment

Commitment is both temporal (i.e., a sense of permanence) and personal (i.e., an awareness of responsibility for others). This community demonstrates both types of commitment, although there is considerable variation within households. Nevertheless, commitment within the community as a whole appears to be increasing. At the outset of this community in 1973, the commitment was essentially economic among relative strangers. As members and households have evolved into a more cohesive whole, the commitments have focused more on interpersonal relationships with a sense of permanence of residence. In a sense, community commitment has been akin to "marriage until death do us part." Residents indicate their degree of commitment by their efforts to maintain good relations with other residents and by their decisions to remain in the community. Couples who divorce typically stay in the community with their children; old partners and new partners often live side by side. Neighbors watch over and nurture the children as parents in common, and children sleep within their friendship groups in one house or another.

Common Ideology

Community members have no apparent ideology in common. "Social harmony and general agreement . . . must grow organically within the community, with the daily experiences of life, rather than conforming to a certain way of life or philosophy" (Peace, 1980: 24). Members have a generous concern for each other, but no one ideological focus is apparent in terms of religious beliefs, occupational pursuits, or nutritional practices. When someone announces a particular protest of ideological focus, interested individuals cluster. The clusters reflect the ideological trends within the community through such activities as cottage industries, a women's collective, and a winery group.

Degree of Organization

A master plan of organization slowly evolves, particularly at the community level; households maintain a high degree of independence. Three different interlocking corporations have been developed as the legal entities for record-keeping purposes. They were organized as different land parcels were being purchased and are not being consolidated. Households have both exclusive (from one to ten acres) and shared (ninety acres of common land) ownership. The community is organized into seven neighborhoods, including from nine to sixteen households in each. At least one representative from each neighborhood attends monthly Town Council meetings at which decisions of the community are made. The decision-making process is usually consensual, although votes are taken to record important decisions and these are printed in a biweekly newsletter.

Emergent Leadership

Successful intentional communities tend to be those in which there are a few identifiable leaders who have evolved their roles over time. This community has ensured leadership by hiring a part-time Community Coordinator who serves as a contact to the outside world, a coordinator of volunteers, and a researcher of specific issues. However, the real leaders are probably the many individuals who emerge as experts. For example, when a bakery collective was formed, the bakers provided the leadership. Over one hundred individuals have served as community leaders at various times.

Well-Integrated Individuals

The community is composed of individuals who are able to handle their lives reasonably well. On some occasions it has served as a therapeutic community for visitors in need of institutional alternatives; only once in nine years have the residents had to call the sheriff for assistance.

Community members are most "centered" when they are in the process of relationship with each other, wherever they are or whatever they think. Lack of relationship, not conflict, seems to most greatly affect the sense of balance within the community. The sense of spirit mentioned above keeps members in emotional touch with each other. In times of individual and household crises a generalized spirit of community support is mustered, and residents who are mental health professionals are informally identified as listeners and facilitators.

These member/professionals have even considered capitalizing on the overall socioemotional health of the community. Two attempts were made by these residents to sponsor a therapeutic half-way house on the land for populations with specific problems (e.g., abused wives, juvenile offenders). However, several residents voted against the proposals, maintaining that therapeutic environments and personal use structures do not mix.

The success of the dissenting minority in this case demonstrates another point. Only when minority concerns have been resolved do the members recognize that consensus has been reached. This approach is beneficial to every person on the land. Strengthening individuals, by listening to them, strengthens the group.

The Future of Radical Community

Radical communities as family options are not unique either to our time or to our society. However, since most of the population of the United States grew up in nuclear families, there may be resistance to exploring these options even though they reflect our heritage as well as our contemporary situation. Prospects for the future of radical communities are discussed in terms of factors that affect the future, family choices of the future, and relevant research potentials.

Factors Affecting the Future

Factors that affect the future of radical community include the dynamics of the status quo, media exposure, increased longevity, decentralization, and increasing egalitarianism.

Dynamic Status Quo

The status quo of family life changes. Although communitarians can expect resistance to change in family forms (Masnick and Bane, 1980), Constantine and Constantine (1973) predicted that the future of the family is pluralistic. Traditional forms of family will continue (Adams, 1980) amid an ever-enlarging array of nontraditional family models (Eiduson, 1981; Sussman, 1979), including radical communities. The status quo evolves as the media expose more Americans to alternatives (Berger, 1981).

Media Exposure

As the popular press publicizes radical communities more often, and as more connections between communal groups and their surrounding communities are made, the number of persons who choose a variation of communal life may well increase. Influencing these choices may be what Berger (1981) conceptualized as "desocialization of sensibility," in this case, the gradual resocialization of personal standards. With more visibility, a social custom or pattern that was formerly unacceptable may become, over time, acceptable.

Increased Longevity

The population of older citizens continues to increase, having a major impact on housing and the "shape and feel of communities" (Masnick and Bane, 1980). The extent to which older persons will become part of the communal movement is uncertain, but there is interest in such forms as "cooperative families" Streib and Hilker, 1980) and "house sharing" (Usher and McConnell, 1980; see the chapter by Dressel and Hess in this volume).

Decentralization

Harris (1981), an anthropologist, recommended decentralization as a return to the American ideal of initiative, improving the quality of life. Many decades earlier, communitarians Ralph Bersodi and Mildred Loomis made similar recommendations (Bouvard, 1975). Today, specialists in systems ecology (Odum and Odum, 1976) predict smaller families whose social needs are provided through interdependence with other small family units in communal networks. "Small is beautiful," Schumacher (1973) argued, maintaining that people organized in small groups take better care of their land while resisting greed and envy and and embracing nonviolence in an atmosphere of egalitarianism.

Increasing Egalitarianism

Individuals are becoming more androgynous (DeFrain, 1979; Knox, 1980). Communes encompass egalitarianism in their worldview (Eiduson, 1981); the gender role models of radical communities change, except in cases of creedal communes (Weisner and Martin, 1979). Radical communities will actualize and then extend their role-sharing values affecting family choices of the future. Members of radical communities that espouse and practice egalitarian values parent the egalitarians of tomorrow.

Family Choices of the Future

A given individual experiences several family forms in a life time (Mesnick and Bane, 1980), and these variant forms bridge the gap between the acceptable and the radically different. Family choices of the future include those that are traditional, variations of the traditional, and radical forms.

Using the broadest definitions of family, variant forms can be categorized by the number of generations involved (from one to three or more). Each of the family form options can then be placed on another axis denoting degree of acceptance by society, as interpreted from the literature (see Table 11.3).

Traditional Choices

Americans accept the traditional nuclear family of two generations as the standard, with the husband as the chief source of income. The wife

TABLE 11.3 Family Form Choices by Generation and Acceptance

	One Generation	Two Generations	Three (or more) Generations
Traditional Choices (accepted)		Nuclear family	Extended family
	Dual-worker		Kin network
Variations of Traditional Choices (increasingly accepted)	Singlehood	Single-parent	
		Family networks	
	Cohabitation	Family cluster	
	Dual-career		
	Commuter		
	Voluntary childlessness	Stepfamily	Affiliated family
	Divorce and remarriage	Binuclear family	
Radical Choices (rarely accepted)	Commune [urban]	Commune [urban, rural]	Commune [rural]
	Gay/Lesbian couple	Gay/Lesbian parent	Intentional community
	Polygyny after sixty		
	Sexually open marriage		
	Group marriage		

SOURCE: Adapted from Sussman (1979); Adams (1980).

may work, as in a "dual-worker" marriage (Berger et al., 1978) with or without children. Extensions of the traditional family with three or more generations include kin networks and extended families. These bloodline intergenerational groups develop "historic continuity" by focusing on important aspects of the life cycle (Kemplar, 1976). The emphasis is on the biological *family* and on the the well-being of that unit.

Variations of Traditional Choices

Family pluralism is increasingly accepted, becoming more of a conscious choice than a result of circumstance, and may replace the nuclear family as the conceptual base for study in the 1980s (Sussman, 1979). Some choices encompass only one generation, such as singlehood (Stein, 1981), cohabitation (Macklin, 1978), and voluntary childlessness (Veevers, 1980). In all of these cases, desire for personal happiness and *individual* success affects the choice of relationships with others, including the decisions to marry and raise children. Also basing choices on individual success are professionals in dual career (Berger et al., 1978) and commuter (Farris, 1978) marriages with one or two generations within the family group. Single parenthood (Klein, 1973) and binuclear (two households, one family resulting from divorce; Ahrons, 1979) families demonstrate family restructuring to resolve malfunctions.

Where blood ties are minimal, individuals choose synthetic forms of family. Sussman (1979) predicted close friends in neighborhoods, schools, and worksites will be the significant primary group of the future for such needs as intimacy, emotional support, companionship, role models for children, and help when needed. Three generational versions of these synthetic kinship groups include family networks, family clusters, and affiliated families. *Family networks* are composed of three or four nuclear families, living in the same neighborhood, who meet regularly for a reciprocal sharing of values, problems, and leisure activities, as well as for an exchange of services (Stoller, 1970). *Family clusters,* based on Stoller's notion of intimate networks of families, are usually closed, short-term, spiritually focused family enrichment groups that meet regularly with trained facilitators who lead experimental activities (Otto, 1971b; Pringle, 1974; Sawin, 1979, 1982). As defined by Clavan and Vatter (1972), the *affiliated family* includes any combination of husband/father or wife/ mother and children plus one or more nonkin members who are informally adopted by the family. These persons need not necessarily live in one household, but they establish a bond of voluntary commitment to treat each other as family.

Radical Choices

In the past, certain collections of families in community have been considered radical by society and rarely accepted as options (see historical accounts by Bestor, 1950; Kanter, 1972; Mayer, 1978; Caan, 1979; and Zablocki, 1980). Currently, communes and intentional communities are available radical options for two- and three-generational family groups. Although they are the least likely options to be chosen by the majority of the population, radical communities offer considerable possibilities for research.

Research Potentials

Radical communities provide settings for study of the cutting edge of change in family life. The many possibilities for study include the existential power of radical communities and the networking among them.

The attracting and holding power of radical communities stands out as an important topic for research. This power might be designated as *meaningfulness,* or what Zimbardo (1982) interpreted as the "candy" of cult (i.e., love, pride in work, a sense of place, and spiritual purpose), and what

Zablocki (1980) studied as "charisma" (associating self-interests with collective interests).

Investigation of the *connections* among radical communities is another important avenue of research. Communes and intentional communities are more a movement than a collection of groups in specific locations. To borrow a notion from Bateson (1979), understanding not only the "patterns" (i.e., the distinctive nature of each communal group) but also the "patterns that connect" those patterns (i.e., the networking) highlights the signficance of the movement.

Radical communities, the various choices of family for a changing but stable minority of Americans, have been, are, and will continue to be options in group living. For Rose and other communitarians, radical community evolves in a "wholeness, an organic building process that fosters stability in a very rich life" (Van Oss, 1980: 26). Radical community represents a small but strong voice in the evolution of American society.

References

ADAMS, B. N. (1981) The Family: A Sociological Interpretation, Chicago: Rand-McNally.
AHRONS, C. R. (1979) "The binuclear family: two households, one family." Alternative Lifestyles 2, 4: 499-515.
ALEXANDER, J. (1976) "Alternative Lifestyles: relationship between new realities and practice." Clinical Social Work Journal 4, 4: 289-301.
BANE, M. J. (1976) Here to Stay: American Families in the Twentieth Century. New York: Basic Books.
BATESON, G. (1979) "Man and Nature." Omni 1, 9: 54-56, 106.
BERGER, B. M. (1981) The Survival of a Counterculture: Ideological Work and Everyday Life Among Rural Communards. Berkeley: University of California Press.
——— M. FOSTER, and B. WALLSTON (1978) "Finding jobs," in R. Rapoport and R. Rapoport (eds.) Working Couples. New York: Harper & Row.
BERGER, B., B. HACKETT, and R. M. Millar (1972) "The communal family." Family Coordinator 21, 4: 419-427.
BESTOR, A. E. (1950) Backwoods Utopias: The Sectarian and Owenite Phases of Communitarian Socialism in America, 1663-1829. Philadelphia: University of Pennsylvania Press.
BLANTON, J. (1980) "Communal child rearing: the Synanon experience." Alternative Lifestyles 3, 1: 87-116.
BOUVARD, M. (1975) The Intentional Community Movement: Building a New Moral World. Port Washington, NY: Kennikat.
BRUDENELL, G. (1982) "Hidden families in an intentional community." (unpublished)
CAVAN, R. S. (1979) "Communes: historical and contemporary." International Review of Sociology 6 (Spring): 1-11.
CLAVAN, S. and E. VATTER (1972) "The affiliated family: a continued analysis." Family Coordinator 21, 4: 499-504.
COFFMAN, C. (1979) "Intentional communities," in P. Freundlich, C. Collins and M. Wenig (eds.) A Guide to Cooperative Alternatives. New Haven, CT: Community Publications Cooperative.
CONOVER, P. W. (1975) "An analysis of communes and intentional communities with particular attention to sexual and genderal relations." Family Coordinator 24, 4: 453-464.

254   RADICAL COMMUNITY

CONSTANTINE, L. and J. CONSTANTINE (1973) Group Marriage: A Study of Contemporary Multilateral Marriage. New York: Macmillan.

DAMMERS, L. S. (1974) "Integration within a commune." Youth and Society 5, 4: 475-496.

EIDUSON, B. T. (1981) "The child in the non-conventional family," pp. 281-316 in M. Lewis and L. A. Rosenblum (eds.) The Uncommon Child. New York: Plenum.

—— (1980) "Changing sex roles of parents and children in alternative family styles: implications for young children," in E. J. Anthony and C. Chiland (eds.) The Child in His Family, Vol. 6. New York: John Wiley.

—— and J. W. ALEXANDER (1978) "The role of children in alternate family styles." Journal of Social Issues 34 Spring: 149-167.

FARRIS, A. (1978) "Commuting," in R. Rapoport and R. Rapoport (eds.) Working Couples. New York: Harper & Row.

de FRAIN, J. (1979) "Androgynous parents tell who they are and what they need." Family Coordinator 28, 2: 237-243.

FRESE, C. (1979) "Housing solutions through local cooperation: a case study." Housing Science 3, 4: 295-304.

HARRIS, M. (1981) America Now: The Anthropology of a Changing Culture. New York: Simon & Schuster.

HAYS, W. C. and C. H. MINDEL (1973) "Extended kinship relations in Black and White families." Journal of Marriage and the Family 35, 1: 51-57.

JAFFE, D. T. and R. M. KANTER (1976) "Couple strains in communal households: a four-factor model of the separation process." Journal of Social Issues 32, 1: 169-191.

JEROME, J. (1974) Families of Eden: Communes and the New Anarchism. New York: Continuum.

JOHNSON, C. M. and R. W. DEISHER (1973) "Contemporary communal child rearing: a first analysis." Pediatrics 52, 3: 319-326.

KANTER, R. M. (1972) Commitment and Community: Communes and Utopias in Sociological Perspective. Cambridge, MA: Harvard University Press.

—— D. JAFFE, and D. K. WEISBERG (1975) "Coupling, parenting, and the presence of others: intimate relationships in communal households." Family Coordinator 24, 4: 433-462.

KEMPLAR, H. L. (1976) "Extended kinship ties and some modern alternatives." Family Coordinator 25, 2: 143-149.

KINKADE, K. (1973) A Walden Two Experiment: The First Five Years of Twin Oaks Community. New York: William Morrow.

KLEIN, C. (1973) The Single Parent Experience. New York: Walker.

KNOX, D. (1980) "Trends in marriage and the family in the 1980s." Family Relations 29, 2: 145-150.

LEVINE, S., R. CARR, and W. HORENBLOS (1973) "The urban commune: fact or fad, promise or pipedream?" American Journal of Orthopsychiatry 43, 1: 149-163.

MACKLIN, E. D. (1982) Personal communication. January 26.

—— (1980) Nontraditional family forms: a decade of research." Journal of Marriage and the Family 42, 4: 905-922.

—— (1978) "Non-marital heterosexual cohabitation: a review of research." Marriage and Family Review 1 (March/April): 1-12.

MAROTZ-BADEN, R., G. R. ADAMS, N. BUECHE, B. MUNRO, and G. MUNRO (1979) "Family forms or family process? Reconsidering the deficit family model approach." Family Coordinator 28, 1: 5-14.

MASNICK, G. and M. J. BANE (1980) The Nation's Families: 1960-1990. Boston: Auburn House.

MAYER, H. T. (1978) Pastoral Care: Its Roots and Renewal. Atlanta: John Knox.

ODUM, N. T. and E. C. ODUM (1976) Energy Basis for Man and Nature. New York: McGraw-Hill.

OTTO, H. A. (1971a) "Communes: the alternative lifestyle." Saturday Review (April 24): 16-21.

—— (1971b) The Family Cluster: A Multi-Base Alternative. Beverly Hills: Holistic Press.

PEACE, R. (1980) "Miccosukee land cooperative: private ownership and community." Communities, No. 42: 24, 25.

PRINGLE, B. (1974) "Family clusters as a means of reducing isolation among urbanites."
    Family Coordinator 23, 2: 175-179.
RAIMEY, E. (1979) Shared Houses, Shared Lives: The New Extended Families and How
    They Work. New York: St. Martin's.
———— and M. WENIG (1979) "Family life and relationships," pp. 83-84 in P. Freundlich,
    C. Collins, and M. Wenig, A Guide to Cooperative Alternatives. New Haven, CT:
    Community Publications Cooperative.
RAMEY, J. W. (1976) "Muli-adult household: living group of the future?" Futurist
    10, 2: 78-83.
SAWIN, M. (1982) Hope for Families. New York: William H. Sadlier.
———— (1979) Family Enrichment With Family Clusters. Valley Forge, PA: Judson.
SCHUMACHER, E. G. (1973) Small Is Beautiful: Economics As If People Mattered. New
    York: Harper & Row.
STEIN, P. [ed.] (1981) Single Life: Unmarried Adults in Social Context. New York: St.
    Martin's.
STOLLER, F. H. (1970) "The intimate network of families as a new structure," in H. A. Otto
    (ed.) The Family in Search of a Future. New York: Appleton-Century-Crofts.
STREIB, G. F. and M. A. HILKER (1980) "The cooperative 'family': an alternative lifestyle
    for the elderly." Alternative Lifestyles 3, 2: 167-184.
SUSSMAN, M. B. (1979) "Actions and services for the new family," in D. Reiss and H. A.
    Hoffman (eds.) The American Family: Dying or Developing. New York: Plenum.
U.S. Bureau of the Census (1981) Household and Family Characteristics: March 1980.
    Current Population Reports, Series P-20, No. 366. Washington, DC: Government
    Printing Office.
U.S. Department of Labor (1980) Occupational Outlook Handbook, 1980-81 Edition
    (Bulletin 2075). Washington, DC: Superintendent of Documents.
USHER, C. E. and S. R. McCONNELL (1980) "Housesharing: a way to intimacy?" Alter-
    native Lifestyles 3, 2: 149-166.
VAN OSS, R. (1980) "A personal view of living at the land cooperative," Communities,
    No. 42: 26.
VEEVERS, J. (1980) Childless by Choice. Scarborough, Ontario: Butterworths.
WEISBERG, K. D. (1977) "The cinderella children." Psychology Today 10, 11: 84-
    86, 103.
WEISNER, T. S. and J. C. MARTIN (1979) "Learning environments for infants: communes
    and conventionally married families in California." Alternative Lifestyles 2, 2: 201-
    242.
WERNICK, R. (1974) Human Behavior: The Family. Boston: Little, Brown.
WOODROW, P. (1981) "Forming a communal household." Communities, No. 46: 25-27.
YORBURG, B. (1975) "The nuclear and extended family: an area of conceptual confu-
    sion." Journal of Comparative Family Studies 6, 1: 5-14.
ZABLOCKI, B. D. (1980) Alienation and Charisma: A Study of Contemporary American
    Communes. New York: Macmillan.
ZIMBARDO, P. G. (1982) "Understanding psychological man." Psychology Today
    16, 5: 58-59.

CHAPTER 12

Contemporary Traditional Families: The Undefined Majority

SARA B. TAUBIN

Drexel University

EMILY H. MUDD

University of Pennsylvania

The terms "traditional marriage" and "traditional family" have no clear, generally accepted meaning and elicit a wide range of emotional reactions. They are sometimes used derogatorily to denote a way of life that is seen as passé, limits human growth and potential, and inhibits individual expression. Using selected census figures to document their case, supporters of this view argue that what was traditional is now vestigial, finished, and representative of only a small percentage of today's households. At the other extreme are those who deplore the changes that have occurred and argue that human survival depends on unquestioning adherence to the established way (see Skolnick and Skolnick, 1980: 1-16, for overview).

In between these extremes are the great numbers of persons who respect and practice those conventions, customs, and ideals that seem relevant and functional to their present well-being, while adapting those that no longer seem to fit. Politically, economically, and socially they live in the present, while attempting to preserve the accumulated experience and wisdom of the past. "Contemporary traditional" is the term that will be used in this chapter to describe this group, the clear majority of American adults.

Many of the current family forms in this country fall under the broad category of "contemporary traditional." Mace and Mace (1977) are talking about "contemporary traditional" when they describe "companionate marriages," where the emphasis is on equality and a sharing of responsibilities and intimacy within a context of commitment and exclusivity.

Most modern couples, struggling to make the necessary accommodation to the demands of a changing time, reject a marriage based on male dominance and female submission, concepts that the Maces (1980) relegate to "the ancient world." Those, in their view, were the "old traditional" patterns, no longer functional for most in today's society. "Contemporary traditional" also characterizes the two-paycheck family (Bird, 1979), in which the wife typically takes time out for child rearing and then reenters the labor market — below where she might have been had she continued without a break, but still making a significant contribution to the family income and to her own sense of self.

Bane (1976) documents the existence of contemporary traditional families when she states that census data "provide convincing evidence that family commitments are likely to persist in our society." It seems clear to her that family ties are not "archaic remnants of a disappearing traditionalism," and that human needs for stability, continuity, and unconditional affection remain unchanged. Macklin (1980) reiterates the point when, after a review of research on nontraditional family forms, she concludes that the dominant pattern continues to be very traditional. The great majority continue to marry, have children, and desire a permanent, heterosexual, exclusive relationship in a home of their own. Although the divorce rate is increasing, most divorcees remarry, still hoping for a happy, permanent relationship. Although increasing numbers of women are in the labor force, the great majority of households are still organized around traditional family roles. Macklin (1980: 916) states:

> The 1970s have brought an increased awareness of the stresses associated with complex relationship systems and a healthy respect for human limits. . . . It is now clear that most, at least at this stage of our societal development, find complex relationship systems, such as multilateral marriage, sexually-open marriage, and communal life, too stressful to allow for long-term participation.

This continuation of themes from the past must be borne in mind as one reads the research on the many variants of the common pattern that are reviewed in this book.

Fallacies About the Concept "Traditional"

Misconceptions about the past, and about transitions from past to present, are prevalent in family study. Gusfield (1967) has identified a number of such fallacies that serve to distort our view of societal change:

Fallacy 1: Traditional culture and society were consistent and homogeneous.

Fallacy 2: Values and customs are inevitably displaced by social change.

Fallacy 3: Existing beliefs and behaviors are antagonistic to and in conflict with changing beliefs and practices.

Fallacy 4: Tradition and change are mutually exclusive.

Fallacy 5: Contemporary values and behaviors undermine traditions.

Gusfield suggests that viewing past and present as discontinuous entities — setting up polarities of traditional and nontraditional — wastes the accumulated worth of the past, thus undermining the supporting base for current enterprises. The reality is that traditions persist, in varying forms, and permeate and influence the direction of change. Their very strength lies in their pragmatic malleability.

Additional confusion arises from the tendency to equate traditional with ideal. Masnick and Bane (1980) note that Americans hold onto a nostalgic ideal of traditional family, of how families were and ought to be, that is often far from actuality, either past or future. Ideal is in fact, by definition, a mirage or fantasy that rarely conforms to past, present, or future reality (Hutter, 1981). Moreover, this rigid conceptualization of the "ideal" family often results in "either/or" labels (good/bad, success/ failure, whole/broken) that serve only to distort and alienate.

Yet ideal images do express human striving for perfectability, and an ideal family type does provide a hypothetical model toward which humans can aspire. For example, a bronze sculpture of a family group of heroic proportions was recently placed on a busy business street corner in Philadelphia. A local art critic describes the work by Timothy Duffield as "a rather ecstatic scene of a nude mother and father with a nude son and daughter standing above them on the parents' outstretched arms" (Hine 1982). He continues, "Because the bronze will endure, the sculpture does stand as a moral statement, a celebration of the family." However, Hine sees a "disquieting element" in "this conservative message." By celebrating this particular configuration, there may be an implicit and perhaps unfortunate message that others are less than ideal and, hence, less acceptable.

This chapter will not try to trace the history of the family to its present point. Excellent reviews are available elsewhere (e.g., Ariès, 1962; Burgess and Locke, 1945; Goode, 1963; Hareven, 1978; Laslett, 1972; Shorter 1975; Skolnick and Skolnick, 1980). Suffice it to say, there has been no golden age of the family, and traditional family life as we conceptualize it in this society has been a fairly recent development in human history, brought about by industrialization, urbanization, the growing ideology of individualism, and a movement toward democratic thought (see Buunk in this volume for a review of the changing norms with regard to family life over the past several centuries). The movement from the institutional family to the companionate family more characteristic of the contemporary traditional is even more recent. Burgess and Locke (1945) saw the transition as beginning in the mid-1940s, with the movement from an authoritarian rigid, sex-roled system to a concern for interpersonal relations (it was

1955 that Foote and Cottrell coined the term "interpersonal competence") and "family togetherness." However, although the goals for families had begun to change, the behaviors lagged behind, and there were few role models and little understanding of the prerequisites for this new way (Mace and Mace, 1977). Much knowledge has been gained in the ensuing decades, but it has yet to filter down to the general public.

How Traditional Is the Contemporary Family?

By what criteria should we define traditional? How far back in time should we look for our model? Macklin (1980: 905) has suggested that the most recent traditional family pattern in this society is that of "legal, lifelong, sexually exclusive marriage between one man and one woman, with children, where the male is primary provider and ultimate authority." How different is the average family today from this criterion?

Most Are Married with Children

Census data (Glick, 1979; U.S. Bureau of the Census, 1981) document continuing conventional choices and a surprising stability in family patterns. Permanent marriage is still, for most, both the ideal and the reality. Although persons may be marrying somewhat later than in the recent past, over 95 percent of the adult population still marry at some point in their life, and more than 60 percent of all married couples remain married. Although the divorce rate has been steadily rising, the great majority of divorced men and women remarry, with the rate depending somewhat on their age at divorce.

Lifelong mutual sexual fidelity has been and is still preferred (Glenn and Weaver, 1979; Yankelovich, 1981), although evidence suggests that clandestine affairs and occasional indulgence in sexual opportunities are common and apparently nondisruptive of many marriages (e.g., Bell et al., 1975). What is new is that wives are increasingly as likely as husbands to have had such an "outside" relationship (Levin, 1975). Sexually open marriages designed for personal growth continue to be far more rare and few couples find it a lifestyle that they prefer to continue over time (Watson, 1981).

Over 90 percent of all married couples have children, although the number of children per couple has declined. Moreover, more than three-quarters of all children under 18 (excluding those who are maintaining their own households) are living at any given time in a household with two parents, at least one of whom is their natural or adoptive parent. Even when children live in a single-parent household, they often have a very significant relationship with the nonresidential parent. The biggest difference for children may be in the number of children living in stepfamilies and the nature of that experience. Unlike earlier years when stepfamilies usually resulted from remarriage after the death of a spouse, most step-families today result from divorce. The result is that the children are often part of two households and have more than one set of functional parents.

An increasing percentage of households consist of a married couple without children present, or a single adult living alone, but it would be misleading to conceive of them all as nontraditional families. Because of increased longevity and smaller families, couples who are in every other way quite traditional are likely to spend more time living together without children. It is true that more persons are living as never-married singles or as unmarried couples, but these numbers still remain a small percentage of the whole, and most of them eventually move into a more traditional family form. Although large numbers of mothers work, many dual-worker families go through an "employed father, mother at home with young children" stage, and at any given time, about one-fifth of all families are in this situation.

Marriage, child rearing, loss of a spouse, remarriage, and finally the death of that spouse — this is the customary sequence of life stages for large numbers of people and it has been for some time, although more of initial loss today is due to divorce than to death. Legal, heterosexual marriage in separate households with children is the way most of us still live, at least at some point in our lives. However, there is no reason to either idealize this form or to label it pejoratively as prototypically traditional.

The Male Is Still the Primary Provider

A major evolutionary change is reflected in the fact that the dual-worker family has become the norm and more than half of all mothers are now employed outside the home. However, it is important that this not immediately be used to document the nontraditional nature of contemporary families. Wives and mothers have worked throughout our national history — on farms, in blue, pink-, and white-collar jobs, and in the professions. Moreover, even though more wives are working, they still tend to earn less than men (U.S. Department of Labor, 1980). Although the wife's contribution to family income is likely to increase over the next decade, and her earnings will be an increasingly important determinant of the family's standard of living, current estimates are that husbands will continue to be the primary providers in most families most of the time. The two-career family, with approximately equal salaries and equal weight given to both careers, is still an exception to the norm and has sufficient built-in costs that it is unclear how many familes will opt for this lifestyle (Hill and Philliber, 1982; Skinner, 1980).

It has long been assumed that the male's source of power in the traditional family was largely due to his status as breadwinner, and that as women gained more access to external resources, power would become more equal. It appears now that this analysis may be too simplistic and that

much remains to be understood, both about actual power in family relationships and about the sources of that power. This point is well made by
McDonald in his Decade Review on power within the family:

> While comparative socioeconomic resources, such as education, occu-
> pation, income, and the employment status of wives, play a role in
> influencing marital power and decision-making patterns, socioeconomic
> variables are increasingly recognized as only one type of resource. In
> order to increase explanatory potential, a wide range of resources has to
> be considered. . . . Socioeconomic resources, especially educational
> status, may relate to the power structure to the degree that they reflect
> interpersonal skills, expertise, and competence brought into the family
> from the outside. As such, these socioeconomic resources may be merely
> reflective of the individual's relative level of social competence in the
> family [1980: 849].

Families themselves are often ambivalent and unclear about the origins and uses of power and authority within their households. Interviews of
families in the early 1950s (Mudd et al., 1965) reveal this confusion,
document the tendency of families to interpret their behavior as consistent
with tradition, and record the transition in family patterns that was already
occurring at that time. Although half of the wives worked, when asked
about the authority within their families:

> Both husbands and wives voiced overwhelming allegiance to the tra-
> ditional view that the man should be the chief bread-winner for the
> family, and that he should have the main say-so in family matters. The
> wives assert more strongly than the husbands that this is the way they
> want it. However, these views are immediately qualified. Only one-third
> of the marital partners agree that the husbands should have the deciding
> vote when it comes to disciplining the children and less than 20 percent
> think that he should have a greater voice in saying how the household
> money should be spent. They also flatly reject the notion that the hus-
> band should influence his wife's vote because he knows more about such
> matters.

> [Although there appears to be some contradiction between reported
> attitudes and facts], perhaps one should substitute the word flexibility for
> contradiction to appreciate the nature of successful family ways. Tra-
> ditional values are not easily discarded when they are inbred and are an
> accepted part of the culture, but the rigid adherence to outmoded
> methods defies good judgment in daily practice. Our families are very
> human, trying new ways, testing alternative courses of action as these
> seem comfortably practical, yet clinging to many familiar values and
> attitudes [1965: 63].

In point of fact, even though in the past decade persons have tended to
espouse more egalitarian attitudes, the majority still tend to hold to fairly
traditional values (e.g., Yankelovich [1981], found in the mid-1970s that
77 percent still thought a woman should put her husband and children

ahead of her own career). Moreover, household behaviors, especially after the birth of the first child, are in fact quite traditional in the majority of families (Scanzoni and Fox, 1980). Sex role behaviors have, in fact, shifted much more slowly than sex role attitudes, with women continuing to carry much of the responsibility for child rearing and household tasks. Men tend to be more traditional than women, and less-educated persons more traditional than the better educated.

Stability and Quality Are Still Primary Goals

The need for stability and the hope for quality are still strong motives underlying family formation, with less emphasis placed on stability than in previous generations and more emphasis on quality. It is increasingly clear that the two variables do not necessarily go hand in hand, and that many quite stable families do not experience a high quality of relationship. Spanier and Lewis (1980) conceive of the two variables as separate, intersecting continua, with different determinants. Intradyadic factors, such as degree of attraction to partner and degree of marital tension, will affect quality, and extradyadic factors, such as available alternatives to the marriage and external pressures on the marriage, will affect stability. In many ways, the factors related to marital quality appear to be quite traditional, for example, premarital homogamy, support from significant others, social-economic adequacy, positive regard for spouse, and role fit.

Whether couples experience more or less quality in their marital relationships than previously is not known. Since spousal satisfaction with lifestyle will be highly dependent on the expectations that spouses bring into their marriage, the answer would seem to rest on the nature of the marital expectations then and now, and on their relative probability of being met. It is often said that because contemporary couples expect a higher level of intimacy in their marital relationship than was previously true, and yet are given little help to achieve this, they are likely to experience less conscious satisfaction with their relationship than in previous generations. However, there are few comparative data to document this. Family historians do report that expectations of deep personal satisfaction from marriage and family date only from the eighteenth century (Aries, 1962). Others have suggested that given the relative ease with which dissatisfied couples can now divorce, a higher percentage of marriages may at any given time be characterized by greater levels of mutual satisfaction than was previously the case.

It is clear that there is less stability in contemporary relationships, presumably because there are fewer external pressures to remain married and more available alternatives. However, even in the case of divorce, few persons elect to follow nontraditional lifestyles for more than a short period of time, and remarriage is often a renewed effort to seek once again the desired permanence and happiness.

Increased Concern with Family Functioning

An important development in the field of marriage and family studies is the research attention being devoted to identifying those factors associated with successful family functioning (see Ammons and Stinnett, 1980; Cole and Goettsch, 1981; Cuber and Harroff, 1965; Lewis et al., 1976; Olson et al., 1979; Stinnett et al., 1979; Stinnett et al., 1980; Stinnett et al., 1981).

After a review of the family therapy literature, Barnhill (1979) identified eight dimensions of healthy family functioning: individuation versus enmeshment, mutuality versus isolation, flexibility versus rigidity, stability versus disorganization, clear versus unclear or distorted perception, clear versus unclear or distorted communication, role reciprocity versus unclear roles or role conflict, and clear versus diffuse or breached generational boundaries. Concerted efforts must now be made to operationalize and measure these variables if research on well-functioning families is to progress.

In the late 1950s, the Division of Family Studies of the Department of Psychiatry, School of Medicine, University of Pennsylvania, initiated a study of a carefully selected national sample of 100 middle-income families who were perceived to be functioning well (see Mudd et al., 1965). In 1979, 59 of these families completed the latest set of follow-up questionnaires. By then, their average length of marriage was 37 years and the majority of their grown children were married with children of their own. Approximately half of the wives had been gainfully employed outside of the home, in the various patterns characteristic of contemporary women who work. Many of the husbands had had periods of illness and unemployment, gone back to school, and changed careers.

The responses are exceptionally detailed, candid, and revealing. Consistency over the two decades is a dominant theme of the family profiles. Mudd and Taubin (1982) summarized some of the major findings:

> Family histories are marked by pragmatic, flexible adaptation. Family dynamics are equalitarian in the marital dyad, democratic with regard to the sons and daughters. Relations with adult children are frequent, reinforced by a thriving transfer economy. Close friendships and active community involvement are cited as important sources of strength. While severely troubling situational events affecting family members are enumerated, few are defined as problems. Perceived problems are most often resolved within the family or in lesser degree with appropriate professionals. Husbands and wives express continuing satisfaction with marriage and family. They are optimistic about the future and through careful planning anticipate positive later-year development.

> The work history of the wives is confused by the interruptions in childbearing and job, and by persistent ambivalence. Some women worked steadily as teachers, in a family business, as self-employed artists or writers. By today's standards, most had jobs not careers. The wives say they worked "most" of their married lives for "personal satisfaction," for

"necessities," and to "improve the standard of living." The husbands' responses are fewer in number and less certain why wives work. Yet the voluntary comments of the husbands express pride in accomplished wives and appreciation of the efforts behind the family benefits. More men than women admitted the wife as an equal or major wage earner at times. These families struggled with the issues of the incipient women's movement but were not ideological leaders. They adapted pragmatically to changing individual and family needs, and maintained their marriages [1982: 62-64].

One may wonder whether families who survive and flourish have done so because in some way they have been favored, shielded, or exempt from misfortune, but apparently not so. Illness, accidents, death, financial reverses, dislocations and relocations, lawsuits, invalided parents, and affairs were all mentioned by the respondents. Clearly these families were not immune to the exigencies of ordinary living, yet they continued to be optimistic and consider themselves fortunate. "We are just an average family" is the self-assessment of the wife of the family judged to be the outstanding family in the original study. Yet her youngest son, now in graduate school, recalls: "I was six years old in 1960 when our family was interviewed. I have only a fleeting remembrance of the events surrounding that moment of my life. I can remember feeling proud of being part of the family. The pride, despite the intervening years, has not drastically diminished." The strength provided by a quiet pride in family was a common theme.

Findings from the above study suggest that the crucial factors leading to cohesive, durable, high-quality contemporary family life include at least the following: low-keyed adaptation (as opposed to rigid adherence to ideology); cooperation and mutual support (as opposed to competition); belief in marriage and a willingness to work at maintaining the marital relationship; commitment to and pleasure in family and in helping the children to grow as individuals; a democratic approach to family interaction; a lifestyle characterized by planning, work, and education; and a sense of being embedded within the community.

The Future: The Pragmatic 1980s

What can be predicted for the decade to come? It is obvious that family units — parents and children — will continue. They seem to be compatible with ingrained human inclinations and with prevailing social structures. Utilitarian in nature, they are bolstered by millenia of ethical and religious traditions (Gaylin, 1980). Variations on this norm — alternative lifestyles and individual experiments — will also continue, are to be expected, even welcomed, and cautiously encouraged. Homoerotic liaisons, polygamy, and communal living have existed in the past as well as in the present, appeal to, and are functional for some. Archaic family structures will also continue to flourish in small ideological enclaves where personal growth is deemed secondary to family and group cohesion.

What changes are foreseen? Will new demands be placed on marriage and family? Will lifelong sexual satisfaction and unlimited personal gratification be seen as the new entitlements? To a degree, yes. But the major factors determining the direction of change will be the realities of economics and demographics. Masnick and Bane (1980: 2) have observed the following trends in family patterns:

(1) Far from being abnormal, the low marriage, high divorce, and low fertility rates of today's generation of young adults are consistent with long-term trends, though inconsistent with the pattern established by their parents' generation.

(2) Between now and 1990, households made up of married couples will increase dramatically.

(3) Fewer and fewer households will have children present.

(4) Although more wives are working, their contribution to family income is small and has not changed.

(5) A revolution in the impact of women's work is on the horizon.

The above trends demonstrate the evolutionary nature of the changing American family and the large role played by economics and demography. Increased longevity and a higher proportion of older adults in the population has already accounted for much of the dramatic increase in single-person and child-free households. The increasing number of women employed outside the home will continue to have an impact on the pattern of child care and care for the elderly, the spousal relationship, and the division of labor within the home.

The decade of the 1980s will be a practical decade. Employment, monetary policies, education of children, care of aging family members, and environmental and nuclear degradation will be central and profound family issues. Contemporary families, with both spouses working, will have to devise for themselves a new balance of work and play, sex and satiety, tradition and innovation. Quality and stability will continue to be important goals. One hopes that society will be more willing to invest the resources necessary to help individuals and families develop the competencies we now know to be necessary to achieve these. Preoccupation with personal happiness and narcissistic self-indulgence at the expense of long-term committed relationships will prove for most to be sterile, dead-end adventures, incapable of fulfilling the basic human needs for connectedness and continuity, and inappropriate in a time when economics, environmental, and global survival issues are dominant.

Conclusion

Pluralism best describes families today in this land of regional, racial, ethnic, and religious diversity. To seek to categorize contemporary families into traditional or nontraditional is far too simplistic and fosters an undesirable and unrealistic polarity. It does an injustice to the enormous complexity of the modern American family.

The human family has been in slow evolution since the beginning of time, changing its structure and norms to fit with the realities of its environment, the basic needs of its members, and its inherited past. So too, today, contemporary families are evolving and adapting old traditions to fit with modern realities and, in the process, creating new traditions. Because other structures are changing more rapidly than has been true in the past, the family, as a subsystem within the larger system, is also changing more rapidly. Hence, the change can appear more dramatic and more alarming than might previously have been the case. But the process is essentially the same as has existed for centuries.

Individuals and collections of individuals called families, when they can, choose a way of life that best meets their needs. They choose, experience, reconsider, and choose again, as they seek some integration of the learnings from their past, the pragmatics of their present, and their dreams for the future. Contemporary families are no different. They refer to the past but they refuse to be left behind. Their choices are based on a core of common needs that unites all humans and all human families. Their resulting actions are their best response to the present, and the future will build on the lessons learned from their experience. It has ever been thus.

References

AMMONS, P. and N. STINNETT (1980) "The vital marriage: a close look." Family Relations 29 (January): 37-42.

ARIÈS, P. (1962) Centuries of Childhood: A Social History of Family Life. New York: Knopf.

BANE, M. J. (1976) Here To Stay: American Families in the Twentieth Century. New York: Basic Books.

BARNHILL, L. R. (1979) "Healthy family systems." Family Coordinator 28 (January): 95-100.

BELL, R. R., S. TURNER, and L. ROSEN (1975) "A multi-variate analysis of female extra-marital coitus." Journal of Marriage and the Family 37 (May): 375-384.

BIRD, C. (1979) The Two-Paycheck Marriage. New York: Rawson, Wade.

BURGESS, E. W. and H. J. LOCKE (1945) The Family: From Institution to Companionship. New York: American Book Company.

COLE, C. L. and S. L. GOETTSCH (1981) "Self-disclosure and relationship quality: a study among nonmarital cohabiting couples." Alternative Lifestyles 4 (November): 428-466.

CUBER, J. F. and P. B. HARROFF (1965) Sex and the Significant Americans. New York: Penguin.

FOOTE, N. and L. S. COTTRELL (1955) Identity and Interpersonal Competence. Chicago: University of Chicago Press.

GAYLIN, N. L. (1980) "Rediscovering the family," pp. 5-16 in N. Stinnett, B. Chesser, J. DeFrain, and P. Knaub (eds.) Family Strengths: Positive Models for Family Life, Vol. 2. Lincoln: University of Nebraska Press.

GLENN, N. D. and C. N. WEAVER (1979) "Attitudes toward premarital, extramarital, and homosexual relations in the U.S. in the 1970s." Journal of Sex Research 15: 108-118.

GLICK, P. C. (1979) "Future American families." The Washington COFO Memo 2 (Summer/Fall): 2-5.

GOODE, W. J. (1963) World Revolution and Family Patterns. New York: Macmillan.

GOUGH, K. (1971) "The origin of the family." Journal of Marriage and the Family 33 (November): 760-770.

GUSFIELD, J. R. (1967) "Tradition and modernity: misplaced polarities in the study of social change." American Journal of Sociology 72: 351-362.

HAREVEN, T. K. (1978) "Family time and historical time," pp. 57-70 in A. S. Rasse, J. Kagan, and T. K. Hareven (eds.) The Family. New York: W. W. Norton.

HILLER, D. V. and W. W. PHILLIBER, (1982) "Predicting marital and career success among dual-worker couples." Journal of Marriage and the Family 44 (February): 53-62.

HINE, T. (1982) The Philadelphia Inquirer, March 7.

HUTTER, M. (1981) The Changing Family. New York: John Wiley.

LASLETT, B. (1978) "Family membership, past and present." Social Problems 25 (June): 476-490.

LASLETT, P. [ed.] (1972) Household and Family in Past Time. Cambridge: Cambridge University Press.

LEVIN, R. J. (1975) "The Redbook report on premarital and extramarital sex: the end of the double standard?" Redbook (October): 38-44, 190-192.

LEWIS, J. M., W. R. BEAVERS, J. T. GOSSETT, and V. A. PHILLIPS (1976) No Single Thread: Psychological Health in Family Systems. New York: Brunner/Mazel.

MACE, D. and V. MACE (1980) "Enriching marriages: The foundation stone of family strength," pp. 89-110 in N. Stinnett, B. Chesser, J. DeFrain, and P. Knaub (eds.) Family Strengths: Positive Models for Family Life, Vol. 2. Lincoln: University of Nebraska Press.

——— (1977) "Counter-epilogue," pp. 390-396 in R. W. Libby and R. N. Whitehurst (eds.) Marriage and Alternatives. Glenview, IL: Scott, Foresman.

MACKLIN, E. D. (1980) "Nontraditional family forms: a decade of research." Journal of Marriage and the Family 42 (November): 905-922.

MASNICK, G. and M. J. BANE, (1980) The Nation's Families: 1960-1990. Boston: Auburn House.

McDONALD, G. W. (1980) "Family power: the assessment of a decade of theory and research, 1970-1980." Journal of Marriage and the Family 42 (November): 841-854.

MUDD, E. H., H. E. MITCHELL, and S. B. TAUBIN (1965) Success in Family Living. New York: Association Press.

MUDD, E. H. and S. B. TAUBIN (1982) "Success in family living: does it last? A twenty-year followup." American Journal of Family Therapy 10 (Spring): 59-67.

OLSON, D. H., D. H. SPRENKLE, and C. RUSSELL (1979) "Circumplex model of marital and family systems: I. cohesion and adaptability dimensions, family types, and clinical applications." Family Process 18: 3-28.

SCANZONI, J. and G. L. FOX (1980) "Sex roles, family and society: the seventies and beyond." Journal of Marriage and the Family 42 (November): 743-756.

SHORTER, E. (1975) The Making of the Modern Family. New York: Basic Books.

SKINNER, D. A. (1980) "Dual-career family stress and coping: a literature review." Family Relations 29 (October): 473-482.

SKOLNICK, A. S. and J. H. SKOLNICK, [eds.] (1980) Family in Transition: Rethinking Marriage, Sexuality, Child-Rearing, and Family Organization. Boston: Little, Brown.

SPANIER, G. B. and R. A. LEWIS (1980) "Marital quality: a review of the seventies." Journal of Marriage and the Family 42 (November): 825-839.

STINNETT, N., B. CHESSER, and J. DeFRAIN [eds.] (1979) Building Family Strengths: Blueprints for Action, Vol. 1. Lincoln: University of Nebraska Press.

——— and P. KNAUB [eds.] (1980) Family Strengths: Positive Models for Family Life, Vol. 2. Lincoln: University of Nebraska Press.

STINNETT, N., J. DeFRAIN, K. KING, P. KNAUB, and G. ROWE [eds.] (1981) Family
    Strengths: The Roots of Well-Being, Vol. 3. Lincoln: University of Nebraska Press.
U.S. Bureau of the Census (1981) Marital Status and Living Arrangements: March 1980.
    Current Population Reports, Series P-20, No. 365. Washington, DC: Government
    Printing Office.
U.S. Department of Labor (1980) Employment in Perspective: Working Women — 1979
    Summary. Report 587. Washington, DC: U.S. Department of Labor, Bureau of Labor
    Statistics.
WATSON, M. A. (1981) "Sexually-open marriage: three perspectives." Alternative Life-
    styles 4, 1: 3-21.
YANKELOVICH, D. (1981) "New rules in American life: searching for self-fulfillment in a
    world turned upside down." Psychology Today (April): 35-91.

PART II

LIFESTYLE PERSPECTIVES AND ISSUES

CHAPTER 13

Alternatives for the Elderly

PAULA L. DRESSEL
Georgia State University

BETH B. HESS
County College of Morris

Alternative lifestyles are not just for young people anymore. Actually, they never were. Variant family forms, that is, departures from the single life-long spouse natural children nuclear ideal, are not particularly recent phenomena. Uhlenberg (1974) has convincingly demonstrated that the marital history of contemporary American women is in many respects *less* diverse than that of earlier cohorts. For example, in the nineteenth and early twentieth centuries, variations in age of marriage and remarriage, and in ages at which widowhood and nest emptying occurred, were much greater across a birth cohort than is the case today, as was the possibility of not marrying, infertility, and raising the offspring of kin. Those women who survived to old age reached that point from many different marital paths, as, indeed, did their male counterparts. Once again, the myth of the "classical family of Western nostalgia" has obscured a realistic assessment of family life in the past as well as in the present.

Nonetheless, social and demographic trends in our society today make alternative lifestyles increasingly likely for the elderly and may eventually evoke patterns far more radical than those of an earlier era. Many of the variants of the past could be considered "normal": singlehood, remarriage after the death of a spouse, and families composed of step- and half-siblings or of nieces and nephews untimely orphaned or deserted. But today there is also the possibility of various communal arrangements, nonmarital cohabitation (which has not been infrequent among the less affluent at any historical moment), and such exotica as polygyny. As the

Authors' Note: The authors wish to thank Sylvia Clavan, Harold Feldman, Margaret Feldman, Helen Hacker, Elizabeth W. Markson, and Ethel Vatter for their comments on an earlier draft of this chapter.

sexual revolution comes of age, literally, we can expect to find more elderly households composed of persons unrelated by blood or marriage, based on either heterosexual or homosexual intimacies, or remaining resolutely nonsexual (Cavan, 1973).

In this chapter we shall note pertinent theoretical models for understanding the emergence of alternative lifestyles among the elderly, examine the limited evidence currently available, discuss life course and cohort differences, consider the implications of these differences, and gaze tentatively into the future. As an overview of this relatively unexplored topic, our chapter is not meant to be exhaustive. Nor does it examine in any detail the variations that may occur among subgroups of old people. As yet, there is so little empirical research on alternative lifestyle differences among older people that there are few data that can be reported. Only recently has the literature even acknowledged alternatives among the elderly as a category, much less recognized the great diversity within the aged population.

Theoretical Perspectives

Under what circumstances can we expect the emergence of alternative patterns for meeting the needs of intimacy, sexual expression, and caring in the later years? Befitting our subject matter, theoretical insight can be gained from two "golden oldies" of the sociological canon. Particularly relevant is Wilbert Moore's classic (1960) work on the roots of social change, in which he identifies tensions and flexibilities in the social system that both encourage and permit the development of functional alternatives to existing structures. Moore cites three general conditions that have obvious and direct implications for today's aged: (a) lack of specificity in role expectations, (b) demographic imbalance, and (c) scarcity of desired goods and services.

With respect to role expectations, it is probably safe to suggest that current cohorts of elderly are pioneering the norms that will come to govern the behavior of those who have outlived major productive and reproductive roles in our society. This lack of clear normative prescription may not have been perceived as an important impetus to social change when relatively few individuals survived their productive years and when active roles in family, community, and work remained available to those few who did survive. Today, of course, most Americans can expect to live a decade or more beyond retirement. Yet it can be argued (e.g., Rosow, 1974) that the absence of effective channels of socialization leads to a situation of relative rolelessness, that, whatever its drawbacks, does permit considerable behavioral latitude to this pioneering generation of elderly.

As for demographic imbalance, this century has witnessed increasing divergence in life expectancy by gender. In 1900, average life expectancy at birth for both males and females was approximately 50 years. Today it is about 70 years for White males and 78 years for White females, and only slightly lower for non-Whites, whose life expectancy doubled in this century, though with the same differential by sex. In the year 2000, moreover, this discrepancy in life expectancy by gender is projected to result in a sex ratio imbalance of 66 males aged 65+ for every 100 elderly women (Soldo, 1980). Furthermore, remarriage rates for men are higher than those for women at all adult ages, but especially so at the older ages. Even never-married men at these ages are six times more likely to marry than are single older women (Treas and Vanhilst, 1976).

The bottom line, then, is that old men, even at ages 75+, are over three times as likely as their female age peers to be living with a spouse, 68 percent and 21 percent, respectively. Conversely, in 1978 there were, among the noninstitutionalized aged, over 10 million old people (2 million men and 8 million women) whose intimacy needs were not being met within a marriage relationship. This figure is roughly 40 percent of all old people (U.S. Bureau of the Census, 1979). Of course, not all *married* persons are enjoying need gratification, either because of longstanding marital difficulties or through illness and incapacity of a partner (e.g., Butler and Lewis, 1976; Pfeiffer and Davis, 1974).

Moore's third causal condition for the emergence of functional alternatives is the scarcity of resources relative to human desires. In this case we are speaking of both affective and material resources. Income, health, friends, and family are resources that become especially scarce in old age, varying somewhat with gender and race. Affection, caring, protection, and emotional support are, of course, important to individuals of all ages, but old people in general have less energy to pursue such goods and relatively little with which to bargain for such inputs (Dowd, 1980). A shortage of affordable private housing, along with other material deprivations, may interfere with an older person's ability to maintain independent residence. In spite of having many of the same needs as younger persons, therefore, the probability of gratification is considerably lessened in later life. Consequently, the possibility of nonnormative behaviors increases.

Another classic conceptual model that would predict innovative responses on the part of the elderly is Merton's paradigm of anomie (1964, 1967), which suggests that individuals who subscribe to culturally validated goals but who are systematically denied legitimate opportunity to achieve these ends will experiment with other means of goal attainment. Innovative lifestyles, then, in the jargon of sociology, are behavioral adaptations to social structural constraints. Note that both Merton and Moore are concerned with social system or macrolevel phenomena, not with personal motivations or socially constructed meanings.

A more recent perspective is that of age stratification (Riley et al., 1972), which describes the processes whereby role players with particular attributes are articulated into a role structure of age-graded statuses. In this case, the factors of interest are the differential life expectancy of males and females leading to an oversupply of older women relative to men, on the one hand, and the paucity of legitimate nonfamily roles for meeting intimacy and caring needs on the other. As Riley and her colleagues have noted, the normal progression of different birth cohorts through a social system is an independent source of social change. When cohorts are marked by extreme demographic shifts, the resulting "disordered cohort flow" creates the conditions for institutional change (Waring, 1975). The same model can be applied to demographic shifts that occur within a cohort's life courses as well as to intercohort differences. Thus when the numbers of men and women were quite similar, and when fewer nonmarried elderly were living independently from kin, the question of alternatives was rarely broached in terms other than those of individual idiosyncrasy. Today, however, a critical mass of widowed and other nonmarried old people exists, exerting pressure on structural arrangements in the taken-for-granted world of the elderly.

We ought to note here that whether or not alternative lifestyles are actually adopted by old people depends to a large extent on the degree to which unmet material and intimacy needs are recognized or acknowledged by the individual. How individuals define their situations varies greatly from person to person, and recognizing one's needs is not the same as viewing them as legitimate. It is not unlikely, for example, that many older people lower their expectations to fit their circumstances, thus reducing cognitive dissonance and potential frustration. Although much of the literature takes the needs of the elderly as a given, the extent of their perceived need must be treated as an empirical question in future research on this topic.

Nonetheless, a certain proportion of elderly men and women today have discovered, constructed, or continued to maintain what are decidedly nontraditional arrangements for ensuring companionship and care. And bearing in mind that those currently old were socialized into a more restrictive view of appropriate living styles, we should perhaps marvel at the variety of alternatives that have evolved, regardless of how few actually participate in them. Cohort considerations lead us to expect that these numbers will increase in the future as more people experience nontraditional living arrangements in their early and middle years, as tolerance of these variations increases, and as those currently old successfully experiment with alternatives.

It is important that a distinction be drawn between alternative lifestyles and alternative statuses. Persons who are widowed or divorced are by definition not in a traditional marital relationship (hence they are in an alternative status), but may or may not adopt a nonnormative living arrangement. In old age, traditional living alternatives for the unmarried are those of living alone or living with close kin. Our discussion of alterna-ive lifestyles for the elderly will emphasize unconventional living arangements. Alternative marital statuses of old people will be mentioned irst since it is one's marital status that is primarily responsible for determing lifestyle options.

Alternative Marital Statuses

The Unmarried

Never-Married Singlehood

The proportion of the U.S. population that had never married by age 5 in 1978 was slightly over 5 percent (almost 6 percent of the females and bout 4.5 percent of the males) compared with over 7.5 percent just a lecade ago (USDHEW, 1979a). Clearly, we are a marrying nation — more o today than ever before. The growing popularity of extended singlehood among young adults should not obscure the powerful pressures toward narrying at least once.

Many of this 5 percent will have always been loners who long ago made the adaptations that will cushion them in old age. Never having lepended upon family, they will have fewer interpersonal resources to shield them from such effects of age as reduced control over one's life, or to mitigate the absence of daily contacts that once provided "location" and meaning (Gubrium, 1975). It is through conversations with others that humans create reality (including the definition of one's self) and exchange expectations of role-appropriate behavior. Persons without family ties or intact friendship networks are, therefore, particularly vulnerable in old age. t should not surprise us, then, that the never married are disproportionately represented in the institutionalized population.

In general, the few available studies of never-married elderly have found that they are somewhat less happy than the married but more so than the widowed and divorced (Scott, 1979; Ward, 1979). However, it must be noted that people still married at age 65 are the selected survivors of a marriage cohort that has been winnowed of its unhappy members. Here also, cohort differences cannot be overlooked: Incoming elderly, women particularly, will be much better equipped than in the past to avoid negative outcomes of singleness, especially in terms of personal resources such as education, income, and experience in independent achievement.

Divorced Persons

In 1978, fewer than 4 percent of persons 65 years of age were categorized as "divorced" (as opposed to single, married, or widowed). Because of differential survival and remarriage rates for men and women, this consisted of 269,000 men and 425,000 women. These figures are likely to increase within the next decade, since the number of divorced persons aged 55 to 64 in 1978 was 500,000 men and almost 700,000 women. Although many of these will remarry (the men at a rate four times that of the women), it seems safe to conclude that the proportions of divorced and never-remarried older people will continue a gradual upward trend due to the increased divorce rate in our society and the decline of remarriage rates with age, particularly in the case of women (USDHEW, 1979b).

Widowed Persons

At ages 65 to 74, fewer than 10 percent of men are widowers, compared to over 40 percent of women; at age 75+, these figures increase to 23 percent and almost 70 percent, respectively. The oldest and frailest of the widowed will either join the household of an adult offspring or enter an institution, but the majority will maintain independent residence. In several respects — income, life satisfaction, and support networks — widowed old people fare less well than those who have never married or who have terminated unhappy marriages. At all ages, the widowed are less likely than the divorced to remarry, although widowed men are eight times more likely than their female counterparts to remarry at age 65+ (Treas and Vanhilst, 1976; USDHEW, 1973).

For many widows, the process of "sanctification" of the dead spouse (Lopata, 1979) impedes establishing intimacy with another man. Conversely, the large number of similarly bereaved women makes it easier to create friendship networks than is the case for either younger widows or divorced elderly women. At least for the concurrent cohort of old people, widowhood is a more legitimated status than is that of divorcée.

The Remarried

Although not literally in an alternative structure since they are still members of a nuclear family, the *remarried* parents and children of divorce or widowhood enter old age with several nontraditional kinship relationships: for example, ties to stepchildren, half-siblings, ex-spouses, and noncustodial parents. Furthermore, if one's own offspring have remarried, an old person might have grandchildren in a large number of different families, including a courtesy relationship with a former daughter- or son-in-law who has remarried.

It could be argued in this respect that the family ties of tomorrow's elderly may actually be richer, and certainly more complex, than is suggested by those who fear the imminent demise of family life in America. These Jeremiahs should be heartened rather than dejected over the continual reconstruction of family links. Perhaps we will soon follow the example of most simple societies by elaborating a system of kinship terminology capable of expressing the uniqueness of each relationship. At any rate, it is those who are in this alternative status whose intimacy needs in old age are most likely to be met, given the variety of kin who can be mobilized for support.

Alternative Living Arrangements

The above alternatives to the life-long nuclear ideal are similar to those of the historical past, with the exception that divorce is a more frequent disrupter of conjugal households than was previously the case. In a sense, these can be considered "legitimated" alternatives. Singlehood, though often deplored, is nonetheless accepted as an individual's choice or fate. Widowhood is perceived as beyond one's control, although the widow may be subtly stigmatized. (The widower, to the contrary, is a sought-after prize on the remarriage market.) Divorce and family reconstitution are tolerated today, if not fully approved.

But what of the less legitimate alternatives? The professional literature is long on discussion but woefully short on empirical evidence regarding the antecedents, meanings, and consequences of many of these nontraditional lifestyles for the elderly. On the assumption that future cohorts of old people will be less inexperienced or inhibited in their choices of living arrangements, and, at the same time, will be as likely to be nonmarried as those currently old, it should prove instructive to survey the evidence and speculation on alternative lifestyles in old age.

Nonmarital Heterosexual Cohabitation

This is a lifestyle option for the elderly that received a great deal of publicity before the 1977 changes in Social Security regulations. Prior to that date, older persons who remarried typically lost their claim to a former spouse's benefits. The new regulations permit a person over 60 who remarries to continue to receive a widow or widower's benefit or half the benefit of the current spouse, whichever is larger. One other major barrier to the remarriage of elderly widows and widowers remains: obstruction by offspring concerned about inheritance. However, this appears to be of decreasing importance for old people; many aging women, for instance, are more independent than was the case before, including having a degree of independence from offspring. Rosenfeld (1979) has documented a tendency for old people who live in retirement communities to leave bequests to their new-found friends and companions rather than to off-spring. That is, they reward those who are providing interpersonal supports at this moment. Many elderly feel that their children are making it on their own and ought not to depend on an inheritance from parents.

Nonetheless, between 1970 and 1977, there was a threefold increase (from 26,000 to 85,000) in the number of households occupied by non-married couples in which the primary householder was 65 or older (Glick and Norton, 1977). This represents 1.3 percent of all elderly households. Although some of these 85,000 households include landlord/tenant or householder/employee units, the similarity in ages of the individuals involved suggests that the great majority are elderly men and women living together without benefit of clergy, even though this is no longer necessary for financial reasons.

In an analysis of 1978 marriage licenses in Fulton County, Georgia, Dressel (1980) found that 28 percent of the older couples applying for a marriage license gave the same address, compared with 36 percent of the younger couples. When multifamily dwelling units were removed from the data base, approximately 25 percent of both young and old applicants had apparently been living together before applying for a marriage license.

It remains to be seen whether the 1977 revisions of the Social Security regulations will lead to a significant reduction in cohabitation among the elderly, or whether changing characteristics of old people, coupled with increasing acceptance of nontraditional arrangements, will lead to ever increasing numbers of households composed of nonmarried men and women over the age of 65.

Multiadult Households

This category includes both intentional and nonintentional communities. The former have typically been associated with religious groups or the young (Kanter, 1972; Streib and Streib, 1975) and are usually characterized by an ideological commitment that supports and sustains the community. The latter, unintended communities, "just grow" out of daily interactions of persons who live in the same building (see Hochschild, 1973) or the same retirement community. The intended/unintended continuum is also characterized by degrees of formality in the relationships, from those that are purely voluntary and unstructured, as in the case of persons who find themselves in the same residential setting, to the highly formalized arrangements of those who enter into an agreement to pool resources, share responsibilities, and, in some cases, hire a manager, as in the Share-a-Home system examined by Streib and Hilker (1980).

Multiadult residences offer both instrumental and expressive rewards, at the cost, of course, of some loss of independence and autonomy. But these latter costs may not weigh so heavily with older persons whose abilities to function on their own are increasingly being undermined by the social and physical decrements of aging. In fact, sharing may enhance independent functioning, particularly in the more formalized settings where basic care is ensured. Indeed, Streib and Hilker (1980) found that declines in health and income were a primary motivation for entering into the Share-a-Home arrangement. Thus, as we have noted elsewhere (Hess, 1976), "necessity makes communards of those who least acknowledge such impulses." In the absence of zoning regulations restricting the number of unrelated individuals who can share a residence, cooperative households of several elderly persons who jointly purchase and maintain the dwelling hold great promise for relieving loneliness and stretching limited resources.

A logical extension of these observations would be to suggest that many elderly homeowners might find it to their advantage to rent space to other unrelated individuals. The very limited evidence on this point (see, for example, Usher and McConnell, 1980) indicates that older people in poor health and those anticipating income problems were most receptive to the idea of sharing their homes, but not necessarily with an old person. Rather, a middle-aged individual was perceived as better able to meet the instrumental needs of the homeowner for services and additional income. Homesharers were not primarily motivated by needs for affiliation or affective need gratification. In the Usher and McConnell sample, for example, it was those homeowners who were *most* socially integrated within communities who expressed the greatest interest in sharing.

The prospects of younger couples sharing a home with an unrelated older person, an arrangement that Clavan and Vatter (1972) have called the "affiliated family," also appear limited unless impelled by necessity. The advantages of additional help with child care and household tasks or in meeting mortgage payments are still outweighed by the desire for privacy. But times may change this balance. There is, in fact, growing interest on the part of the federal government in the placement of older people in foster homes of younger adults who are not necessarily related to the older person (e.g., Sussman, 1979). The Veterans Administration, for example, currently places released psychiatric patients in households that then receive income supplements and free medical care in return for caring for the older individual. This arrangement may prove to be less expensive than either institutionalization or the provision of community-based services for independent living, despite the fact that it appears to run counter to the desire of most older persons to remain in their own homes.

Another form of multiadult household, more honored in the speculative literature than in fact, is the polygynous family structure. Kassel (1966) argues that polygyny is a time-tested and widely used solution to problems generated by skewed sex ratios. Although designed to increase reproduction and to reinforce systems of social stratification in other societies, he argues that polygyny could provide material and socioemotional benefits to the elderly, including group health insurance, division of household labor, care for the ill, improved diet and housing, and better grooming, not to mention "sexual outlet" (in Kinsey's immortal term). However, as Rosenberg (1970) points out, polygyny requires ideological support, which is highly unlikely in a society based on ideals of conjugality and monogamy, or among a population socialized to more traditional family values. It is even debatable whether incoming cohorts of elderly will be greatly attracted to this alternative.

In sum, older people appear to entertain the notion of formalized multiadult living arrangements when they can perceive an instrumental payoff in terms of health care and income. Since neither of these conditions is going to improve significantly among old people in the immediate future, the multiadult household will continue to offer an alternative to maintenance of an independent residence or the more drastic step of institutionalization. Since it is currently the oldest segments of the elderly population that are increasing at the fastest rate, there will be many more nonmarried old people at risk of health and income problems, adding greatly to the pool of potential adopters of the multiadult household option. If, as current directions seem to indicate, public policy is redirected toward community-based living arrangements for the elderly, some relief might be expected in zoning regulations, utility costs, assistance with renovation, and other factors leading to safe and comfortable group dwellings.

Alternatives to Exclusive Heterosexuality

There are no current systematic data on *extramarital sexuality* among the elderly. The Kinsey et al. (1948) findings of three decades ago indicate only a slight decline in the older years in the proportion of men engaged in such activity, but the sample was highly selective and very skewed toward respondents at higher income and education levels. There will undoubtedly continue to be older men who find it both erotically satisfying and ego gratifying to be sexually involved with women other than their wives. Interestingly, in literature on sexuality in later life, one fairly consistent finding is that a decrease in sexual activity among married persons is typically attributed to the husband's lack of interest rather than to the wife's (Pfeiffer and Davis, 1974). However, there is no evidence as yet that frustrated sexual needs are driving older women in any large numbers into the extramarital marketplace.

Given the current rate of extramarital experience among younger cohorts, greater numbers of both men and women will be entering old age with a history of extramarital relationships, thus increasing the likelihood of such relationships in later life. On the other hand, we must keep in mind that in later-life marriages, the unions that have survived are typically characterized by satisfaction and closeness. Also, despite the reams of hortatory calls for sexual liberation of the elderly, the spirit is likely to be far more willing than the flesh (Cleveland, 1976). Lastly, extramarital sex is a moot issue for the overwhelming majority of women aged 65 and over, given the few available men.

What about *homosexual relationships* in old age? In some respects this alternative will be as foreign to today's older women as that of polygyny. Although many women may develop close emotional ties to one another in widowhood, it does not seem likely that these relationships will become eroticized. Whether or not such inhibitions will also characterize older women of the future is a debatable question. Since we do not yet know the actual incidence of homosexuality in the female population, we cannot know if there has been any significant increase. It is safe to say that tolerance of homosexuality is greater with each birth cohort, and that openness in displaying one's sexual object choice is also cohort related. Thus although the actual proportion of male and female homosexuals may not have changed greatly over time, the probability of their living openly with a same-sex lover has increased. Higher proportions of elderly lesbian households in the future, then, may not indicate an increase in homosexual preference among older women as much as a relaxation of inhibiting forces.

What of those older persons, male and female, who have lived as homosexuals in earlier adulthood? A review of the literature on homosexuality and aging by Dressel and Avant (1983) suggests the following:

(1) Homosexuals, like never-married persons, may be less affected by role losses in later life through the early development of coping patterns for dealing with isolation, loneliness, and stigmatization. Nonetheless, for those who have established ties with a particular lover, the loss of a partner can be as devastating as heterosexual widowhood.

(2) Again, similar to the never married, homosexuals experience less role discontinuity throughout adulthood than do people with family responsibilities. By the same token, their life course is less varied.

(3) Homosexuals do not necessarily experience greater isolation or diminution of social networks in later life than do heterosexuals.

(4) The unbalanced sex ratio and double standard of aging actually favor the older lesbian in contrast to heterosexual women; that is, the pool of potential partners is relatively greater for the homosexual than the heterosexual woman. But it is also a rather small pool of eligibles.

(5) To the extent that homosexuality is associated with gender role flexibility, adaptation to aging may be facilitated. One of the most fascinating research findings in the recent literature has been the reduction of stereotypic gender role orientations and behaviors among aging men and women — androgynous tendencies that correlate with successful adjustment to the vicissitudes of old age (Sinnott et al., 1980; Livson, 1983).

(6) The literature is less clear on the issue of whether or not gay men experience an accelerated aging; that is, do homosexual men identify themselves as old at earlier ages than do heterosexual males? Some researchers have noted such an effect while others have not.

Generalizations about older homosexuals are no more accurate than generalizations about older heterosexuals, or about homosexuals at earlier ages, for that matter. Sexual orientation is not the sole, and perhaps not even the primary, basis of identity for most people. Moreover, the aged as a category are more diverse in attitudes, behaviors, and lifestyles than any other age group. Thus the lives of older homosexuals are as varied as those of any other group of elderly (see, for example, Bell and Weinberg, 1978; Raphael and Robinson, 1980). Dressel and Avant (1983) suggest that how and with whom one lives and shares the vagaries of aging is probably more important in determining quality of life in old age than is sexual orientation per se.

Alternative Lifestyles Across the Life Course

From the foregoing review of nontraditional statuses and lifestyles, several life course considerations are evident. First and most obviously, the adoption of alternatives among the elderly is most often a response to necessity. If there are not enough husbands to go around, one must willy-nilly construct an alternative support network. There is certainly very little of an ideological commitment to a different way of life (except perhaps among homosexuals), or much evidence of a voluntary espousal of non-traditional living arrangements. Rather, "making do" appears to be the most accurate description (Kieffer, 1977).

In contrast, many young people are actively engaged in creating alternatives to what they perceive as constricting structures of work and family life. In terms of the Mertonian paradigm, they reject both legitimate goals and means, and either retreat or seek to "restructure" the society. It remains to be seen how many young people will remain never married or childfree or members of communes through adulthood. Our guess, tentatively based on the currently low percentages of never marrieds and involuntarily childless couples, is that over 90 percent of young adults will eventually fit into the standard patterns of our society for some portion of their life courses: they will marry and become parents within a conjugal household; they may also divorce, remarry, and reparent.

If today's old people are uncomfortable with nontraditional arrangements because of their early socialization and relatively low tolerance of deviation from the norm, then clearly tomorrow's old people will be less resistant. If such cohort differences make alternative choices more likely, aging effects make them more necessary. It is difficult, however, in the absence of longitudinal data from successive birth groups to predict much about the impact of early lifestyles on later ones. There are simply too many contingencies over the course of four or more decades of adulthood and too many historical events with differential effects on various age groups to permit easy generalizations.

Although we are not yet able to say much about the consequences of earlier choices for later lifestyles, the examination of alternatives over the life course can tell us something about the social structural determinants of lifestyle choices. Young people have voluntary, ideologically based choices precisely because they are young and have not yet encumbered themselves with the obligations that channel individuals into traditional forms. Old people turn to less traditional lifestyles when, for economic and demographic reasons, they cannot meet their needs through traditional forms. But there are also other categories of persons whose lifestyle choices are constrained by structural factors: the poor and minority groups, most obviously. The individualistic bias in so much social science research, including that on alternative lifestyles, focuses attention on the characteristics, family experiences, and motivations of the chooser, while obscuring the institutional and historical dynamics that expand or limit lifestyle choices. Whether they actually wish to or not, the poor, for example, often find that they must share households and pool resources in order to survive. The female-headed family is an adaptation to particular conditions of existence imposed by such forces as the economic system and public policy, including urban planning (see Cazenave, 1980).

At the moment, professional and popular interest in alternative life-styles for the elderly may have outstripped the actual incidence of such arrangements. But given the potential need and the increasing pool of eligibles, this attention may not be misplaced. In some fashion, the current publicity and experimentation will change the atmosphere in which future choices are made.

The subject of alternative lifestyles among the elderly still evokes much resistance — from the adult offspring of old people, who may oppose even conventional remarriage of their parent, and from old people themselves, whose attitudes toward nonmarital sexuality or homosexuality, for exam-ple, were formed in the early part of this century. Unconventional ex-pressions of intimacy among the aged still evoke ridicule if not clear negative sanctions, as when cohabitation or lesbianism are given as grounds for involuntary institutionalization of an older parent (Miller et al., 1975).

Nor is there any apparent widespread public support for relaxation of sexual standards in the society as a whole; to the contrary, restrictive legislation by the new moral entrepreneurs of the radical right could well affect older people. Laws regulating private behavior between consenting adults, or limiting civil rights of homosexuals, or controlling the number of unrelated individuals sharing a household are all distinct possibilities. So, too, are contractions of Medicaid benefits to those who remarry individuals with personal assets.

We have argued throughout, however, that cohort differences could presage liberalization of both attitudes and behavior by the time the youth of the 1960s reach old age, around the turn of the century. Certainly, the sex ratio imbalance will not change greatly, nor will the incidence of affective and material scarcity among the aged, although these may occur at later ages than at present. Some might argue that the precipitating conditions for functional alternatives will actually be exacerbated in the decades ahead; such factors as inflation, energy shortages, and structural unemployment may make home sharing a common occurrence (at least with one's own kin, if not with unrelated persons).

Are there any implications from the foregoing for researchers, educators, practitioners and policymakers? Most obviously, the research gaps are enormous, and what little data are available are neither cumulative nor theoretically based, but, rather, anecdotal, individualistic, and cohort-centric. We do not know the incidence of most alternative arrangements, the social background correlates or life history of participants, the meanings attached to lifestyle choices in old age, the processes whereby such options are selected, the socialization process (including sanctions, supports, and role models), or the opportunity structures involved. The links between social system variables and personal outcomes remain unexplored and, hence, unexplained.

Research also should be guided by basic theoretical issues. In this regard, each of the major theoretical perspectives in contemporary sociology can be fruitfully applied. For example, structural functionalism directs our attention to variables such as differential opportunity, structural dislocation, demographic changes, and age stratification. From a conflict perspective, the unequal allocation of societal and personal resources in old age should be examined, along with their effect on an individual's range of choice of lifestyle. Intergenerational conflicts or tensions should also be explored. The insights of the exchange model could illuminate the tradeoffs between traditional and nontraditional choices. The macrosystem perspective would lead one to be interested in the effects that alternative lifestyles among the elderly have on the social system as a whole and in particular, on the range of choices available to incoming cohorts of old people.

At the microlevel, little is known about the meanings attached to their unconventional behavior by the elderly in alternative relationships and settings. There are few symbolic interactionist accounts of the processes by which old people enter, maintain, and remove themselves from such situations. This information would be of value to counselors, physicians, and other service providers, as well as to the general public, in place of the rather sensationalistic or patronizing presentations typically found in the media. Nor can it be said that family life educators are any more well informed on the issues raised in this chapter: Dressel and Avant (1978), in a content analysis of twelve textbooks in family sociology, found that fewer than half mentioned alternatives to marriage for the elderly other than a titilating reference to polygyny, the most unrealistic and least prevalent possibility. Three texts discussed cohabitation, only two mentioned institutionalized communal settings such as the Israeli Kibbutz, and none mentioned what will probably become the most common alternative — voluntary group home sharing along the model described by Streib (1978).

Finally, social policies must be examined for the impact, both manifest and latent, that they have on the elderly in their "freedom, independence, and the free exercise of individual initiative in planning and managing their own lives" (Older Americans Act of 1965, as amended). Policies falling under this mandate include a broad scope of issues, from local zoning regulations to state laws concerning sexual behavior to federal regulations related to such problems as income maintenance and health care provision.

Lifestyle options are contingent upon the ability to make other kinds of choices — having available residential options, adequate personal resources, freedom from health and energy constraints — all of which are rendered problematic in old age in our society. Unlike those nations with a full range of publicly funded income, health, housing, and social service programs, the United States has enshrined its work-oriented, individualistic value system in programs providing for security in old age. It is an unintended triumph of our Social Security System that it has evolved into the major income support of most older Americans, while Medicare (less than two decades old) protects the elderly against instant poverty in case of illness. The outcome is that the vast majority of old people can remain independent of their kin, live in homes of their own, in communities of their choosing. This independence, however precarious for many (very old widows especially), is the basic condition for the exercise of lifestyle choices. Therefore, if we seek to extend the range of acceptable behaviors for meeting affective and affiliative needs in old age, we must first secure the elderly's entitlements to adequate income and health care, to affordable housing, and to community provision of social services. Each of these programs is currently in jeopardy of reduced funding if not of complete phasing out. Accompanied by a renewed emphasis on familial rather than public responsibility for the welfare of old people, these cutbacks will severely affect the older person's freedom of choice at all levels. Particularly vulnerable are widowed women, whose income and health status are already constraining factors. Between the new Puritanism and the retreat from social welfare activism at the federal level, the life space of many older people will probably shrink rather than expand in the near future.

In the long run, however, we suspect that the liberating currents of the past several decades will ultimately enhance the ability of old people as well as young to create satisfying interpersonal networks in a variety of lifestyles. In sum, alternative lifestyle options for the elderly should command the attention of social scientists, educators, service practitioners, and policymakers, as well as concerned citizens of all ages.

References

BELL, A. P. and M. S. WEINBERG (1978) Homosexualities. New York: Simon & Schuster.
BUTLER, R. N. and M. I. LEWIS (1976) Sex After Sixty. New York: Harper & Row.
CAZENAVE, N. A. (1980) "Alternate intimacy, marriage, and family lifestyles among low-income Black Americans." Alternative Lifestyles 3 (November): 425-444.

CAVAN, R. S. (1973) "Speculations on innovations to conventional marriage in old age."
    The Gerontologist 13: 409-411.
CLAVAN, S. and E. VATTER (1972) "The affiliated family: a continued analysis." Family
    Coordinator 21: 499-504.
CLEVELAND, M. (1976) "Sex in marriage: at 40 and beyond." Family Coordinator
    25: 233-240.
DOWD, J. J. (1980) Stratification Among the Aged. Monterey, CA: Brooks/Cole.
DRESSEL, P. L. (1980) "Assortive mating in later life: some initial considerations." Journal
    of Family Issues 1 (September): 379-396.
——— and W. R. AVANT (1983) "Range of alternatives," in R. Weg (ed.) Sexuality in the
    Later Years: Roles and Behavior. New York: Academic.   •
——— (1978) "Aging and college family textbooks." Family Coordinator 27
    (October): 427-435.
GLICK, P. C. and A. J. NORTON (1977) Marrying, Divorcing, and Living Together in the
    U.S. Today. Population Bulletin 32 (5). Washington, DC: Population Reference
    Bureau.
GUBRIUM, J. (1975) "Being single in old age." Aging and Human Development 6: 29-41.
HESS, B. B. (1976) "Self help among the aged." Social Policy 7, 3: 55-62.
HOCHSCHILD, A. R. (1973) "Communal lifestyles for the old." Transactions 10, 5: 50-
    57.
KANTER, R. M. (1972) Commitment and Community. Cambridge, MA: Harvard Univer-
    sity Press.
KASSEL, V. (1966) "Polygyny after 60." Geriatrics 21 (April): 214-218.
KIEFFER, C. (1977) "New depths in intimacy," pp. 267-293 in R. W. Libby and R. N.
    Whitehurst (eds.) Marriage and Alternatives. Glenview, IL: Scott, Foresman.
KINSEY, A. C., W. POMEROY, and C. MARTIN (1948) Sexual Behavior in the Human
    Male. Philadelphia: W. B. Saunders.
LIVSON, F. (1983) "Sexuality and sex roles: implications of change," in R. Weg (ed.)
    Sexuality in the Later Years: Roles and Behavior. New York: Academic.
LOPATA, H. Z. (1979) Women as Widows: Support Systems. New York: Elsevier.
MERTON, R. K. (1967) On Theoretical Sociology. New York: Macmillan.
——— (1964) Social Theory and Social Structure. New York: Macmillan.
MILLER, M. B., H. BERNSTEIN, and H. SHARKEY (1975) "Family extrusion of the aged
    parent: family homeostasis and sexual conflict." The Gerontologist 14
    (August): 291-296.
MOORE, W. (1960) "A reconsideration of theories of social change." American Sociologi-
    cal Review 25 (December): 810-818.
Older Americans Act of 1965, as amended (Public Laws 89-73, 90-42, 91-69, 92-258,
    93-29).
PFEIFFER, E. and G. C. DAVIS (1974) "Determinants of sexual behavior in middle and
    old age," in E. Palmore (ed.) Normal Aging II. Durham, NC: Duke University Press.
RAPHAEL, S. M. and M. K. ROBINSON (1980) "The older lesbian: love relationships and
    friendship patterns." Alternative Lifestyles 3 (May): 207-230.
RILEY, M. W., M. JOHNSON, and A. FONER (1972) Aging in Society. Vol. 3: A Sociology
    of Age Stratification. New York: Russell Sage.
ROSENBERG, G. S. (1970) "Implications of new models of the family for the aging
    population," pp. 171-181 in H. A. Otto (ed.) The Family in Search of a Future. New
    York: Appleton-Century-Crofts.
ROSENFELD, J. (1979) The Legacy of Aging. Norwood, NJ: Ablex.
ROSOW, I. (1974) Socialization to Old Age. Berkeley: University of California Press.
SCOTT, J. P. (1979) "Single rural elders." Alternative Lifestyles 2 (August): 359-378.
SINNOTT, J. D., M. R. BLOCK, J. D. GRAMBS, C. D. GADDY, and J. L. DAVIDSON
    (1980) Sex Roles in Mature Adults: Antecedents and Correlates. Technical Report
    NIA-80-1. College Park, MD: Center on Aging, University of Maryland.
SOLDO, B. J. (1980) "America's elderly in the 1980s." Population Bulletin 35, 4.
STEIN, P. J. [ed.] (1981) Single Life. New York: St. Martin's.
STREIB, G. F. (1978) "An alternative family form for older persons: Need and social
    context." Family Coordinator 27 (October): 413-420.

———— and M. A. HILKER (1980) "The cooperative 'family': an alternative lifestyle for the elderly." Alternative Lifestyles 3 (May): 167-184.

STREIB, G. F. and R. B. STREIB (1975) "Communes and aging: utopian dream and gerontological reality." American Behavioral Scientist 19 (November/December): 176-189.

SUSSMAN, M. B. (1979) Social and Economic Supports and Family Environments for the Elderly. Final Report to the Administration on Aging, AOA Grant No. 90-A-316 (03), January.

TREAS, J. and A. VANHILST (1976) "Marriage and remarriage rates among older Americans." The Gerontologist 16 (April): 132-136.

UHLENBERG, P. (1974) "Cohort variations in family life cycle experiences of U.S. females." Journal of Marriage and the Family 36: 284-292.

U.S. Bureau of the Census (1979) Social and Economic Characteristics of the Older Population, 1978. Current Population Reports: Special Studies. Series P-23, No. 85 (August). Washington, DC: Government Printing Office.

U.S. Department of Health, Education and Welfare (1979a) Divorces by Marriage Cohort. DHEW Publication No. (PHS) 79-1912, August. Washington, DC: DHEW.

———— (1979b) First Marriages: United States, 1968-1976. DHEW Publication No. (PHS) 79-1913, September. Washington, DC: DHEW.

———— (1973) Remarriages. DHEW Publication No. (HRA) 74-1903, December. Washington, DC: DHEW.

USHER, C. E. and S. R. McCONNELL (1980) "House-sharing: a way to intimacy?" Alternative Lifestyles 3 (May): 149-166.

WARD R. A. (1979) "The never-married in later life." Journal of Gerontology 34: 861-869.

WARING, J. (1975) "Social replenishment and social change: the problem of disordered cohort flow." American Behavioral Scientist 19: 237-256.

CHAPTER 14

The Present and Future of Alternative Lifestyles in Ethnic American Cultures

MARIE F. PETERS
University of Connecticut

HARRIETTE P. McADOO
Howard University

The term "alternative lifestyles," when applied to family life in the United States, implies that the traditional or preferred style of family living in this country is the independent and residentially isolated nuclear family with extreme differentiation in parental roles (i.e., husband/father expected to fill the economic provider role and wife/mother assigned the homemaker/child caregiver role). Concommitantly, alternative lifestyles imply that other families, such as single-parent families or dual-career families — the choices and preferences many contemporary families are now making — are new, nontraditional, and optional. This is misleading. Many so-called alternative lifestyles, which seem so modern and bold to middle-class Americans, are merely variant family patterns that have been traditional within Black and other ethnic communities for many generations. Presented as "the new lifestyles" of the young mainstream elite, they are in fact the same lifestyles that have in the past been discounted as pathological, deviant, or unacceptable when observed in Black families (Peters, 1974). The structures and patterns of ethnic families, although presented here within the perspective of alternative lifestyles, are not necessarily viewed by Blacks themselves as alternative but as available, traditional, and logical life choices. Because of the economic and social imperatives of technology in the Western world, the nuclear patriarchal family was indeed the American middle-class ideal family structure during the first part of this century (Ogburn and Nimkoff, 1955). However, in the past decade the escalating demands of cybernation and the psychologically attractive ideological preferences of an expanding educated elite have allowed affluent and socially advantaged middle-class White Americans some flexibility and choice with regard to marriage and family living patterns. This increased opportunity for choice of lifestyle has caused family sociologists and other observers of the middle-class American family to label nontraditional (i.e., nonnuclear, nonmale/female role specific) family arrangements "alternative lifestyles."

This chapter discusses issues related to research on lifestyles within the Black community. To review the literature on all ethnic groups is too vast a task to permit adequate coverage in one short chapter; therefore, the decision was made to concentrate on one ethnic group, and to use it as illustrative of research on ethnic family patterns in general. A more logical choice would have been to include information on ethnic families within each chapter of this volume. However, awareness of ethnic families is usually so limited that unfortunately it has become customary to set aside one chapter to cover all ethnic families.

Alternative or Diverse Lifestyles in the Black Community

There are more reports on the alternative lifestyles of Black families than on those of other ethnic groups because Blacks are the largest ethnic minority and their family forms have been consistently documented over the past generations (McAdoo, 1982). Historians such as Blassingame (1972) and Gutman (1976) as well as many biographies and autobiographies have described family life of Black people during and after slavery, providing evidence of a long heritage of alternative lifestyles. Sociologists similarly have studied Black families — urban, rural, in the North, and in the South. In 1908 W.E.B. DuBois, the eminent Black sociologist, published a study of Black American families living in Philadelphia that emphasized the many diverse family patterns found among Black families at that time. Charles S. Johnson (1934), E. Franklin Frazier (1939), and Davis (1940), along with the more recent works of H. Lewis (1955), Billingsley (1968), Young (1970), Hill (1971), Scanzoni (1971), Staples (1973), Nobles (1974), Peters (1974), Stack (1974), Aschenbrenner (1975), D. Lewis (1975), Willie (1976), Martin and Martin (1978), Scott (1980), McAdoo (1981), and Peters and Massey (1981), all have documented the continued creativity, variety, and diversity of Black family life.

More recently, other groups of color have begun the process of documenting the unique, and yet in many ways similar, family values and patterns that are found in their various ethnic and immigrant family groups. These patterns include flexible husband/wife roles (shared income-producing and child care chores), employed mothers (with preschoolers who need day care), female-headed (single-parent) families, never-married mothers (often nonmarried by choice and children not considered to be illegitimate), extended families, augmented families, nonrelatives as kin, nonmarried cohabitants, and polygyny. High divorce and separation rates, low pay (especially for women), chronic unemployment, poor and expensive housing, and other stresses that many Black families face have often demanded creative and resourceful lifestyles.

The publications of the above authors are a rich source of information for researchers and others who are interested in understanding the evolution of alternative lifestyles. Much insight could also come from an exploration of the experiences of Black families who are developing new lifestyles to adapt to current economic pressures and population imbalances. As Cazenave (1980: 427) has written:

> Because of the increasing availability of opportunities, or the persistent lack of them, a large proportion of Blacks do not live in traditional marital and familial arrangements. If present family demographic trends continue, we can expect that Black American families will be *pushed* (e.g., via economic restraints) and *pulled* (e.g., via ethnic subcultural preferences) into an even greater variety of lifestyles.

The various patterns of contemporary Black American ethnic cultures are partly the result of particular economic/social structural forces that impinge on their lives, and their involvement in alternative living patterns is not necessarily the result of philosophical preferences. For the 40 percent of Blacks whose family income is below or near the poverty level, the so-called alternative lifestyles are an indication of the "increasing challenges to their mere physical and social survival" (Cazenave, 1980: 427). As more non-Black families are facing some of these same economic pressures with the present economic slowdown, more of them are adopting the variant living patterns characteristic of Black American lifestyles.

However, many of the living patterns of Afro-Americans reflect their cultural history (Nobles, 1974). Traditionally, there has been a more ready acceptance of viable diverse family living arrangements by the Black community and, hence, more permission for personal lifestyle choices than is characteristic of the majority culture. The cultural history of Afro-Americans, which differs from that of Euro-Americans, influences Black family life in basic ways that are evident in the lifestyles of Black families regardless of social class background or economic vicissitudes (Aschenbrenner, 1975). To attribute the variety of lifestyles seen in the Black community solely to coping responses to the harsh economic constraints low-income Blacks face is an ethnocentric perspective that ignores the validity of the Afro-American experience. As Aschenbrenner (1975: 463) writes, "Black family organization (is) fundamentally different from that of Euro-Americans . . . reflecting a value difference that cuts across economic lines in Black communities."

The Status of Research on Ethnic Minority Families of Color

Research and theory on Black and other ethnic families, based on a view that such families evidence a viable and distinct cultural pattern of family and kinship, have not progressed as rapidly as would be desired. This is partially due to the difficulty that Black family researchers uniquely face in achieving professional recognition. In addition, Black families are practically invisible to most Americans, and American social scientists typically view Black Americans from a problem-oriented perspective (Billingsley, 1968; Peters, 1974; Cazenave, 1980). The humanitarian and politically motivated War on Poverty that excited America during the 1960s ultimately resulted in what amounted to documentation by social scientists of inadequacies, deviances, and pathologies that they perceived to be characteristic of Blacks. Much funded research involved developing programs designed to eliminate observed differences by transforming the behavior and lifestyles of Black parents and their children into those preferred by mainstream American families (Peters, 1977a). If economic and social demands and constraints had a similar impact on Black American as they do on White American families, perhaps a case might be made for this approach. However, as long as Blacks in America have not assimilated completely into mainstream American culture (considered by Billingsley [1968], Lyman [1973], Nobles [1974], and others to be theoretically and culturally unlikely, if not impossible), or continue to be oppressed by covert and subtle institutional racism, creative alternative family lifestyles will characterize the Black community.

As has been seen, diversity in Black culture has been documented and analyzed by scholars in the past and continues to be studied by Black social scientists. However, the work of Black social scientists studying Black families is virtually ignored by the scientific community, and Black sociologists face a serious problem in getting their research published. In general, professional journal editorial boards have no more than token Black representation, if any at all, a situation that adversely affects the publication selection process for Black family researchers.

The low status of Black family research can be seen in the limited and often pejorative coverage given Black families in the current professional literature in the family field. In the current 1000-page decade review issue of the *Journal of Marriage and the Family* (1980), ten years of productive research on minority families, including Black, Chicano, Asian-American, and Native American families, were condensed into sixteen pages, the same space allotted to each of the individual chapters devoted to topics associated with marriage and family in mainstream America. Only a few of the other articles recognized the contributions of Black or other minority scholars.

The introductory article of the decade review exemplifies the confusion of many social scientists in interpreting the situation of Blacks in this country. After carefully and correctly commenting on the "negative stereotypes and pejorative terms" that researchers have used in their "depictions" of Black families in the past, the author (Berardo, 1980: 726) observed that in the 1970s researchers adopted a "more positive" perspective. He then promptly slipped into the ethnocentric perspective of most of White America by viewing current developments among Blacks negatively.

Although Macklin (1980), in her review in the same issue of the journal, describes never-married singlehood as "an important development of the 1970s," and although Price-Bonham and Balswick (1980) in their article referred to divorce, desertion, and remarriage as "major life transitions" whose "consequences" social scientists are investigating, the editor of the decade review (Berardo, 1980) termed single-parent households, marital dissolution, and similar developments in Black family life "disturbing shifts." Research on Black American families need "more sophisticated conceptual refinements," concluded the editor. However, in the subsequent paragraph, he called for family researchers in the 1980s to focus on "innovations" such as the dual-career and the two-paycheck family, topics that have been well-documented in the Black family literature (Hill, 1972; Scanzoni, 1971; Staples, 1973; Willie, 1976; Peters, 1977b; Harrison and Minor, 1978; McAdoo, 1978).

To better understand alternative lifestyles, theories must be developed that go beyond an either/or dichotomy (e.g., traditional or nontraditional, single-parent or two-parent) and that provide for an analysis and understanding of the conditions that determine the lifestyles of American families. These theories must account for the impact of race, culture, and intercultural conflict on minority family lifestyles and they must accommodate the reality of discrimination and prejudice in minority families' access to economic and educational opportunities.

Cultural Context of Diverse Family Forms

Cazenave (1980: 439-440) wrote that a socioethnic, rather than a normative/comparative, model "assumes that families are similar or different according to the socio-historical forces affecting them. Such an approach can address the issues of change and conflict, and can provide an analysis of Black family life within the context of ethnicity, class, culture, and the larger social structure."

Sudarkasa (1981) stated that there is a cultural, historical basis for the reason Black family organization differs from that of other groups, even when political and economic factors are held relatively constant. The cultural differences result in differential family forms. The groups that originally came from Western Europe will, therefore, differ from those coming from West Africa or Asia. African families are traditionally organized around consanguineous cores of adult siblings, while European families are based on conjugal family cores.

The major differentiation in alternative lifestyles between African and European descendant families today is a reflection of their differential emphasis on consanguinity and conjugality, in addition to the roles and influence of women. European extended families were of two or more nuclear families united through parent/child or sibling ties, while African extended families were united around consanguineous cores (Sudarkasa, 1981). The enslaved Africans came from the Western part of the continent where there had been a long history of cultural contact and assimilation. Sudarkasa further illustrated that some features of kin organization were universal in West Africa: lineages, coresidential domestic groups, and polygynous marriages.

The concept of single-mother units was practically nonexistent in Africa and was rare among enslaved Africans (Gutman, 1976). The adaptive nature of the cultures of enslaved Africans responded to the context in which they found themselves. Marriages were usually monogamous, and separate, female-headed households were attached to extended families. In reality, the White slave master was actual head of the households within societally condoned interracial polygynous family arrangements that often continued over generations.

The present growth in single parent-family units and informal neopolygynous arrangements are not African continuities, but rather are the result of cultural adaptation to adverse economic and social conditions. The cultural patterns that have helped the adaptation to these conditions have been the extended kin support networks, the performance of family roles regardless of sex of the adult, and the absorption of nonkin within the family.

Using the perspective of a culture-based model, diverse lifestyles are not compared to some ideal or norm. Instead, they are systematically examined from a functional and historical view that analyzes the cultural and environmental forces that affect families and observes subsequent family characteristics and behavior.

Black Family Patterns

Family lifestyles develop out of the variant types of family structure in the Black community. Billingsley (1968: 16) in his study of Black family life provided a fairly comprehensive framework for classifying the various family lifestyles in the Black community. Beginning with a definition of family "as a group of persons related by marriage or ancestry, who live together in the same household," he broadened his perspective to include extended families related by marriage or ancestry who are geographically separated. A more comprehensive definition states: two or more persons related by marriage or ancestry who live together in the same household or extended households, or two or more persons unrelated by marriage and ancestry who share reciprocal emotional/economic supportive relation ships and live together in the same household or in extended households.

According to Billingsley, there are four types of extended families in the Black community. McAdoo (1978) has summarized these as follows (1) simple extended (married couple with own children plus one or more live-in relatives); (2) incipient extended (married couple without children plus one or more live-in relatives); (3) attenuated extended (single mother or father with own children plus one or more live-in relatives); and (4) modified extended or neolocal (two or more nuclear families in a reciprocal emotional/economic supportive relationship who are geograph ically distanced from each other).

Billingsley's basic typology, which allows for additional subtypes, has helped to unify subsequent research on Black families (Hays and Mindel 1973; Hill and Shackleford, 1978; McAdoo, 1978; Shimkin et al., 1978 Cazenave, 1980). An adaptation of Billingsley's categories of family struc ture provides a useful way to conceptualize contemporary lifestyles in the Black community without the sense of deviation from a norm that is implied by the term "alternative." When the definition of family is broadened to accommodate patterns of Black family lifestyles, i.e., to include unmarried and unrelated persons who live together in a house hold, as well as to include kin who live in separate households, the definition becomes descriptive of the lifestyles traditionally characteristic of Black families and of current lifestyles that appear to be gaining popular ity among non-Blacks in the United States today. These variant lifestyles might be more accurately termed, as Aschenbrenner and Carr (1980) have suggested, "alternate" lifestyles instead of "alternative" lifestyles.

Everyone is born into one of the many possible family forms. As relationships dissolve and become reconstituted over the life span, most people will live in more than one of these family forms. Figures that cite the number of single-parent families or extended families or unmarried cohabitants are aggregated figures only, descriptive of family living styles at a point in time. They do not document the movement from one marital status and family living pattern to another that most people will experience during their lifetime.

The 1980 U.S. Census reported the following Black family household composition (Glick, 1981: 113-114):

	Percentage
Two-parent families (with children)	33
Single-parent families (with children)	25
Married couples (no children)	16
Adults living alone	8
Unmarried couples	3
Other arrangements (including institutions)	16

Social Class and Black Family Lifestyles

In recent years the diversity in Black families is often described in terms of social class categories with careful distinctions made between lower- and middle-class Black families (Rainwater, 1966; Scanzoni, 1975; Willie, 1976; Wilson, 1980; McAdoo, 1981). In the opinion of some observers of Black family life, the impact of economic forces on Black families is the determining influence in their lifestyles. Remove the economic barriers and Black families will be little different from White families of similar socioeconomic status, they postulate (Scanzoni, 1975; Stack, 1974; Wilson, 1980). Critics of this economic-based perspective suggest that the narrow emphasis on economics as a determinant of family lifestyle ignores the influence of social/cultural forces in the lives of Afro-Americans, historically and contemporarily (Nobles, 1974, 1981; Willie, 1976; Peters and Massey, forthcoming).

It is most probable that both cultural influences on the lives of Black Americans, as discussed at the beginning of this chapter, and economic realities have an impact on Black family lifestyles. Willie (1976), who acknowledges the influence of race and culture on Black family lifestyles, studied Black families at three socioeconomic class levels: middle class, working class, and lower class. Upper-class, upper-middle-class, and under-class Black families were omitted from his sample. Fully 75 percent of Black families fell into one of the three socioeconomic classes he studied (Willie: 1976: 12). It was found that both middle-class and working-class Black families tended to be nuclear households, consisting of husband, wife, and two or three children. The working-class Black family was likely to be larger, with five or more children, was "broken" more often than those in the middle class, and was more likely to have a relative or boarder in the household. Lower-class Black families were more likely to be a one-parent household and more likely to include a grandparent than middle-class or working-class Black families.

Willie found that family values varied according to social class. Working-class Black families emphasized "morality and clean living," and children were assigned household chores and other responsibilities. Children of middle-class Black families, in contrast, "are taught music and recreational skills and are encouraged to do household chores for an allowance" (1976: 13). Children in lower-class families were expected to be independent. They were taught how to prepare their own meals and encouraged to be on their own at an early age. Willie concluded that, in general, "different and distinct styles of life among blacks of different class levels [were] associated with family composition, childrearing, and community participation" (1976: 15).

The Effect of the Sex Ratio on Family Patterns

The rising number of out-of-wedlock births among Black teenagers and their subsequent drift into diverse living arrangements illustrates how an imbalance of men and women in the marriage age range may be influencing demographic developments in Black communities across the United States. Among Blacks this imbalanced sex ratio is accounted for by the smaller proportion of Black male births, a high death rate in the 18 to 26 age range among Black males, and the higher rate of incarceration of Black males. To this loss of males in the marriage eligibility pool can be added Black men who marry White women, a phenomenon that has increased sharply in the last decade (Glick, 1981; Heer, 1974; Porterfield, 1977).

Almost 40 years ago, Cox (1940) called attention to the connection between the sex ratio and marital status among American Blacks. In addition to finding a declining sex ratio, Cox also found that as the sex ratio declined, the number of married females declined. In examining contemporary Black families, it becomes important to ascertain if the sex ratio has continued to decline. Jackson (1971), in a study of these phenomena, found correlations so revealing that it is surprising so few demographers working with Black family census data have followed up on the sex-ratio hypothesis.

Jackson (1971) reported the following:

(1) Since 1940, the Black sex ratio has decreased progressively.

(2) The supply of available Black males eligible for marriage has decreased progressively.

(3) In 1970 alone, there were over a million more Black females than Black males.

(4) In 1970, there was the greatest deprivation of unmarried Black males in the 25 to 44 age bracket, prime childbearing ages for females; from 25 to 34, the sex ratio of number of males to females was 84 per 100; from 35 to 44, it was 83 per 100.

(5) As the Black sex ratio has decreased, the proportion of Black female-headed households has increased.

(6) In conclusion, there was indeed a significant connection between the proportion of Black female-headed households and the supply of marriage-aged, Black males.

The decreased number of Black males of marriageable age has had untold effects on the Black marriage marketplace. Staples (1973) reported an increase in competition among Black women for the scarce desirable males. He also corroborated Jackson's findings of the connection between the rise in female-headed households and the fall in the Black sex ratio. Furthermore, he has found that man sharing is beginning to appear in some Black communities. This pattern will be discussed later in the chapter.

Perhaps the most corroborating evidence to date has been that presented by Farley and his colleagues (see Bianchi and Farley, 1979; Farley, 1971; Farley and Hermalin, 1971). Although they too have completely ignored the impact of the declining sex ratio on family household formation in the Black community, they have nevertheless provided supporting evidence for that thesis. In one of Farley's (Bianchi and Farley, 1979) most recent articles, he reported the following:

(1) There is an increasing number of Black families headed by a woman rather than a married couple.

(2) The proportion of persons living in husband/wife families is declining faster among Blacks than among Whites. The proportion of husband/wife families stood at 55 percent for Blacks and 80 percent for Whites in 1976.

(3) There has been a substantial decrease in the proportion of adult Black women who are classified as wives.

(4) There has been a modest decline in the proportion of adult Black women who live outside households or who are children or other relatives of household heads.

Singlehood, Cohabitation, and Homosexuality in the Black Community

Although marriage is the preferred status for most Black Americans, Staples (1981) in his recent book on Black singles pointed out the startling fact that increasingly large proportions of Black adults, 18 or older, are single. This status includes the never married, divorced, separated, and widowed. The Black singles population has been little studied, perhaps because of the transient status of singlehoodness. Most Black single adults expect to marry and most eventually do marry. Singlehood appears to be a temporary alternative lifestyle for many Black adults for a considerable number of years (Staples, 1981).

The group of Blacks most likely to remain unmarried are lower-class men (Staples, 1981). The middle-class Black young men in Staples's study, while professing to enjoy the "single life," nevertheless admitted that they planned to eventually marry. Black women in the study indicated that they "harbor a desire to marry at some point in their lives" (Staples, 1981: 187). Staples noted that most of the middle-class Black unmarried women had a "singles career" consisting of several stages. Few claimed not to have ever been in a committed relationship. Many had had several serious relationships in their "singles career."

Nevertheless, Staples found loneliness to be a special problem for "individuals with a long tenure in the single status. . . . The most common solution to this feeling . . . is heterosexual cohabitation" (Staples,1981: 190-191). Living together without being legally married, although once quite common in low-income Black families in the South, appears today to be much more favored by Black men than by Black women, according to Staples (1981). Jacques and Chason (1978) reported that 21 percent of the Black women in their study, compared to 49 percent of the Black men, had practiced cohabitation. For most couples heterosexual cohabitation is a transient stage, according to Staples (1981), inasmuch as most of them either marry or break up. He therefore does not consider it to be an alternative lifestyle.

Heterosexual living together without sex is another strategy singles use against feelings of loneliness. Staples found this pattern, along with "mixed threesomes," to be uncommon among Black singles. Similarly, communes and other cooperatively shared living arrangements are rare among middle-class Black singles. Staples found that many middle-class Black singles prefer to live alone.

Homosexuality as an alternative lifestyle is an option some Black singles have chosen. Little is known about Black homosexuals, however. The best source to date is the Bell and Weinberg (1978) study, which included Black homosexuals. Although this study found both Black and White homosexuals were more satisfied with their jobs than heterosexual men, and half of them stated that they experienced no regret concerning their homosexuality. Black homosexuals find acceptance difficult in the Black community (Staples, 1981). Black female homosexuals are less visible in the Black community than Black male homosexuals, and Staples (1981) observes that, unlike male homosexuals, the majority of Black lesbian relationships tend to be stable and caring. In spite of popular concern about the shortage of men in the Black community, Staples concluded that his study indicated "that most Black women live primarily heterosexual lives" (1981: 205).

Single-Parent Families

One-half of all Black children are now being raised by single mothers. While non-Black single families are frequently formed by divorce, Black units are increasingly formed because of out-of-wedlock births to young women. These early births, lack of education, and the wage differentials earned by Black women result in the "feminization of poverty" in these families (Pearce and McAdoo, 1981). In addition to the stresses of single parenting, the economic vulnerability of these units is an important issue. Financial support from the fathers is limited, although fathers and their families have been found to remain part of the life of the child in approximately half of the cases. While male roles within the family are often played by relatives within the extended family and by friends, the main parenting falls chiefly upon the mother's shoulders. White single mothers usually enter a second marriage, but because of the sex-ratio imbalance, this single status is more likely to become permanent for the Black woman since there are no alternatives to this status.

Extended and Augmented Families

Adaptations of Black families to the imbalanced sex ratio can be seen not only in the increase in female-headed Black families and in nontraditional polygamous families, but in the incidence of extended and augmented families. Extended family living, i.e., multigenerational households, has traditionally been a resource-sharing mechanism that has allowed Black families to survive under conditions of exploitation, discrimination, and limited resources (Hill, 1972; Stack, 1974; Hill and Shackleford, 1978; Martin and Martin, 1978). Many extended families contain an adult male and two or more adult females and their children. Stack (1975) has described in interesting detail how sisters and brothers in low-income families regularly share home, automobile, paycheck, child care, information, or any other help or resources that may be needed.

Billingsley (1968) estimated that approximately one-fourth of all Black families contain relatives in addition to the immediate family, and Hill (1977) reported that over a third of Black families include related or nonrelated (informally adopted) minor children. It has been estimated that over half a million Black persons are currently living in families to whom they are unrelated by ancestry, marriage, or adoption (Hill and Shackleford, 1978).

The phenomenon of nonrelatives living within households as members of the family (characteristic of a substantial number of Black families) has, with few exceptions (e.g., Stack, 1974; Hill, 1977; Shimkin et al., 1978), been largely overlooked. Traditionally, for Black families, the hope of a better future has centered on their children. Children are highly valued and cherished. The parent/child relationship is the most important bond in many Black families (Bell, 1970; Shimkin et al., 1978; Aschenbrenner and Carr, 1980). Cazenave (1980: 430) in a review of this literature concluded, "Among Blacks, consanguine ties often take precedence over conjugal relations." Families feel that the welfare of the child must be maintained and children whose parent(s) cannot care for them properly are readily cared for by kin or nonkin, temporarily or permanently. Holloman and Lewis (1980) described this sharing of responsibilities for the care of children by others as "co-rearing" on the part of "a core group of kin or nonkin, resulting in close interaction in the childrearing group" (Aschenbrenner and Carr, 1980: 468). In contrast to the formal adoptions of mainstream Americans, many Black families "adopt informally" so that the child retains his or her biological parentage (Hill, 1977).

Within the family support network of Black families with Southern roots, along with child fosterage, are adult nonkin or fictive kin. Referred to as "play daughter/son," "play mother/father," or "play sister/brother," special reciprocal relationships — whether originating in childhood or not — are acknowledged and identified. Who is "in" or "not in" a family's kin/nonkin network can often be seen in the assignment of responsibilities at family rituals such as funerals, weddings, or reunions (Kennedy, 1974). Fictive kin, whether part of an individual's social interaction or involvement in a family's kin/friend support system, often maintain reciprocal obligations within interlocking families (McAdoo, 1978).

Black extended families are usually viewed as a coping strategy for low-income Blacks (Rainwater, 1966; Billingsley, 1968; Gibson, 1972; Hill, 1972). However, researchers have found that extended family support networks also exist in many Black middle-income families, although they may not share their physical space with kin (McAdoo, 1978; Shimkin et al., 1978). McAdoo (1981) found in her study of urban and suburban Black families that the majority of two-parent and female-headed families in this middle-income sample lived within thirty miles of close kin. The families in McAdoo's study viewed family members as "the most important source of outside help." Some 80 percent had a reciprocal involvement with relatives, giving and receiving help with child care, financial aid when necessary, and, most importantly, emotional support.

Dual-Income Families

Publications of the U.S. Census Bureau (1972, 1974, 1975, 1979) have consistently revealed the Black employed wife to be an important factor in the labor force, as well as a consistent contributor to the family income and to the maintenance of a higher level of living in Black families. In Black families, the wife is likely to be employed in a full-time job, although, contrary to popular belief, the wife's earnings are usually significantly less than her husband's. Hill (1972: 13-15) pointed out a decade ago that the Black working wife is "a primary factor in keeping many Black families out of poverty . . . [and] the additional income contributed by the wife is essential for the survival and stability of many of these families."

The fact that Black mothers and wives at all income levels continue to enter and remain in the labor force in large numbers indicates an aspect of female roles in Black families that has been institutionalized in the Black community (Scanzoni, 1975). Unlike the newly developing lifestyles in White middle-class families currently being studied by many contemporary social scientists, two adult earners in a family are not a recent development within the Black families. After a five-state survey of Black and White marriages, Scanzoni (1975 reported a "phenomenon," long taken for granted within the Black community, that for Blacks, the employed wife/mother role is common. Encouraged historically to work steadily in domestic labor because the American economic system denied decently paid employment to Black men, Black women have traditionally been employed outside the home, even when there were young children living at home. Scanzoni (1975: 130-131) suggests that "both men and women have come to value the rewards and accept its costs as acceptable, necessary, or inevitable." Scanzoni's research (1975) has documented the participation of Black wives in the labor force at all stages in the family life cycle.

Here again, however, in spite of the social science scramble to investigate the modern working wife/mother of the 1980s, White researchers have rarely studied Black dual-earner families. Recently, however, a number of Black scholars have begun to investigate the lifestyles of dual-earning Black families where the sharing of home and economic responsibilities is expected of husband and wife and of children throughout the family life cycle. They are noting the coping strategies of these families, how they orchestrate their multiple roles, the problems and pressures these families face in the process, as well as the satisfactions parents may receive as they cooperatively combine and share the homemaking, child care, and provider roles (Peters, 1977a; Harrison and Minor, 1978; Landry and Jendrek, 1978).

As mentioned earlier, dual-income-producing parents in Black families do not regard themselves as creating a new lifestyle. Peters (1977a), in a study of working-class, dual-income Black families, found that for these Black working mothers, employment in the labor force was viewed as an integral part of the mother role. Although some husbands in Peters (1977a) study said that their wives did not have to work and that working was their wives' own choice, wives felt that they must work if the family were to get ahead. For them, the provider role was as much the wife's responsibility as it was the husband's. Husbands indicated that they were supportive of their wives' employment. Men felt that they were performing the husband/father role adequately in providing for some or most of the basic financial needs of the family. However, if the wife worked to supplement the family income, husbands not only appreciated it, but they helped to make it possible by assisting with or assuming responsibility for certain household or child care chores.

The division of household and child care tasks that these families evolved appear to be pragmatic solutions to the realities of parental working hours and preferred or available child care arrangements. The particular pattern of division of household/child care tasks is the particular response a family has made at one point in time to the exigencies of (1) job hours of both parents (i.e., whether tandem or conjoint), (2) age of children, and (3) available child care arrangements. As these change, the particular division of household/child care tasks change. For most of these families, however, the ultimate responsibility for housekeeping and child care remains with the mother.

Black Polygamous Family Formation

A variant lifestyle more controversial in the Black community than homosexuality, developed in response to the imbalanced sex ratio discussed earlier in this chapter, is the polygynous family where two women share one husband. This family type, although not widely practiced in the Black community, is, perhaps, the only newly developing lifestyle in the Black community that fits the popular conception of alternative lifestyles. Although limited in occurrence, research on polygynous Black families will be discussed in some detail because of its uniqueness and the interest that has been recently generated on this topic.

Joseph Scott (1980) summarized the research on Black polygamous family formations and reported an in-depth study of 22 young Black women aged 18 to 32 (11 legal wives and 11 consensual wives) who had drifted into polygynous (man-sharing) relationships. All of the women in this study were either still in a polygynous relationship or had been in that situation for some considerable period of time (2 to 12 years) prior to the interview.

The evolution of the neopolygynous relationship has been explained by developmental task theory. This theory (as advanced by Magrabi and Marshall, 1965, and Aldous, 1978) postulates that there are specific tasks associated with the various developmental stages in life, which, if success-fully performed, lead to satisfaction as well as success with subsequent tasks at later stages. The inability or incapacity to accomplish these de-velopmental tasks leads either to failure or to difficulty with later tasks and, at times, to disapproval by society.

When the life histories of the 22 women were analyzed, it became clear that decisions made at crucial developmental stages (i.e., regarding virgin-ity, the onset of sexual intercourse, the practice of birth control, pregnancy, childbirth, and, finally, parental home leaving and independent residency) were responsible for their present family pattern. Failure to manage suc-cessfully the developmental tasks at each of these decision points had preconditioned their choices at the next and subsequent stages. For example, the initial inability to manage their peer relations with the oppo-site sex led them into early intercourse. Early sexual intercourse without the successful application of birth control and preventive medical care led to unwanted teenage pregnancies. These pregnancies led to either teen-age marriages with weak adult/adult affective bonding or to single-parent households devoid of adult/adult affective bonding. Given the sex ratio and the economic dependency of these young women, the natural out-come was entanglement in polygynous family relations (Scott, 1980).

A striking factor in these families is the fact that these women had most of their life choices determined for them. They were born into cir-cumstances where there were limited options available to them, and they made their choices based on their understanding of these options. Each of these choices helped to structure the set of circumstances they were to confront at a later stage. Each stage's circumstances resulted from the combination of choices made at earlier stages, choices over which the woman had had little control (Scott, 1980).

Scott's contention that polygymy is a functional answer to imbalanced sex ratios and single-mother parenting among Blacks has been widely commented upon by social science researchers (Allen and Agbasegbe, 1981; Jack, 1980; McAdoo, 1980). Although this research has encountered considerable criticism for a number of reasons, including the fact that only women were interviewed, it is interesting to note that Black male researchers seem unanimous in their fascination with this alternative, while female researchers are almost equally unanimous in their opposition to this as a viable family alternative. While demographically it may be a logical solution to the lack of adult Black males in urban settings, many are concerned about the vulnerability of the mother/child units in "man sharing" and see the pattern as one more instance of the exploitation of poor women.

The Future of Alternative Family Patterns for Ethnic Groups

Any discussion of future alternative or alternate lifestyles must take into account the bleak national economic picture. According to various demographic predictions, the present economic situation is not expected to improve dramatically within this present decade. Thus a short period of relative economic improvement in the financial conditions of many citizens has come to an end. Often Blacks and other minorities do not make a conscious, deliberate decision to participate in an alternative lifestyle, but are forced to do so out of economic necessity.

Patterns of alternative lifestyles among Black Americans will not only be influenced by the economic conditions, but also by traditional ethnic family values. Two very significant factors in ethnic family values are:

(1) Black families and other ethnic families of color often hold more traditional, conservative views than majority groups. This is often based on the wider influence of the churches within Black and ethnic communities.

(2) Among ethnic groups there is greater involvement of extended kin and community support networks in the functioning of the family unit.

The traditional system of the extended family often results in residential compounding, with members rendering aid to one another and the exchange of goods and services. This cultural pattern is found at all economic levels among ethnic groups, even after some families have attained middle-class status and maintained that status over several generations. Some researchers have suggested that continued working- and middle-class status is felt to be so precarious that even persons at this level need the reassurance of an extended family support network.

There is likely to be an increase in extended family residential arrangements, as elder family members find themselves unable to remain independent because of the decrease in such benefits as social security and the diminution of pension plans with spiraling inflation. Unable to maintain their own residences, senior family members will be forced to live with relatives. Demographic predictions also indicate that adult children are returning home because of their financial inability to maintain separate residences.

For the present and immediate future, single women will find it difficult to marry because of the imbalanced sex ratio. However, in the 1990s, a shift in the sex ratio may lead to a decline in single-parent homes. Fewer children will, therefore, be born in one-parent households, with fewer Black out-of-wedlock children. According to trends documented by census data (McAdoo, 1981), during the 1970s the number of one-parent families increased at a faster rate for Blacks than for non-Blacks. However, the number of children in one-parent families grew at a slower pace in Black than in other families. This convergence between Blacks and Whites is due primarily to a smaller increase in the already high proportion of Black children with separated or never-married parents. Thus racial differences in statistics will be blurred.

In the future, it can be expected that there will be greater involvement in ethnicity movements. It is evident that the "melting pot" orientation to ethnicity has not worked, for ethnic family members have increasingly sought cultural and emotional support in continuing their involvement within their own ethnic cultures.

To reiterate, there are six safe predictions that can be made about future family lifestyles among ethnic groups:

(1) There will be an increase in extended family residential arrangements due to elder members and adult children being unable to remain financially independent.

(2) There will be a subsequent increase in extended family mutual support networks.

(3) A shift in the 1990s sex ratio should result in a decline in the number of single-parent homes and in the number of children born in one-parent homes and out of wedlock.

(4) There will be a greater convergence in the statistics between ethnic and nonethnic families.

(5) There will be a greater involvement by minority group members in their own ethnic groups.

(6) There will be increased diversity of ethnic family lifestyles due to the economic spread predicted for the late 1980s.

As more nonethnic (i.e., White, middle-class, mainstream) families adopt the alternative lifestyles that have existed in greater proportion over generations in ethnic families of color, such as single parenting, serial mate sharing, and formation of nonfamilial support networks, there may be a growing diversity within nonethnic families and more similarity between ethnic and nonethnic families. It is hoped therefore that researchers will have less need of the ethnocentric crutch that leads to the use of negative stereotypes in evaluating ethnic lifestyle trends.

References

ALDOUS, J. (1978) Family Careers. New York: John Wiley.

ALLEN, W. and B. ABASEGBE (1980) "A comment on Scott's 'Black polygamous family formation.'" Alternative Lifestyles 3 (November): 375-381.

ASCHENBRENNER, J. (1975) Lifelines: Black Families in Chicago. New York: Holt, Rinehart, and Winston.

—— and C. CARR (1980) "Conjugal relationships in the context of the Black extended family." Alternative Lifestyles 3: 463-484.

BELL, R. (1970) "Comparative attitudes about marital sex among Negro women in the United States, Great Britain, and Trinidad." Journal of Comparative Family Studies 1: 71-81.

BELL, A. and M. WEINBERG (1978) Homosexualities. New York: Simon & Schuster.

BERARDO, F. M. (1980) "Decade review: some trends and directions for family research and theory in the 1980s." Journal of Marriage and the Family 42 (November): 723-728.

BIANCHI, S. and R. FARLEY (1979) "Racial differences in family living arrangements and economic well-being: an analysis of recent trends." Journal of Marriage and the Family 41 (August): 537-551.

BILLINGSLEY, A. (1968) Black Families in White America. Englewood Cliffs, NJ: Prentice-Hall

BLASSINGAME, J. W. (1972) The Slave Community. New York: Oxford University Press.

CAZENAVE, N. A. (1981) "Alternative lifestyles in minority ethnic cultures." Presented at the Workshop on Alternative Lifestyles in Minority Ethnic Cultures, Groves Conference on Marriage and the Family, Mt. Pocono, Pennsylvania.

—— (1980) "Alternative intimacy, marriage and family lifestyles among low-income Black Americans." Alternative Lifestyles 3 (November): 425-444.

COX, O. (1940) "Sex ratio and marital status among Negroes." American Sociological Review 49: 1129-1135.

DAVIS, A. (1940) Children of Bondage. Washington, DC: American Council on Education.

DuBOIS, W.E.B. (1908) The Negro American Family. Cambridge: MIT Press.

FARLEY, R. (1971) "Family types and family headship: a comparison of trends among Blacks and Whites." Journal of Human Resources 6: 275-296.

FARLEY, R. and A. HERMALIN (1971) "Family stability: a comparison of trends between Blacks and Whites." American Sociological Review 36: 1-17.

FRAZIER, E. F. (1939) The Negro Family in the United States. Chicago: University of Chicago Press.

GIBSON, G. (1972) "Kin family network: overheralded structure in past conceptualization of family functioning." Journal of Marriage and the Family 34, 1: 13-22.

GLICK, P. (1981) "A demographic picture of Black families," pp. 106-126 in H. McAdoo (ed.) Black Families. Beverly Hills, CA: Sage.

GUTMAN., H. G. (1976) The Black Family in Slavery and Freedom: 1750-1925. New York: Random House.

HARRISON, A. and J. MINOR (1978) "Interrole conflict, coping strategies, and satisfaction among Black working wives." Journal of Marriage and the Family 40 (November): 799-805.

HAYS, W. and C. H. MINDEL (1973) "Extended kinship relations in Black and White families." Journal of Marriage and the Family 35 (February): 51-57.

HEER, D. (1974) "The prevalence of Black-White marriage in the United States, 1960 and 1970." Journal of Marriage and the Family 36 (May): 246-258.

HILL, R. (1977) Informal Adoption. Washington, DC: National Urban League Research Department.

—— (1972) The Strengths of Black Families. New York: National Urban League.

HILL, R. and L. SHACKLEFORD (1978) "The Black extended family revisited," pp. 201-206 in R. Staples (ed.) The Black Family: Essays and Studies. Belmont, CA: Wadsworth.

HOLLOMAN, R. E. and F. E. LEWIS (1978) "The 'clan': Case study of a Black extende family in Chicago," pp. 201-238 in D. Shimkin, E. Shimkin, and D. Frate (eds.) T Extended Family in Black Societies. The Hague: Mouton.
JACK, L. (1980) "Friendship: a refutation." Alternative Lifestyles 3 (November): 38 394.
JACKSON, J. (1971) "But where are the men?" Black Scholar 3: 30-41.
JACQUES, J. and K. CHASON (1978) "Cohabitation: a test of reference group theo among Black and White college students." Journal of Comparative Family Studi 9: 147-165.
JOHNSON, C. S. (1934) Shadow of the Plantation. Chicago: University of Chicago Press
KENNEDY, T. (1974) "You gotta deal with it: the relationships in the Black domestic unit Ph.D. dissertation, Princeton University.
LANDRY, B. and M. JENDREK (1978) "The employment of wives in middle-class Bla families." Journal of Marriage and the Family 40 (November): 787-797.
LAOSA, L. (1978) "Maternal teaching strategies in Chicano families of varied education and socioeconomic levels." Child Development 49: 1129-1135.
LEWIS, D. (1975) "The Black family: socialization and sex roles." Phylon 26 (Fall): 47 480.
LEWIS, H. (1955) Blackways of Kent: Chapel Hill: University of North Carolina Press.
LONDON, H. (1981) "Comments on Warfield-Coppock/Scott's presentations." Wor shop on Alternative Lifestyles in Minority Ethnic Cultures, Groves Conference Marriage and the Family, Mt. Pocono, Pennsylvania.
LYMAN, S. (1973) The Black American in Sociological Thought. New York: Capricorr
MACKLIN, E. D. (1980) "Nontraditional family forms: a decade of research." Journal Marriage and the Family, 42 (November): 905-922.
MAGRABI, F. and W. MARSHALL (1965) "Family developmental tasks: a resear model." Journal of Marriage and the Family 27: 454-461.
MANNS, W. (1981) Presentation to the Workshop on Alternative Lifestyles in Minori Ethnic Cultures, Groves Conference on Marriage and the Family, Mt. Pocon Pennsylvania.
MARTIN, E. P. and J. M. MARTIN (1978) The Black Extended Family. Chicago: Universi of Chicago Press.
McADOO, H. P. [ed.] (1981) Black Families. Beverly Hills, CA: Sage.
——— (1980) "Commentary on Joseph Scott's 'Black polygamous family formation.
Alternative Lifestyles 3 (November): 383-387.
——— (1978) "Factors related to stability in upwardly mobile Black families." Journal Marriage and the Family 40 (November): 761-776.
——— (1977) "The impact of extended family variables upon the upward mobility Black families." Final Report. Washington, DC: Department of HEW, Office of Chi Development.
NOBLES, W. (1981) "African-American family life: an instrument of culture," pp. 77-86 H. P. McAdoo (ed.) Black Families. Beverly Hills, CA: Sage.
——— (1974) "African root and American fruit: the Black family." Journal of Social a Behavioral Sciences 20 (Spring): 66-77.
OGBURN, W. F. and M. F. NIMKOFF (1955) Technology and the Changing Family. Bosto Houghton Mifflin.
PEARCE, D. and H. McADOO (1981) Women and Children: Alone and in Pover Washington, DC: National Advisory Council on Economic Opportunity.
PETERS, M. F. (1977a) "Nine Black families: a study of household management a childrearing in Black families with working mothers." Dissertation Abstracts Interr tional (January): 4648-A.
——— (1977b) "Sharing tasks or juggling roles: Black women as working wives/worki mothers." Presented at Annual Meetings of the Eastern Sociological Society.
——— (1974) "The Black family — Perpetuating the myths: an analysis of family soci ogy textbook treatment of Black families." Family Coordinator 23 (October): 34 357.
——— and G. C. MASSEY (forthcoming) "Chronic vs. mundane stress in family stre theories: the case of Black families in White America," in H. McCubbin (ed.) Stress Families. New York: Haworth.

———— (1981) "Normal stress and coping in contrasting young Black families: two case studies." Alternative Lifestyles 4 (May): 156-180.

PORTERFIELD, E. (1977) Black and White Mixed Marriages. Chicago: Nelson-Hall.

PRICE-BONHAM, S. and J. O. BALSWICK (1980) "The noninstitutions: divorce, desertion, and remarriage." Journal of Marriage and the Family 42 (November): 959-992.

RAINWATER, L. (1966) "The crucible of identity: the lower class Negro family." Daedalus 95 (Winter): 258-264.

SCANZONI, J. (1975) "Sex roles, economic factors, and marital solidarity in Black and White marriages." Journal of Marriage and the Family 37 (February): 130-144.

———— (1971) The Black Family in Modern Society. Boston: Allyn & Bacon.

SCOTT, J. W. (1981) Presentation to the Workshop on Alternative Lifestyles in Minority Ethnic Cultures, Groves Conference on Marriage and the Family, Mt. Pocono, Pennsylvania.

———— (1980) "Conceptualizing and researching American polygyny — and critics answered." Alternative Lifestyles 3 (November): 395-404.

SEMAJ, L. (1980) "Meaningful male/female relationships in a state of declining sex ratio." Black Books Bulletin 6: 4-10.

SHIMKIN, D., G. LOUIE, and D. FRATE (1978) "The Black extended family: a basic rural institution and a mechanism of urban adaptation," pp. 25-147 in D. Shimkin, E. Shimkin, and D. Frate (eds.) The Extended Family in Black Societies. The Hague: Mouton.

STACK, C. B. (1974) All Our Kin: Strategies for Survival in a Black Community. New York: Harper & Row.

STAPLES, R. (1981) The World of Black Singles. Westport, CT: Greenwood.

———— (1973) The Black Woman in America: Sex, Marriage, and the Family. Chicago: Nelson-Hall.

SUDARKASA, N. (1981) "Interpreting the African heritage in Afro-American family organization," pp. 37-53 in H. McAdoo (ed.) Black Families. Beverly Hills, CA: Sage.

U.S. Bureau of the Census (1979) The Social and Economic Status of the Black Population in the United States: A Historical Review, 1790-1978. Series P-23, No. 80. Washington, DC: Government Printing Office.

———— (1975) The Social and Economic Status of the Black Population in the United States, 1974. Series P-23, No. 54. Washington, DC: Government Printing Office.

———— (1974) The Social and Economic Status of the Black Population in the United States, 1973. Series P-23, No. 48. Washington, DC: Government Printing Office.

———— (1972) The Social and Economic Status of the Black Population in the United States, 1971. Series P-23, No. 42. Washington, DC: Government Printing Office.

WARFIELD-COPPOCK, N. (1981) Presentation to the Workshop on Alternative Lifestyles in Minority Ethnic Cultures, Groves Conference on Marriage and the Family, Mt. Pocono, Pennsylvania.

WILLIE, C. V. (1976) A New Look at Black Families. New Bayside, NY: General Hall.

WILSON, W. (1980) The Declining Significance of Race. Chicago: University of Chicago Press.

YOUNG, V. (1970) "Family and childhood in a southern Negro community." American Anthropologist 72 (April): 269-288.

CHAPTER 15

Alternative Lifestyles from an International Perspective: A Trans-Atlantic Comparison

BRAM BUUNK

University of Nijmegen, The Netherlands

North Americans often believe that social changes occur sooner and at a higher rate in their society than in other Western countries. This general American bias can even be seen among researchers in the field of alternative lifestyles. For example, in a well-conceived paper published by Cogswell (1975: 398), it is stated that "the United States and Canada seem to be the locus of most variant forms." The fact is that in some Western European countries movement toward the acceptance and practice of alternative lifestyles has been faster than in the United States. This is particularly interesting considering that there has been a higher rate of marital stability in Western Europe than in the United States.

With the exception of single-parent and stepfamilies, this review will focus on those lifestyles that, according to Macklin (1980), deviate from the structural characteristics of the traditional nuclear family. Because it is impossible in the available space to do an adequate analysis of worldwide patterns, the focus will be on the Netherlands and on a comparison of Dutch trends with trends in other European countries and the United States.

Author's Note: Thanks are due to Jim and Cynthia Richardson, Gerrit Kooy and Bernard Murstein, Joan Constantine, Jeri Hepworth, Roger Libby, Penina Okul, and Darwin Thomas.

Changes in Marriage and Family Patterns
Since the 1960s

After World War II, partly due to factors associated with economic recovery in Europe as well as in the United States, "the myth of the idealized nuclear family" was prevalent and rarely questioned. It is still prevalent, but on both sides of the Atlantic it has been challenged by a number of demographic developments and attitudinal shifts. However, despite the similarities in cultures, the change has been more noticeable in the Netherlands than in the United States. Although some alternative forms, such as "dual-career" marriage, are more prevalent in the United States than in the Netherlands, generally speaking, Dutch attitudes toward most alternatives, such as cohabitation, voluntary childlessness, homosexuality, and extramarital sex, are much more positive. As Dutch family sociologist Kooy (1977: 102) has put it, talking about the Nether-lands: "A society which had distinguished itself by constant reflection upon the restrictive traditional teachings of orthodox theology became a very permissive society within a few years." The changes that have occurred, and the apparent reasons for these changes, are discussed below.

Some General Patterns

Marriage

From the end of the 1940s until the beginning of the 1970s, the rate of first marriage in the United States, after a temporary increase, gradually decreased (Norton and Glick, 1979). During the same period in the Netherlands, the rate of first marriage remained about the same. However, recently, there has been a rather sudden decrease in rate of first marriage, dropping about 35 percent from 1970 to 1977 (van Poppel, 1979). This is a much larger decrease than occured during the same time period in the United States. A similar development began earlier in 1967 in Sweden and Denmark (Trost, 1977). In this respect, the Netherlands was behind the Scandinavian countries, but, according to Straver et al. (1980), ahead of England and France, where the same development still is not obvious. Parallel with the decreasing rate of first marriage, the average age at marriage has stopped declining. In 1978, this was 25 years for men and 23 years for women (van Poppel, 1979), figures that are a year or two higher than in the United States.

Divorce

Except for the temporary post-World War II increase, the Dutch family has always been characterized by a low divorce rate compared with most other Western European countries such as Denmark, Sweden, England and Wales, Austria, and France. However, after slowly increasing during the 1960s the divorce rate turned upward in a rather dramatic way at the beginning of the 1970s. A similar development took place in several other

Western European countries, especially Sweden, Finland, England, and Wales, countries that now have the highest Western European divorce rates. This change did not occur to the same extent in Roman Catholic countries, such as France and Austria (Chester, 1977; Frinking, 1975).

Despite the increase, European divorce rates are, compared with the United States, still low. For example, in 1972 the divorce rate per 1000 married women was 4.6 in the Netherlands and 10.9 in Denmark (the highest Western European rate at that time), while the United States had a divorce rate of 17.5 (Terstegge, 1978). However, the increase during the 1970s in the United States was less dramatic than it was in some Western European countries (Norton and Glick, 1979). For instance, by 1979 in the Netherlands, the divorce rate had risen to 6.9 percent, which while still less than in the United States, is one and a half times as much as in 1972.

Alternatives to Marriage

Singlehood

Because of the developments described above, since the 1960s there has been an increase in the Netherlands in the percentage of unmarried persons (both never married and once married). In 1979, the majority of Netherlands' males and females between 20 and 24 years old were unmarried, with men more likely than women to be single. However, above the age of 30 this pattern is reversed: 16 percent of the males and 28 percent of the females in that age group were unmarried. Of the total population of persons 18 years and older, nearly a third were unmarried (Statistical Yearbook, 1979). These figures seem similar to those reported for the United States (Macklin, 1980). However, the composition of the unmarried group is probably different in each country, with more divorced persons in the United States and more persons not yet married in the Netherlands.

Although being unmarried does not necessarily imply living in a one-person household, as will be shown below when cohabitation is discussed, many singles do practice this lifestyle. Since the beginning of the 1960s, the percentage of one-person households rose from 14 percent in 1960 to 22 percent in 1977 (Statistical Yearbook, 1979), which is similar to figures reported for the United States (Ramey, 1978). With an increasing number of people in the Netherlands consciously choosing singlehood, it is not unusual to find persons having a "living apart together" kind of relationship (i.e., two persons who have an intimate, sexual relationship, but do not live together). In a study of singles, it was found that of the unmarried persons younger than 56 years of age who were living alone, 37 percent (more women than men) could be labeled as "creative singles" who professed no feelings of deprivation concerning the lack of a partner (de Jong-Gierveld and Aalberts, 1980).

Nonmarital Cohabitation

In the Netherlands and the Nordic countries, unmarried cohabitation has become a preferred lifestyle for many never-married and divorced people. For example, in 1979, of the total number of one-household couples of all age groups in Sweden, approximately 15 percent were cohabiting nonmaritally. In the Netherlands, this proportion was about 7 percent, against an estimate of 2.3 percent in the United States (Glick and Spanier, 1980). Among the younger people, cohabitation is widespread: In the Netherlands, it is estimated that more than 50 percent of the never-married people in the age group 18-25 years live together. Similar figures can be found in Sweden and Denmark, with somewhat lower figures in Norway (Straver et al., 1980; Trost, 1979).

The acceptance of cohabitation in the Netherlands is further illustrated by the fact that in a recent representative sample of Dutch youth, 37 percent had positive attitudes toward cohabitation as long as there were no children, and 13 percent chose cohabitation as their future lifestyle (Straver and de Boer, 1977). The following factors possibly account for the relatively high Dutch and Scandinavian cohabitation rate compared with that of the United States: the high degree of acceptance of premarital sex in these European countries, the tendency toward earlier independence of youth (Shorter, 1975), the traditional inclination to postpone marriage in Western Europe, and the fact that young people tend to leave their parental home at a younger age.

Communes

As Jansen (1980) has pointed out, the first communes in the 1960s in Western Europe originated from the radical student movement. They combined Marxist societal criticism with a radical criticism of bourgeois-Christian ethics. As in the United States, other types of communes emerged, such as the counterculture and religious communes. Although this lifestyle became clearly visible by the end of the 1960s, only a small minority of the Western European population was in fact living in such groups at that time. In the sole Dutch research project on communes during that time period, only 72 such groups could be detected in the entire country (Jansen, 1980). Even taking into consideration the smaller Dutch population, this number is still comparatively lower than in the United States, where Conover (1975) estimated 15,000 communes during the same time period.

Since the beginning of the 1970s, the above pattern seems to have changed. Communes came to be called *woongroepen* — a more modest term, referring to a group of people who live together and share a common household but do not necessarily have common ideological goals. These groups exist especially among students and are often of a temporary nature. One indication of the increasing number of such groups is the fact that the percentage of nonfamily, multiperson households grew during the 1970s from 3.1 percent of all households in 1971 to more than 5.4 percent in 1979 (Statistical Yearbook, 1979). Based on a recent survey, the number of *woongroepen* is estimated to be no less than 7000 (Jansen et al., 1982). A recent study by Sanders (1980) shows the positive attitude among young heterosexuals toward such groups: 28 percent regarded living with a number of people in one house with the possibility of sexual relationships as an attractive alternative.

Homosexuality

Many persons in the Netherlands still hold prejudices against, and ambivalent attitudes toward, homosexuals (see Straver, 1976, for a review). Nevertheless, there have been dramatic changes since the 1960s toward greater acceptance of homosexuality as a lifestyle. Middendorp (1974, 1975) compared responses in representative samples of the Dutch population in different years. He found that, whereas in 1965, 56 pecent believed that homosexuals should be allowed to live as they saw fit, this percentage rose to 70 percent in 1970 and to 83 percent in 1974. Although in some areas in the United States, such as San Francisco and New York City, homosexuality seems rather well accepted, Dutch attitudes concerning homosexuality are much more liberal than is the case in the United States, where in 1974 no less than 73 percent of the population considered sexual relations with a same-sex partner to be always wrong (Glenn and Weaver, 1979).

In passing, it must be pointed out that the Dutch homosexual liberation movement rejects the homosexual "marriage," an idea that is apparently more popular in the States (see Murstein, 1974: 540-542). Equal rights for homosexual lifestyles are claimed in the Netherlands, but this struggle is largely seen as an opposition to the current heterosexually biased marriage and family ideology and not as an adoption of a positive attitude toward homosexual marriage.

Alternatives in Marriage

Gainfully Employed Wives

A striking feature of Dutch family life during this century has been the low number of gainfully employed wives. This pattern has been strongly supported by the powerful Christian political parties, which in the past have successfully tried to expel and keep married women out of jobs. Although in recent years an increasing number of married women are working outside the home, the basic Dutch pattern has undergone only a modest change, especially when these changes are compared with those in other countries.

In 1960, only 4 percent of married women in the Netherlands were gainfully employed; in 1973, this percentage had risen to no more than 11 percent (Boelmans-Kleinjan, 1977). This is still much lower than in most other Western European countries or the United States, where, for example, in 1974 the comparable figure was 43 percent (Locksley, 1980). In contrast to the United States, the large majority of marriages in the Netherlands are still characterized by a rather traditional pattern. Even among 20 to 24 year olds, 68 percent of the married women did not have an outside job, which is all the more remarkable when one considers the declining birth rate and the tendency to postpone the birth of the first child (Boelmans-Kleinjan, 1977).

A majority (67 percent) of Dutch women feel that having children means that they must stop their paid work outside the home (den Bandt and Veenhoven, 1979). Studies of Dutch attitudes show that in 1975, nearly half of the Dutch population was opposed to outside gainful employment of the wife with school-aged children. Although this percentage is lower than the 84 percent reported in 1965 (Meijer, 1977), it is high compared to such countries as Norway and France (see Fransella and Frost, 1977). On the whole, marriage is experienced as an unequal situation, providing more rewards and fewer costs for the husband than for the wife (Buunk, 1980a).

Voluntary Childlessness

In the past, the birthrate in the Netherlands has been considerably higher than in the rest of Europe, apparently reflecting highly pronatalist attitudes consistent with the Dutch tendency to see the home as the place for women. Although the birthrate started to drop at the end of the nineteenth century, its decline was much slower than in comparable countries. However, in 1969, an acceleration in this decline developed in the Netherlands (den Bandt, 1980). The mean duration of marriage before the birth of the first child increased, and the birthrate, which was 84.4 in 1969, dropped to 69.5 in 1975. A similar trend could be observed in West Germany, England and Wales, but not in South European Roman Catholic countries (Frinking, 1977).

Parallel with the decreasing birthrate has been an increase in the number of voluntarily childless marriages among persons who married after 1966. For those marrying in 1976, it is estimated that 18 percent of the marriages will be voluntarily childless (den Bandt, 1980). This figure seems to be higher than in the United States (see Veevers, 1979), but about the same as in West Germany (Niphuis-Nell, 1979b).

The increasing acceptance by the Dutch of marriage without children is clearly reflected in public opinion polls: In 1965, only 22 percent approved of this lifestyle, but in 1974 no fewer than 65 percent did so (Middendorp, 1974, 1975). Den Bandt (1980) has pointed out that, considering the traditional Dutch pronatalist attitudes, the change in marriage and fertility patterns in the last ten years can be called revolutionary. Nevertheless, as in the United States (e.g., Blake, 1979), many stereotypes about voluntarily childless people still exist, with such individuals being seen as selfish, in discord with life, and immature (Bierkens et al., 1978).

Extramarital Sex

In the Netherlands, attitudes toward extramarital sex changed considerably during the 1960s, although not as much as the attitude toward voluntary childlessness. In 1965, 78 percent of the adult population considered extramarital sex for a man to be wrong in all cases; in the 1970s, the comparable proportion was about 50 percent (Middendorp, 1974, 1975). It is quite clear that the Dutch have a much more tolerant attitude toward extramarital sex than do the North Americans, where even in 1977, 73 percent of the population considered such behavior to be always wrong (Glenn and Weaver, 1979). Despite the relatively liberal Dutch attitudes, the majority of the Dutch people say they would experience negative feelings if their spouse had sexual contact with someone else, especially if this contact occurred in a long-term affair (Buunk, 1978).

Further information about differences between the United States and Europe comes from Christensen (1973), who compared opinions on extramarital sex of students at nine universities in different countries. Although the responses date from 1968 and changes may have occurred with variable speed in different countries, the findings are still illustrative. Except for one American Black university, the percentage of people giving unqualified disapproval to extramarital coitus was much higher in *all* the American universities than in the Danish, Swedish, and Belgian universities. Furthermore, in Denmark and Sweden, students were much more tolerant of extramarital sex than in Belgium. No Dutch students were included, but it can be assumed that the Dutch were more liberal in this respect than the Belgians, but possibly not as tolerant as the Scandinavians.

Because no reliable figures on the incidence of extramarital sex in the Netherlands are available, a comparison with the United States is not possible. It is important to note, however, that because of the relatively positive Dutch attitudes, more people in the Netherlands than in the United States engage in extramarital sex with the knowledge and consent of their spouse (Buunk, 1980b; Hunt, 1974). On the other hand, in the Netherlands, "swinging" never became the kind of movement it seems to be in the United States, probably because the Dutch do not like such highly structured ways of relating. They also never developed anything akin to the American "dating system."

Conclusion

Since the 1960s, in Western society, a number of assumptions underlying the prevalent marriage and family model have come under attack as manifested by the growing attention given to so-called alternative life-styles. Compared with the United States, the Dutch have more rapidly adopted liberal attitudes toward departures from the "traditional" nuclear family, such as homosexuality, cohabitation, voluntary childlessness, and extramarital relationships. However, in Sweden and Denmark, cohabita-tion is even more common. In the Netherlands, there seems to be more resistance to the use of the word "marriage" to refer to group living and homosexual arrangements than is the case in the United States.

The number of communal arrangements increased dramatically in the Netherlands during the 1970s, possibly more so than in the United States. The growth in the number of singles is parallel in both countries. On the other hand, the divorce rate in the Netherlands — for years one of the lowest in Europe, but radically increasing since the 1960s — is still much lower than in the United States. The percentage of gainfully employed married women is also low, making the dual-career marriage an excep-tional arrangement in the Netherlands.

A Tentative Historical and Typological Interpretation

A cross-cultural comparison of contemporary developments in West-ern Europe and the United States makes sense only when the different historical backgrounds of existing marital and family practices are taken into account. However, a thorough comparison of Western European and American developments is difficult. According to Shorter (1975), less is known in the United States than in Europe about the life of people in the past. Moreover, the Dutch historical development is in certain respects different from that in other Western European countries. Therefore — and because of space limitations — only a tentative and global description can be presented.

Building on the typologies presented by Weeda (1978) and Douma (1976), three types of marriage and family life can be distinguished histori-cally. It is argued that alternative lifestyles are not so much to be viewed as new forms, but rather, despite the formal differences among them, as indicative of a historically new value pattern concerning intimate relation-ships. This commonality in value pattern is perhaps more significant than any differences in structure, and it is the variations in values underlying marriage and family patterns that form the basis for the typology to be presented here. Thus any specific living pattern is viewed not as charac-teristic of a particular family *form,* but of a particular family *value pattern.* The criterion determining whether a certain lifestyle falls under a specific type is, therefore, not its structure, but the *attitudes* and *values* the partici-pants have concerning marriage, family, and intimacy. For example, sin-glehood can exist in all three types, but the values of a man who remains single because he and his brother could not both take over his father's farm are obviously quite different from the middle-class intellectual who prefers singlehood to the obligations and restrictions of marriage. Of course, there are many borderline and transitional cases, so the typologies are not to be seen as clear cut. Moreover, even within a certain historical phase, when a given type may be dominant, pronounced differences in ideology can be found, as, for example, among social classes (see Rubin, 1976).

Type I: Functional, Patriarchal, and Community Dependent

According to Shorter (1975), in Western Europe until the end of the eighteenth century (before the Industrial Revolution), a variety of family and marital forms existed simultaneously. In the cities, the larger the income, the larger and more complex the household. In the higher classes, people often had other family members, their children, and their employees living in their house. In the lower classes, the households were much smaller. In the rural areas, three patterns could be distinguished. The stem family, consisting of father, mother, children, and one pair of grand-parents was the dominant pattern in many Western European areas. A second pattern was the large family household where several affiliated couples of the same generation lived together with one pair of grand-parents. This type rarely existed in Western Europe after the Medieval Ages. Both types of households included occasional other personnel. In some respects these living groups had more in common with contempo-rary communal arrangements than with the nuclear family household, the third important family form in pre-industrial Europe (Pickett, 1978a).

Despite the different household arrangements, European marriage as an institution had certain definite characteristics in the period under con-sideration. It was mainly formed on economic and rational grounds. The continuation of family property and the expected instrumental role fulfill-ment by the spouses were the main factors taken into consideration. The decision of whom to marry was largely made by the parents, and marriage was primarily a unity for production and reproduction. The structure was patriarchal; the wife was viewed as subordinate to her husband and often of less worth than the cattle. There was not much affection between the spouses or between the parents and children (see Douma, 1976; Shorter, 1975; van Ussel, 1968). Nevertheless, the wife often had a certain domain of her own where she could act more or less independently and, in contrast to most contemporary housewives, was often directly involved in produc-tive work (Wieringa et al., 1975). There was no domestic intimacy. Accord-ing to Shorter (1975), sex was not an important aspect of life, premarital sex and masturbation hardly existed at all, and biologically mature people had a relatively sexless existence during a long time of their life. Marriage and family were integrated into and controlled by the larger community.

Family patterns in the United States during the same period seem to have differed considerably from the Western European pattern. Gordon (1972) has emphasized that historical evidence is increasingly supportive of the position that the nuclear family was already the prevailing residential unit in the United States long before the Industrial Revolution. The extended family forms, characteristic of many European areas, seem hardly to have existed in the United States. Unlike Europe, Puritan America offered a model of nuclear family organization (Pickett, 1978b). Families were spatially and socially more isolated from the surrounding community, the houses were larger, facilitating private sexual relations, and, because of better economic and health conditions, marriages lasted longer (Shorter, 1975). Therefore, even before the American revolution, the majority of the American population could, much more than in other Western countries, lead a sexual and emotional life that was not controlled by outsiders.

Another typical feature of the American pattern was the low age at marriage and the fact that most people married. Because of the necessity of producing offspring, singlehood was not acceptable and was often a penalized lifestyle (Murstein, 1974). In contrast, in traditional Western Europe, people married late and many people remained unmarried. In the nineteenth century in the Netherlands, widespread poverty often prevented people from founding a family (Wieringa et al., 1975) or forced them to postpone one. So the average age at marriage for the people born about 1820 was nearly 30 for men and more than 28 for women, and about 14 percent of the people born before 1880 never married at all (Frinking and van Poppel, 1978, 1979). Many of these differences between Europe and the United States were a consequence of the large amount of land that was available in the United States, making it possible to leave home early and to start a farm elsewhere (Gordon, 1972; Shorter, 1975). This system of relatively isolated farm families further facilitated the nuclear family formation.

Type II: Affectionate, Private, and Male Dominated

Beginning with the end of the eighteenth century in Western Europe, a new pattern of marriage and family life gradually evolved, starting in the upper classes and becoming more widespread with the increase in industrialization. Increasingly, the nuclear family household, consisting of father, mother, and children, became the preferred lifestyle. However, this particular form was not the most characteristic feature of the new pattern. Probably the most significant change was the important role that personal feelings started to play. According to Shorter (1975), there were three aspects to this development. First, romantic feelings for another person, rather than functional considerations, gradually became the primary motive for marrying a given individual. Parallel to this development, the direct influence of the community on courtship patterns diminished. Second, love of one's children, especially in the case of the mother, became a core feature of the family. As van Ussel (1968) has concluded, this had a clear societal cause. Because of the increasing social necessity for people to learn to control their own feelings and behavior, education of children became more important. This development created a new source of fulfillment for wives in the upper class who, at the end of the eighteenth century, were leading a boring life of doing nothing (Wieringa et al., 1975). Third, domesticity came into existence, that is, the awareness of the family as an emotional unit that had to be protected against interference from the outside. Gradually, the family became a socioemotional enclave, separated from the surrounding community (Douma, 1976; van Ussel, 1968), with the affective bond between spouses becoming the cornerstone of the marriage. With time, this bond gradually became more sexualized (Shorter, 1975).

This new, by now well-known, type of marriage and family has been given many names, such as traditional monogamous marriage (Libby, 1978), modern family (Douma, 1976), and closed marriage (O'Neill and O'Neill, 1972). Whatever the label, the ideology underlying this marriage pattern is still prevalent in Western society. Primary emphasis is placed on permanency (i.e., the marriage is lifelong) and exclusivity (i.e., the spouses do as much as possible together, keep secrets within the family, and are only sexual with one another). Extramarital sex is seen as a threat to the exclusive bond of the spouses and is therefore unthinkable. Male dominance and division of labor is characteristic; that is, the husband provides the money, the wife takes care of the children, and, although decisions are formally made together, the husband has the final word in case of disagreement (Perrucci and Targ, 1974). Another feature is the disapproval of premarital sex, although premarital sex with the future spouse gradually has became accepted (Kooy, 1975). According to Shorter (1975), the incidence of premarital sex, starting in the lower social classes, gradually increased, beginning with the end of the eighteenth century and stabilizing in the first half of the twentieth century. All behavior deviating in one or more aspects from the features of this traditional marriage, such as homosexuality, voluntary childlessness, cohabitation, and extramarital sex, were condemned.

An important difference between the United States and Western Europe is that this pattern became widespread in Western Europe only with the introduction of industrialization, while, as Shorter (1975) suggests, it existed earlier in the United States. Furthermore, because American pioneer conditions demanded the maximum participation of both husband and wife, a rough kind of equality existed in the United States, even in the days of the colonies. Finally, unique to the Netherlands was its late industrialization and its neutrality in World War I, which limited the need for women to participate in the labor market. This undoubtedly strengthened the emphasis on the housekeeping role of the house wife, already present in the nineteenth century Dutch family (Wieringa et al., 1975).

Type III: Individualized, Open, and Equal

The changes occurring in Western countries since the 1960s concerning marriage, family, and alternative lifestyles grew out of a value and attitude pattern that is quite different from those just described. While it is unlikely that everyone choosing a variant family form is rejecting of all facets of the traditional middle-class nuclear family, many do appear to find this form inadequate, restrictive, or counter productive to achieving their individual goals and aspirations.

The value pattern underlying the alternatives to the traditional family is apparent in much that has been written on relationships during the last decade. (A clear example is *Open Marriage* by O'Neill and O'Neill, 1972). Several features of this new orientation can be noted (see Buunk, 1975, 1980d). While subordination to the community was taken for granted in the first type, and personal interests were secondary to the survival of marriage and the family in the second, in the third type, *individual* interests and feeling are given the highest priority. An analysis of the advices given by the Dutch lady's journal *Margriet* clearly demonstrates this orientation, which started to prevail rather suddenly at the beginning of the 1970s (Brinkgreve and Korzec, 1978). In the most radical sense, this attitude means that a relationship is only continued as long as it serves the individual's interests. This means that permanency is no longer a self-evident feature of the relationship, as is apparent in the research of Straver (1981). The growing divorce rate and the acceptance of voluntary childlessness, sexually open marriage, and singlehood as viable options all follow from this increased emphasis on the individual and on personal choice. One's sexual life is considered ultimately a matter of individual preference. Formal aspects of the relationship, such as engagement and marriage, become relatively unimportant.

Another aspect is the strong emphasis on close relationships with peers outside the couple relationship (Cogswell and Sussman, 1972), whether one is married or cohabiting. It is interesting to compare this attitude with the other marriage types discussed earlier. In the first type, the husband and probably the wife had independent same-sex friendships outside marriage. The friends were not met at home, but in certain given settings and contexts (Shorter, 1975). A similar pattern can still be observed in the lower working classes (Allan, 1979). In the second type, the couples had friends on a couple-to-couple base, with certain areas considered inappropriate for discussion or sharing outside the couple bond. Independent friendships with people of the other sex were considered unwise and undesirable (see Buunk, 1978). In the third type, independent friendships outside the marital or cohabiting relationship are valued. Intimate information is disclosed and sometimes sexual contact occurs (Buunk, 1980b). Extramarital sex is not always easily accepted, but it is not condemned on a moral level, and a high degree of emotional exclusivity is seen as undesirable. This is especially true for communes, which can be seen as attempts to institutionalize friendships. Openness to the community and to the outside world is a characteristic shared with the first pattern.

Another important feature of this pattern is the emphasis on male/female equality with regard to sexual behavior, household tasks, gainful employment, and responsibility for the children. The close relationship between female liberation and alternative lifestyles is stressed by many scientists: "Until the society as a whole began to accept the right of the female to be a peer, such excursions into marriage alternatives could only fail" (Ramey, 1972: 437). When there are children, an ideal for many is the shared role pattern (Bernard, 1973) in which both parents work, perhaps part time, and share equally in care of the children.

The attitude toward children is also changing. From minimal nurturance in the first type to dependence on motherly care in the second, the attitude is evolving toward an emphasis on independence of the child in the third type. Simultaneously, the value attached to motherhood seems to be decreasing, making the choice for singlehood and voluntary childlessness relatively easier for women (den Bandt and Veenhoven, 1979).

It is assumed that the third pattern is, historically speaking, relatively new. It is perhaps more appropriately seen as a natural consequence of trends within the second type. For example, when personal feelings and preferences are accepted as the basis for marriage, the logical next step is to accept such feelings as the reason for not marrying, for not having children, or for having extramarital relationships. When premarital sex with one's future spouse is accepted, it is hard for young people to see what is wrong with cohabitation with that potential spouse.

There has been a more rapid departure from the second type to this third type in the Netherlands and Scandinavia than in the United States. This is related to several factors. First, the Dutch historically have been less puritanical. Second, in general, the Dutch have been more tolerant of deviant behavior, possibly as a consequence of having traditionally been a more liberal, commercial, capitalistic country. Third, the influence of peer groups as opposed to the family seems stronger in Western Europe than in the United States (Shorter, 1975). Fourth, within the Dutch Catholic and Protestant churches there have been influential people advocating liberal ideas about sex and marriage (Kooy, 1977), resulting in a relatively low degree of social pressure for traditional patterns.

Conclusion

In the United States, a marriage type that can be designated as affectionate, private, and male dominated seems to have existed earlier than in the Netherlands and other Western European countries. Only in this century has this model come to replace the functional, patriarchal, and community-dependent marriage and family patterns more characteristic of Europe. Recent changes in the Netherlands suggest that there is now movement toward a third pattern, the individualized, open, and equal intimate lifestyle, and that this evolution is occurring more rapidly in the Netherlands than in the United States. This may be because the Netherlands has traditionally been a more urban, liberal country and because nonreligious intellectuals have established considerable political power in that country.

Selected Research on Alternative Lifestyles in the Netherlands

The following is a review of the most important studies on Dutch alternative lifestyles, several of which were presented in a special issue of *Alternative Lifestyles* (Buunk, 1980c). This review is confined to those lifestyles that seem to be more easily accepted in the Netherlands than in the United States, i.e., cohabitation, communes, homosexuality, voluntary childlessness, and extramarital sex. Therefore, research on dual-career marriages and singlehood is excluded from this review (for some findings concerning singlehood in the Netherlands published in English, see de Jong-Gierveld and Aalberts, 1980). In all the lifestyles discussed, aspects of the third type of family value pattern described above are clearly visible, most specifically in th emphasis placed on independence and sex role equality.

Nonmarital Cohabitation

When Dutch scholars have compared cohabiting and married couples, cohabiting couples have been found to report somewhat better intracouple communication, but to be less satisfied with their relationship (Buunk and Nijskens, 1980). There were no differences between married and cohabiting couples with regard to intention to engage in sexual contacts outside the relationship (Buunk, 1980b), or in the kind of groundrules they developed to protect their relationship against the possible negative effects of extramarital relationships. Unlike men, cohabiting women appeared to be more jealous than married ones (Buunk, 1980d), possibly reflecting the still manifest influence of traditional norms and concomitant sex role socialization. As Bernard (1973: 55) has noted, "Women have internalized the norms prescribing marriage so completely that the role of wife seems the only acceptable one."

The most extensive study of cohabiting persons in the Netherlands was conducted by Straver et al. (1980); it represented a joint effort by specialists in the field of family sociology and law, subsidized by the Dutch government. In total, 75 homosexual and heterosexual couples from different social backgrounds were interviewed. One of the assumptions of the study was that cohabiting people irrespective of whether or not they are married, must work out how they want to relate to one another with regard to five basic functions: affection, provision of shelter, housekeeping, care of children, and provision for financial needs. The findings indicated that while society expects a marital union to fulfill *all* of these functions, there is

a wide range of opinion among nonmarital cohabiting persons with regard
to whether they consider themselves responsible for fulfilling these basic
functions. For example, a couple may agree to share household responsibilities, but not to support each other financially; or a couple may no
wish to share responsibility for the parenting of their respective children
but may see living together in one house as desirable.

The degree to which cohabiting persons are willing to fulfill basic
functions for each other seems to be related to the economic contrac
underlying the relationship. Couples may vary from sharing everything
together to remaining independent of one another (Straver, 1981). Based
on this, four categories of cohabiting couples can be distinguished:

- the *traditional role* model — the woman brings up the children and is
  economically dependent on the man;

- the *complete togetherness* model — the couple does many things
  together, has friends together, brings up the children as a joint
  responsibility, and the relationship is seen as permanent;

- *tendency toward independence* — there is less restriction on the
  relationship, and a possibility for outside sexual contact; there is a striving
  toward equal financial contributions; and the relationship is not
  necessarily permanent;

- *independence* — the couple shares no economic responsibility for one
  another; both contribute to the upkeep of the house; they have separate
  possessions; the continuity of the relationship is dependent on its meaning
  to the individuals involved; self-development is a central value.

As can be seen, only the last two categories clearly fit the third type of
marriage and family value pattern discussed above, with the second
category of cohabitation being transitional between types.

Communes

Only one research project has been conducted on communes in the
Netherlands. This project was initiated in 1972 by the late Jos van Ussel
(1970, 1977), one of the leading Dutch researchers on intimate relation
ships. He saw the commune as potentially overcoming some important
structural disadvantages of the nuclear family, such as excessive emotional
interdependence of the spouses, overdependence of young children on
the mother, and the subjugation of women. In this sense, van Ussel has
been a clear proponent of the third value pattern described above.

The project investigated 52 communes, probably the majority of Dutch
communes in 1972 (see Jansen, 1980; van Ussel, 1977). Nearly all groups
were urban communes, subsisting by means of work outside the com
mune and study grants. Most consisted of small groups of young students
primarily males, and intellectuals from middle- and upper-class families
The majority had a joint household income arrangement, with most con-
sumer goods, such as household machinery, furniture, records, and books

owned individually and used collectively. About half of the participants had a regular sexual partner within the group. About a quarter of the total had more than one sexual partner, usually their regular partner within the group and another partner or partners outside. Although this situation seemed to cause jealousy and conflict, groups in which one or more members had multiple sexual relationships were *not* less stable than groups practicing exclusivity. Stability of the commune was strongly related to the degree of organization and group integration, and to group size, with the large groups being more stable.

What Jansen (1980) has called "relational self-actualization" appeared to be the most important motive for joining a commune, with nearly half of the communards giving this as their primary reason. Enjoyable company and possibilities for social contact and intimate peer relationships were sought by about a quarter of the respondents. Not surprisingly, more than half of the participants saw the commune as an alternative to the closed, isolated family. Although marriage itself was not rejected, the closed type of marriage that is prevalent in Dutch society was rejected by the majority of respondents. The majority of the communes studied fit clearly the third type of marriage and family value pattern described earlier.

Homosexuality

Most Dutch research since the 1960s has been concerned with the difficulties that homosexuals, young ones in particular, experience in acquiring a social identity and arranging their lives (see Straver, 1976, for a more expanded review of these studies). On the basis of their studies, several Dutch authors (Moerings and Straver, 1970; Sanders, 1968; Sanders and Buunk, 1969) have identified two important stages in the process of accepting one's homosexual lifestyle: the first, an often vague awareness of being different from one's peers, which makes its appearance somewhere between twelve and fifteen years of age, and the second, the realization that this feeling is labeled by others as homosexuality, which leads to guilt and fear of rejection. Not surprisingly, young people usually wait a long time before discussing their feelings with others.

In a large Dutch project on homosexuality conducted by Sanders (1977, 1980), 267 self-defined homosexual and 239 heterosexual men and women between 18 and 26 years of age were interviewed. This project confirmed the earlier findings mentioned above and demonstrated that heterosexual young people also encounter difficulties in the acceptance of their sexuality, although there were fewer communication barriers for them than for the homosexuals. Not surprisingly, self-esteem and acceptance of one's own homosexual feelings were clearly linked. The study also showed the conflict many experience between the predominantly male, intensely sexual climate of the homosexual subculture and the personal preference for living with one partner. Males report having discovered their homosexual feelings earlier than females and are more likely than females to report feelings of personal insecurity and social isolation. Females are more likely to indicate that the discovery of their homosexuality took place within an emotional context. Homosexual young people were more likely than heterosexuals to be in favor of alternative lifestyles, and were more likely to find cohabitation and group-living situations an attractive alternative.

Voluntary Childlessness

In the 1970s, several Dutch studies were conducted on voluntarily childless couples. As in the United States, this lifestyle was found more often among the higher educated, nonreligious couples in which both the husband and wife are gainfully employed (Bekius et al., 1975; Niphuis-Nell, 1979a). However, den Bandt (1980), in a recent study, found no relationship between voluntary childlessness and educational or occupational level. Den Bandt (1980: 344) suggests that possibly "the idea of voluntary childlessness moved from an elite to a more general level."

The study of Niphuis-Nell (1979a) showed that, predictably, voluntarily childless couples saw lower satisfactions and higher cost for having children than did mothers, women delaying parenthood, and women who were undecided. Personal freedom, the opportunity to work out of the home, and the chance to do things spontaneously with one's spouse were very important goals for the voluntarily childless women (den Bandt, 1980). These findings show the close link betwen the voluntarily childless lifestyle and the third type of marriage and family value pattern.

Extramarital Sex

In the beginning of the 1970s, several studies were done on persons practicing mate exchange, or swinging, as it is referred to in the United States (IPM, 1971; Jacobsen et al, 1971). Such persons were found mostly in the middle and upper-middle classes, had strict rules governing their behavior, a positive attitude toward the institution of marriage, and often a negative attitude toward other alternative lifestyles such as communes. Mate exchangers, or swingers, frequently had difficulty finding suitable partners, and were rather positive about the effects of their activities on their marriage. These findings are largely in line with comparable American studies (see Bartell, 1971). Building on arguments outlined more fully elsewhere (Buunk, 1979, 1980e; van Ussel, 1970), mate exchange as it is practiced can hardly be considered an example of the third type of marriage and family value pattern because it rests on rules and regulations that hamper individual expression and autonomy.

One study (Buunk, 1980b) showed that extramarital sexual and erotic involvement was more common among people with higher educational backgrounds and little or no church attendance. The social-psychological variables that appeared most predictive of intent to engage in extramarital sex were: a facilitative social context, a need for intimacy, marital need deprivation, approval by the spouse, and, among women, sex role egalitarianism. The importance of these variables illustrates that extramarital sex in the Netherlands is a product of the third type of marriage and family value pattern.

In a study of couples with sexually open marriages (Buunk, 1980d, 1980f), one-third reported an extramarital relationship that lasted longer than eighteen months. About a quarter reported feelings of guilt and ambivalence about their extramarital involvements. A common problem was difficulty in apportioning time between the spouse and extramarital partner. However, in spite of problems, most subjects found their extramarital relationships emotionally and sexually satisfying. Five different types of strategies or groundrules to keep the marriage intact could be distinguished:

- *marriage primacy:* loyalty to the spouse was a central value;
- *restricted intensity:* contacts were to be short and not too intense, and would be terminated at the request of the spouse;
- *visibility:* the extramarital involvement was as open as possible, with the knowledge of the spouse;
- *mate exchange:* extramarital involvement was allowed only as long as both partners were simultaneously and jointly involved;
- *invisibility:* extramarital relationships were permitted only as long as the spouse was not aware of them.

None of these patterns proved effective in preventing jealousy (Buunk, 1981), but divorced respondents mentioned more conflicts and jealousy than did couples who were still together (Buunk, 1980d). Persons with high marital satisfaction communicated more openly concerning their extramarital involvements (Buunk, 1982). The main effect of extramarital sex on marriage seemed to be an intensification of the marital relationship, with the result dependent upon the way in which the conflicts were managed (Buunk, 1980d).

Conclusion

An increase in the scientific study of alternative lifestyles has paralleled the rapidly changing attitudes toward such lifestyles, but the number of studies in the Netherlands is small. Nevertheless, what data are available confirm the assumption that the third type of family value pattern described above is common to the various alternatives. Features of this new value pattern, such as the importance attached to intimate relationships, independence, and sex role equality, can be found with different emphases in such divergent contexts as sexually open marriage, cohabitation, and communal living.

Concluding Remarks

The acceptance of some alternative lifestyles has occurred more quickly in the Netherlands than in the United States. Rather than spending

considerable time constructing complicated models describing these individual lifestyles, it is suggested that efforts be directed toward identifying
those elements that are common to these lifestyles and to linking them to
broader changes in society. When viewed in this way, the growing acceptance of alternative lifestyles is seen as indicative of the emergence of a new
value pattern emphasizing individualized, open, and equal relationships.

It is also important to note, as Cogswell (1975) suggests, that many
family forms that appear nontraditional and characteristic of the new value
pattern may not be as "progressive" or "emancipatory" as they first appear. For example, as Straver (1981) has shown, cohabitors often practice
traditional sex role patterns, although the myth is that they are very
"liberated." On the other hand, this does not mean that the emerging
alternatives are merely "old wine in new skins." Indeed, one of the tasks of
the social scientist will be to examine critically the differences and
similarities between the traditional and the evolving lifestyles.

Furthermore, one must look at evolving family patterns from a world
perspective (see Marciano, 1975). For example, although it is improbable
that the new value pattern concerning marriage and the family will become
widely accepted within the next few years, the chances for this seem
greater in the Netherlands than in the United States. An understanding of
why particular patterns evolve may come more easily when one compares
patterns across cultures.

An important task for future research will be to determine whether the
third type of marriage and family value pattern proposed here is really a
separate, internally coherent pattern. While the various lifestyles have
been studied separately, no empirical research has been conducted on the
commonalities across lifestyles. In so doing, it would be of great advantage
if such research could be conducted cross-culturally from the start. While
demographic figures are often comparable across nations, attitude researchers usually have devised their own questionnaires, making cross-
cultural comparisons difficult. Before designing new questionnaires for
cross-cultural usage, researchers would be advised to search out and
translate questionnaires from other countries, especially if they have been
used with similar samples.

As far as the Netherlands and the rest of Western Europe are concerned, there is a clear need for more research on evolving alternative
lifestyles such as creative singlehood (Libby, 1977). Especially in Western
Europe, research on alternatives has not been as extensive as European
developments seem to deserve. Moreover, many family sociologists seem
to respond slowly to societal developments, continuing to concentrate
their research on manifestations of the second type of marriage and family
value pattern and on its practice by the middle classes. Intimate lifestyles in
the lower socioeconomic strata (see Rubin, 1976) and among various
ethnic groups (see Cazenave, 1980) also deserve much more attention.

It is important that there be a broader understanding of the wide range of family ideologies that exist simultaneously, both within any given country and across countries. Looking at family value patterns from an international perspective may help to remove many of the myths about old and evolving family patterns that are so prevalent in contemporary middle-class culture.

References

ALLAN, G. A. (1979) A Sociology of Friendship and Kinship. London: George Allen & Unwin.

BANDT, M. L., den (1980) "Voluntary childlessness in the Netherlands." Alternative Lifestyles 3, 3: 329-349.

—— and R. VEENHOVEN (1979) "Achtergronden van verandering," in Veenhoven (ed.) Vrijwillige Kinderloosheid. Rotterdam: Kooyker.

BARTELL, G. D. (1971) Group Sex: A Scientist's Eyewitness Report on the American Way of Swinging. New York: Wyden.

BEKIUS, R., I. DELLEMAN, R. ROZEBOOM, and T. van de VONDERVOORT (1975) Motieven voor Vrijwillige Kinderloosheid. Groningen: Instituut voor Algemene Psychologie.

BERNARD, J. (1973) The Future of Marriage. New York: Bantam.

BIERKENS, P. B., A. S. F. BUSSER, J. P. I. GOMMERS, and F. M. W. SCHIKS (1978) "Attitude tegenover vrijwillige kinderloosheid: een onderzoek." Medisch Contact 33, 3: 1045-1050.

BLAKE, J. (1979) "Is zero preferred? American attitudes towards childlessness in the seventies." Journal of Marriage and the Family 41, 2: 245-257.

BOELMANS-KLEINJAN, A. C. (1977) "Ontwikkelingen in de beroepsarbeid door vrouwen," in C. J. M. Corver, A. M. van der Heiden, C. de Hoog, L. Th. van Leeuwen (eds.) Gezin en Samenleving. Assen/Amsterdam: Van Gorcum.

BRINKGREVE, C., and M. KORZEC (1978) "Margriet Weet Raad": Gevoel, Gedrag, Moraal en Nederland 1938-1978. Utrecht: Het Spectrum.

BUUNK, B. (1982) "Strategies of jealousy: styles of coping with extramarital involvement of the spouse." Family Relations 31, 1: 13-18.

—— (1981) "Jealousy in sexually open marriages." Alternative Lifestyles 4, 3: 357-372.

—— (1980a) "Sociale vergelijking en liefdesrelaties: Ervaren ongelijkheid en relatiesatisfactie," in H. Wilke and J. B. Rijsman (eds.) Sociale Vergelijkingsprocessan: Theorie en Onderzoek. Deventer: Van Loghum Slaterus.

—— (1980b) "Extramarital sex in the Netherlands: motivations in social and marital context." Alternative Lifestyles 3, 1: 11-39.

—— (1980c) "Alternative lifestyles in the Netherlands: introduction to the issue." Alternative Lifestyles 3, 3: 251-254.

—— (1980d) Intieme Relaties Met Derden: Een Sociaal Psychologische Studie. Alphen aan den Rijn/Brussel: Samson Sociale en Culturele Reeks.

—— (1980e) "Buitenechtelijke seks," in J. Frenken (ed) Seksuologie, Een Interdisciplinaire Benadering. Deventer: Van Loghum Slaterus.

—— (1980f) "Sexually open marriage: groundrules for countering potential threats to marriage." Alternative Lifestyles 3, 3: 312-328.

—— (1979) Seksuele Relaties Buiten het Huwelijk: Een Overzicht van Recent Onderzoek Naar Comaritaal en Extramaritaal Gedrag. Zeist: NISSO, literatuurrapport nr. 12.

—— (1978) "Jaloezie 2/Ervaringen van 250 Nederlanders." Intermediair 14, 12: 43-51.

———— (1975) Jaloezie: Een Orienterend Onderzoek Naar Jaloezie en Relaties. Den Haa
Uitgeverij Bert Bakker.

———— and J. NIJSKENS (1980) "Communicatie en satisfactie en intieme relaties.
Gedrag 4: 240-260.

CAZENAVE, N. A. (1980) "Alternate intimacy, marriage, and family lifestyles amor
low-income Black Americans." Alternative Lifestyles 3, 4: 425-444.

CHESTER, R. [ed.] (1977) Divorce in Europe 3. Leiden: Martinus Nijhoff Social Science
Division.

CHRISTENSEN, H. T. (1973) "Attitudes toward marital infidelity: a nine-culture samplin
of university student opinion." Journal of Comparative Family Studies 4: 197-214.

COGSWELL, B. E. (1975) "Variant family forms and lifestyles: rejection of the tradition.
nuclear family." Family Coordinator 24, 4: 391-406.

———— and M. B. SUSSMAN (1972) "Changing family and marriage forms: complication
for human service systems." Family Coordinator 21, 4: 505-516.

CONOVER, P. W. (1975) "An analysis of communes and intentional communities wit
particular attention to sexual and gender relations." Family Coordinator 24, 4: 453
464.

DOUMA, W. H. (1976) "Gezinsveranderingen sinds 1960." Intermediair 12, 16: 1-7.

FRANSELLA, F. and K. FROST (1977) On Being a Woman: A Review of Research on Ho
Women See Themselves. London: Tavistock.

FRENKEN, J. (1976) Afkeer van Seksualiteit. Deventer: Van Loghum Slaterus.

FRINKING, G. A. B. (1977) "Kinderloosheid in cijfers," in R. Veenhoven and E. van de
Wolk (eds.) Kiezen voor Kinderen. Assen: Van Gorcum.

———— (1975) "Echtscheiding in Europa." Demografie 14.

———— and F. W. A. van Poppel (1979) Een Sociaal-Demografische Analyse van d
Huwelijkssluiting en Nederland. 's-Gravenhage: Staatsuitgeverij.

———— (1978) "Huwelijkssluiting en Nederland," in C. J. M. Corver, A. M. van der Heider
C. de Hoog, and L. Th. van Leeuwen (eds.) Gezin en Samenleving. Assen
Amsterdam: Van Gorcum.

GLENN, N. D. and C. N. WEAVER (1979) "Attitudes toward premarital, extramarital an
homosexual relations in the U. S. in the 1970's." Journal of Sex Research 15, 2: 108
118.

GLICK, P. C. and G. B. SPANIER (1980) "Married and unmarried cohabitation in th
United States." Journal of Marriage and the Family 42, 1: 19-30.

GORDON, M. [ed.] (1972) The Nuclear Family in Crisis: The Search for an Alternative
New York: Harper & Row.

HUNT, M. (1974) Sexual Behavior in the 1970's. Chicago: Dell.

I. P. M. Kontaktadvertenties voor en Door Echtparen: Rapport van een Onderzoek Naar he
Verschijnsel "Echtparenadvertentie." Zeist: NISSO, 1971.

JACOBSEN, R. et al. (1971) Wie Doen er aan Partnerruil en Waarom? Een Exploratie
Onderzoek. Amsterdam: Psychologisch Laboratorium.

JANSEN, H. A. M. (1980) "Communes." Alternative Lifestyles 3, 3: 255-277.

———— R. KNOOPE, and S. SPREEUWENBERG (1982) "Woongroepen," in B. Buun
(ed.) Andere Leefvormen. Deventer: Van Loghum Slaterus.

JONG-GIERVELD, J., de and M. AALBERTS (1980) "Singlehood: a creative or a lonel
experience." Alternative Lifestyles 3, 3: 350-368.

KOOY, G. A. (1977) "The Netherlands," in R. Chester (ed.) Divorce in Europe 3. Leiden
Martinus Nijhoff Social Sciences Division.

———— (1975) Seksualiteit, Huwelijk en Gezin en Nederland: Ontwikkelingen en Vooruit
zichten. Deventer: Van Loghum Slaterus.

LENERO-OTERO, L. [ed.] (1977) Beyond the Nuclear Family Model: Cross-Cultura
Perspectives. Beverly Hills, CA: Sage.

LIBBY, R. W. (1978) "Introduction to the journal." Alternative Lifestyles 1, 1: 3-8.

———— (1977) "Creative singlehood as a sexual lifestyle: beyond marriage as a rite o
passage," pp. 37-61 in R. W. Libby and R. N. Whitehurst (eds.) Marriage and Alterna
tives: Exploring Intimate Relationships. Glenview, IL: Scott, Foresman.

LOCKSLEY, A. (1980) "On the effects of wives' employment on marital adjustment an
companionship." Journal of Marriage and the Family 42, 2: 337-346.

MACKLIN, E. D. (1980) "Nontraditional family forms: a decade of research." Journal of Marriage and the Family 42, 4: 905-922.

MARCIANO, T. D. (1975) "Variant family forms in a world perspective." Family Coordinator 24, 4: 407-420.

MEIJER, J. L. (1977) Social Atlas van de Vrouw. 's-Gravenhage: Staatsuitgeverij.

MIDDENDORP, C. P. (1975) "Verdere culturele veranderingen en Nederland? De periode 1970-1974." Intermediair 11, 19: 1-5.

——— (1974) "Culturele veranderingen en Nederland 1965-1970." Intermediair 10, 11: 5-9.

MOERINGS, M. and C. J. STRAVER (1970) Homofiele Jongeren en Relatie Tot Hun Omgeving. Zeist: NISSO Onderzoeksrapport nr. 3.

MURSTEIN, B. I. (1974) Love, Sex, and Marriage Through the Ages. New York: Springer.

O'NEILL, N. and G. O'NEILL (1972) Open Marriage: A New Lifestyle for Couples. New York: Evans.

NIPHUIS-NELL, M. (1979a) "Kenmerken van vrijwillig kinderloze vrouwen en Nederland." Bevolking en Gezin 2: 201-226.

——— (1979b) "Hoeveel huwelijken blijven kinderloos?" in R. Veenhoven (ed.) Vrijwillige Kinderloosheid. Rotterdam: Kooyker.

NORTON, A. J. and P. C. GLICK (1979) "Marital instability in America: Past, present and future," in G. Levinger and O. C. Moles (eds.) Divorce and Separation. New York: Basic Books.

PERRUCCI, C. C. and D. B. TARG (1974) Marriage and the Family: A Critical Analysis and Proposals for Change. New York: David McKay.

PICKETT, R. S. (1978a) "Monogamy on trial: an analysis of historical antecedents to monogamy and its alternatives. Part I, the premodern era." Alternative Lifestyles 1, 2: 153-190.

——— (1978b) "Monogamy on trial: an analysis of historical antecedents to monogamy and its alternatives. Part II, the modern era." Alternative Lifestyles 1, 3: 281-302.

POPPEL, F. W. A., van (1979) "Huwelijksfrequentie en Nederland blijft dalen." Demografie 38.

RAMEY, J. W. (1978) "Experimental family forms — the family of the future." Marriage and Family Review 1, 1: 1-9.

——— (1972) "Emerging patterns of innovative behavior in marriage." Family Coordinator 21, 4: 435-456.

RUBIN, L. B. (1976) Worlds of Pain. New York: Basic Books.

SANDERS, G. J. E. M. (1980) "Homosexualities in the Netherlands." Alternative Lifestyles 3, 3: 278-311.

——— (1977) Het Gewone en het Bijzondere van de Homoseksuele Leefsituatie. Deventer: Van Loghum Slaterus.

——— (1968) De Zelfbeleving als Uitdagingssituatie. Groningen: Instituut voor Sociale en Bedrijfspsychologie.

——— and B. BUUNK (1969) De Levenslopen van 28 Homofielen. Groningen: Instituut voor Sociale en Bedrijfspsyhologie.

SCANZONI, J. (1972) Sexual Bargaining: Power Politics in the American Marriage. Englewood Cliffs, NJ: Prentice-Hall.

SHORTER, E. (1975) The Making of the Modern Family. New York: Basic Books.

Statistical Yearbook of the Netherlands: 1979 (1980) Gravenhage: Staatsuitgeverij.

STRAVER, C. J. (1981) "Unmarried couples: different from marriage?" Alternative Lifestyles 4, 1: 43-74.

——— (1976) "Research on homosexuality in the Netherlands." Netherlands Journal of Sociology 12: 121-137.

——— and J. de BOER (1977) Toenaderingsgedrag van Jongens en Meisjes. Zeist: NISSO Onderzoeksrapport nr. 18.

STRAVER, C. J., A. M. van der HEIDEN, and W. J. ROBERT (1980) Tweerelaties, Anders dan het Huwelijk? Alphen aan den Rijn/Brussel: Samson.

SUSSMAN, M. B. and B. E. COGSWELL (1972) "The meaning of variant and experimental marriage styles and family forms in the 1970's." Family Coordiantor 21, 3: 375-381.

TERSTEGGE, M. (1978) Literatuurrapport Echtscheiding. Zeist: NISSO Literatuurrapport nr. 11.

TROST, J. (1979) Unmarried Cohabitation. Vasteras: International Library.

——— (1977) "Sweden," in R. Chester (ed.) Divorce in Europe 3. Leiden: Martinus Nijhoff Social Sciences Division.

USSEL, J. M. W., van (1977) Leven en Communes. Deventer: Van Loghum Slaterus.

——— (1970) Afscheid van de Seksualiteit. Meppel/Den Haag: Bert Bakker, Boom, N.V.S.H.

——— (1968) Geschiedenis van het Seksuele Probleem. Meppel: Boom.

VEEVERS, J. E. (1979) "Voluntary childlessness: a review of issues and evidence." Marriage and Family Review 2, 2: 1-24.

WEEDA, I. (1978) Echtscheiding en Huwelijksideologie: Een Theoretische Orientatie voor een Onderzoek. Wageningen: Landbouwhogeschool, afd. Sociologie.

WIERINGA, F., S. LEYDESDORFF, and J. OUTSHOORN (1975) "Huis uit, huis in." Jeugd en Samenleving 5: 248-269.

CHAPTER 16

Clinical Issues in Alternative Lifestyles

ROBERT A. PHILLIPS, Jr.
University of Maryland

In the past decade a growing number of women and men have become engaged in the exploration of alternatives to traditional marriage and family forms. Clinicians can now expect to encounter numerous clients who are questioning traditional relationships or who find themselves thrown by circumstance into a nontraditional lifestyle. It is no longer unusual to find one's clients participating in or considering a wide range of living patterns, such as singlehood, open and multiple relationships, intimate friendship, group marriage, communal living, bisexual or lesbian or gay relationships, childfree marriage, nonmarital cohabitation, dual-career marriage, stepparenting, and/or single parenthood.

Yet the therapy literature yields few articles or books that deal with the issues facing the clinician who is working with clients involved in alternative lifestyles. Therapy journals rarely contain articles that explore nontraditional relationship forms in nonjudgmental terms. Most clinical training continues to reflect the assumption that psychotherapists will deal with persons in traditional family forms and gives scant attention to the evolving variations on these forms. Thus therapists today are inevitably faced with numerous issues for which they are inadequately prepared. This chapter will explore these issues in order to sensitize clinicians to the kinds of problems they may face when working with persons in nontraditional relationships.

Issues for Clinicians and Clients

A basic issue for the individual therapist is whether or not he or she is able to work effectively with persons who have chosen to explore or live in

Author's Note: Special credit is due to the following for their participation in the workshop on Clinical Issues at the 1981 meetings of the Groves Conference on Marriage and the Family, and for their critical discussion of the issues that form the basis for this chapter: consultants Frederick Humphrey, Anthony Jurich, and Willis Willard and participants Judith Felton, Joseph Hoernick, Carol Love, Hal Minor, Louis Poetter, Robert Ryder, and Ernest Stricklin.

alternative types of relationships (Constantine and Constantine, 1972; Elbaum, 1981; Knapp, 1975; Macklin, 1978, 1981; Pendergras, 1975; Price-Bonham and Murphy, 1980; Riddle and Sang, 1978). Persons in nontraditional living patterns often experience great difficulty in finding therapists who will deal with their concerns in a nonjudgmental manner. For example, Knapp (1975), after a survey of clinical members of the American Association of Marriage and Family Counselors (now the American Association for Marriage and Family Therapy), reported that one-third of the clinicians who completed questionnaires indicated that persons in sexually open marriages are neurotic or have personality disorders. A number of these professionals indicated that they would engage in efforts to influence such clients to abandon such behavior.

Traditionally, psychotherapists have reflected the major recognized value systems of the cultural groups in which they live and have seen alternative lifestyles to be either pathological or immoral. Because of this bias, they are often tempted to focus on changing the lifestyle rather than on alleviating the specific problems that motivated the individual to seek therapy to begin with. In such cases, the client is likely to leave the therapeutic interaction even more conflicted, alienated, and frustrated than when she or he came. Since therapists in general practice have often failed to respond to the needs of clients in alternative lifestyles, numerous specialized services developed, such as feminist therapy collectives and gay and/or lesbian therapy centers.

It has been suggested that the clinicians who will be most effective with clients involved in alternative lifestyles are those who are able to focus on what is best for the client from the client's perspective rather than their own (Constantine and Constantine, 1972). They will possess the degree of flexibility necessary to tune into the values and life goals of the client and to work with the client to assess and actualize these. They will seek to focus on the potential of the client's lifestyle and work to help clients find ways of preserving and enriching their chosen relationships. They will be willing to go beyond ready-made or customary solutions and to explore what may well be uncharted territory, to put aside traditional scripts, and to help the client write his or her own script, preferably in conjunction with the significant others in the relationship (Macklin, 1981). They will be able to see alternative family patterns as "unique, possibly new, potentially very productive family models" rather than viewing them from a "conventional pejorative perspective" (Constantine and Constantine, 1972: 539). They will be adept at creating an atmosphere in which clients feel free to explore, find understandings, and make choices appropriate to them. To do otherwise serves only to put clients on the defensive, where instead of being free to evaluate their decisions, they are forced into the position of justifying their decisions.

The permission giving and acceptance implicit in the above can only come if the therapist is truly supportive of pluralism and individual lifestyle choice. To assess one's readiness to do this requires that the therapist be willing to make a commitment to personal awareness and self-exploration. An honest examination of one's own values and definition of normality is necessary if one is to understand one's emotional reactions and evaluate their bases. Often upon reflection the therapist finds her or his reactions to be based more on her or his socialization to favor traditional family forms than on a careful exploration of the lifestyle in question. Since traditional values tend to support assumptions that describe certain lifestyles as intrinsically unhealthy and indicative of disturbance, they often blind the therapist to the particular problems that may be troubling that client.

In order to understand how much of what one believes is ideological myth and how much is fact, the therapist must seek to become familiar with empirical research based on samples that adequately reflect the general population, and to rise above her or his own experience with clinical samples. Classically, research on nontraditional lifestyles has been based on small samples of persons exhibiting pathology, and it is only recently that efforts have been made to obtain nonclinical or nonproblematic samples. A conscious effort to become familiar with the current literature requires a willingness to explore the validity of one's assumptions and to redefine one's belief system on the basis of factual data. Not all therapists are willing or able to do this and, hence, not everyone should feel obligated to work with such clients. Clinicians need to be honest about their limitations and give themselves permission not to accept someone as a client. Otherwise, their clinical work may involve value conflicts and/or require specialized knowledge with which they may not desire to deal. An honest explanation and a supportive referral is often the best alternative in such cases.

There is also the danger that therapists who support the exploration of alternative lifestyles will tend to romanticize such nontraditional approaches. For some, their involvement as therapist may border on voyeurism or a form of vicarious participation in a lifestyle in which they do not dare to participate themselves. Enthusiastic support of a given lifestyle, or of lifestyle experimentation in general, can cause the loss of objectivity necessary to enable clients to assess the dynamics of their particular relationships. Those clinicians who themselves participate in an alternative lifestyle must be particularly conscious of the danger of the politicization of therapy, that is, ideological stances that make critical examination secondary to political statements about the inherent "goodness" of the lifestyle. Such statements often link personal acceptability with participation in a specific lifestyle lived in a prescribed way. Again, clinicians must make a conscious effort to avoid any stance that denies the opportunity to clients to explore their own needs and goals.

In working with persons in alternative lifestyles, it is important for the goals of the therapy to be those of the client rather than those of the therapist. To do this requires that therapists seek to help clients articulate their goals and facilitate the necessary communication between participants to achieve this. In the process, clients may find themselves struggling with unanticipated conflicts regarding values, motivations, and expectations. As always, this is much more likely to happen if the therapist can begin with an acceptance of a specific lifestyle decision and focus primarily on the problematic dynamics within that lifestyle for the specific client.

It is not unusual for participants in alternative lifestyles to experience a range of internal conflicts of which they may not be initially aware, and which the therapist must help them to examine. For example, it is important to determine whether the participants have internalized an acceptance of the lifestyle on an emotional level, or whether they have merely accepted it intellectually. Persons who for philosophical reasons have decided to engage in an alternative lifestyle may well find that they have difficulty in dealing with their emotional response once they begin to live that lifestyle and experience a sense of personal inadequacy and guilt because of this. Or they may have agreed to participate out of fear that if they refused to do so they would lose their lover or spouse. Clients must be helped to explore their own value systems and their impact on their feelings about themselves. Does participation in a particular lifestyle create a state of incongruence between internalized values and expressed values? Do they experience their decisions as responsible or do they question their validity? Have they internalized religious or philosophical beliefs that condemn their lifestyle (as in the case of gay men who may experience a great deal of anxiety and guilt because they believe this lifestyle to be inconsistent with religious teachings that are important to them)? The therapist must be sensitive to these internal conflicts and help clients gain some awareness and acceptance of their own psychological reality and personal limits.

Clients may also be struggling with certain external realities that create stress. They may be experiencing fear of rejection by other family members whom they believe will disapprove if they discover their participation in a particular lifestyle. They may fear the reactions of coworkers and superiors and potential negative repercussions for their careers. Since certain nontraditional lifestyles involve behaviors that are considered in some states to be illegal, the risk of character assassination or the selective enforcement of those laws can lead to anxiety. Such fear of criticism, rejection, and recrimination may lead to attempts to keep the lifestyle participation a secret and to severe problems within the relationship. Therapists must be aware that dysfunction within a nontraditional relationship may well be due to stresses resulting from these internal/external value conflicts and not necessarily from the relationship per se.

A frequent problem experienced by persons in alternative lifestyles is the lack of appropriate scripts. Participants may not have available role models to which they can turn as they work out the interaction patterns within their lifestyles, or they bring with them different role models and expectations from their past, leading to much trial and error, insecurity, and role conflict within the relationship. This is exemplified by families dealing with divorce and remarriage, where there may be a need for ex-spouses to continue to relate as coparents, for new spouses to deal with ex-spouses, and for children to deal with natural parents and stepparents. It is also frequently experienced by dual-work and, in particular, dual-career families, where the traditional sex role patterns become increasingly dysfunctional.

There has been some suggestion that therapists must have participated in a particular lifestyle themselves in order to be able to empathize and work effectively with persons in that lifestyle. For example, some argue that in order to work effectively with women struggling with sex role issues one must be a woman, or only therapists who are gay or lesbian should work with gay or lesbian clients. Others argue that a therapist who is sensitive, aware of his or her value biases, and well informed about a variety of lifestyles can work with persons regardless of their lifestyles (Macklin, 1978). Debate on this issue frequently elicits strong feelings, both pro and con, with much of the discussion based on ideological positions rather than on empirical findings. Knapp's survey (1975) did find that those therapists who expressed the most positive attitudes toward clients involved in sexual relationships outside of marriage were therapists who either had had sexual experiences outside marriage or who were open to them for themselves. The extent to which actual experience with a given lifestyle is related to effectiveness in counseling persons in that lifestyle remains an open question.

Therapists (Constantine and Constantine, 1972; Macklin, 1978) often report that once they are able to deal with and accept a given lifestyle, client couples in nontraditional relationships tend to present issues that differ little from those brought by couples in more traditional relationships. Issues such as inadequate communication, differing degrees of commitment, conflicting expectations, and the search for a balance between autonomy and intimacy are common in both. Constantine and Constantine (1972: 551) indicate that work with clients involved in marriages that include a multilateral element is in many cases "merely an extension of dyadic counseling." Macklin (1978: 135) presents an excellent summary of the most common presenting problems of couples in nontraditional relationships:

(a) inadequate communication with partners; (b) inadequate problem-solving skills; (c) feelings of guilt about the lifestyle or its effect on others; (d) feelings of possessiveness and jealousy, e.g., feeling left out or excluded; feeling that insufficient time is spent with partner; fear of loss of power or control over partner; fear of loss of partner (Francis, 1977); (e) discrepancy between degree of intellectual and emotional liberation (i.e., the individual finds him/herself unable to live out comfortably the intellectual ideal s/he has adapted); (f) disapproval from significant others; and (g) lack of an external support group with whom one can openly share the details of one's personal lifestyle, and the feelings of isolation, alienation, loneliness, and self-doubt which result from this.

Specific Lifestyle Issues

Although one can identify problems that are common to many life-styles, each individual lifestyle raises its own unique set of issues for both participants and therapists. The following is a description of some of the clinical issues that arise in selected nontraditional lifestyles. It is not meant to be exhaustive but as exemplary of the types of issues that are associated with various nontraditional lifestyles as reported in the literature to date. (It must be recognized that there are relatively few data that would enable us to understand adequately the experience of minority persons or persons in various economic groups. See the chapter by Peters and McAdoo in this volume for a review of what is known.)

Open and/or Multilateral Relationships

Much has been written about the issues associated with "open" and/or multilateral relationships (e.g., Constantine and Constantine, 1972, 1973, 1977; Ellis, 1972; Hunt, 1969; Knapp, 1975; Libby, 1977, 1978; Macklin, 1978; Neubeck, 1969; and Ramey, 1976). The Constantines (1972, 1973) note that communication problems and personality differences are the most frequently reported, but issues related to commitment, need satisfaction, possessiveness and jealousy, fear of abandonment, guilt, and the nature of sexual activity are common. Persons in multilateral relationships have special problems related to the formation of such relationships and the integration of participants. These include the time and energy required to engage in continual processing and search for consensus, availability of sufficient "alone" time, territoriality, the reality of the prior dyads, and issues related to differential personal growth. For some there may be problems that arise from reluctant or demanding spouses, and, in some cases, a variety of legal questions to be considered.

Often people who explore open or multilateral relationships find themselves in internal conflict because they experience emotions and fears that the ideology of the "new openness" tells them they should not have. On one hand, they may experience guilt based on their more traditional socialization, which condemned nonmonogamous lifestyles, and, on the other, guilt from new value systems, which define jealousy and a desire for monogamous commitment as "immature." The therapist therefore may need to help the client explore the meaning systems by which she or he has been influenced.

Nontraditional Sex Roles

When therapists work with men and women who are exploring alternatives to traditional male and female roles, there may be issues regarding the therapeutic relationship itself. As noted earlier, there is much controversy over whether a female client should work only with a female therapist (and conversely, male with male) in order to allow that person-free exploration without the complicating factor of cross-sex interaction. Many would argue that only a woman can effectively help a woman in her critical period of self-exploration. The same issue can be raised for men who are questioning their socialization into traditional expectations of what it means to be masculine. Once again, the value bias of the particular therapist may well be the crucial factor.

With the increased interest in women's roles, collections of articles dealing with women and psychotherapy have become available (Rawlings and Carter, 1977; Hill et al., 1979). A primary concern has been sexism in psychotherapy. At the 1978 meeting of the American Psychological Association, the Division 17 Ad Hoc Committee on Women presented thirteen "Principles Concerning the Counseling and Therapy of Women" (Hill et al., 1979: 21). These include the need for therapists to have more information about women, a recognition that assumptions about mental health may be differentially applied to men and women, a sensitivity to the various forms that sexism and sexual oppression can take, an awareness of one's values regarding male and female roles, and an acceptance of the fact that neither women nor men have intrinsic limits on their ability to change and grow.

Much of contemporary therapy for women seeks to help them explore the nature of power and the societal attitudes that limit their sense of power. Numerous books and articles have been written about the dynamics of assertiveness and nonassertiveness and methods to enable women to gain a greater sense of their own power and of how to express it (Alberti and Emmons, 1974; Bloom et al., 1975; Jakubowski-Spector, 1973; Phelps and Austin, 1975).

The literature on the special issues facing men has been less prolific but a steadily growing list of resources is available. Descriptions of the special problems of growing up male focus on the implications of male socialization for healthy self-esteem and for the ability to engage in intimate relationships (Balswick and Peek, 1971; Farrel, 1974; Fasteau, 1974: Goldberg, 1976, 1979; Jourard, 1964; and Phillips, 1977, 1978). A number of collections describe the issues that men face and provide insight into the special problems of men (Cooke, 1978; Lewis, 1981; Petras, 1975; and Pleck and Sawyer, 1974). Pleck (1981) presents a summary of the major research literature on the male role and concludes that traditional roles contain harmful characteristics that undercut psychological health. The most critical problems appear to stem from the lack of emotional awareness and expressiveness resulting from traditional male socialization (Phillips, 1977). This factor affects not only the ability of men to communicate in relationships in ways that create intimacy but also sexual functioning (McCarthy, 1977; Phillips and Laube, 1978; Zilbergeld, 1978). Men also can benefit from assertiveness training in order to increase their interpersonal effectiveness (Phillips, 1977, 1978).

Gay/Lesbian Relationships

There has been a recent upsurge in literature dealing with therapeutic issues for persons in gay and lesbian relationships (e.g., Escamilla-Mondanaro, 1977; McCandlish, 1982; McWhirter and Mattison, 1982; Pendergras, 1975; Riddle and Sang, 1978; Woodman and Lenna, 1980; Zeiger, 1982). Because of the homophobic nature of our society (Weinberg, 1973), gay clients raise a number of issues for the therapist. Can the therapist focus on the problems that the individuals or couples present or is he or she blinded by the fact that the persons seeking psychotherapy live a lesbian or gay lifestyle? Can a heterosexual therapist help gay or lesbian clients as effectively as a gay or lesbian therapist (Rochlin, 1982)? Will a heterosexual therapist be aware of the extent to which simply living in a society that defines gay/lesbian/bisexual as immoral or perverted may be responsible for the self-esteem and identity problems experienced by the client? Can a male therapist who has been socialized traditionally help gay male clients learn to express feelings and develop intimacy with other males?

Issues for lesbian and gay clients include: (a) low self-esteem due to internalized homophobia as well as to the oppression from societal homophobia (Deyton and Zeiger, 1978a, 1978b; Maylon, 1982); (b) questions of sexual identity and sexual orientation; (c) whether and when to come out; and (d) the special problems of gay men and lesbian women who desire to be parents in a society that seeks to deny gay and lesbian persons the opportunity to parent (e.g., Bozett, 1981; Clark, 1977; Green, 1978; Hall, 1978; Maddox, 1982; Miller, 1979; Pagelow, 1978; Voeller and Walters, 1978).

Because of the emphasis placed on intimacy within lesbian relationships, lesbians often face the problem of fusion in their couple relationships (Krestan and Bepko, 1980), and the therapist who works with lesbian couples must seek to help the participants maintain healthy boundaries and balance intimacy with individuality. Gay males often deal with issues stemming from the traditional male socialization, which stresses emotional inexpressiveness and supports sexual nonexclusivity. Male couples may need help in learning how to establish intimacy and commitment to an ongoing relationship, how to communicate effectively, and how to deal with jealousy and desire for autonomy. Therapists must be aware of how gay male couples become established and the ways in which males can express commitment in a relationship (Harry and Lovely, 1979; Lewis et al., 1981; McWhirter and Mattison, 1982; Tuller, 1978).

Because gays and lesbians often come out after they have attempted to follow society's pressure to establish heterosexual marriages, therapists report increased numbers of men and women who seek help in revealing their homosexuality to their heterosexual marriage partners. Therapists must be prepared to deal with the complex constellation of feelings on the part of both the heterosexual and the gay or lesbian partners (Coleman, 1982). Such clients often struggle with feelings of anger, hurt, grief, and guilt, and need support as they deal with the reality of their situation.

Stepfamilies

Divorce and remarriage have given rise to an increasing number of stepfamilies, often involving the blending of two sets of children. A number of problem areas are commonly found when parents remarry (Visher and Visher, 1979). There is always the risk of competition between the step-parent and the biological, same-sex parent. Because the role of stepparent is ill-defined and there are few models, stepparents often experience a great deal of role ambiguity and resulting insecurity. Children may feel torn in their loyalty to biological parents and stepparents and, where they are members of two households (as in joint custody or coparenting), may have difficulty dealing with the continual transition involved in dual residency. The new couple relationship must evolve in a household in which there are "instant children" and little opportunity for normal bonding to occur. Members of new stepfamilies often have unrealistic expectations about the relationship and are unprepared for the numerous adjustment problems. Since blended families come from diverse backgrounds with a variety of histories, they must be helped to develop a tolerance for differences and to realize that conflict, jealousy, guilt, and anger are frequent and to be expected. The therapist must be sensitive to the fact that stepfamilies will have issues that are different from those experienced by intact nuclear families and be prepared to differentiate between problems that are normal for this family form and those that are symptomatic of more serious dysfunctions.

Single-Parent Families

Single-parent families can be expected to report a number of equally predictable problems: role overload, conflicting home and job respon-sibilities, the stress of having to make parenting decisions alone, lack of time and privacy for a separate social life, loneliness, lack of adequate finances and child care facilities, and, in the case of single fathers, lack of experience regarding the parental/housekeeping role. Unless the parent works to prevent this, there is the danger of enmeshment between the parent and child subsystems, with the parent turning to the child for social/emotional support and companionship (see chapter by Thompson and Gongla in this volume for further discussion).

Dual-Career Families

Skinner (1980), in her analysis of the dual-career family, reminds therapists of the need to differentiate between stressors that are internal to the family and those that are external to the family. In this case, external stressors include such factors as occupational demands for geographic mobility and full-time commitment to the job, and lack of time for social interaction with friends and kin. Internal stressors include conflicting demands from the parent, spouse, and professional roles, conflicts between gender socialization and present lifestyle, and gender role conflicts between spouses. Price-Bonham and Murphy (1980) indicate that role overload is a major problem faced by couples in dual-career marriages, which in turn creates severe individual and relationship strain. Couples thrust into commuting relationships because of professional aspirations and career requisites experience considerable personal and relationship stress due to such factors as lack of sharing on a day-to-day basis, continual transition, and loneliness (see chapter by Gerstel and Gross in this volume). It is important to identify the source of stress in each individual case and to recognize that it may be inherent in the lifestyle rather than in the participants or their particular relationship.

Conclusion

The above are only a few of the issues that arise when clinicians begin to deal with persons in alternative lifestyles. In preparing to work with such clients the therapist must resolve basic questions regarding the purpose and practice of psychotherapy. If psychotherapy is to enable persons to explore options and life experience in a neutral or supportive, affirming environment that encourages self-responsibility, then we as psychotherapists need to deal with the ways in which our personal value systems may sabotage that goal. Only then can we facilitate the self-exploration, personal growth, and responsible decision making of all who seek psychotherapy.

References

ALBERTI, R.E. and M.L. EMMONS (1974) Your Perfect Right. San Luis Obispo, CA: Impact.
BALSWICK, J.O. and C.W. PEEK (1971) "The inexpressive male: tragedy of American Society." Family Coordinator 20 (April): 363-368.
BLOOM, L.Z., K. COBURN, and J. PERLMAN (1975) The New Assertive Woman. New York: Dell.
BOZETT, F. (1981) "Gay fathers." Alternative Lifestyles 4 (February): 90-107.
CLARK, D. (1977) Loving Someone Gay. New York: New American Library.
CONSTANTINE, L. and J. CONSTANTINE (1977) "Sexual aspects of group marriage," pp. 186-194 in R. Libby and R. Whitehurst (eds.) Marriage and Alternatives. Glenview, IL: Scott, Foresman.
——— (1973) Group Marriage. New York: Macmillan.
——— (1972) "Counseling implications of comarital and multilateral relations," pp. 537-552 in C. Sager and H. Kaplan (eds.) Progress in Group and Family Therapy. New York: Brunner/Mazel.

COLEMAN, E. (1982) "Bisexual and gay men in heterosexual marriage: conflicts and resolutions in therapy." Journal of Homosexuality 7 (Winter/Spring): 93-103.

COOKE, C. [ed.] (1978) The Men's Survival Resource Book. Minneapolis, MN: M.S.R.B. Press.

DEYTON, B. and R. ZEIGER (1978a) "Mental and emotional wellness, part 1: some problems." The Blade (January): 14.

—— (1978b) "Mental and emotional wellness, part 2: seeking solutions to problems." The Blade (February): 15.

ELBAUM, P. (1981) "The dynamics, implications and treatment of extramarital sexual relationships for the family therapist." Journal of Marital and Family Therapy 7 (October): 489-495.

ELLIS, A. (1972) The Civilized Couple's Guide to Extramarital Adventure. New York: Pinnacle.

ESCAMILLA-MONDANARO, J. (1977) "Lesbians and therapy," pp. 256-265 in E. Rawlings and D. Carter (eds.) Psychotherapy for Women: Treatment Toward Equality. Springfield, IL: Charles C. Thomas.

FARRELL, W. (1974) The Liberated Man. New York: Random House.

FASTEAU, M. (1974) The Male Machine. New York: McGraw-Hill.

FRANCIS, J.L. (1977) "Toward the management of heterosexual jealousy." Journal of Marriage and Family Counseling 3 (October): 61-69.

GOLDBERG, H. (1979) The New Male. New York: William Morrow.

—— (1976) The Hazards of Being Male. New York: Nash.

GREEN, R. (1978) "Sexual identity of 37 children raised by homosexual or transsexual parents." American Journal of Psychiatry 135, 6: 692-697.

HALL, M. (1978). "Lesbian families: cultural and clinical issues." Social Work 23, 5: 380-385.

HARRY, J. and R. LOVELY (1979) "Gay marriages and communities of sexual orientation." Alternative Lifestyles 2 (May): 177-200.

HILL, C.E., J.M. BIRK, C.A. BLIMLINE, M.M. LEONARD, M.A. HOFFMAN, and M.F. TANNEY [eds.] (1979) Counseling Women III. Special issue of the Counseling Psychologist 8, 1.

HUNT, M. (1969) The Affair: A Portrait of Extramarital Love in Contemporary America. New York: World.

JAKUBOWSKI-SPECTOR, P. (1973) "Facilitating the growth of women through assertive training." The Counseling Psychologist 4, 1: 75-86.

JOURARD, S. (1964) The Transparent Self. Princeton, NJ: D. Van Nostrand.

KNAPP, J.J. (1975) "Some non-monogamous marriage styles and related attitudes and practices of marriage counselors." Family Coordinator 4 (October): 505-514.

KRESTAN, J. and C.S. BEPKO (1980) "The problem of fusion in the lesbian relationship." Family Process 19 (September): 277-289.

LEWIS, R.A. [ed.] (1981) Men in Difficult Times: Masculinity Today and Tomorrow. Englewood Cliffs, NJ: Prentice-Hall.

LEWIS, R.A., E.B. KOZAC, R.M. MILARDO, and W.A. GROSNICK (1981) "Commitment in same-sex love relationships." Alternative Lifestyles 4 (February): 22-42.

LIBBY, R.W. (1978) "Introduction to the journal." Alternative Lifestyles 1 (February): 3-8.

—— (1977) "Extramarital and comarital sex: a critique of the literature," pp. 80-111 in R. Libby and R. Whitehurst (eds.) Marriage and Alternatives: Exploring Intimate Relationships. Glenview, IL: Scott, Foresman.

MACKLIN, E.D. (1981) "Education for choice: implications of alternatives in lifestyle for family life education." Family Relations 30 (April): 567-577.

—— (1978) "Counseling persons in non-traditional relationships," pp. 134-139 in C. Simpkinson and L. Platt (eds.) 1978 Synopsis of Family Therapy Practice. Olney, MD: Family Therapy Practice Network.

MADDOX, B. (1982) "Homosexual parents." Psychology Today 16 (February): 62-69.

MAYLON, A.K. (1982) "Psychotherapeutic implications of internalized homophobia in gay men." Journal of Homosexuality 7 (Winter/Spring): 59-69.

McCANDLISH, B.M. (1982) "Therapeutic issues with lesbian couples." Journal of Homosexuality 7 (Winter/Spring): 71-78.

McCARTHY, B. (1977) What You (Still) Don't Know About Male Sexuality. New York: Thomas Y. Crowell.

McWHIRTER, D. P. and A. M. MATTISON (1982) "Psychotherapy for gay male couples." Journal of Homosexuality 7 (Winter/Spring): 79-91.

MILLER, B. (1979) "Gay fathers and their children." The Family Coordinator 28 (October): 544-552.

NEUBECK, G. [ed.] (1969) Extra-Marital Relations. Englewood Cliffs, NJ: Prentice-Hall.

PAGELOW, M. D. (1978) "Lesbian and straight mothers: comparative study of mothers of variant sexual preference," pp. 208-218 in K. Henry (ed.) Social Problems: Institutional and Interpersonal Perspectives. Glenview, IL: Scott, Foresman.

PENDERGRAS, V. E. (1975) "Marriage counseling with lesbian couples." Psychotherapy: Theory, Research and Practice 12 (Spring): 93-96.

PETRAS, J. (1975) Sex: Male/Gender: Masculine. Port Washington, NY: Alfred.

PHELPS, S. and AUSTIN, N. (1975) The Assertive Woman. Fredericksburg, VA: Bookcrafters.

PHILLIPS, R. A., Jr. (1978) "Men as lovers, husbands and fathers: explorations of male socialization and the implications for marriage and family therapy," pp. 142-147 in C. Simpkinson and L. Platt (eds.) 1978 Synopsis of Family Therapy Practice. Olney, MD: Family Therapy Practice Network.

——— (1977) "Assertion training for men: impact on selected interpersonal behaviors, self-description, and concepts of gender role." Ph.D. dissertation, University of Minnesota.

——— and H. H. LAUBE (1978) "Sexual problems of men," pp. 87-96 in C. Cooke (ed.) The Men's Survival Resource Book. Minneapolis, MN: M.S.R.B. Press.

PLECK, J. H. (1981) The Myth of Masculinity. Cambridge: MIT Press.

——— and J. SAWYER (1974) Men and Masculinity. Englewood Cliffs, NJ: Prentice-Hall.

PRICE-BONHAM, S. and D. C. MURPHY (1980) "Dual-career marriages: implications for the clinician." Journal of Marital and Family Therapy 6 (April): 181-183.

RAMEY, J. (1976) Intimate Friendships. Englewood Cliffs, NJ: Prentice-Hall.

RAWLINGS, E. and D. CARTER [eds.] (1977) Psychotherapy for Women: Treatment Toward Equality. Springfield, IL: Charles C. Thomas.

RIDDLE, D. I. and B. SANG (1978) "Psychotherapy with lesbians." Journal of Social Issues 34, 3: 84-100.

ROCHLIN, M. (1982) "Sexual orientation of the therapist and therapeutic effectiveness with gay clients." Journal of Homosexuality 7 (Winter/Spring): 21-29.

SKINNER, D. A. (1980) "Dual-career family stress and coping: literature review." Family Relations 29 (October): 473-481.

TULLER, N. R. (1978) "Couples: the hidden segment of the gay world." Journal of Homosexuality 3 (Summer): 331-343.

VISHER, E. B. and J. S. VISHER (1979) Stepfamilies: A Guide to Working with Stepparents and Stepchildren. New York: Brunner/Mazel.

VOELLER, B. and J. WALTERS (1978) "Gay fathers." Family Coordinator 27, 2: 149-157.

WEINBERG, G. (1973) Society and the Healthy Homosexual. New York: Doubleday.

WOODMAN, N. J. and H. R. LENNA (1980) Counseling with Gay Men and Women: A Guide for Facilitating Positive Lifestyles. San Francisco: Jossey-Bass.

ZEIGER, R. (1982) Personal communication about lesbian lifestyle.

ZILBERGELD, B. (1978) Male Sexuality: A Guide to Sexual Fulfillment. Boston: Little, Brown.

CHAPTER 17

The Law and Alternative Lifestyles

NOEL MYRICKS

University of Maryland

Most social scientists and other observers of human behavior are aware of the fact that in the past quarter of a century the United States has undergone a significant change in social attitudes and behaviors, which in turn have been reflected in judicial decisions. This chapter will describe the judicial responses to issues raised by persons who have chosen to pursue an alternative lifestyle, and review the societal implications of these decisions. Topics are chosen because of their timeliness and controversy, and include: nonmarital cohabitation, the effect of the parents' lifestyles on custody decisions, adoption between adult homosexuals, the effect of the woman's lifestyle on alimony decisions, the rapidly expanding right of grandparents to visit and to obtain custody of their grandchildren, divorce and distribution of property, and rights of stepparents to adopt.

Nonmarital Cohabitation

According to Census Bureau data, the number of unmarried couples living together tripled between 1970 and 1980. In 1970 it was estimated that 523,000 unmarried couples (i.e., households occupied by two unrelated adults of the opposite sex, with or without children under the age of 15) lived together. By 1980 these statistics had increased to 1,560,000 (U.S. Bureau of the Census, 1981). Myricks and Rubin, writing on alternative lifestyles and the law, stated, "Alternative lifestyles have surfaced and the concept of traditional monogamy with one and the same person 'til death do you part' seems on the wane" (Myricks and Rubin, 1977: 357). This trend emerged in dramatic fashion when the California Supreme Court ruled in the case of *Marvin* v. *Marvin* that nonmarital partners had a right to have any express agreements enforced unless the agreements rested on an unlawful meretricious consideration. Indeed, the Court said:

Adults who voluntarily live together and engage in sexual relations are nonetheless as competent as any other persons to contract respecting their earnings and property rights. Of course, they cannot lawfully contract to pay for the performance of sexual services, for such a contract is, in essence, an agreement for prostitution, and unlawful for that reason. But they may agree to pool their earnings and to hold all property acquired during the relationship in accord with the law governing community property [Marvin v. Marvin, 1976: 106].

The Court added:

We believe that the prevalence of nonmarital relationships in modern society and the social acceptance of them marks this as a time when our courts should by no means apply the doctrine of the unlawfulness of the so-called meretricious relationship to the instant case. . . . To equate the nonmarital relationship of today to such a subject matter is to do violence to an accepted and wholly different practice [Marvin v. Marvin, 1976: 106].

As if the point had to be emphasized, the Court also said:

The mores of the society have indeed changed so radically in regard to cohabitation that we cannot impose a standard based on alleged moral considerations that have apparently been so widely abandoned by so many [Marvin v. Marvin, 1976: 106].

This decision and subsequent judicial decisions make it clear that nonmarital cohabitation has become an increasingly acceptable alternative lifestyle. The presence of such de facto families poses serious challenges to legal doctrines in various jurisdictions in the country. Yet not all courts are eager to follow the direction of the California Supreme Court. When confronted with the issue as to whether a woman, who alleged she lived with a man from 1960 to 1975 in an unmarried, familylike relationship into which three children were born, could recover from him "an equal share of the profits and properties accumulated by the parties" during that period, the Supreme Court of Illinois said *No!* (Hewitt v. Hewitt, 1979: 1204). The Court said:

It is apparent that the *Marvin* Court adopted a pure contract theory, under which, if the intent of the parties and the terms of their agreement are proved . . . recovery may be had unless the implicit sexual relationship is made the explicit consideration for the agreement. . . The increasing incidence of nonmarital cohabitation referred to in *Marvin* and the variety of legal remedies therein sanctioned seem certain to result in substantial amounts of litigation, in which whatever the allegations regarding an oral contract, the proof will necessarily involve details of the parties' living arrangements. . . . We are aware, of course, of the increasing judicial attention given the individual claims of unmarried cohabitants to jointly accumulated property, and the fact that the majority of courts considering the question have recognized an equitable or contractual basis for implementing the reasonable expectations of the parties unless sexual services were the explicit consideration. . . . Of substantially greater importance than the rights of the immediate parties is the impact of such recognition upon our society and the institution of marriage.

. . . Judicial recognition of mutual property rights between unmarried cohabitants would, in our opinion, clearly violate the policy of our recently enacted Illinois Marriage and Dissolution of Marriage Act. . . . The policy of the Act gives the State a strong continuing interest in the institution of marriage and prevents the marriage relation from becoming in effect a private contract terminable at will. This seems to us another indication that public policy disfavors private contractual alternatives to marriage [Hewitt v. Hewitt, 1979: 1204].

Notwithstanding the *Hewitt* decision, courts in several jurisdictions have followed the lead of the 1976 California Supreme Court decision in *Marvin* (Marvin v. Marvin, 1976: 106). It is important to note that although the *Marvin* decision gave judicial recognition to the rights of nonmarital partners to have any express agreements enforced unless such agreements rest on a meretricious consideration, a monetary award may or may not be forthcoming. In a 1981 decision, the California Supreme Court ruled that the Los Angeles Superior Court erred when it gave a rehabilitative award to Michelle Triola Marvin. The award, referred to by the press as "palimony," was denied on the rationale that the award did not protect the expectations of both parties; Lee Marvin had no obligation to support Michelle Marvin, who had benefited from the relationship; and Lee had not acted wrongfully with regard to terminating the relationship, and he had not enjoyed any unjust enrichment (Marvin v. Marvin, 1981: 2661).

Cohabitation and Child Custody

When a court determines the best interests of a child in custody decisions, it considers factors such as the fitness of persons seeking custody; the adaptability of the prospective custodian to the task; the age, sex, and health of the child; the physical, spiritual, and moral well-being of the child; the child's preference; and the environment and surroundings in which the child will be reared.

Generally, courts have allowed a child to remain with its mother regardless of her conduct, unless it can be clearly demonstrated that she has engaged in illicit conduct and such conduct is detrimental to the physical, mental, and/or emotional health of the child. The question has been raised whether living with a parent who is cohabiting nonmaritally is detrimental to the well-being of the child. The Supreme Court of Montana ruled that the trial court abused its discretion by modifying the custody provision of a divorce decree in such a way as to transfer custody of the child from the mother to the father because the mother was cohabiting with a man. The Supreme Court said that the trial court did not have sufficient evidence to show the moral environment of the home had been adversely affected because of the cohabitation (Foss v. Leifer,

1976: 1309). The Alaska Supreme Court came to a similar conclusion when it held that without evidence of adverse effects on the child, the fact that a former wife and her son lived in the same house with another man who was not her husband was not sufficient per se to deny her continued custody (Bonjour v. Bonjour, 1977: 667). The Court said that too much weight was attributed to the mother's sexual conduct without clearly demonstrating its impact on the child. Indeed, the Court stressed the point that "the partner's sexual relationship is of importance only as it may affect the best interest of the child" (Bonjour v. Bonjour, 1977: 667).

There are cases that hold contra. Often these cases rely on violations by the custodial parent of state statutes that prohibit fornication. In a case that received national attention, Jacqueline Jarrett, an Illinois mother of three daughters, lost the custody of her children shortly after she permitted her boyfriend to move in with her family (Jarrett v. Jarrett, 1979: 421). The majority of the court ruled that the kind of conduct exhibited by Jacqueline Jarrett and her live-in lover not only violated the statutorily expressed moral standards of the State, but encouraged others to do the same. Such behavior in the court's opinion "debases public morality" (Jarrett v. Jarrett, 1979: 421). The court divested Jacqueline Jarrett of custody and awarded custody to her ex-husband, and when this case was appealed to the U. S. Supreme Court, the Court refused to reverse the decision of the Illinois Supreme Court.

The Illinois Supreme Court had made a special point to reaffirm the view of the trial court, which concluded that the children's daily presence in such an environment was injurious to their moral well-being and de-velopment (Jarrett v. Jarrett, 1979: 421). Indeed, the Court said that societal rules enacted for the governance of its members are not limited to those who agree with them; "they are equally binding on dissenters" (Jarrett v. Jarrett, 1979: 421). As if to add strength to its opinion the Court pointed out that the Illinois General Assembly had refused to enact a new Illinois Marriage and Dissolution of Marriage Act *that would have sanctioned nonmarital relationships.* The Assembly's rationale was that by refusing to enact such legislation it would "strengthen and preserve the integrity of marriage and safeguard family relationships" (Jarrett v. Jarrett, 1979: 423).

This decision may signal an ominous warning to unmarried couples who have a child in the house with them either to get married or be prepared to be deprived of custody. Although no harm to the children could be discovered, the majority of the Court found this irrelevant. They said they were not convinced that such open cohabitation would not affect the mental and emotional health of the children. According to one judge, "It is difficult to predict what psychological effects or problems may later develop from their efforts to overcome the disparity between their con-cepts of propriety and their mother's conduct" (Jarrett v. Jarrett, 1979: 426).

It appears that in the majority of jurisdictions, visitation restrictions are upheld when it can be shown that cohabitation has affected the child. Contrary to the Illinois Supreme Court's approach in *Jarrett,* in which custody was removed entirely, the Connecticut Supreme Court upheld a modified restriction with regard to children and their cohabitating parents (Gallo v. Gallo, 1981: 2499). The Court approved a lower court's ban on overnight visitation between a father and son for as long as the father continued to live with a woman to whom he was not married. The judgment, however, was modified so that the restriction applied only to the particular woman with whom the father was living at the time of the hearing. The Court found no basis for extending the restriction to any other woman. This restriction, interestingly, was not based solely on the fact of cohabitation. The Court discussed the small size of the living quarters and the father's failure to further the boy's religious education. The Court concluded that it would be in the child's best interest to impose visitation restrictions rather than have no restrictions whatsoever (Gallo v. Gallo, 1981: 2499).

In a Maryland case that attracted national attention, an Annapolis Circuit Court judge issued an innovative order in a custody case involving a father who was living with a woman (Studham v. Studham, 1980). The judge awarded custody of the children to the father on the condition that he either marry the woman with whom he was living or move her out of the house. The judge defended the "marry or move" condition as protection of the interests of the children, who "should not be subjected to people living together who are not married" (Studham v. Studham, 1980). The judge based his decisions (this was the second time he had issued such an order) on *his* notion of morality. In the opinion of some local attorneys, these decisions will be overturned on appeal. However, these same attorneys find consolation in the fact that the judge showed a willingness to consider awarding custody to a parent who had been living in an adulterous relationship.

An Illinois ex-wife who allowed her married paramour to move in with her and her children discovered this was sufficient cause to lose custody of her children (DeFranco v. DeFranco, 1978: 997). When the mother began cohabiting with a married male in the residence occupied by her and her minor children, her ex-husband moved for a modification of the custody order on the grounds that his former wife had created an unhealthy environment for the children, and, further, that such an enivironment would seriously endanger the minor children's mental, moral, and emotional health. The wife argued that the court should place minimal importance on the adulterous aspects of her relationship because she and her paramour planned to marry when he obtained a divorce. Further, she argued that a mother's sexual improprieties are irrelevant, unless proven to have a negative effect on her children.

The Court said that "the abhorrence of adultery is more than a public policy of the State of Illinois. It is a concern central to most civilized cultures and a fundamental tenet of Judeo-Christian law and religious beliefs" (DeFranco v. DeFranco, 1978: 997). The Court added that it would be hard pressed to countenance expressly or provide tacit toleration of this illegal conduct by holding that it has no effect on the minor children or their relationship with their mother. The Court also said that it is inconceivable that the Court could sanction adultery because one partner *might* soon be divorced, since such result could serve to severely undermine any attempt at reconciliation between the paramour and his wife.

The Court ruled that the type of flagrant adulterous relationship involved in this case did indeed affect the relationship of the mother and children within the meaning of the applicable Illinois Statute, and it negatively impacted on the moral health of the children. Custody was awarded to the father (DeFranco v. DeFranco, 1978: 999).

Custody and the Career Woman

Approximately 3 million single mothers are pursuing careers. Some recent decisions suggest that courts may penalize them for their efforts to obtain economic independence by denying them custody of their children.

Generally, to determine who should receive custody of children when there is a dispute, the "best interests of the child" test is used. Essentially, this means that the claims of parents are subordinate to the right of their children to grow to maturity in a proper environment. In a recent case that involved a custody dispute over two children, the father prevailed in the lower court, and the mother, Linda, appealed (Tresnak v. Tresnak, 1980: 109). The lower court said:

> Linda at this time in life now desires to continue her education by attending law school at the University of Iowa. While this is commendable insofar as her ambition for a career is concerned, it is not necessarily for the best interest of the children who are now ten and eight years old. Anyone who has attained a legal education can well appreciate the time that legal studies consume. Although Linda was able to care for the children during her undergraduate work . . . the study of law is somewhat different, in that it usually requires library study, where reference material is required. Also, other than time in class during the day, there will be study periods during the day in the library . . . as well as in the evening, all of which would necessarily require the children being in the hands of a babysitter for many hours a day when not attending school. Weekends are usually occupied by study periods . . . and additional activities will be bestowed upon her, such as becoming a member of a law review, which is time-consuming. On the other hand, the father has a stable position in the school system, is president of the teachers' association and so far as known now, can remain so in the future. His salary is adequate to maintain the children properly, and give them the necessities of life [Tresnak v. Tresnak, 1980: 109].

The trial court added that the father would be able to engage in various activities with the boys, such as athletic events, fishing, hunting, mechanical training, and other activities of interest to his boys.

The appellate court reversed the decision of the lower court. The court said that there had been no evidence introduced at trial that supported the court's assumptions about law school and the children's activities. The facts on which the lower court based its decision were assumed facts, and therefore not a valid basis for deciding the case. Further, the appellate court said the lower court's statement represents a stereotypical view of sexual roles that should have no place in child custody adjudication cases.

> Child custody cases are to be decided upon what the evidence actually reveals in each case, not upon what someone predicts it will show in many cases . . . the real issue is not the sex of the parent but which parent will do better in raising the children [Tresnak v. Tresnak, 1980: 111].

The appellate court also pointed out that there was no basis for depicting the wife's law school years as unstable. Facts were adduced that demonstrated that the wife could control the time she spends on her studies just as her ex-husband can control the time he spends on his work. The significance of this decision is that whether a mother is in college or pursuing a career should be irrelevant to the issue of custody unless it can be demonstrated that the father can provide more quality time for the child than his wife.

Lesbians and Child Custody

In December 1973, the American Psychiatric Association adopted a resolution that homosexuals be given all protections now guaranteed to other citizens (American Psychiatric Association, 1973). This organization also voted to remove homosexuality from its official list of mental disorders. Inspired by new attitudes toward homosexuals and enhanced feelings of gay pride, some mothers at the risk of great personal loss are admitting their lesbianism and at the same time requesting custody of the children born during their heterosexual marriages.

Historically, homosexuals have had to face a combination of fear, hatred, and ignorance that resulted in extensive persecution. Such prejudices have often influenced legislative and judicial responses to homosexuals' demands for equal rights. The acceptance of homosexuality as variant rather than deviant behavior, and the impetus toward decriminalizing all private consensual adult sexual activity, is a relatively recent trend (People v. Onofre, 1980: 568).

Courts, when confronted with cases involving child custody and lesbian mothers, have varied in their judicial response. Some have automatically decreed the woman to be unfit. Others have taken the position that homosexuality is only one of the relevant factors to be considered in deciding what is the "best interest of the child." In some instances, there has been judicial recognition that lesbianism and lesbian relationships have no bearing on the issue of fitness. One of the first major decisions that dealt with the issue of a lesbian's fitness to have custody of her children was the case of *Nadler* v. *Superior Court* (1967: 523). The California Court of Appeals vacated a lower court order that had held that homosexuality as a matter of law rendered a parent unfit. At the rehearing, the Superior Court again granted custody to the father, but the mother was given visitation rights every Sunday with the proviso that another adult be present at all times. This decision seemed to suggest that a lesbian mother, if left alone with her children, would use undue influence and get them to adopt a similar sexual preference to her own.

In a recent Michigan Circuit Court decision, the Court ruled that the father of two minor children, aged four and six years, was a more fit and able parent than their lesbian mother (Hall v. Hall, 1979: 243). The Court said that while it has not been "overwhelmed" by the fact of the mother's lesbianism, nonetheless, homosexual behavior is "not within the purview of our modern concepts of morality" (Hall v. Hall, 1979: 2543). Indeed, the Court disagreed with the mother that there is nothing detrimental in children being raised in an atmosphere frequented by homosexuals of both sexes. It appeared to the Court that the chief priority in the woman's life at the time was her lesbian relationship and all other considerations were secondary. The Court perceived the mother as self-centered and felt the interests of the children would be subverted.

In an entirely different ruling, the New York Supreme Court, Nassau County, said that it was in the best interest of four minor children that they remain in the custody of their lesbian mother whose lover was part of the household. Liberal visitation rights were granted to the father (Armanini v. Armanini, 1979: 2501). This court said that the mother's sexual preference in itself does not make her unfit, and noted that, aside from her sexual preference, the mother appeared to be a good parent. This decision met with the approval of both the Nassau County Probation Department and the Nassau County Medical Center, and reflects a marked change in attitudes toward homosexual parents. Whether it is indicative of a new trend is speculative.

A concern uppermost in the minds of many is how homosexuals in general influence the young, and, in particular, how homosexual parents might influence their children. Many also believe homosexuals have a tendency toward child molestation (pedophilia) and seducing youth, and use this as justification for keeping homosexuals out of touch with the young. These tendencies are no more characteristic of homosexuals than of heterosexuals, and the vast majority of heterosexuals as well as homosexuals neither approve of nor want to be associated with such behavior. To believe otherwise would be prejudicial toward the homosexual. The concept of personal freedom includes a broad and unclassified group of values and activities related generally to individual repose, sanctuary, and autonomy, and to the individual's right to develop personal existence in the manner he or she sees fit (People v. Onofre, 1980: 566). Personal sexual conduct is a fundamental right, protected by the right of privacy because of the transcendental importance of sex to the human condition, the intimacy of the conduct, and its relationship to a person's right to control his or her own body (People v. Onofre, 1980: 567). The New York Family Court, Kings County, appeared to recognize this when it refused to thwart an adult adoption between two competent consenting adults that was sought for valid legal and economic reasons, notwithstanding the homosexual relationship involved (see below).

Adoption Between Adult Homosexuals

Generally, adoption is defined as the legal process by which a child acquires parents other than his or her biological parents and parents acquire a child other than their biological child. When an adoption occurs, the legal rights and obligations that formerly existed between the child and his or her biological parents come to an end, and are replaced by similar rights and obligations with respect to adoptive parents.

The New York Family Court, Kings County, said recently that just as *People* v. *Onofre* eliminated consensual homosexuality as a crime, public morality would not be advanced by judicial interference with the statutory right of adult adoption albeit the parties involved are homosexual (In Re Adult Anonymous, 1980: 528). The Court emphasized the fact that no public policy or public morality considerations operate as a bar to adult adoption. In the case before it, two unmarried adult males, both in their twenties, testified that they sought the adoptions to establish a legally cognizable relationship to facilitate such legal and economic matters as inheritance, the handling of their insurance policies and pension plans, and the acquisition of suitable housing. Since these individuals would be committing neither adultery nor incest, and given that consensual homosexuality is not a crime in New York, there was no basis on which to bar adoption.

The trend in most jurisdictions in recent years has been to ease restrictions and to deemphasize the benefits to the parties and the motive for adoption when the adoptee is an adult. State legislatures generally recognize distinctions between the adoption of adults and minors (Wadlington, 1969: 566). This distinction was aptly expressed by a New Jersey Court, which said:

> In an adult adoption the relation between the parties is different. The motivation can be quite varied, and such adoptions are treated differently

in the statutes. Adoption of adults is ordinarily quite simple and almost in the nature of a civil contract [Matter of the Estate of Griswold, 1976: 171].

Thus New York appears to be in the mainstream of jurisdictions in its simplified approach to adult adoptions since it has almost no statutory procedural restrictions for such adoptions.

Alternative Lifestyles and the Termination of Alimony

The decision to reduce or terminate alimony on the grounds of an ex-wife's misconduct is left to the discretion of the court. Within the past ten years there has been a noticeable trend by the courts not to interfere with separation agreements on the basis of the private sexual conduct of the ex-wife. A case typical of this trend came before the Arkansas Supreme Court (Sturgis v. Sturgis, 1974: 2042). A husband had agreed to provide his wife with monthly alimony payments until "remarriage or death." He later stopped payments contending that since she was living with another man, she was de facto remarried and he was absolved of his support obligation. The trial court disagreed with him, but did agree that an injunction should be issued preventing her from living with a man to whom she was not married. The Arkansas Supreme Court disagreed on both counts and ruled that the husband continued to be obligated for support under his contractual agreement with his ex-wife, and that the trial court did not have the authority to regulate the divorced wife's morals (Sturgis v. Sturgis, 1974: 2042).

Courts in several jurisdictions have ruled that a divorce settlement that requires the husband to provide alimony until the wife is remarried will not be terminated because the wife admittedly lives with another man (Vaughn v. Vaughn, 1976: 2586; Fleming v. Fleming, 1977: 329; Bates v. Bates, 1977: 706; Northrup v. Northrup, 1978: 1221). However, where an ex-wife is using alimony to support her lover, or where it can reasonably be inferred that the lover is contributing to her support, most jurisdictions hold that the alimony award should be modified or terminated (Garlinger v. Garlinger, 1975: 799; Suozzo v. Suozzo, 1938: 475). Generally termination occurs when it can be shown that the ex-wife's lover is being supported by the alimony payments (Latzky v. Latzky, 1976: 2168; Taake v. Taake, 1975: 449). A minority of courts take the position that the wife's postdivorce immoral conduct is sufficient to justify termination of alimony.

With present-day morals changing in the direction of greater sexual freedom, wives who become legally separated or divorced from their husbands are likely to cohabit or engage in sexual relations with other persons. In most instances, those other persons are men. When postdivorce sexual relations are with another woman, this poses a slightly different test of values and problems, as illustrated in the following case (Anonymous v. Anonymous, 1978: 2127).

The parties were divorced in Ohio in 1972. Custody of the children was awarded to the wife, but in December 1973, at the husband's request, the wife returned to the marital home where they lived with their two children until October 1975. The parties never remarried. In early 1976, the ex-husband introduced his former wife to a single woman. The three became close friends and socialized together. One afternoon in 1976, the ex-husband came home to find his former wife and her friend in a compromising position in the bedroom. The ex-husband agreed to leave the home and to allow the other woman to stay there with the couple's two boys. A 1972 separation agreement, which had been incorporated into a final divorce decree, specified that the husband would pay his ex-wife, who was aged 30 at the time, $130.00 per month "until such time as she remarries or dies, which ever occurs first." Payments would not extend beyond July 1, 1980, a reasonable date by which the ex-wife would be financially independent. In September 1976, the couple signed a property agreement that provided that the ex-husband would lease the marital home to the two women, and that he would pay $120.00 per month in child support. After the children told their father in January 1977 that they did not like their living arrangement, the father returned to the home on February 1, 1977, and the two women moved out, leaving the children behind.

The ex-husband sued his former wife for permanent custody of the children, child support, and forgiveness of past and future alimony. The former wife sought arrearages, permanent custody, and confirmation of her right to future alimony. The general rule of law with regard to the termination of alimony is that alimony that has been awarded pursuant to stipulation will be terminated only on the basis of a substantial change in circumstances in one or both parties (Ramsay v. Ramsay, 1975: 729). A Minnesota District Court judge said that there had been a basic change in the assumptions of the 1972 stipulation. The Court stated that when the husband signed the separation agreement, he did not realize that remarriage would not be a realisitic possibility for his ex-wife. Indeed, if he had anticipated his wife's postdecree lesbianism, he would not have entered into an agreement to pay alimony until she remarried or died, since remarriage would be impossible. The Court ruled that the aforementioned represents the kind of change of circumstances necessary to warrant ending contractual alimony because the assumptions of the agreement are no longer valid (Hardwick v. Hardwick, 1979: 2478). The Court also ruled that the ex-husband was a fit and proper person and should be awarded custody of his two children with reasonable visitation by the mother (Hardwick v. Hardwick, 1979: 2478).

Rights of Grandparents

Historically, grandparents have participated in child rearing and leisure activities with their grandchildren. Increasing divorce and remarriage rates have loosened some of the close ties that heretofore permitted grandparents to have frequent contact with their grandchildren. In response to this phenomena, grandparents have taken political and judicial action to protect what they feel are their visitation and custodial rights.

Visitation

Most states over the last decade have considered legislation to establish procedures by which grandparents and other family members could petition for visitation rights. Prior to 1979, 16 states had enacted such statutes. Between 1979 and 1980, at least 18 additional states passed laws conferring visitation rights on grandparents, bringing the total number of jurisdiction to 34. In 1981, the legislatures of 7 more states addressed the issue. Of those 7 Indiana and Maryland passed grandparent visitation legislation. The states of Hawaii, Ohio, Utah, and Virginia decreed that any person or relative with an interest in the welfare of the child may obtain visitation privileges if the Court determines it is in the child's best interest. The proposed legislation died in the Nebraska State Senate.

By the end of 1982, statutes conferring rights that will enable grandparents to visit their grandchildren should be in effect in as many as 40 states. Generally, grandparents are guaranteed visitation rights only if it can be established in any given case that it is in the best interest of the child. In Alabama, Arkansas, Florida, New Hampshire, and West Virginia, visitation rights are restricted in that grandparents may petition to be heard only in the context of a divorce or custody proceeding.

The courts have not agreed as to whether the adoption of a child by a stepparent or other third party terminates a grandparent's visitation rights. Statutes in Montana and New Mexico specfically deny rights to grandparents after adoption unless the adoptive parent is a stepparent or a grandparent. The legislatures in Missouri and Oklahoma have bills before them that would prevent adoption from terminating grandparents' rights to visitation. The Oregon legislature has a bill under consideration which, if passed, would provide that if a stepparent is the adoptive parent, the rights of grandparents are not terminated.

There is no legislation enacted or pending that would confer visitation rights on grandparents in the states of Arizona, Kentucky, Maine, Massachusetts, Nebraska, North Dakota, South Dakota, Vermont, and Wyoming. Decisions from various jurisdictions suggest that, absent a statute, grandparents have no common-law rights of visitation. All rights are derivative through the child's natural parents. It is a prerogative of parenthood to determine with whom the child will associate. Where parents have custody, courts will not undertake to give visitation rights to a grandparent or any nonparent over the parents' objection.

This was recently demonstrated when the Virgina Supreme Court ruled that a lower court had erred when it granted visitation privileges to the grandmother (West v. King, 1980: 386). When the child's parents divorced, custody had been awarded to the natural mother, and the paternal grandmother sued for visitation rights with her four-year-old grandson. The mother objected on the grounds that she wanted a new life for herself. Shen did not want her former husband's family included in this new life because when her son visited his paternal grandmother, he was difficult to manage when he returned home. The court ruled that the rights of the custodial parent are paramount (West v. King, 1980: 387). The Missouri Court of Appeals also ruled that a child's paternal grandparents had no visitation rights after the child was adopted by the new husband of the natural mother (Aegerter v. Thompson, 1980: 308). The Court reasoned that where a statute terminates the rights of natural parents on adoption, it also terminates the rights of natural grandparents.

In summary, where states have a visitation law in effect, there appears to be a trend to extend the law to include not only grandparents, but other relatives (such as stepparents or half-siblings, or any other interested persons, especially those who may have become a child's "psychological" parents). The major consideration is what is in the child's best interests. This ambiguous phrase invariably means judges can use their own values in deciding what they feel is best for the child. Historically, the best interests rule was formulated by Justices Cardozo and Brewer. Its intent was to repudiate the rule that affirmed the parents' primary right.

According to Foster and Freed (1980: 1933), in addition to the child's best interests, the following factors should be considered by the court when granting visitation or custody when such is not conferred by statute: (a) an agreement or stipulation regarding visitation made incident to a divorce proceeding, (b) previous residence of the child with the person seeking visitation, and (c) evidence that the parent seeking custody is "unfit" under the prevailing notions of the time. According to these scholars, in instances where grandparents have had de facto custody, it may be easier for grandparents to retain custody than to obtain visitation rights.

Custody

Generally, grandparents have no common-law right to custody. However, where courts decide that the best interests of the child would be served, they have ruled otherwise. The Superior Court in Delaware ruled "so long as the preservation of the best interests of the child remains the paramount concern, there is no reason to exclude grandparents or other interested third parties from participation in custody proceedings" (R.A.D. v. M.E.Z., 1980: 211). In this case the maternal grandmother was awarded custody of a 15-year-old girl even though neither parent was found unfit, nor was neglect shown. In California, the maternal grandparents were permitted to adopt their grandchild when the child's father killed the child's mother (In Re Geoffrey G., 1979: 412). Such an act according to the court proved the father's unfitness to have future custody and control of the child. In the case, *In Re Adoption of Tachick,* the Supreme Court of Wisconsin overruled a lower court decision that had denied grandparents' the right to adopt because of their age (In Re Adoption of Tachick, 1973: 865). The lower court had ruled that because of the grandparents' age, health, and other factors, they were unsuitable to adopt their grandchild over whom they had had custody from birth. In overruling this decision, the State Supreme Court said that since the child had lived with the grandparents all its life, looked upon the grandparents as psychological parents, and identified with them for its sense of security, the sole issue was whether the grandparents could provide food, shelter, clothing, love and affection, education, and training that would aid the child to develop his full potential as a human being. The Supreme Court justified its decision on the basis that the age of the grandparents was offset by the fact that *they are grandparents* who could give natural love and affection, and were inclined by ties of blood and human nature to raise the child in the child's best interests.

A case so novel in approach that it was made into a television show was *Painter v. Bannister* (1966: 152). This case involved a custody dispute between the child's maternal grandparents and the child's father, with the issue being the father's *lifestyle.* When the child's mother died, the child's father, Howard Painter, a resident of Marin County, California, left his son in temporary custody of the Bannisters, the child's maternal grandparents. The child remained with his grandparents for two years, and when his father remarried and sought to regain custody, the grandparents refused. The father was depicted as either agnostic or atheist, with no formal religious training. He was alleged to have read a lot of Zen Buddhism, and to have been substantially influenced by it. His approach to finances and life in general was described as "Bohemian" and his main ambition was to be a freelance writer and photographer. It was also alleged that his income from these efforts was negligible. Since leaving college he had allegedly changed jobs seven times in ten years (twice because he was asked to leave, twice because he did not like the work, twice because he wanted to devote more time to writing, and once for better pay). He was also described as a political liberal who supported the American Civil Liberties Union, and as a man who had had "two funerals" for his wife (one in the basement of his home where he alone was present, and for which he conducted the service and wrote her a long letter; the second for the benefit of her friends, which he attended in a sport shirt and sweater). A psychiatrist classified him as a "romantic and somewhat of a dreamer" (Painter v. Bannister, 1966: 152). As a result of his father's influence, his son, Mark, was described as a youngster "who knew where his freedom was and didn't know where his boundaries were "(Painter v. Bannister, 1966: 154).

The Iowa Supreme Court ruled in favor of the grandparents. The Court justified its decision on the rationale that the grandparents had become the child's psychological parents. The grandparents were college graduates, prominent citizens in their community and their home was well kept, roomy, and comfortable. The Court also said Mark was happy, well-adjusted, and progressing nicely in his development, and it did not believe it was in Mark's best interest to take him out of this stable atmosphere. An interesting footnote to this case was that after several visits to his father's home in California, Mark expressed a desire to stay with his father. Two years after the Iowa Supreme Court decision, the father moved for custody in a California Court, and the grandparents did not oppose the change of custody.

Although there has been an increased recognition of the rights of grandparents, courts are not as sympathetic as one might mistakenly assume. The Court of Appeals in Ohio decided that where the custodial grandparents were approaching their sixties, and the father and step-mother were established, the grandparents should return the child to his father and stepmother (Jackson v. Jacobson, 1981: 2218). This ruling was justified on the basis that the father and stepmother would be better equipped to deal with teenage problems than would aging grandparents. The Court of Appeals in Louisiana, applying the rule that governs custody disputes between biological parents and third parties, said that where natural parents are engaged in custody disputes with third parties, the natural parents are entitled to preference in any contest between them and a nonparent absent exceptional circumstances (LaCroix v. Cook, 1980: 59).

Divorce and Property Distribution

All American jurisdictions except Illinois and South Dakota had some form of "no-fault" divorce legislation by the end of 1980. Moreover, an increasing number of states have given judicial recognition to both the monetary and nonmonetary contribution of the spouse with regard to the distribution of property. By the end of 1981, at least 31 states had guidelines for a determination of property distribution and/or mainte-nance that took into consideration the contribution of the homemaker. There is a significant trend to minimize the importance of marital miscounduct. According to Freed and Foster (1981: 229), no fewer than 18 states and the Virgin Islands have either expressly or implicitly excluded marital fault from consideration in awarding alimony or distributing property. There are 12 states that regard marital fault as a discretionary factor that may be considered in the distribution of property or alimony (Freed and Foster, 1981: 230).

The shift or trend to no-fault divorce has caused a change in the concept of alimony. According to Weitzman and Dixon (1980: 183), by the end of 1980, 48 states retained statutory provisions for some form of postdivorce support. The most significant factors in determining whether there should be an alimony award, as well as the amount of the award, is need and length of marriage. According to these authors, "The priniciple of punishing marital wrongdoing by requiring or denying wife support regardless of her financial need appears to have disappeared" (Weitzman and Dixon, 1980: 183). There is also a clear shift "from permanent to temporary awards among those awarded alimony. (Weitzman and Dixon, 1980: 184-185). With the increasing employment opportunities for women, many courts are loath to hold the man responsible for maintaining his ex-wife's lifestyle. Weitzman and Dixon (1980: 185) make a poignant comment that all family social scientists and practitioners would be well advised to remember:

> Judges who are themselves more sympathetic to the position of divorced men consider the earnings of most divorced men too low to support two households adequately, or even to provide half of the support for the husband's children who are in the custody of their former wives. They therefore decide that it is better to leave most of the family's postdivorce income with the husband — viewing it as his rather than theirs. And even when the husband can afford to support his former wife and children, he is rarely required to help them sustain a standard of living that is half as good as his own.

Stepfamilies and the Right to Adopt

Approximately one-half million stepfamilies are formed each year. When a custodial parent remarries, there will often be an attempt by a stepparent to adopt the child. Generally, courts will use as their guideline the doctrine of "the best intersts of the child." In cases decided from 1972 through 1979, the U.S. Supreme Court held that due process required natural fathers to be given notice of the proceedings to adopt and an opportunity to be heard before their rights could be terminated. This precedent began with *Stanley* v. *Illinois* (1972: 645), a case involving three children who had been born out of wedlock to parents who had lived together periodically over an 18-year period. When the natural mother died, the children were declared wards of the state and placed with a state agency for adoption. An Illinois statute created the legal presumption that unwed fathers were unfit and not entitled to a hearing before the child could be placed for adoption. When this statute was challenged, the U.S. Supreme Court ruled it unconstitutional, reasoning that by denying a fitness hearing to unwed fathers and granting it to others, the statute violated the equal protection clause of the fourteenth amendment.

Under Georgia law, only consent of the mother was required for the adoption of a child born out of wedlock. In *Quolloin* v. *Walcott* (1978: 246), the U.S. Supreme Court was asked to rule on the constitutionality of Georgia's adoption laws as applied to deny an unwed father authority to prevent adoption of his illegitimate child. When the mother in the case consented to adoption of the child by her husband, the child's stepparent, the child's natural father filed a petition to block the adoption and to secure visitation rights. Interestingly, he did not seek custody or object to the child's continuing to live with his mother and her husband. The Court granted the adoption even though the natural father was not found to be an unfit parent. The Court reasoned that the natural father did not petition for legitimation of his child at any time during the eleven years between the child's birth and the filing of the adoption petition. Further, the child had expressed a desire to be adopted and to take the stepparent's name. The Court found the stepparent to be "a fit and proper person to adopt the child," and concluded that it would be in the best interests of the child to grant the adoption (Quollin v. Walcott, 1978: 246). The Court reasoned that since the natural father had never exercised actual or legal custody over the child, and had never agreed to accept "any significant responsibility with respect to the daily supervision, education, protection, or care of the child . . . and even now does not seek custody of the child," there was no real commitment to the welfare of the child (Quolloin v. Walcott, 1978: 248).

In *Caban* v. *Mohammed,* a New York statute was held to be unconstitutional because of the distinction made between the rights of unmarried mothers and the rights of unmarried fathers (1979: 380). An unwed father and mother had lived together for approximately five years during which time two children were born. The mother left the children's father and moved in with someone whom she eventually married. The mother and her new husband filed for adoption, and the children's natural father cross-petitioned for adoption. The natural father lost in the lower court, but when he appealed to the U.S. Supreme Court he prevailed. The Court ruled that the New York statute violated the father's equal protection rights since the gender-based distinction served no legitimate governmental objective. The Court said:

> Even if unwed mothers as a class were closer than unwed fathers to their newborn infants, this generalization concerning parent-child relations would become less acceptable as a basis for legislative distinctions as the age of the child increased. The present case demonstrates that an unwed father may have a relationship with his children fully comparable to that of the mother [Caban v. Mohammed, 1979: 380].

Conclusion

Most social scientists would agree that we are now living in what is probably the most rapid period of change in the history of the world. Single-parent families have increased from 12 percent in 1970 to 20 percent in 1980. The number of unmarried cohabitants tripled from 1970 to 1980. Divorces increased from 2.5 per 1000 population in 1965 to 5.3 in 1979. These changes, and others like them, have posed serious challenges to previous legal precedents. This chapter has reviewed some of the major legal developments in the past decade that have developed out of these changing lifestyles.

It is clear that with an increasing divorce rate, and a concomitant increase in the number of stepparents who want to adopt the children living with them, this area of the law will continue to be a source of future litigation for parents and stepparents. It is equally clear that grandparents and other interested parties who have become "psychological parents" to children will continue their initiatives in both the political and judicial forums to enhance and protect visitation and custody rights.

During the past quarter of a century there has been an increased recognition of the contribution of the homemaker. This has had an effect on property distribution and/or maintenance. In many jurisdictions even though the property may be titled in the husband's name, if he was married at the time the property was acquired, the wife is presumed to have a half interest in the property. Further, there is a noticeable trend to minimize the importance of marital misconduct in awarding alimony or distributing property. It is also evident that alimony is increasingly rehabilitative in nature, in that the period of time during which a party can expect to receive alimony is becoming progressively shortened. There are instances of alimony being awarded to males, especially in those states that have their own equal rights amendments, even though, historically, alimony was intended to be exclusively for women.

To understand and appreciate fully the significance of the judicial decisions discussed herein, and the trends suggested by them, one has to see them as a reflection of dramatic change in values and morality. Historically, the United States has been dominated by the Protestant ethic values of its ancestors, and accordingly has been one of the most antisexual of countries. Nonetheless, the United States has been undergoing a revolution in social and sexual attitudes and behavior. When the California Supreme Court gave judicial recognition to the rights of unmarried cohabitants in the precedent setting *Marvin* decision, it also gave judicial recognition to a change in the mores of society.

Cases

Aegerter v. Thompson, Mo. 610 S.W. 2d 308 (1980)

Anonymous v. Anonymous, Ramsey County Minnesota District Court, 2d Dist. 5 Family Law Reporter 2127 (1978)

Anonymous, In Re Adult, 435 N.Y.S. 2d 527 (1980)

Armanini v. Armanini, New York Supreme Court, Nassau County, 5 Family Law Reporter 2501 (1979)

Bates v. Bates, 560 P.2d 706 (1977)

Bonjour v. Bonjour, 566 P.2d 667 (1977)

Caban v. Mohammed, 441 U.S. 380 (1979)

DeFranco v. DeFranco, 384 N.E. 2d 997 (1978)

Fleming v. Fleming, 559 P.2d 329 (1977)

Foss v. Leifer, 550 P.2d 1309 (1976)
Gallo v. Gallo, Connecticut Supreme Court, 7 Family Law Reporter 2499 (1981)
Garlinger v. Garlinger, 347 A.2d 799 (1975)
Geoffrey G., In Re, 98 Cal. App. 3d 412, 159 Cal. Rptr. 460 (1979)
Hall v. Hall, Circuit Court, Macomb County, 5 Family Law Reporter 2543 (1979)
Hardwick v. Hardwick, 5 Family Law Reporter 2478 (1979)
Hewitt v. Hewitt, 394 N.E. 2d 1204 (1979)
Jackson v. Jacobson, 7 Family Law Reporter 2218 (1981)
Jarrett v. Jarrett, 400 N.E. 2d 421 (1979)
LaCroix v. Cook, 383 So. 2d 59 (1980)
Latzky v. Latzky, 2 Family Law Reporter 2168 (1976)
Marvin v. Marvin, 557 P.2d 106 (1976)
Marvin v. Marvin, 7 Family Law Reporter 2661 (1981)
Matter of the Estate of Griswold, 35 A.2d 171 (1976)
Nadler v. Superior Court, 255 Cal. App. 2d 523 (1967)
Northrup v. Northrup, 373 N.E. 2d 1221 (1978)
Painter v. Bannister, 140 N.W.2d 152 (1966)
People v. Onofre, 424 N.Y.S. 2d 566 (1980)
Quolloin v. Walcott, 434 U.S. 246 (1978)
R.A.D. v. M.E.Z., 414 A.2d 211 (1980)
Ramsay v. Ramsay, 233 N.W. 2d 729 (1975)
Stanley v. Illinois, 405 U.S. 645 (1972)
Studham v. Studham, No. 25870, Circuit Court for Anne Arundel County, Maryland
      (1980)
Sturgis v. Sturgis, 1 Family Law Reporter (1974)
Suozza v. Suozza, 16 N.J. Misc. 475 (1938)
Taake v. Taake, 233 N.W. 2d 449 (1975)
Tachick, In Re Adoption of, 210 N.W. 2d 865 (1973)
Tresnak v. Tresnak, 297 N.W. 2d 109 (1980)
Vaughn v. Vaughn, 2 Family Law Reporter 2586 (1976)
West v. King, VA 263 S.E. 2d 386 (1980)

References

American Psychiatric Association (1973) "Resolution on homosexuality." Press release,
      December 15.
FREED, D. J. and H. H. FOSTER (1981) "Divorce in the fifty states: an overview." Family
      Law Quarterly 14: 229-284.
———— (1980) "Grandparent visitation: vagaries and vicissitudes." National Law Reporter
      1, 5: 1929-1961.
MYRICKS, N. and R. RUBIN (1977) "Sex laws and alternative lifestyles." Family Coor-
      dinator 26, 4: 357-360.
U.S. Bureau of the Census (1981) Marital Status and Living Arrangements: March 1980.
      Current Population Reports. Series P-20, No. 365. Washington, DC: Government
      Printing Office.
WADLINGTON, W. (1969) "Adoption of adults: a family law anomaly." Cornell Law
      Review 54: 566-584.
WEITZMAN, L. J. and R. B. DIXON (1980) "The alimony myth: does no-fault divorce
      make a difference?" Family Law Quarterly 14, 3: 141-185.

CHAPTER 18

Teaching About Alternative Family Forms and Lifestyles

ANTHONY P. JURICH

CATHERINE A. HASTINGS

Kansas State University

Students frequently ask, "Why is the American family suddenly changing?" We smile and answer that their question is predicated upon the mistaken assumption that the family traditionally has been stable and unchanging. We try to explain that the family has always been in a state of transition. Even the American family has been in a continual state of evolution.

However, there is no doubt that in the past 20 years the rate of change has indeed accelerated. Numerous statistics, such as divorce rate and the percentage of couples who choose to be childless, have demonstrated the changing nature of the American family. Ramey (1977) has indicated that, based on an extrapolation from census data, only 13 percent of American families in 1975 were living in a "traditional" American family with a single breadwinner, two parents, and one or more children under the age of 18. The average person is much more likely to come into contact with someone living in an alternative family form and may even become part of such an alternative lifestyle him- or herself. This situation is creating a new clientele and new content for family life education. No longer is the family life educator able to focus only upon the "traditional American family." Regardless of one's personal views and moral stance, today's family life educator must recognize the existence of such alternative family forms and help students explore the "pros" and "cons" of such lifestyles, both academically and personally (see Macklin, 1981).

The changing situation has led in the last ten years to a plethora of books dealing with alternative family forms (e.g., Butler, 1979: Cox, 1972; DeLora and DeLora, 1975; Gordon, 1972; Libby and Whitehurst, 1977; Murstein, 1978; Otto, 1970), two special issues of *The Family Coordinator*

(October 1972, October 1975), and a new professional journal, *Alternative Lifestyles*. Courses on alternative family forms have sprung up on college campuses and, once in a while, one even surfaces in a high school. Alternative lifestyles and family forms are popular topics for seminars, speeches, workshops, and early morning television programs. To meet the demands of the public for information and discussion about alternative family forms, educators in general and family life educators in particular are frequently asked to offer programs and courses that deal with alternative lifestyles. However, with the exception of the articles by Macklin (1981) and Van Meter (1973), little has been written on teaching about alternative lifestyles. Therefore, much of the subsequent information has been extrapolated from articles dealing with teaching other similarly controversial materials, such as sex education.

Jump on the Bandwagon or Criticize the Deviants?

As with the sex education movement of the late 1960s and early 1970s (Schulz and Williams, 1968), the teaching of alternative family lifestyles is occasionally motivated by a "hidden agenda." Some instructors are less interested in "teaching" and more interested in "advocacy." These instructors, for either personal or philosophical reasons, attempt to sell a specific type of lifestyle or family form to their students. In fact, "students" is a misnomer, because such instructors are actually more interested in "followers" than in "students." They do a disservice to education because they present an incomplete picture to the student, pressure the individual into making choices that the instructor considers to be morally correct, and, consequently, restrict the student's freedom of choice.

On the other end of the continuum, some instructors have a suppressive motivation for teaching about alternative family forms. They seek to emphasize only the negative aspects of alternative family forms in an effort to reinforce their students' faith in the traditional nuclear family. Such instructors foster, in both overt and covert ways, the message that the student should "play it safe," restrict his or her choice of family style to the more traditional forms, and follow limited and very specific guidelines. Similar to the advocate, these instructors also restrict the education of their students and do an equally inadequate job of preparing students to deal with the complexity of modern American families. Instead, they send their students into their life decisions armed with incomplete knowledge and few tools for making informed choices.

Between these two extremes are a group of instructors who have "jumped on the bandwagon" of education about alternative family forms. Because of the excitement of the subject matter, these instructors seek to accomplish as much as possible with a minimum of planning and effort. They frequently describe their course or program as a panacea that will solve all the problems of the American family. This is similar to the bandwagons that arose in the areas of Head Start and sex education (Shultz and Williams, 1968). They may spend a lot of time developing interesting classroom sessions and assignments, but little time on other crucial aspects of a successful program, such as community acceptance, delineation of goals and objectives, selection of instructors, development of instructional techniques, and evaluation. An ill-conceived and under-planned program may leave the students, their parents, and the whole community disillusioned, thereby discrediting alternative family forms as a legitimate field of study and exploration.

The successful instructor attempts to give complete information on each alternative family form, including the costs and benefits involved in each. Armed with that knowledge base, the student is then helped to articulate his or her own needs and value system and to evaluate the extent to which any given lifestyle will be congruent with them. In this way, the student not only explores the "degree of fit" between his or her own needs and values and the available alternatives, but also develops skills in evaluation and decision making, with freedom to choose. Having been well prepared to make intelligent choices and to respect the choices of others, it is hoped that these students will be better prepared to help the system of marriage and family in America continue to evolve in directions that are functional for contemporary society.

Community Acceptance — How to Get the Foot in the Door

The first step in good family life education about alternative family forms is to work on community acceptance. It is important for the educator to be aware of the attitudes of the general public and it is important to have the community support. Several studies have explored public attitude toward and interest in alternative family forms (Jurich and Jurich, 1975; Strong, 1978; White and Wells, 1973). All three studies found that interest and willingness to participate in alternative family forms was greatest for the more traditional lifestyles (i.e., traditional marriage, egalitarian marriage, cohabitation). Interest, feasibility (as a realistice lifestyle) ratings, and expressed willingness to participate all went down as the type of alternative family became more extreme and less traditional. Mate swapping, group marriage, polyandry, and polygymy all received fairly low scores.

In fact, family forms seem to be able to be placed into four groups: (1) traditional family forms (traditional marriage and egalitarian marriage); (2) family lifestyles that are based upon the traditional family with normative variations (dual-career families, child-free marriages, one-child families, role-reversal marriages, homosexual marriages, single-parent families, cohabitation, stepfamilies, and singlehood); (3) family forms that violate the permanence aspect of the traditional family (divorce and serial monogamy, open-ended or time-limited contract marriages); and (4) family forms that violate the exclusivity (especially sexual) aspect of the traditional family (mate swapping, traditional affairs, group marriage, sexually open marriage, polygamy, and communes).

For the most part, the greatest acceptance is of the traditional family styles. The family forms based upon normative variations receive the next highest ratings of "willingness to participate." Exceptions are single-parent families, which are mostly nonvoluntary; role-reversal marriages, which are more highly favored by women than men; and homosexual marriages, which still bear the stigma associated with homosexuality, and are, therefore, the least favored of any lifestyle, although as a family form, they are relatively traditional. Family forms that violate the permanence aspect of marriage are fairly well accepted by nonparticipants. As a group, the alternative family forms that violate the exclusivity aspect of the family are the least accepted and considered the least feasible of all alternatives. However, group marriage and communal living arrangements were seen as growth producing by a large minority of respondents.

The family life educator must keep in mind the degree of general acceptance for each alternative lifestyle. A fairly open discussion about cohabitation may shut down in a hurry if homosexuality is mentioned. Students who would be willing to role play a dual-career family situation may balk at participating in a role-play situation about mate swapping. In these more volatile situations, the instructor may have to allow the student more distance from the subject matter. This may be accomplished by posing hypothetical role-play situations at first and gradually working into the student's "here and now" feelings. It is not being suggested that the instructor ignore specific topics, but that one take into the account the students' preexisting feelings about any specific family lifestyle when developing a format for presentation.

The studies by Jurich and Jurich (1975), Strong (1978), and White and Wells (1973) mentioned previously give the educator some clue as to the general community acceptance of a course about alternative lifestyles. All three studies found male/female differences in the acceptance of alternative family forms. Although, in most cases, the male and female samples placed the alternative family styles in a similar ordinal position, males generally were more acceptive of less traditional lifestyles, especially those involving nonexclusivity. Exceptions to this were role-reversed marriages (Strong, 1978), homosexual marriages (White and Wells, 1973), and polyandry (Jurich and Jurich, 1975), where the women in each sample were more positive about feasibility than were the men.

Strong (1978) found that persons who grew up in urban environments were more likely to indicate willingness to participate in such nonexclusive alternatives as consensual extramarital sex and mate swapping. Similarly, Strong found the frequency of church attendance to be negatively related to the willingness to participate in nontraditional forms involving premarital or extramarital sex. Jurich and Jurich (1975) found the university-related populations of two different cities to be much more accepting of cohabitation, open-ended marriage, communal marriage, group marriage, polyandry, and polygyny than their nonuniversity counterparts. Conversely, the nonuniversity population, when asked to rank order their preferences among ten family lifestyles, ranked monogamy, affairs, and mate swapping higher than did their university-oriented counterparts. These studies indicate the need for family life educators to study their audience and to be aware of the particular preferences and prejudices. A church audience in a rural area will require a different approach than a secular audience at an urban university.

After the family life educator is informed about the characteristics of the potential students, attention must be given to obtaining the support of the larger community. Communities differ with respect to size, composition, sophistication, and readiness to accept change. Regardless of the source of the impetus for a program or course on alternative family lifestyles, the educator should invite the participation of civic leaders, school teachers and officials, ministers, parents, and concerned citizens in the planning of the course. "Their views should be solicited, their doubts and concerns sympathetically listened to, their suggestions carefully considered — for their support is absolutely essential if the program is to be a success" (Schulz and Williams, 1968: 8). The family life educator must not only attempt to incorporate input from each of these groups but also try to keep each of the above groups from alienating one another. This is not always easy in a large group, where special interest groups may be particularly vocal.

An excellent way to create community liaison with a minimum of disruption is through the use of a community advisory committee. Respected local leaders should be recruited to provide a sympathetic ear, diversity of opinion, and a liaison with specific community groups. Such a committee will serve to develop community trust in both the family life educator and the specific course material. The people of the community know the persons on the committee and should have relatively ready access to them in order to both voice concerns and receive information. Such a committee can troubleshoot potential problems *before* they occur. This type of committee process gives the educator more knowledge about both the community and the potential audience. However, the most important function of such a committee is its existence as a symbol of the educator's regard for community opinion, setting the stage for a climate of mutual respect.

Philosophy of Education — The Seed for the Tree of Knowledge

Most of the literature on family life education deals with "what" to teach and some literature addresses "how" to teach. Very few educators and scholars address the more basic question of "Why teach about alternative family forms at all?" Some of the more covert and political reasons were elucidated earlier; they are seen as inappropriate for true educators. If the intention is to genuinely educate, the careful articulation of goals and objectives is of crucial importance. They become the cornerstone upon which the curriculum is built, the teachers selected, and the instructional techniques developed and they form the basis for eventual evaluation.

The first goal of education is *the transfer of accurate knowledge about alternative family forms to the student.* On the surface this may appear to be simple, but in fact it is a very complex task. It requires more than simply providing demographic statistics and incidence rates. The educator must present the range of possible variations within each lifestyle, the typical as well as the atypical. Students will want to know "why" a certain lifestyle is selected, and so there must be some review of research and speculation as to the motivations for any particular alternative. There must also be some consideration of the satisfaction and problems commonly experienced by participants in a given lifestyle. Unlike mathematics or the natural sciences, the students themselves will have feelings and attitudes about the incidence, practices, and motivations surrounding each alternative family form (Van Meter, 1973). Some students will affirm the rationale for choosing a given lifestyle, and others will find such a choice inconceivable. Regardless of whether the student is in favor of or against a specific alternative family form, the numerous myths surrounding each lifestyle pattern will have to be dispelled.

The second goal of education about alternative family forms is to *help students clarify their value positions and to make responsible lifestyle decisions based upon these values* (Englund, 1980; Helm and Irvine, 1980). To achieve this, the instructor must focus much of his or her attention on the attitudes and feelings that the student has concerning the course content, the learning process, and the required self-appraisal and self-application (Olson and Moss, 1980). Because of the volatile and often controversial nature of the subject matter, the students will bring strong feelings and long-held values to the classroom experience, which they must be helped to articulate and explore (Helm and Irvine, 1980). In addition, the learning process itself may evoke a high degree of affect. A student who may sit contently through a lecture may balk at the thought of being involved in a role-play situation, where he or she might become threatened by his or her own vulnerability. For many students, particularly those in their middle and late adolescence, the material on alternative family lifestyles will have a significant impact upon their self-definition and, ultimately, on their self-concept (Tharp, 1980). Finally, the students may find it threatening or difficult to apply the knowledge they are gaining about variant lifestyles to their own personal life situations. It is crucial that the teacher work to create a supportive learning environment in which students will feel safe to explore and express their own ideas, and experience their personal reactions (Helm and Irvine, 1980; Olson and Moss, 1980).

The third goal is to *help students become more accepting of the lifestyle choices of others.* It is not surprising that, in a society as complex and multifaceted as our own, pluralism of family lifestyles has become the norm (Ramey, 1977). Therefore, a course on alternative family forms should produce a flexibility within its students that will allow them to better cope with the range of lifestyles which they will experience in their professional (e.g., teacher, lawyer) and personal (e.g., spouse, parent, child) lives (Van Meter, 1973). Regardless of the student's own personal like or dislike of a given family lifestyle, the flexibility gained by academic and personal exploration of alternatives should enable the student to become a more effective force in strengthening family relationships in all societal variants.

The Teacher — The Primary Ingredient

It will be impossible to achieve any of the above goals if the right teacher with the proper training and attitudes is not found to implement the course. Any teaching job is demanding, but teaching about family relations, with its intertwining of cognitive and affective components, is particularly stressful (Tharp, 1980). Educating about a volatile topic, such as alternative family forms, puts extreme demands upon the instructor. In a survey of sex education teachers, the instructors themselves worried about whether they were adequately prepared to teach about such controversial subject matter (Herold and Benson, 1979). Teachers of courses or workshops on alternative family forms face a similar situation.

One of the most crucial characteristics of a good teacher is a thorough grasp of the subject matter (Schulz and Williams, 1968). This is particularly true for the instructor of a course on alternative family forms, where students come to class with preconceived notions, myths, a lack of information, and experiences that may have prejudiced them either for or against a given lifestyle. These students may pose a major threat to the educator who is not well enough informed to handle a detailed discussion or field difficult or combative questions. It is *not* important that the teacher know all the answers. Nothing destroys the credibility of a teacher as much as trying to fake knowledge about something about which he or she has little knowledge. It *is* important to know and acknowledge the limitations of one's knowledge and to differentiate between fact, speculation, and personal opinion.

In order to prevent bias, the instructor must be aware of his or her own feelings about alternative family lifestyles. This requires a considerable amount of self-evaluation. The educator must be careful not to interject his or her own biases into an objective presentation. He must evaluate his or her own need system in order to determine his or her strengths and weaknesses, both personal and academic. He or she must also be aware of the image that he or she projects to students. It will be important to present a model of a warm, empathetic, genuine person, who is able to openly discuss feelings and views, carry on an unbiased discussion, and be tolerant of a variety of viewpoints (Schulz and Williams, 1968; Tharp, 1980). The educator must be able to transcend his or her professional role and become a "person" to his or her students. When a teacher becomes comfortable with both the content of the material and his or her own feelings about it, he or she will be better able to apply classroom methodology, facilitate an objective discussion, and field challenging questions which may arise. With the periodic assistance of colleagues, other supporting staff, and administrators, such an instructor should be able to provide a viable learning experience.

The Curriculum — What Do We Teach?

There are two aspects to the curriculum question: (1) What alternative family forms should be covered? (2) What aspects of each family lifestyle should be focused upon? Beginning the course with a focus upon the traditional nuclear family is an excellent starting point (see Van Meter, 1973). It provides the students a familiar lifestyle with which they may more easily identify, which helps in turn to build a supportive classroom atmosphere. It allows the students to understand the pressures affecting the traditional family that prompted the rise in alternative family forms. It serves as a basis for comparison with other family forms to be discussed later in the course. A discussion about egalitarian marriages (Forisha, 1978) could be included as the traditional marriage's most frequent alternative. It is suggested that one then present a section on alternatives that are variations upon the traditional family structure. These would include: *dual-career families* (Gross, 1980; Hopkins and White, 1978; Skinner, 1980); *child-free marriages* (Russell et al., 1978; Veevers, 1973, 1975, 1979); *one-child marriages* (Hawke and Knox, 1978); *role-reversal* marriages (Lyness, 1978); *single-parent families* (DeFrain and Eirick, 1981; Rosenthal and Keshet, 1978; Weiss, 1979); *singlehood* (Staples, 1981; Stein, 1976, 1978); *nonmarital cohabitation* (Clayton and Voss, 1977; Greenwald, 1970; Macklin, 1972, 1978; Ridley et al., 1978); *stepfamilies* (Visher and Visher, 1979); and *homosexual marriages* (Bell and Weinberg, 1978; Harry and Lovely, 1979; Peplau and Amaro, 1982). Except for the homosexual marriage, these are the family lifestyles that are most easily accepted by students (Jurich and Jurich, 1975; Strong, 1978; White and Wells, 1973); hence, there are several advantages to presenting them first. They are most similar to the traditional family and, consequently, are easiest for the student to link to his or her previous experience. Except for the homosexual marriage, they require the fewest value judgments, enabling the student to work gradually into the process of confronting values and formulating value decisions. The curriculum then becomes a series of successive approximations which, on one level, deliver content to the student and on another enable the student to learn gradually to analyze feelings and the values underlying these feelings.

The next section of the course should include those alternative family forms that violate the permanence aspect of the traditional family. These include *time-limited contract marriages* (Weitzman, 1981; White and Wells 1973) and *serial monogamy* (Alpenfels, 1970). These variants change the time structure of the family and force the student to revise a basic universal tenet of most marriages.

The last group of family forms covered would be those based upon the violation of the exclusivity aspect of the traditional family. Since most marriages and families have some sort of exclusivity as a foundation for their existence, these family forms are the most radical, are the most difficult to accept, and require the most effort to integrate cognitively into the student's preexisting mental schema. These include: *open marriage* (O'Neill and O'Neill, 1972), including *sexually open marriage* (Buunk 1980; Knapp and Whitehurst, 1977; Ramey, 1976); *traditional affairs* (Atwater, 1979; Bernard, 1977; Clanton, 1977; Hunt, 1969; Libby, 1977) *mate swapping* (Bartell, 1971; Denfield and Gordon, 1970; Gilmartin 1978); *communes* (Bradford and Klevansky, 1980; Eiduson and Alexander, 1978; Kanter, 1972; Kanter et al., 1975; Talmon, 1972); *group marriage* (Constantine, 1978; Constantine and Constantine, 1973), and *polygamy* (Kassel, 1970; Neubeck, 1970). Among these family forms those that do not mandate a violation of sexual exclusivity, such as open marriages and communes, will meet the least value resistance. Variants involving numbers of persons, such as communes and group marriages are cognitively complicated and violate many exclusivity boundaries while alternative forms such as mate swapping and traditional affairs violate sexual exclusivity but keep the other interpersonal boundaries intact. It is suggested that the instructor, in planning the curriculum, program in sufficient flexibility to allow the agenda to respond to the feedback that students provided earlier in the course. If the students are generally "uptight" about sexual exclusivity, the teacher may want to discuss communes before mate swapping. However, if the class appears to have little difficulty discussing sexual nonexclusivity, the instructor may wish to postpone a discussion of communal living because of its cognitive complexity. Thus the curriculum becomes merely a guide and the instructor is able to avoid being tyranized into rigidity by her or his own curriculum.

The educator must then turn his or her attention to what will be taught about each alternative family form. There must be a description of the family lifestyle and its interpersonal dynamics (Van Meter, 1973), including the psychological, social, and transactional elements of the family system a presentation of statistics regarding incidence and growth rates, and overview of reasons for entry into an alternative lifestyle, and a discussion of the personal and societal pressures that impact upon persons within that particular family form. Such a presentation should serve to generate a discussion of the "pros" and "cons" of each family form and, eventually, a discussion of the possible consequences and products, both societal and personal, of each.

Somewhere within this process, the class will be forced to deal with the issue of values. In many traditional sex education programs the value issue was avoided in an effort not to intrude upon the students' value systems (Schulz and Williams, 1968). This has been shown to be extremely dysfunctional in the field of sex education (Herold and Benson, 1979), and it is now acknowledged that values must be discussed within the classroom context (Englund, 1980; Schulz and Williams, 1968; Tharp, 1980). Without any discussion of values, students are presented with choices and then forced to make decisions in a vacuum. That is unfair, unethical, and poor teaching. Instead, the educator should seek to teach cognitive coping skills that will aid the student in clarifying his or her own values, and to provide a forum within which the students may voice their opinions in open, nonthreatening discussion (Englund, 1980).

Teaching Techniques — How to Translate Content into Learning

During the first session, the instructor must lay down the "ground rules" governing class discussion, and inform the class as to the goals, structure, and content of the course. There must be an explicit effort made to create a supportive and nonjudgmental atmosphere (Tharp, 1980). By indicating the linkage of the affective and cognitive components of the course (Olson and Moss, 1980), and by designating the students' feelings as a legitimate concern of the course, students will come to realize that the instructor views them as people as well as students.

Helm and Irvine (1980) list four guidelines that will help the instructor create and maintain a supportive atmosphere: (1) everyone deserves the right to be heard; (2) accentuate the positive; (3) disagree with a student's ideas or actions but always reaffirm the student as a person; and (4) protect the privacy of both the students and the teacher. These guidelines will enhance both the safety and supportive atmosphere of the class environment. They allow the student to be heard and his or her ideas to be evaluated authentically without the threat of being put down. There should also be an understanding that no one will be pressed to disclose against his or her will.

Most family life education courses are conducted either through lecture or discussion group techniques. It is suggested that both of these techniques be utilized. If the course consists solely of lectures, students seldom get involved other than cognitively. On the other hand, when the subject matter is as controversial and volatile as alternative family lifestyles, discussion groups often get sidetracked, and it becomes difficult to cover each lifestyle adequately. Lectures are an effective way to present basic facts and set the tone for group discussions (Olson and Moss, 1980; Schulz and Williams, 1968). While lecturing, the teacher can model the necessary qualities of warmth, empathy, genuineness, and unconditional positive regard (Englund, 1980; Singer and Weissman, 1974). This should then carry over into the students' behavior in the discussion groups. The content of the lecture should be more than simple facts and figures. A figure means little to students unless they are given something with which to compare it. Bare facts and lists of characteristics come alive when peppered with case studies and examples (Helm and Irvine, 1980; Olson and Moss, 1980; Schulz and Williams, 1968). By presenting specific problems and situations, one can more easily blend the cognitive and affective components of the course. Examples and case studies also stimulate analytical thought among the students, give them a chance to identify with persons in the various lifestyles (Schulz and Williams, 1968), and set the stage for group discussion.

Educational films on alternative family forms, movies, videotapes, records, and examples from popular movies and television shows can serve to enliven the class and draw the students into the affective dimensions of the material (Herold and Benson, 1979; Lieberman and Lieberman, 1977; Schulz and Williams, 1968; Van Meter, 1973). Humor interjected into a course on alternative family forms makes the material more human, adds realism, and helps the student to identify with the lifestyle participants (Adams, 1974; Bryant et al., 1980).

After the lectures have set the tone and established a basic foundation of knowledge, it is time for group discussion. Group discussion has often been listed as the single most important technique used to study the American family (Englund, 1980; Herold and Benson, 1979; Russell et al., 1978; Schulz and Williams, 1968; Singer and Weissman, 1974; Tharp, 1980). There are certain things that can only be gained through interactions that encourage self-disclosure and provide opportunities for feedback (Tharp, 1980). Group discussion allows students to learn from the experiences and feelings of their fellow classmates, integrate material collectively in the group, and utilize their interpersonal relationship skills to explore their own thoughts and feelings. The interaction and reactions of a group of self-motivated students creates an atmosphere of support, nurturance, and reality testing that is unparalleled in a lecture class (Singer and Weissman, 1974).

Within this unique environment, students soon discover that there is more than one way to approach a situation (Schulz and Williams, 1968). Evidence accepted by one person may not be considered valid or even relevant by another. By listening to and evaluating alternative viewpoints, the students add to their understanding of themselves and of each alternative family form.

To fully accomplish the above goals, the teacher must actively engage in the group process (Tharp, 1980). The instructor who asks his or her students to risk self-involvement, but refuses to do so him- or herself, will often receive little or no response from the students. It is relatively easy to lecture about subject matter content while hiding behind a lecturn and then to require students to regurgitate specific answers on a multiple choice test. However, this process of teaching assumes that there is a "right" answer and that the only one in the class who "knows" the "right answer" is the teacher. In an area as controversial as alternative family forms, that attitude becomes folly. Only the educator who is willing to become part student and to ask of him- or herself the same risk taking that he or she asks of the students is able to draw from those students the kind of true learning that is required.

There are many techniques for initiating the discussion of alternative family forms. Some educators ask their students to fill out questionnaires at the beginning of class and then use the answers as a springboard for discussion (Herold and Benson, 1979; Russell et al., 1978; Schulz and Williams, 1968). Others use field trips, panel debates (Herold and Benson, 1979), and guest speakers (Helm and Irvine, 1980; Schulz and Williams, 1968; Van Meter, 1973) as discussion starters. The latter has the advantage of bringing into the classroom someone intimately connected with an alternative lifestyle who can provide insights that otherwise could only be gained second hand. Moreover, someone who has actually participated in a given lifestyle has a degree of veracity that cannot be approached by the teacher, regardless of how highly respected that individual may be.

Role playing is another frequently used technique to elicit student involvement (Herold and Benson, 1979; Olson and Moss, 1980; Russell et al., 1978; Schulz and Williams, 1968; Singer and Weissman, 1974). In a situation in which the subject matter may be foreign to a great many students, as it is when studying alternative family forms, role-playing techniques may help one gain insight into the feelings and behaviors of others. In this way, the student gains empathy for those in an alternative lifestyle. Role playing also allows the students to explore different solutions to the problems posed by alternative family lifestyles (Schulz and Williams, 1968). The role-playing technique of role reversal is particularly fruitful, for example, having a male play the role of a communal woman who feels "stuck" in menial labor tasks. In order to more fully explore role playing as a learning experience, Singer and Weissman (1974) recommend videotaping the role-play situations and replaying them for the group's subsequent discussion.

Sooner or later the discussion group will have to deal with values, and here the instructor is often on the horns of a dilemma. He or she may either tell the students what to believe or avoid the topic of values and morality all together. Both are unacceptable alternatives if true learning is to occur. Helm and Irvine (1980) suggest that the educator cope with controversial issues by asking questions of the students that encourage their own thought processes. In this manner, the content of the discussion comes from the students themselves. The process outlined by Englund (1980), utilizing Kohlberg's concept of cognitive moral development, is another excellent approach to the topic of values. By presenting material in a series of vignettes and asking students to logically justify their choices, they are trained to think at higher cognitive levels of thought. One may remain within his or her original value system if he or she desires, or change that value system in accord with the new information. Regardless of the level of cognitive sophistication, all choices of morality or values reside within the individual. It becomes the teacher's job to present to the students the widest spectrum of information so that they can make the most informed choices possible.

In addition to classroom experience, students may be assigned tasks to perform outside of class. Cognitive homework, such as reading, should be supplemented by homework in the affective area (Russell et al., 1978; Schulz and Williams, 1968; Singer and Weissman, 1974). Assignments involving reports on novels or movies may encourage the student to explore the world outside the classroom. Russell et al. (1978) achieved success when they had students interview other classmates. The experience brought the class together and the dyadic interchange provided for a quality of exchange that would be difficult in a larger group. A standard assignment is to require students to interview all members of a family engaged in an alternative lifestyle. The student is required to do library research on the family form, construct a structured interview (which must be evaluated by the instructor ahead of time), find an alternative lifestyle family, conduct the interview, write up the results of the interview, and compare and contrast the results with available literature and with his or her own thoughts, attitudes, and feelings. Regardless of the assignment used, it is crucial to design tasks that encourage the student to reach beyond the classroom. The class that is talked about after class is the class in which learning occurs.

Evaluation — Where Do We Go from Here?

If we are to leave a legacy to others who will teach after us there must be some evaluation of the success of our efforts at education. However, this is an extremely difficult task. It is easy to assess pure information (Van Meter, 1973), but this is the least of the goals for which we are striving. Therefore, the traditional and relatively easy evaluation methods of effective teaching, such as objective testing, become relatively useless. Subjective methods that inquire into the student's perceptions and feelings about both the subject matter and his or her own learning process are most often recommended (Olson and Moss, 1980). It is suggested that a broad subjective evaluation, followed by several pointed, open-ended questions, is a reasonable method for obtaining an evaluation of the learning experience. The first question might ask the student which of the educational experiences was the most valuable for him or her. Second, students should be asked to indicate in what way their expectations were not met or what changes they would recommend. Whatever method is used, it should be remembered that the real evaluation, the true "acid test," will only be possible several years after the student has completed the course. Only after the present generation of students have lived their lives for a few years can we truly know if we have been successful. The best possible evaluation would be some long-term follow-up of these students to see if in fact they are more understanding, more tolerant, and better able to make lifestyle choices than a similar group of persons who had not had the course. Only then can we really say that our teaching has borne the fruit for which we sowed the seeds.

References

ADAMS, W. J. (1974) "The use of sexual humor in teaching human sexuality at the university level." Family Coordinator 23: 365-372.

ALPENFELS, E. J. (1970) "Progressive monogamy: an alternate pattern?" pp. 67-73 in H. A. Otto (ed.) The Family in Search of a Future. New York: Appleton-Century-Crofts.

ATWATER, L. (1979) "Getting involved: women's transition to first extramarital sex." Alternative Lifestyles 2, 1: 38-68.

BARTELL, G. (1971) Group Sex. New York: Signet.

BELL, A. P. and M. S. WEINBERG (1978) Homosexualities: A Study of Diversity Among Men and Women. New York: Simon & Schuster.

BERNARD, J. (1977) "Infidelity: some moral and social issues," pp. 131-146 in R. W. LIBBY and R. M. WHITEHURST (eds.) Marriage and Alternatives: Exploring Intimate Relationships. Glenview, IL: Scott, Foresman.

BRADFORD, D. and S. KLEVANSKY (1980) Non-utopian communities — the middle-class commune," pp. 131-139 in K. Kammeyer (ed.) Confronting the Issues. Boston: Allyn & Bacon.

BRYANT, J., J. CRANE, P. COMISKY, and D. ZILLMAN (1980) "Relationship between college teachers' use of humor in the classroom and students' evaluation of their teachers." Journal of Educational Psychology 72: 511-519.

BUTLER, E. W. (1979) Traditional Marriage and Emerging Alternatives. New York: Harper & Row.

BUUNK, B. (1980) "Sexually-open marriages: ground rules for countering potential threats to marriage." Alternative Lifestyles 3, 3: 312-328.

CLANTON, G. (1977) "The contemporary experience of adultery: Bob and Carol and Updike and Rimmer," pp. 112-130 in R. W. Libby and R. N. Whitehurst (eds.) Marriage and Alternatives: Exploring Intimate Relationships. Glenview, IL: Scott, Foresman.

CLAYTON, R. R. and H. L. VOSS (1977) "Shacking up: cohabitation in the 70s." Journal of Marriage and the Family 39: 273-284.

CONSTANTINE, L. L. (1978) "Multilateral relations revisited: group marriage in extended perspective," pp. 131-147 in B. I. Murstein (ed.) Exploring Intimate Life Styles. New York: Springer.

———— and J. M. CONSTANTINE (1973) Group Marriage. New York: Macmillan.

COX, F. D. (1972) American Marriage: A Changing Scene? Dubuque, IA: Brown.

DeFRAIN, J. and R. EIRICK (1981) "Coping as divorced single parents: a comparative study of fathers and mothers." Family Relations 30, 2: 265-274.

DeLORA, J. S. and J. R. DeLORA (eds.) (1975) Intimate Life-Styles: Marriage and Its Alternatives. Pacific Palisades, CA: Goodyear.

DENFIELD, D. and M. GORDON (1970) "The sociology of mate-swapping." Journal of Sex Research 6: 85-100.

EIDUSON, B. T. and J. W. ALEXANDER (1978) "The role of children in alternative family styles." Journal of Social Issues 34, 2: 149-167.

ENGLUND, C. L. (1980) "Using Kohlberg's moral developmental framework in family life education." Family Relations 29: 7-13.

FORISHA, B. L. (1978) Sex Roles and Personal Awareness. Morristown, NJ: General Learning Press.

GILMARTIN, B. G. (1978) The Gilmartin Report. Secaucus, NJ: Citadel.

GORDON, M. [ed.] (1972) The Nuclear Family in Crisis: The Search for an Alternative. New York: Harper & Row.

GREENWALD, H. (1970) "Marriage as a non-legal voluntary association," pp. 51-56 in H. A. Otto (ed.) The Family in Search of a Future. New York: Appleton-Century-Crofts.

GROSS, H. E. (1980) "Dual-career couples who live apart: two types." Journal of Marriage and the Family 42, 3: 567-576.

HARRY, J. and R. LOVELY (1979) "Gay marriages and communities of sexual orientation." Alternative Lifestyles 2, 2: 177-200.

HAWKE, S. and D. KNOX (1978) "The one child family: a new life style." Family Coordinator 27: 215-220.

HELM, G. and A. IRVINE (1980) "An approach to teaching family life education: tell it like it is, but keep it safe," pp. 455-471 in N. Stinnett, B. Chesser, J. DeFrain, and P. Knaub (eds.) Family Strengths: Positive Models for Family Life. Lincoln: University of Nebraska Press.

HEROLD, E. S. and R. M. BENSON (1979) "Problems of teaching sex education — a survey of Ontario secondary schools." Family Relations 28: 199-203.

HOPKINS, J. and P. WHITE (1978) "The dual-career couple: constraints and supports." Family Coordinator 27: 253-259.

HUNT, M. (1969) The Affair. New York: World.

JURICH, A. P. and J. A. JURICH (1975) "Alternative family forms: preferences of nonparticipants." Home Economics Research Journal 3: 260-265.

KANTER, R. M. (1972) Commitment and Community. Cambridge, MA: Harvard University Press.

———— D. JAFFEE, and D. K. WEISBERG (1975) "Coupling, parenting, and the presence of others: intimate relationships in communal households." Family Coordinator 24: 433-452.

KASSEL, V. (1970) "Polygyny after 60," pp. 137-143 in H. A. Otto (ed.) The Family in Search of a Future. New York: Appleton-Century-Crofts.

KNAPP, J. J. and R. N. WHITEHURST (1977) "Sexually open marriage and relationships: issues and prospects," pp. 147-160 in R. W. Libby and R. N. Whitehurst (eds.) Marriage and Alternatives: Exploring Intimate Relationships. Glenview, IL: Scott, Foresman.

LIBBY, R. W. (1977) "Extramarital and comarital sex: a critique of the literature," pp. 80-111 in R. W. Libby and R. N. Whitehurst (eds.) Marriage and Alternatives: Exploring Intimate Relationships. Glenview, IL: Scott, Foresman.

———— and R. N. WHITEHURST [eds.] (1977) Marriage and Alternatives: Exploring Intimate Relationships. Glenview, IL: Scott, Foresman.

LIEBERMAN, L. and L. LIEBERMAN (1977) "The family in the tube: potential uses of television." Family Coordinator 26: 235-242.

LYNESS, J. F. (1978) "Androgyny," pp. 16-34 in B. I. Murstein (ed.) Exploring Intimate Life Styles. New York: Springer.

MACKLIN, E. D. (1981) "Education for choice: implications of alternatives in lifestyles for family life education." Family Relations 30, 4: 567-577.

——— (1978) "Non-marital heterosexual cohabitation: a review of the research." Marriage and Family Review 1, 2: 1-12.

——— (1972) "Heterosexual cohabitation among unmarried college students." Family Coordinator 21: 463-472.

MURSTEIN, B. I. [ed.] (1978) Exploring Intimate Life Styles. New York: Springer.

NEUBECK, G. (1970) "Polyandry and polygyny: viable today?" pp. 99-109 in H. A. Otto (ed.) The Family in Search of a Future. New York: Appleton-Century-Crofts.

OLSON, T. D. and J. J. MOSS (1980) "Creating supportive atmospheres in family life education." Family Relations 29: 391-395.

O'NEILL, N. and G. O'NEILL (1972) Open Marriage. Philadelphia: J. B. Lippincott.

OTTO, H. A. (ed.) (1970) The Family in Search of a Future. New York: Appleton-Century-Crofts.

PEPLAU, L. A. and H. AMARO (1982) "Understanding lesbian relationships," in J. Weinrich and W. Paul (eds.) Homosexuality: Social, Psychological, and Biological Issues. Beverly Hills, CA: Sage.

RAMEY, J. W. (1977) "Alternative life styles." Society 14, 5: 43-47.

——— (1976) Intimate Friendships. Englewood Cliffs, NJ: Prentice-Hall.

RIDLEY, C. A., D. J. PETERMAN, and A. W. AVERY (1978) "Cohabitation: does it make for a better marriage?" Family Coordinator 27, 2: 129-136.

ROSENTHAL, K. M. and H. F. KESHET (1978) "The impact of childcare responsibilities on part-time or single fathers: changing patterns of work and intimacy." Alternative Lifestyles 1, 4: 465-492.

RUSSELL, M. G., R. N. HEY, G. A. THOEN, and T. WALZ (1978) "The choice of childlessness: a workshop model." Family Coordinator 27: 179-183.

SCHULZ, E. D. and S. R. WILLIAMS (1968) Family Life and Sex Education: Curriculum and Instruction. New York: Harcourt, Brace, Jovanovich.

SINGER, L. J. and J. WEISSMAN (1974) "Action process teaching: a multidimensional, experiential, learning approach." Family Coordinator 23: 115-122.

SKINNER, D. A. (1980) "Dual-career family stress and coping: a literature review." Family Relations 29, 4: 473-481.

STAPLES, R. (1981) The World of Black Singles. Westport, CT: Greenwood.

STEIN, P. J. (1978) "The lifestyles and life chances of the never-married." Marriage and Family Review 1, 4: 1-11.

——— (1976) Single. Englewood Cliffs, NJ: Prentice-Hall.

STRONG, L. D. (1978) "Alternative marital and family forms: their relative attractiveness to college students and correlates of willingness to participate in nontraditional forms." Journal of Marriage and the Family 40: 493-504.

TALMON, Y, (1972) Family and Community in the Kibbutz. Cambridge, MA: Harvard University Press.

THARP, L. (1980) "Applying the process of humanistic psychology to the facilitating of family life education," pp. 485-497 in N. Stinnett, B. Chesser, J. DeFrain, and P. Knaub (eds.) Family Strengths: Positive Models For Family Life. Lincoln: University of Nebraska Press.

VAN METER, M.J.S. (1973) "Teaching about changing life styles." Family Coordinator 22: 171-176.

VEEVERS, J. E. (1979) "Voluntary childlessness: a review of issues and evidence." Marriage and Family Review 2, 2: 1-26.

——— (1975) "The moral careers of voluntarily childless wives: notes on the defense of a variant world view." Family Coordinator 24: 473-487.

——— (1973) "Voluntary childlessness: a neglected area of family study." Family Coordinator 22: 199-205.

VISHER, E. B. and J. S. VISHER (1979) Stepfamilies: A Guide to Working With Stepparents and Stepchildren. New York: Brunner/Mazel.

WEISS, R. S. (1979) Going It Alone: The Family Life and Social Situation of the Single
    Parent. New York: Basic Books.
WEITZMAN, L. J. (1981) The Marriage Contract: Spouses, Lovers, and the Law. New
    York: Macmillan.
WHITE, M. and C. WELLS (1973) "Student attitudes toward alternate marriage forms,"
    pp. 280-295 in R. W. Libby and R. N. Whitehurst (eds.) Renovating Marriage. Dan-
    ville, CA: Consensus.

CHAPTER 19

Religious Reactions to Alternative Lifestyles

ROBERT T. FRANCOEUR

Fairleigh Dickinson University

The twenty years between 1960 and 1980 are increasingly being viewed as a watershed era in the history of Western civilization and the Judaeo-Christian culture. In the early 1960s, the general conservativism and sexual repression of the previous decades began to show signs of relaxation (Francoeur, 1982: 30-38).

Many factors helped trigger this shift. The advent of rock'n'roll music mixed the quivering reverence of Deep South gospel music with the earthy, raw, Black rhythm of the blues, and quickly achieved white respectability as symbolized by the teenagers' adulation of Elvis Presley. The popularization of the bikini, miniskirts, hot pants, and the hormonal contraceptive pill were signs of the trend. The civil, women's, and gay rights movements and the Vietnam War controversy reinforced the self-orientation of the "flower children" and "hippie generation." The increasing permissiveness and new acceptance of nudity created "go-go" discotheques, theatrical productions such as *Hair, Oh Calcutta!* and *Let My People Come!*, sex-oriented magazines such as *Playboy*, and the liberalization of obscenity laws by the U.S. Supreme Court. With Kinsey's statistics on the sexual behavior of American men and women already a matter of public record, the laboratory studies of the human sexual response by William Masters and Virginia Johnson (1966) made sex a legitimate topic for the mass media. The growing affluence and leisure of the American middle class made it possible for large numbers of people to indulge themselves in once taboo activities and lifestyles. The incidence of premarital and extramarital sex rose significantly. Sexually active singlehood,

Author's Note: The author wishes to acknowledge the contributions of Jon Alston (Texas A & M University), Mary Burton (University of Arkansas), Margaret Feldman (Cornell University), Virginia Heffernan (Washington, D.C.), Roger Rubin (University of Mary-

open marriage, and swinging became the lifestyles of many (Francoeur, 1982: 372-377, 454-505).

The churches responded to these social developments with a series of important national and international conferences. Simultaneous with the much heralded "window opening" by Pope John XXIII at the Catholic Church's 1963 Second Vatican Council, there were several less publicized but equally important national Protestant conventions. All these dealt openly with the need for a new application of traditional principles and values to the social realities of the 1960s, particularly the increasing tendency to separate sexual intercourse from procreation, the rising incidence of divorce, remarriage, and single-parent families, and the growing tolerance and acceptance of premarital sex (Genne, 1975).

Developments in the 1970s continued this trend toward a more open, more tolerant, and more pluralistic culture. The gay rights movement became politically visible. Concern over world population led to the formation of the National Organization of Non-parents and Zero Population Growth. The age of first marriage pushed into the early twenties and the annual divorce rate passed the million mark. Reproductive and embryo technologies became realities with the birth of the world's first test-tube baby. *Open Marriage* (O'Neill and O'Neill, 1972) and *The Joy of Sex* (Comfort, 1972) were trend-setting best sellers, while swingers and massage parlors became part of the middle-class scene (Francoeur, 1982: 38-41).

Behind this social turmoil, a major dichotomy began to surface in all the major church groups and religious traditions. This dichotomy was not new to human consciousness, but the social upheaval of the 1960s and 1970s brought the split into sharp focus.

Every human effort at creating a philosophy or theology as a support for a religious or humanist belief system starts with the way the person or group views the world in which they live. Theologies and philosophies that attempt to explain and systematize religious or humanist beliefs grow out of a specific *Weltanschauung*, world perspective, or cosmology.

Historically, the human mind seems to have been unable to think of more than two ways of viewing the world. For centuries the dominant cosmology has been based on a cyclic concept of time, on an absolutist, fixed philosophy of nature that believes everything was created perfect and complete in the beginning of time, after which the human race fell

---

land), and Darwin Thomas (Brigham Young University), who participated in the workshop on Religion and Alternative Lifestyles at the 1981 meetings of the Groves Conference on Marriage and the Family. Timothy Perper, a behavioral geneticist from Philadelphia, and Richard Kropf, a Catholic theologian, were particularly helpful in adding precision to the interpretation of the first six paradigms and their relationship to the religious paradigm.

from grace and began a painful, guilt-ridden, penitential return to Eden. From earliest Chinese and Greek times, there were those few "heretics" who held a different world view, based on a linear conception of time and on the evolving or process-oriented character of the world and human nature, moving toward some utopian goal.

Europeans began to take the process view seriously with the advent of the evolutionary geology proposed by Hutton and Lyell in the early 1800s. Darwin's application of the process view to animal species and the human animal in the late 1800s marked an irreversible turning point in human consciousness. But it would take another hundred years for the process picture to emerge in full detail with Einstein's quantum mechanics and relativity, the space age, and genetic engineering.

The process view began to penetrate the religious world in the 1960s, when it brought into focus the longstanding tensions between the two perspectives (Francoeur, 1965, 1970). Rituals, theological statements, and moral judgments based on an absolutist, fixed philosophy of nature cannot be simply transported into a pluralistic, process-oriented mentality. Herein lies the key to understanding what has happened to all religious traditions in the last two decades, and to appreciating the tensions, changes, and conflicting views often endorsed by a particular religious tradition struggling to adjust to the radically changed social ecosystem.

The dichotomy represented by a fixed philosophy of nature on one end and a process-oriented consciousness on the other is apparently deeply rooted in human nature. Its concrete expression in American culture today has been documented by Daniel Yankelovich's 1981 longitudinal study of changing American values between 1940 and 1980. Yankelovich has found a tripartite split among Americans that clearly fits the fixed philosophy/process-oriented dualism, with one in five Americans situated at either end of the spectrum and the rest straddling the middle.

Some 20 percent of the adult Americans in Yankelovich's (1981) study remain unaffected by the recent shifts in majority culture and never question the merits of traditional values, goals, and rules. This group, approximately 34 million Americans, is predominantly older and rural. But it includes Americans of all ages who are conservative in their cultural outlook, oriented to preserving the "good old days." It also includes some poor, both Black and White.

The second subculture, about 17 percent, is deeply and openly committed to the emerging new person-oriented values. Younger than average, with professional careers, liberal politics, and some college education, these Americans often agonize over their commitment to the quest for self-fulfillment in an ever-changing world.

The clear majority of Americans range between the unchanging traditionalist 20 percent and the 17 percent openly committed to creating new rules and goals. For this majority, self-fulfillment with the freedom to choose from many options and lifestyles is not the primary or only goal of life, but it is a reality. Although they worry about the death of old values and goals, they question these traditions and wonder where to draw the line.

What does it imply about the human mind that we seem compelled to divide or categorize human behavior and sexual morality into two such clear-cut opposites as the absolutist fixed philosophy and the process-oriented world view? What does it mean that we can so easily detect and describe the ends of this spectrum?

The task of this chapter will be to try to answer these questions and to understand the response of religious traditions in recent years to changing lifestyles and sexual morality. The argument will be made that the Judaeo-Christian tradition, Western civilization, and in fact, all cultures today, are being forced by a convergence of irreversible social currents to replace an absolutist, fixed philosophy of nature morality with a pluralistic, process-oriented morality and sexual value system. This is the dilemma the churches have begun to face in recent decades. They will continue to grapple with it as they encounter the growing pluralism of sexual and family lifestyles. Jonathan Gathorne-Hardy touched on the essence of the situation when he wrote in *Marriage, Love, Sex and Divorce* (1982: 3):

> "We are all engaged in the first confused moves in an experiment to let people live and love and explore as they think fit, however bold or foolish or dangerous; to explore as far as they like into powers which may or may not exist; to try to lead the huge variety of lives of which they are capable or of which they dream; to let them change and suffer and explore as far as is humanly possible.

In trying to understand what is happening in religious traditions today as they respond to social changes, we need to begin with the most basic expressions of the two ways humans organize their world and construct their *Weltanschauung*. The rest of this chapter attempts to do this by bringing together seven distinct paradigms. Each paradigm is dichotomous in the sense of presenting a spectrum ranging from a list of views and behaviors consistent with the fixed philosophy of nature on one end and a second list emerging out of a process view. These paradigms were developed independently by specialists in widely divergent fields who have felt compelled to bring their many years of study together in models that sum up the main conclusions of their research. The seven paradigms focus on: (1) primate and human social structures, (2) an analysis of English and French culture, (3) nurturance patterns and attitudes toward body pleasure, (4) technological and economic structures, (5) sexual values and behaviors, (6) marital values and patterns, and (7) theological perspectives and ecclesiastical structures.

A Behavioral Paradigm Based on
Primate and Human Social Structures

There is a clear suggestion in the ethological studies of the higher primates that the tendency to dichotomize our views of the world and visualize two distinct worlds with two distinct moralities is perhaps deeply rooted in the ways primates socialize. "In the nearest relatives of man," as (Chance 1979: 617) tells us, "social cohesion is achieved by attention to a spatially central, focal individual. These are the centric societies which are of two types depending on how the centric attention is brought about," either by controlled aggression and threat, or by the reassurance of touching and stroking. Chance, a professor of ethology at the Medical School of Birmingham (U.K.), calls these two types of societies "agonic" and "hedonic." His paradigm based on 40 years of primate research is summarized in Figure 19.1.

Chance has briefly noted strong similarities between the agonic social structures of the macaques and baboons and the highly structured centric character of large corporations such as IBM and American Telephone and Telegraph, the military, and hierarchical churches.

A Cultural Moral Paradigm Based on
an Analysis of French and English Societies

Gordon Rattray Taylor (1972), a British science writer and philosopher, has derived a dichotomous paradigm from his examination of British and French art, fashions, politics, lifestyles, and social structures in the seventeenth, eighteenth, and nineteenth centuries. In what he terms "patrist" cultures, artists depicted highly ordered scenes of nature and sailing ships riding at anchor with their sails furled. Architects designed geometric formal gardens and men and women dressed in highly distinct and stereotyped fashions. In the "matrist" eras, artists painted wild nature scenes with fallen, rotting trees and ships conquering stormy seas. Informal country gardens were popular. Matrist fashions tended to be androgynous with flamboyant styles for both men and women. Figure 19.2 is drawn from Taylor's 1972 work, *Rethink: A Paraprimitive Solution.*

A Cross-Cultural Behavioral Paradigm Based on
Somatosensory Affectional Deprivation

Laboratory experiments and cross-cultural analyses pioneered by Harry and Margaret Harlow, and extended by James Prescott, indicate a clear causal relationship between lack of somatosensory pleasuring during infancy, childhood, and adolescence and a high level of adult violence. In societies that encourage body pleasuring and somatosensory nurturance for their youth, one finds a very peaceful adult society. A wide variety of values, attitudes, and behavioral patterns show definite correlation with

Agonic Societies	Hedonic Societies
Highly structured, fixed hierarchy	Flexible social structure
Aggressive dominate male controls by protecting and demanding attention	Social coherence maintained by periodic display, touching, and calling to one another
Fixed social relationships maintained by constant attention to physical distance and personal space	Flexible social relationships maintained by physical and vocal contact
Stereotyped ritualized behavior	Considerable flexible behavior
Limited threats from dominate male attract others but keep them at appropriate distance	
Constant alertness except when asleep. Protracted states of inhibited startle focus attention on constant danger response	Lack of need for constant attention to leader and ranking allows creative, inventive activities
Intellectual activity pre-occupied with resolution of social conflict	Intellectual activity has optimal conditions for wide variety of interests and time to devote to these
Emphasis on badges, uniforms, and possessions as extensions of the individual for group identification and social status definition	Frequent body contact within the group is interspersed with on-going shared activities that reduce arousal and produce frequent excitement modulation for socializing and other interests
Frequent confrontations in and outside the group	
Individual self-awareness defined by position in hierarchy	Self-awareness arises out of concern for others in the group.
Limited time, energy, and potential for inventiveness and creativity	Expanded time, energy and potential for inventiveness and creativity
Learning is motivated by avoidance of negative incentive (punishment)	Learning motivation is positive reward
— Macaques, baboons	— Chimpanzee, gorilla

SOURCE: Adapted from Chance (1979).

Figure 19.1   A Behavioral Paradigm

the absence or presence of nuturance and body pleasuring in any given culture. The dichotomous paradigm presented in Figure 19.3 is based on extensive statistical studies of correlations by neurophysiologist James Prescott. Prescott's basic thesis is contained in a 1975 article in *The Futurist*.

Patrism	Matrism
Restrictive, especially sexually	Permissive, especially sexually
Authoritarian	Democratic
Hierarchic	Egalitarian
Woman: low status	Woman: high status
Conservative	Adaptable
Looks to past	Looks to present or future
Pessimistic, depressive	Optimistic, euphoric
Self-control valued	Spontaneity valued
Homosexuality taboo	Incest taboo
Sexual jealousy	Lack of jealousy
Sky-father	Earth-mother or pantheistic religion

SOURCE: Adapted from Taylor (1972).

Figure 19.2   A Cultural/Moral Paradigm

The extended version presented in Figure 19.3 was kindly provided by Prescott for use here.

A Paradigm Based on Lifestyles and Values Related to Technological and Economic Structures

The relationship of lifestyles and values as a direct outcome of a culture's economic theory and technological focus is the source for a paradigm developed by Mario Kamenetzky (1979, 1981), an economist and engineer with worldwide experience, and Sophia Kamenetzky, a gynecologist and specialist in Latin American population issues. The Kamenetzkys see a hard-technology/high-consumption value system at one end of the spectrum, pursued by decision makers of both the capitalist free market and centrally planned Marxist economies (see Figure 19.4). The soft-technology/voluntary-simplicity approach has not had many followers until recently, when futurists called attention to the need for appropriate technologies and a down-scaling of the developed nations' reliance on raw materials and resources from the Third World (Elgin et al., 1977).

A Paradigm Based on Sexual Values and Behaviors

In 1967, Marshall McLuhan, a communications analyst, and George B. Leonard, an educational theorist, suggested a dichotomous model of sexual values. The model was based on McLuhan's conception of "hot" communications media with high definition (photographs and printed media) and "cool" media with a low definition and high involvement of the observer/participant (cartoons and television). In 1974 this basic insight was extended to create a fully developed model of *Hot and Cool Sex: Cultures in Conflict* (Francoeur and Francoeur, 1974). This is summarized in Figure 19.5.

Low Nurturance Cultures	High Nurturance Cultures
(1) Patrilineal.	(1) Matrilineal.
(2) Polygyny has high incidence.	(2) Polygyny has low incidence.
(3) Women's status inferior.	(3) Women's status not inferior.
(4) High avoidance of in-laws.	(4) Low avoidance of in-laws.
(5) High incidence of mother/child households.	(5) Low incidence of mother/child households.
(6) High community size.	(6) Small community size.
(7) High societal complexity.	(7) Low societal complexity.
(8) Small extended family.	(8) Large extended family.
(9) Wives are purchased.	(9) Wives are not purchased.
(10) Slavery present.	(10) Slavery absent.
(11) Grandparental authority over parents is present.	(11) Grandparental authority over parents is absent.
(12) Subsistence is primarily by food production.	(12) Subsistence is primarily by food gathering.
(13) High class stratification.	(13) Low class stratification.
(14) Low infant physical affection.	(14) High infant physical affection.
(15) High infant physical pain.	(15) Low infant physical pain.
(16) Low infant indulgence.	(16) High infant indulgence.
(17) Low reduction of infant needs.	(17) High reduction of infant needs.
(18) Delayed reduction of infant needs.	(18) Immediate reduction of infant needs.
(19) High infant/child crying.	(19) Low infant/child crying.
(20) Breastfeeding less than 2½ years.	(20) Prolonged breastfeeding over 2½ years.
(21) High child anxiety over performance of responsible behavior.	(21) Low child anxiety over performance of responsible behavior.
(22) High child anxiety over performance of obedient behavior.	(22) Low child anxiety over performance of obedient behavior.
(23) Low smiling, laughter, humor.	(23) High smiling, laughter, humor.
(24) High anxiety over transition: infancy/childhood.	(24) Low anxiety over transition: infancy/childhood.
(25) Low or no food taboos during pregnancy.	(25) High number of food taboos during pregnancy.
(26) Abortion highly punished.	(26) Abortion permitted.
(27) Strength of desire for children is high.	(27) Strength of desire for children is low.
(28) Postpartum sex taboo greater than one month.	(28) Postpartum sex taboo less than one month.
(29) Premarital coitus punished.	(29) Premarital coitus permitted.
(30) Extramarital coitus punished.	(30) Extramarital coitus permitted.
(31) Female initiation rites present.	(31) Low or absent female initiation rites.
(32) Sex disability present.	(32) Sex disability absent.
(33) Castration anxiety is high.	(33) Castration anxiety is low.
(34) High sex anxiety.	(34) Low sex anxiety.
(35) Narcissism is high.	(35) Narcissism is low.
(36) High exhibitionistic dancing.	(36) Low exhibitionistic dancing.

Figure 19.3   A Cross-Cultural Behavioral Paradigm

(37) High display of wealth.	(37) Low display of wealth.
(38) Contracted debts are high.	(38) Contracted debts are low.
(39) High adult physical violence.	(39) Low adult physical violence.
(40) Bellicosity is extreme.	(40) Bellicosity is low.
(41) High killing, torture, mutilation.	(41) Low or absent killing, torture, mutilation.
(42) High personal crime.	(42) Low personal crime.
(43) Incidence of theft is high.	(43) Incidence of theft is low.
(44) High warfare.	(44) Low or no warfare.
(45) Military glory emphasized.	(45) Low military glory.
(46) Superordinate justice present.	(46) Superordinate justice absent.
(47) Supernaturals are aggressive.	(47) Supernaturals are benevolent.
(48) Fear of supernatural rather than fear of humans.	(48) Fear of humans rather than fear of supernatural.
(49) High God is present.	(49) High God is mainly absent.
(50) High religious activity.	(50) Low or no religious activity.
(51) Belief in reincarnation present.	(51) Belief in reincarnation absent.
(52) High asceticism in mourning.	(52) Low asceticism in mourning.
(53) Witchcraft highly present.	(53) Witchcraft low or absent.
(54) Religious specialists are full time.	(54) Religious specialists are part-time.
(55) Political integration at state level.	(55) Political integration at community and family level.
(56) Metal working is present.	(56) Metal working is absent.

SOURCE: Adapted from Prescott (1975).

Figure 19.3   Continued

A Paradigm Based on Open and Closed Marital Values

For several years after its publication and best-seller status, *Open Marriage,* by George and Nena O'Neill (1972), was a common topic of discussion in the mass media. The paradigm has now become part of family and marriage theory and practice (see Figure 19.6). Below is the dichotomous model developed by the O'Neills independently of the other models previously mentioned. The self-evident convergence and overlapping will be explored in the next section of this chapter when these various models are integrated with the response of the churches to alternative lifestyles.

A Paradigm Based on Opposing Theological Perspectives and Ecclesiastical Structures

In the early 1960s when the Second Vatican Council was bringing fresh creative life to the Catholic world, the author devoted considerable time to the evolutionary synthesis of science and theology proposed by Pierre Teilhard de Chardin (1959). Teilhard turned out to be a prophetic spirit in

Hard technology/High consumption	*Soft technology/Voluntary simplicity*
(1) Concentration of the means of production and, hence, of power in public administrators or private owners.	(1) Decentralization of power and ownership.
(2) Nature is the source of resources to be exploited and dominated by human beings.	(2) Nature is the nurturing environment and human beings are part of its equilibria.
(3) Human beings are factors of production and consumers.	(3) Human beings are unique and distinct, one from another with only a few biological and psychological needs in common, which they try to satisfy by using their bodies and their minds.
(4) The human body is a piece of equipment formed by a set of interconnected parts with the mind acting as a mechanism of control.	(4) Each individual body/mind system is at the same time a physical structure, a set of chemical reactions, and a field of energy.
(5) Using the means of production, or fighting for their possession, requires men to be tough.	(5) Tenderness is strength for both men and women.
(6) All forms of sexuality non-conducive to reproduction and pure sensuality are repressed and punished because they would reduce the present flow rate and the accumulation of reserves of human energy for production.	(6) All forms of sexuality and sensuality are accepted because of respect for the uniqueness and diversity of human beings. Relational, recreational, and reproductive aspects fo sex are combined in different proportions by each individual and these proportions vary from one moment of life to another.
(7) Male and female roles are sterotyped because men of all social classes are needed in the production units, while women are needed at home for either reproduction and management of the means required for replenishing the energy lost by men in production (lower classes) or as clear and secure channels for the transfer of the means of production concentrated in the family (upper classes.)	(7) Androgynous families.

Figure 19.4   A Technological/Economic Paradigm

| (8) | The size of production units is constantly enlarged, seeking for economies of scale. Participation, when allowed, is only intended for workers and understood as sharing a small percentage of the benefits, the capital, or both. It never is a sharing of the power of public administrators or private owners. | (8) | Most of the production units are kept small in order to allow for decentralization and for participation of the beneficiaries (workers and consumers) in the establishment of objectives, the control of their accomplishment, and the ownership of the means of production. |

Figure 19.4 Continued

the often fevered debates of the Council Fathers and theological experts as the traditionalist and the process views of religion, morality, and theology met head on at the Vatican. Teilhard had once spoken of the human race as living on a raft in the middle of the ocean. Most of the people he knew in the 1930s were "looking at their feet and stoutly claiming that nothing was changing" while a few others watched the horizon with fascination and shouted with joy as they watched everything changing. By 1980, as Yankelovich (1981, 1982) documented, the proportion had shifted, with one in five Americans embracing the dynamism of change, and three in five moving in the direction of process. But this shift in balance and perspective has brought with it a sharpening of the dichotomous values, attitudes, and behaviors made clear in the preceding six models. The split is now even more evident than it was in the 1930s or 1960s. The paradigm pictured in Figure 19.7 is an attempt to put the many details of this split in a simple model encompassing various aspects of religious concern.

The dimensions of this religious paradigm can easily be expanded beyond the Christian dimension. With necessary modifications it can be applied to the hassidic/liberal Jewish spectrum of values and attitudes. It is also helpful in understanding the fundamentalist Moslem perspective endorsed by the mullahs who overthrew the Shah of Iran and the Moslem fundamentalists who assassinated Egypt's Anwar Sadat because of his "heretical" interpretation of the Koran.

The Implications of Paradigm Convergence

The reoccurrence of certain attitudes, values, and behaviors in these seven independent paradigms makes a persuasive case for their validity and usefulness. There are unique features in each paradigm traceable to its author's discipline and primary concern, but the similarities and overlapping features are clearly evident and striking, particularly if one visualizes the seven models arranged in transparencies ready for simultaneous display on an overhead projector.

Hot Sex	Cool Sex
Definitions	
High definition of sex.	Low definition of sex and sex roles.
Reduction to genital sex.	Sexuality coextensive with personality.
Genitally focused feelings.	Diffused sensuality/sexuality.
Time and place arrangements.	Spontaneous.
Highly structured games.	Lightly structured with few games.
Clear sex role stereotypes.	Little if any role stereotyping.
Many strong imperatives from socially imposed roles.	Few imperatives, self-actualizing encouraged.
Value Systems	
Patriarchal.	Egalitarian.
Male domination by aggression.	Equal partnership as friends.
Female passivity.	
Double moral standard.	Single moral standard.
Behavioral Structures	
Property oriented.	Person oriented.
Closed possessiveness.	Open inclusiveness.
Casual, impersonal.	Involved, intimate.
Physical sex segregated from life, emotions and responsibility.	Sex integrated in whole framework of life.
Nonhomogeneous, grossly selective of playmate.	Homogeneous, finely selective in all relationships.
Screwing sex objects for conquest.	"Knowing" sexual persons.
Genital hedonism.	Sex as communication.
Concerns	
Orgasm obsessed.	Engaging, pleasuring communications.
Performance pressures, sex obligatory when possible.	Sexual relations truly optional.
Fidelity = sexual exclusivity.	Fidelity = commitment and mutual responsibility.
Extramarital relations as escape.	Comarital relations a growth reinforcement of primary bond.
Fear of emotions and senses.	Embracing of emotions and senses.
Nudity a taboo, prelude to sex.	Nudity unrelated to sex.
Sexuality feared, tenuously situated.	Sexuality accepted, securely situated.
Entopic relations, viewed as "property" that can be lost or used up.	Synergistic relations, mutually reinforcing.
Frequent alcohol and drug use.	Few drug-altered states.
Territory and personal distance.	"Grokking."

SOURCE: Adapted from Francoeur and Francoeur (1974).

Figure 19.5   A Sexual Values and Behaviors Paradigm

Closed Marriage	Open Marriage
Definitions	
Static framework.	Dynamic framework.
Threatened by change.	Adaptable to change.
Rigid role prescriptions.	Flexibility in roles.
Calculating.	Spontaneous.
Value Systems	
Unequal status.	Equality of stature.
Selfhood subjugated to couplehood.	Personal identity.
Bondage.	Freedom.
Behavioral Structures	
Locked together, closed in on one another.	Open to each other.
Limited potential.	Infinite potential.
Smothering togetherness.	Privacy for self-growth.
Possession of the other.	Individual autonomy.
Shuts out others — exclusivity limits growth.	Incorporates others — grows through companionship with others.
A closed self-limiting energy system.	An open, expanding energy system.
Concerns	
Deception and game playing.	Honesty and truth.
Limited love.	Open love.
Conditional static trust.	Open trust.
Inhibitive, degenerative.	Creative and expanding.
Shuts out others.	Incorporates others.
Substractive.	Additive.
Closed self-limiting energy system.	Open expanding energy system.

SOURCE: Adapted from O'Neill and O'Neill (1972).

Figure 19.6   Open and Closed Marital Values Paradigm

The challenge, then, becomes one of ascertaining what these paradigms can tell us about the organization of human society and the current history of religious responses to changing lifestyles and growing pluralism in sexual relationships. Using details from these seven models, we can construct a composite world view extending the two ends of the spectrum in logical and consistent fashion into every dimension of social and personal life. Both ways of looking at the world claim deep and abiding roots. In the past and present this has resulted in an inevitable tension, often warfare, as the absolutist conservers of past traditions fought to restrain or suppress the advocates of change.

In the 1980s a resolution of this tension appears to be possible, perhaps inevitable, because of the irreversible character of changes in our ecosys-

	Christian Religions Type A	Christian Religions Type B
Basic Vision	COSMOS — A finished universe.	COSMOGENESIS — An evolving universe.
Typology	Like the universe, humankind is created perfect and complete in the beginning. Theological understanding of humans emphasizes *Adam*.	Like the universe, humankind is incomplete and not yet fully formed. Theological emphasis has shifted to *The Adam, Christ*, at the end of time.
Origin of Evil	Evil results from primeval "fall" of a perfect couple who introduce moral and physical evil into a paradisical world.	Evil is a natural part of a finite creation, growth, and the birth pains involved in our groping as imperfect humans struggling for the fullness of creation.
Solution to the Problem of Evil	Redemption by identification with the crucified Savior. Asceticism, mortification.	Identification with *The* Adam, the resurrected but still fully human transfigured Christ. *Re-creation*, growth.
Authority System	Patriarchal and sexist. Male dominated and ruled. Autocratic hierachy controls power and all decisions; clergy vs. laity.	Egalitarian — "In his kingdom there is neither male nor female, freeman or slave, Jew or Roman."
Concept of Truth	Emphasis on one true Church as sole possessor of all truth.	Recognition that other churches and religions possess different perspectives of truth, with some elements of revelation clearer in them than in the one true Church.
Biblical Orientation	Fundamentalist, evangelical, word-for-word, black-and-white clarity. Revelation has ended.	Emphasizes ongoing revelation and reincarnation of perennial truths and values as humans participate in the creation process.
Liturgical Focus	Redemption and Good Friday, Purgatory, Supernatural.	Easter and the creation challenge of incarnation. Epiphany of numinous cosmos.
Social Structure	Gender roles clearly assigned with high definition of proper roles for men and women.	There being neither male nor female in Christ, gender roles are flexible, including women priests and ministers.

Figure 19.7   A Cognitive and Normative Continuum of Sexual Values and Behavior

Ecological Morality	Humans are stewards of the earth, given dominion by God over all creation.	Emphasis on personal responsibility in an ongoing creation/incarnation.
Self-Image	Carefully limited; isolationist, exclusive, Isaias' "remanent." Sects.	Inclusive, ecumenical, catalytic leader among equals.
Goal	Supernatural transcendence of nature.	Unveiling, Revelation of divine in all.
Human Morality	Emphasis on laws and conformity of actions to these laws.	Emphasis on persons and their interrelationships. We create the human of the future and the future of humanity.
Sexual Morality	The "monster in the groins" that must be restrained.	A positive, natural, creative energy in our being as sexual (embodied) persons. "Knowing," Communion.
	Justified in marriage for procreation.	An essential element in our personality, in all relationships.
	Genital reductionism.	Diffused, degenitalized sensual embodiment.
	Heterosexual/monogamous.	"Polymorphic perversity."
	Noncoital sex is unnatural, disordered.	Noncoital sex can express the incarnation of Christian love.
	Contraceptive love is unnatural and disordered.	Contraception can be just as creative and life-serving as reproductive love.
	Monolithic-celibate or reproductive-marital sexuality.	Pluralistic-sexual persons must learn to incarnate chesed/agape in all their relationships, primary and secondary, genital and non-genital, intimate and passing.
Energy Conception	*Competitive.* Consumerist. Technology-obsessed.	*Synergistic.* Conservationist. Concerned with appropriate technologies.

Figure 19.7   Continued

tem. In *The Two Biologies,* John Pringle (1963; cited by Chance, 1979: 611) shares his vision of our situation today as one in which "the stabilizing role of superstitious fear has been replaced by a global conscience and a general acceptance of personal restraint in the interest of mankind." Working from his paradigm of primate behavioral patterns and social structures, Michael Chance (1979: 611) believes

> This task means replacing existing "in built" biological control mechanisms [of patriarchal authoritarian models designed to conserve the past] by [conscious cooperative] human artifact. . . . The task amounts to no less than constructing [a new ethic and] new social relations; so we first of all have to become aware of how existing soical relations constrain us; to resist existing tendencies to construct models in advance on old-fashioned lines and to be aware of the insidious influence of unconscious social processes by revealing their current forms.

In essence, this task requires a definitive shift in the balance of human thinking with the creative, future-oriented process perspective gaining dominance over and eventually replacing the absolutist, past-oriented fixed philosophy of nature. No system in power willingly relinquishes its control over human minds without a battle. In the 1980s, the battle lines are already drawn and warfare declared on such issues as abortion, contraceptive services for teenagers, and the rights of gays and other sexual minorities. If Yankelovich is correct in his statistical analysis, the balance rests with the 63 percent of Americans caught in the middle of the spectrum but inclining with each passing year more and more in favor of a pluralistic future.

Jean Piaget and Lawrence Kohlberg have both pictured this shift in terms of the process of moral development. Piaget (1965) talks of the amoral infant evolving into an egocentric child who lacks any real morality, bends the rules, and reacts instinctively to his or her environment. As the child develops, a new sense of heteronomous morality emerges, based on total acceptance of a morality imposed by others. In a final stage of moral development the adult develops an autonomous sense of morals based on an internalized morality of cooperation. Kohlberg (1969) has a similar vision of moral development, moving from the preconventional, to a conventional "good boy/nice girl" orientation of law and order, and on to a postconventional or autonomous moral sense based on ethical principles that have been internalized.

Piaget's heteronomous morality and Kohlberg's conventional morality are very congenial to, and functional in, a culture or society variously described as being agonic, patrist, low nurturant, concerned with hard technology and high consumption, and devoted to hot sexual values, closed monogamous marriage, and Type A religions rooted in a fixed philosophy of nature. Piaget's autonomous morality and Kohlberg's postconventional moral sense are more functional in hedonic, matrist cultures with high nurturance, a concern for pluralistic, person-oriented sexual values, synergistic open relations, soft technology/voluntary simplicity, and Type B religious perspectives involved in the ongoing creation of the human. Society appears to be slowly, painfully evolving to ever higher levels of consciousness.

Religious Views and the Response to Alternative Lifestyles

Recent statements on sexual morality and human relations from various religious groups, can easily be sorted out in terms of the concerns and values expressed in the seven paradigms outlined above (Genne, 1975). This ease of categorization needs a cautionary note, however. No society, group, or individual will express all the characteristics one finds at one or the other end of these seven spectrums. The extremes in these paradigms are abstractions, characterizations, and, therefore, unreal to some extent.

With this caution in mind, one can sort out the person- and relation-oriented morality endorsed in *Human Sexuality: New Directions in American Catholic Thought* (Kosnick et al., 1977), which is cautiously open to the moral acceptability of premarital sex, gay relations, sexually open marriages, and even multilateral relations. This contrasts with the Vatican's position, at the other end of the spectrum, which condemns all masturbation and both homosexual and contraceptive intercourse, as disordered, unnatural, and irrevocably immoral. The same range of views can be found in the person-oriented United Presbyterian workstudy document, "Sexuality and the Human Community" (1970), or in the United Church of Christ's "Human Sexuality: A Preliminary Study" (1977) on one side, and in the fundamentalist biblical definitions of male/female relations, patriarchal monogamous marriage, and reproductive/marital sex endorsed by the advocates of Total Woman, Fascinating Womanhood, the Moral Majority, and FLAG (Family, Life, America and God) on the other (Francoeur, 1982: 661-695). The American Humanist statement of 1976 (Kirkendall, 1976) clearly falls on the future, pluralistic side of the spectrum, but without any organized opposing view in the humanist tradition unless one decides it is appropriate to locate areligious political and economic conservatives at the same end of the values spectrum as the Vatican, Moral Majority, and political New Right.

There is an interesting convergence of views and basic agreement among those groups at the two ends of the spectrum. Fifty years ago, the fractionation was along denominational lines drawn between Protestants, Catholics, Jews, and the unchurched. Today process-oriented Catholics,

Protestants, Jews, and humanists can often agree on basic issues. Similarly, Protestants, Jews, humanists, and Catholics who follow a fixed
philosophy of nature often agree more among themselves than they do
with members of their own groups on the process end of the spectrum. The
authors of the Catholic Theological Society report on sexuality (Kosnick et
al., 1977) are more in agreement with the views of the United Church of
Christ, United Presbyterian, and humanist statements than they are with
the formal statements of the Vatican. The Moral Majority, the New Political
Right, the advocates of "total woman" marriages, Protestant fundamentalists, and the Vatican are very much in accord in condemning any and all
deviations from traditional monogamous marriage and marital/
reproductive sex. The alliance on the right is vehemently opposed to
divergent values and pluralism in lifestyles. Their absolutist authoritarian
conviction is that there is only one right path to which everyone must
conform if they are to be Christian and saved.

In some respects the New Right alliance appears to be more politically
and economically motivated, with religous beliefs brought in where convenient to support conservative secular concerns. Regional factors and
differences in ages and social class appear to be more important than
religion in explaining the responses of the New Right to changing sexual
values and alternative lifestyles. Yankelovich (1981) described the conservative 20 percent as predominantly older, rural, middle class, with high
school education. The 17 percent committed to change were predominantly young, college educated, and urban.

In the 1960s, the flexible pluralism of arisotocratic/bohemian lifestyles
began to filter into the middle class and to create social turmoil based on
the perceived threat of the contraceptive pill to the moral fabric of American society. Today the same pluralizing currents are reaching into the
blue-collar community, creating similar social earthquakes. The reaction is
typical. In some respects, the blue-collar community feels its whole lifestyle
and value system is in jeopardy. Its members feel powerless and manipu-
lated by events beyond their control or influence. They are pushed and
pulled in every direction. In desperation they have found one area in which
they can set their feet down for "traditional" values, and that is in the family
life education of their children. The big brother of federal government can
at least be fought on such issues as parental rights to prohibit secular
agencies from giving contraceptives to their children, abortion and the
"right to life," sex education in the schools, gay rights, and the defense of
traditional marriage and family. Whether the blue-collar community will
adjust to the winds of change as the middle class did in the 1970s remains
to be seen.

Prospects for the 1980s

The ethnographic paradigm suggested by Michael Chance (1979) and
the other models cited earlier do not explain why humans have been so

consistently dualistic and dichotomous in their views and values, but they do give us some crucial clues to understanding the opposing moralities attached to the two ends of the spectrum. The key is in the function these moralities serve in the control of sexuality and the freedom of sexual expression they allow. As long as human sexual relations and reproduction were inextricably associated, the absolutist moralities maintained a distinct functional advantage. They reflect overpowering *social* demands. The very social order itself could be claimed to arise from and depend on obedience to a personal sexual morality that stabilizes the family, maintains sex roles with the female submissive to the male and her maternal nature, protects inheritance by controlling reproduction, and restricts the spread of sexually transmitted diseases. An authoritarian, monogamous, patriarchal, reproductive, act-oriented, and guilt-motivated morality has proven functional and well suited to the social needs of the human race until recent years.

But the situation has changed. Contraceptives and antibiotics have severed the traditional linkage between sex and reproduction. This irreversibly alters the traditional dichotomies and moves Western society — ultimately all human societies — away from the need to *control sexual behavior* in order to control reproduction and in turn protect the well-being of families and their members. The emphasis can now afford to shift toward *personal freedom* in sexual relations and *autonomy* in human reproduction. It is now functional for morality to recognize and accept the relational and pleasuring functions of sex, and responsibility and self-determination in reproduction.

In fifty years we have moved from a predominantly static conception of a permanent and irreconcilable opposition between sexual freedom and social regulation to a dynamic and fluid conception in which the needs of both society and the individual can develop along independent, if congruent, tracks according to the dictates of internal logic and according to a new, person-oriented moral formula. Not too long ago a biological link necessitated the association of sexuality with reproduction. This made every act of sexual intimacy that occurred outside the marital bond a potentially lethal threat to the ordained rules of legitimacy, kinship, and alliance. With this link broken for the first time in human history, a wide range of alternative lifestyles now becomes not only conceivable but also socially and morally acceptable.

Once the sex/reproduction connection is severed, the logic for, and consistency of, values, attitudes, and behaviors at the traditional end of the spectrum is shattered once and for all. To many this is a frightening possibility. Even though in effect it has already occurred, the psychological and social awareness of the revolution has only reached two in every five Americans. Half of these are thrilled and challenged by the separation of sex from reproduction. The other half are terrified by it. The key to how the churches and formal religious traditions will respond to alternative lifestyles and the need for new ethics to guide sexual relations and reproduction depends on the continued pressures of our changing ecosystem on the three out of five Amricans wavering in the middle of the spectrum. Religious reactions in the near future will depend on whether this 60 percent is willing to move further away from the agonic, patrist, low nurturant, closed monogamous, hot sex, hard technology/high consumption, and Type A religions on the traditional side, and closer to the hedonic, matrist, high nurturant, open pairing, cool sex, soft technology/voluntary simplicity, and Type B religions end of the spectrum. It they do so, we can look to a future with a more humane form.

Whether the 1980s brings a dialogue, with accommodations on both sides, or a head-on confrontation between individuals and groups of the conservative religious and political New Right and the process-oriented majority, the philosophical and behavioral analysis offered here will be critical in appreciating the issues at stake. If one can remember that the disagreements between the two factions are based on an outmoded, but once realistic, need to protect the family from sexual freedom by calling on a heteronomous authority, it will be easier to understand why emotions often ride so high. It will also be easier to appreciate why so many find the personal responsibilty of an autonomous lifestyle and morality so frightening when contrasted with the security of the traditional religious position.

References

CHANCE, M.R.A. (1979) "The behavioral dimensions for the operation of intelligence," pp. 611-636 in The Re-Evaluation of Existing Values and the Search for Absolute Values, Vol. 2. Proceedings of the Seventh International Conference on the Unity of the Sciences. New York: International Cultural Foundation Press.

COMFORT, A. (1972) The Joy of Sex. New York: Crown.

ELGIN, D., A. MITCHELL, and R. GREGG (1977) "Voluntary simplicity." Coevolution Quarterly 14 (Summer): 4-27.

FRANCOEUR, R. T. (1982) Becoming a Sexual Person. New York: John Wiley.

——— (1970) Evolving World, Converging Man. New York: Holt, Rinehart & Winston.

——— (1965) Perspectives in Evolution. Baltimore: Helicon.

——— and A. K. FRANCOEUR (1974) Hot and Cool Sex: Cultures in Conflict. New York: Harcourt, Brace, Jovanovich.

GATHORNE-HARDY, J. (1982) Marriage, Love, Sex and Divorce. New York: Summit Books.

GENNE, W. H. (1975) A Synoptic of Recent Denominational Statements on Sexuality. New York: National Council of Churches.

KAMENETZKY, M. (1981) "The economics of the satisfaction of needs." Human Systems Management 2: 101-111.

——— (1979) "Development for the people." Bulletin of the Atomic Scientists 35 (June): 45-49.

KIRKENDALL, L. A. (1976) "A new bill of sexual rights and responsibilities." The Humanist 36, 1: 4-6.

KOHLBERG, L. (1969) "Stage and sequence: the cognitive-developmental approach to socialization," in D. Goslen (ed.) Handbook of Socializaton Theory and Research. Chicago: Rand McNally.

KOSNICK, A., W. CARROLL, A. CUNNINGHAM, R. MODRAS, and J. SCHULTE (1977) Human Sexuality: New Directions in American Catholic Thought. New York: Paulist Press.

MASTERS, W. and V. JOHNSON (1966) Human Sexual Response. Boston: Little, Brown.

McLUHAN, M. and G.B. LEONARD (1967) "The future of sex," pp. 15-25 in R.T. Francoeur and A.K. Francoeur (eds.) The Future of Sexual Relationships. Englewood Cliffs, NJ: Prentice-Hall.

O'NEILL, N. and G. O'NEILL (1972) Open Marriage: A New Lifestyle for Couples. New York: Evans.

PIAGET, J. (1965) The Moral Judgement of the Child. New York: Macmillan.

PRESCOTT, J.W. (1975) "Body pleasures and the origins of violence." The Futurist 9, 2: 64-74.

PRINGLE, J.W.S. (1963) The Two Biologies: An Inaugural Lecture Delivered before the University of Oxford, October, 24, 1963. Oxford: Clarendon.

TAYLOR, G.R. (1972) Rethink: A Paraprimitive Solution. New York: Dutton.

TEILHARD de CHARDIN, P. (1959) The Phenomenon of Man (B. Wall, trans.). New York: Harper & Row.

United Church of Christ, Board of Home Ministries (1977) Human Sexuality: A Preliminary Study. The Eleventh General Synod.

United Presbyterian Church in the U.S.A. (1970) Sexuality and the Human Community. Philadelphia: UPC Press.

YANKELOVICH, D. (1982) New Rules: Searching for Self-Fulfillment in a World Turned Upside Down. New York: Random House.

———— (1981) "New rules in American life." Psychology Today 15, 4: 35-91.

Epilogue:
Families and Alternative Lifestyles in an Age of Technological Revolution

ROGER H. RUBIN
University of Maryland

> The times they are a changin'. *
> — *Bob Dylan*

This mid-1960s refrain from a popular song reflects a fundamental reality of life in the twentieth century. Never before in recorded history has change been so swift and dramatic. Toffler's (1971) "future shock" challenges individuals and interpersonal relationships. Americans find themselves in a world of altered states. They face the spectre of a rootless and uncertain future.

Simultaneously, accelerated change brings forth a quotient of opportunity. Francoeur observes that today we can control much of what we could not overcome in the past. People are healthier and living longer than ever before. Birth control technology and legalized abortion has created a third sex: females who govern their fecundity. An economic revolution has made the individual self-sufficient and has redefined traditional gender roles and the meaning of parenthood. A majority of married women work outside the home. Computers, household devices, and flexible work schedules provide new opportunities for time management. The personnel policies of government and the private sector are increasingly recognized as having an impact on the quality of family life. Mass communication and the information explosion promote competing values and ideologies. Liberalized divorce laws provide new options to the maritally oppressed. Rapid transportation conveys us to locations our ancestors could only dream about. Insidiously, mobility has "modified" the extended family and "isolated" the nuclear family. Urbanization places us physically closer and emotionally farther apart, while suburbanization draws us physically apart and intensifies our emotional neediness. Housing patterns increasingly segregate us by age and lifestyle. And our education and affluence make it more possible than ever before to contemplate and study these changes.

The Technological Revolution

Technology has nurtured a new and revolutionary age. The opportunities created provide choices and require decisions unknown to previous generations. Social relationships once considered unusual have become commonplace. A review of some of these changes follows.

In 1900 the life expectancy of an American man or woman was approximately 47 years. Over the next eight decades, growing numbers of people would survive into their seventies and eighties. For both sexes, increasing longevity and health would be a blessing and a harbinger of new interpersonal issues. Today, the marital vows of "until death do you part" mean a longer relationship for more couples than ever before. This reality forms the basis for the greatest social experiment of our time. The test is whether or not marriages that emphasize individual, personal feelings and romantic notions can successfully sustain themselves over such an extended period. This desire to achieve emotional and affectional satisfaction should not be underestimated. Yankelovich (1981) reports that personal fulfillment is more important for contemporary Americans than is worldly success.

Historically, marriage served the needs of the individual for physical and mental survival. It furnished an environment for economic and social exchange between the sexes. A husband provided for the feeding, sheltering, and clothing of his spouse and their offspring, while a wife offered domestic services, child care, and sex. Although this was not always the reality, it established the image of a socially cohesive, economically interdependent unit. The family was referred to as the building block of society. Today, this traditional arrangement has been undermined by an expansion of economic opportunities and technological advances. A variety of alternative living arrangements currently compete for the attention of individuals, offering rewards once reserved almost exclusively for the married. Ramey (1976) maintains that the individual has now become society's foundation.

As the economic basis for marriage eroded, the importance of companionship and personal needs increased. The gender role equation changed. Traditionally, male roles had emphasized a detached, unemotional stance. This was a personality requisite for someone whose primary ego identity was represented by economic success, prestige, and power. In contrast to the financial provider role of men, women were to be economically and emotionally dependent. Today this legacy of gender roles proves to be the antithesis of what is necessary for successful communication directed at intrapsychic needs.

Sexual issues may also vitiate male/female relationships. Advances in the variety, availability, and effectiveness of contraception, coupled with the 1973 Supreme Court decision legalizing abortion, have resulted in a new sexual consensus. No longer does the behavioral double-standard prevail. Females are rapidly achieving equity with males in their participation in sexual activities before, during, after, and without marriage. However, the schism between sexual behavior and values remains a source of personal stress and social cost. For example, females still tend to desire a higher degree of emotional commitment prior to their sexual indulgences than do males. Such differences still lead often to misunderstanding and exploitation.

Consistent conflict or the incompatability of personal goals between individuals may culminate in divorce. A popular debate has arisen as to whether or not liberalization of divorce laws encourages divorce or just facilitates the termination of an already existing dissatisfaction. Whatever their source, the 1970s movement from adversarial to no-fault divorce laws is recognition of the price to be paid for the modern social experiment in marriage we are presently experiencing.

Much attention has been focused on male/female relationships and employment. Industrialization separated work from the home and drew men away from the family domicile. Technology made possible the movement of unprecedented numbers of women into the paid work force. Today the relationships between the world of work and our personal lives are being rediscovered and reconciled. Let the workplace accommodate itself to the needs of families and individuals, rather than vice versa, is the common plea. Nine-to-five work regimens become suspect as restrictive or oppressive. Thus for men and women struggling to redefine their relationships to one another, alternative work schedules such as flextime, pressed time, core time, and job sharing become attractive. These are viewed as possible solutions to family conflicts over child care, leisure, and intimate time.

There is also a growing awareness of the unplanned consequences of government and private sector policies on family life. The impact of a new highway on a community, the closing of a post office, the creating of a new tax law, or the geograpical transferring of an employee are more likely to be critically appraised.

A revolution in mass communication has kept us in touch with our changing world. Television, radio, telephones, movies, tapes, records, newspapers, magazines, and books create a media blitz. Imbedded in these mass-communicated messages are images, models, and guidelines for interpersonal relationships. Diversity abounds with the portrayal of romance, love, infidelity, autonomy, commitment, selfishness, altruism, jealousy, violence, hostility, individualism, familism, careers, parenthood, sexism, ageism, racism, homosexuality, heterosexuality, religion, humanism, secularism, and ad infinitum. It is contradictory, confusing, exciting, and representative of the plethora of contemporary experiences.

Some of us escape or pursue this cacophony by moving. One out of five American families changes residence each year. Americans are among the most mobile people on earth. Henry Ford's automobile assembly line fostered a revolution the impact of which has not yet been fully recognized. Our consanguine and affinal relatives may be scattered about. Grandparents, grandchildren, aunts, uncles, and cousins become little more than vacation time playmates. Teenagers are more likely to run away from home when they can no longer seek refuge with nearby kin. Practical knowledge of child care declines with increasing isolation from the daily observing of our family group. These are additional prices we pay for economic opportunity, personal autonomy, and the enrichment of a chosen environment.

Recently, the cities were pronounced dead, the fittest people fled to the suburbs, and the future of the republic shifted to the sunny South, once known primarily to sharecroppers and destitute Indians. Then there was an energy crisis and the corpse of the city was resurrected. Gentrification was the key to rebirth. These fickle shifts in predictions are only the latest convulsions in the century-long phenomenon of urbanization. Today Americans are concentrated in sprawling urban complexes. As this process has evolved, the community social controls found in rural areas have diminished, individual freedom and autonomy have increased, secular ideas have spread, and strangers have had to decide on the extent of their cooperativeness. Urbanization has brought forth the social acceptance of modern dating and courtship. Interpersonal relationships have been revolutionized.

Access to the cities has been encouraged by the availability of transportation for the masses. The automobile contributed as much to a revolution in lifestyles as any other invention. The areas we can work in and settle have expanded. Cars provide the opportunity to meet new people and a place to entertain some. Automobile entrepreneurs assisted more in the uprooting of American sexual standards than Alfred Kinsey or William Masters and Virginia Johnson ever could. An extraordinary highway system has been built to accommodate this vehicle and its driver's insatiable appetite to explore, relocate or express an ego. Simultaneously, air travel has made great distances an irrelevant obstacle in the quest for increased mobility. Families can now live far apart, yet be only hours away.

With migration came new residential patterns. Segregation by lifestyle appears to be an ascendant trend. There are landlords who ban families with children and housing complexes with child-free zones. Singles enclaves have blossomed in every major city. Senior citizens find themselves trapped in decaying inner cities or joining their peers in retirement communities.

Finally, affluence has served as both producer and product of the technological revolution. Yankelovich (1981) claims it has changed lifestyles and attitudes. When people were freed from the daily struggle to survive, they were granted the time to create new opportunities for themselves. Stein's distinction between lifestyles and life chances is of related importance. The former describes how one lives his or her life. The latter pertains to the opportunities that money, prestige, status, and connections provide. Therefore, lifestyle choices may be dependent on the options made available through life chances, which increase during periods of affluence. Similarly, Dressel and Hess distinguish between lifestyles, which are chosen, and statuses, like widowhood, which are not. As life chances grow there are more lifestyles to select from.

Time also has an ominous dimension. We have extended our lifespan, yet it remains finite. These realities may have profound consequences for interpersonal lifestyles. Nena O'Neill (1981) states that technology impels people to freedom and choice, but not necessarily to the achievement of happiness. With all the new opportunites available to individuals for travel, relationships and work, will we become too frantic partaking? Yankelovich (1981) reports that people cherish the freedom to make mistakes even when it means broken marriages or unhappy careers. People today can take the risks their parents were unable or unwilling to take, including not following the adage about "making the best" of a bad marriage. This risk-taking impulse is the epochal experience of our time, according to Yankelovich (1981). Is it reasonable to expect a person to share the bulk of their life with one other individual and forsake other ventures? The circumstances are new to us. Only time will tell.

Interpersonal Relationships and the Technological Revolution

Catherine Chilman poses several questions at the end of her prologue to this book. Whatever the answers, they will be cast in the context of the new technological age. Yankelovich (1981) describes dramatic shifts in norms in the past 20 years. The effects of this revolutionary period on families and alternative lifestyles are extensively documented in this volume. At least three major trends are identifiable.

First, there has been the inevitable emergence of an increased heterogeneity of lifestyles. Longevity contributes to this, according to Dressel and Hess. They describe the greater number of elderly, many of whom are retired, and the variety of behavioral patterns among this group. Previously the few who lived to advanced ages fit into the society. Today new roles must be forged to meet the needs of this expanding population. Further diversity can be anticipated, given Buunk's observation that if marriage is to be based on personal feelings and preferences then these also serve as a rationale for not marrying, avoiding parenthood, and indulging in extramarital sex.

Second, the struggle between the personal freedom of the individual and the integrity of societal institutions will continue. Buunk notes that lifestyle changes are an international phenomenon and emphasizes the increasing importance of the individual's interests and feelings. He describes this as a movement toward an individualized, open, and equal pattern in relationships. The suggestion was made that the need for intimacy, independence, and gender equality may be the common thread in a wide variety of lifestyles. In some respects this type of relationship is a product of the process-oriented world described by Francoeur. It reflects the enormity of the revolution in individual opportunities and the increasing control people exert over their own destinies. This is in sharp contrast to the two more traditional and historically prevalent marriage and family patterns described by Buunk: the functional, patriarchal, and community-dependent relationship and the affectionate, private, and male-dominated pattern. Hicks, Hansen, and Christie's examination of dual-career/dual-work families illustrates the capacity of external institutional changes in the economy and education to create stress and strain in marriage, yet provide personal reward and expanded options for the individual.

Third, conflict will persist between the two different views of nature discussed by Francoeur: the absolutist, fixed philosophy versus a process-oriented consciousness. The former conceptualizes a human origin of perfection and completion from which humanity fell and to which it must return, and the latter an evolutionary scheme in which the human race plods toward a more utopian future. It is a helpful paradigm for understanding reactions to the changes created by technology. Arguments over abortion, sex education, and traditional family values may stem from different interpretations regarding the locus of control over one's own life. The adversaries represent those who adapt, however reluctantly, to societal changes brought about by technology and those who resist social change by maintaining that the personal consequences of technology can be controlled and even reversed. It is a paradox that at a time when people have unprecedented control over their lives, many fear the opportunity to exercise it. The secular humanism or social pluralism that seems so objectionable to some essentially means that the individual can select his or her own life (Yankelovich, 1981). This contrasts with an absolutist, fixed philosophy of human potential. It is unlike the traditional sex roles, exclusivity, and "togetherness" advocated by writers like Marabel Morgan (1973), who emphasize the nuclear family and romantic love expressed only in the confines of marriage. Weis stated that it is reasonable to expect "traditionalists" to resist nonexclusive relationship models since they represent a radical departure from what most Americans have been socialized to anticipate. However, the social environment of the 1960s led to a challenge of these basic concepts of marriage. A process-oriented view of marriage emerged and publications like *Open Marriage* by George and Nena O'Neill (1972) reflected the change.

Finally, Francoeur's dichotomy is useful in recognizing cultural bias when studying minority ethnic group marriages and family life. For example, Peters and McAdoo believe that the greater prominence of nontraditional or alternate lifestyles in minority cultures is partially a result of racism and discrmination. These living patterns were strategies for economic and social survival. Dual-career/dual-work couples and egalitarian relationships are not "new alternatives" in the Black community. Nor are cohabitation, single-parent families, and sexual nonexclusivity, which were once negatively evaluated by the dominant society and seen as justification for criticizing and punishing minority groups. As these patterns became more common and accepted in the majority community, they began to lose their pejorative meaning. This reflects a somewhat greater acceptance of the process-oriented view when it applies to the majority community. Evidently, there has been another standard for minorities.

Implications for Theory and Research

Human relations specialist Lydia Walker-Savasten (1977: 8) stated that

> the ultimate goal of our search as adults exploring alternative lifestyles is to find meaning in life, to know the freedom of being in love and the freedom to love others to the depths and lengths of our spiritual, mental, emotional, and physical potential as human beings.

The contributors to this volume recognize the search for personal growth and happiness as the unifying element in all lifestyles. To achieve this goal more individuals are experiencing a greater number and variety of interpersonal relationships over their lifespan (Masnick and Bane, 1980). For example, Price-Bonham, Wright, and Pittman view divorce as transitional in a life cycle of different lifestyles. Chilman notes that stepfamilies start at a different developmental stage than do first-marriage families. Studying this increasing diversity of interpersonal experiences, instead of simply identifying family structures, is urged by Thompson and Gongla, and by Brudenell. They cite literature that promotes the importance of family process over family structure and the significance of the psychosocial interior of the family rather than counting, for instance, the number of available parents.

Complex taxonomical problems that challenge the lifestyles researcher arise from this proliferation of experiences. Establishing meaningful and descriptive categories and labels has proven difficult. An example is defining who is voluntarily childless. As Veevers notes, the consequences of childlessness are different depending on whether it involves achieving a major life goal or the frustration of one. The ultimate question is: Did the individual get what he or she wanted? In this case, did they or did they not want children? In addition, Veevers suggests that research on childlessness should also include the study of singles as a subpopulation of the voluntary childless, including those who want children but do not want to marry and reject an out-of-wedlock pregnancy. Ordinarily only married couples are referred to in childlessness studies. By ignoring singles we oversimply. Veevers recommends an unraveling of the links tying together marriage and parenthood decisions.

Classification of lifestyles into homogeneous groups is a common conceptual error that researchers make. Taubin and Mudd discussed the ambiguity of the term "traditional family" and the failure to distinguish longitudinal from cross-sectional perspectives. Stein has developed a typology of singlehood according to whether it is voluntary or involuntary and stable or temporary. Macklin discusses the persistent problem of categorizing cohabitors. The meaning of single-parent family remains unclear, and Thompson and Gongla emphasize the need to indicate the extent to which other adults in fact assist in the parenting function. Brudenell reflects on the changing nature of communes and the difficulty in determining a meaningful terminology. He makes an important distinction between communes and intentional communities. The communal focus affirms the group as more fundamental than the family. The commune in essence defines the family. Although members of intentional communities identify with the group, they retain the authority to make individual household decisions.

Finally, labels influence public acceptance or rejection of a lifestyle. Peters and McAdoo note that unmarried Black motherhood has been discussed in the context of "broken" homes, whereas as single-parent White households increase, researchers refer to single parenthood as an "alternative" lifestyle. The term "cohabitation" lent increased respectability to "living in sin." Stereotyping of gay individuals and couples continues. Harry notes the legal problems of gays and lesbians wishing to marry or obtain custody of their children. Concern that alternative arrangements by definition are harmful to children is still often expressed, according to Thompson and Gongla.

Beyond taxonomy, other research issues abound. Chilman indicates how little we know about the consequences of alternative lifestyles. The contradictions she reports in the stepparenting literature are prevalent elsewhere. Weis deplores the lack of knowledge regarding how social factors like alienation affect lifestyle choices. The absence of consistent operational definitions persists. For example, Veevers suggests distinguishing between de facto versus de jure lengths of marriage. On the other hand, definitional agreement may create conceptual limitations. Illustrative of this is the willingness of social scientists to accept common residence as a characteristic of familiies. Yet, as Gerstel and Gross write, this linking together of the "intact" marriage with the spouses' occupancy of a single household is called into question by commuter marriages.

Greater sensitivity to research issues affecting minority groups is needed. Stein's discussion of the relationship between upward mobility and singlehood among educated Black women exemplifies a growing awareness. Weis calls for more non-Whites to be included in research samples. Phillips criticizes the scarcity of clinical data regarding persons other than White, middle-class clients. Peters and McAdoo believe that Black social scientists still face difficulties in getting their works published and recognized in a climate dominated by the ethnocentric perspectives of White American researchers.

Lastly, lifestyle research may prove valuable to society through its applicability to public policy, law, and clinical work. Myricks describes the preeminence of the legal doctrine of "the best interests of the child," yet it is often the personal beliefs of a judge that are used to make such a determination. Perhaps by utilizing the increasing clinical understanding of alternative lifestyles, as urged by Phillips, it will be possible to make decisions that are in fact in "the best interests of the individuals" involved.

The Future

As we speculate about the future of families and alternative lifestyles in an age of technological revolution there are two essential points to consider. First, we must not lose our perspective. In spite of all the discussion about change, the vast majority of Americans marry, remain married, bear and rear children, and are primarily provided for by male breadwinners. These conventional choices, made by "contemporary traditionals," remain the dominant themes in American family life, and stability and quality are the two ingredients most sought after in a relationship (see Taubin and Mudd). Only those who remain permanently single and/or never have children will ever really experience a totally alternative lifestyle.

Second, we must not replace old myths about the family with new myths. Dressel and Hess write that the "classical family of Western nostalgia" is just that — nostalgic, but untrue. There were many variations in Western family living in the past. Americans can still recall boarding houses, orphan asylums, and middle-class families with sleep-in maids. Buunk speaks of rich Europeans with their servants and family members living in households, a form that is rarely visible today. People commonly delayed marriage in nineteenth-century Western Europe. Many remained single. The explanations are rooted in the poverty and lack of opportunity at the time. Thompson and Gongla remind us that between 1870 and 1970 the proportion of single-parent families in the United States was virtually unchanged. Sociologist Arlene Skolnick (1980) reports that in 1790 a typical American household included 5.6 members. In the mid-1700s, men married at 24 and women at 21. Ten percent of all first births were out of wedlock in eighteenth-century America. None of these figures differs dramatically today. Ramey (1981) states that common-law cohabitation involved one in five couples during the 1920s. Taubin and Mudd caution that even the conventional facade of the 1950s was deceiving. Wives who were having babies had earlier worked to support those very husbands who were now launching their careers to become the primary bread-winners.

As we more accurately assay the past we must not glorify the present. Just as nostalgic reminiscences about a perfect past cannot forge realistic solutions to contemporary problems, neither should today's lifestyles be seen as necessarily "progressive" or "emancipatory" (Buunk). For example, divorce may be simply a modern compromise in the struggle between personal autonomy and family commitment. One marries, has children, and divorces, thereby gaining both a family and autonomy. Cohabitation is also a compromise according to Levine (1981: 75), who said, "Young adults who do not want to live alone hedge against solitude and marriage by living together. . . thereby, tentatively, overcoming the misgivings and apprehensions about marriage."

In conclusion, perhaps some of the pessimism expressed in Catherine Chilman's prologue is premature. "Social Luddites" cannot turn back time. I doubt the "moral majoritans" described by Yankelovich (1981) can lead a successful counter-revolution. The momentum of the new technological age is inexorable. The Gallup Poll reports a growing tolerance among Americans. What was once considered outrageous is now mundane: cohabitation, homosexuality, coed dormitories. Pluralism has gained respectability and we teach about it (see Jurich and Hastings). The only reason for pessimism is the shadow of nuclear war. But then, even on doomsday, to borrow from Ralph Linton, the last persons will undoubtedly spend their final moments searching for their family members.

References

LEVINE, E. M. (1981) "Middle-class family decline." Society 18: 72-83.

MASNICK, B. and M. J. BANE (1980) The Nation's Families: 1960-1990. Boston: Auburn House.

MORGAN, M. (1973) The Total Woman. Old Tappan, NJ: Revell.

O'NEILL, N. (1981) Presentation to Groves Conference on Marriage and the Family, Mount Pocono, Pennsylvania.

O'NEILL, N. and G. O'NEILL (1972) Open Marriage. New York: Evans.

RAMEY, J. (1981) Presentation to Groves Conference on Marriage and the Family, Mount Pocono, Pennsylvania.

——— (1976) Intimate Friendships. Englewood Cliffs, NJ: Prentice-Hall.

SKOLNICK, A. (1980) "The American family: the paradox of perfection." American Educator 4: 8-11, 23.

TOFFLER, A. (1971) Future Shock. New York: Bantam.

WALKER-SAVASTEN, L. (1977) "Children and alternative lifestyles." (unpublished)

YANKELOVICH, D. (1981) "New rules in American life: searching for self-fulfillment in a world turned upside down." Psychology Today 4: 35-91.

About the Contributors

Gerry Brudenell, Ed.D., is Associate Professor of Childhood Education at Florida State University, Tallahassee. His Ed.D. was earned in Psychology, Counseling, and Guidance at Colorado State College (now the University of Northern Colorado), with post doctoral study in early childhood education at Bank Street College, New York City. He writes in the areas of early childhood education and family life. His current research is on home play materials and environments, and relationships among persons in homes, schools, and communities. Since 1973, Dr. Brudenell has been a resident of a rural intentional community.

Bram Buunk, Ph.D., is Associate Professor of Social Psychology at the University of Nijmegen, The Netherlands. He received his Ph.D. in the social sciences from the University of Utrecht. Dr. Buunk has published three books and numerous papers, in Dutch as well as in English, mainly in the areas of interpersonal attraction, love, jealousy, extramarital relationships, marital satisfaction, and alternative lifestyles. Currently, he is finishing a book and several papers on friendship. In 1982, Dr. Buunk served as Honorary Fellow at the Family Study Center of the University of Minnesota. He also serves on the boards of several Dutch professional organizations.

Catherine S. Chilman, Ph.D., is Professor of Social Welfare at the University of Wisconsin—Milwaukee. She received her Master's degree in social work from the University of Chicago and her Ph.D. in psychology from the University of Chicago. She has served on the boards of numerous national and international organizations and is past president of the Groves Conference on Marriage and the Family. Her experience includes direct social work practice, university teaching, research and administration in the federal government and curriculum development concerning population planning with schools of social work around the world. Her numerous scholarly books and articles include such areas as poverty and families, parent satisfactions, family planning, and adolescent sexuality.

Leo A. Christie, Ph.D., is a therapist at the Daniel Memorial Residence for Adolescent Boys in Jacksonville, Florida. He received his Ph.D. in family therapy from the Interdivisional Program in Marriage and Family at the Florida State University. He also maintains a limited private practice in Jacksonville, and is Adjunct Professor at the University of Northern Florida.

His primary interest is in developing systems theory, with particular emphasis on changing role relationships between men and women.

Paula L. Dressel, Ph.D., is Associate Professor of Sociology and a faculty member with the Gerontology Center at Georgia State University in Atlanta. Her doctorate is from the University of Georgia. She has published primarily in the areas of family and aging, community development, and social planning. Her current research focuses on social welfare issues from the perspective of human service providers.

Robert T. Francoeur, Ph.D., ACS, is Professor of Human Sexuality and Embryology at Fairleigh Dickinson University, Madison, NJ. With graduate degrees in theology, genetics, and experimental embryology, he is also a charter member of the American College of Sexologists. Among his books are *Eve's New Rib* (1972), *Hot and Cool Sex* (1974), *The Future of Sexual Relations* (1974), and the college text, *Becoming a Sexual Person* (1982). His main research interest is in changing value paradigms associated with reproductive technologies and alternate lifestyles.

Naomi Gerstel, Ph.D., is Assistant Professor of Sociology at the University of Massachusetts, Amherst. She received her Ph.D. in sociology from Columbia University. She has published in the areas of gender and the family and on the New Right and the family. Presently, she is conducting research on the relationship between marital dissolution, social networks, and mental health and is writing a book (with Harriet Gross) on commuter marriage.

Patricia A. Gongla, Ph.D., is Assistant Research Sociologist at the Neuropsychiatric Institute, University of California, Los Angeles, and is also Research Sociologist at the Veterans Administration Medical Center, Brentwood. She received her Ph.D. in sociology from Case Western Reserve University. Divorce and single-parent families have been major interests for research and publication, as has the more general area of adjustment to stress. Currently, she is directing research on posttraumatic stress among Vietnam veterans and is also working in evaluation research, specializing in the mental health field.

Harriet Gross, Ph.D., is University Professor of Sociology, College of Arts and Sciences, Governors State University, Park Forest, Illinois. She received her Ph.D. in sociology from the University of Chicago. She has published in the areas of sex roles, deviance, and the family. She is presently doing research on Merchant Marine families and is writing a book (with Naomi Gerstel) on commuter marriage.

Sally L. Hansen, Ph.D., is Associate Professor of Home Economics Education at the Florida State University, Tallahassee, Florida. She received her Ph.D. in family relations and child development from Florida State and her B.S. and M.S. in Home Economics Education from the University of

Wisconsin—Madison. She has published in the areas of dating and mate selection, education/curriculum for the handicapped, and adolescence. Her most recent research grant has been in the area of adolescents. She is active in numerous professional organizations and is currently serving on a national committee to develop standards and certification for family life education.

Joseph Harry is Associate Professor with the Sociology Department of Northern Illinois University. He received his Ph.D. at the University of Oregon in 1968. His major publications include *The Social Organization of Gay Males,* with William DeVall (Praeger, 1978) and *Gay Children Grown Up: Gender Culture and Gender Deviance* (Praeger, 1982). His principal areas of interest include deviance, criminology, and sexual orientation.

Catherine A. Hastings is Assistant Professor of Marriage and Clinical Director of the Marriage and Family Unit at Kansas State University. She is a marriage and family therapist certified by the American Association for Marriage and Family Therapy. Her research interests include the effects of chronic illness on families, aging in the family, the applications of family therapy to the medical field, and the effects of father absence on children of divorced parents.

Beth B. Hess is Professor of Sociology at County College of Morris, Randolph, N.J. She received her Ph.D. from Rutgers—the State University of New Jersey. A Fellow of the Gerontological Society, she has written several textbooks in social gerontology, as well as numerous articles on such aspects of aging as self-help, friendship, politics, family relationships, older women, the social consequences of medical advances, and the effects of Reaganomics. Dr. Hess is senior author of *Sociology* (Macmillan, 1982) and associate editor of *Contemporary Sociology, Research on Aging,* and *Society.* She has also held offices in the Gerontological Society of America, the Eastern Gerontological Society, the Society for the Study of Social Problems, and Sociologists for Women in Society.

Mary W. Hicks, Ph.D., is Professor of Home and Family Life at the Florida State University, Tallahassee, Florida. She received her Ph.D. in family relations and child development from the Pennsylvania State University. She has published in the areas of dating and mate selection, marital satisfaction, dual-work/dual-career, and family systems. Her most current interest is in the area of systems theory and family therapy. She is active in numerous professional organizations at the local, state and national levels.

Anthony P. Jurich is Professor of Family and Child Development at Kansas State University. He is a marriage and family therapist and supervisor certified by the American Association for Marriage and Family Therapy and a sex therapist certified through the American Association of Sex

Educators, Counselors, and Therapists. He has published numerous research articles on such topics as marriage and family therapy, adolescence, family crisis, alternative lifestyles, and family forms. He is coeditor of *New Perspectives in Marriage and Family Therapy* (forthcoming from Human Sciences Press) and was the 1976 recipient of the Kansas State University Teacher of the Year Award.

Eleanor D. Macklin, Ph.D., is Associate Professor, Department of Child and Family Studies, Syracuse University, Syracuse, New York. She received her Ph.D. from Cornell University, and is known for her pioneering work on nonmarital cohabitation. She is a clinical member and approved supervisor of the American Association for Marriage and Family Therapy, and is accredited as a sex educator by the American Association of Sex Educators, Counselors, and Therapists. She was program chairperson for the 1981 Groves Conference on Marriage and the Family, and authored the chapter on "Nontraditional Family Forms: A Decade of Research" for the 1980 Decade Review, *Journal of Marriage and the Family.*

Harriette P. McAdoo is Professor in the School of Social Work, Howard University, and Research Associate at Columbia Research Systems. She received her Ph.D. from the University of Michigan with postgraduate work at Harvard. She has published on racial attitudes and self-esteem in Black children, mobility patterns of Blacks and support networks of single mothers. Her primary interests include Black upward mobility, single parenting stress and coping strategies, and race and self-attitude of Black and Chinese children. She is a Director of the National Council on Family Relations and the Society for Research in Child Development.

Emily H. Mudd, M.S.W., Ph.D., is Professor Emeritus of Family Study in Psychiatry, Consultant and Staff, Human Behavior Unit, Department of Obstetrics and Gynecology, School of Medicine, University of Pennsylvania. She has published and edited six books and over 200 articles on marriage and family therapy, evaluative research, and adolescent fertility problems. Dr. Mudd is past president of the American Association for Marriage and Family Therapy and currently serves on the Executive Committee of the World Academy of Art and Science, the American Orthopsychiatric Association, and Marriage Council of Philadelphia, and holds numerous positions at the international, national, state, and local levels.

Noel Myricks, J.D., Ed.D., is Associate Professor in the Department of Family and Community Development at the College Park campus of the University of Maryland. He is also an attorney-at-law. He has published extensively in the area of children's legal rights, with recent articles appearing in the *Children's Legal Rights Journal.* His most recent article, "Brown

Revisited," appears in the *Black Law Journal* published by UCLA. His primary research interests are in family law.

Marie F. Peters, Ed.D., is Associate Professor, Human Development and Family Relations, at the University of Connecticut, Storrs. She received her doctorate in human development from Harvard University. Her publications and research have been concerned with child socialization and parent-child interaction in Black families, coping and stress in dual-income families, and intergenerational relationships. Active in professional organizations on the national level, Dr. Peters is currently secretary of the National Council on Family Relations.

Robert A. Phillips, Jr., is Assistant Professor in the Family and Community Development Department at the University of Maryland, College Park, and a therapist on the clinical staff of the Human Sexuality Institute in Washington, D.C. His current research interests include male sexuality, incest, and more specifically, the development of multiple personalities in women as a coping response to incest. Dr. Phillips is an approved supervisor of the American Association for Marriage and Family Therapy and a member of numerous professional organizations including the American Association of Sex Educators, Counselors, and Therapists, and the Society for the Scientific Study of Sex. He received his Ph.D. from the University of Minnesota.

Joe F. Pittman, M.A., is a Ph.D. student in child and family development at the University of Georgia, Athens. He received his M.A. in counseling from the University of Georgia. Before returning for his Ph.D. studies, he worked as a mental health counselor. Presently, he is doing research on family cohesion and divorce.

Sharon Price-Bonham, Ph.D., is Associate Professor of Child and Family Development at the University of Georgia, Athens. She received her Ph.D. in sociology at Iowa State University. She has published in the areas of divorce, sex roles, marital decision making, father and child relationships, dual careers, and adolescence. She is currently conducting research on the relationships of former spouses. She has held offices in the Southeastern Council on Family Relations, American Home Economics Association, and the National Council on Family Relations.

Roger H. Rubin, Ph.D., is Associate Professor of Family and Community Development at the University of Maryland, College Park. He received his Ph.D. in child development and family relationships from the Pennsylvania State University. He has published in the areas of Black family life, interpersonal lifestyles, and income maintenance programs. Presently, he is doing research on divorce. Professor Rubin has been elected and appointed to numerous positions in professional family life organizations at the national, state and local levels. He served as Associate Chairperson for the 1981 Groves Conference on Marriage and the Family.

Robert G. Ryder was originally trained as a clinical psychologist at the University of Michigan, going from there in 1961 to what became the Family Development Section of the National Institutes of Mental Health. In 1963 he became the chief of the section, responsible for research on recently married couples. In 1974, Ryder left NIMH to become Head of the Department of Child Development and Family Relations at the University of Connecticut. He is now Dean of Family Studies at the University of Connecticut. Ryder's association with the Groves Conference goes back into the 1960s. He was Program Chair for the Myrtle Beach meetings in 1973 and President of the Conference from 1979 to 1981.

Peter J. Stein, Ph.D., is Associate Professor of Sociology at William Paterson College of New Jersey. He received his Ph.D. from Princeton University. He is the author of *Single Life: Unmarried Adults in Social Context* (St. Martin's, 1981); *Single* (Prentice Hall, 1976); and co-author of *Sociology* (Macmillan, 1982); *The Family: Functions, Conflicts and Symbols* (Addison-Wesley, 1977); and *The Marriage Game* (Random House, 1977). He is active in several professional organizations, including the Executive Board of the Eastern Sociological Society, the Program Committee of the Groves Conference on Marriage and the Family, Chair of the Family Division of the SSSP, and the NJCFR Executive Committee.

Sara B. Taubin, Ed.D., is Associate Professor in the Department of Human Behavior and Development at Drexel University, Philadelphia. She received her doctorate from the University of Pennsylvania and has published in the areas of successful family functioning, fathers, family strengths, marriage in the later years, and human sexuality. Her current research is concerned with child care needs and parent education in two-career families. She brings family information to the public through lectures, radio, and television.

Edward H. Thompson, Jr., Ph.D., is Assistant Professor of Sociology at Holy Cross College, Worcester, Massachusetts. He received his Ph.D. in sociology from Case Western Reserve University, with specialities in family and medical sociology. He has published in the areas of family burden and interpersonal lifestyles. His present research concerns women's subjective experience of pregnancy.

Jean E. Veevers is Professor of Sociology at the University of Victoria, Canada. She received her Ph.D. from the University of Toronto and for a number of years taught family sociology at the University of Western Ontario. She has published extensively concerning couples who are *Childless by Choice.* Her research interests have now shifted from family studies to gender roles. Her current concern is with the possibility that changing roles for women may have negative consequences for their health, with the result that some women literally may be *Dying To Be Equal.*

David L. Weis, Ph.D., is Assistant Professor of Home Economics at Cook College, Rutgers University, New Brunswick, New Jersey. He received his

Ph.D. in family studies from Purdue University. He has published in the areas of adolescent sexuality, extramarital relationships, and educational programs. He is currently doing research on exclusivity attitudes and adolescent contraceptive behavior. Professor Weis has been elected and appointed to several positions in professional organizations, chiefly in the areas of family life and human sexuality.

David W. Wright, M.A., is a doctoral student in child and family development at the University of Georgia, Athens, GA. He received his Master's degree in marriage and family counseling from Chapman College, Orange, California. He has published in the area of divorce and is currently involved in a longitudinal study of former spouses. Other research interests include stepfamily functioning, family power, and the training of family therapists.